Cisco
Network
Professional's
Advanced Internetworking Guide

Cisco®
Network
Professional's
Advanced Internetworking Guide

Patrick J. Conlan

Wiley Publishing, Inc.

Acquisitions Editor: Jeff Kellum
Development Editor: Mary Ellen Schutz
Technical Editor: Tim Boyles
Production Editor: Eric Charbonneau
Copy Editors: Cheryl Hauser and Kim Cofer
Production Manager: Tim Tate
Vice President and Executive Group Publisher: Richard Swadley
Vice President and Publisher: Neil Edde
Media Project Supervisor: Laura Moss-Hollister
Media Development Specialist: Josh Frank
Media Quality Assurance: Shawn Patrick
Book Designer: Judy Fung
Compositor: Craig Woods, Happenstance Type-O-Rama
Proofreader: Nancy Bell
Indexer: Ted Laux
Project Coordinator, Cover: Lynsey Stanford
Cover Designer: Ryan Sneed

Conlan, Patrick J., 1978-
  Cisco network professional's advanced internetworking guide / Patrick J. Conlan. — 1st ed.
    p. cm.
  ISBN-13: 978-0-470-38360-5 (paper/cd-rom)
  ISBN-10: 0-470-38360-7 (paper/cd-rom)
  1. Internetworking (Telecommunication) I. Cisco Systems, Inc. II. Title. III. Title: Advanced internet-
working guide.
  TK5105.5.C6625 2009
  004.6—dc22
                                    2009009767

Dear Reader,

Thank you for choosing *Cisco Network Professional's Advanced Internetworking Guide*. This book is part of a family of premium-quality Sybex books, all of which are written by outstanding authors who combine practical experience with a gift for teaching.

Sybex was founded in 1976. More than thirty years later, we're still committed to producing consistently exceptional books. With each of our titles we're working hard to set a new standard for the industry. From the paper we print on to the authors we work with, our goal is to bring you the best books available.

I hope you see all that reflected in these pages. I'd be very interested to hear your comments and get your feedback on how we're doing. Feel free to let me know what you think about this or any other Sybex book by sending me an email at nedde@wiley.com, or if you think you've found a technical error in this book, please visit http://sybex.custhelp.com. Customer feedback is critical to our efforts at Sybex.

Best regards,

Neil Edde
Vice President and Publisher
Sybex, an Imprint of Wiley

To my parents, who gave to me the love and the drive to always learn and succeed.

To the innumerable people who have taught and helped me, thank you.

Finally, to my two Labrador retrievers, for waking me up in the middle of the night, sound asleep at my desk, so that I could go to bed.

Acknowledgments

Tim Boyles, contributing author and technical editor, added Chapters 12 and 15 to the book. Tim has an unbelievable amount of knowledge and a superb way of explaining and passing that knowledge on. In his role as technical editor, he always had the missing piece of information or idea that I needed. Tim caught the tiniest of errors and suggested changes that made the book that much better.

Mary Ellen Schutz, developmental editor, gets her own paragraph. She may not like it this way, but she does. Without Mary Ellen this book would be a garbled heap of strewn together words that no one could read. I cannot thank her enough for the help she gave me on this book and for making me an infinitely better writer. For the many late nights editing, giving me ideas for examples, and making sure my technical words come out in intelligible English, I give her the sincerest Thank You!

Jeff Kellum, acquisitions editor, thank you for giving me the opportunity to write this book and staying on me to get it done! Thanks also to Kim Cofer and Cheryl Hauser, the copy editors, who made sure that even my grammar and spelling were perfect; and Eric Charbonneau, production editor, who worked hard against an impossibly tight timetable to make sure everything flowed through the production process. Thanks also to the compositor, Craig Woods; Nancy Bell, proofreader; and the indexer, Ted Laux. The book couldn't happen without them.

Finally, I would like to thank Todd Lammle. I work with Todd and he is a great friend. He definitely helped me through the writing process and helped so that I had the time to complete this book.

About the Authors

Patrick J. Conlan spent 10 years in the U.S. Navy as a communications technician operating, maintaining, and designing communication systems of diverse types, including radio, satellite, non-IP and IP communication systems. The last four years of his naval career were spent as an IT instructor and curriculum developer. He taught numerous courses ranging from basic computer networking to advanced IP system integration and design. Pat was also in charge of developing a new and updated IT curriculum that the U.S. Navy continues to use today to train their IT personnel.

After the Navy, Pat started his own consulting company where he delivered network assessment, design, IT instruction, and curriculum development services.

Pat is currently employed by GlobalNet Training as a full-time senior staff instructor and consultant. He teaches a wide range of curriculum, focusing primarily on Cisco certifications, including the CCNA, CCDA, CCNP, and CCSP courses. In addition, he provides consulting services including design and implementation of networks to large companies of all types.

Tim Boyles is a senior consultant with BT Global Services and is the south central region security practice lead. Tim has over 20 years experience in networking and security and is an author, speaker, and occasional instructor in the security field.

Tim has held positions with the U.S. Navy, Rockwell Automation, International Network Services, and others in addition to his current position. He currently holds CISSP, CISM, CISA, CCNA, GCIH, and GAWN certifications.

Contents at a Glance

Introduction			*xxv*
Chapter	**1**	Enterprise Network Design	1
Chapter	**2**	Switching	29
Chapter	**3**	Spanning Tree Protocol (STP)	67
Chapter	**4**	Routing Concepts and Distance Vector Routing Protocols	111
Chapter	**5**	Advanced Distance Vector Protocols	145
Chapter	**6**	Link State Routing Protocols	191
Chapter	**7**	Exterior Gateway Protocols	247
Chapter	**8**	Multicast	291
Chapter	**9**	Internet Protocol Version 6 (IPv6)	313
Chapter	**10**	Redundancy Protocols	337
Chapter	**11**	WAN and Teleworker Connections	375
Chapter	**12**	Virtual Private Networks	429
Chapter	**13**	Device Security	469
Chapter	**14**	Switch Security	515
Chapter	**15**	Cisco IOS Firewall	539
Chapter	**16**	Cisco IOS IPS	573
Chapter	**17**	Voice	601
Chapter	**18**	DiffServ Quality of Service (QoS)	623
Chapter	**19**	Wireless Devices and Topologies	669
Chapter	**20**	Wireless Management and Security	707
Appendix		About the Companion CD	745
Glossary			**749**
Acronyms			**813**
Index			*825*

Contents

Introduction   *xxv*

Chapter 1   Enterprise Network Design   **1**

The Three-Layer Hierarchical Design Model   2
Enterprise Composite Network Model   4
    Enterprise Campus   5
    Enterprise Edge   7
    Service Provider Edge   9
IIN and SONA   9
Case Study: FutureTech Corporation   10
    Book Organization   10
    FutureTech Company Background   11
    Test Network   16
    Wireless Equipment   21
Summary   23
Review Questions   25
Answers to Review Questions   27

Chapter 2   Switching   **29**

Layer 2 Switching   30
    Address Learning and Forwarding   31
VLANs   32
    Link Types   34
    Trunk Protocols   35
    Implementing VLANs   38
    VLAN Trunk Protocol   40
    Configuring VLANs   43
Inter-VLAN Routing   51
    Router on a Stick   51
    Configuring Router on a Stick   52
    Multilayer Switching   53
    Cisco Express Forwarding (CEF)   54
    Configuring Inter-VLAN Routing   56
EtherChannel   57
    Automatic Bundling Protocols   58
    Configuring EtherChannel   60
Summary   62
Review Questions   63
Answers to Review Questions   65

Chapter	3	**Spanning Tree Protocol (STP)**	**67**
		STP Operation	68
		STP Components	69
		Switch Identification	71
		Determining Paths	72
		Configuring Spanning Tree Protocol	76
		History of STP	81
		PVST+	82
		Rapid Spanning Tree Protocol (RSTP)	90
		Multiple Spanning Tree (MST)	93
		Protecting Spanning Tree	96
		BPDU Guard	97
		Root Guard	97
		BPDU Filtering	98
		Loop Guard	100
		UniDirectional Link Detection (UDLD)	100
		Verifying and Troubleshooting	102
		Checking the STP Process	102
		Checking Port Details	104
		Checking STP Features	105
		Checking the Root and Port Properties	105
		Determining UplinkFast and BackboneFast Status	106
		Summary	106
		Review Questions	107
		Answers to Review Questions	109
Chapter	4	**Routing Concepts and Distance Vector Routing Protocols**	**111**
		Routing Fundamentals	112
		Basic Routing	112
		Administrative Distance	116
		Static Routing	117
		Dynamic Routing	121
		Route Information Protocol (RIP)	128
		RIP Timers	129
		Configuring RIP Routing	129
		RIP Version 2	130
		Summarization with RIP	132
		Verifying Your Configurations	132
		Interior Gateway Routing Protocol (IGRP)	137
		Route Manipulation	138
		Passive Interface	139
		Distribute Lists	139

Summary   141
Review Questions   142
Answers to Review Questions   144

Chapter 5   Advanced Distance Vector Protocols   145

EIGRP Terms and Features   146
    EIGRP Capabilities   147
    Terms   148
    Message Types   153
    Tables   155
Enabling EIGRP   158
    Autonomous System Numbers   158
    Configuring EIGRP on a Router   159
    Controlling Interfaces Placed in the Routing Process   161
    Configuring EIGRP on a Switch   163
    Configuring the Rest of the Network   163
Improving EIGRP Operations   166
    Changing the EIGRP Metric   166
    Default Routing   167
    Summary Routes   169
    Stub Routers   171
    Load Balancing   173
    Using EIGRP over WANs   176
Verifying and Troubleshooting   179
    show ip eigrp neighbors   179
    show ip eigrp topology   180
    show ip route   182
    show ip protocols   184
    show ip eigrp interfaces   185
    show ip eigrp traffic   186
Summary   187
Review Questions   188
Answers to Review Questions   190

Chapter 6   Link State Routing Protocols   191

Introduction to Link State Protocols   192
    Link State Protocol Improvements   192
OSPF   193
    OSPF Tables   195
    OSPF Packet Types   196
    Link State Advertisements (LSA)   198
OSPF Operation   199
    Neighbor Discovery   200
    BangRtr4Router Identity (RID)   203

Designated Router (DR) Elections   204
The Link State Database   208
The Routing Table   211
OSPF Cost   212
OSPF Features and Benefits   213
OSPF Hierarchy   214
OSPF Link Types   215
Stub Type Areas   218
Configuring OSPF   224
Verifying OSPF   227
Integrated IS-IS   234
IS-IS Features   235
IS-IS Compared to OSPF   238
Configuring IS-IS   240
Summary   241
Review Questions   243
Answers to Review Questions   245

Chapter   7   Exterior Gateway Protocols   247

BGP Operations   248
When Not to Use BGP   249
When to Use BGP   249
Ways to Connect a Network   250
Path Vectors   252
BGP Transmissions   253
BGP Tables   254
BGP Messages   254
Types of BGP Connections   257
BGP Attributes   262
Choosing a Path   268
Route Maps   270
Configuring BGP   274
Basic Setup   275
Example Configuration   280
Verifying BGP   283
Summary   286
Review Questions   287
Answers to Review Questions   289

Chapter   8   Multicast   291

What Is Multicast?   292
Transmission Types   292
Multicast Pros and Cons   294
Multicast Addressing   295

Multicast Protocols 299
Internet Group Management Protocol (IGMP) 299
Protocol Independent Multicast (PIM) 302
Multicast Operation and Configuration 305
Verify Multicast 307
Summary 309
Review Questions 310
Answers to Review Questions 312

Chapter 9   Internet Protocol Version 6 (IPv6)   313

Operating Internet Protocol Version 6 314
The Benefits of IPv6 315
IPv6 Addressing 316
Using IPv6 in an Internetwork 320
Interoperating IPv6 with IPv4 329
Dual Stacking 329
Tunneling 330
NAT-PT 332
Summary 333
Review Questions 334
Answers to Review Questions 336

Chapter 10   Redundancy Protocols   337

Client Redundancy Issues 338
Introducing Redundancy Protocols 340
Hot Standby Router Protocol 341
HSRP Timers 341
Group Roles 342
Virtual MAC Address 343
HSRP States 343
HSRP Group Communication and Configuration 344
Improving HSRP Operations 353
Virtual Router Redundancy Protocol 362
VRRP and HSRP Comparison 362
VRRP Redundancy Characteristics 364
VRRP Timers 365
VRRP Transition 366
Configuring VRRP 366
Gateway Load Balancing Protocol 367
GLBP Functions 367
GLBP Features 368
GLBP Per-Host Traffic Balancing 369
Configuring GLBP 371

		Summary	371
		Review Questions	372
		Answers to Review Questions	374

Chapter	**11**	**WAN and Teleworker Connections**	**375**
		Introduction to the Campus Edge	376
		Enterprise Branch	376
		Enterprise Teleworker	378
		Cable Technologies	379
		DSL Technologies	389
		ADSL in Detail	395
		Configuring the CPE as a PPPoE Client	402
		Configuring the CPE with PPPoE and an ATM Interface	408
		Configuring the CPE as a PPPoA Client	409
		Minimizing Dropped Packets	412
		Enterprise WAN	413
		MPLS	413
		Switching Types	414
		Router Architecture	416
		Using Labels in MPLS	417
		Summary	425
		Review Questions	426
		Answers to Review Questions	428

Chapter	**12**	**Virtual Private Networks**	**429**
		Introduction to Virtual Private Networks	430
		IPsec	431
		Generic Routing Encapsulation (GRE)	434
		VPN Operation	435
		Cisco-Specific Operation	435
		Configuring Site-to-Site VPN	436
		Verify and Troubleshoot VPN	442
		Cisco Easy VPN	452
		Summary	464
		Review Questions	465
		Answers to Review Questions	467

Chapter	**13**	**Device Security**	**469**
		Why Secure Your Devices?	470
		CLI-Based AutoSecure	472
		SDM-Based Security Audit Wizard	482

AAA   495
    RADIUS   498
    TACACS+   500
    Configuring AAA   503
Securing Management Functions   508
    SNMP   508
    Syslog   508
    TFTP   509
    NTP   509
Summary   510
Review Questions   511
Answers to Review Questions   513

Chapter   14   Switch Security   515

Introduction to Layer 2 Security   516
    Rogue Devices   517
    Layer 2 Attacks   517
Securing Layer 2   526
    Port Security   526
    AAA   528
    802.1x   528
    VACLs   530
    Private VLANs   531
    DHCP Snooping   533
    IP Source Guard   533
    Dynamic ARP Inspection   534
Summary   535
Review Questions   536
Answers to Review Questions   538

Chapter   15   Cisco IOS Firewall   539

Function of the Cisco IOS Firewall   540
    Authentication Proxy   540
    Transparent Firewall   541
    Stateful Packet Inspection   541
Configure Cisco IOS Firewall with SDM   545
    Basic Firewall   545
    Advanced Firewall   552
Verify Cisco IOS Firewall Configurations   560
    Basic Firewall   560
    Advanced Firewall   564
Summary   569
Review Questions   570
Answers to Review Questions   572

Chapter	**16**	**Cisco IOS IPS**	**573**
		Securing Networks with IDS and IPS	574
		Basic Functions of the Intrusion Detection System (IDS)	574
		Basic Functions of the Intrusion Prevention System (IPS)	576
		Using IDS and IPS Together	577
		Benefits and Drawbacks of IPS/IDS Sensors	578
		Types of IDS and IPS Sensors	578
		Working with Signatures	581
		Configuring IOS IPS	585
		Summary	597
		Review Questions	598
		Answers to Review Questions	600
Chapter	**17**	**Voice**	**601**
		Introduction to Voice Networks	602
		Converging Voice Traffic	603
		Voice Components	604
		Making a Phone Call	606
		Call Control	606
		Converting and Transmitting Voice	609
		Introduction to QoS for Voice	611
		Configurations for Voice	614
		Switch Configuration	614
		Gateway Configuration	616
		Summary	619
		Review Questions	620
		Answers to Review Questions	622
Chapter	**18**	**DiffServ Quality of Service (QoS)**	**623**
		Introducing QoS	624
		The Problems You Face	625
		Bandwidth	626
		Delay	628
		Packet Loss	630
		Preparing to Implement QoS	631
		Identifying Traffic	632
		Classifying Traffic	633
		Models for Implementing QoS	635
		QoS Mechanisms	637
		Traffic Marking	637
		Queuing	644
		Traffic Conditioning	645
		Congestion Avoidance	646

Configuring QoS	647
Modular QoS CLI	649
SDM QoS Wizard	656
Summary	665
Review Questions	666
Answers to Review Questions	668

Chapter 19   Wireless Devices and Topologies   669

Wireless Fundamentals	670
The 802.11 Standards	672
2.4GHz (802.11b)	674
2.4GHz (802.11g)	676
5GHz (802.11a)	677
5GHz (802.11h)	677
2.4GHz/5GHz (802.11n)	678
Wireless LAN Modulation Techniques	679
Range Comparisons	680
Wireless Devices	681
Wireless Access Points	681
Wireless Network Interface Card (NIC)	681
Wireless Antennas	681
Wireless Topologies	684
Client Access	685
Service Areas	686
Configuring Wireless Clients	687
Installing Cisco Client Adapters	687
Configuring a Profile	691
Checking the Status of Your Connection	694
Diagnostics	695
Wireless Implementation Strategies	698
Autonomous Solution	698
Lightweight Solution	699
Summary	702
Review Questions	703
Answers to Review Questions	705

Chapter 20   Wireless Management and Security   707

Wireless Security	708
Open Access	709
Older Wireless Security Types	710
Temporal Key Integrity Protocol (TKIP)	711
WPA and WPA 2 PSK	712

Wireless QoS   713
   Queuing and Marking for Wireless   713
   Implementing Wireless QoS   715
Configuring Wireless Management Devices   718
   The Wireless Control System   718
   The Wireless LAN Controller   734
Summary   739
Review Questions   741
Answers to Review Questions   743

Appendix   **About the Companion CD**   **745**

What You'll Find on the CD   746
   Sybex Test Engine   746
   PDF of the Book   746
   Adobe Reader   746
System Requirements   747
Using the CD   747
Troubleshooting   747
   Customer Care   748

Glossary   **749**

Acronyms   **813**

Index   *825*

Introduction

When I started this project, I had two requirements and I strived throughout the book to balance both of them. My first requirement comes from being an instructor and consultant for 10 years now. In that time, I have found a consistent void with most of my students and clients. It is not that clients are unwilling to implement new technologies. It is not that students are unable to learn about new technologies. The void is between those two. You learn about new technologies, but often the knowledge you gain does not provide a solid understanding of where in the network the new technology resides. You get design models, learn commands to turn features on and off, but you don't know where to locate the device or why to implement a particular application or feature.

For this reason, I have written this book in the form of a single case study that runs through the entire book. The case study revolves around a single, fictitious company that I created for the sole purpose of explaining where and why technologies should be placed in a real network. I hope that they do not become just objectives in a book for you to memorize. The Real World Scenarios are designed to trigger your thought process and allow you to find practical applications in your own networks.

Speaking of objectives, this brings me to the second requirement for the book. That requirement is to fill a hole in having a single source of information, a place to learn about all of the common technologies used by network engineers today.

To provide an outline for those common technologies, I used the objectives in place as of January 2009 for the Cisco Certified Network Professional (CCNP) certification. It would be difficult to cover every single objective from this certification track in one book, but you will find I have covered a vast majority of the objectives. My hope is that you will find this book a valuable supplemental guide in your studies as you endeavor to attain the coveted CCNP certification.

The challenge was getting as many technologies into the book with enough detail so you would to know where and how to use them. There is not enough room in a single book to cover every possible solution or every single command and option you could use to accomplish a task. I do recommend some of the best and most common ways to accomplish the tasks.

On that note, I hope that my coverage of wireless technologies in the last two chapters of the book will pique your interest in the exciting new technologies in wireless LANs. If you want a more in-depth fundamental look at how wireless networks operate and all of the fun, new toys (I mean wireless devices) that you can use to implement them, then watch for the new CCNA wireless book that Todd Lammle and I are currently writing for Sybex.

Who Should Read This Book

I highly recommend to anyone reading this book to have their CCNA certification or a firm understanding of the objectives and concepts covered. I put so many technologies into this one book, and covered as much of the CCNP material as possible that I didn't have the space required to review all of the CCNA material.

How to Use This Book

This book not only covers many exciting and complex networking topics but shows you the steps required to design a full corporate internetwork. If you follow the chapters in order, I walk you not only through building single VLANs and subnets but through the security, voice, QoS, and wireless technologies you need to implement an entire campus network.

How This Book Is Organized

In Chapter 1, I provide for you an explanation of Cisco's current design methodologies. This includes a discussion on Cisco's Enterprise Composite Design Model and how that model has evolved over the years. Even a little bit about where it may go in the future.

Following the design section of Chapter 1, I break down for you in detail what you can expect to accomplish in each chapter of the book and explain why I organized the book the way I did.

After that, I describe for you the case study that is the framework for the book. This includes background of FutureTech, Inc., the network layout that the company has, and the technologies you are going to implement over the course of the book. You will be acting as the senior network engineer for the company (or the highly paid expert consultant that helps them through the process, if that sounds better to you).

The last thing that I cover in Chapter 1 is the equipment and lab setup you can use to test and practice the technologies and topics you go through in the book. I will give you a breakdown of the topology that I will be using and supplemental equipment that can be used in exchange for the equipment that I have in my setup.

With those details out of the way, I jump right into helping you build your network. Chapter 2 provides the lowdown on switching. Here you get a look at Layer 1 and Layer 2 functionality and access layer devices, creating a strong foundation from which to build the rest of the network. Then, I get into some Layer 3 functions with inter-VLAN routing. In Chapter 3, I walk you through controlling the topology and your connections. By the time you've finished Chapter 3 you will understand all of the functions of STP and how it prevents broadcast storms, multiple frame copies, and protects the stability of the MAC address table.

In Chapters 4 through 7, you learn specifically about the routing process itself and how to give routers the information they require. I cover both static and dynamic routing protocols in depth, along with ways to filter and control the propagation of routing information between routers and routing domains. I also provide you with the means to verify and troubleshoot your network connections.

Chapters 8 through 10 teach you about protocols and functions that make your network more reliable and efficient. In Chapter 8, I cover multicast. Here you learn what makes multicast work and see some of the configurations available to help you cope with increased use of applications and programs that send large amounts of data to a whole group of users. Continuing in this vein in Chapter 9, I give you the nuts and bolts of Internet Protocol version 6 (IPv6). In Chapter 10, I show you how to provide redundancy and load balancing features to your network using just your routers. You learn to configure and use HSRP, VRRP, and GLBP.

In Chapters 11 and 12, I show you how to set up WAN connections, both for small and home offices and major corporate connections. In particular in Chapter 11, I cover DSL and broadband cable technologies, as well as basic frame mode MPLS. In Chapter 12, you learn about Virtual Private Networks (VPN) and use the graphical tool Cisco Security Device Manager to configure a Site-to-Site VPN, a GRE tunnel, and I introduce you to Cisco Easy VPN.

Securing your network is the emphasis in Chapters 13 through 16. In Chapter 13, you learn about the built-in features that are available to secure routing devices, how to use AutoSecure to lock down CLI services, and try out the SDM the Security Audit and One-Step Lockdown wizards. Chapter 14 provides a solid foundation in Layer 2 security. In Chapter 15, I walk you through configuring the firewall with Cisco Security Device Manager (SDM). Chapter 16 takes you into the exciting and ever-changing world of intrusion detection and intrusion prevention.

Voice traffic is introduced in Chapter 17. The primary focus of this chapter is understanding the requirements for carrying voice traffic on the data network that you have been building. In Chapter 18, I cover Quality of Service (QoS). This framework of multiple protocols and mechanisms allows you to control the flow and timing of traffic across your network.

Wireless services, topologies, management, and security are the focus of Chapters 19 and 20. In Chapter 19, I take you through some of the basic devices, wireless clients, and wireless access points (APs), and show you how to configure and operate them. I show you the newest implementation strategy for wireless devices. To wrap things up in Chapter 20, I take you through a whole new line of management devices and software that have been created to help you implement and control the wireless LAN.

At the end of the book you will find two glossaries. I hope that you find them useful. The first glossary is a list of terms and their definitions. The second glossary is a list of acronyms and what they mean. I always tell my students at the beginning of a class to make a vocabulary and acronym list, or if they need more than a list I suggest flash cards. So many times a simple term or abbreviation has prevented a student from understanding or answering a question.

The Book's CD

In addition to a digital copy of this book, the included CD contains many text files from the actual configurations included in the book. It also has a couple of bonus exams so that you can review and ensure that the concepts from the book are sticking with you.

Chapter

1

Enterprise Network Design

IN THIS CHAPTER, YOU WILL LEARN HOW TO DO THE FOLLOWING:

- ✓ Compare methodologies used to design a network
- ✓ Identify network requirements to support the organization
- ✓ Describe the Enterprise Composite Network Model
- ✓ Describe the Cisco Services-Oriented Network Architecture

I start off by showing you the components and practices that will allow you to design and implement a network—not just any network, but the perfect network for a given situation. It will be properly sized and have high availability features throughout. All of the devices will be chosen with the proper resources for the load they will carry. I introduce some design models to help you understand how to connect those devices together and help you ensure that it can grow and remain stable in the future. Basically, you will find out how to make a network that is high speed, low drag, and leaves you the hero. Hopefully with a raise!

For up-to-the-minute updates on this chapter, check out www.sybex.com/go/CiscoProGuidetoInternetworking or www.lammle.com.

The Three-Layer Hierarchical Design Model

For years, the three-layer model has been used to design and evaluate networks with a good amount of success. The three-layer model, as shown in Figure 1.1, provided you with three design areas. The three layers are the access, distribution, and core layers. Using a layered approach allows a network designer to logically define the network in terms of functions and devices. The result is a network that can be easily managed and has deterministic failure built in.

Concept: Deterministic Failure

Although no one wants a device or link to fail, every seasoned network administrator knows that failures occur. Deterministic failure allows you to implement secondary or standby devices to take over for a failed primary or permits a redundant link to relieve the traffic load for a downed link. Deterministic failure allows you to predict exactly how a network will respond when a device or link fails.

FIGURE 1.1   Three-layer hierarchical design model

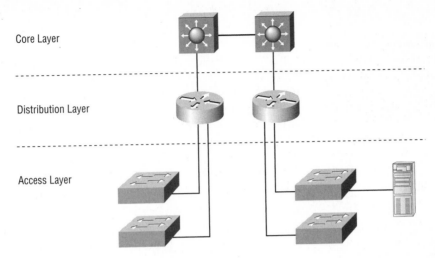

Access Layer   The access layer connects all of the hosts and user workstations. This layer uses switches with high port density or the lowest cost per port device. The switch devices in this layer should also have the ability to make or use higher speed uplinks to the other layers. Depending on the switch platform that is used, there might be built-in uplink ports that have greater bandwidth capacity. It may also be necessary to create and use EtherChannel links from the access layer to the other layers. Those uplinks should be redundant so that the loss of any one link does not prevent the traffic from getting out of the access layer. Normally, the redundant connections in the access layer are Layer 2 connections, which means Spanning Tree Protocol (STP) controls the forwarding and blocked links preventing loops in this area of the network. I discuss STP in Chapter 3, "Spanning Tree Protocol."

Concept: EtherChannel

EtherChannel is a feature that allows you to bind together more than one interface, which gives the switch a higher bandwidth connection between devices. I cover EtherChannel later in Chapter 2, "Switching."

Distribution Layer   The distribution layer serves as the aggregation point for all of the access layer networks and devices. Filtering and security are implemented here. It is the point in the network where routing and filtering decisions are made. Features such as quality of service (QoS) policies, access control lists (ACLs), and route filtering should also be placed at this layer.

Distribution layer devices must have the capacity to process and forward traffic from all of the connected devices. Here, you will find all the redundant connections from access layer devices, as well as redundant connections to the core layer.

Core Layer   The core layer primarily provides high-speed transport for data. There should be very little manipulation of the data in this layer. No filtering or access lists are found here. All of the connections in and out of the core layer should be redundant for high availability. The redundant links in the core layer and down to the distribution layer devices are usually routed or Layer 3 links. Having a routing protocol determine which links are used makes the time to transition from the primary link to the secondary link much shorter than when STP is being used. I discuss this difference later in the chapter.

You might be asking right now, "What if my network isn't large enough for all of those layers?"

Well, that is a very good point. Not all networks require all three layers. In fact, many small- and medium-sized networks are designed with only two. The functions of all three layers still exist and are still necessary. In these networks, the distribution and core layers are pushed together in what is called a collapsed core design. The collapsed core design allows for a simplified and cost effective network.

The three-layer model has been very successful due to its simplicity. However, the requirements for networks today have increased tremendously and require a more detailed and feature-rich model for design. This complexity has brought about the Enterprise Composite Network Model.

Enterprise Composite Network Model

The Enterprise Composite Network Model was introduced to provide a more detailed strategy for designing networks. Previous design models did not define how to make specific connections or how the network should expand over time. Networks, therefore, grew with no direction. Network administrators had little control over the way networks reacted to change.

To ensure that this doesn't happen to your network, I'm going to show you some design practices and components that will give you a scalable and highly available network for years to come. We all need job security and these techniques will make you the rock star of your network!

The Enterprise Composite Network Model is based on the three-layer model. The new model is broken into more pieces, so we can more easily define their function and physical connections. Figure 1.2 shows the areas of the model that I'll cover.

In the Figure 1.2, you can see that the design model has three main pieces or modules.

- Enterprise Campus
- Enterprise Edge
- Service Provider Edge

Each of these pieces is further divided to define specific distinct functions for the network.

FIGURE 1.2 Enterprise Composite Network Model

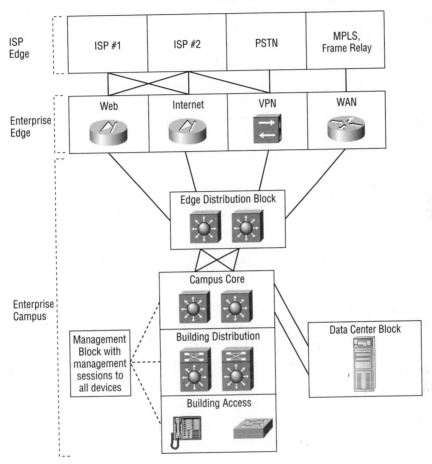

Enterprise Campus

The Enterprise Campus section of the network is the real meat and potatoes in the design. It houses all of the local area networks (LANs). LANs start by connecting the users and end devices. Connecting LANs gives a path through the network to the core or backbone, which provides a central connection point for everything in the network. In the following sections, I'll introduce you to each of the components that make up this area of the network. Figure 1.3 shows the components in the Enterprise Campus Module.

FIGURE 1.3 Enterprise Campus Module

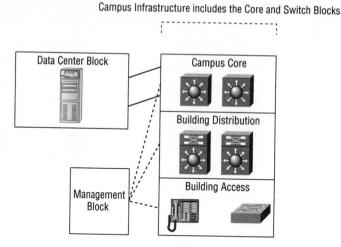

Campus Infrastructure includes the Core and Switch Blocks

Campus Infrastructure Module

The Campus Infrastructure Module is really made up of two primary building blocks for a network: the switch block and the campus core.

A switch block is often referred to as a building switch block because a campus with multiple buildings often has a separate switch block for each building. The switch block is a combination of the access layer and the distribution layer for a particular part of the network. The part of the network that a switch block represents depends on a couple of things, first of which is the number of users or end devices in the switch block. The second major factor is the type and amount of traffic that will be transmitted through it. I'll cover the different types of traffic and the effects on the network in much greater detail later in the book.

The second piece of the Campus Infrastructure Module is the campus backbone. Like the core block described in the three-layer model, the campus backbone is in place to transport data as quickly and efficiently as possible. It is the central point in the network and carries all of the traffic from the building switch blocks, edge block, and server farm block. Since it will carry all of that traffic, the backbone must be sized to handle at least the sum of traffic that all of the distribution switches carry. The backbone of a network today is often implemented as a Layer 3 (the network layer in the open-systems interconnection (OSI) model) or routed core. With the vast improvements in multilayer switches in recent years, there is not the huge performance loss using a routed solution. I'll tell you about the benefits of multilayer switches in Chapter 2, "Switching." A routed core provides link redundancy and failover. Routing protocols have the ability to load balance across multiple links and utilize whatever path may be left after a failure. The benefit of using multiple links is not the only thing a Layer 3 core provides. Routing protocols give much more control in determining what links will be used when a failure occurs, and the time a routing protocol takes to fail over the link is much shorter than what spanning tree protocol (STP) can provide in a Layer 2 solution.

Network Management Block

The next component in the Enterprise Campus is the Network Management Block. Enterprise networks today, with their vast number of devices and services, must be managed with a management tool or an entire suite of tools and applications. In the past, a management network or virtual local area network (VLAN) that spanned the entire network was setup for monitoring and management. In today's networks, however, spanning a single network or VLAN across the entire network is considered poor practice. It provides no way to control the amount of traffic that would be going across every layer of the enterprise. To prevent this practice, it is now recommended that management addresses and subnets be assigned to all of the devices being monitored. Some devices can be configured specifically with the addresses and names of the management devices that will be monitoring them. Others though will have to be configured with access lists and filtering so that they only allow management devices from a specific subnet to access them. This allows all of the management applications to be located within the management block and still be capable of monitoring the devices across the enterprise. Some of the most common items included in the management block are:

- Monitoring applications
- Security management, policy, and intrusion detection
- Alarm and logging servers
- AAA servers (for authentication, authorization, and accounting)

Server Farm Block

The Server Farm Block allows for the physical collocation and consolidation of most, if not all, of the servers and applications that the vast majority of users in the enterprise will access. The Server Farm Block, like the other blocks, needs redundant connections between the access switches and the distribution switches, and between the distribution switches and the core switches. However, with the high availability of the servers and applications in this block, the hosts, which are the servers in this case, will also have redundancy built in. Most servers today can be multihomed. A multihomed server has at least two separate connections to the network. In this case, the server could have a separate connection to two different switches in the block, allowing it to have redundant paths should any one device fail.

Enterprise Edge

The Enterprise Edge is truly another switch block. It connects to the campus core in the Enterprise Infrastructure with redundant links and redundant distribution switches, just as any other switch block in the network would. The difference between this block and the other blocks is in the devices that you put into the Enterprise Edge. The Enterprise Edge provides connections out of the Enterprise network. Those connections fall into a few different categories and each category defines the type of device that will be placed there. Let's take a look at each of the different categories that make up the foundation for this block.

Internet Connection   The first and most common type of connection in and out of the enterprise is an Internet connection. This connection provides access for all enterprise users to external web servers, e-mail, and any other public service. Depending on the importance and the amount of traffic going in and out to the Internet this connection can be redundant. The amount of bandwidth that you get for this connection is most often determined by the amount of money that you are willing to spend. The bandwidth of a connection is determined by the service provider and usually comes in increments—the more you pay, the wider the bandwidth.

WAN Connection   The wide area network (WAN) connection provides access to other locations throughout the enterprise. Branch offices and other remote sites, located too far away to install and maintain your own cables, will have WAN connections installed between them and the rest of your enterprise. Again, bandwidth and connection types vary based on the amount of money that you want to spend, but they can also differ based on the type of connection available from a service provider in the city where the branch office is located. Many types of WAN connections can be purchased today; some of them have been around for a very long time. They can include frame relay, asynchronous transfer mode (ATM), leased lines, integrated services digital network (ISDN), and multi-protocol label switching (MPLS). I tell you about MPLS in Chapter 11, "WAN and Teleworker Connections." I don't spend a lot of time describing the other technologies, but you should have learned about frame relay and leased lines when you were studying for the Cisco Certified Network Associate (CCNA) certification.

Remote Access Connections   The remote access connections usually refer to dial-up connections that can be made into the network. These connections allow remote workers to gain access to enterprise resources while away from the office. This type of connection is made over the public switched telephone network (PSTN).

VoIP Connections   Since I am talking about telephone lines and connections made to a phone company, it is important to realize that the internal enterprise phone system still requires external phone line connections. External phone connections will be made at this location in the network if you have a voice over IP phone (VoIP) system. The VoIP system still requires you to have outside lines connecting it to the outside world. These lines allow calls made to a number that is not internal or on the enterprise phone system.

VPN Connections   The last type of connection I want to mention is hopefully replacing most of the dial-up connections that users have made for years. Virtual private network (VPN) connections provide a secure tunnel in which to pass data from a remote site or user to the enterprise edge. The secure tunnel is carried over an unsecure or untrusted network. Most often, that network is the Internet. Using a VPN, a simple and cheap connection can be made to the office. The flexibility it gives users is also a huge benefit. Almost anywhere a user can get a connection to the Internet, they can have a secure tunnel back to the office to access e-mail and other resources. Now, whether they view this ability as a benefit or a leash connecting them 24/7 to work, that is up for discussion.

Service Provider Edge

The service provider edge is often a network engineer's favorite part of the entire network design. This piece of the design model is here to signify where the physical connections to various service providers terminate. There is very little or no equipment in this module that must be maintained by you or your enterprise network engineering team. Other than the occasional disagreement with a service provider about whose fault an outage was, there shouldn't be anything that you have to do or maintain here.

IIN and SONA

IIN or Intelligent Information Network is more of a vision for future design and implementation strategy in a network. IIN combines the functions of applications and the network, allowing the network to make better and smarter decisions about how to move and direct traffic. By placing some of the intelligence in the network, it reduces the amount of influence any one application has to have on the network. The enterprise composite model is the basis for the IIN to be built on. The IIN adds functionality to what the network already does. IIN is described in a three-phase approach.

Phase 1   Integrated system describes the intelligent movement of data, voice, and video across a system of networks. It is where the underlying composite designed network is used.

Phase 2   Integrated services describe virtualized networking resources. Their usefulness has become apparent in the shift to using virtual servers and storage. It also extends past just the use of virtualized servers and moves into network devices. You can already begin to see single devices such as routers and firewalls with the ability to appear and operate as multiple virtual instances, replacing what would have been a group of many individual devices.

Phase 3   Integrated applications or application-aware networks and services are the parts of phase 3. We can already witness the beginning of where this exciting idea can go. Through the use of Network Admission Control (NAC), the network can detect a host machine attaching to the network. From the point of connections, NAC can authenticate; scan the host for antivirus software, which can be checked to make sure it is up to date; and then configure the physical port to access the appropriate VLAN to which the device should be connected. This process enables the network devices to grant and authorize access only when a device authenticated. All of those functions can be controlled through central policies. In the past, each of those functions would have been controlled and configured separately, making their management an administrative nightmare.

SONA or Services-Oriented Network Architecture is the true implementation strategy for IIN. SONA has three layers of implementation that correlate to the three phases on IIN. Those layers are listed here in order respective to phase 1 through 3 of the IIN.

- Network system layer
- Integrated network service layer
- Application layer

Case Study: FutureTech Corporation

In today's networks, you have to know many different technologies and functions. Keeping track of where in the network items are used and deployed can become difficult. Many of the functions have dependencies, so you'll need to track those relationships to each function. Some of the processes you run can be on independent devices, and keeping track of the fact that they may not play well with other devices can be a real pain in the neck. To aid you in keeping track of where in the network you plan to deploy and implement all of the technologies covered in this book, I'm going to use a single enterprise network example. For this purpose, I created a fictional company named FutureTech Corporation. The name and all examples of this company are entirely fictitious and do not in any way represent a real company, named or otherwise.

FutureTech will serve as the basis of our case study. As I move you through each topic in the book, I will relate back to this overall network example to better show you where in a real network a technology can be used and for what specific purpose.

I am going to ask you, the reader, to put yourself in the place of a senior network engineer for FutureTech. As I move through the technologies in this book, you can think about designing this network, basically from the ground up. The design process that I am going to take you through will be somewhat of a parallel path using two design guides everyone should be now familiar with. I am going to use the OSI model as the first guide, starting off at Layers 1 and 2, then moving through the layers to add applications and new technologies to the network.

As I start building the network with the OSI model, the second guide will be the Enterprise Composite Network Model. Since the fundamental building block of the enterprise model is the switch block, my discussion starts there. I'll show you how the different types of switch blocks will be built layer by layer.

Book Organization

With that in mind, this book begins with the OSI model. I start with switching (Layer 2) that has Layer 1 connections and cables scattered through it. Then, I go through the routing and all of the routing protocols. The routing chapters help tie the layers of a switch block, allow me to show you how the switch blocks will be linked, and ultimately bring you into the core of the network.

Following the routing protocols, I cover a couple of other Layer 3 functions that, if not now, will soon be placed into all enterprise networks. These topics include Internet Protocol version 6 (IPv6) and multicast routing. I immediately follow those protocols with WANs, VPNs, and remote access connections. This will tie another switch block, the Enterprise Edge, into the network. You will see how all of those services are provided and brought into the enterprise.

After all of the switch blocks have been built, I continue up the OSI model, adding services and higher layer functions into the network. Some of the later topics may actually reside or use protocols in lower layers of the OSI; however, you need a good foundation in the network design before you can add them into your network.

At this point, you will add security to the network. Most of the network's framework will be constructed, and you need to make sure that it is secure and protected from possible attack. I cover securing Layer 2 and the associated devices followed by the same for Layer 3 and the devices found there. You will learn how to configure the internetwork operating system (IOS) Firewall and intrusion prevention system (IPS) services on a router.

Once your security is in place, I take you through some network convergence and traffic management topics. Many of you have or soon will be adding voice traffic and applications to your network and you will have to understand the effects of that traffic to properly finish the design.

Finally, I round out the book with wireless local area network (WLAN) functions. I discuss WLAN last not because it is a higher layer protocol or function, but because again not everyone uses or implements wireless technologies. However, a lot of new and exciting enhancements can be made to networks today with the use of wireless devices.

FutureTech Company Background

FutureTech is a globally scaled, advanced, technology company. The company designs, develops, and distributes thousands of products for businesses and government agencies all over the world.

Figure 1.4 gives you an overall view of where the company headquarters, primary offices, branch offices, manufacturing plants, and remote offices are located. Notice that the FutureTech enterprise network includes:

- VPN connections for branch offices and remote users
- Multi-protocol label switching (MPLS) connections for its WAN connections
- Redundant connections to separate Internet service providers (ISP) that provide high availability to the enterprise

Enterprise Network Design Details

From that broad overview, the company can be broken into smaller pieces with the different technologies applied. By technologies, I mean all of the concepts I cover through the course of this book. I start at the bottom of the OSI model and in the Enterprise Campus module of the composite design model. The enterprise network will have multiple switch blocks, but most of them have similar design topics and all of them have access and distribution layer devices and protocols.

Layers 1 and 2

Using a global company gives the ability to use and see just about every technology that a network administrator could want. I start out by showing you a small single piece of the network. That small piece is typically called a switch block. Remember that a switch block is usually a single building on a campus setting or a whole floor in a large building. It might even be a branch office or department-size piece of the network.

FIGURE 1.4   FutureTech VPN Connections and Physical Plant Locations

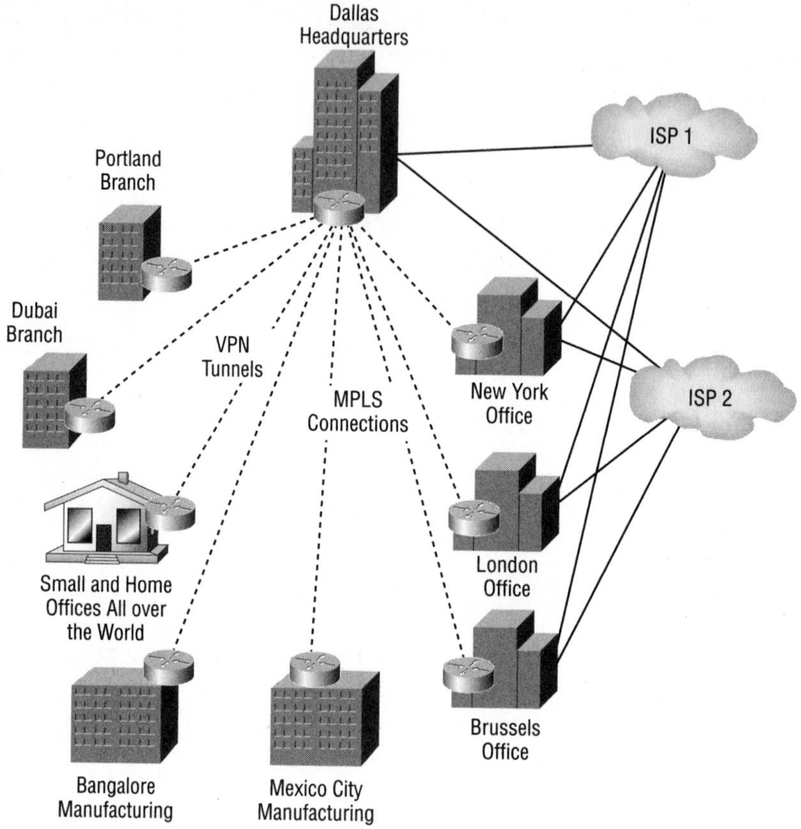

Starting in this small setting, you will be able to explore access and distribution layer devices. I can also begin showing you Layer 2 functions, since the access layer is primarily made up of Layer 2 switches. I'll show you the protocols and functions that you can use to connect them and provide resiliency and availability. Through the course of the book, I will cover the most common network devices in detail and show you how to configure them.

In the access layers of the network, port density—meaning the number and amount of users and data that can be taken into the network—is the issue that most concerns network administrators. Many different types of switches can be used to address this issue.

Each of the different parts of the network has different numbers of users. The headquarters building, for instance, could have as many as 25,000 users. With that number of people, a network could have between 10 and 50 switch blocks depending on how you break up the users. Moving through the other size buildings, offices, and the branch offices, the number of users is obviously going to be different. Each could have as few as 100 to 500 users; with this number of users the network may require only a single switch block to connect the entire building.

As you go through the book, I show you how to configure even these Layer 2 devices for security, quality of service (QoS), redundancy, voice, and other types of converged traffic conditions. You will see how these devices handle different types of traffic, as well as the effects on all of the other devices you implement. You will also have to think about the load each device will have to accommodate.

Layer 3

Moving from the access layer specifically into the distribution layer brings other challenges and more protocols to explore. Most common will be the wide range of routing protocols. Routing protocols allow you to connect all of the networks and VLANs in the access layer. I will walk you through the most common routing protocols, starting off with distance vector protocols such as routing information protocol (RIP) and interior gateway routing protocol (IGRP). You will see how they can be used in smaller networks or in places where you need to keep the overhead on a router's processor down.

In areas of the network where administrators have to plan for much larger deployments with more routers and more connected networks, I show you how to use enhanced interior gateway routing protocol (EIGRP), open shortest path first (OSPF), and integrated intermediate system to intermediate system (IS-IS). Each of these protocols has distinct benefits and drawbacks. For example, EIGRP has the ability to provide fast convergence and loop-free operation, as well as routing for multiple network layer protocols. However, it is a Cisco proprietary protocol and can only be run in a homogeneous Cisco environment.

Core Layer or Backbone   The backbone of the network is supposed to move data as fast as possible without changing it. So at this point, I'll show you the different ways to configure the core of the network and the advantages and disadvantages of each. In the past, the core of the network was always a Layer 2 structured design. I will show you some of the ways a Layer 3 setup can provide a more deterministic flow of traffic and increase reliability when there is a failure. You will see how STP handles a link that has gone down, and then compare that to the way a routing protocol handles the same link failure.

Enterprise Edge   Moving out of FutureTech's primary internal infrastructure into the service provider's network requires an understanding of how and where to make external connections. Those external connections fall into the Internet, WAN, and remote access/VPN categories. Many companies today use connectivity that differs from the traditional WANs of years past. One of the most common types of new connections is the VPN. VPNs can be used to connect branch offices and home offices to the primary enterprise. VPN client software loaded on almost any personal computer or laptop can give a single user the ability to connect to the enterprise from all most anywhere they have an Internet connection.

Internet Connectivity   Internet connectivity might require you to route between your network and the ISP. In this case, I'll show you the uses and complexities of border gateway protocol (BGP). You're probably already aware that BGP is a routing protocol that falls into the exterior gateway protocols (EGP) category. With the decision to use BGP comes a much larger responsibility and the need for a working knowledge of its operation. Being that FutureTech has redundant Internet connections and multiple ISPs, the use of BGP will allow the network a much more consistent presence on the Internet, as well as higher availability.

Wide Area Network (WAN) Of course, while considering ISP connections, I will talk about ways to connect parts of the FutureTech network. Traditionally, these connections are made using WAN protocols such as frame relay or dedicated circuits like T1 and T3. I'll help you explore a newer and nontraditional connection type; that newer type of WAN offering is MPLS. MPLS isn't available in all geographic areas or through all service providers, but it can be obtained from more and more ISPs all the time. MPLS has many of the same characteristics of older protocols but with a bunch of new benefits. Some of the benefits are not immediately apparent to the customer or even in your network, but they allow the ISP to make service offerings that were either not possible before or were much more costly and complex to implement. These services allow users to make connections and move data between sites and other companies in ways that were not possible with other protocols.

Virtual Private Network (VPN) Many of you, I am sure, have at least heard of VPNs, but maybe you haven't used them. You will see how they connect people and networks like never before. VPNs provide a way to connect remote users and offices with much greater bandwidth and service than they ever had with dial-up. You'll also get a look at how a VPN can provide a different way to make a WAN connection. These VPN connections can serve as a primary connection or a backup connection to an already existing WAN circuit of a different type. How and where to use them depends on load constraints and the importance of dedicated bandwidth.

Concept: VPNs

I want to make a quick distinction between the two different types of VPNs. Most people are at least vaguely familiar with a security VPN, a VPN that is secured with the use of a protocol such as internet protocol security (IPSec). There is another type of VPN, primarily used by service providers, that is a multiprotocol label switching (MPLS) VPN. Service providers use MPLS VPNs to separate and manage traffic as it travels across their network to different customers.

Security, Convergence, and Upper Layer Applications

At this point in the design, you will learn to add features to the framework that you have built up to now. The complexity and high use of networks today requires that you efficiently manage and keep secure every piece of the network. The different kinds of traffic that you could experience on a network will have their own challenges and requirements. I will explain the many different security, management, and convergence features that are available.

Network Management and Security Because there are so many types of traffic to be handled and many new regulations to be adhered to, the topic of security is more important than ever. So, to make the task of securing your network easier and less error prone, new features are built right into the routers and switches that you use every day. These new features include one-step lockdown wizards, fully configurable stateful firewalls, and intrusion prevention systems. All of these run on our good ol' routers and switches.

In addition to the configurable security features, routers and switches now have the ability to generate alerts and warnings when less than desirable conditions exist. All of those messages can be sent to management stations for proper action and documentation. To get these messages sent, you have to add a few other configurations, so I will show you how to set up logging, authentication, authorization, and accounting. The authentication, authorization, and accounting functions are also known as AAA for short. Additional protocols facilitate their actions. I will cover remote dial-in user service (RADIUS) and terminal access control access control service plus (TACACS+).

Converged Data and Traffic Management   I have already mentioned a couple of the other exciting things that are going to be added into the FutureTech network. Voice traffic will require some extra configurations on the switches and routers. It will most likely require the use of quality of service (QoS). There will also be some discussion about where all the backend voice equipment will be placed and the requirements for those devices.

Looking to the Future

FutureTech as a whole will have to consider and plan for other types of traffic, as well as changes that are coming in the information technology (IT) industry. The requirement to provide more data and different kinds of data is becoming more important and more of a challenge every day. Like your fictional counterparts, you have to be on top of all things that are changing and new. A huge change that is not far on the horizon is Internet Protocol version 6 (IPv6). We work in a great field that is always giving way to better things and new ways to do them. It can be exciting if you like a challenge or get bored doing the same thing all of the time like I do!

Multicast and Video   With a global company, you know there are going to be a bunch of meetings (pointless or otherwise). It will be up to you to make sure everyone can attend. That could mean some new cool video equipment to play with! Along with video and some other cool applications, like online training and webcasts, comes the need to transmit data a little differently. It requires sending a large amount of data out onto the network so many people can access and use it. A ton of bandwidth will be needed unless we use something called multicast. Multicast provides just what is needed; it sends a large volume of data to a group of end users or devices in a single stream of data.

Internet Protocol version 6 (IPv6)   Internet Protocol version 6 (IPv6) is the next generation of network layer protocols. It provides many benefits over the current Internet Protocol version 4 (IPv4) that is in use today. The most prevalent of the improvements is the size and number of available addresses in the address space. IPv4 uses 32-bit addresses that provide a maximum of 4.29 billion addresses and, out of those addresses, fewer than half are actually usable. With IPv6 you have a 128-bit address, which provides a maximum number of 3.4×10^{38} addresses. Yes, that is a ton of addresses. In fact, it is thousands of addresses for every person. You will be able to have your computers, phones, cars, televisions, refrigerators, and toasters on the Internet. Well, maybe we don't need the toaster, but if I could remotely make toast that could be cool!

I show you how to implement IPv6 into enterprise networks. It is going to take more than a one-night maintenance window to get this done. For that reason, I show you a few migration techniques that you can use to help make the transition less painful and more deliberate. Three of them will be covered in a little more detail:

- Dual stacking
- Tunneling (manual and automatic called 6t04 tunneling)
- Network Address Translation - Protocol Translation (NAT-PT)

Concept: NAT-PT

This type of NAT is not like the NAT in IPv4, where one IPv4 address is translated to another. This is protocol translation that allows translation between IPv4 addresses and IPv6 addresses.

Wireless Local Area Network (WLAN)   Another fast-growing area in enterprise networking is the use of wireless local area networks (WLANs). Wireless networks have more presence and available devices than ever before. I will help you explore the entire new line of devices that make configuration and management of WLAN environments much simpler and consistent to implement. As with anything, but especially for WLAN, security is a huge concern. The transmission of data on a wireless network is unbounded. There is less control over where the transmission is being sent. You don't have to worry about an attacker sitting in the parking lot and just listening to data that is passing over a wire like you do with wireless data. I'll help you look closely at the security considerations of deploying wireless devices.

Test Network

Now, you can't just start turning on all of these things in a production network. A test environment suitable for practicing and testing is needed. For the purpose of a test network for FutureTech, I have set up a network topology. The test network, as I will refer to it from here on out, is primarily a group of routers and switches that are connected, basically in a full mesh setup. This configuration allows all the different configurations and technologies to be tested without messing up any real production networks. Figure 1.5 shows you a network diagram of the primary test network.

The information in Table 1.1 will help you keep track of all of the connections between the devices.

FIGURE 1.5   FutureTech Test Network Diagram

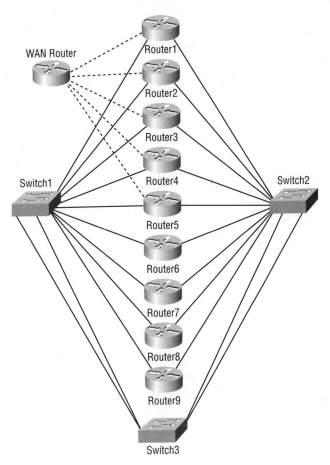

TABLE 1.1   Connections between Devices for Test Network

Source Device and Interface	Destination Device and Interface
Switch1 - Fa0/1	Router1 - Fa0/0
Switch1 - Fa0/2	Router2 - Fa0/0
Switch1 - Fa0/3	Router3 - Fa0/0
Switch1 - Fa0/4	Router4 - Fa0/0
Switch1 - Fa0/5	Router5 - Fa0/0

TABLE 1.1 Connections between Devices for Test Network *(continued)*

Source Device and Interface	Destination Device and Interface
Switch1 - Fa0/6	Router6 - Fa0/0
Switch1 - Fa0/9	Router7 - Fa0/0
Switch1 - Fa0/10	Router8 - Fa0/0
Switch1 - Fa0/11	Router9 - Fa0/0
Switch2 - Fa0/1	Router1 - Fa0/1
Switch2 - Fa0/2	Router2 - Fa0/1
Switch2 - Fa0/3	Router3 - Fa0/1
Switch2 - Fa0/4	Router4 - Fa0/1
Switch2 - Fa0/5	Router5 - Fa0/1
Switch2 - Fa0/6	Router6 - Fa0/1
Switch2 - Fa0/9	Router7 - Fa0/1
Switch2 - Fa0/10	Router8 - Fa0/1
Switch2 - Fa0/11	Router9 - Fa0/1
Switch1 - Fa0/19	Switch2 - Fa0/19
Switch1 - Fa0/20	Switch2 - Fa0/20
Switch1 - Fa0/21	Switch3 - Fa0/21
Switch1 - Fa0/22	Switch3 - Fa0/22
Switch2 - Fa0/7	Switch3 - Fa0/7
Switch2 - Fa0/8	Switch3 - Fa0/8

TABLE 1.1 Connections between Devices for Test Network *(continued)*

Source Device and Interface	Destination Device and Interface
WAN Router - S1	Router1 - S0/0/0
WAN Router - S2	Router2 - S0/0/0
WAN Router - S3	Router3 - S0/0/0
WAN Router - S4	Router4 - S0/0/0
WAN Router - S5	Router5 - S0/0/0
WAN Router - S6	Router6 - S0/0/0
WAN Router - S9	Router7 - S0/0/0
Router1 - S0/0/1	Router3 - S0/0/1
Router7 - S0/0/1	Router8 - S0/0/0

In Table 1.2, you can see a list of the actual device models that I use in the test network.

TABLE 1.2 My Equipment List

Test Network Device Name	Device Model or Type
Routers 1 through 9	Cisco 2811 ISR with WIC-2T interfaces
Switches 1 through 3	Cisco Catalyst 3560 24 port
WAN router	Cisco 2522 router with 8 serial ports

A caveat about the devices that I used in the test network: if you don't have access to exactly the models of routers that I have used, that is okay. I am going to give you some pointers about other devices that you can use as replacements. I have chosen this topology and these devices for flexibility and the gear's ability to be used for most any test configuration you might need. By that, I mean this network allows you to test all the configurations in this book, and is perfect for future studies all the way to Cisco Certified Internetwork Expert (CCIE) Routing and Switching and CCIE Service Provider.

Switches   I used the 3560 switches because they will support all the functions you might need, even for CCIE. You could use a 3550 switch, but it won't support all of the QoS and

IPv6 functions needed for the CCIE. The switches in your test setup must be multilayer switches with the proper code to support all the routing protocols.

Here is one thing that might save you just a little cash. Cisco has made a great 3560 switch that only has eight ports. It has all the same functionality, but costs less because it is smaller. However, you only have eight ports and an uplink, so with the number of routers I use in the examples and trunk links to the other switches, you won't have enough ports. You could scale down the size of the test network, though, to make this switch a cost-effective solution.

Routers   The routers are a little more difficult. By more difficult, I mean it is harder to explain why I chose these particular models and present all of the options to consider when choosing your router models. There are quite a few router models that are okay for use. This is good as, hopefully, it means having more of them available to you.

The biggest differentiator to look for is whether the router runs a 12.4 version of code. Version 12.4 is the newest version of code and supports all of the functions you need to study. The other big thing, both for the exercises in this book and for studying for your Cisco Certified Network Professional (CCNP) certification, your router will have to support the Secure Device Manager (SDM).

Concept: The Secure Device Manager

The SDM is a router flash memory resident graphical user interface (GUI). SDM supports a wide range of Cisco IOS software releases and is available free of charge on Cisco router models from Cisco 830 series to Cisco 7301. The SDM can be accessed by making a hypertext transport protocol (HTTP) or hypertext transport protocol secure (HTTPS) connection to the router. A Java-based applet will then open in your browser and allow you to configure and modify the router. Some CCNP objectives must be accomplished through this interface. I include explanations of this interface and how to use it where applicable.

Other routers that can meet your needs   Table 1.3 is a list of alternate routers that support both the SDM and version 12.4 code requirements.

TABLE 1.3   Alternative Routers

Router Model	SDM	Version 12.4 code
830 Series	Can be run	At least one version can run
850 series	Preinstalled	Preinstalled
870 series	Preinstalled	Preinstalled
1700 series	Can be run	At least one version can run

TABLE 1.3 Alternative Routers *(continued)*

Router Model	SDM	Version 12.4 code
1800 series	Preinstalled	Preinstalled
2800 series	Preinstalled	Preinstalled
2600 XM series	Can be run	At least one version can run
3600 series	Can be run	At least one version can run
3700 series	Can be run	At least one version can run
3800 series	Preinstalled	Preinstalled
7200 VXR series	Can be run	At least one version can run
7301 series	Can be run	At least one version can run

Buyer Beware

I have a couple of things you should look out for when choosing different models of routers. First, the 800 series models of routers don't always include a full version of the SDM. There is a "lite" version of the software called Express SDM. It does not provide all of the functionality that the full version does.

The second caution that I offer to you, and I know this is hard because you might have to buy the equipment yourself: Don't just buy the cheapest model that you can get. For instance, the 800 series again are pretty much a fixed interface router. They don't have any module bays so you can't add other interfaces or functionality. Even the 1700 and 1800 series routers don't have all the necessary module bays. Depending on the model, they have between one and four WAN interface card (WIC) slots that allow the installation of high-performance WAN interface cards (HWIC) and voice WAN interface cards (VWIC). They don't, however, have network module (NM) bays. Depending on your needs and what you plan to configure, this may or may not be a big deal. It is something you should look at though.

Wireless Equipment

I add a few more things to this network before all of the testing is done. For example, when I get to the wireless sections, I include much of the new equipment for practice. You will get look at the new Wireless LAN controller devices, as well as the new lightweight access points.

You'll even get a glimpse of a few really cool new devices and management suites that make a WLAN run smoother and much easier to manage. The management suite for Cisco WLANs is the Wireless Control System (WCS). This is a great GUI that provides central management of all your lightweight wireless equipment. If you are not familiar with the lightweight solution, fasten your seatbelt. I cover all the new protocols and setup for this exciting new offering.

The other new device I mentioned is the 2710 Location Appliance. The location appliance allows you to track clients and active radio frequency identification (RFID) tags. The great thing about this device is that it allows you to track, in real time, all of the devices on your network.

I show you how all of these things work and what they look like under the hood. Table 1.4 provides a list of devices that I will use for examples in this book.

TABLE 1.4   Wireless Test Equipment

Type	Device
Wireless LAN controllers (WLC)	4402 series controller
	2006 series controller
	NM-WLC embedded controller
Lightweight access points (LAP)	1242 series
	1000 series
Mesh access points	1510 series
	1522 series
Location appliance	2710 series
Wireless Control System (WCS)	WCS Location version for Windows Server 2003

That sums up my discussion on devices for now. Remember, this is just a brief introduction to get you started. Now, hopefully, you can start to gather some gear to begin testing the topics I am going to cover in this book. It is imperative that you have some real equipment to practice and test configurations on—not only for testing and certification purposes but to test that you are able to properly implement new technology into your network.

Alternative Wireless Hardware

If you don't have any of the APs I'm using in the test network, you might be able use ones that you already have. Some of the access points (APs) that have been out on the market from Cisco for a while can be upgraded to act as a lightweight AP. These APs can be controlled by a WLC. I am going to show you some of them. Both the 1100 and 1200 series access points are upgradeable.

There is also a new series of APs and WLCs that you can get. They are called the express versions. These controllers and APs are for smaller deployments, in small- and medium-sized businesses (SMB). They typically support a smaller number of APs and don't offer all of the functions that would be used in a large enterprise implementation. The express devices can be a good place to start in learning about lightweight WLANs. They are included in the objectives for the CCNA Wireless concentration certification.

Here is a list of those devices:

- Cisco 526 Wireless Express Mobility Controller
- Cisco 521 Wireless Express Access Point

Summary

Wow, the first chapter is down! You have covered quite a few things here already. Remember, the chapter started off looking at how networks used to be designed with the three-layer hierarchical design model. You'll want to remember the three layers (access, distribution, and core) and their basic functions in a network.

From the basic three-layer model, you moved on to the Enterprise Composite Network Model. The enterprise model provides a much more detailed explanation of which devices should be used and how they should be connected. The easiest way to remember the enterprise model is to start out with the three major areas—Enterprise Campus, Enterprise Edge, and Service Provider Edge. You learned about the pieces that make up the Enterprise Campus because that is where network administrators spend most of their time and money. The Enterprise Campus is made up of the Campus Infrastructure Module, Server Farm Block, and the Network Management Module. Now, with that better understanding of both the design models, you can see that the original three-layer model is still used but it's called the Campus Infrastructure piece of the larger enterprise model.

Don't forget about the Enterprise Edge. Without that piece, your network would not be connected to any one outside of your company. The edge has subsections as well. If you remember, there is the Internet module, WAN module, and the remote access/VPN module.

Each module provides a separate and distinct connection in and out of the enterprise, each with its own services.

Next, I briefly introduced you to the SONA and IIN strategies, both of which are used to help bring about change and future implementation ideas for the networks of tomorrow. With an idea for future paths and where to go, we can provide smarter networks and more compatible technologies for later.

Finally, I gave you a broad overview of the FutureTech case study that will be built on for the duration of this book. At this point, you should have a basic understanding of the areas of the network that I'll help you work through. The test network provides a great way to ensure that everything placed in the network works together and a good understanding of effects they have on other devices, protocols, and applications.

Get ready for a ride through some of the newest, most exciting, and essential topics for network engineers today.

Review Questions

1. What is the fundamental building block of a network design?

   A. Switch block

   B. Core

   C. Campus infrastructure

   D. Edge

2. What was Cisco's original design model called?

   A. IIN

   B. SONA

   C. Three-layer hierarchical model

   D. Enterprise composite

3. What part of the Enterprise Campus design model does most of the network fall into?

   A. Enterprise Campus

   B. Data Center

   C. Network Management

   D. Edge

4. What is the bottom component in a switch block?

   A. Edge

   B. Core

   C. Access layer

   D. Data center

5. What piece of the network has always been characterized as just needing to move data as fast as possible without data manipulation?

   A. Edge

   B. Core

   C. Access layer

   D. Data center

6. The Enterprise Edge typically contains firewalls.

   A. True

   B. False

7. SONA is the implementation strategy for what process?

   A. SWAN

   B. IIN

   C. WDS

   D. ITIL

8. What area of the enterprise composite model has very little configuration for enterprise administrators?

   A. Core

   B. Network Management

   C. Customer Edge

   D. Service Provider Edge

9. VPNs are not implemented in the Enterprise Edge?

   A. True

   B. False

10. The name of my made up company is FutureTech Inc.?

    A. True

    B. False

Answers to Review Questions

1. **A.** A switch block is the fundamental building piece to the network; it is where all of the users connected and data is brought into the network.

2. **C.** The three-layer hierarchical model is the original name..

3. **A.** The Enterprise Campus contains all of the primary switch blocks and the data center and management block.

4. **C.** The access layer is the bottom layer in a switch block; it is where users connect to the network.

5. **B.** The core of the network has always had the goal of not changing the data and to move it across the network as fast as possible.

6. **A.** True. The Enterprise Edge contains firewalls to protect the network from external connections.

7. **B.** SONA is the true implementation for the IIN process.

8. **D.** The service provider edge has devices controlled and configured by the ISP, not the enterprise administrators.

9. **B.** False. VPNs are typically implemented in the edge of the network to protect data over unsecured networks.

10. **A.** True. This was supposed to be funny!

Chapter

2

Switching

IN THIS CHAPTER, YOU WILL LEARN HOW TO DO THE FOLLOWING:

✓ Describe Layer 2 switching functions components

✓ Explain the functions of VLANs in a hierarchical network

✓ Configure VLANs (e.g., native, default, static, and access)

✓ Describe Layer 3 switching and routing functions

✓ Explain and configure VTP

✓ Describe EtherChannel, Layer 2 and 3

Now that I have given you a broad design methodology of the FutureTech Corporation's network, it is time to begin a more granular look at the design so the implementation process can begin. A logical place to begin is at the bottom, so to speak. I start with Layer 1 and 2 functionality and access layer devices, laying a strong foundation from which to build the rest of the network. Then, I get into some Layer 3 functions with inter-VLAN routing. For the most part, this chapter covers the functions and operations of the devices within a single switch block. This means that you are going to look at small piece of FutureTech's network. I build and use as an example a single switch block in FutureTech's headquarters building.

So, this chapter covers the most common Layer 2 and Layer 3 switching functions including VLANs, trunk encapsulations, VTP, and port aggregation. You will configure your test network and round out the chapter by making sure that you can troubleshoot problems that might arise.

For up-to-the-minute updates on this chapter, check out www.sybex.com/go/CiscoProGuidetoInternetworking or www.lammle.com.

Layer 2 Switching

Whenever network administrators talk about the access layer and connecting devices to the network, the discussion of collision domains and broadcast domains always arises. Old devices like hubs do not provide separation of traffic on the network. The bridge, which provided for collision domain separation, followed the use of hubs. But bridges did so slowly with a lot of processor time and fewer ports than are needed on a network today. For your current design needs, an extensive selection of Layer 2 Ethernet switches provides a wide variety of choices and offers many benefits over older network access devices.

Smaller Collision Domains   Every port on the switch is a collision domain. This means the only devices in the collision domain are the switch port and the device directly connected to it. This could still be extended if there were a hub placed on the port, but I don't recommend the use of hubs as a good design practice.

Full-Duplex Mode   A host now can have a direct connection to the switch, which means there is no contention on the segment. This mode allows the effective doubling of throughput because communication can occur in both directions at the same time.

Dedicated Bandwidth   Dedicated bandwidth means no more shared bandwidth that divides the throughput up by the number of hosts on the segment. Each switch port can provide dedicated bandwidth to the device in which it is connected. The media rate can be dynamically adjusted by the switch to the device that is connected.

Management and Security   Switches today provide a multitude of management and security functions, which help you in your everyday network needs.

In this chapter, I also discuss multilayer switching functions. In the next chapter, I'll cover the Spanning Tree Protocol (STP) functions and the improvements that have been made over the years to that protocol. Later, in Chapter 14, "Switch Security," I'll show you filtering and security measures that you can put in place for switches.

No matter how many management functions and security functions are added to a switch, it still has three primary functions that make it a switch. The first two functions, address learning and forward filtering, are covered in the next section. I'll get to the third function, loop avoidance, in Chapter 3, "Spanning Tree Protocol (STP)."

Address Learning and Forwarding

The most native and primary function that a switch performs is address learning. Address learning makes intelligent forwarding decisions possible. Without the ability to make forwarding decisions, the switch would be a hub. Hubs do not learn any information about the network and, therefore, they can only flood traffic out every port—except of course the port that the frame was received on.

Bridges made the first leap by creating a media access control (MAC) forward filter table. On switches, this table is also called the MAC address table and the content-addressable memory (CAM) table. By looking at the source MAC address of a frame when it is received, the bridge can learn where all of the host devices are located in relationship to its own ports. Switches do exactly the same thing, but they can forward the frames much faster than a bridge because the switch can perform the lookup and forwarding process in hardware instead of the slower software lookup a bridge must perform.

For example, let's say you have a switch with two hosts connected to it. Host A is connected on Fast Ethernet 0/1 and Host B is connected on Fast Ethernet 0/2. When a switch is powered up, there are no dynamically learned addresses in the table. If Host A sends a frame to the switch, the switch will take the incoming port number and the source MAC address and place that information into the MAC address table. But, whatever the destination of this frame, the switch will not know it, yet. When the switch does not know where the destination is located, the switch must flood the frame. Now for the benefit of this process, when Host B sends a frame back to Host A, the switch would again receive the frame and place the incoming port and source MAC address into the MAC address table. However, this time when the switch makes its forwarding decision, it knows what port Host A is located on and can forward the frame out Fast Ethernet 0/1 only. One additional thing to remember is that this process applies only to unicast traffic. All broadcast and multicast traffic by default is flooded by the switch.

VLANs

For years, networks have been designed in a flat architecture. By *flat* I mean they have consisted of multiple hubs or bridges that reside in a single broadcast domain. If any device sent a broadcast packet, every system on the network would have to read the data, even if it was not meant for that device. At that point in history, a switch was treated as a single broadcast domain. Having a single broadcast domain limits the number of devices you can connect to the network. There are other downsides in addition to just having one huge broadcast domain. One large broadcast domain limits your ability to secure the network because any end station could connect into any switch port and have access to all of the other devices. Making separate broadcast domains also allows you to more easily manage where and even if a device can connect to the network; this also makes making moves, adds, or changes (also called MACs, not to be confused with MAC address, if you haven't heard this term) for hosts easier on you.

Well, not to fear, we can configure VLANs on switches now. VLANs provide a way to separate a switch into individual broadcast domains. Think about the example in Figure 2.1; it shows a part of the network that FutureTech wants to implement. In the headquarters building, three of the floors house three different research departments that do separate work and have separate network resources. In the past, each of the departments would have been located on a separate floor and the resources that they needed to access would be located on the department's network segment.

FIGURE 2.1   Network without VLANs

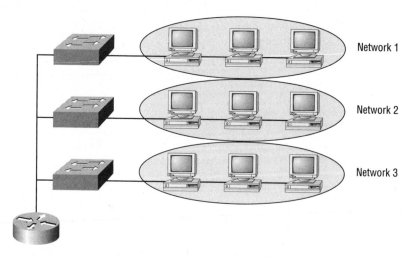

In networks and companies of today, not all users sit together isolated from other departments and the resources they need to access aren't necessarily located on their segment any more. In fact, you now know that most resources will be collocated or in some remote data center. Well, if switches operated the same way as they used to, you would need to have three separate physical switches on each floor so that users from each one of the subnetworks could connect into the appropriate network. Not only that, each one of those switches would have to have a separate connection into the router. With three floors and three switches, there would have to be nine connections into the router. Not to mention that nine switches—ridiculous—is a waste especially if that much port density is not needed. This configuration would not be an efficient use of ports or the router and switch resources.

Instead of using so many switches and ports, FutureTech can create VLANs on the switches. By creating additional VLANs on each switch, the switch can be logically divided into multiple logical switches, so to speak. When you create a VLAN on a switch and assign ports into that VLAN, you create another broadcast domain. Now, even though hosts are plugged into the same switch, if the ports they are connected to are in different VLANs, they will be unable to communicate directly through the Layer 2 switch. In order for devices in different VLANs to communicate, they must be routed by a Layer 3 device.

So, back to the example. The same three departments are now connected into the same switch. Their ports can be assigned to the different VLANs, which represent their individual subnets. This setup allows them to access the resources on their subnet. You can see an example of the network with VLANs in Figure 2.2.

FIGURE 2.2   Network with VLANs

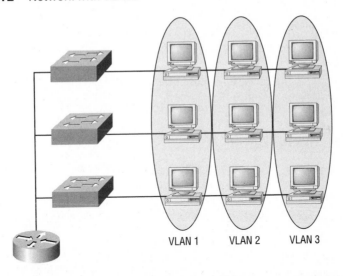

VLAN 1   VLAN 2   VLAN 3

Now, you are probably asking, "What about traffic and connections between the switches?" Well, that is the very good question, which I'm going to answer in the next section. I'll tell you about link types and what they do for us. But before we move on, a few more details about VLANs still need to be reviewed.

Notice, earlier I said that you could create an additional VLAN. Well, I was specific in saying an additional VLAN because every switch has a default VLAN called VLAN 1. VLAN 1 is always there and cannot be deleted. By default, every switch port is in VLAN 1, which is why the switch represents one broadcast domain. Finally, the maximum number of VLANs you can have on a switch is 4096. Typically, only the first 1005 are used; above 1005, the VLANs are called extended VLANs.

Link Types

In a switched environment, each port can be configured into one of two types of links, either an access port or a trunk port—not both. Since switches remove all VLAN information from the frame before it's forwarded out to an access-link device, access-link devices can't communicate with devices outside their VLAN unless the packet is routed. So you've got to choose one or the other, and know that if you make a port an access port, that port can be assigned to one VLAN only.

Access Ports

An access port can generally belong to only one VLAN. (There is an exception for voice; I'll tell you about that in the next section.) Therefore, an access port can only carry traffic for that one VLAN. Traffic is both received and sent, unchanged, as it was sent from the end station or host. It contains no VLAN tagging or encapsulation whatsoever. The switch assumes any traffic that arrives on an access port belongs to the VLAN to which that port is assigned.

The assigned VLAN is referred to as the configured *VLAN* of the port. Any device attached to an *access link* is unaware of a VLAN membership—the device only knows or assumes it's part of the same broadcast domain, but it doesn't have the big picture so it doesn't understand the physical network topology at all.

So, what do you think will happen if an access port receives a tagged packet? Well, if you said that the frame would be dropped, you are right! Why? An access port doesn't look at any information except the destination MAC address, so tagged traffic can only be understood by trunk ports. I will be discussing trunk ports in the section, "Trunk Ports," later in the chapter.

Voice Traffic Considerations

One thing that you have to get used to in networking is that as soon as you make a rule, you have to make a new rule to break the first one. I just said that an access port can only be assigned to one VLAN. That is true most of the time, except in a voice VLAN configuration. With so many networks today becoming converged (by converged I mean a network that carries more than just application data like Hyper Text Transfer Protocol (HTTP) or email), most switches allow you to add a second VLAN to an access port for voice traffic. The second VLAN must be specified as the voice VLAN though. The voice VLAN used to be called the auxiliary VLAN. This allowed it to be overlaid on top of the data VLAN and enabled both types of traffic through the same port. Even though this is technically considered to be a different type of link (a trunk link, to be discussed next), it's still just an access port that can be configured for both a data and a voice VLAN. Using this configuration, you can connect both a phone and a PC device to one switch port and still have each device in a separate VLAN. I talk much more about the use and configuration of voice traffic later in Chapter 17, "Voice."

Trunk Ports

The name *trunk port* came from the telephone companies. Phone company systems had trunk lines that could carry multiple telephone conversations at a time. So, the name makes sense. Trunk ports on network switches can carry multiple VLANs at the same time.

A trunk link is usually at least a 100 Mbps or 1 Gbps link (10 Gbps links are now in use as well) between two switches, between a switch and router, or even between a switch and server. They carry the traffic of multiple VLANs—from 1 to 4096—at any given time. (Remember, it's really only up to 1005 unless you're going with extended VLANs.)

A trunk link can be very useful in a network because with it you get to carry the data for a whole bunch of different VLANs at the same time. This is really cool because it means you can actually set things up to have a server in two separate broadcast domains simultaneously so your users won't have to cross a Layer 3 device (router) to log in and access it. If the traffic were to be routed between the VLANs, a router would be necessary, and it would not be very efficient if you have an access link from each one of your VLANs going to a separate port on the router. So instead, a trunk link can be created to the router. Then, subinterfaces you create on the router port will route the traffic between VLANs while only using one physical interface. This is called "router on a stick." I love the name of that configuration—every once in a while an engineer is actually creative in naming something!

It's good to know that all VLANs send information on a trunked link unless you remove the VLAN from the allowed list. I'll go through how to remove individual VLANs from a trunk.

Trunk Protocols

Trunk ports don't allow switches to carry data from multiple VLANs by magic; you must configure a trunking protocol to identify the VLANs from one switch to the next. Individual switches identify the VLANs using the VID or VLAN ID field in their headers. Each switch maintains its own VLAN database, so it is in essence locally significant to the switch. When data is sent from one to switch across to another, the sending switch must identify which VLAN owns the data. The receiving switch then knows how to handle the data and can identify only VLAN the data can be forwarded into.

For this process to properly occur, a trunking protocol, also called an encapsulation protocol, must be configured on the trunk link. Generally, two trunk protocols are used for Ethernet networks. Those protocols, ISL and 802.1Q, will be covered in detail in the next sections. The 802.1Q protocol is usually referred to as dot1q, pronounced "dot-1-q."

ISL Encapsulation

ISL, Inter-Switch Link, is a Cisco proprietary protocol; it was released and used before the standards-based dot1q protocol. ISL is actually not used much in production networks today. ISL has some limitations that were improved on by dot1q. Here are those limitations:

- ISL only carries 1000 VLANs—dot1q can carry 4095
- ISL encapsulates the frame, which adds more overhead

- ISL must be point to point

- ISL does not have a separate QoS standard field

ISL is truly an encapsulation protocol, as it takes the original frame and places a new ISL header on the front. Then, the protocol recalculates the cyclic redundancy check (CRC) and places the new trailer on the end. No modification of the original frame occurs. Figure 2.3 shows you what a frame that has been encapsulated with ISL looks like.

FIGURE 2.3 ISL Encapsulated Frame

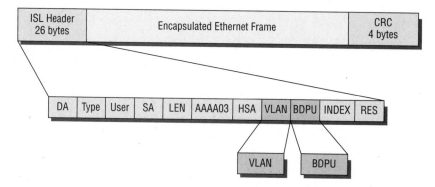

In addition to not modifying the original frame, ISL encapsulates every frame and therefore does not use a native VLAN. I'll tell you about native VLAN in the dot1q next section. Because it encapsulated the entire frame, ISL can support other Layer 2 protocols besides just Ethernet. It can support Token Ring, Fiber Distributed Data Interface (FDDI), and Asynchronous Transfer Mode (ATM). It also supports Per VLAN Spanning Tree (PVST), which I will discuss in Chapter 3, "Spanning Tree Protocol (STP)."

802.1Q Tagging

The standards-based alternative to ISL, 802.1Q, can configure dot1q between switches and routers from different vendors. Rather than encapsulating the entire frame as ISL does, dot1q adds a tag to the existing Ethernet header. It then recalculates the frame check sequence (FCS) at the end of the frame. The tag that is inserted into the header is 4 bytes. If you take a look at Figure 2.4, you can see the tag that has been added to the standard frame.

FIGURE 2.4 802.1Q Tagged Frame

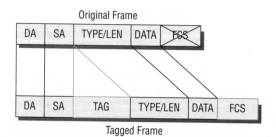

Dot1q does offer some features the ISL does not. The dot1q header includes a priority field called the 802.1P field, which provides richer QoS support. Because of the QoS support, dot1q has become the standard for IP telephony networks.

Dot1q also has support for a wider variety of networks and protocols, including:

- Ethernet
- Token Ring
- 4095 VLANs
- Common Spanning Tree (CST)
- Multiple Spanning Tree (MSTP)
- Rapid Spanning Tree (RSTP)

Dot1q also supports a point-to-multipoint topology and allows untagged traffic to be sent over the trunk link via the native VLAN.

The native VLAN allows frames that are not tagged with a VID to be sent across a trunk link. By default on Cisco switches, the native VLAN is set to VLAN 1 and you can only have one native VLAN. On a dot1q segment, all the trunk ports must be configured with the same native VLAN to operate correctly. Otherwise, you will get a message on your console screen telling you that there is a native VLAN mismatch.

Dynamic Trunking Protocol

While the recommended method of creating trunk links is to configure them manually, the process can be accomplished dynamically through a protocol called Dynamic Trunking Protocol (DTP). DTP is a Cisco proprietary protocol that runs only on Cisco Catalyst switches. With DTP enabled, which is the default setting for all ports, frames can be sent to a connected device to negotiate the trunk link status. However, if a port has been manually configured as either an access or trunk port, then the negotiation attempt of DTP may not have any effect. A port that is manually configured as access or trunk stays in the mode. It is never recommended to connect a manually configured access port to a trunk port, as there will be a lot of dropped frames.

Now, knowing that, let's look at the two dynamic operating modes that DTP uses. Dynamic desirable is the default mode for DTP. When desirable is enabled, the port actively sends out DTP frames, soliciting the connected port to be a trunk link.

The second dynamic mode is dynamic auto; this mode works a little differently. With dynamic auto, no DTP frames are sent out from the port, but if the other end sends DTP frames, the auto port will accept them and become a trunk link. So, again, dynamic desirable sends out DTP solicitations; dynamic auto does not.

The last configuration option for DTP is nonegotiate. The nonegotiate option prevents the port from sending or receiving DTP frames. So if you want a trunk link to be formed, you are going to have to manually configure it with the trunk option. Take a look at the switches in Figure 2.5; the links between each of the switches have the DTP setting for each specific link. Using this type of diagram, you can see exactly which combination can become a trunk and which cannot.

FIGURE 2.5   Possible DTP Port Configurations

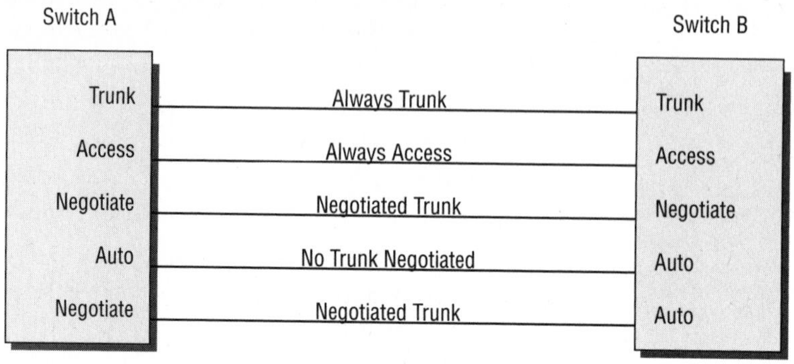

Implementing VLANs

Now that you've reviewed the basic components of VLANs and how they work, we need to discuss how they will be implemented. When I say how they can be implemented, I mean where in the network a VLAN will be physically located and how far across the network the VLAN will span. When thinking about the implementing VLANs, you also have to think about what kind of traffic the VLAN will be carrying.

Over the years, the way that networks have been designed has changed a few times. As I stated already, there was a time when all the users from a department worked and sat together. All of their resources were located on their local subnet with them. When those users started being geographically separated, the technical answer was to extend the VLAN to a switch physically located where those users are located. This type of design is called end-to-end VLAN.

I am sure that you can guess from this lead up, things have changed. Today, most of the networks resources are centrally located in a data center. The data center is sometimes referred to as a server farm, but there can be much more than just servers in this location. Since network resources are now located off the local subnets, the vast majority of traffic is now also traveling off the local subnet. Due to the significant change in how and where data flows on the network, a change in the boundaries and control of the data was needed. This led to the creation of local VLANs, which are much more efficient than end-to-end VLANs.

Local VLANs are defined as being contained within a single switch block. You can attempt to keep local VLANs in a single switch, but more important is maintaining the VLANs to a within a geographic area and not letting broadcast and other unnecessary traffic cross WAN and other bandwidth-limited links.

End-to-End VLANs

You will remember that the term *end-to-end VLAN* refers to a single VLAN that has associated switch ports on switches that are dispersed throughout an enterprise network.

Important to remember is that traffic for this VLAN is carried throughout the network, wherever there are switch ports in the VLAN. In order for multiple VLANs to be carried end to end, trunk links are required between switches to carry the traffic from all the different VLANs.

Important features of end-to-end VLANs are:

Geographic Dispersal   An end-to-end VLAN is geographically dispersed across the network. This can be done for security to allow access to resources or to apply quality of service (QoS) settings.

Membership   Users can be grouped into the VLAN regardless of physical location. End-to-end VLANs may be beneficial for purposes of a user's moving around the network and maintaining the same membership. It can also be useful for traffic or users where routing their data needs to be avoided such as in a client/server relationship some broadcast or non-routable traffic is required to get back and forth between the two communication devices.

IP Subnet Address   Devices on a VLAN typically have addresses on the same IP subnet. This can be useful again for applying QoS or for management reasons. Special purpose VLANs can also take advantage of this configuration. An example of such a VLAN could be a voice VLAN, wireless roaming VLAN, multicast VLAN, and even a VLAN setup for security to separate visitors and guest users on the network.

A few important considerations should be looked at when implementing end-to-end VLANs. When a user needs access to a VLAN at a given location, the switch ports are provisioned for that user and associated with the given VLAN. Since users on an end-to-end VLAN can be located anywhere in the network, all switches must be aware of the end-to-end VLANs. All switches carrying traffic for these VLANs have to have identical VLAN databases.

You should also consider that flooded traffic for the VLAN, including broadcast and multicast traffic, is by default passed to every switch, even if you have not currently configured any active ports in the particular end-to-end VLAN. The last thing you want—and what can cause hours of hair-pulling work—is troubleshooting devices on a network with end-to-end VLANs. This can be very difficult because the traffic for a single VLAN can traverse multiple switches in a large area of the campus.

Local VLANs

In the past, end-to-end VLANs were typically used because network designers attempted to implement the 80/20 rule—the idea that most of the user data stayed on the local subnet. Generally, about 80 percent of the traffic was passed locally, and only about 20 percent of the traffic left for a remote network.

But now network engineers typically consolidate servers into a data center on the network and provide access to external resources such as the Internet. The design rule now is closer to a 20/80 split, in which the greater amount of traffic leaves the local segment. This shift in traffic characteristics has made local VLANs be the more efficient solution.

End-to-end VLANs worked very well when IP address configuration was a manually administered and burdensome process. Anything that reduced this burden as users moved between networks was an improvement. Now though, with the ease and wide spread use of Dynamic Host Configuration Protocol (DHCP), the process of configuring IP information at each desktop is no longer a significant issue. As a result, there are few benefits to extending a VLAN throughout an enterprise.

It is often more efficient to group all users in a geographical area or local switches into a single VLAN, regardless of the organizational function of those users, especially from a troubleshooting perspective. VLANs that have boundaries based on campus geography rather than organizational function are called local VLANs. Local VLANs are generally confined to a switch block.

Important features of local VLANs are:

Geographic   Local VLANs should be created around geographic boundaries rather than the job or department functions of the users on the end devices.

Predetermined Traffic Flow   Traffic from a local VLAN is routed at the distribution layer when traveling to destinations on other networks. This design provides what is called deterministic traffic flow. In other words, the path that traffic is going to take is predictable and if there is a failure, then it is easy to track down and fix.

Highly Available   In most cases, a VLAN does not extend beyond the distribution layer. This makes the all devices highly available and provides easy to implement redundancy controlled by either STP or routing. There can also be a redundant router for each of the VLANs, providing failover should any one fail. Having redundant routers requires setup and is controlled by a protocol such as Hot Standby Router Protocol (HSRP), which I discuss in Chapter10, "Redundancy Protocols."

Scalable   VLANs on a given access switch should not be advertised or configured on all the other switches in the network. Controlling the scope of the VLANs allows the network to be more scalable because now adding a new switch is easy and does not require reconfiguring other devices.

VLAN Trunk Protocol

VLAN Trunk Protocol (VTP) is a Cisco proprietary protocol that allows automation of updating and managing the VLAN database across multiple switches. Switches that share the same VLAN database are grouped into what is called a VTP domain. The VLAN database is propagated to all the switches in the same VTP domain. VTP information is only propagated over trunk links. All the switches in the same domain can then maintain exactly the same, up-to-date database. You can have a domain with only one switch in it, but VTP will allow you to add more switches later.

Only part of the VLAN database is exchanged, however. The VLAN number, name, and description are exchanged. The data about which ports are associated to what VLANs is configured and maintained only on the local switch. This means that if you need to add an additional port into a given VLAN, you must do that on the local switch.

Switches can only be in one domain at a time. The updates that VTP sends can only be applied by switches in the same domain. By default, the domain name on a switch is null, meaning it belongs to no domain. The domain name is typically configured on each of the switches that will be in the domain.

VTP Modes

It is possible for you to configure a switch into one of three different VTP modes:

- Server mode
- Client mode
- Transparent mode

The mode you configure will affect how VTP sends and communicates its updates.

Server Mode   The default mode for VTP is server mode. In server mode, the switches VLAN database can have VLANs added, changed, or removed. The server mode switch will also be a transmitting switch of the VTP data. You are typically going to have a primary and secondary server mode switch within the switch block. Finally, server mode saves the VLAN information permanently in flash; all of the VLAN information is saved in the vlan.dat file. Note, by default all switches save their VLAN information in the vlan.dat file. The exception is the VTP client mode switch.

Client Mode   Client mode will be the setting for most of the switches in the switch block. This mode accepts the advertisements from the server mode switches. It does not store the VLAN information it receives in flash, only in RAM. The biggest difference is that you cannot add, change, or delete VLANs on a switch in client mode. In fact, if you try to do so, the switch will give you a big fat error message saying that you are in client mode and the action cannot be completed. I will show you that in the test network a little bit later. Last, a client mode switch will forward the advertisements it receives out through its trunk lines, onto other switches. It does this to make sure that all the switches in the switch block receive the updates.

Transparent Mode   A transparent mode switch listens to no other switch; it does whatever it wants. Well, whatever you configure it to do, that is. A transparent mode switch does not update its database with VTP advertisements. You can add, change, and delete VLANs directly to the local database. The VLAN database is stored in flash in the vlan.dat file. A transparent mode switch is nice enough to still forward on the advertisements so that the other switches in the block can still receive them. This mode can be useful if you have a switch that needs completely separate VLANs that you don't want to propagate to the rest of the switch block. I have used this feature for separating research or development type hosts on the network. I also recommend putting new switches in transparent mode. This removes the risk of adding a switch that could wipe out the VLAN database.

VTP Operation

VTP uses a configuration revision number to track changes and allow other switches to verify they are up to date. A newly configured server in a new VTP domain will have a revision number of 0. When information in the database is modified, the revision number is incremented. When there is a new change, then the server where the change was made originates the change and sends out an advertisement telling the other switches there is a change. The other switches verify the revision number against their own. The advertised revision number should now be one higher than their own, indicating the other switches should take the change. VTP then synchronizes the change on all of the other switches. The advertisements are sent as multicast frames so that only a switch listening for the VTP advertisements will process them. If there are no changes for a while, VTP by default sends out an update every 5 minutes to maintain contact with the client switches.

A critical point here is the revision number. In the transparent mode section, remember that I said that when you add a new switch to an existing domain it should be added in transparent mode. This removes the risk of the database being unintentionally overwritten. If you add a server mode switch to the network and its revision number happens to be higher than the current revision number of the domain, this new switch would overwrite the domain database, which could corrupt or delete part of or an entire database. Unfortunately, this happens to far too many administrators. So I can't stress the point enough: don't take this lightly; you could take down all the devices in an entire switch block. I typically call this sort of mistake RUE: Resume Updating Event!

VTP Pruning

Pruning can be used to make the use of bandwidth more efficient. It does this by reducing the amount of flooded traffic. Pruning uses the advertisements to determine whether the traffic is being flooded to switches that don't need it. What do I mean by switches that don't need it? Well, let's say I have a typical switch block in the FutureTech headquarters building; this switch block consists of two distribution layer switches and connected to them are two access switches. Take a look at Figure 2.6.

FIGURE 2.6   VTP Pruning

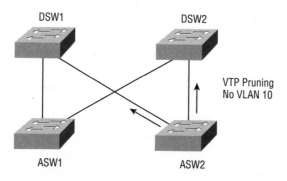

DSW1   DSW2

VTP Pruning
No VLAN 10

ASW1   ASW2

Normally, broadcast traffic would be carried to all the switches for a VLAN, if that VLAN existed on all of the switches. But, what if one of the access switches didn't have any ports in a given VLAN? There would be no use in sending broadcast traffic to that switch because it has no hosts to send the broadcast to.

Look at Figure 2.6 again. I enabled pruning on all of the switches and created VLAN 10 in the VLAN database of the VTP server. The server, then, propagated VLAN 10 to all of the other switches. Notice, however, that only ASW1, DSW1, and DSW2 from the diagram have ports in VLAN 10. Since ASW2 doesn't have any ports in VLAN 10, it will tell DSW1 and DSW2 that it does not have any hosts. Now, when a host on ASW1 sends a broadcast frame, that frame will only be propagated to DSW1 and DSW2. ASW2 will not receive the frame since it has no hosts to send the traffic to.

Configuring VLANs

Now that I have described the function and operation of VLANs, links, encapsulations, DTP, and VTP, I show you the commands to configure each function and the common options to modify their operation.

For the next few sections of configuration, I am going to use the following network setup (see Figure 2.7). It is similar to the setup you saw for the VTP example. In Figure 2.7, I show you the network that I use. From the test network, I use three switches. I know the diagram has four switches in it, but that is so the switch block looks fuller. If you have four switches, then that is great, but this setup doesn't require a fourth.

FIGURE 2.7   Switch Configuration Network

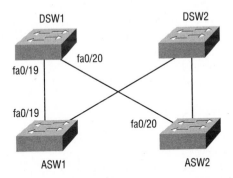

The configurations in this section give you flexibility in the type of switches that you can use. If you have the 3560 switches that I mentioned in the test network setup, then you are good to go. For this section, if you have 2950s, 2960s, or 3550s, you also will be just fine. When you get down to the inter-VLAN routing configuration, you will have to have at least one 3550 or 3560 to use as a distribution layer switch.

You have seen the diagram and know the switches that you need. Now you just have to know where and what you are going to be doing.

Let's look at the setup of the basic functions and implement the features from the case study.

Real World Scenario

Connecting Sales

FutureTech has added a new sales group at the Dallas headquarters. The network administrator assigns you the task of installing a new switch block, designated DSW1, to support that group. Both workstation and telephone connections need to be supported. Unnecessary broadcast traffic is to be kept to a minimum.

Two trunk links connect DSW1 to the rest of the network through another switch, identified as ASW1. According to the plans, the trunk links are to run from port fa0/19 on DSW1 to fa0/19 on ASW1 and from fa0/20 on DSW1 goes to fa0/20 on ASW1. By configuring a trunk link, data can be passed from the group's multiple VLANs and allow the hosts connected to ASW1 to access the rest of the network.

Setting Up VLANs

1. View the VLAN database for DSW1 in your test setup.

   The command to view the database is **show vlan**. The output from this command looks like the listing produced from DSW1 on my test pod equipment. Notice in the output that under the default VLAN 1, all of the ports for the switch are associated by default.

```
DSW1#sh vlan
VLAN Name Status Ports
---- ----------------------- --------- ------------------------------
1 default active Fa0/1, Fa0/2, Fa0/3, Fa0/4
Fa0/5, Fa0/6, Fa0/7, Fa0/8
Fa0/9, Fa0/10, Fa0/11, Fa0/12
Fa0/13, Fa0/14, Fa0/15, Fa0/16
Fa0/17, Fa0/18, Fa0/20, Fa0/21
Fa0/22, Fa0/23, Fa0/24, Gi0/1
Gi0/2
1002 fddi-default act/unsup
1003 token-ring-default act/unsup
1004 fddinet-default act/unsup
1005 trnet-default act/unsup
VLAN Type SAID MTU Parent RingNo BridgeNo Stp BrdgMode Trans1 Trans2
---- --- ---- ---- ------ ------ -------- ---- -------- ------ ------
1 enet 100001 1500 - - - - - 0 0
1002 fddi 101002 1500 - - - - - 0 0
```

```
1003 tr 101003 1500 - - - - - 0 0
1004 fdnet 101004 1500 - - - ieee - 0 0
1005 trnet 101005 1500 - - - ibm - 0 0
Remote SPAN VLANs

------------------------------------------------------------------------

Primary Secondary Type Ports
------- --------- ----------------- ------------------------------------
DSW1#
```

2.   Create a new VLAN on the switch.

The first thing that I want you to configure is an additional VLAN. Remember, VLAN 1 was created by default. We want to create VLAN 10 now. From global configuration mode, use the vlan command. Be sure to include the ***vlan-id*** or VLAN number after the command. Your output should be similar to the listing:

```
DSW1>enable
DSW1#configure terminal
DSW1(config)#vlan 10
DSW1(config-vlan)#
```

Now that you have created the VLAN in the database, you can see that you are in VLAN configuration mode. There are a few options that you can configure here. One of the most common options allows you to give the VLAN a name for reference and administration ease.

If you were to issue the show vlan command again you would see that VLAN 10 is created and exists in the database. The show vlan command will have to be issued from privileged exec mode.

A separate note that I would like to point out is the use of the do command. Since the inception of the Cisco IOS you have had to enter specific commands in the proper mode. For example, the show vlan command above must be entered at privileged exec mode and cannot be entered in the VLAN configuration mode. Engineers have complained about this setup for years. In the mainline 12.3 router code, this was finally changed. About the same time, the command was introduced in the switch IOS as well. The benefit of this command is that you don't have to back out all the way to a different mode to verify a configuration or issue a different command. While you are still in VLAN configuration mode, use the command do show vlan. This will work with a majority of the commands I will be showing you.

3.   Name the VLAN.

```
DSW1(config-vlan)#name TestVLAN
```

Again, at this point if you were to look at the VLAN database, you would see that VLAN 10 is now named, TestVLAN. When you name a VLAN, it is for reference only, the name cannot be used as a variable in a command syntax to identify the VLAN.

4. Remove the VLAN.

    If you need to remove a VLAN from the VLAN database, use the no version of the VLAN command. After you issue this command, you can view the VLAN database and see that it has been removed.

    ```
    DSW1(config)#no vlan 10
    ```

Configuring Access Ports

At the end of the last section, you removed VLAN 10 from the database. So, let's reestablish VLAN 10 and assign a port so we can get on about the business of configuring.

> I would like to show you a little shortcut that combines adding a VLAN to a port and then subsequently creates that VLAN, if it doesn't already exist. If you know that you need to create a new VLAN and you know what ports are going to be placed into that VLAN, you can create both with the command you use to place a port into the VLAN. The command to move a port association is switchport access vlan *vlan-id*. This command must be executed from the interface configuration mode of the interface that you are moving.

1. Recreate VLAN 10 and assign port fa0/1 using the switchport access vlan *vlan-id* command.

    ```
    DSW1(config)#int fa0/1
    DSW1(config-if)#switchport access vlan 10
    % Access VLAN does not exist. Creating vlan 10
    ```

    Now, if you look at the VLAN database again, you will see that VLAN 10 has been created again and port fa0/1 is associated with the VLAN.

2. Add the voice VLAN.

    Remember that some of our end stations are phones, so you need to manage voice traffic. Well, you can create a voice VLAN, so that the voice traffic can be placed into it. Remember a few things about the voice VLAN:

    - It is a special case data VLAN
    - A port can be placed into a voice and a data VLAN
    - It is created when you assign port to it

So, let's say that the powers that be at Future Tech specified that voice VLAN be VLAN 12. You would configure that on the interface with the `switchport voice vlan 12` command. Like this:

```
DSW1(config-if)#switchport voice vlan 12
% Voice VLAN does not exist. Creating vlan 12
```

3.   Secure the port for host use only.

Now let's ensure that the port is an access port. By making the port an access port, only an end station can connect to the port. This is especially important on access layer switches that have their ports physically accessible by users or anyone in offices or conference rooms. The wall plugs in cubicles and offices all run back to a switch closet somewhere and plug into a switchport. Configuring the ports of your switches prevents one of these people from walking into an office, unplugging the phone or host, plugging in a switch, and creating a trunk port. If an attacker or unknowing person were to do this, they could have access to all of the VLANs and the traffic passing across them. The command to configure a port into access mode is `switchport mode access`.

```
DSW1(config)#int fa 0/1
DSW1(config-if)#switchport mode access
```

I talk about voice configurations and the options in much more detail in Chapter 17, "Voice."

Configuring Trunk Links

Now that you have configured basic functions on a single switch, such as access ports for the end stations, the VLANs those ports go into, and even a voice VLAN, it is time to figure out how this traffic is going to get from one switch to a different one. Once data from a host enters into a switch that data must be able to get somewhere. Needing to move data off of a single switch brings you to the configuration of trunk links; this way the data can be passed up to distribution switches and to a routing process to be routed toward another VLAN or switch block.

You will still be using the network shown in Figure 2.7 for this section of configuration, except now you will be using two of the switches. You will continue to use DSW1 and now you are going to use ASW1 as well. The two switches are connected with two links, port fa0/19 on DSW1 goes to fa0/19 on ASW1 and fa0/20 on DSW1 goes to fa0/20 on ASW1. By configuring a trunk link between the two switches, you can pass data from multiple VLANs and allow the hosts connected to ASW1 to access the rest of the network. Also, in the next section when you configure VTP, a trunk link is required to carry the VTP data.

1.   Configure the trunk encapsulation.

Now, you must configure the trunk encapsulation protocol before you can configure a port to be a trunk link.

There is, however, an exception to this configuration rule. On Cisco's access layer switches (the 2950 and 2960 series), trunk encapsulation configuration is not required because those switches only support the dot1q protocol. Remember dot1q has become the standard protocol used on networks today, and now Cisco doesn't even support ISL on some of their switches.

The encapsulation command is switchport trunk encapsulation **type**, where the type option is either dot1q or isl. Both commands are entered from the interface configuration mode.

```
DSW1(config)#int fa0/19
DSW1(config-if)#switchport trunk encapsulation dot1q
```

2. Create the trunk port.

Now that the encapsulation is configured we can make the port a trunk port. The command is very similar to making a port an access port, but the option is trunk. The command is then switchport mode trunk.

```
DSW1(config-if)#switchport mode trunk
DSW1(config-if)#
00:45:58: %LINEPROTO-5-UPDOWN: Line protocol on Interface FastEthernet0/19,
changed state to down
00:46:01: %LINEPROTO-5-UPDOWN: Line protocol on Interface FastEthernet0/19,
changed state to up
```

3. Verify the trunk link.

Notice after we put interface fa0/19 into trunk mode, the interface went down and then came back up. Why did that happen? Well, if you said, "It is because the port was made a trunk, and by default, the switch on the other end of the link was still an access port," you were right about why the port went down.

But why did the port come back up? Remember the negotiation process and how DTP works. When the port on Switch1 became a trunk, DTP frames started to be sent to the other end. By default, all switch ports are in desirable mode, which means the port on ASW1 was negotiated into being a trunk link. Then, the link on DSW1 came back up. You can verify that the interface is in trunk mode with the show interface trunk command.

```
DSW1(config-if)#do sh int trunk
Port Mode Encapsulation Status Native vlan
Fa0/19 on 802.1q trunking 1
Port Vlans allowed on trunk
Fa0/19 1-4094
Port Vlans allowed and active in management domain
```

```
Fa0/19 1,10,12
Port Vlans in spanning tree forwarding state and not pruned
Fa0/19 none
```

Look at the show interface trunk command on ASW1. The mode says "negotiated." Configure fa0/19 on ASW1 with the same commands you used on DSW1 to make it permanently a trunk link. The console messages from ASW1 will be the same as it was for DSW1. Then, run the show interface trunk command again on ASW1. You can now see that the mode changed to ON.

4. Configure the DTP options.

If you want to change the DTP options for a given port, you can do that with a couple of very simple commands on the interface. Remember that you set the DTP mode to ON by placing the port into trunk mode, and can turn it off by placing the mode into access mode. Those options look like this:

```
DSW1(config-if)#switchport mode ?
access Set trunking mode to ACCESS unconditionally
dot1q-tunnel set trunking mode to TUNNEL unconditionally
dynamic Set trunking mode to dynamically negotiate access or trunk mode
private-vlan Set private-vlan mode
trunk Set trunking mode to TRUNK unconditionally
```

To change the dynamic mode from the default of desirable to auto, use the command switchport mode dynamic [auto | desirable]:

```
DSW1(config-if)#switchport mode dynamic ?
auto Set trunking mode dynamic negotiation parameter to AUTO
desirable Set trunking mode dynamic negotiation parameter to DESIRABLE
```

Configuring VTP

Now that you understand how to create a VLAN and assign ports to it, I need to show you VTP configuration. VTP, you'll remember, is the protocol that allows you to synchronize the VLAN database across multiple switches. The first thing that you need to configure on the switch is a VTP domain name. Let me show you the options that are available with the vtp command.

```
DSW1(config)#vtp ?
domain Set the name of the VTP administrative domain.
file Configure IFS filesystem file where VTP configuration is stored.
interface Configure interface as the preferred source for the VTP IP updater
address.
mode Configure VTP device mode
```

```
password Set the password for the VTP administrative domain
pruning Set the adminstrative domain to permit pruning
version Set the adminstrative domain to VTP version
```

1. Set the VTP domain name.

   Now the domain is set with the vtp domain **domain-name** command. Notice again the default domain name is NULL.

   ```
   DSW1(config)#vtp domain Test
   Changing VTP domain name from NULL to Test
   ```

2. Establish a VTP password.

   The next thing that you can configure is the VTP password. Remember this makes sure that only the switches you want and have configured will take and give updates.

   ```
   DSW1(config)#vtp password futuretech
   Setting device VLAN database password to futuretech
   ```

3. Set the VTP mode for each switch in the VLAN.

   Next, you want to make sure that only the switch or switches that you choose are in server mode and all the others are in client mode. To change the mode of the switches' VTP process, the command is **vtp mode [server | client | transparent]**. Let's take a look. Remember the default mode is server.

   When you try to set a switch that is still configured as default to server, it responds with a message that tells you it already is a server. I am going to change my switch's mode back and forth so that you can see the output it gives me.

   ```
   DSW1(config)#vtp mode server
   Device mode already VTP SERVER.
   DSW1(config)#vtp mode client
   Setting device to VTP CLIENT mode.
   DSW1(config)#vtp mode server
   Setting device to VTP SERVER mode
   ```

   For you, to continue with the example and the switch block that you are building, you need to place your DSW1 switch into server mode and your ASW1 switch into client mode.

4. Turn on VTP pruning.

   Finally, you're ready to enable VTP pruning, which saves the amount of unnecessary broadcast traffic that is sent across your switches. Enable VTP pruning on all of the switches in the switch block. The command to enable VTP pruning is simply vtp pruning. To disable pruning, you only need to put no in front of the same command.

The command option no in the Cisco IOS always negates the default action of a command. Sometimes you have to pay very close attention to this option because the command may be a double negative. You might actually be turning something ON using the no option.

```
DSW1(config)#vtp pruning
Pruning switched on
DSW1(config)#no vtp pruning
Pruning switched off
```

Now that the access switches are configured with the items necessary to get them connected to other switches and to the host devices, we can move on to making them connect and route through the distribution devices.

Inter-VLAN Routing

In most networks today, switches support multiple VLANs. But if those switches have no Layer 3 capabilities, then packets cannot travel between VLANs. Without Layer 3 capabilities, the switch or switches must be connected to an external router. The best and most efficient way to set this up employs a single trunk link between the switch and the routing device. That way, the trunk can carry the traffic for multiple VLANs. When the traffic reaches the router, either a router or multilayer switch, it can then be routed. This single physical link, the trunk, must be Fast Ethernet or greater to support Inter-Switch Link (ISL) encapsulation. The 802.1Q trunking protocol is supported on 10 Mb Ethernet router interfaces.

Router on a Stick

When you use an external router to perform the inter-VLAN routing functions, the configuration is typically called "router on a stick." As mentioned earlier, every once in a while an engineer creates something really useful and actually gives it a cool name; this is one of those times. A trunk link connects the router to the switch. The router can then receive packets from one VLAN and forward them to any other VLAN or subnet that is connected or known by the router.

To perform the inter-VLAN routing function, the router must know where and how to reach all the connecting VLANs. Each of the VLANs represents a separate IP subnet, which requires its own router connection. I can hear you asking me, "Didn't we just say that we are going to have single trunk interface to the router?" You are right, so here is how you are going to do that.

The router must have a separate connection for each IP subnet, not necessarily a separate physical connection. A separate logical connection or subinterface for each VLAN will work just fine. The router will run a trunking protocol, such as ISL or 802.1Q, just like the switch. Take a look at Figure 2.8 and you can see how this is going to look physically.

FIGURE 2.8   Router on a Stick

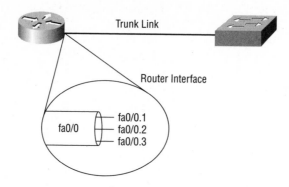

The routing table on the router will show directly connected subnets that are associated with each of the VLANs. They are just configured on the router's subinterfaces. The router must still learn routes to networks that are not directly connected via a dynamic routing protocol.

There are advantages and disadvantages of using the router on a stick configuration for inter-VLAN routing.

Advantages:

- Pretty easy to configure and implement
- Layer 3 switch not required
- Provides the inter-VLAN communication

Disadvantages:

- Can become a single point of failure
- With a single trunk link there may be congestion
- Switch that connects to the router may introduce latency

Configuring Router on a Stick

Now I will show you how to configure routing with an external router—the router on a stick configuration. This type of configuration isn't that common anymore. It is possible that you could use it in a small branch office somewhere that has a few VLANs and where you don't want to spend the money for a multilayer switch. For example, you might do this configuration for a development team that is setting up test networks and needs routing. You would not buy a new router, so you would configure router on a stick. You only need a single switch and a router for this setup. Connect fa0/1 switch to the fa0/0 interface of a router—called Router1 for this exercise.

When you set up this kind of routing, part of the configuration will be on your switch. (You have learned the switch side of the configuration already by configuring a switch port as a trunk that goes to a router.)

On the router, you have to configure the interface with a subinterface for each of the VLANs that you wish to have routed. The additional command will be the `encapsulation` command on each of the subinterfaces. Let's take a look at what the configuration would be if we have the default VLAN 1 and VLANs 10 and 20.

The use of the `encapsulation` command is just like this: `encapsulation [dot1q | isl] vlan-id`.

```
Router1>enable
Router1#configure terminal
Router1(config)#interface Fa0/0.1
Router1(config-if)#ip address 192.168.1.1 255.255.255.0
Router1(config-if)#encapsulation dot1q 1 native
Router1(config-if)#int Fa0/0.10
Router1(config-if)#ip address 192.168.10.1 255.255.255.0
Router1(config-if)#encapsulation dot1q 10
Router1(config-if)#int Fa0/0.20
Router1(config-if)#ip address 192.168.20.1 255.255.255.0
Router1(config-if)#encapsulation dot1q 20
```

We can see from this configuration that each of the VLANs has a subinterface from which to be routed. Notice though in the `encapsulation` command, we specified the protocol being used and the VLAN ID, which is the same ID as is configured on the switch. The router must include the VLAN ID for the encapsulation just like the switch.

Multilayer Switching

Multilayer switching is a function performed by a multilayer switch. A multilayer switch brings the functions of a switch and a router together in one device. Traditionally, a switch forwards traffic based on Layer 2 information and a router forwards traffic based on Layer 3 information. With a multilayer switch, the device can forward traffic that is in the same VLAN at Layer 2 and that same device has the ability to do inter-VLAN routing and forward traffic between VLANs at Layer 3.

Multilayer switches can forward traffic at line speed. (Line speed is a nice way of saying that it forwards the traffic with very little delay.) The forwarding lookups are done in hardware rather than in software. Software lookups require that the forwarding decisions be made by the central processor, a process that takes considerably longer. The hardware that is used to accomplish this is called an application-specific integrated circuit (ASIC).

The routing and required forwarding information are held in the hardware. The information is built into tables that are stored in content-addressable memory (CAM) and ternary content-addressable memory (TCAM). Having this information readily available in hardware makes the forwarding process much more efficient, hence the reason for multilayer switches having wide spread use. In devices today, Cisco Express Forwarding (CEF) is the mechanism that performs this forwarding and uses these tables. We are going to look at CEF in a little more detail in the next section.

In order for a multilayer switch to have the ability to route, it needs a route processor. However, remember that on routers each interface is a separate subnet; this is a fundamental part of its functionality. A router routes traffic from one network or subnet to another. On a switch, when we think about the physical ports, they are Layer 2 ports and cannot have an IP address configured on them. So where do we put Layer 3 information on a switch?

Well, if you think back to your CCNA days of studying, you always assign the management IP address for a switch to the VLAN 1 interface. This interface exists by default on all switches. The interface itself is called a switched virtual interface (SVI). The SVI provides the Layer 3 path and default gateway for hosts in the VLAN. These SVI are the Layer 3 interfaces that the route processor uses to route between subnets. On a Layer 2 switch such as 2950 or 2960, there is only one SVI that can be used at a time. On a multilayer switch, however, you can create an SVI for each of the VLANs that you wish to route to. The maximum number of SVIs that you can have on a switch depends on a few things:

- Switch platform

- Number of supported VLANs

- Processing overhead

Processing overhead isn't so much a hard limit but something you will have to watch. If your switch is acting slow or has a constantly maxed out processor, then you may have too many interfaces configured or too much data being routed across the device.

Multilayer switches can also be configured with true routed ports, which means you can configure the port to act just as a port on a real router would. You can place the IP address and router interface commands directly on the interface. The port when configured this way is no longer part of any VLAN; it represents a subnet just as a router interface would.

Cisco Express Forwarding (CEF)

CEF is the newest Cisco proprietary switching or forward type. CEF makes the forwarding process in multilayer switches and routers much faster and more efficient. The history of switching includes a couple of different forwarding types.

Routing The lineage of switching really started in routers. When you hear switching, you typically think Layer 2 switches; however, switching is really moving a piece of data from one interface to another. So, when a router moved a packet from one interface to another internally, it is really switching the traffic. Routing was the process the router used to determine which interface had to be the outgoing interface to move the data toward its destination.

Process Switching The first switching was just process switching; all of the data packets had to be processed through the central processor. Process switching was very time consuming and delayed the packets.

Cache-Based Switching Cache-based switching has had a few different names—Netflow switching, "route one switch many"—but they refer to the same thing. When the first packet enters the device, it is process switched so that all the appropriate information can be determined. Once the device has the forwarding information, it is cached in a fast lookup table. When the rest of the packets in the flow enter the device, the forwarding lookup can be accomplished in RAM by looking at the information in the cache table.

Cisco Express Forwarding The current forwarding type is CEF. CEF is also called topology-based switching. CEF allows for fast forwarding of data at Layers 2 and 3 by building new tables to hold the information in hardware.

Building the Forwarding Information Base (FIB) Table

CEF builds a new routing table called the forwarding information base (FIB). The FIB table holds all of the routes the same way the routing table does; the FIB is constructed from the routing table. CEF is not a routing protocol itself. It relies on a routing protocol to build and update the routing table from which the FIB is built. When CEF is enabled, the FIB table has the same authority as the routing table. If a destination network is not in the FIB when a packet comes into the device, then the packet is dropped just as it would be with the standard routing table.

Building the Adjacency Table

CEF also builds an adjacency table that houses the Layer 2 information for forwarding decisions. The adjacency table is stored in CAM and lookup time is improved through the use of search algorithms. A key is created to compare the frame to the table content. Let me give you an example. The destination MAC address and VLAN ID (VID) of a frame constitute the key for Layer 2 table lookup. This key is fed into a hashing algorithm, which produces a pointer into the table. The system uses the pointer to access a smaller specific area of the table without requiring a search of the entire table.

Preparing to Transmit

Once the forwarding decision has been made and the packet has been switched across the routing device, the frame must be rewritten to be transmitted on the new network. IP unicast packets are rewritten on the output interface like this. First, the device must change the source MAC address from the sender's to its own. Second, the device must change the destination MAC address from its address to the next hop's address. Third, the time to live (TTL) must be decremented by one, which means that the IP header checksum must be recalculated. Last, the frame checksum must be recalculated.

Configuring Inter-VLAN Routing

To configure an inter-VLAN, I am going to go back to the network in Figure 2.7. For this example, your DSW1 switch must use a multilayer switch (3550, 3560, or 3750). Also, the switch block you are creating will use VLANs 10 and 20, so if you have not created them in your VLAN database, you will need to create them.

I will show you how to turn on routing in your multilayer switch. Then, you have to configure the interfaces to route from. Finally, I will show you how to create routed ports on your multilayer switch.

First, we need to enable routing on your multilayer switch. By default, routing is not enabled; a multilayer switch is still a switch first. The command to enable routing is nothing more than ip routing.

```
DSW1>enableDSW1#configure terminal
DSW1(config)#ip routing
```

Now that routing is enabled, you have to give the switch, and more important the VLANs, a Layer 3 interface from which to route. The feature is called an SVI. The SVI is configured with the interface vlan **vlan-id** command. Because VLAN 10 and VLAN 20 are the VLANs used in this switch block, you have to create an SVI for each one.

 If you have not created the VLAN in the VLAN database, creating an SVI for a VLAN will not create the VLAN in the VLAN database. The VLAN and the SVI for a VLAN are completely separate items.

```
DSW1(config)#interface vlan 10
DSW1(config-if)#ip address 192.168.10.1 255.255.255.0
DSW1(config-if)#no shutdown
DSW1(config-if)#interface vlan 20
DSW1(config-if)#ip address 192.168.20.1 255.255.255.0
DSW1(config-if)#no shutdown
```

Notice that once the SVI has been created, enabling the interface and setting the IP address is done just like on a router interface.

Finally, you're ready to create a routed interface on the switch. A routed interface will function just like a router port. It isn't part of a VLAN. You can use it to connect a single system such as a server or firewall. This will give you a network that has only one system and only one switch port is needed, which you can compare with a network where you have multiple hosts and each of them use their own port as part of a VLAN.

The command for this configuration is just no switchport. The switchport command is used to configure most of the Layer 2 functions for the switch, so by saying no switchport you take away the Layer 2 functions and leave a Layer 3 port.

```
DSW1(config)#interface Fa0/1
DSW1(config-if)#no switchport
```

So, now you have configured the functionality for inter-VLAN routing. This gives you the routing ability you need inside the switch block and ultimately out of the switch block to the rest of the network.

EtherChannel

Everyone knows that networks always need more bandwidth. End users want fast responses and more applications. So many applications today are huge bandwidth suckers. With the wider use of video, audio, and intensive web applications, the requirement for bandwidth keeps getting higher. To combat this growing need, Cisco developed EtherChannel. EtherChannel is a switch-to-switch technique that inversely multiplexes multiple Fast or Gigabit Ethernet switch ports into one logical channel. Its major advantage is being cheaper than higher-speed media while utilizing existing switch ports.

EtherChannel can be used for other reasons. It can increase the bandwidth to a single server. EtherChannel is used this way quite a bit today with the growth of virtual servers and so much data coming and going from a single system.

EtherChannel is also very useful as an upgrade path instead of having to immediately upgrade switches to newer more expensive devices. For example, think about the switch block that you have been building in this chapter. The hosts connect to the switches on Fast Ethernet connections and the access switch connects to the distribution switch with a Gigabit Ethernet connection. That may be fine right now, but in a couple of months when the number of users on the switch has grown and the amount of data they generate has increased, it probably won't be enough. What are you going to do?

You could buy more expensive switches that have 10 Gigabit Ethernet uplinks to the distribution switches. You might get hung for asking to buy them too! You could buy more switches so that you could spread out the users more, but again you are buying more equipment.

Here is where EtherChannel comes in. You can add an additional Gigabit Ethernet connection between the switches and bundle them together, essentially doubling the throughput you have between the switches. EtherChannel is a cross-platform method of load balancing between servers, switches, and routers. EtherChannel can combine two, four, or eight ports (depending on the switch platform) into one logical connection that can deliver redundancy.

EtherChannel doesn't just do round-robin frame-by-frame forwarding on each link like many other load-balancers. The load-balancing policy or frame distribution can use multiple pieces of data to perform the load balancing (depending on the switch platform used). For example, the load-balancing operation could perform an X-OR calculation on the two lowest-order bits of the source and destination MAC address. The X-OR operation between a given pair of addresses uses the same link for all frames. This can be an advantage, but it can also be a disadvantage.

One of the benefits of the X-OR operation is that it prevents out-of-order frames on the receiving switch. Another advantage is redundancy. If the active channel that a connection is using goes down, the rest of the traffic flow can travel over a different active link on that EtherChannel. The disadvantage to X-OR operation is that there is less control in guaranteeing the load on the channels will be equal. This is because the load-balancing policy is using a specific header value, a value that can be defined by the platform or by the user.

Remember the following requirements when configuring EtherChannel:

- All ports in the EtherChannel must be configured to operate at the same speed and in the same duplex mode.

- If an interface in the bundle gets shut down, the switch treats it as a link failure. With a link failure, traffic will traverse other links in the EtherChannel.

- An EtherChannel will not form if one of the interfaces is a SPAN destination port.

- If this is to be a Layer 3 EtherChannel, then the Layer 3 addresses must be configured on the port-channel logical interface, not to the physical interfaces in the channel.

- All ports in the EtherChannel bundle must be assigned to the same VLAN or be configured as a trunk.

- An EtherChannel must have the same allowed range of VLANs on all the interfaces in a trunked Layer 2 EtherChannel. If the allowed range of VLANs is not the same, the interfaces do not form an EtherChannel.

- For Layer 2 EtherChannel bundles, either assign all interfaces in the EtherChannel to the same VLAN or configure them as trunks.

In the "Configuring EtherChannel" section, I cover all the configuration options. For now, let's get a look at the differences in the automatic association protocols (PAgP and LACP) that can be used for EtherChannel setup.

Automatic Bundling Protocols

Cisco has developed a proprietary protocol for creating EtherChannel bundles; it functions much like DTP does for trunk negotiation. The protocol for EtherChannel is called Port Aggregation Protocol (PAgP). PAgP packets are sent between switches on EtherChannel-capable ports. These packets are used to negotiate the forming of a channel. When PAgP finds Ethernet links that match all their settings, it groups or bundles the links into an EtherChannel. The EtherChannel is then added to the spanning tree topology as a single bridge port.

PAgP uses the same type of settings for negotiation as DTP does—ON, desirable, and auto. Table 2.1, shows you each of the modes for PAgP and describes their actions.

TABLE 2.1   PAgP Negotiation Mode Settings

Setting	Description
ON	ON works the same as setting the trunk option in DTP; it forces the negotiation of the EtherChannel and only operates as an EtherChannel.
Desirable	Desirable is the active negotiator. It sends out the PAgP packets to tell the other side of the link it wishes to be an EtherChannel.
Auto	Auto works the same way as it did in DTP. The port passively listens for EtherChannel negotiations and will become part of a bundle if asked.

The other part of the PAgP configuration creates the EtherChannel virtual interface. The virtual interface acts as the single point of entry and exit for data instead of using the physical interfaces. When the switch processor forwards frames to a connected device but the device is connected by an EtherChannel, the virtual interface acts as the single connection for the forwarding process. The virtual interface is also where you can make configuration changes for all of the ports that are in the bundle.

The other automatic negotiation protocol is the Link Aggregation Control Protocol (LACP). LACP is an open standard and part of the 802.3ad specification. LACP, like PAgP, allows multiple ports to be automatically bundled into a single EtherChannel. The biggest difference is that LACP can be used in mixed vendor environments because it is an open standard. The three options for negotiation are listed in Table 2.2. They operate the exact same way, but they have different names.

TABLE 2.2   LACP Negotiation Mode Settings

Setting	Description
ON	ON works the same as setting the trunk option in DTP; it forces the negotiation of the EtherChannel and only operates as an EtherChannel.
Active	Like desirable in PAgP, active is the active negotiator. It sends out the PAgP packets to tell the other side of the link it wishes to be an EtherChannel.
Passive	Passive works the same way as auto did in DTP and PAgP. The port passively listens for EtherChannel negotiations and will become part of a bundle if asked.

In order for LACP to function properly, a couple of other parameters have to be set. The parameters can be set automatically or through manual configuration.

System Priority   Each switch running LACP must have a system priority. The switch automatically uses the MAC address and the system priority to form the system ID.

Port Priority   Each port in the switch must have a port priority. The port priority and the port number form the port identifier. The switch uses the port priority to decide which ports to put in standby mode when a hardware limitation prevents all compatible ports from aggregating. A hardware limitation could be something as simple as the switch only allows four ports to be placed in a bundle.

Administrative Key   Each port in the switch must have an administrative key value. The administrative key defines the ability of a port to aggregate with other ports, determined by a few factors. The port has physical characteristics, such as data rate, duplex capability, and point-to-point or shared medium.

So, basically, setting up an EtherChannel is a pretty painless process. It's especially useful if you need to have more bandwidth from one device to another and don't want to shell out the money for new switches or routers. Now, you may be able to use EtherChannel as a solution before equipment upgrade is mandatory.

Configuring EtherChannel

So, let's configure EtherChannel on a switch. Configure DSW1 from the same test network setup you have been using. Again, refer back to Figure 2.7 if you need to refresh your memory.

1. Configure the port-channel interface.

   The first thing that you have to configure for the EtherChannel is the virtual interface that the switch will use instead of the individual ports. This virtual interface is called a port-channel. The command to configure it is `interface port-channel` **channel-group number**.

   ```
   DSW1(config)#interface port-channel 1
   ```

2. Assign physical ports to the port-channel interface.

   Now that you have created the port-channel interface, you can associate physical ports to it for use in the bundle. To do that, simply go into the interface configuration mode on an interface.

> You can now specify more than one switch port at a time for configuration. To do this, use the `interface range` command. This command was introduced in the 12.1(19)EA1 version of IOS.
>
> Using the `interface range` command, specify ports fa0/19 through fa0/20 on switch DSW1.
>
> ```
> DSW1(config)#interface range Fa0/19 - 20
> ```
>
> Notice when you are specifying the ports, you only have to specify the slot (the fa0/ part of the port number) once. Then, you specify the actual port numbers 19–20. This is because you cannot span across a slot in a switch that has more than one module or blade. If you are using the range command, the ports you are selecting must be on the same module.

3. Associate the ports with a port-channel.

   Now that you have selected a port or range of ports, you can move on to the EtherChannel configuration. The next thing to do is tell the ports what port-channel they are going to be associated with. Use the `channel-group` command on the interface for this step. The channel group number that you specify must match the port-channel interface number that you already created. This number match is what associates the two features together.

   ```
   Switch1(config-if)#channel-group 1
   ```

4.   Set the bundling protocol.

If you wanted to change the channeling or bundling protocol from the default of PAgP to LACP, you can use the `channel-protocol [pagp | lacp]` command. You may have to do this if you are connecting to a different vendors' equipment or a server device that doesn't support Cisco's PAgP.

```
Switch1(config-if)#channel-protocol lacp
```

5.   Set the port negotiation mode.

You can also change the mode in which the port will act in. Remember auto is the default for PAgP and passive is the default for LACP. The command to change the mode is the `channel-group` command that you used already; the mode is appended to the end of the command. So now the command is `channel-group 1 mode [active | on | auto | desirable | passive]`.

```
Switch1(config-if)#channel-group 1 mode desirable
```

You have now created a regular Layer 2 EtherChannel bundle. You can also configure a Layer 3 EtherChannel bundle. When the network includes a Layer 3 core, Layer 3 bundles connect your distribution switches to the core switches. I'll cover the benefits and drawbacks of Layer 2 versus Layer 3 in Chapters 4 through 6 when I cover routing protocols. But, for now, let's take a look at the Layer 3 configuration.

Most of the configuration is the same as what you have already done for EtherChannel. You have to create a port-channel interface, but now on the interface you have to make it a Layer 3 port. How do we do that on a switch? If you said, "Use the `no switchport` command," you are right! When we add physical ports into the bundle, we will also have to make those ports into Layer 3 ports. You are going to see these configurations in my next example. You will make the EtherChannel bundle that you currently have that is a Layer 2 bundle into a Layer 3 bundle.

So let's run through creating a sample Layer 3 EtherChannel.

```
Switch1(config)#interface port-channel 1
Switch1(config-if)#no switchport
Switch1(config-if)#ip address 192.168.30.1 255.255.255.0
Switch1(config-if)#interface range Fa0/19 - 20
Switch1(config-if)# channel-group 1
Switch1(config-if)#no switchport
```

That is the minimum configuration that you need to create a Layer 3 EtherChannel. The only thing that I threw in there on you was the `ip address` command. Since it is Layer 3 interface, it has to have an IP address.

There are a couple of good commands that you can use to verify the configuration and operation of an EtherChannel. First, use the `show running-config` command to check your configuration. You can also use the `show etherchannel channel number port-channel` command to see some statistics on the interface. You can also look at the individual port statistics with the show interfaces fastethernet 0/1 etherchannel command. Try them out once you have your EtherChannel up and running; you can get good information. Hopefully, your configuration is working, but these commands can really help you out if it is not.

Summary

I have discussed and configured tons of great things—many very important things. Most of the topics in this chapter covered items used on a daily basis in the average network. I started off talking about VLANs and how to configure them, and it won't be every day that you make a new VLAN. But you will need to know different ways to create VLANs in the database. Remember, when you associate a port with a VLAN, if the VLAN doesn't exist in the database, it will be created when you try to put the first port into it. So, knowing all the ways that you can create a VLAN is very important. Chances are you could be placing and removing ports from VLANs on a near daily basis, and if you do it incorrectly you could be adding VLANs you don't need or placing ports into a VLAN that will get them nowhere.

You learned about the different modes that you can configure your ports into. Remember that, for security, it is best to have all of your ports in access mode. Only place the ports in trunk mode if they are going to be trunks. Configure trunk links so they are always trunks and not negotiating that mode. DTP can be a useful protocol but, unfortunately, useful protocols are often security threats.

VTP is great for maintaining your VLAN database between many switches, but make sure when you are adding new switches that you add them into the network in client mode at least and, better yet, use transparent mode. If the switch is in transparent mode, the revision number is reset and you won't overwrite your existing database. No RUEs please! There are quite a few options for VTP that can make your network safer and work more efficiently. Don't forget about the password you can set, and be sure to turn on pruning so you don't waste bandwidth.

When it is time to make sure that traffic can go from one VLAN to another, you now have a couple of ways to configure inter-VLAN routing. The router on a stick method works great for smaller areas in your network, such as branch offices, but most of your larger switch blocks are probably going to have a multilayer switch. Remember, there is a difference between an SVI and a routed port. The SVI is the Layer 3 function for the VLAN. Multilayer switches have routing turned off by default. Many people can't get traffic between VLANs simply because they didn't enable it.

Finally, you now have EtherChannel in your arsenal to use against low bandwidth. You can configure Layer 2 and 3 bundles, depending on where they are going and how the link needs to function. The configuration for EtherChannel is pretty easy; don't let something silly like one of the prerequisites prevent you from getting the channel to come up. Remember the list. You have to have the same duplex, speed, VLANs allowed, SPAN ports, and port type. They must all be the same!

Again, practice the configurations that I walked you through. It is important for your practical work on the network and is covered by objectives for certification exams as well. All very important!

Review Questions

1. What feature in a switch provides separate broadcast domains?
   - **A.** STP
   - **B.** Broadcast domain
   - **C.** VLAN
   - **D.** PortFast

2. What type of link on an Ethernet switch is a host connected to?
   - **A.** Trunk link
   - **B.** Access link
   - **C.** EtherChannel
   - **D.** Token Ring

3. What is the IEEE standard for a trunking protocol?
   - **A.** 802.11
   - **B.** 802.3
   - **C.** 802.1Q
   - **D.** 802.5

4. What is the Cisco proprietary trunking protocol?
   - **A.** ISL
   - **B.** dot1q
   - **C.** Token trunk
   - **D.** SS7

5. How many VLANs can an ISL trunk carry?
   - **A.** 4096
   - **B.** 500
   - **C.** 1000
   - **D.** 64

6. What is the default port configuration for DTP?
   - **A.** Dynamic auto
   - **B.** Dynamic desirable
   - **C.** Trunk
   - **D.** Access

7. Will a trunk be formed if both ends are configured for dynamic auto?

    A. Yes

    B. No

    C. Don't know

    D. All of the above

8. End-to-end VLANs are the recommended way to configure VLANs in today's networks?

    A. True

    B. False

9. VTP maintains what database across all of your switches?

    A. VLAN

    B. Port

    C. EtherChannel

    D. Port security

10. A feature to route between VLANs using just one router port and a VLAN trunk is called what?

    A. Routing

    B. Inter-VLAN

    C. Router on a stick

    D. Impaled router

Answers to Review Questions

1. C. VLANs provide separate broadcast domains on switches by logically dividing the switch.

2. B. Hosts are typically connected to access links.

3. C. The IEEE standard for trunking is 802.1Q.

4. A. The Cisco proprietary trunking protocol is ISL.

5. C. ISL can only carry 1000 VLANs as compared to dot1q carrying 4095.

6. B. Dynamic desirable is the default for Cisco switch ports.

7. B. If both ends are set to auto, then no trunk will be formed because no DTP request packets are being sent.

8. B. False. VLANs are recommended to be configured as local VLANs.

9. A. VTP maintains the VLAN database across all of your switches.

10. C. Router on a stick is the feature with this setup to provide inter-VLAN routing.

Chapter

3

Spanning Tree Protocol (STP)

IN THIS CHAPTER, YOU WILL LEARN HOW TO DO THE FOLLOWING:

- ✓ Describe the operation of STP

- ✓ Explain the functions and operations of the Spanning Tree Protocols (i.e., RSTP, PVRST, MSTP)

- ✓ Configure RSTP (PVRST) and MST

- ✓ Describe and configure STP security mechanisms (i.e., BPDU Guard, BPDU Filtering, Root Guard)

- ✓ Configure and verify UDLD and Loop Guard

- ✓ Verify and troubleshoot Spanning Tree Protocol operations

Well, you might have thought you were done with switching, but there is more. In this discussion, I talk about how you control the topology and your connections. In the last chapter, I mentioned Spanning Tree Protocol (STP), which is used to verify that your switched infrastructure does not have loops. You want to have redundant links between switches. You want those extra links so that if one goes down, there is a second to take its place.

The goal in this chapter is to understand all of the functions of STP and how it prevents broadcast storms, multiple frame copies, and protects the stability of the MAC address table. I'm going to give you a look at a few different types of STP, as there have been upgrades to the protocol over the years. Those upgrades include port fast and what I like to call the guard functions: BPDU Guard, Root Guard, Loop Guard, and BPDU filtering. STP is very important to the operation of your switched network, so pay attention.

NOTE   For up-to-the-minute updates on this chapter, check out www.sybex.com/go/CiscoProGuidetoInternetworking or www.lammle.com.

STP Operation

The first thing to look at is the original IEEE 802.1d STP protocol. Under this standard, when STP starts up on a switch, which by default is automatic when a switch boots, it sends out information so that each of the switches can compare themselves to one another for the purpose of finding who has the best bridge ID. The information is basically a hello frame. Specifically, in STP the hello is called Bridge Protocol Data Unit or BPDU. The BPDU allows all of the switches to see what the best switch is in order to elect a root bridge and how (on what links) they are connected to each other. This comparison ultimately allows each switch to become part of the shortest path tree. A single tree structure is built, starting at the root bridge and working down through the rest of the switches, and is used to prevent loops in the network.

I'm going to introduce you to each of the components that make up the shortest path tree including the Root Bridge, root ports, and designated ports. I'll also cover the comparison or election process and, finally, the full operation of STP in your network.

STP Components

It's time to take a closer look at all of the components that STP uses to perform its job. As I already mentioned, one of the first things that must be done is allow all of the switches to communicate to each other about their seniority in the network. Seniority is determined by the switch's Bridge ID (BID). I'll cover the way a switch finds its BID in the next section. The BID must be communicated to each of the switches in the connected switch fabric. By *switch fabric* I mean all of the switches that are connected in a broadcast domain. BPDUs are only propagated within a broadcast domain. The STP Hello frame is called a BPDU, and it contains a switch's BID. Take a look at Figure 3.1 and Table 3.1, where I show you the other fields in a BPDU.

FIGURE 3.1   BPDU Fields

Protocol Identifier (2 bytes)	Version (1 byte)	Message Type (1 byte)	Flags (1 byte)	Root ID (8 bytes)	Root Path Cost (4 bytes)	Bridge ID (8 bytes)	Port ID (2 bytes)	Message Age (2 bytes)	Maximum Age (2 bytes)	Hello Time (2 bytes)	Forward Delay (2 bytes)

TABLE 3.1   BPDU Field Descriptions

BPDU Field	Description
Protocol Identifier	The Protocol Identifier field indicates the type of protocol. This field contains the value zero.
Version	The Version field indicates the version of the protocol. This field contains the value zero.
Message Type	The Message Type field indicates the type of message. This field contains the value zero.
Flags	The Flags field includes one of the following:
	Topology change (TC) bit, which signals a topology change
	Topology change acknowledgment (TCA) bit, which is set to acknowledge receipt of a configuration message with the TC bit set
Root ID	The Root ID field indicates the root bridge by listing its 2-byte priority followed by its 6-byte ID.
Root Path Cost	The Root Path Cost field indicates the cost of the path from the bridge sending the configuration message to the root bridge.
Bridge ID	The Bridge ID field indicates the priority and ID of the bridge sending the message.

TABLE 3.1   BPDU Field Descriptions *(continued)*

BPDU Field	Description
Port ID	The Port ID field indicates the port number from which the configuration message was sent. This field allows loops created by multiple attached bridges to be detected and corrected.
Message Age	The Message Age field indicates the amount of time that has elapsed since the root sent the configuration message on which the current configuration message is based.
Maximum Age	The Maximum Age field indicates when the current configuration message should be deleted.
Hello Time	The Hello Time field indicates the time between root bridge configuration messages.
Forward Delay	The Forward Delay field indicates the length of time that bridges should wait before transitioning to a new state after a topology change. If a bridge transitions too soon, it is possible that not all network links will be ready to change their state and loops can result.

BPDUs are sent out to all ports that are not in blocking mode, on all switches every two seconds. This default two second duration is controlled by the hello timer. I talk more about timers coming up when I take you through the operating steps of STP.

Once the seniority of all the switches as been determined, then the best switch makes itself the Root Bridge. The best switch is the switch that has the lowest BID.

NOTE   Fact: The "bridge" in Root Bridge is a leftover from the days when STP that ran on bridges and switches didn't yet exist.

The Root Bridge is now going to act as the root of the shortest path tree. Every other switch will determine its best path to the root bridge. Once the best path for every other switch is determined, the tree structure starts to take form with each of the non–root bridge switches forming a branch in the tree.

At this point you need to understand what port states are. For this first version of STP, various ports play specific roles: root, designated, or nondesignated. It is through these port roles that the branches of the tree are found.

Root Port   A port is designated as the root port of a switch when it is connected to the path or segment that is the best path back to the root bridge. Each switch has one—and only one—root port, with the exception of the root bridge, which does not have a root port. The root port is always the path out of the switch leading to the root bridge.

Designated Port Every network segment must have one designated port. The designated port is the port that is in forwarding mode. To make sure you understand, there must be one—and only one—designated port on every segment. The exception to this rule is the root bridge; every port on the root bridge is placed in the designated port state.

Nondesignated Port A nondesignated port is a port that is in blocking mode. You can have one nondesignated port on a segment, but a nondesignated port is not always needed, like in the case of a root port's being connected to the designated port of the root bridge.

Now let me take you back to the STP process. The root bridge has all of its ports set as designated ports. All of the other switches find the port that is connected to their best path to the root bridge, and assign that port role of Root Port. At this point, the rest of the tree is determined and all other segments place their ports in designated and nondesignated status. I'll tell you more about the process of figuring out all of those paths in the "Determining Paths" section later in this chapter. First, I'll show you how the root bridge is determined.

Switch Identification

As I told you earlier, the switches determine seniority, but we need to know how they do this. It is an election process. So, what determines which one the best is? Do all of the switches submit votes? Well, sort of. Each switch sends out its BID, which is a field in the BPDUs, for comparison. Each switch must have a BID. Okay, so on to the next question you are asking. How does a switch determine its BID? Every switch basically determines its own BID based on two values already in the system; you can configure one value and the other you generally cannot.

The BID is then made up of two pieces. The first is the system priority. By default, every switch's priority is 32768. You can change this value, but only in increments in 4096. So, the lowest value is 0 and the next is 4096, then 8192, and so on. The full range runs from 0 to 65536. The lower you set the value, the higher the switch raises in the election results.

Now you have the first part of the BID, the second half of the BID is the switch's MAC address. The MAC address used is the system MAC address, and the system MAC address is the MAC address assigned to the switch. It would also use this MAC address to send traffic that is sourced from the switch itself.

Now once you have both of these pieces, you can make the BID. You essentially just write them together. First, write the priority then a dot like this: 32768.; then you add the MAC address written in three groups separated by dots. So the whole thing would look like this: 32768.00c0.004c.3451. Now you have the whole BID.

You may be asking yourself, "Okay, great, now I have the BID. What is done with it now?" Well, here's where the election process I mentioned comes in.

During the election process all of the switches compare their BIDs and the switch with the lowest BID wins and becomes the root bridge. Yes, that's right—the lowest number wins. Now, just so that you understand how to compare the BID, first the priority is looked at. If all the switches carry the default priority of 32768, then nothing is decided at this point.

You must next look at the MAC address. The MAC address is compared bit by bit, and the switch with the lowest MAC becomes the root bridge. Once the root bridge is identified, then each of the other switches determines their best path to the Root Bridge and that starts forming the shortest path tree. The next thing I show you is how the paths are chosen and how the redundant paths are blocked.

Determining Paths

A switch uses a series of three factors to determine the best path between switches. Those three factors are:

- Path cost
- BID
- Port ID

All three factors are not necessarily used in every instance of path selection but at least one of them will. They are, however, always used in the order I just listed.

Path Cost Over the years, the standard by which the path cost is determined has changed. The old scale used to be a very easy to calculate value that was based on a linear scale. Those linear scale values were determined by dividing a reference bandwidth (1,000,000,000 bits per second) by the real bandwidth of the link. The new standard for STP path cost is a nonlinear scale assigned based on the standard path speeds. There isn't a nice easy way to calculate the cost anymore, but you get to memorize some fun random numbers now! (I hope you can hear the sarcasm in my voice.) The path cost is the total sum of all the segments in the entire path. The path with the lowest cost is selected. Each segment has a cost based on its speed. Table 3.2 lists the breakdown.

TABLE 3.2   Spanning Tree Protocol Path Costs

Link Bandwidth	Old Cost	New Cost
4 Mbps	250	250
10 Mbps	100	100
16 Mbps	63	62
45 Mbps	22	39
100 Mbps	10	19
155 Mbps	6	14
1 Gbps	1	4
10 Gbps	0	2

BID   The BID is used to compare two bridges on a segment. A switch compares its BID to its designated bridge's BID. A designated bridge is the bridge that the local switch considers its directly connected neighbor along the root path; traffic must go through this neighboring bridge to get to the root bridge along the root path.

Port ID   Port ID is the last criteria in the list, the final tie breaker. If the other two factors have not produced a winner, then the port with the lowest port number is selected.

I always make a joke about elections in IT-related topics; this last tie-breaking value in a series of values seems to almost always be a case of "My mom is prettier than your mom." It's almost as if we were fighting about it on the play ground at school. The port ID is that value for STP, and that seems to help me remember it.

Let's take a look at a few examples. I want to start out simply. To help you understand where you might to see this, let's look at the FutureTech network. For these basic STP examples, you will see them anywhere you have more than one switch connected together. You will also see as I go through the examples that it only takes two or three switches to examine the basics of STP. So, it is very easy to recreate a situation and practice configuring them. Think about where you probably spend most of your time, in the access layer of the network, places where there are users to mess things up for you! The access layer or a switch block isn't the only place in the network to think about of course; if you have a Layer 2 network core, you will see the exact same things happen there.

Look at the first example shown in Figure 3.2. For this example, you are one of the lead network engineers in the corporate headquarters of FutureTech. So here is the situation.

 Real World Scenario

Super Widget XT

The sales staff for one of the most popular new products, Super Widget XT, has almost doubled in the last few months. This growth requires the implementation a new switch in the access layer of the switch block that services the sales group. The switch will be physically cabled to two distribution switches.

Once the new switch is in place, look at where it fits into the network and what its STP role is. Just look at the new switch and the distribution switches that it is connected to. (In later examples, I will show you some of the effects of having more switches and not having STP configured properly.)

For right now, three switches are connected. The two switches, DSW1 and DSW2, at the top of the figure represent the distribution layer switches in a switch block. The switch, ASW1, on the bottom of the diagram represents the new access layer switch that you recently added to the network.

FIGURE 3.2   Determining STP Root Ports with Path Cost

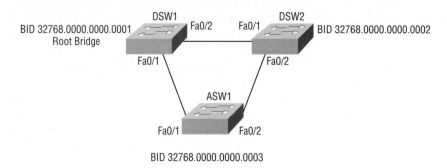

When you examine the BID on each of the switches, you see that DSW1has been elected as the root bridge because it has the lowest BID. (Later in this chapter, I show you the output from the show spanning-tree command where you can see the BID for a switch.) You will have to look at the BID on each of the individual switches and compare them.

Write It Down

When I am doing this for real, say at a client's office doing a network assessment, I create a diagram. (It would be nice if the company had a diagram of the network, but that is rarely the case.) On the diagram, I put down the seniority of each switch. There is no use in figuring out where in the pecking order all of the switches are multiple times.

You should always have a diagram of the network. Just write down which switch is the Root Bridge and which switch is the second best, third best, and so on. I just write a number directly on the switch. That number indicates the order of the switch. This way, when I am trying to figure out the other links between the switches, I don't have to keep looking at the BIDs to figure which switch is the best. A simple diagram will save you a bunch of time.

The next step is to figure out the root port for the other two switches, DSW2 and ASW1. The root port, again, is the port that connects them on the best path to the root bridge. In order to figure out the root ports, you have to determine the path costs for each of the non–root bridges. Notice all of the segments between the switches are 100 Mbps links, so each segment has a cost of 19. For each of the non–root switches, the path through fa0/1, the port directly connected to the root bridge, has a path cost of 19.

Now, notice that each switch has an alternate route to the root bridge, through their fa0/2 port. But, if either of the non–root switches was to choose the fa0/2 interface as its root port, the path cost would increase to 38. The path cost goes up because along that path to the root bridge, traffic must cross two segments, each with a cost of 19.

Take a look at Figure 3.3. In this segment, there are just two switches. To determine the port status for each of the switches, first check the MAC address in the BID. DSW1, based on the MAC address in the BID, is the root bridge. The root bridge's ports all become designated ports. To determine the port status for the non–root bridge, begin by checking the path cost. Both of the links between the switches are 100 Mbps links, which means that the path cost between them is the same at 19. The next determining factor is the BID. Since there are only two switches and the root bridge has all of its interfaces as designated already, this won't determine the root port, the final and determining factor becomes the port ID. Since the two ports are ports fa0/7 and fa0/8, the port with the lower port ID becomes the root port. In this case, port fa0/7 becomes the root port and fa0/8 becomes the nondesignated port and is placed in blocking mode.

FIGURE 3.3   Determining STP Root Ports with Port ID

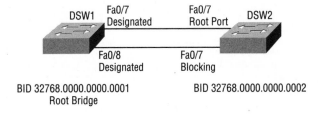

Now, consider what would happen in that same two-switch network segment if switch DSW2 had a 10 Mbps link connected to fa0/7 and the link connected on fa0/8 was 100 Mbps link. Would the root port be different? If you said, "Yes," then you are right. When the path costs are different for the links, the path cost becomes the determining factor. Since the slower 10 Mbps link has a cost of 100 and the 100 Mbps has a cost of 19, the 100 Mbps link, port fa0/8, becomes the root port.

But what if neither of the switches is the root bridge? You have to go a step further and figure out the port states between two switches when neither is the root bridge. Look at Figure 3.4. Here you see three switches. DSW1 is again the root bridge. This time look specifically at the link between the two non–root switches, ASW1 and ASW2. Once again, you must determine which port will be designated and which will be in the blocking mode.

Again, go back to the three factors for determining roles: path cost, BID, and port ID. This time, the path cost for both of the switches is the same, as both are 100 Mbps links. Each carries a path cost of 19 when traffic travels across the link. The second factor is the BID. Now you'll see a difference between the switches' BIDs in this case. You can see the BID of switch ASW1 is lower than the BID of switch ASW2, which means that ASW1 will have the designated port and ASW2 will have the nondesignated port.

FIGURE 3.4   Determining Port Roles for Non–roots

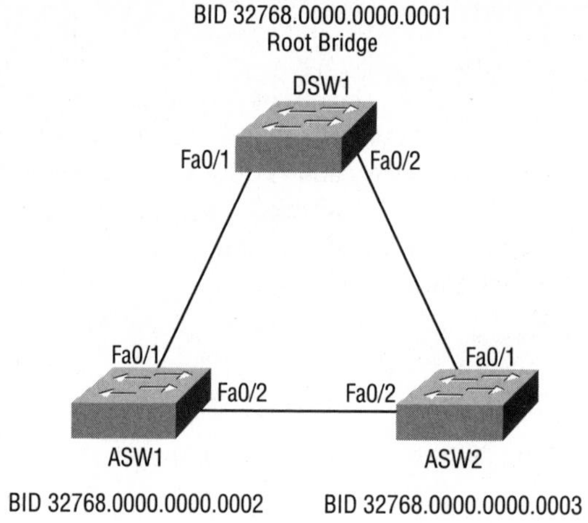

Configuring Spanning Tree Protocol

So, now you know how the switches automatically elect a root using the BID. However, leaving the election to the automatic method may leave something to be desired in your production network. Remember, using the automatic method, the only thing a switch needs to be elected root bridge is the lowest BID. This means that the oldest slowest switch in your network could end up being the root because it could very well have the lowest MAC address on the network. I have seen an old 1900 series switch become the root in a network with new, great 3560 and 4500 series switches. If the traffic load is high, then having this old slow switch as your root bridge will not be a good thing. Not only will load be an issue but if the switch fails or goes down, there is no clear definition of the backup switch is going to be. Both of these things can be addressed with a couple of fairly simple configurations. Let's take a look. I show you how you can configure one or two things to prevent this. You can configure the newer switches to win the election and become the root bridge or make sure that the old switch will never be elected by configuring it so that it can never win.

Setting Priorities Manually

The command for setting priorities manually is spanning-tree [*VLAN number* | *VLAN list*] priority *value*. It would look something like this.

```
Switch1(config)#spanning-tree vlan 1, 10-20 priority 4096
```

Notice with this command after the VLAN 1, I added 10-20. This option is a VLAN list. You can use commas to separate individual VLAN numbers or the hyphen to specify a range of VLANs. Then, I configured the bridge priority to 4096. The next thing that you should do is specify a backup root, that can be done like this.

```
Switch2(config)#spanning-tree vlan 1, 10-20 priority 8192
```

🌐 Real World Scenario

When You Want It Done Right . . .

There are many reasons why you might want to designate which switch is going to be the root bridge. I run into all sorts of problems caused by automatic elections in client networks. Believe me, they can be a pain to troubleshoot when the network goes down. Fortunately, the fix is very easy; all you have to do is manually set your STP topology. Here are some of the things that I have seen; they aren't in any order of significance.

- Poor direction or flow of traffic

- Overwhelmed old switch

- Switch with slow links being the root

- No backup root configured

Like I mentioned, you can specify the VLANs that you want to configure in more of a real list fashion. To show you an example of this, consider: what if you didn't want to set the priority for all the VLANs between 10 and 20 and you had other VLANs outside that initial range that needed to be configured? You can configure just the VLANs that you want. Check this configuration out.

```
Switch2(config)#spanning-tree vlan 1, 10, 13, 17, 19-23 priority 8192
```

Using a Macro to Set Priorities

Another way to configure the root and backup is to use a built-in macro.

Concept: Macros

Just so that you have a little information on the use of macros, I want to tell you about macros and how you can use them. You have the ability in the Cisco IOS to create your own macros. Macros for the most part just make it easier for you to do multiple mundane tasks. You can configure a macro to run four or five commands to set up a new interface, for example. Instead of having to type in all of those separate commands, you could use a macro and it will run them for you.

Quite a few macros are built into the IOS. With many of them, you may not realize that they are macros. Most people think that it is just the command they have to use to accomplish a task.

One of these macros, the STP macro, has the ability to configure a couple of things. First, you can use the macro to configure the STP priority for the primary and secondary switches in the network, or what will be the root bridge and the backup root bridge. The second configuration is optional; it allows you to change the values of all the STP timers. This is what the macro commands look like.

```
Switch1(config)#spanning-tree vlan 1, 10-20 root primary {diameter diameter}
Switch1(config)#spanning-tree vlan 1, 10-20 root secondary {diameter diameter}
```

Now, the problem with using this STP macro is how and when it configures the priority for each switch you use it on. By default, it sets the priority of the primary switch to 24,576, unless there is an existing switch in the network that has a priority lower than that already. If there is a switch with a lower priority, the macro makes the primary switch's priority 4096 lower than the lowest priority existing in the switched network. For the secondary switch the macro makes the switch's priority 28672, unless there is a switch with a lower priority in the network.

Now configuring the priorities in this way is okay, as long as you don't put another switch into the network with a lower priority. Adding the lower priority switch will negate the fact that you ran the macro at all. Why? Because the macro will not run again after the new switch is put into the network, so it will lose the election like any other switch would that has a higher priority.

One additional issue that you could run into is if another switch is configured at 4096 already. I said that running the macro will set the priority to 4096 lower than whatever the lowest value is, but it will not set the priority to 0. The macro doesn't set the priority to 0 and therefore fails. When the macro fails, you have to set the priority manually like you did above with the priority option. In most cases, it is safer to set both the primary and the secondary with the manual configuration. That way you are sure which switches are taking the root and backup root roles and you can modify those devices if you wish to.

I said that you could use this macro to change the values of the STP timers as well. It does this by using the diameter option. The `diameter` option is a way for STP to calculate all of the timers at once using the size of the network as a reference. Remember the timers I am talking about:

- Hello timer
- Max age timer
- Forward delay timer

These timers define how long it will take the STP topology to converge following a change. By default, the timer values are determined by assuming that the network has a diameter of 7. You may be wondering what I mean by diameter; it is simply the number of switches traffic could go through as it moves from one side of the switch fabric to the other. The diameter value can be set to anything between 2 and 7. Changing this diameter value allows all of the timers to be calculated at one time, ensuring that they are set properly and will not conflict with each other. Configuring the STP diameter value is the best way to change the timers.

Configuring the Path Cost

Remember that the path cost is the sum of each of the link costs along a path. That link cost is basically the inverse of the link bandwidth. It is possible to artificially select or control the path that might be chosen by changing the link cost between switches on an interface-by-interface basis. Now, before I show you this, I have to tell you that great care must be taken in calculating the path costs before you make any changes. If you just start changing costs on a port for a path, it is still possible that another path could be chosen or, even worse, you could just start making lower bandwidth links appear to be better links! I know you aren't going to do that, now are you? Not after all of this STP discussion.

Here is how you change the path cost. The last *cost* parameter in the command has a range of 1 to 65,535.

```
Switch1(config-if)#spanning-tree vlan 1 cost cost
```

Configuring the Port ID Value

If the path cost and the BID are the same for two switches, then the last determining factor is the port ID. Well, the truth about the port ID is that there is more to it than just the port number itself. The port ID value is really made up of two things: the port priority and the port ID. The second part of the port ID really is the port number I've already discussed. The first half of the value is what is called the port priority. Because of the priority field, you can actually have an effect on how the port ID value is used in determining which port and path is used in the STP tree. Lowering the value in the priority field indicates to the STP that the path is preferred.

Here is how you can change the priority on the port. You must configure this parameter an individual port basis on the ports that you want to manipulate. By default the port priority is 128, but you can change the port-priority value to any number between 0 and 255. The command would look like this:

```
Switch1(config-if)#spanning-tree vlan 1 port-priority port-priority
```

Load Balancing Using Port Priority

Modifying the port-priority value is a good way of configuring load balancing across redundant links between switches.

Why would I do this you ask? Think about how you get to use the available bandwidth when STP is running. You now know that there should be redundant links between switches for failover purposes, but it is a great advantage to have them for load balancing as well. You can use the bandwidth across both of the links that already are connected between switches.

Let's take a look at Figure 3.5 and I will show you what I mean. Put yourself back into the FutureTech network. I told you before that the number of employees in one of sales departments had almost doubled in the past few months. Well, FutureTech is doing very well in other areas too. The Portland Branch office has experienced a good deal of growth as well.

Real World Scenario

Load Balancing in the Lab

The Portland office designs and engineers IP-based security devices, including video cameras, infrared scopes, motion sensors, and an array of other products. Sometimes in a real network, the perfect design principles that I have told you about don't get used like they should. In engineering environments, like the one the Portland office, you can be faced with a lab situation where a large number of devices are added and removed from the network with little warning. You might end up with switches that are just connected in a daisy chain. It isn't a perfect situation and you need to control the number of switches that are added like this, but it happens. I see setups like this in networks all the time.

Now my point for a situation like this is that you need to ensure that there is enough upstream bandwidth. When I say *upstream bandwidth* I mean bandwidth from one switch to another. Take a look at Switch 1 in Figure 3.5; it's daisy-chained to Switch 2. There are a couple of ways that you can accomplish the task of creating more bandwidth between the two switches. EtherChannel is one option, but you could load balance as well.

FIGURE 3.5   Load Balancing between Switches

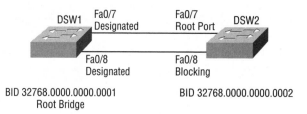

Load-balancing configuration can be accomplished by separating out the VLANs. Remember the *VLAN list* option in the command. Say, for instance, we have 10 VLANs and two interfaces between two switches, ports fa0/7 and fa0/8. If you change the port priority for VLANs 1–5 to something lower on port fa0/7 and change the priority for VLANs 6–10 to something lower on port fa0/8, then the traffic in VLANs 1–5 would take the preferred path through fa0/7, and for VLANs 6–10, the preferred path would be through fa0/8. If one of the links failed, STP would converge and the VLANs assigned to the failed link would begin using the other port. Pretty cool, huh!

The actual configuration would be like this.

```
Switch1(config)#interface fa0/7
Switch1(config-if)#spanning-tree vlan 1-5 cost 64
Switch1(config-if)#interface fa0/8
```

```
Switch1(config-if)#spanning-tree vlan 6-10 cost 64
Switch2(config)#interface fa0/7
Switch2(config-if)#spanning-tree vlan 1-5 cost 64
Switch2(config-if)#interface fa0/8
Switch2(config-if)#spanning-tree vlan 6-10 cost 64
```

History of STP

Now that you understand the operation of 802.1d STP and its primary functions, it is time to take a look at the shortcomings of this original standard. Possibly the biggest problems arose around the amount of time it takes to converge the network, to move a port into forwarding state, and to allow a host to send traffic.

Another major issue arose when VLANs were included in the network topology. IEEE 802.1d STP operates at Layer 2. When the switch or bridge topology only had Layer 2 boundaries, 802.1d worked well. It did not have to deal with Layer 3 borders or the possibility of a different topology with each VLAN. Cisco saw many of these needs before an open standard change was made to the protocol.

Cisco saw the need to improve on the default functions that existed in the original 802.1d standard of STP. Those improvements are in the Cisco-proprietary standard known as PVST. PVST's being a Cisco protocol requires the use of ISL trunk links between the switches.

Cisco also enhanced STP to speed topology convergence. In PVST, Cisco created features, such as PortFast, BackboneFast, and UplinkFast, that aid in time-sensitive events.

PortFast   PortFast allows an access link to transition to forwarding state immediately instead of waiting for STP to converge. This functionality allows host machines that will not cause a loop to begin communicating faster.

BackboneFast   BackboneFast allows for a shortened convergence time by determining whether there are additional paths to the root bridge; by doing this it can find an indirect link failure.

UplinkFast   UplinkFast allows a switch that loses its root path to begin forwarding on a predetermined backup path within just a few seconds rather than waiting for a full STP convergence.

The first open standard change to STP came in the 802.1q standard. This STP type is referred to as Common Spanning Tree (CST), but it required the use of dot1q trunks and implemented a single spanning tree topology that was carried in untagged frames over the native VLAN. Because PVST and CST each required the use of different trunking protocols, there was no interoperability between them. To resolve this problem, Cisco made an enhancement to PVST called PVST+. PVST+ is a standard that allows 802.1d and PVST to interoperate in a switched network.

The next sections cover each of these changes and features.

PVST+

Per-VLAN Spanning Tree Plus (PVST+) effectively supports three groups of STP operating in the same campus network. It allows switches running PVST, switches running PVST+, and switches running CST over 802.1Q to interoperate. For this to work, PVST+ acts as a middleman between groups of CST switches and groups of PVST switches. PVST+ can communicate directly with PVST over ISL trunks.

The communication with CST is a bit different. PVST+ exchanges BPDUs with CST as untagged frames over the native VLAN. BPDUs from other instances of STP are propagated across the CST portions or an instance of the network through tunneling. PVST+ uses a multicast group address to send these BPDUs. Using multicast, the CST switches can send the BPDUs to neighbors that won't have to interpret them. The tunneled BPDUs will ultimately reach other PVST+ switches where they will be read and used.

PortFast

PortFast is a wonderful feature that allows you to connect a workstation or user host device to a switch and have the port transition to forwarding almost immediately. This is particularly important for workstations that get their TCP/IP information from a DHCP server. By default, PortFast is not enabled. Without PortFast, when an access port goes up or down (say, from a workstation being cycled or turned on) then the port must transition through the STP states. This process takes at least 30 seconds. The default timers for listening and learning modes are each 15 seconds, finally getting to the forwarding state after their expiration. If the port is configured with PAgP for EtherChannel, then an extra 20 seconds could be added on to that time, resulting in a possible 50-second delay before the host could send or receive traffic. With PortFast enabled, the transition to forwarding is immediate, which lets a host begin communicating right away.

As long as only end user devices that cannot create bridging loops are connected to a PortFast-enabled port, things will be okay. If a switch or hub were to be connected to a PortFast port, it is possible that a loop could be formed.

PortFast can be enabled on a switchport in two different ways.

1. You can send the enabling command directly to an individual port from interface configuration mode. The command to enable PortFast on the port is `spanning-tree portfast`.

2. You can enable PortFast for every port that is configured as an access link with the `global` command. In the global method, you can configure PortFast with the single global configuration mode command `spanning-tree portfast default`. PortFast is then enabled on every port that is not trunking. Even if you configure a port as an access link later, the PortFast configuration will automatically be applied to the port.

The PortFast configuration is a major benefit the topology as a whole. As I described already, every time a workstation reboots or gets shut down the port status changes. This triggers a topology change notification (TCN) BPDU to be sent. TCNs then force the entire topology to verify status with the root bridge even though, in this case, none of the paths really changed.

You can configure PortFast on any port where you have an end host that won't cause a bridging loop. If you think about this in terms of our example network for FutureTech, this could be on hundreds of switches. However, you can easily pick out the switches pretty that are going to get this configuration. If the network is designed properly, PortFast should be configured on the access layer switches. So thinking about that, you could have it configured in every switch block on all the access layer switches.

 Real World Scenario

Speeding Up the Sales Team

Let's use a specific example—the new switch that you implemented earlier for the sales team in the headquarters building at FutureTech. The sales force is complaining that it takes "centuries" to bring up their workstations. Remember that the new switch was specifically added for connecting user machines and voice traffic. So just about all of the ports on that switch (the ports that have users on them) can have PortFast enabled without causing any looping problems.

So, is there an easy way to configure PortFast? You may have to configure PortFast on hundreds of switches (which means thousands of ports). That is a perfect question. The answer is yes and no. Let me show you two different ways to configure PortFast:

- Globally for a whole switch
- Individually for a per port basis

Let's take a look at the PortFast configurations on a switch. The first configuration globally enables PortFast on all nontrunking interfaces.

```
ASW1(config)#spanning-tree portfast default
```

 This command enables portfast by default on all interfaces. You should now disable portfast explicitly on switched ports leading to hubs, switches, and bridges as they may create temporary bridging loops.

The really nice thing about this global configuration is that you don't have to go to each one of the individual ports and configure PortFast separately. Another major benefit to configuring PortFast globally is that any time you make an individual port an access port, the PortFast configuration will be automatically added to the port and there is nothing else that you have to configure. This is a great feature because it prevents you from forgetting to add the command on the port.

Next, let's configure PortFast on individual interfaces. There are again many places that you could use this type of configuration. Think about the Portland office situation discussed earlier. In cases where you are connecting many different types of devices to the network, you may not always configure every port to have PortFast enabled. To best serve the lab, you must enable and disable the feature on each port individually.

You can enable and disable the feature on an interface basis with the following commands.

```
ASW1(config)#int fa0/2
ASW1(config-if)#spanning-tree portfast ?
disable Disable portfast for this interface
trunk Enable portfast on the interface even in trunk mode
<cr>
ASW1(config-if)#spanning-tree portfast
%Warning: portfast should only be enabled on ports connected to a single host.
Connecting hubs, concentrators, switches, bridges, etc. . . . to this interface
when portfast is enabled, can cause temporary bridging loops. Use with CAUTION
%Portfast has been configured on FastEthernet0/2 but will only
have effect when the interface is in a nontrunking mode.
Switch1(config-if)#spanning-tree portfast disable
```

> Remember, you can use the interface range command for PortFast configuration, too. Any time you want to configure the same feature on more than one port on a switch, you can use the range command and save yourself a good amount of time.

BackboneFast

BackboneFast is a Cisco-proprietary feature that can save a switch up to 20 seconds (max_age timer) when it recovers from an indirect link failure. It does this by having the switch figure out whether or not there is an alternate path to the root bridge.

Look at Figure 3.6. Here you can see how a switch normally functions when an indirect link failure occurs. Three switches, CSW1, DSW1, and DSW2, are connected. CSW1 is the root bridge and DSW1 is the backup root bridge. DSW2 blocks its port fa0/7 and DSW1 is the designated bridge for the segment between DSW1 and DSW2.

The BackboneFast feature saves max_age (20 seconds). In order to do this, Backbone-Fast will immediately age out the known BPDU on a port after the port receives an inferior BPDU. An inferior BPDU is a BPDU that is received and has a root bridge BID that is not as good as the switch's current listed root bridge. In order for BackboneFast to do this and get rid of the max_age timer delay, it has to do a couple of things differently.

First, BackboneFast can detect an indirect link failure as soon as the failure happens. It does this by tracking the inferior BPDUs that a designated bridge (its current upstream bridge) sends when it experiences a direct link failure. Second, BackboneFast introduced a mechanism to allow for immediate verification of whether the BPDU information stored on a port is still valid. This specific check is implemented with a new message called a Root Link Query (RLQ).

 Real World Scenario

Connecting the Super Widget XT Team to the Core Network

You are still one of my network engineers in the headquarters building of FutureTech, and you implemented a switch block and switch for the sales team that sells the Super Widget XT product. Now you have to start thinking about how that switch block will be connected to the core of the network. This will be the beginning of my discussion on the difference between having a Layer 2 core compared to a Layer 3 core.

In Figure 3.6, you can see that CSW1 switch is a core switch and the DSW1 and DSW2 switches are distribution layer switches. For this example, you are going to be looking at a Layer 2 core. The root bridge is now moved into the core as CSW1. Having a design like this extends your VLANs into the core and, if not limited, to the rest of the network (you can end up with end-to-end VLANs).

The most important issues to look at are the flow of traffic and what happen when a link fails. Even with BackboneFast and other STP improvements, the amount of time to recover from a link failure can still be pretty high.

If the segment between CSW1 and DSW1 goes down, DSW1 immediately detects the failure and assumes it is the root. It starts to send BPDUs to DSW2 saying it is the new root. When DSW2 receives this new BPDU from DSW1, it ignores it because it realizes that the BPDU is inferior to the one it had stored for port fa0/7. After the max_age timer expires (20 seconds by default), the BPDU stored on DSW2 for port fa0/7 ages out. After this age-out, the port goes into listening and DSW2 sends its better BPDU to DSW1. As soon as DSW1 receives the BPDU from DSW2, it stops sending its BPDU, the BPDU that claimed it was the new root. Port fa0/7 on DSW2 transitions to the forwarding state after going through the listening and learning states.

Remember the transition through listening and learning takes twice the fw_delay value, which is 15 seconds for each state, an additional 30 seconds total. Only now will full connectivity be restored. This entire process took the max_age value (20 seconds) plus twice the fw_delay value (2 × 15 seconds) to recover from this indirect link failure. That is 50 seconds by default, which is an excruciating amount of time.

FIGURE 3.6   STP 802.1d Indirect Link Failure

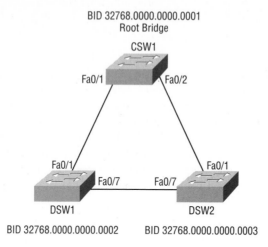

BID 32768.0000.0000.0001
Root Bridge

CSW1

Fa0/1   Fa0/2

Fa0/1   Fa0/1
       Fa0/7   Fa0/7

DSW1   DSW2

BID 32768.0000.0000.0002   BID 32768.0000.0000.0003

To see these functions in action, let's go back to Figure 3.6. Now, look at this scenario with BackboneFast enabled on all of the switches.

In order for this to work, BackboneFast must be enabled on all of the switches. Because of the second and active function that is the RLQ transmission, all of the switches must know what these messages are and what to do with them.

Let's look back to the diagram. Now, if the link between CSW1 and DSW1 fails, with BackboneFast enabled, DSW1 immediately sends a BPDU to DSW2 saying that it is the new root. DSW2 then sees that this BPDU is inferior to the one that it had stored on the port. DSW2 will age out the stored BPDU right away. It does this because it knows there must have been a failure along that path.

Now on its own path to the root bridge, DSW2 is going to send a RLQ to verify that its path to the real root bridge is still active. Once that path is verified, DSW2 skips the max_age timer on port fa0/7 and goes right to listening and then learning. DSW2 only had to wait the 30 seconds for the port to transition to forwarding. Once the port has transitioned to forwarding, DSW1 has a good path to the root through DSW2 and 20 seconds of waiting was saved.

The only thing left now, like always, is to look at the configuration for this feature. As I told you before, this feature must be enabled on all of your switches. Each switch must be able to send and understand the RLQ messages and know to age out the BPDUs when there is an indirect link failure.

```
CSW1(config)#spanning-tree backbonefast
DSW1(config)#spanning-tree backbonefast
DSW2(config)#spanning-tree backbonefast
```

You can verify the configuration of BackboneFast with the show command.

```
CSW1(config)#show spanning-tree backbonefast
BackboneFast is enabled
CSW1(config)#
```

Now, I want to finish analyzing this scenario. As I mentioned, this was partially to describe the difference between a Layer 2 and Layer 3 core. In a Layer 2 core, even with the enhancements that you are learning now, the amount of time to recover from a link failure is at least 30 seconds. That is a very long time on a network to have potentially no traffic being forwarded to parts of the network. Even with redundant links between the switches, STP is going to be blocking one of the links. With STP controlling the topology, you are always going to incur a significant delay while the network converges around a failure.

The amount of delay that STP introduces to the network is one of the primary reasons that Layer 2 cores are not used as much in networks today. There is another reason that I briefly mentioned in this example: the fact that you want to maintain your VLANs inside your switch blocks and not let them extend across the entire network.

UplinkFast

You can set up UplinkFast to accelerate the choice of a new root port when a link or switch fails. UplinkFast also speeds up things when the spanning tree instance reconfigures itself. UplinkFast is only available when a switch is configured for PVST+. When rapid PVST+ or Multiple Spanning Tree (MST) mode is turned on, you can configure a switch for Uplink-Fast, but it remains disabled until you change the spanning tree mode to PVST+.

When you enable UplinkFast, you enable it for the entire switch. It cannot be enabled for individual VLANs. UplinkFast is typically only configured on access switches because they are the switches down line from the root bridge. This means that this protocol should be used in switch blocks down in the access layer only. For UplinkFast to work properly, you want to reduce the chance that the switch will become the root switch. To ensure that this happens, when UplinkFast is enabled, the switch priority and the path cost are automatically changed to higher values. With UplinkFast enabled:

- The switch priority of all VLANs is set to 49152.
- If the path cost is a value less than 3000, the path cost of all interfaces and VLAN trunks is increased by 3000.
- If you change the path cost to 3000 or above, the path cost is not altered.
- When you disable UplinkFast, the switch priorities of all VLANs and the path costs of all interfaces are set to default values, unless you modified them from their defaults.

Now take a look at how UplinkFast operates in a real situation. I am going to put you right back in the same switch block you have been building the whole chapter. Figure 3.7 shows the setup.

FIGURE 3.7   Using UplinkFast

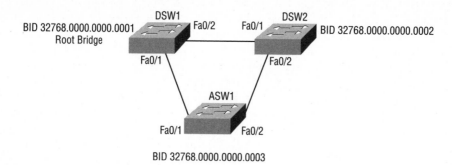

 Real World Scenario

Keeping Sales Up and Running

The sales team that resides in the switch block needs to have access to the network and Internet all of the time with the least amount of interruption possible. They are salespeople, making money for the company; you want to make their job easier! UplinkFast will reduce the recovery time for a failure so that the salespeople can keep doing their jobs.

Look at Figure 3.7. You can see the distribution switches (DSW1 and DSW2) and the access layer switch (ASW1) connected to them. ASW1 is the new switch that you implemented into the network. Since DSW1 is the root bridge, ASW1's fa0/1 port is its root port. If the link or port connecting ASW1 to DSW1 went down, ASW1 would not be able to forward traffic until the STP topology converges. This could mean that the users on ASW1 could be without a connection for between 30 and 50 seconds. That is way too long for them to wait.

With UplinkFast configured, ASW1 could immediately switch over to an alternate root port, changing the new root port directly to forwarding state. During this time, a topology change notification is sent. This allows the topology to swap over in about 5 seconds or less. That means the users on ASW1 will be sending traffic in just a few seconds. They may not even know anything changed, which of course is the goal; the users shouldn't know or see any change in the network. Their experience should be consistent and as timely as possible.

   Do not enable Root Guard on interfaces that will be used by the UplinkFast feature. (I cover Root Guard later in this chapter.) With UplinkFast, the backup interfaces (usually, in the blocked state) replace the root port in the case of a failure. However, if root guard is enabled, all the backup interfaces used by the UplinkFast feature are placed in the root-inconsistent state (blocked) and prevented from reaching the forwarding state.

One last very cool feature of UplinkFast is the max-update-rate option. The option specifies how many packets per second can be sent. By default it is set to 150. The entire configurable range changed in IOS version 12.1(13). For earlier versions, the range was 0–65535. For versions 12.1(13) and higher, the range is 0–32000.

What is this option for? UplinkFast has the ability to automatically update the local switch's MAC address table when the uplink port changes, so that all of the destination hosts are forwarded correctly. It also has the ability to give the upstream switches this information by sending out fake multicast frames to those switches. These multicast frames include the source MAC addresses of all the hosts that are connected downstream or in the access block. By doing this, the switch updates the other switches with the link change and the fact that those hosts can now be reached over the new link. In cases where the MAC address table is very large, you can control how many of these packets are sent with the max-update-rate option.

Many options such as the max-update-rate option can be difficult to judge exactly how high you should set the value. In the case of this option that is true as well. Every network and every case could be a little different, but just to give you an idea of what to think about, here are my two cents. The default value may work very well for you if the size of your MAC address table is not very big. However, if the size of the table is large, you may want to increase the value. A value too low and the tables aren't being updated fast enough and traffic is not flowing properly anyway. A value too big and you could overload the buffers on the receiving switch. If the switch that is receiving the frames is dropping them, then you aren't doing any good either. So the primary thing to check: make sure the frames are not being dropped. If they are being dropped, then you will know to decrease the value you have set.

Now the configuration of the UplinkFast feature is very straightforward. As I mentioned earlier, when you enable the feature, it is turned on for the entire switch. So, it stands to reason the UplinkFast configuration will be done from the global configuration mode. The UplinkFast feature must be enabled on each of the access switches in the switch block, so that each can independently make use of the feature. Here is what the command looks like.

```
ASW1(config)#spanning-tree uplinkfast {max-update-rate packets-per-second}
```

The current configuration of UplinkFast can be verified with the show command.

```
ASW1#show spanning-tree uplinkfast
UplinkFast is enabled
Station update rate set to 150 packets/sec.
UplinkFast statistics
-----------------------
Number of transitions via uplinkFast (all VLANs) : 0
Number of proxy multicast addresses transmitted (all VLANs) : 0
```

```
Name Interface List
------------------- -----------------------------------
VLAN0001 Fa0/21(fwd), Fa0/22
VLAN0010
```

Rapid Spanning Tree Protocol (RSTP)

Rapid Spanning Tree Protocol (RSTP) was created to help a network converge faster than it could under the original version of STP IEEE 802.1d. RSTP is the common name for the IEEE 802.1w standard. You'll remember that with the original version a change to the topology can take at least 30 seconds to propagate and begin forwarding properly again. This amount of time is basically unacceptable in most networks today. RSTP can be used in a couple of different ways. Cisco has added RSTP to its proprietary PVST+ protocol. You guessed it: this means that you create a RPVST+ or Rapid Per-VLAN Spanning Tree. RSTP can also be used with 802.1s Multiple Spanning Tree (MST), but I cover that in the next section.

RSTP does some things just like the original 802.1d STP did. It elects a Root Bridge the same way, using the lowest BID, and all of the switches know and accept this role. But 802.1d made all of the switches propagate the BPDUs from the root only and that is how they determined the topology. Now, with RSTP, each switch can communicate directly with its neighbors on every port. In order for RSTP to do this, it had to define the port roles a little bit differently than before. Here are the RSTP roles.

Root Port   The root port is actually the exact same in RSTP as is in 802.1d STP. This port has the best path back to the root bridge.

Designated Port   A designated port is very much the same as well. It is still defined as the port on a segment that has the best path back to the root. Remember there has to be one and only one of these ports on each segment.

Alternate Port   An alternate port has a path to the root; it just isn't as good as the root ports path. The switch keeps track of this port so that it can be swapped if there is a failure. This is much like the UplinkFast feature that Cisco added on to 802.1d standard. You would use it the same way, too. Think of an access switch in the FutureTech switch block that has multiple ports up to the distribution layer; one of the ports will be forwarding and under RSTP one of them will be the alternate port.

Backup Port   This type of port is also a redundant link, but its path goes to a segment or switch that is not directly the root bridge.

RSTP ports handle traffic a little differently as well. Under 802.1d, port states transition through blocking, listening, learning, and finally forwarding. Of course, there was also a disabled state, but we would have to turn the port on anyway.

RSTP just cuts to the chase. It says, "Well, disabled, blocking, and learning—all of those states just drop traffic and don't do anything else with it. So let's just put those states together into one state, discarding. That is what we do with the traffic anyway."

Now, RSTP still has a learning state because the switch still needs to learn where all of the hosts are connected and populate its MAC address table, but in this state the switch is still dropping the traffic. Finally, the third and last RSTP state is forwarding, and it does just that. It forwards traffic based on the MAC addresses it's learned. Of course, under RSTP, the switch continues to learn MAC addresses as well.

As an RSTP network begins to converge, the root bridge is elected, and then all of the ports determine whether their state is forwarding or discarding. RSTP uses a Hello timer similar to the one used under 802.1d. Every two seconds each port sends out a BPDU. These BPDUs are backward compatible with 802.1d so, if switches are running the old version, they can be communicated down to. The RSTP port would just begin running as though it was 802.1d port.

For normal operation between RSTP ports, though, the switches exchange the Hellos and determine their roles as root, designated, and so on. If a neighbor switch is not heard from within three intervals of the Hello timer (6 seconds), then the switch is assumed to be gone or down and removed from the topology—right then. Under RSTP, there is no waiting for a timer like the 20 second max_age timer.

RSTP also takes a new stance on determining the topology of the tree. When a new or changed switch is introduced, the switch is allowed to join the topology. The new switch then bases its decisions on the type of port connection it has. The RSTP port types are edge port, root port, and point-to-point port.

Edge Port   An edge port is defined by its location. It is a port that has only an end device, such as a host, connected to the port. Think about the access switches in the switch block; they are the ports that are at the bottom or edge of the network. You must configure a port with PortFast for it to act as an edge port in RSTP. To ease the transition into RSTP, Cisco kept the way you configure an edge port the same as the you configured access ports to skip STP, using the `feature` and `configuration` commands for PortFast.

Root Port   This should be an old familiar term by now. The root port is the single best port with regard to its path to the root bridge. There can be more that one port with a path to the root, but those ports are then flagged as alternate or backup ports. Alternate and backup ports can be put into place and used if the real root port were to go down.

Point-to-Point Port   Point-to-point ports allow switches to determine the status of segments that connect to another switch. The switches exchange a small message or proposal that tells the switch on the other end that it will have the designated port. The opposite switch will agree or disagree based on the BID of the two switches; the opposing switch sends back an agreement message if it has a worse BID or a message saying it is better.

Now, when it comes to point-to-point ports in RSTP, RSTP looks at two different states. A port is treated as point to point if the segment is in full duplex. Being in full duplex means no other switches can be on the segment and the abbreviated negotiation of RSTP is fine to use. If the ports are in half-duplex mode, called *shared* instead of point to point, then there is a possibility that other switches exist on the segment. In this situation, the ports must go through a 802.1d type of negotiation and standard timers are put into place.

The abbreviated RSTP process for communicating with neighbors is called synchronization and involves RSTP switches sending BPDUs through the network, layer after layer, until the topology is determined. The process starts at the top (where the root bridge is located) and moves out to the edge of the network (where all of the edge or access switches are located). So, each switch begins by communicating with its neighbor to learn whether that switch is the root bridge. The switches continue to learn about superior BPDUs until the root is found. Each switch must then determine which ports are edge ports and which are non-edge ports. The edge ports, the ports connected to end devices, can begin forwarding immediately.

Non-edge ports must continue through the agreement process. The first step is again sending the proposal message to a switch neighbor. If the opposite switch agrees, then the local switch will have the designated port. But, if the neighbor switch has a superior BPDU, then the neighbor becomes the designated port for the segment. While this is happening, all non-edge ports are in the discarding mode.

Once the root port has been determined, it can go to forward mode. All other non-edge ports continue through this process of proposal and agreement until all the ports have determined their state of forwarding or not. This process continues down through all of the switches until each of the ports has been set.

If you really think about where and when you would want implement RSTP, you'll come to the conclusion that the only good reason not to enable RSTP on your switches is if a switch does not support it. Table 3.3 lists the versions of IOS and switch models that support RSTP on a model-by-model basis.

TABLE 3.3   RSTP Support by Switch Model and IOS

Switch Model	Version of IOS with Support
Catalyst 2940	12.1(20)EA2
Catalyst 2950/2955/3550	12.1(13)EA1
Catalyst 2970/3750	12.1(14)EA1
Catalyst 3560	12.1(19)EA1
Catalyst 4000/4500 IOS	12.1(19)EW
Catalyst 6000/6500 IOS	12.1(13)E

Now, let's look at configuring RSTP on our switches. The default STP mode on a Cisco switch is PVST+, which uses 802.1d rules. In order to use RSTP, the STP mode has to be changed to either Rapid Per-VLAN Spanning Tree Plus (RPVST+) or to Multiple Spanning Tree (MST). RPVST+ is also known as PVRST+. The command, issued from global configuration mode, to change the switch to RPVST+ is `spanning-tree mode rapid-pvst`. This configuration must be set on each of the switches that you are upgrading and support it.

```
Switch1(config)# spanning-tree mode rapid-pvst
```

To place the switch back into default PVST+ mode, the command is **spanning-tree mode pvst**, again at global configuration mode.

The other things that you can configure for RSTP are the port types. The first one that you will look at is making a port and edge port. For the sake of consistency, Cisco kept the command the same from 802.1d. What was the command to make a port in 802.1d change immediately to forwarding state? If you said the command is **spanning-tree portfast**, you would be correct!

```
Switch1(config-if)#spanning-tree portfast
```

The other port configuration that we can set is to make a port into a point-to-point type. By default, RSTP uses all the ports that are in full duplex, but if you have a port that is not in full duplex but only goes between switches with nothing else on the segment, then you can configure it to act like a point-to-point link. The command to do so is **spanning-tree link-type point-to-point**.

```
Switch1(config-if)#spanning-tree link-type point-to-point
```

Multiple Spanning Tree (MST)

It can be useful to have the flexibility to run more than one instance of STP. This flexibility can be used to setup a type of load balancing. I mentioned this briefly in the section, "Configuring Spanning Tree Protocol," earlier in this chapter, when you learned about changing the port priority so that a group of VLANs could be carried across one link and another group could be carried across a different link.

If you think about the switch block that you have been building throughout this chapter, how many different topologies will really be present there? Only a couple will really be there, right? Think about the access layer switches. They have redundant links to the distribution switches. Only if you implemented the load-balancing feature and some VLANs traverse one link and other VLANs traverse a different link will you have more than one topology. Why then do you need your switches to run a separate instance of STP for every single VLAN?

The answer is you don't. You could instead map a group of VLANs to one instance of STP and another group of VLANs to a different instance, and save all the processing of extra BPDUs, the extra table and cache space used to store redundant information, and the processing to create and send all the extra data. So now, you just have to figure out how you can do all of this and save the resources. That is where Multiple Spanning Tree (MST) comes in. Lucky for you, there is a standard, 802.1S MST, that was created to just this task. It allows you to map multiple instances of STP together into one.

The first thing that you have to plan is the number of instances that need to be created to support the network. Then, you can figure out which VLANs to map to each of those instances.

MST was created so that it can interoperate with all other forms of STP. So it can support instances from each type of STP. You have to think about the MST region as one big switch. All of the switches that you configure into the region will appear as the same switch to any switches that are outside of the region. The STP instance that is running outside of the region doesn't care what is going on inside; in fact, it doesn't understand that anything else is going on inside. It is only given the information it needs. The switch on the edge of the region gives it all it needs to know about what state to put its port into. That information is calculated by an instance of MST, called the Internal Spanning Tree (IST), within the region. If the outside switches are running CST, then the information is given to them over the native VLAN. If they are running PVST+, then the information is replicated into each and every VLAN on the trunk.

Now, within the region there is a separate instance of MST that works out the topology for the internal region called the MST instance (MSTI). An MSTI exists for each of the instances that you created or mapped a set of VLANs to. You can have 16 total instances of MST running; the IST instance is always identified as MSTI 0. From there, you can make or map instances 1 through 15 for your individual instances.

RSTP made the convergence of STP faster. With MST, however, it isn't speeding the convergence but making it more efficient for the switches on the network. If you have a small number of VLANs in each switch block and they all have the same topology, then adding MST is probably not necessary for you. However, if you have quite a few VLANs (not a set number, but maybe 40 or 50) and those VLANs don't have the same topology, then MST could save you some resources. Again, the most common reason for not having the same topology between STP instances is because you are grouping VLANs together to make use of redundant links.

 Real World Scenario

Growth Is Good, but Expensive

Let's look at the sales team again, and imagine that it is a few months down the road. Things have changed. There are more people and not all of the salespeople are located in the same switch block anymore. The number of VLANs that you have now has grown to about 50. You have already implemented the redundancy configuration that I discussed with you earlier, so you have more than one topology of STP. You want to get a little more life out of the switches that you have before you upgrade them, but they are starting to be taxed in the amount of processing that they are doing. This would be the perfect time for you to implement MST.

Table 3.3 lists the switches and versions of IOS that support MST features on model-by-model basis.

TABLE 3.3 MST Support by Switch Model and IOS

Switch Model	Version of IOS with Support
Catalyst 2940	12.1(20)EA2
Catalyst 2950/2955/3550	12.1(19)EA1
Catalyst 2970/3750	12.1(14)EA1
Catalyst 3560	12.1(19)EA1
Catalyst 4000/4500 IOS	12.1(12c)EW
Catalyst 6000/6500 IOS	12.1(11b)EX, 12.1(13)E, 12.2(14)SX

To configure MST, you must complete a series of commands on every single switch that will be in each region. The commands establish the MST configuration name, configuration revision number, and the VLAN instance mapping. Here's what the process for an individual switch looks like.

1. First enable MST on the switch. Use the `spanning-tree mode mst` command from global configuration mode.

   DSW1(config)#**spanning-tree mode mst**

2. Next, enter the MST configuration mode. The command is `spanning-tree mst configuration` from the global configuration mode.

   DSW1(config)#**spanning-tree mst configuration**

3. Once you are in the configuration mode, you have to give the instance a name. This is done with the `name` command.

   DSW1(config-mst)#**name** *name*

4. Then, you need to assign the revision number.
   The command to set the revision number is `revision` *version*.

   DSW1(config-mst)#**revision** *version*

> Unlike VTP, there is no automatic way to update an MST region. When you need to update, you have to update the configuration on every switch manually. Assigning a revision number for each instance helps you keep track as you make changes to the network, so every time you make a change you should increment the revision number. But remember, all the parameters must be the same on all switches in the region, so you have to update and configure consistently on every switch.

5. The next step is the whole point of this feature and that is to map the VLANs to the instance of MST. This is done with the `instance` *instance-id* `vlan` *vlan-list* command.

    ```
    DSW1(config-mst)#instance instance-id vlan vlan-list
    ```

6. Now, verify everything that you have set with the `show pending` command. Verification allows you to check and ensure that what you set is really what you want done.

    ```
    DSW1(config-mst)#show pending
    ```

7. To make all of the changes and save work that you have done, you have to exit MST configuration mode. This will look much like it did when we used to use the VLAN database and you exited out of the mode and it told you that the changes were saved.

    ```
    DSW1(config-mst)#exit
    ```

Protecting Spanning Tree

STP primarily uses BPDUs to ensure that the switch network is maintained loop free. When all is working well, STP should maintain the topology of the network. As you know, this happens for the most part on its own. There can be times, however, when this harmony can be interrupted. Some ports like edge or PortFast ports should never receive any BPDUs. If they do receive BPDUs, this could mean that a loop as been formed in the network, which would, to say the least, make your network operate undesirably. Now on the flip side, when ports that should be receiving BPDUs stop receiving BPDUs, STP can again make decisions, like unblocking a port that should still be blocked, that would have your network create a loop and not operate optimally.

To prevent these problems, I introduce you to a few features that have been added to assist STP and ensure that the topology is maintained the way you would like it to be. These features include:

- BPDU Guard
- Root Guard
- BPDU Filtering

- Loop Guard
- UniDirectional Link Detection (UDLD)

BPDU Guard

BPDU Guard was specifically made for PortFast-enabled ports. You know that you can enable PortFast on access ports where end devices will be connected to the network. When you do this, the port immediately moves to forwarding mode and skips the STP process for determining whether or not there is a loop on the port. But what if a switch was plugged into a port that it shouldn't have been? The introduction of a loop or new switch on a PortFast-enabled port could cause a loop. BPDU Guard is a great feature for preventing an accidental loop from being formed. Therefore, you should use the BPDU Guard function on all ports where PortFast is enabled.

BPDU Guard works like this: if an enabled port receives a BPDU, which it should not, then the port is placed into err-disable state. That port is then effectively shut down until you manually reenable it. Even if the port stops receiving BPDUs, the port remains in this down state until you enable it.

The natural location to enable this feature is on access ports where the end devices are, but care should be taken to not enable the feature on uplink ports that go to the root bridge, as these ports can and should receive BPDUs. Even if there are multiple links that go to the root and they are in blocking mode, BPDUs will still be received on those ports and will be put into err-disable state if BPDU Guard is enabled.

This feature can be configured in a couple of ways. By default, BDPU Guard is disabled on all switch ports. You can enable BPDU Guard globally with the `spanning-tree portfast bpduguard default` command. This command will enable the feature automatically whenever a port is placed into PortFast mode.

You can also enable or disable BPDU Guard on a port-by-port basis from the interface configuration mode using the `spanning-tree bpduguard enable` command.

I bet you can't guess where my example is going now. Think about the switch block from earlier when you were enabling PortFast on the access ports. The exact same ports and switches where you enabled PortFast are where you should enable BPDU Guard. There is no reason not to enable it as it helps you prevent the formation of loops in your network. The configuration is going to look like this.

A global command is entered at the configuration mode.

```
ASW1(config)#spanning-tree portfast bpduguard default
```

The interface-specific command is enter in the interface configuration mode.

```
ASW1(config-if)#spanning-tree bpduguard enable
```

Root Guard

When STP is done converging, each of the ports will be in a specific port role. That port role depends on where the port is in the topology. We want root ports and alternate ports to receive

BPDUs from the root bridge as this maintains the topology. However, what happens when a new switch with a better (read lower) BID is plugged into the network? Well, if you said that it will become the new root bridge, you are correct. That is how STP works—the best switch wins. But what if you don't want the topology to change? Well, if you have the priorities configured correctly, it may not. But, if priorities are set to the default or you don't catch it before a switch is plugged in, then there could be a problem. (Of course you would never let that happen, but someone else could plug one in.)

Even though STP would operate the way it should, you may not want the change. It could cause a very inefficient topology for data flow, and it may make parts of the network inaccessible while the topology is changing.

Root Guard was designed to prevent a switch from being added to the network and taking over. Root Guard can also be very useful for isolating your network from a service provider or partner network if they make connections right into a switch. (I am going to discuss a connection like this more in the next section with BPDU filtering.) Root Guard learns the BID of the current root bridge. Then, if a BPDU that advertises a switch with a superior or better BID is received on any port that has Root Guard enabled, the port is placed into root-inconsistent state. This state prevents the port from sending or receiving any data. The port will listen, though, for another switch that may be advertising itself to be the root bridge.

> Enable Root Guard only on ports where you will never receive BPDUs from the root bridge. That means that those ports should not be hearing the root at all on any VLAN. The port itself is placed into the root-inconsistent or down state, so it won't matter what VLAN or instance of STP this occurs on; they will all be affected.

Root Guard is disabled by default on all interfaces. It can only be enabled on a specific interface from the interface configuration mode. The command to enable Root Guard is `spanning-tree guard root`. It will look like this.

```
ASW1(config-if)# spanning-tree guard root
```

BPDU Filtering

By default, STP runs on all of your switch ports. This is a good thing because it makes sure that you don't have any loops, which of course you don't want. But there may be a very special case where you don't want STP to run on a port. Perhaps you have a host or other device that can't receive any BPDUs. Whatever your reason, there is one good way to effectively disable STP on a port and prevent it from sending out or processing any BPDUs. BPDU Filtering effectively disables STP on a port.

Now by default, of course BPDU Filtering is disabled on all ports. You can enable it in one of two ways. The first is to enable BPDU Filtering globally. If you enable it globally, then all ports that are configured with PortFast will also be configured with BPDU filtering.

BPDU filtering feature is useful on every switch where you have hosts and ports where someone could connect a device to the network. One benefit to BPDU filtering over BPDU Guard is that if a port were to receive a BPDU, instead of the port being placed into err-disabled mode (as it is with BPDU Guard) with BPDU filtering the ports PortFast feature is disabled, forcing it to resume normal STP operations. STP will then be responsible for ensuring a loop is not formed.

BPDU filtering can also be very useful when used in conjunction with the Root Guard feature. I mentioned in the Root Guard discussion that in some service provider connections one of your switches might be directly connected to an ISP switch. If you look at Figure 3.8, you can see the type of situation I am talking about. This happens with Layer 2 switched connections such as Metro Ethernet. (I am not going to talk about Metro Ethernet, but it is a type of connection you can get in some areas.)

FIGURE 3.8   Switch Connections with the ISP

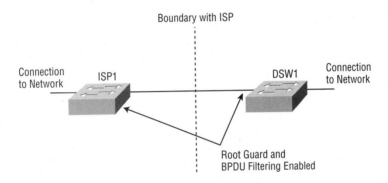

You can see from the diagram that switch DSW1 is connected to ISP1. You don't want your STP topology to be effected by the ISP's topology and vice versa. So, you and the service provider can enable Root Guard on the connected ports. This way if a superior BPDU was received on either side, it wouldn't change your topologies. Now, you also don't want your port to be in root-inconsistent state either because then you aren't passing any data. To prevent that, you and the service provider will enable BPDU filtering. This keeps both of the ports from sending BPDUs in the first place.

The command for globally enabling it is `spanning-tree portfast bpdufiltering default` and it is executed from global configuration mode. The command looks like this.

```
DSW1(config)#spanning-tree portfast bpdufiltering default
```

You can also enable the BPDU Filter feature on an interface-by-interface basis. This is done from the interface configuration mode with the `spanning-tree bpdufilter enable` command. It looks like this when configured on a switch.

```
DSW1(config-if)#spanning-tree bpdufilter enable
```

Loop Guard

I think of the Loop Guard feature as a type of enforcer. It forces a port to maintain a hold pattern when it is supposed to be in blocking mode. Let me explain. Normally a port that is redundant would be in blocking mode. It is kept in blocking mode because it received BPDUs from the designated port on the other end of the link, its upstream switch. If the port for whatever reason stops receiving those BPDUs, it holds on to the last BPDU it received until the max_age timer expires. When the timer expires, the port goes through the stages of STP and becomes a designated port. The designated port status would allow it to forward traffic and cause a loop. This situation would cause a loop because the port stopped receiving BPDUs erroneously for some reason.

When it is enabled, Loop Guard prevents loops by listening on nondesignated ports. When STP is running fine, Loop Guard does nothing. But if a port stops receiving BPDUs, then Loop Guard steps in and puts the port into a loop-inconsistent state. In this state, the port is effectively blocking, which prevents it from making a loop. That is the holding pattern that I talked about. Now something of note here: this feature is only blocking the instance of STP that is behaving badly. So, if other instances are running, they are not affected and continue to run. Loop Guard can take itself out of the holding pattern once it starts to receive BPDUs again.

Loop Guard is disabled by default on all ports. It can be enabled two ways, globally or on a particular interface. To enable Loop Guard globally, again from the global configuration mode, use the `spanning-tree loopguard default` command. It looks like this.

```
Switch1(config)#spanning-tree loopguard default
```

To enable Loop Guard on a particular interface, use the `spanning-tree guard loop` command.

```
Switch1(config-if)#spanning-tree guard loop
```

UniDirectional Link Detection (UDLD)

You've looked at the way devices are connected; here I discuss our switches. In switch blocks, most of the switches have uplinks connecting them to upstream switches. Many of those uplinks today are fiber connections because fiber optics offer high-bandwidth, low-loss connections. They can carry data a greater distance than Ethernet if need be as well. But with a fiber connection, you can encounter a problem that you don't ever worry about with an Ethernet or twisted pair cable—a unidirectional link.

A unidirectional link occurs when one of the fibers in a pair goes down. Because there are separate transmit and receive cables, the switches on each end may not detect that the interface is down. How could something like this happen? Well, one of the interface modules could be damaged or simply not working. If this happens, then the switches could still send data in one direction. If the switch port that is supposed to be blocking stops receiving BPDUs, then that blocking switch will begin forwarding after the port transitions through STP. This situation would then cause a loop in the one direction.

Fact: Fiber connections today generally use one of two types of modules, gigabit interface converters (GBIC) or small form-factor pluggable (SFP) modules.

To prevent these loops, Cisco developed the proprietary UniDirectional Link Detection (UDLD) feature. This feature has to be enabled on both ends of the link. It monitors the port to ensure that it maintains bidirectional communication. Each switch independently sends Layer 2 UDLD frames to the switch on the other side. The frames include the sending switch port ID and a request for a reply. If no reply arrives, then the link is assumed to be unidirectional and faulty.

UDLD messages are sent at regular intervals, by default every 15 seconds. It takes the switch about three intervals to detect the link, about 45 seconds depending on your configuration. This timing is important because UDLD needs to detect the failure before STP begins forwarding on the port. Remember, STP will begin forwarding on the port after about 50 seconds, a sum of the max_age timer (20 seconds) and two intervals of the forward delay timer (30 seconds total).

UDLD operates in two different modes, normal or aggressive. In normal mode, UDLD doesn't do anything to the port when a unidirectional state is detected. It merely marks the port as such and generates a log message. But in aggressive mode, UDLD takes an active role is trying to reestablish communication on the port. It sends out eight UDLD messages, one per second for 8 seconds. If none of the messages get a reply, then the port is placed into err-disabled state so that it cannot be used.

It is worth mentioning at this point that it is nice that this feature runs separately on each individual interface, especially in the case of an EtherChannel. If UDLD puts one of the links into err-disabled state, the other links in the bundle remain unaffected.

As far as the configuration goes, I am sure you can almost guess at this point what I am going to say. UDLD can be configured in two ways, either globally or on an individual interface.

If you enable globally, then UDLD will be enabled on all fiber interfaces. The command is udld {enable | aggressive | message time *seconds*} and it is run from global configuration mode. Use the *enable* option to configure normal mode, and the *aggressive* option to enable aggressive mode. The *message time* option configures the interval in which the messages are sent between switches. The configurable range is 7 to 90 seconds.

The UDLD feature is good to use on any switch were you have fiber links. The biggest difference will be what mode you place the feature into. In normal mode, nothing is actively done about the situation, but you can have the log message or alert sent to a management station so that you can do something about it yourself. This is fine if you have something like this set up and someone to always check out these situations. The problem is if you don't have someone to check it out, then you could possibly be leaving a loop condition in the network.

In aggressive mode, you don't have to be there right away when the situation occurs. The switch will try to resolve the problem, and if it cannot, then the port is put into err-disabled mode and you don't have to worry about a loop being created.

```
DSW1(config)#udld enable
DSW1(config)#udld aggressive
```

UDLD configuration on the interface is very similar. The command is udld {enable | aggressive | disable} and is run from the interface configuration mode.

```
DSW1(config-if)#udld enable
DSW1(config-if)#udld aggressive
DSW1(config-if)#udld disable
```

Verifying and Troubleshooting

Now that you have gone through so many of the configurations for STP, it is time to look at how you can verify and troubleshoot any issues. Any changes to the network can cause a shift in the topology. These shifts ultimately may prevent you from knowing exactly what the topology is, at least the topology you thought you had. If you know for sure that something changed or you are trying to determine whether something changed, you have to know where to find that information. You can use commands and outputs from the command line interface of a switch to determine the topology of STP. You can also figure out which switch is the root bridge and get the status of the ports. Let take a look at some of these commands.

Checking the STP Process

The first and most obvious command is to look at the STP process itself. We can do this with the show spanning-tree command.

```
Switch1#sh spanning-tree
VLAN0001
Spanning tree enabled protocol ieee
Root ID Priority 32769
Address 0015.6342.8c80
Cost 3019
Port 23 (FastEthernet0/21)
Hello Time 2 sec Max Age 20 sec Forward Delay 15 sec
Bridge ID Priority 49153 (priority 49152 sys-id-ext 1)
Address 001c.575e.c880
Hello Time 2 sec Max Age 20 sec Forward Delay 15 sec
Aging Time 300
Uplinkfast enabled
Interface Role Sts Cost Prio.Nbr Type
---------------- ---- --- --------- -------- --------------------------------

Fa0/3 Desg FWD 3019 128.5 P2p Edge
```

```
Fa0/4 Desg FWD 3019 128.6 P2p
Fa0/5 Desg FWD 3019 128.7 P2p
Fa0/6 Desg FWD 3019 128.8 P2p
Fa0/9 Desg FWD 3019 128.11 P2p
Fa0/10 Desg FWD 3019 128.12 P2p
Interface Role Sts Cost Prio.Nbr Type
---------------- ---- --- --------- -------- --------------------------------
Fa0/11 Desg FWD 3100 128.13 Shr
Fa0/19 Altn BLK 3019 128.21 P2p
Fa0/20 Altn BLK 3019 128.22 P2p
Fa0/21 Root FWD 3019 128.23 P2p
Fa0/22 Altn BLK 3019 128.24 P2p
VLAN0010
Spanning tree enabled protocol ieee
Root ID Priority 32778
Address 001c.5783.3900
Cost 3019
Port 21 (FastEthernet0/19)
Hello Time 2 sec Max Age 20 sec Forward Delay 15 sec
Bridge ID Priority 49162 (priority 49152 sys-id-ext 10)
Address 001c.575e.c880
Hello Time 2 sec Max Age 20 sec Forward Delay 15 sec
Aging Time 300
Uplinkfast enabled
Interface Role Sts Cost Prio.Nbr Type
---------------- ---- --- --------- -------- --------------------------------
Fa0/1 Desg FWD 3019 128.3 P2p Edge
Fa0/2 Desg FWD 3019 128.4 P2p Edge
Fa0/19 Root FWD 3019 128.21 P2p
```

You can see from this output it contains many pieces of very useful information. Starting at the top of the output, you will find that the output is for VLAN 1 and that the original IEEE version is currently running.

Now, take a look at the output section titled Root ID. This section lists all the information for the root bridge. It is followed by the Bridge ID section, which lists the information for the local switch to which you are connected. The bottom section of this output gives you the port status information. There you will find listings (in columns from left to right) for:

- Each port in the current VLAN's instance of STP
- The port's role
- The status of that port

- The port cost
- The port priority and port ID
- The port type

Notice in this output, UplinkFast is enabled so the cost has the 3000 addition to it.

Checking Port Details

Now, take a look at is the output from the show spanning-tree detail command.

```
Switch1#show spanning-tree detail
VLAN0001 is executing the ieee compatible Spanning Tree protocol
Bridge Identifier has priority 49152, sysid 1, address 001c.575e.c880
Configured hello time 2, max age 20, forward delay 15
Current root has priority 32769, address 0015.6342.8c80
Root port is 23 (FastEthernet0/21), cost of root path is 3019
Topology change flag not set, detected flag not set
Number of topology changes 18 last change occurred 2d00h ago
from FastEthernet0/19
Times: hold 1, topology change 35, notification 2
hello 2, max age 20, forward delay 15
Timers: hello 0, topology change 0, notification 0, aging 300
Uplinkfast enabled
Port 5 (FastEthernet0/3) of VLAN0001 is designated forwarding
Port path cost 3019, Port priority 128, Port Identifier 128.5.
Designated root has priority 32769, address 0015.6342.8c80
Designated bridge has priority 49153, address 001c.575e.c880
Designated port id is 128.5, designated path cost 3019
Timers: message age 0, forward delay 0, hold 0
Number of transitions to forwarding state: 1
The port is in the portfast mode
Link type is point-to-point by default
BPDU: sent 3232577, received 0
<Output cut>
```

This output shows the finite details about the instance of STP that is running, including timer values and associated costs. You can thank me now for cutting the output after just one port. When you run the command, you will see the details for each of the ports in the VLAN instance.

Checking STP Features

The next command will show you the ports that are in each of the instances of STP, which features are enabled and which are not. The command is show spanning-tree vlan *vlan-id* summary.

```
Switch1#show spanning-tree vlan 1 summary
Switch is in pvst mode
Root bridge for VLAN0001 is 32769.0015.6342.8c80.
Extended system ID is enabled
Portfast Default is disabled
PortFast BPDU Guard Default is disabled
Portfast BPDU Filter Default is disabled
Loopguard Default is disabled
EtherChannel misconfig guard is enabled
UplinkFast is enabled
BackboneFast is disabled
Configured Pathcost method used is short
Name Blocking Listening Learning Forwarding STP Active
-------- -------- --------- -------- ---------- ---- -------
VLAN0001 3 0 0 8 11
```

Checking the Root and Port Properties

The **show spanning-tree vlan *vlan-id* root** command shows all of root properties. Using this command, you can find the root bridge, root port, root cost, and timer values.

```
Switch1#show spanning-tree vlan 1 root
Root Hello Max Fwd
Vlan Root ID Cost Time Age Dly Root Port
----------- -------------------- ----- ----- ---- --- ----------
VLAN0001 32769 0015.6342.8c80 3019 2 20 15 Fa0/21
```

The command, **show spanning-tree vlan *vlan-id* bridge**, gives you information about the local switch, including its BID and timers.

```
Switch1#show spanning-tree vlan 1 bridge
Hello Max Fwd
Vlan Bridge ID Time Age Dly Protocol
-------- ---------------------------- ----- --- --- --------
VLAN0001 49153(49152,1) 001c.575e.c880 2 20 15 ieee
```

Determining UplinkFast and BackboneFast Status

The next couple of outputs show the status of UplinkFast and BackboneFast operation on the local switch. The commands are **show spanning-tree uplinkfast** and **show spanning-tree backbonefast**.

```
Switch1#show spanning-tree uplinkfast
UplinkFast is enabled
Station update rate set to 150 packets/sec.
UplinkFast statistics
-----------------------
Number of transitions via uplinkFast (all VLANs) : 0
Number of proxy multicast addresses transmitted (all VLANs) : 0
Name Interface List
-------------------- ------------------------------------
VLAN0001 Fa0/21(fwd), Fa0/19, Fa0/20, Fa0/22
VLAN0010 Fa0/19(fwd)
Switch1#show spanning-tree backbonefast
BackboneFast is disabled
```

Summary

You've covered a considerable number of topics in this chapter. Of course, it depends on what version of STP you run in your network as to which ones you find the most important. It is key that you are able to configure and work with all of them. You must be intimately familiar with STP for that purpose. Most important is STP's use in the network. You got a look at the operation of STP going back to the original version, IEEE 802.1d. You saw what had to happen for STP to operate. You reviewed the modifications and standard changes that have occurred to STP over time. There was 802.1q, also known as CST, and the changes that Cisco initiated, including PVST and PVST+. You also looked at enhancements, including PortFast, BackboneFast, and UplinkFast.

Finally, you looked at 802.1s (MST) and 802.1w (RSTP). Both of these standards brought their own enhancements. MST allows you to map multiple instances of STP together to conserve resources and minimize the number of topologies that have to be maintained. RSTP gave you the ability to save a great deal of time in network convergence.

Then, you looked at some features that provide some protection to the STP instance, including BPDU Guard, BPDU Filtering, Root Guard, Loop Guard, and UDLD.

The last things covered were some of the commands that can be used to determine the operation and help you troubleshoot STP. You should practice using these commands and be sure that you understand their use and outputs. The better your understanding of these commands, the easier it will be to operate STP in the future.

Review Questions

1. What IEEE standard is the original version of STP defined in?

   A. 802.2

   B. 802.1d

   C. 802.11

   D. 802.3

2. What piece of information is used by switches to determine the root bridge?

   A. Port ID

   B. Port number

   C. BID

   D. Path cost

3. What value is used to determine the root port of a switch?

   A. Path cost

   B. port ID

   C. BID

   D. Switch name

4. What Cisco-created feature allows a switch to transition a port immediately to forwarding?

   A. UplinkFast

   B. UDLD

   C. PortFast

   D. max_age timer

5. What is the name of the message switches send to determine the topology for STP?

   A. BPDU

   B. Update

   C. Status

   D. PDU

6. What Cisco-proprietary feature was added to speed convergence when a root port is lost?

   A. BPDU Guard

   B. PortFast

   C. UplinkFast

   D. BackboneFast

7. What feature prevents a superior BPDU that is received from affecting the current STP topology?

   A. BPDU Guard

   B. Loop Guard

   C. PortFast

   D. Root Guard

8. What value can be changed by the administrator of a switch to make the switch more likely to become the root bridge?

   A. Priority

   B. Port priority

   C. Port number

   D. MAC address

9. What feature allows a switch to verify that a fiber optic link has not partially failed?

   A. Loop avoidance

   B. UDLD

   C. Root Guard

   D. PortFast

10. What feature prevents the sending and receiving of BPDUs on a switch port?

   A. PortFast

   B. BPDU Guard

   C. BPDU filtering

   D. Priority

Answers to Review Questions

1. B. The original version of STP is defined in the IEEE 802.1d standard.

2. C. The BID is used by the switches to determine the root bridge; the lowest BID is the winner of the election.

3. A. The path cost is used to determine the root port; the lowest total path cost for all of a switches ports becomes the root port.

4. C. The Cisco-proprietary feature of PortFast allows a switch port to move immediately to forwarding without having to transition through any other states.

5. A. The BPDU (Bridge Protocol Data Unit) is sent every 2 seconds by switches and contains the information to determine the topology.

6. C. UplinkFast was added by Cisco, and allows the loss of root port to be converged around in about 5 seconds.

7. D. Root Guard prevents a superior BPDU from changing the current STP topology by placing the port where it was received into root-inconsistent state.

8. A. The priority can be changed for each VLAN on a switch to affect the root bridge election. The priority value can be changed in increments of 4096.

9. B. UDLD allows a switch to verify whether the switch on the other end is still present or whether the link has failed in one direction.

10. C. BPDU filtering effectively disables STP on the port because it prevents the port from sending or receiving BPDUs.

Chapter 4

Routing Concepts and Distance Vector Routing Protocols

IN THIS CHAPTER, YOU WILL LEARN HOW TO DO THE FOLLOWING:

✓ Describe basic routing fundamentals

✓ Describe RIP version 1

✓ Describe RIP version 2

✓ Describe route filtering with distribute lists

Without routing, data would never get beyond its own subnet; it is the true backbone and strength to internetworking. The routing process gives a router its abilities, from the most basic (a broadcast domain boundary) all the way through its most advanced routing protocol interaction (a gateway to the Internet and the world). Of course, there are rules to be followed and information that routers must have to make this happen.

In this chapter, you will learn specifically about the routing process itself and how to give routers the information they require. I'll cover a couple of primary forms: static routing and dynamic routing. For dynamic routing, this chapter is only the beginning. The next three chapters will be devoted to dynamic routing protocols as well.

Additionally, you will learn ways to filter and control the propagation of routing information between routers and routing domains.

For up-to-the-minute updates on this chapter, check out www.sybex.com/go/CiscoProGuidetoInternetworking or www.lammle.com.

Routing Fundamentals

To begin, you need to understand the routing function itself and what happens during the process. In this section, I show you how a router makes its decisions about where and how to send data. You'll learn about the information that a router needs in order to make these decisions. Then you'll delve into the ways that the router gets this information—both static routing (you, as the administrator, will give this to the router) and dynamic routing. You will look at administrative distance and some of the functions that help a router determine which routing information is the best. You will see how dynamic routing protocols are categorized and the features each provides.

Basic Routing

At this point we have discussed connecting hosts and wiring up the network for use. With routing, you go beyond the network connections. You have figure out how the router is going to pass data between subnets. Start off by thinking about the information a router needs to make a routing decision. Routers care only about networks when they are routing, not about individual host IP addresses. Every router must know about every destination network to which it can send data. If a router has a packet to route but the destination network is not in its routing table, then the packet will be dropped. The information that a router needs to route are:

- Destination address
- Possible routes to all remote networks
- The best route or path to a destination network
- Neighbor routers from which it can learn routes and send data
- A way to learn, update, and maintain route information

For this chapter, I am going to have you building and upgrading the Brussels office. Business in Europe has been growing steadily over the past couple of years. The number of people, hosts, applications, and networks in the Brussels office has grown with it.

 Real World Scenario

The Brussels Office

In the beginning of the chapter, I start you off as if it were a couple of years ago in the Brussels office. There weren't enough people or resources for a full switch block design. The person who set up the office at that time wouldn't have known to use the design methods you now know anyway. I will show you how the network looked with just a single router and a few subnets connected to it. Then, you will learn what must happen when a second router is added to the network.

As the chapter progresses, you will add more subnetworks and more routers to the Brussels network. Once you have more than a few routers, you will see that the need for a dynamic way to update the network is needed. This will lead my discussion right into dynamic routing protocols, and you will be adding more routers to the network. Once I get you through some of the basics of routing, I will then be expanding (even over the next couple of chapters and other routing protocols) the network and showing you how the routing devices that are located in the distribution layer update one another. I just say routing devices here, because they can often be multilayer switches as well as routers.

So now, let me begin by examining a single router in the FutureTech Brussels office. Take a look at Figure 4.1. You can see that the router (BrusRtr1) has four separate interfaces. Each, obviously, represents its own network and broadcast domain. In order for traffic to pass between the two hosts BrusPC1 and BrusPC2, the router must route the data. Now the router is only configured with the interface IP addresses and the interfaces are enabled. So, what information does the router have in its routing table? If you said, "The routing table includes each of the four networks and it shows them as directly connected," you are exactly right! A router always knows about the networks that are directly connected. Those networks show up in the routing table as long as the interface is enabled and active.

FIGURE 4.1   Routing with a Single Router

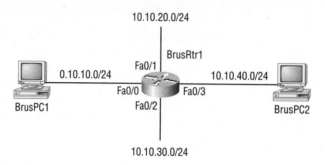

So, what happens when BrusPC1 pings BrusPC2? Well, BrusPC1 creates an Internet control message protocol (ICMP) packet, frames it at the data link layer, and then sends the frames across the network to the router. At the data link layer, the destination address is the router because it is default gateway for BrusPC1 and the packet is destined for a remote network. Once the frame reaches the router, the router tears off the frame and looks into the IP packet header. It needs the destination IP address for the route lookup. The router finds that the destination network is 10.10.40.0/24. Looking at the routing table of BrusRtr1 you can see where the packet is going to go.

```
BrusRtr1#show ip route
[output cut]
Gateway of last resort is not set
C       10.10.10.0/24 is directly connected, FastEthernet0/0
C       10.10.20.0/24 is directly connected, FastEthernet0/1
C       10.10.30.0/24 is directly connected, FastEthernet0/2
C       10.10.40.0/24 is directly connected, FastEthernet0/3
```

After the router has determined that the packet will go out to interface fa0/3, it must switch the packet from incoming interface of fa0/0. Because this is meant to be a short review, I review a few key things but not every little detail.

Take note. The term that I used above was switch. The router must switch the packet from the incoming to the outgoing interface. Many people confuse the processes involved in routing and switching when they talk about the internal processes on a router. The routing process made the decision about where the packet had to be sent to move along the path to the destination. The process that actually moves the packet from one interface to another is switching.

Switching is often looked at as something only a Layer 2 switch does. This is not the case. A switch moves or switches frames at Layer 2, while a router switches packets at Layer 3. In both cases, a chunk of data is being moved from one interface to another, but the difference is the type of data and at what layer the exchange occurs. Switching is always this process of moving data from one interface to another, whether it happens at Layer 2, 3, or 4. Think back to the Cisco Express Forwarding (CEF) information I reviewed with you in Chapter 2, "Switching." That should help imprint the concept on your memory.

Now that the packet is on the outgoing interface, it must be passed back down to Layer 2. Here it will be reframed and sent out to the destination. In this case, the destination is BrusPC2.

So, now you can move a packet from one host to another across a single router. What happens when there is another router in the network? Take a look at Figure 4.2 while you are thinking about the question. As the business grew and staff increased at the Brussels office, a single router could no longer handle the load. There are now two routers and the second router, BrusRtr2, has networks of its own. At this point, BrusRtr1 still knows about the networks that are directly connected. But what does BrusRtr2 know about? If you said, "It knows about its directly connected networks," once again you are correct. Here is the routing table for BrusRtr2.

```
BrusRtr2#show ip route
[output cut]
Gateway of last resort is not set
C       10.10.40.0/24 is directly connected, FastEthernet0/0
C       10.10.50.0/24 is directly connected, FastEthernet0/1
C       10.10.60.0/24 is directly connected, FastEthernet0/2
C       10.10.70.0/24 is directly connected, FastEthernet0/3
```

What about our first question? What will happen when we add another router to the network? Will BrusPC1 now be able to communicate with BrusPC3? Well, that is what you are going to figure out.

FIGURE 4.2   Routing with Two Routers

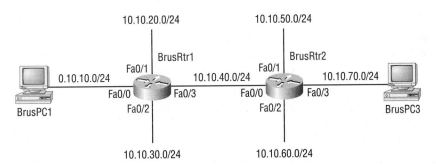

Looking at Figure 4.2 again, let's go through the process of BrusPC1 pinging BrusPC3. Again, BrusPC1 is going to create the ICMP packet, frame it, and send it out onto the network. When BrusRtr1 receives the frame, it again tears off the frame header to see the IP packet header. Once it finds the destination IP address, BrusRtr1 can do a lookup in the routing table for the network. You know that the destination network for BrusPC3 is 10.10.70.0/24 because that is the subnet the host is located on. Now, remember that the routing table for BrusRtr1 includes information about networks that are directly connected. You can check the routing table output from BrusRtr1 on the last page if you have forgotten the addresses. Is there an entry for the 10.10.70.0/24 network in the routing table of BrusRtr1? No, there is not. So, what will happen to this packet on the incoming interface of BrusRtr1? If you answered, "It will be dropped," then you are correct. This is one of the most basic rules of routing: If the router does not have the destination network in its routing table, then the packet is dropped.

Now what can be done to get BrusRtr1 the information that it needs to route the packets to BrusPC3? What are the ways that a router can learn, update, and maintain its routing information? As discussed before, the administrator can give the router the information manually through static routing, or you can configure an automatic method through a routing protocol. In the next section, I'll specifically discuss the manual way. After that, for the next few chapters, I discuss in detail the dynamic routing protocol methods.

Administrative Distance

Before I get too far into the details of each type of routing, you need to take a look at something called administrative distance. It is fairly common to have more than one type of routing within an internetwork. As I show you each of the types of routing, you will see that some have strengths for one particular application while another type may be better for another situation. With this in mind, if the router is getting information from multiple sources, you have to give the router a way to determine which source of information is best. You have to do this because every single routing protocol uses different information (called a metric) to determine its own best path to networks.

A router has no way of equally balancing or comparing the routes that it receives from different protocols. This means that you need to assign a weight or value to every type of routing information that a router may receive. This value or scale is called administrative distance. The lower the number in the administrative distance scale, the better the information is to the router.

So, what is the best information that a router could have? If you said, "A directly connected network is the best," you are correct! An individual router always knows about directly connected networks and for that reason, they are the best. In terms of administrative distance, a directly connected network has a value or distance of 0. This is the best distance that a route can have. If you configure a router with a static route, it has a distance of 1. You are going to learn how to create static routes in the next section.

In the next few chapters, I discuss each of the routing protocols in detail. For now though, here is Table 4.1, with the administrative distances for each routing protocol.

TABLE 4.1   Administrative Distance Values

Protocol or Route Source	Administrative Distance
Directly connected interface	0
Static Route	1
EIGRP Summary Route	5

TABLE 4.1   Administrative Distance Values *(continued)*

Protocol or Route Source	Administrative Distance
External BGP	20
Internal EIGRP	90
IGRP	100
OSPF	110
IS-IS	115
RIP v1, v2	120
EGP	140
External EIGRP	170
Internal BGP	200
Unknown	255

Static Routing

It is now time to pick up where we left off before we talked about administrative distance. It is time to start looking at how you are going to give the router what it needs to route, beginning with manual or static routing configurations. Now, there are many reasons that you would use static routing. Often, you will use static routing to fix a small problem or hole in the network that is left by a dynamic routing protocol solution. You can also use static routes to help chose a backup path when a primary fails. This is called a floating static route. Static routing can also be used to configure a default route.

Let's figure out how you can configure a static route. Refer back to Figure 4.2. BrusRtr1 was trying to send a packet from BrusPC1 to BrusPC3, but the packet was dropped because the destination network was not in the routing table. So, you need to add a route in the routing table. You are going to do that with a static route. The command to put a static route in the routing table is `ip route` *prefix mask {ip-address | interface-type interface-number } [distance]*.

The command starts with `ip route` and must be followed by the prefix and mask of the destination network that is being placed in the routing table. The next piece of the command is either the next hop IP address or the exit interface. If you choose the next hop address, use the IP address of the neighboring router that the local router is connected to. This IP address and neighbor must be in the direction of the destination network. Instead of using a next hop IP, you can use the exit interface of the local router.

The exit interface can be used just for simplicity, but I recommend that you only do it with non-broadcast interfaces such as serial interfaces. If you configure this on a broadcast interface such Ethernet, the route will only be added when the interface is up. The bad thing is that the router will think that any destination host it doesn't know about through some other router to be directly connected to that Ethernet interface. This can cause a huge amount of ARP traffic, a huge ARP cache, and even make the router crash and reload!

The last option I have listed is the distance. This stands for the administrative distance of the routing information. If you do not include this option, the default will be used. We discussed what the administrative distance does in the last section. Remember, the administrative distance for static routes are 1. If you use a directly connected interface for a static route, the router in the routing table considers them to be directly connected. The impact differs depending on the routing protocol, but has its biggest effect when you do redistribution. I will cover this more when I talk about redistribution for each of the dynamic routing protocols.

Let's take a look at what the configuration would look like for Router A if we put a static route in the routing table for the 10.10.70.0/24 subnet. This first example uses the next hop IP address for where the data is to be sent.

```
BrusRtr1(config)#ip route 10.10.70.0 255.255.255.0 10.10.40.2
```

This next example shows you the command using the exit interface of the local router for where the data is to be sent.

```
BrusRtr1(config)#ip route 10.10.70.0 255.255.255.0 Fa0/3
```

Now, there is more than one use for a static route. You can use a static route for giving a router default routing information, or a default route as it is typically called. There are a few reasons that we might give a router default route information. The two most common are to give a stub router a route to send all of its data to or to give an edge router the route it needs to send all of its data to a service provider, for instance. Now when I say *all of its data*, I specifically mean all the data the router doesn't have a specific route for. Let's first look at Figure 4.3. In this diagram, you can see that BrusRtr1 is connected to the rest of the internetwork and BrusRtr2 only has a connection to BrusRtr1. Because BrusRtr2 has only one place that it can send data, this router is considered a stub router. It isn't necessary for BrusRtr2 to know about every network in the internetwork because BrusRtr1 knows how to route beyond itself. BrusRtr2 must send all of its data to BrusRtr1 and it is BrusRtr1's problem to move it further along the path.

FIGURE 4.3   Static Default Route for a Stub Router

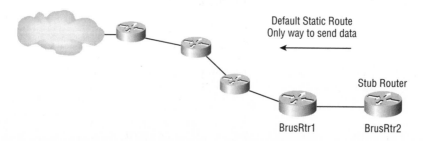

The second reason for a default route is to send all unknown data to an Internet Service Provider (ISP).

 Real World Scenario

Adding Internet Access

If you look at Figure 4.4, you will see that we now have BrusRtr1 that is connected to the service provider network. It is a common practice to have remote sites with their own Internet access. If they did not, then all of their Internet data would have to be carried across the WAN link to the headquarters building in Dallas. Once in Dallas, the data would then be routed out to the Internet, and the return traffic from the Internet would have to take the reverse path back to the Brussels office. This would not only be very inefficient but it would eat up way too much valuable and expensive WAN bandwidth. Just as in the last example, it is not required that BrusRtr1 know all of the networks that are in the ISP network. For that to happen, BrusRtr1 would have to know about all of the networks on the Internet. That could be hundreds of thousands of routes. In most cases, that would be way too many routes for the routers to handle. So, again from the diagram, you can see that you are going to route all of the unknown data toward the ISP router or network.

FIGURE 4.4 Default Route for an Edge Router

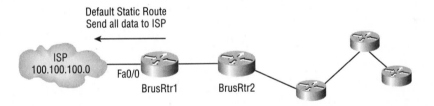

For both of these cases the actual configuration is the same. You use the same command you used for static routing. Only now, we are going to replace the destination network prefix and mask with all zeros. This tells the router to send the data destined for any network with any mask that it does not have knowledge of down this path. The route will show up in the routing table with all zeros. Here are the configuration commands.

```
BrusRtr1(config)#ip route 0.0.0.0 0.0.0.0 100.100.100.2
BrusRtr1(config)#ip route 0.0.0.0 0.0.0.0 Fa0/0
```

The other situation where you could use a static route is to advertise a redundant link, but you don't want to always advertise the link. Let me explain.

 **Real World Scenario**

Keeping Connected

FutureTech has redundant wide area network (WAN) connections from their headquarters office in Dallas to the Brussels branch LAN. If one of those connections is the primary, maybe because it has a higher bandwidth, you would want that to be the route that is in the routing table of your routers. Only when that primary link goes down would you want the other link, the link with the lower bandwidth, to be used. The network is running Enhanced Interior Gateway Routing Protocol (EIGRP) as its dynamic routing protocol. (I know that I haven't discussed EIGRP but you have enough basic knowledge from CCNA or other reading for this example, so not to worry.)

Look at Figure 4.5. You can see the two WAN links between the sites; one of them is a MPLS and the other is an IPSec VPN connection. You want the MPLS link to be used and the route for that path to be found by EIGRP. The secondary link will be configured with a static route so that it will only be used if the primary link goes down. This type of static route is called a floating static route. It is called this because you modify the administrative distance of the static route so that it floats right above the route for whatever dynamic routing protocol you might be using. In this case, since FutureTech is using EIGRP and the administrative distance for EIGRP is 90, the administrative distance of the static route must be set to something above that value.

FIGURE 4.5 Floating Static Route

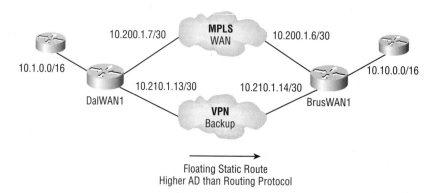

Floating Static Route
Higher AD than Routing Protocol

For this example, the only routing protocol FutureTech is running on the network is EIGRP, so you can make the distance anything above 90. Let's make it 95 for the example. You need to tell the DalWAN1 router what the redundant path to get to all the destination subnets in Brussels is. The subnets that exist in Brussels, as you have seen from the previous examples, are summarized into the range of 10.10.0.0/16. In this, case the static route configuration would look like this:

```
DalWAN1(config)#ip route 10.10.0.0 255.255.0.0 10.210.1.14 95
```

You should be pretty comfortable with static routing, so it is time to move on to dynamic routing, which will allow you to more easily route more networks without so much administrative burden.

Dynamic Routing

As you start down the dynamic routing protocol path here, I want to start off with a caution. Everyone is always worried about how a particular protocol operates and what all the little details of its use are. But do you ever stop to think about the downside of running a dynamic protocol? Just to make sure that you don't think I am trying to talk you out of using them, I am not. I would not administer most networks without the use of a dynamic routing protocol. I am merely stating that some issues created by using dynamic protocols deserve your consideration.

You have probably heard people talk about the obvious ones. Dynamic routing protocols require the router to use more CPU time, and they require more memory to store their tables and information. Those are things that network engineers have to think about, yes, but they can be easily overcome by making sure that you use a router model that handles the processing load. The issue that I want to make sure you think about is the amount of bandwidth that a protocol uses.

Now, bandwidth won't be an issue in every instance. If your internetwork has all of the devices connected with Gigabit Ethernet or fiber optic connections, no problem. Bandwidth will become an issue when you start talking about WAN links and Quality of Service (QoS). In the case of a WAN link, you don't always have a bunch of extra bandwidth. For some of the protocols that I will show you, there are configurations that we can use to help you control the amount of bandwidth that is allowed. Not all of the protocols have this feature though. This can be a determining factor in deciding which protocol to use and the determination of which protocol to use is going to be the topic of other discussions.

Why is this important you ask? Well, let's take a look at another part of the FutureTech network.

The other instance that I mentioned was QoS. This will be something to think about when the QoS discussion comes around in Chapter 18, "QoS." For now though, it's enough to know that the purpose for QoS is to control and manage bandwidth and how data is to be sent. With that in mind, you will have to remember that to consider routing protocols and other management data when you do your configuration.

Now that we have static routing out of the way, let's talk about all of the great things that dynamic routing protocols do for you. The thing that comes to mind first is the amount of time and energy that you save configuring your routers. Unlike a static route, you don't have to go to every single router and configure it for every destination network. If manual static routing was the only way to configure routing, there would probably be a lot fewer of us interested in working as a network engineer for a living. Thankfully, routing protocols do much of the work for us. You still have to know what the protocol is going to do and how it will do it, but the routing protocol will take care of most of the updating and sending information between the routers.

 Real World Scenario

Timbuktu's Inventory Connection

The FutureTech network diagram from Chapter 1 didn't include some smaller sites that are connected to the Dallas headquarters network through an old legacy frame relay network. The committed information rate (CIR) that is being purchased for these connections is very small. Most of these sites are only connected to an old mainframe application that keeps FutureTech's inventory data up to date. So the issue is that these connections are small for the reason of not sending much data. If a dynamic routing protocol were running, then a significantly higher amount of data would have to be sent basically for no reason. This is a perfect place to have static routes. Most current networks today don't have to worry about this sort of thing, because even a VPN connection going over the Internet can have more bandwidth than old frame relay connections like this.

Like I said, you have to know how and why the protocols are going to do these things. You have to choose between the protocols and decide which of them is able to do all of the things that you need accomplished on your network. To make that decision, you have to know all the choices and their characteristics. For that purpose, I have created what I call the routing tree. For years, I have seen my students struggle with all of the different categories of routing protocols and where each protocol fits into the mix. So, I simply put all of the categories and protocols into a tree structure. You can see the routing tree in Figure 4.6. Use the tree to track the categories and which protocols fall into each one.

You can see that I start off with routing at the top. Routing breaks into two different means of updating a router's information, static and dynamic routing. Static routing ends there; it is just the manual means of giving the router information. The other branch of the tree just begins there. You can see that dynamic routing protocols break up into many different categories or types of protocols. The first split in the dynamic protocol branch is the division of Interior Gateway Protocols (IGP) and Exterior Gateway Protocols (EGP). I talk about each protocol and category coming up in the next few sections, but for now the difference is interior or exterior routing of an Autonomous System (AS).

An autonomous system is a collection of networks or subnets that are in the same administrative domain. Another way of saying administrative domain is "within your company's network." You control or administer the network and all of the subnets within it. You control and set the policy for what happens in an autonomous system.

An IGP operates and routes within an AS; an EGP works outside or between systems.

FIGURE 4.6   Routing Tree

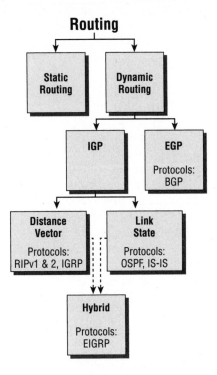

That is the end of the EGP branch of the tree, but the IGP branch continues to split out as you go down further. At the IGP split, you can see that there are two primary categories, Distance Vector and Link State routing. You'll get a chance to work with all of these types of protocols over the next couple of chapters. In the Distance Vector category, you will find Routing Information Protocol (RIP) and Interior Gateway Routing Protocol (IGRP). Under the Link State category, there is Open Shortest Path First (OSPF) and Intermediate System to Intermediate System (IS-IS).

Now, there is a third category shown in the diagram. This category is called Advanced Distance Vector Protocol. The only protocol under this one is Enhanced Interior Gateway Routing Protocol (EIGRP). It is Cisco proprietary and has characteristics of both Distance Vector and Link State. Sometimes, EIGRP is sometimes called a hybrid protocol but you will see it called an Advanced Distance Vector Routing Protocol, which is more correct. So, let's look a little more closely at each of the categories and protocols that fall under each one.

Interior Gateway Protocols (IGP)

IGPs operate inside of autonomous systems. This means that they route and determine paths for an internetwork that you control or administer. I have not gone through all the details of each category, but each type and protocol has its own distinct features. One of the major things that you will need to consider is whether the protocol is classful or classless. The difference is huge and determines how you can address the network and where and when you can use summarization and variable length subnet masking (VLSM). As I discussed with you in the introduction of this book, VLSM and summarization fall into those objectives from the CCNA you should have a good understanding of at this point. If you are not sure of how to configure summarization, you don't need to worry about that. As I go through each of the protocols, I'll show you how to configure summarization for that particular protocol.

Distance Vector Protocols

As you saw in the routing tree diagram (Figure 4.6), a couple of protocols fall under the distance vector category. The primary protocol that you are going to look at is the Routing Information Protocol (RIP). RIP has long been an open standard protocol and most equipment vendors support it. It is useful not just for routers; in many cases, RIP is the only protocol supported by devices such as UNIX servers. The fact that you have devices that only support RIP can be a reason that RIP must still be used in a particular network.

Two versions of RIP, version 1 and version 2, work for IPv4 addressing. The primary difference between the versions is that version 1 is a classful routing protocol and version 2 is a classless routing protocol. I give you all of the details of the two versions a little later in this chapter.

The other distance vector routing protocol that you see in the routing tree is IGRP. I don't discuss this protocol in great detail, as it has been removed from the IOS in version 12.3 and it is no longer supported by Cisco. IGRP is a proprietary protocol that was only supported by Cisco equipment anyway, so removing the protocol does not impact other vendor's devices.

Distance vector protocols, by their very name, operate only a small amount of information about the network. They need basic information about destination networks. To successfully route information, distance vector protocols must know a specific distance and direction (or vector) to each destination network, hence the name of the protocols. These protocols really know very little about the network otherwise. They don't keep track of neighbor routers or which routers are connected to which networks. Keeping track of that type of information is what a link state protocol does.

Distance vector routing protocols keep track of changes to the internetwork by broadcasting periodic routing updates out all active interfaces. Each broadcast includes the complete routing table. This can work okay, but the amount of CPU process and link bandwidth can be more than you might want. And if a network outage happens, real problems can occur. Plus, the slow convergence of distance vector routing protocols can result in inconsistent routing tables and routing loops.

Routing loops occur because every router isn't updated simultaneously, or even close to it. Here's an example. You are still in the Brussels office and the network has grown to the point of having four routers. You can see in Figure 4.7 that the four Brussels routers are in the network. To make this example easier, I used letters to signify the networks instead of a bunch of numbers. Let's start off by saying that you have configured RIP on all of the routers and each one of the four routers knows about all of the networks A through E. Now for a routing loop to occur, a sequence of events would have to happen in perfect timing. I am sure that you can guess that the engineer who made one of these first routing protocols didn't anticipate that loops could occur or the engineer would have just built in mechanisms from the start to prevent the loops. After I go through this sequence, I will describe for you the mechanisms that are now in place to prevent this from happening.

You have to be aware of one other piece of information. RIP uses a very simple metric of hop count. Hop count is simply the number of routers that must be traversed to get to a destination network. For a network that is directly connected, the hop count is 0. In the diagram, network E has a metric of 0 for BrusRtr4, a hop count of 1 for BrusRtr3, a hop count of 2 for BrusRtr2, and a hop count of 3 for BrusRtr1.

1. At the starting point, all of the routers are up to date and updates are being sent normally.

2. Network E now goes down for some reason (such as a failed interface or cut link), but the point is that the network is now down for BrusRtr4 and removed from the routing table. This is where the timing comes into play. If BrusRtr4 had sent its last update 1 second before network E went down, then BrusRtr4 is not due to send another update for 29 more seconds. (RIP's update timer is 30 seconds.)

3. If BrusRtr3's timer expires before that 29 seconds is up for BrusRtr4, then BrusRtr3 will send out its update.

4. The problem is that when BrusRtr4 receives that update, it will add a route back into its table. Because the route from BrusRtr3 had a hop count of 1 (which was the correct hop count when BrusRtr3 learned the route from BrusRtr4), BrusRtr4 knows nothing else to do but add 1 to that metric and place the route with a count of 2.

5. When the timer expires for BrusRtr4 and it sends its update to BrusRtr3, BrusRtr3 will see that there is a change to the hop count from what it had originally. Now BrusRtr3 must update its hop count to 3.

6. When BrusRtr3 sends out its next update the problem will extend in the other direction as well.

7. BrusRtr2 will add 1 to its hop count and send out an update.

8. BrusRtr1 will add 1 to its hop count and send out an update.

9. This is going to continue forever. It is called counting to infinity and is the reason for the first loop avoidance mechanism called maximum hop count.

FIGURE 4.7   Routing Loop Example

Mechanisms are built into routing protocols to prevent routing information from causing loops or other problems in the network. Some of these mechanisms are used in other protocols, such as EIGRP and OSPF. I will talk about those cases later, when we look at those protocols specifically. Well, let's look at distance vector routing loop avoidance mechanisms.

Maximum Hop Count   The routing loop problem just described is called counting to infinity. It's caused by gossip (broadcasts) and wrong information being communicated then propagated throughout the internetwork. Without some form of intervention, the hop count increases indefinitely each time a packet passes through a router.

One way of solving this problem is to define a maximum hop count. RIP permits a hop count of up to 15, so any network that requires 16 hops is deemed unreachable. In other words, if network E were to go down with a hop count of 15 (whether any other messages were received or not), network E will be considered down. Thus, the maximum hop count will control how long it takes for a routing table entry to become invalid or questionable.

Split Horizon   Split horizon reduces incorrect routing information and routing overhead in a distance vector network. It enforces a very simple rule: It is never useful to send routing information back in the direction from which it was learned. In other words, the routing protocol identifies the interface a network route was learned on and won't advertise the route back out that same interface. Split horizon would have prevented any of the routers from sending the updated information it received back toward the source of network E.

Route Poisoning   Another way to avoid problems caused by inconsistent updates and stop network loops is route poisoning. For example, when network E goes down, router D initiates route poisoning by advertising network E as 16, or unreachable (sometimes referred to as infinite). Poisoning the route to a downed network keeps other routers from being susceptible to incorrect updates. When a router receives a poisoned route, it sends an update, called a *poison reverse,* back to the notifying router. This ensures all routers on the segment have received the poisoned route information.

Why send this special poison reverse message? This message ensures that the source router will know the route was received and is indeed poisoned, but think about where the message is going. BrusRtr3 would be sending it back to BrusRtr4. So what rule would be broken by sending this update? If you said "split horizon," you are exactly correct.

Holddowns   A holddown prevents regular update messages from reinstating a route that is going up and down (called flapping). Typically, this happens on a serial link that's losing connectivity and then coming back up. If there wasn't a way to stabilize this, the network would never converge, and that one flapping interface could bring down the entire network!

Holddowns prevent routes from changing too rapidly by allowing time for either the downed route to come back up or the network to stabilize somewhat before changing to the next best route. Holddowns also tell routers to restrict, for a specific period, changes that might affect recently removed routes. This prevents inoperative routes from being prematurely restored to other routers' tables.

Link State Protocols

Link state routing protocols are classless routing protocols. Again, to be a classless routing protocol, the subnet mask information is carried with the routing update so that all of the neighbor routers know how big the advertised network route is. One of the biggest differences between link state and distance vector protocols is the fact that link state protocols learn and maintain much more information about the internetwork. Distance vector routing protocols only maintain a routing table with the destination routes in it. Link state routing protocols maintain two additional tables, a neighbor table and a topology table.

Neighbor Table   A neighbor table is maintained through the use of Hello packets. Hello packets are exchanged by all routers to determine what other routers are available for exchange routing data. All routers that can share routing data are stored in the neighbor table.

Topology Table   The topology table is built and maintained through the use of link state advertisements (LSA) or link state packets (LSP), depending on the protocol. The table contains a listing for every destination network for every neighbor that the router can talk to. It is essentially a map of the entire internetwork, and not just a map of the routes or paths that the local router is going to use but of every single route and network—a complete map of the internetwork. Once all of routing data is shared and each one of the routers has the raw data in their topology table, then the routing protocol runs the Shortest Path First (SPF) algorithm against the raw data so that the best paths to each of the destination networks can be found. I will go into every detail of how the link state protocols do what they do, but not until Chapter 6, "Link State Routing Protocols."

Advanced Distance Vector Protocols

The only Advance Distance Vector Routing Protocol currently in use is Enhanced Interior Gateway Routing Protocol (EIGRP). EIGRP is sometimes called a hybrid routing protocol, but advanced distance vector is a better description of the protocol. EIGRP is a Cisco-proprietary protocol and will only run on Cisco equipment. If you have a multivendor environment, you will not be able to run just EIGRP.

> The issue of running more than one routing protocol can be overcome; I will talk about running more than one routing protocol and how to configure something like redistribution. I'll tell you about how that works specifically for each protocol in Chapters 5 through 7.

If you are running all Cisco gear, then you can run an all EIGRP network. There are many benefits from running EIGRP. It provides a loop-free network through the use of the Diffused Update ALgorithm (DUAL). EIGRP can support multiple network layer protocols (IP, IPX, and Appletalk) through the use of Protocol Dependant Modules (PDMs).

EIGRP can support all of the classless functions, *all* because, again, it carries the subnet mask information in its routing updates. Possibly the biggest thing that sets EIGRP apart from the other categories is that fact that it takes the best of distance vector and link state and puts them together. It is simple to configure and turn on, like a distance vector protocol, but it keeps track of more information.

EIGRP creates and maintains a neighbor table and a topology table just like link state protocols do. The neighbor table is maintained through the use of, you guessed it, Hello packets. The topology table is maintained through EIGRP update packets. The EIGRP topology table is different than a link state protocol topography table. Instead of maintaining all of the networks and neighbor paths in the table and processing the raw data independently, like a link state router would, the EIGRP router passes preprocessed data to its neighbor and doesn't require as much CPU time to fully calculate.

EIGRP is a very fast, scalable, fault-tolerant routing protocol. You will learn all of the details of this protocol in Chapter 5, "Hybrid Routing Protocols."

Exterior Gateway Protocols (EGP)

The last branch on the routing tree left to discuss is the Exterior Gateway Protocols (EGPs) branch. A few protocols have fallen into this category over the years, but only one is authorized to be used on the Internet today. That protocol is Border Gateway Protocol (BGP) version 4. In the past, the Gateway-to-Gateway Protocol (GGP) and the Exterior Gateway Protocol (EGP) were used. In the case of this discussion, EGP is the name of the protocol and not the type on our tree. The EGP name has been repurposed and is now recognized as a protocol type; you should be used to terms being reused in the networking world by now. The basic goal of all of these protocols was to exchange routing information between autonomous systems. They allow administrators to know where destination networks are all across the Internet and in far-reaching internetworks.

You will see when I discuss BGP in detail that it doesn't use a simple metric like most other protocols do. BGP is a path vector routing protocol. It provides the direction of a path, and with that path information you can control and manipulate how the routes and data will be forwarded. This control is enabled through a rich set of attributes that are used to control the protocol. Later in this chapter, you will learn about route maps. You will see that you can use things like route maps and manipulate or control how the attributes are used or even what their values are. We are going to discuss in much more detail how BGP works in Chapter 7, "Exterior Gateway Protocols."

Route Information Protocol (RIP)

The Routing Information Protocol (RIP) is a true distance vector routing protocol. RIP version 1 (RIPv1) broadcasts the complete routing table out to all active interfaces at a set interval, by default every 30 seconds. RIP's only metric, hop count, determines the best path to a destination network. The maximum allowable hop count is 15 by default, meaning that 16 hop destinations are deemed unreachable. RIP works well in small networks, but can quickly become inefficient in a large network. The use of a slow WAN link or a large number of routers installed makes the broadcast nature, or the sending of the entire routing table, inefficient and unable to scale well.

RIPv1 uses classful routing; all devices in the network must use the same subnet mask. RIP version 1 doesn't include subnet mask information in updates. RIP version 2 (RIPv2) provides something called prefix routing and sends subnet mask information with the route updates. In effect, RIPv2 becomes classless routing. I'll tell you more about this in the "RIP Version 2" section a little later in this chapter.

In the next couple of sections, you will learn first about the timers used to regulate RIP performance and then about RIP configuration.

RIP Timers

RIP uses four different kinds of timers to regulate its performance:

Route Update Timer   The route update timer sets the interval (typically 30 seconds) between periodic routing updates. Each routing update sends a complete copy of each router's routing table out to all neighbors.

Route Invalid Timer   The invalid timer determines the length of time that must elapse (180 seconds) before a router determines that a route has become invalid. If a router hasn't heard any updates about a particular route for that period, the router will send updates to all its neighbors, letting them know that the route is invalid.

Holddown Timer   The holddown timer sets the amount of time during which routing information is suppressed. Routes enter into a holddown state when an update packet that indicates the route is unreachable is received. Information is suppressed until either an update packet with a better metric is received or until the holddown timer expires. The default is 180 seconds.

Route Flush Timer   The flush timer sets the time between a route becoming invalid and its removal from the routing table (by default 240 seconds). Before it's removed from the table, the router notifies its neighbors of that route's impending demise. The value of the route invalid timer must be less than that of the route flush timer so the router has enough time to tell neighbors about the invalid route before the local routing table is updated.

Configuring RIP Routing

To configure RIP routing, you must first enable the protocol with the router rip command. Second, you must tell the RIP routing protocol which networks to advertise with the network command.

You can add the RIP routing protocol by using the router rip command and the network command. The network command tells the routing protocol which classful network to advertise. In addition to the network that will be advertised, the network command tells RIP which active interfaces to include in the routing process. Any interface that has an IP address within the range of one of the network commands is then placed into the routing process.

Look at the BrusRtr1 configuration and see how easy this is. I use the same routers from the Brussels office for the configuration examples as well. Right now, the example is a single router showing you the commands to enable RIP.

```
BrusRtr1#config t
BrusRtr1 (config)#router rip
BrusRtr1 (config-router)#network 10.0.0.0
```

That's it. Two or three commands, and you're done—sure makes your job a lot easier than building static routes, doesn't it? However, keep in mind the extra router CPU process and bandwidth that you're consuming.

Notice in the network command you didn't put in each of the subnets. The only information that you had to input was the classful network address with all subnet bits and host bits off. After doing that, the routing protocol takes over and finds the subnets and populates the routing tables. Where do they find the subnets? Well, think about what you've configured already. Each of the interfaces has an IP address and mask on it, right? The router gets all the information that it needs from the interface configurations.

Concept: Building an RIP Routing Table

Remember that RIP uses the classful address when configuring the network address. Because of this, all subnet masks must be the same on all devices in the network (this is called classful routing). To clarify, let's say you're using a Class B network address of 172.16.0.0/24 with subnets 172.16.10.0, 172.16.20.0, and 172.16.30.0. You would only type in the classful network address of 172.16.0.0 and let RIP find the subnets and place them in the routing table.

RIP Version 2

Now, it's time to spend a few minutes discussing RIPv2. RIPv2 is very much the same as RIPv1. Both are distance vector protocols, which means that each router running RIP sends its complete routing tables out all active interfaces at intervals (30 seconds). Also, the timers and loop-avoidance schemes—holddown timers and the split horizon rule—are the same in both RIP versions. Both RIPv1 and RIPv2 are configured with classful addressing (but RIPv2 is considered classless because subnet information is sent with each route update), and both have the same administrative distance (120).

But there are some important differences that make RIPv2 more scalable than RIPv1. Now, a word of advice here before we move on; I'm definitely not swaying you away from or toward RIP. There are cases where v1 must be used, for instance with a UNIX server. The version of the protocol that you use can be very important. If you leave a Cisco router with the default running version and do not issue a version command, then the router will send only version 1 updates. It will, however, receive or listen for version 1 or 2 updates. If you configure the router for specific version, then the router will send and receive only updates of the configured version.

RIP is an open standard; you can use RIP with any brand of router, which can be a major benefit. You can also use OSPF, since OSPF is an open standard as well. RIP just requires much more bandwidth, making it pretty intensive to use in your network, but OSPF is going to require much more understanding and configuration. Later in the chapter, I give you criteria to decide which is better for a given situation.

> ## 🌐 Real World Scenario
>
> ### When RIP Won't Talk to RIP
>
> Let's look at the Brussels office again. Recall that there are some old routers, and the configurations on them haven't been messed with for quite a while. The first and oldest router BrusRtr is still running the default setup of RIP; it will receive either version but only send version 1. The new routers that you have been putting into the network have been configured for RIPv2. You now have devices that are sending and receiving updates that are of totally different versions and the old BrusRtr router would listen and take the RIPv2 updates that are coming from the new routers. However, the new routers that you have installed would ignore the old RIPv1 updates that are coming from BrusRtr. You are now going to have inconsistent routing tables because the new routers won't have the networks that are connected to the old router. In order to fix this, you are going to have to update the old router to version 2.

Table 4.2 lists the differences between RIPv1 and RIPv2.

TABLE 4.2   RIPv1 vs. RIPv2

RIPv1	RIPv2
Distance vector	Distance vector
Maximum hop count of 15	Maximum hop count of 15
Classful addressing	Classless addressing
Broadcast based	Uses Multicast 224.0.0.9
No support for VLSM	Supports VLSM networks
No authentication	Allows for MD5 authentication
No support for discontiguous networks	Supports discontiguous networks

By sending the subnet mask information with the updates, RIPv2 can support variable length subnet masks (VLSMs), as well as the summarization of network boundaries. In addition, RIPv2 can support discontiguous networking.

Configuring RIPv2 is pretty straightforward. Here's an example:

```
RouterA(config)#router rip
RouterA(config-router)#network 192.168.40.0
```

```
RouterA(config-router)#network 192.168.50.0
RouterA(config-router)#version 2
```

That's it; just add the command version 2 at the (config-router)# prompt and you are now running RIPv2.

Summarization with RIP

There is one additional thing that we need to look at for RIP and that is manual summarization. With RIPv1, the routing protocol itself would perform automatic summarization to a classful boundary. That means that if a router has four interfaces and the networks that are attached to those interfaces are 64 blocks of a class C network, then the router would automatically summarize the subnets and send a routing update for only the class C network. With RIPv2, you have the ability to send the classful network, each of the subnets individually, or to craft a new manual summary address that you choose.

There are two configurations that have to be completed in order to send a manual summary route. First, you must tell the routing protocol, which by default sends automatic classful summaries, not to send automatic summaries. Second, you must configure the manual summary command for the routing protocol to create the new summary route. The no auto-summary command tells the router to stop sending automatic classful summary routes. Next, use the ip summary-address rip command to configure the manual summary. Let's take a look at what each of these commands looks like.

```
RouterA(config)#router rip
RouterA(config-router)#no auto-summary
RouterA(config-router)#exit
RouterA(config)#interface fa0/0
RouterA(config-if)#ip summary-address rip 10.0.0.0 255.0.0.0
```

Verifying Your Configurations

As a network professional, you need to be able to troubleshoot the network and verify the things you configure along the way. Every engineer I know likes to think that they won't mess anything up and there won't be any problems, but a history of working with networks tells a different story. I have yet to meet any one who hasn't messed up some kind of configuration. The following list includes the commands you can use to verify the routed and routing protocols configured on your Cisco routers:

- show ip protocols
- debug ip rip

The *show ip protocols* Command

The show ip protocols command displays the routing protocols configured on a given router. Look at the output that follows. Not only can you confirm that RIP is running on the router but you get information about the timers that RIP is using. This output is from the old BrusRtr that I just discussed in the last example.

```
BrusRtr#sh ip protocols
Routing Protocol is "rip"
Outgoing update filter list for all interfaces is not set
Incoming update filter list for all interfaces is not set
Sending updates every 30 seconds, next due in 24 seconds
Invalid after 180 seconds, hold down 180, flushed after 240
Redistributing: rip
Default version control: send version 1, receive version 1
Interface Send Recv Triggered RIP Key-chain
FastEthernet0/1 1 1
Serial0/0/1 1 1
Automatic network summarization is not in effect
Maximum path: 4
Routing for Networks:
10.0.0.0
Passive Interface(s):
FastEthernet0/0
Serial0/0/0
Routing Information Sources:
Gateway Distance Last Update
10.1.11.2 120 00:00:10
10.1.5.1 120 00:00:22
Distance: (default is 120)
```

Notice, in the output above that RIP is sending updates every 30 seconds, which is the default. The timers used in distance vector are also shown.

Notice further down that RIP is routing for directly connected interfaces fa0/1 and s0/0/0. To the right of each interface listing, the version the interface uses is listed—RIPv1.

Fa0/0 and s0/0/0 are listed as passive interfaces (they will not send out RIP information). The neighbors it found are 10.1.11.2 and 10.1.5.1. The last entry is the default AD for RIP (120).

Troubleshooting with the *show ip protocols* Command

Let's use and use the **show ip protocols** command and see what we can determine about routing by looking at the following output from a router on another network:

```
BrusRtr#sh ip protocols
Routing Protocol is "rip"
Sending updates every 30 seconds, next due in 6 seconds
Invalid after 180 seconds, hold down 180, flushed after 240
```

```
Outgoing update filter list for all interfaces is
Incoming update filter list for all interfaces is
Redistributing: rip
Default version control: send version 1, receive any version
Interface Send Recv Key-chain
Serial0/0 1 1 2
Serial0/1 1 1 2
Routing for Networks:
10.0.0.0
Routing Information Sources:
Gateway Distance Last Update
10.168.11.14 120 00:00:21
Distance: (default is 120)
```

Under the show ip protocols output, you can see that RIP routing is being used for network 10.0.0.0.The configuration would have looked like the commands below. I am showing you these so that you know what was configured on the old BrusRtr router.

Router(config)#**router rip**
Router(config-router)#**network 10.0.0.0**

Also, only serial 0/0 and serial 0/1 are participating in the RIP network. And last, our neighbor router is 10.168.11.14.

Let's also look at the show ip interface brief command from the same router and see what we find:

BrusRtr#**sh ip interface brief**
```
Interface IP-Address OK? Method Status
FastEthernet0/0 192.168.18.1 YES manual up
Serial0/0 10.168.11.17 YES manual up
FastEthernet0/1 unassigned YES NRAM Administatively down
Serial0/1 192.168.11.21 YES manual up
```

From the output of the show ip interface brief command, you can see that only serial 0/0 is in the 10.0.0.0 network. This means that the router will only send and receive routing updates with the 10.0.0.0 network and not advertise the 192.168.0.0 networks out any interface.

The *debug ip rip* Command

The debug ip rip command sends routing updates as they are sent and received on the router to the console session. If you are telnetted into the router, you'll need to use the terminal monitor command to be able to receive the output from the debug commands.

You can see in this output that RIP is both sending and receiving. The metric is the hop count.

TIP   If the metric of a route is listed as 16, the 16 is a route poison and the route being advertised is unreachable.

```
BrusRtr#debug ip rip
RIP protocol debugging is on
RouterA#terminal monitor
*Mar 17 19:08:34.371: RIP: sending v1 update to 255.255.255.255 via Serial0/0/1
(10.1.5.2)
*Mar 17 19:08:34.371: RIP: build update entries
*Mar 17 19:08:34.371: subnet 10.1.10.0 metric 1
*Mar 17 19:08:34.371: subnet 10.1.11.0 metric 1
*Mar 17 19:08:34.371: subnet 10.1.12.0 metric 2
*Mar 17 19:08:40.107: RIP: received v1 update from 10.1.5.1 on Serial0/0/1
*Mar 17 19:08:40.107: 10.1.1.0 in 1 hops
*Mar 17 19:08:40.107: 10.1.2.0 in 1 hops
*Mar 17 19:08:40.107: 10.1.3.0 in 1 hops
*Mar 17 19:08:40.107: 10.1.4.0 in 1 hops
*Mar 17 19:08:40.107: 10.1.6.0 in 2 hops
*Mar 17 19:08:40.107: 10.1.7.0 in 2 hops
*Mar 17 19:08:40.107: 10.1.8.0 in 2 hops
*Mar 17 19:08:40.107: 10.1.9.0 in 2 hops
*Mar 17 19:08:47.535: RIP: sending v1 update to 255.255.255.255 via
FastEthernet0/1 (10.1.11.1)
*Mar 17 19:08:47.535: RIP: build update entries
*Mar 17 19:08:47.535: subnet 10.1.1.0 metric 2
*Mar 17 19:08:47.535: subnet 10.1.2.0 metric 2
*Mar 17 19:08:47.535: subnet 10.1.3.0 metric 2
*Mar 17 19:08:47.535: subnet 10.1.4.0 metric 2
*Mar 17 19:08:47.535: subnet 10.1.5.0 metric 1
*Mar 17 19:08:47.535: subnet 10.1.6.0 metric 3
*Mar 17 19:08:47.535: subnet 10.1.7.0 metric 3
*Mar 17 19:08:47.535: subnet 10.1.8.0 metric 3
*Mar 17 19:08:47.535: subnet 10.1.9.0 metric 3
*Mar 17 19:08:47.535: subnet 10.1.10.0 metric 1
*Mar 17 19:08:49.331: RIP: received v1 update from 10.1.11.2 on FastEthernet0/1
*Mar 17 19:08:49.331: 10.1.12.0 in 1 hops
RouterA#undebug all
```

Let's talk about the boldface lines in the output. RIP sends a v1 packet to 255.255.255.255—an "all-hands" broadcast—out interface Serial0/0/1, via 10.1.5.2.

This is where RIPv2 would come in handy. Why? Because RIPv2 doesn't send broadcasts, it uses the multicast 224.0.0.9. So, even though the RIP packets could be transmitted onto a network with no routers, all hosts would just ignore them, making RIPv2 a bit of an improvement over RIPv1. Router A uses a passive interface, so it is not sending broadcasts out to a LAN with no routers connected.

Troubleshooting with the *debug ip rip* Command

Now, let's use the debug ip rip command to both discover a problem and figure out how RIP was configured on a router from a different sample network. Take a look at the output from FutureTech's Bangalore manufacturing plant. It shows a problem that I experienced not too long ago and wanted to share with you.

```
07:12:58: RIP: sending v1 update to 255.255.255.255 via
FastEthernet0/0 (172.16.1.1)
07:12:58: network 10.0.0.0, metric 1
07:12:58: network 192.168.1.0, metric 2
07:12:58: RIP: sending v1 update to 255.255.255.255 via
Serial0/0 (10.0.8.1)
07:12:58: network 172.16.0.0, metric 1
07:12:58: RIP: Received v1 update from 10.0.15.2 n Serial0/0
07:12:58: 192.168.1.0 in one hop
07:12:58: 192.168.168.0 in 16 hops (inaccessible)
```

From the output, you can see from the updates that BangRtr1 is sending out information about network 10.0.0.0, 192.168.1.0, and 172.16.0.0. But both the 10.0.0.0 network and the 172.16.0.0 network are being advertised with a hop count (metric) of 1, meaning that these networks are directly connected. The 192.168.1.0 is being advertised as a metric of 2, which means that it is not directly connected.

For this to happen, the configuration would have had to look like this:

```
BangRtr1(config)#router rip
BangRtr1 (config-router)#network 10.0.0.0
BangRtr1 (config-router)#network 172.16.0.0
```

And there's something else you can find out by looking at the first output: There are at least two routers participating in the RIP network, because the router is sending out two interfaces, but it is only receiving RIP updates on one interface.

Notice that the network 192.168.168.0 is being advertised as 16 hops away. Because RIP has a maximum hop count of 15, a hop count of 16 is considered unreachable, making this network inaccessible. So, what will happen if you try to ping to a host on network 192.168.168.0? You will not be successful, that's what! But if you try any pings to network 10.0.0.0, you should be successful.

There is one more output that you should look at—see if you can find the problem. Both a debug ip rip and a show ip route output are shown from the sample router below:

```
07:12:56: RIP: received v1 update from 172.16.100.2 on Serial0/0
07:12:56: 172.16.10.0 in 1 hops
07:12:56: 172.16.20.0 in 1 hops
07:12:56: 172.16.30.0 in 1 hops
BangRtr2#sh ip route
[output cut]
Gateway of last resort is not set
172.16.0.0/24 is subnetted, 8 subnets
C    172.16.150.0 is directly connected, FastEthernet0/0
C    172.16.220.0 is directly connected, Loopback2
R    172.16.210.0 is directly connected, Loopback1
R    172.16.200.0 is directly connected, Loopback0
R    172.16.30.0 [120/2] via 172.16.100.2, 00:00:04, Serial0/0
S    172.16.20.0 [120/2] via 172.16.150.15
R    172.16.10.0 [120/2] via 172.16.100.2, 00:00:04, Serial0/0
R    172.16.100.0 [120/2] is directly connected, Serial0/0
```

Looking at the two outputs above, can you tell why users can't access 172.16.20.0?

The debug output shows that network 172.16.20.0 is 1 hop away and being received on serial 0/0 from 172.16.100.2. By checking out the show ip route output, you can see that packets with a destination of 172.16.20.0 are being sent to 172.16.150.15 because of a static route. This is wrong because from the output you can see that 172.16.150.0 is directly connected to FastEthernet 0/0. From the update output at the top you can see the router is learning network 172.16.20.0 out serial 0/0. So the traffic is being sent incorrectly out the wrong interface because the static route in wrong.

Interior Gateway Routing Protocol (IGRP)

Interior Gateway Routing Protocol (IGRP) is discussed here simply because you need to know of the protocol's existence and the fact that it is not longer used. It was a Cisco-proprietary distance vector routing protocol. In the past, to use IGRP in a network, all the routers had to be Cisco routers. Cisco created this routing protocol to overcome the problems associated with RIP. It has been replaced by EIGRP and is no longer supported by Cisco.

IGRP has a maximum hop count of 255 with the default being 100 (same as EIGRP). This is helpful in larger networks and solves the problem of 15 hops being the maximum possible in a RIP network.

IGRP also uses a different metric than RIP. By default, IGRP uses the bandwidth and delay of the line as a metric for determining the best route to an internetwork. This is called a composite metric. Reliability, load, and maximum transmission unit (MTU) can also be used, although they are not used by default.

Concept: How Does IGRP Differ from RIP?

The main difference between RIP and IGRP configuration is that when you configure IGRP, you supply the autonomous system number. All routers must use the same number in order to share routing table information.

Table 4.3 shows a list of IGRP characteristics that you won't find in RIP.

TABLE 4.3 IGRP vs. RIP

IGRP	RIP
Can be used in large internetworks	Works best in smaller networks
Uses an autonomous system number for activation	Does not use autonomous system numbers
Gives a full route table update every 90 seconds	Gives full route table update every 30 seconds
Has an administrative distance of 100	Has an administrative distance of 120
Uses bandwidth and delay of the line as metric (lowest composite metric), with a maximum hop count of 255	Uses only hop count to determine the best path to a remote network, with 15 hops being the maximum

Why isn't there anything else in the IGRP section? Because watch what happens when you try to configure IGRP on a router:

```
R3#config t
Enter configuration commands, one per line. End with CNTL/Z.
R3(config)#router igrp 10
              ^
% Invalid input detected at '^' marker.
R3(config)#
```

Route Manipulation

Let's take a look at a couple a ways that you can filter or control the routing information that leaves or enters a router. There are many reasons you may want to do this. I haven't completely covered all of them yet, but not to worry; I'm going to.

One of those big reasons is to control routes coming through a redistribution configuration. Another might be to prevent routing information from leaving the internetwork, say preventing it from going into an ISP network. Sometimes there are links that, because of the bandwidth, you just don't want to have the updates being sent across.

There are a few ways that you can accomplish these filtering affects on the network. These include passive interface configuration, distribute lists, and route maps. The route map discussion in this chapter will just be the introduction. Here I will talk about something called policy-based routing. Later, in Chapter 7 "Exterior Gateway Protocols ,"when you learn about BGP and its attributes, you will learn how to use a route map to manipulate the attributes that gives BGP the ability to provide routing based on policies rather than metrics.

Passive Interface

Sometimes you don't have any choice about including an interface in a `network` command configuration under a routing protocol, whether or not you want the interface to participate in the routing protocol. If you need to prevent a specific interface from sending routing information, you can configure the `passive-interface` command. You can configure a single interface or multiple interfaces to be passive with the `passive-interface` command. If you have a router that has dozens of interfaces and you want to set most or all of them to a passive state, you used to have to issue an individual command for each passive interface. IOS release 12.0 added the `passive-interface default` option. With the default option, every interface is set in the passive mode. Then, you can use the `no passive-interface` command to remove individual interfaces from the passive mode.

Each of the routing protocols handles passive configuration differently. If you are running RIP or IGRP and configure a passive interface, then the only thing that happens is that you prevent that protocol from sending any updates out the specified interface. Updates can still be received if they are sent from the other end of the link, but none will be sent.

If you are running a link state or hybrid routing protocol such as OSPF, IS-IS, or even EIGRP (because EIGRP uses Hellos to establish neighbor relationships as well), the passive interface command blocks Hello messages from being sent. Each of these protocols requires Hello messages to be sent to establish neighbor relationships. Without the Hellos, no neighbor relationships are established and any updates that might be received are dropped because there is no neighbor relationship.

Let's take a look at how a passive interface is configured on a router. I have included the `no passive-interface` command just so that you can see it.

```
RouterA(config-router)#passive-interface fa0/0
RouterA(config-router)#passive-interface default
RouterA(config-router)#no passive-interface fa0/0
```

Distribute Lists

You saw that by using the `passive-interface` command you could block all of the routing updates from coming out of an interface. What if you want to filter only a few of the routes and let others through? You can use something called distribute lists. A distribute list is an access control list that is applied using the `distribute-list` command.

Access list statements are written in the global configuration mode, just as they would be if you were going to apply them to an individual interface. So, why don't we just apply the access list to an interface? Well, in this case, you want to block routing updates from leaving the router. So, what kind of traffic would an access list not block? If you said, "An access list doesn't block traffic that is generated by the router," then you are correct. We can't use an access list to block traffic from leaving the router, because access lists do not block traffic that originates from the router, and routing updates are generated by the router.

You can apply a distribute list in directions, just as you can with an access list. You can apply a distribution list to an interface in the inbound or outbound direction. A distribute list can also be applied to a routing protocol for the purpose of filtering routes when they are redistributed.

At this point I have only mentioned redistribution but discussed it. I've told you that redistribution may be necessary to run more than one routing protocol on your network. For routes to be shared properly between protocols, there must be a translator, or a process that shares the information between the protocols. That process is redistribution. Redistribution ensures that each of the routing protocols understands the other and can share its routes.

There is some danger with redistribution, if it is not carefully configured. This can be especially true in cases where two or more redistribution points exist in the network. If the flow of routes is allowed to be redistributed more than once, you can end up with inconsistent routing tables or worse routing loops that could cause data loss.

The command for applying a distribute list in the outbound direction is `distribute-list` {access-list-number | name} out [interface-name | routing process [routing-process parameter]]. The command is issued from within the routing protocol configuration mode. So, let's breakdown the `distribute-list` command.

The first parameter is the *access-list number* or *name* followed by the direction, in this case out. The next parameter gives you an option that specifies where the command is going to be applied. You can specify a particular interface, such as fa0/0, or a routing protocol and process, such as RIP.

The `distribute-list out` command can be used to filter outgoing routing updates either from an individual interface or to routes being redistributed out into another routing protocol. The command cannot, however, be used with a link state routing protocol to block outbound updates (called link state advertisements, LSA) on an interface.

The command for applying a distribute list in the inbound direction is `distribute-list` [access-list-number | name] | [route-map map-tag] in [interface-type interface-number]. Just as with the outbound version, the command is issued from the routing protocol configuration mode. Again, you begin with the command with `distribute-list`. The first parameter is the access list number or name. If you are using OSPF, there is an optional parameter: route map. You will learn about the creation of route maps in Chapter 7, "Exterior Gateway Protocols." The next parameter specifies the direction for filtering—in this case, inbound. The last parameter specifies the interface to which you are going to apply the list.

Summary

You have again covered quite a few things in this chapter. I started off talking about the routing process and how a router makes its decision about where to send traffic. That led you right into the ways that you can give a router the information that it needs in order to route.

You learned about static routing and a few uses for static routes. You learned about default routes and floating static routes. I then showed you the routing tree, which gave you a way to keep track of all the different routing categories and the protocols that fall under each. I went through the EGP and IGP categories. Under the IGPs, you learned about distance vector, link state, and hybrid protocols.

Along the way, you learned about things that could affect the routing process, like administrative distance and metrics for the protocols. The protocol that I focused on for this chapter was RIP. You learned that there are two versions of RIP and that there are some good reasons for upgrading to the new version.

With RIP came the configuration, which is the "how do you turn it on and make it work" type of thing. Finally, you looked at how to control summarization and how to verify an RIP configuration.

Finally, in the chapter we went through some pretty cool ways to manipulate and control routing updates to and from a router, and sometimes even within the router. We talked about is the `passive-interface` command, which prevents the router from sending out updates from a specified interface. Then, we talked about distribute lists, which allow you to apply an ACL to a routing process for the sake of filtering the updates. These lists can be used on an interface or in the redistribution process.

Review Questions

1. What will a router do with a packet it does not have a destination for in the routing table?
   A. Forward the packet
   B. Drop the packet
   C. Hold the packet
   D. Send the packet back

2. What is the manual method for giving a router routes?
   A. Dynamic routing
   B. Reverse routing
   C. Static routing
   D. ARP routing

3. Administrative distance allows a router to determine which type of routing information is better between different protocols?
   A. True
   B. False

4. What is the default administrative distance for an EIGRP summary route?
   A. 90
   B. 5
   C. 110
   D. 100

5. A static route that has a higher configured administrative distance than a similar dynamic route for the same link is called what?
   A. Static backup route
   B. Next hop static route
   C. Directly connected route
   D. Floating static route

6. Dynamic routing protocols are broken into what two categories? (Choose two.)
   A. Distance vector protocols
   B. Exterior gateway protocols
   C. Interior gateway protocols
   D. Link state protocols

7. What protocol is considered an Advanced Distance Vector Protocol?

    A. IS-IS

    B. OSPF

    C. EIGRP

    D. RIPv1

8. What routing loop avoidance mechanism says that it is never useful to send information back in the direction from which it was learned?

    A. Holddown timer

    B. Split horizon

    C. Max hop count

    D. Poison reverse

9. What is the default update timer for RIP?

    A. 5 minutes

    B. 10 seconds

    C. 30 seconds

    D. 20 seconds

10. What command allows you to configure RIP to operate in version 2?

    A. `router(config)#version 2`

    B. `router(config-if)#version 2`

    C. `router(config-router)#version 2`

    D. `router(config-line)#version 2`

Answers to Review Questions

1. B. By default a router will drop a packet that it doesn't know the destination network for in the routing table.

2. C. Static routing is the type of routing that allows you to give a router manual routing information.

3. A. True. Administrative distance is the value that allows a router to determine which routing data is the best.

4. B. The default AD for an EIGRP summary route is 5.

5. D. A floating static route is a type of route that is used as a backup route and has a higher AD than a dynamic routing protocol that is running for the link.

6. B, C. Dynamic routing protocols are broken into Exterior and Interior Gateway protocols.

7. C. EIGRP is the protocol that is considered to be an Advanced Distance Vector Protocol.

8. B. The routing mechanism that prevents information from being sent back in the source direction is split horizon.

9. C. The default update timer for RIP is every 30 seconds the routing table will be sent out.

10. C. The command to configure RIP for version 2 operation must be done under the routing protocol configuration mode.

Chapter

5

Advanced Distance Vector Protocols

IN THIS CHAPTER, YOU WILL LEARN HOW TO DO THE FOLLOWING:

✓ Explain the functions and operations of EIGRP (e.g., DUAL)

✓ Configure EIGRP routing (e.g., stub routing, summarization)

✓ Verify or troubleshoot EIGRP routing configurations

In this chapter, I delve into the one of the most unique routing protocols that you will ever configure. Enhanced Interior Gateway Routing Protocol (EIGRP) is a Cisco-proprietary protocol that offers capabilities and features far beyond the normal distance vector family from which it came. It does this by employing features from link state routing protocols. It has features from both distance vector and link state protocols.

EIGRP has many features and capabilities to offer. I discuss the messages the routers exchange using EIGRP and show you how they differ from other protocols. EIGRP has the ability to not only load balance across equal cost paths like other protocols but it can do so across unequal cost paths. Then, you learn how to configure EIGRP and make sure that it is operating correctly and efficiently.

For up-to-the-minute updates on this chapter, check out www.sybex.com/go/CiscoProGuidetoInternetworking or www.lammle.com.

EIGRP Terms and Features

Some of the key capabilities that make EIGRP stand out from other routing protocols include:

- Fast convergence
- Variable-length subnet masking (VLSM) support
- Partial update capability
- Multiple network layer protocol support through the use of Protocol Dependant Modules (PDMs)

I am sure that you have heard those terms before. I would like to look at some of the other advanced things that you can do with EIGRP—things you can't do with most other protocols:

- Performing unequal-cost load balancing
- Configuring the stub router
- Performing WAN link optimization
- Changing the metric calculation

Before we can do all of these very cool things, I have to go through how EIGRP works and the processes it uses to perform tasks. First, I take you through all of the terms associated with EIGRP so that you can understand the functions as we progress through them. It is also important to understand the tables where EIGRP information is stored, and the messages types used to send the information from the tables back and forth to other routers. Not to worry, I discuss the full operation of EIGRP in the following sections.

EIGRP Capabilities

Very similar to Interior Gateway Routing Protocol (IGRP), EIGRP is pretty easy to configure and you can use it with a variety of network topologies and types. As I told you, EIGRP includes some link state features, such as dynamic neighbor discovery, which makes EIGRP an advanced distance vector protocol. However, it is called a hybrid protocol because EIGRP uses the Diffused Update ALgorithm (DUAL). Each router calculates the routing information for all neighbors to use, much like a standard distance vector protocol does. The DUAL feature of EIGRP provides rapid convergence and the guarantee of a loop-free topology at all times. Here are the features and capabilities of EIGRP.

Fast Convergence   An EIGRP router stores a list of all its neighbors in a neighbor table. Then, it stores all of the neighbors' routes in a topology table. Based on that information, a routing table is built, allowing each router to quickly adapt to changes in the network and have alternate routes. I discuss the different kinds routing information in just a bit. If there is a change to a destination route and a suitable replacement route doesn't exist, EIGRP queries its neighbors to discover an alternate route. These queries propagate through the network until an alternate route is found.

VLSM Support   EIGRP is a classless routing protocol, which means in its routing updates the subnet mask for each destination network is advertised. Since the subnet mask is advertised in every routing update, EIGRP can support discontiguous networks and VLSM in the internetwork. By default, routes are automatically summarized at classful network boundaries.

Partial Updates   Unlike RIP and IGRP, which send periodic updates, EIGRP sends partial triggered updates. A triggered update is an update that is sent out when the path or the metric changes for a route. These partial updates only contain information about the route or routes that changed. Because one of EIGRP's goals is to always conserve the amount of bandwidth that is used, the partial updates are only sent to the routers that need to be updated with the information. This is different even from the link state protocols that I discuss in the next chapter, but for now know that link state routers send their updates to all of the other link state routes even if they don't need the information.

Multiple Network-Layer Protocol Support   EIGRP can support IP, AppleTalk, and Internet Packet Exchange (IPX) with things called Protocol Dependent Modules (PDMs). These PDMs make it possible for EIGRP to provide the necessary communication to each of the associated network layer protocols. This may be especially beneficial to you when the need arises to route more than just IP. It can decide which routing protocol is easier to use if that is the case.

Seamless Connectivity   One great feature of EIGRP is that it makes the configuration easier for you. It does not require a different or special configuration depending on the data link protocol or connection that is being used. Open shortest path first (OSPF), for instance, requires you to configure connections differently based on the Layer 2 media type. For example, when a network uses OSPF, an Ethernet connection must be configured differently than a frame relay connection. EIGRP can operate on either a LAN or WAN connection. For example, supporting WAN types like point-to-point links and non-broadcast multi-access (NBMA) topologies is automatic for EIGRP and doesn't require a separate configuration like in OSPF. I also show you EIGRP's ability to configure a limit for the amount of bandwidth that may be used on a specific WAN link. I cover this more in the coming section, "Using EIGRP over WANs."

Sophisticated Metric   EIGRP uses the same algorithm for metric calculation as IGRP but represents values in 32-bit format unlike the 16-bit form that IGRP uses; this gives the value more granularity or separation between path values. There will be a full discussion on metric calculation coming up in the metric section.

Unequal Metric Load Balancing   EIGRP support for unequal metric load balancing allows you to better distribute or direct the flow of traffic over links in the network.

Multicast and Unicast   EIGRP uses multicast and unicast, rather than broadcast like RIPv1 and IGRP. The multicast group address used by EIGRP is 224.0.0.10.

Neighbor Discovery/Recovery Mechanism   With the use of Hello packets, routers can dynamically learn about the routers that are on their directly connected networks. Routers can also then discover when a neighbor router becomes unreachable or goes down. As long as a router continues to receive hello packets from its neighbor router, the neighbor is assumed to be functioning and the exchange of routing information should be possible.

RTP   The reliable transport protocol (RTP) is responsible for ensuring the guaranteed, ordered delivery of EIGRP messages to all neighbors. It provides support for either multicast or unicast packets to be transmitted. For efficiency and bandwidth reasons, only specific message types are transmitted reliably. Not all of the messages have to be acknowledged.

DUAL Finite State Machine   DUAL is the no kidding decision maker for all the route processing that happens in EIGRP. DUAL keeps track of all the routes that the neighbors advertise and uses the metric (which by default is a calculation of bandwidth and delay) to select loop-free paths to all destination networks.

Terms

Understanding the primary EIGRP terms is essential to understanding the way EIGRP operates. Some terms, such as *successor* and *feasible successor*, provide specific routing information for each given destination. Other terms, such as *advertised distance* and *feasible distance*, provide information about the metric or cost values that are used to determine which route is the best for an individual network.

Real World Scenario

Future Tech's R&D EIGRP Routing

Let's take a look at a real world application that should help you understand these terms just a little better and see what happens when EIGRP routers share routes to one another. The FutureTech headquarters has many switch blocks in the headquarters portion of the network. Each floor in each of the physical areas of the buildings has at least one switch block. One floor in the building has multiple research and development (R&D) groups. Due to the large number of people in these groups and the different kinds of systems they have connected to the network, there are two switch blocks located here. Each switch block has redundant routers that connect the switch block to the core of the network. So, with these two switch blocks, there are four routers that are connected to two core layer routers, as shown in Figure 5.1.

FIGURE 5.1 FutureTech Headquarters R&D EIGRP Routing

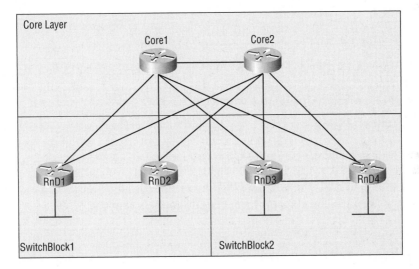

Figure 5.1 shows you all of the connections that would really exist in a production network. You can see that each of the distribution routers has a redundant connection to a separate core layer router. This is how a routed or Layer 3 core would look and I discuss how it will behave. As I go through more EIGRP explanations, I come back to this diagram. For some of the specific examples to amplify a specific point, I modify the diagram slightly—not to change how the production network would look or operate but to make the discussion more clear. I build the smaller specific points back into this whole production network example.

EIGRP's routing algorithm, DUAL, uses many different types of distance information to find or calculate the metric (sometimes called cost). The metric that EIGRP uses is referred to as a composite metric because by default it is calculated using two different values. Bandwidth and delay of the line are the default values. All of this is done so that the best route can be selected efficiently and to ensure the routes to be used are all loop-free paths.

Let's take a look at a list of the terms.

Advertised Distance (AD)   The cost between the next hop or neighbor router and the destination network.

 Both advertised distance and administrative distance are abbreviated with the letters AD. Be careful to not get them confused.

Feasible Distance (FD)   The cost from the local router to the destination network. It is a sum of two distance costs. The first value in the calculation is the cost between the local router and the router that advertised the network. The second value is the cost that was actually advertised to the router for the network—meaning there is an associated cost from the local router to the next hop router, and that next router already told the local router what its cost was to the destination network. When the two values are added together, the total cost for the local router to the destination network is found.

Best Route   The route or path with the lowest cost or FD to the destination.

Successor   Also called current successor, this is the next hop router that has the lowest-cost and loop-free path to the destination.

Feasible Successor   A feasible successor is a backup router with a loop-free path. There is a requirement for a router to be considered a feasible successor—the AD of the feasible successor must be lower than the FD of the successor router.

Now, look at Figure 5.2. Notice that I removed the redundant links between the distribution routers and the core routers. Figure 5.2 shows you the costs and paths a router will use when there are distinctly different routes to a destination network.

FIGURE 5.2   EIGRP Route Propagation

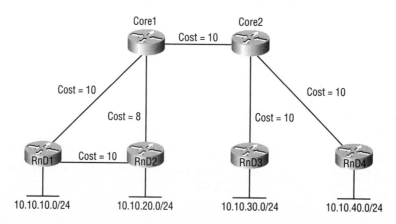

I want you to look specifically at the directly connected networks of the distribution routers. That way you can see how each of the terms that I already discussed comes into play in the FutureTech R&D network. So, I will start with the RnD routers' propagating their routes to their neighbors.

Every network has a cost associated with it, even a directly connected network. By default, a directly connected FastEthernet interface has a cost of 28160 in EIGRP. You can start to see that the cost values in EIGRP are going to be quite high. Large numbers are used on purpose; they allow you finer levels of granularity for cost comparisons between routes. For this example, I use artificially low numbers—just for the sake of easily calculating the costs.

In order for RnD1 to send a packet from itself across the internetwork to subnet 10.10.40.0/24, it must determine the best path to that subnet. A quick glance at Figure 5.2 shows that the subnet is connected to RnD4. You also can see that there are two paths RnD1 could take to RnD4. One path runs through Core1, Core2, and finally to RnD4. The other path runs through RnD2, Core1, Core2, and finally to RnD4. Both routes get you to RnD4 so your packet can be delivered to the directly connected network 10.10.40.0/24. But which is best?

To calculate the path costs for each route, you must start back at RnD4, the router that started the propagation of the network information. Here are the steps the routers go through to get the route information to RnD1.

Using AD and FD to Calculate Route Costs

These are the steps to generate the routes from RnD4 to Core2, Core1, and RnD2. (Remember, I'm assigning artificially low cost numbers to make the calculations easier.)

1. RnD4 has a cost of 10 for being connected to the network. When RnD4 sends this information to Core2, it is advertising this distance. Therefore, this cost is called the advertised distance (AD).

2. When Core2 receives the route, it must add to the AD the cost of getting to RnD4 from itself. This cost is an additional 10, making its FD 20 total.

3. Core2 then takes its new FD and advertises it to Core1. The AD sent to Core1 is 20.

4. Core1 now does the same thing Core2 had to do. It must add to the AD its cost to get to Core2. This cost is an additional 10. Core1 now has a FD of 30.

5. Core1 must now advertise its new route to all of its neighbors. It takes its FD of 30 and sends it to RnD1 and RnD2. The AD sent to them is 30.

6. RnD1 will then receive the route, and add to that AD the cost to get to Core1, which makes the FD of this route 40.

7. RnD2 will also receive the route from Core1, and add to the AD a cost of 8, making its FD 38.

8. RnD2 must then advertise the route to its neighbor, which in this case is an AD of 38.

9. RnD1 will receive the route from RnD2 and have to add to it the cost of getting to RnD2. This will make the route's FD 48.

10. RnD1 must now evaluate the routes that it has to the destination network 10.10.40.0/24. The router determines the best route by looking at FD of each of the routes; the route with the lowest FD is the best route.

Every router in the network will go through a similar process to determine the best route for each destination network. At that point, all of the routers would have their own feasible distance (FD) for each path to every destination network.

Selecting Successor and Feasible Successor Routes

Now that RnD1 has both of the possible routes through the internetwork to network 10.10.40.0/24, it can make its decision about which path is the best route. RnD1 in this case will make the path to Core1 the best route. Since the route through Core1 has the lowest FD, it is the best route and Core1 becomes the successor. Remember that a successor is the neighboring router that advertised the best path to the local router. The successor router or route is copied into the routing table.

The route through RnD2 has higher FD, so it is not the successor. Now I show you how to see whether or not the route through RnD2 is a feasible successor. The rule for a feasible successor is this: If a potential feasible successor route has a lower AD than the FD of the current successor route, it qualifies as a feasible successor. So let's check.

The AD of the route through RnD2 is 38, and the FD of the successor is 40. This means that the route through and RnD2 qualifies as a feasible successor route and router

As defined by Cisco, the neighbor router itself is the successor or feasible successor, not the route. But successors and feasible successors are often explained and examined as though they were the route. So, now you know how to find what successors and feasible successors are and what name to give the router and the routes.

Concept: Feasible Successors

To be a feasible successor, the AD of the potential route must be lower than the FD of the successor route. This is a very important point because the concept will be used again later as I tell you more about EIGRP.

If the route through RnD2 did not have an AD lower than the FD of the successor, it would not have been a feasible successor. This makes a difference in the operation of EIGRP in the event of a failure. For example, let's say the route through Core1 was to go down. If there is a feasible successor, then EIGRP can immediately place that feasible successor route in the routing table. It can do this because, by meeting the feasible successor requirement, a route is proven to not cause a network loop.

If there is no feasible successor route, then the router must go through something called the query process. This process determines whether a loop-free route exists and can be put in the routing table. I discuss the query process later in this chapter, in the "Tables" section. I also cover query messages in the next section.

Message Types

I have told you about a few of the EIGRP messages and what they are used for, but now let's take a look at all of the messages that EIGRP uses. I also will go through how EIGRP sends each of the packets and the reasons for sending them.

Hello   Hello packets are required for neighbor discovery. The packets are sent as multicasts and do not require an acknowledgment. Hellos are sent out periodically based on the hello timer or interval.

Update   Routers use update packets to propagate routes and changes to routes to neighboring routers. Update packets are sent reliably to only the routers that need the information. The updates can be sent as a unicast to a specific router or as a multicast to multiple routers that might be on a network.

Query   When a router loses a route and has to calculate or go "active" for a destination that does not have a feasible successor, it must send a query packet to all of its neighbors. The query determines whether any neighbor has a feasible successor for the destination. Queries are usually sent as multicasts but can be retransmitted as unicast packets in certain cases. Query packets are sent reliably and must be acknowledged because if a reply is not received, then a retransmission will be sent. RTP has a built-in function that tells the neighbor the query must be acknowledged.

Reply   A neighbor router sends a reply packet in response when a query packet is received. Replies are unicast reliably to the originator of the query.

ACK   The acknowledgment (ACK) packet acknowledges update, query, and reply packets. ACK packets are unicast hello packets and contain a nonzero acknowledgment number.

Now I want to go through how each of these packets works a little more. When routers are connected to a multi-access network that has multicast capabilities, such as Ethernet, it is a huge waste to send hello packets reliably to all neighbors individually. So instead, EIGRP sends a single multicast hello packet. The packet contains an indicator that informs the receivers that the hello packet does not need to be acknowledged. Other types of packets, such as updates, include an indicator that acknowledgment is required. Another benefit of RTP is a feature that allows multicast packets to be sent quickly, even when there are unacknowledged packets pending. This helps ensure that convergence time for the network remains low even when there are links with different speeds.

Using Messages to Establish Neighboring Routes

The full process for establishing and discovering neighbor routes occurs simultaneously in EIGRP. Let me show you what would happen in when a new router is added to FutureTech's R&D network.

Real World Scenario

Atlanta Moves In

An entire group of engineers just moved to headquarters from the Atlanta field office. To accommodate the new traffic, a new router (RnD5) is brought up. Figure 5.3 shows the messaging process that takes place as RnD5 learns about its neighbors and is added to the routing tables in the existing RnD2 router.

FIGURE 5.3 Neighbor Establishment

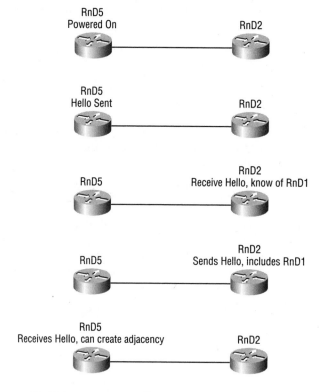

1. The new router (RnD5) comes up on the link and sends a hello packet out all of its interfaces that are configured for EIGRP.

2. Routers on any of those networks receive the hello packet (for this example, let's look at the interaction with RnD2) and reply with update packets.

The update packets contain all the routes that existing routers have in their routing table. The rule of split horizon is enforced, preventing the routes learned on the interface from being sent back out the same interface. Even though RnD2 sends an update packet to RnD5, a neighbor relationship is not formed until RnD2 sends a hello packet to RnD5. The update packet RnD2 sends has something called the initialization bit set; this bit indicates the start of the initialization process. The update packet not only includes the routes that it is aware of but also includes the metric that it has for each destination.

3. When both routers have exchanged hellos, the neighbor adjacency is established, and RnD5 then replies to RnD2 with an ACK packet. This indicates that the route information has been received.

4. RnD5 then puts all of the route information from all the update packets in its topology table. RnD5 learned that RnD2 and Core1 are neighbors, but RnD5 also could have received updates from any number of routers that received hello messages. The topology table includes all destination networks advertised by neighbor or adjacent routers. There is a listing for each destination and, for each destination, there is an entry for all the neighbors that can be reached through that destination and associated metrics.

5. The next step is for RnD5 to update RnD2 and any other neighbors with the destinations that it now knows. This is done by sending update packets to RnD2 and Core1 or any other neighbors it has.

6. When RnD2 and Core1 receive the update packet, each router must send an ACK packet back to RnD5.

After RnD1 and RnD2 successfully receive the update packets from each other and their topology tables are updated, each router is ready to update its routing table with the successor routes from the topology table. Again, a successor route is the best route to a given destination. A new route would be added for any new destinations and possibly an updated route for a destination that now has a better path.

Tables

Now I explain the significance of the tables the EIGRP makes and maintains. Earlier in this chapter, I told you that EIGRP builds three tables very similar to OSPF and other link state routing protocols: the neighbor, topology, and routing tables.

Neighbor Table The neighbor table contains a list of all the routers that can be found and are known as adjacent routers. The table also contains reachability information through hold timers and also information RTP uses.

Topology Table   The topology table is built and maintained through the use of update packets. The topology table is a list of all the routes to every destination that have been learned.

Routing Table   Finally, the routing table lists the best routes or paths to every destination network.

Now I want to show you how you can use this information to understand what EIGRP is doing and how you can make it run better for your network.

Neighbor Table

When a router first gets turned on or the EIGRP process enabled (the more likely situation), it begins by sending out an EIGRP Hello packet. The router will also discover other routers or neighbors by listening for Hello packets that other routers will be sending out. In order for a router to truly have an adjacent neighbor, it must see itself in the neighbor's Hello packet.

When a local router forms an adjacency with a new neighbor, it records the neighbor's address and the interface through which it can be reached as an entry in the neighbor table. The router keeps a separate neighbor table for each network layer protocol or PDM.

Every router includes an advertisement of the hold time it is assigning to its neighbor routers when they send a hello packet. The hold time is the amount of time that a router waits for a response before deciding that a neighbor is not operational. I think of it as one of those annoying little egg timers and you don't want it to go off. If a new hello packet is not received to reset the hold timer before it expires, then when the timer runs out, the DUAL process is told there is a change. In this case, the change would be that a router is no longer a neighbor and any networks that were known through that router will have to have found a different path. The neighbor table also keeps track information that allows it to communicate reliably with each neighbor. I mentioned earlier that EIGRP uses reliable transport protocol (RTP) to reliably transport many of its messages. In order to keep track of those packets, sequence numbers, queued packets, and round-trip timers are stored in the neighbor table. For example, by storing the last packet's sequence number, an EIGRP router can determine whether an out-of-order packet is received and what the last packet sequence number was. A transmission list is also stored in the neighbor table. Using this information, the router knows when a packet needs to be retransmitted. Finally, the round-trip timers are stored so that the interval at which the packets are resent can be modified if it takes a long time to receive the answers.

Topology Table

Now you will remember that when a router was added to accommodate the new engineers moving to the FutureTech headquarters building, that new router (and all the other routers in the EIGRP network) had to update the topology table as routes became known. Update packets were used to populate the table.

The topology table is a complete list of all destination networks that are advertised and learned from neighbor routers.

At this point, it is important to note that EIGRP uses a rule to prevent loops from forming in the network, for example, when the RnD5 router came up as the new router, and its new neighbor, RnD2, advertised routes that helped RnD5 populate its topology table. Here's where the rule comes in: RnD2 could only advertise a destination network that it was already using as a route or path to forward packets. This rule is strictly followed by all distance vector protocols and prevents suboptimal paths from being advertised and used by other routers.

The topology table is the repository that a router uses to store all the routing information it knows for the internetwork. So, RnD1 (see Figure 5.2) keeps all the routes learned from each of its neighbors, in this case RnD2 and Core1. For each of the destination networks learned, a router stores the metric (the AD) that the neighbor advertises. Remember that the AD is the metric or cost for the neighbor router (RnD2 or Core1) to use to get to the destination network. Each router also stores its own metrics (the FD) for reaching the destinations via its neighbors. The FD is the cost for the local router to reach the neighbor router plus the neighbor's metric (AD) to reach the destination.

A couple of different circumstances would trigger an update to the topology table. First, a router can have direct knowledge of changes in the network, such as a directly connected route or interface coming up or going down. Second, a neighboring router sends a change for a route because it had a route or interface come up or go down. Take a look back at Figure 5.2. RnD1 can learn about changes from RnD2 or Core1, since they are the neighbors. The change may not have occurred directly on RnD2 or Core1, though. Maybe, for instance, a change happened beyond RnD2 or Core1. The change could have occurred on Core2. If this were the case, Core2 would update Core1, and Core1 would update RnD1 and RnD2. The point is that all changes originate from a router that has direct knowledge of the route or interface that changed.

Now that the router has routes in the topology table, it keeps track of each destination with one of two states: active or passive. In the passive state, the router isn't recomputing anything for the route. If a route is in the active state, then the router is actively recomputing or finding a path to the destination. Passive state is the state that the router wishes to have all of its destinations in. This is where the feasible successor that I mentioned before comes into play. If there is a feasible successor available, a destination doesn't have to go into the active state and avoids a recomputation. This is because a feasible successor is a verified loop-free path that can be immediately used reach to the destination.

So, what happens when a route goes down and there is no feasible successor? Well, a recomputation occurs; the router has no alternate route that it can automatically use. A router initiates the recomputation by sending a query packet to each of its neighbors. Remember I said that each neighbor has a transmission list and is keeping track of all the packets that are sent to it. The query process works like this then: When a router receives the query and has a good route for the destination, it sends a reply packet giving the path information. If the neighbor router does not have a route, it sends a query packet to its neighbors. This process continues through the internetwork until routing information is found or it is verified that no other route exists. Each of the routers who successively sent the query also placed their route in the active state. As long as the destination is in the active state, a router cannot change the destination's routing table information. Only after the router has received a reply from each neighboring router can it do anything with the destination. When a router receives replies from its neighbors, the topology table entry for the destination can be taken back to the passive state. Once in the passive state, the router has all the route information for that destination and can select a successor, which it knows now is loop free.

What happens when a reply is not received from a neighbor? If a query has to be retransmitted because an acknowledgment was not received, then the route goes into a state called stuck-in-active (SIA). You don't want this condition on your router. If a route is still in SIA when the active time expires (about 3 minutes), then the neighbor that did not acknowledge the query is restarted and goes through a reset state. All of the routes that are known from that neighbor are flushed as well, creating more overhead on the routers.

Routing Table

Once a router has all of the routing information from its neighbors, then it can begin to choose the routes that it will use for forwarding data. A router looks in the topology table and goes through each of the destination networks. For each of the destinations, it compares all FDs to reach that specific network and then selects the route with the lowest FD. That route with the lowest FD is the best and designated the successor. The successor route is copied into the IP routing table. The successor route is stored in both the topology table and the routing table. When the route is copied, it takes the form of a route in the routing table. All of the associated information for that route is copied. The FD for the chosen route becomes the EIGRP routing metric to reach that network in the routing table. If the default administrative distance has not been changed, then the default is added with the route. If it has been changed, then the new modified value is used. The interface from which it was learned is placed with the route.

Enabling EIGRP

Now that I have gone through some of the basics of EIGRP, it is a good time to look at how you can enable or turn on EIGRP. I take you through some basic setup and then some specific configurations might find useful in your network. I use my test network to show you how to configure a few routers to make sure all the routes pass and can send traffic across the network. Follow along using your own test network.

Later in the chapter I show you a few other specific examples, showcasing different areas of the network that might require special configurations. That discussion will follow the features in "Improving EIGRP Operations" section.

I start off on RnD1 in my test network. I want to go through the basic configuration of EIGRP on a single router. Then I will go to RnD2–RnD 4, Core1, and Core2, add configurations, and form a test network.

Autonomous System Numbers

On RnD1 then, I am going to log in and move to global configuration mode. From global configuration mode, I can execute the `router eigrp` command. This command enables and starts an EIGRP routing process on the router. The `router eigrp` command includes an additional parameter that we did not see in either version of RIP configuration, the autonomous system (AS) number. An AS is a collection of networks that is administratively controlled by the same organization. For example, ISPs have AS numbers assigned to them to identify their network to the rest of the Internet. Large organizations and educational institutions like colleges may also have an AS number assigned to them.

The AS number identifies the process of EIGRP running on the router, as well as the AS the router belongs to. The AS number must be the same on all routers that you wish to allow to share routing information. If you accidently put a router into a different AS, then the other routers will treat it like it is in a different network. Routers in one AS will not share routing information with routers in a different AS.

Concept: AS Numbers

AS numbers are assigned from ARIN much the same as IP address ranges are. The possible range for an AS number is between 1 and 65535. The numbers between 1 and 64511 are reserved for public use, meaning they are the numbers assigned to ISPs and organizations. The numbers between 64512 and 65535 are private numbers and can be used for internal networks that do not advertise it to the Internet. For the purposes of this book, we use numbers from the private range so that a number is not used that someone may own and use on the Internet. EIGRP AS numbers shouldn't be advertised to the Internet anyway, so in reality, you could use any number. This policy only applies to IPv4 and IPv6, since they are the only ones being publicly routed. You will see why this matters in Chapter 7, "Exterior Gateway Protocols" when I talk about BGP.

With that said, the entire command to enable EIGRP on a router is `router eigrp [as-number]`. Again, this enables the routing process on the router. At this point, the EIGRP is not aware of any networks or interfaces. It cannot route packets. Now, think about how to tell EIGRP which interfaces and networks are to be routed. This is done with the `network` command. The `network` command can be configured a couple of different ways in EIGRP. I show you both of them. For this example, take a look at Figure 5.4. I use this diagram to move through all the steps as I have you configure the test network. You will configure quite a bit of the network now. This way, everything will be set up when I take you through other features of EIGRP later in the chapter.

Configuring EIGRP on a Router

Let's take a look at configuring RnD1. I have already put the IP addresses on the router. I show you what they are and how to configure EIGRP.

FIGURE 5.4 EIGRP Test Network Configuration

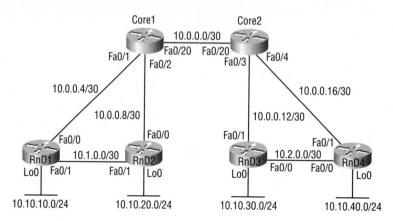

Here is the result of a show ip interface brief command from RnD1 so that you can see the configured IP addresses.

```
RnD1#sh ip interface brief
Interface          IP-Address     OK?  Method  Status                 Protocol
FastEthernet0/0    10.0.0.6       YES  manual  up                     up
FastEthernet0/1    10.1.0.1       YES  manual  up                     up
Serial0/0/0        unassigned     YES  unset   administratively down  down
Serial0/1/0        unassigned     YES  unset   administratively down  down
Loopback0          10.1.1.1       YES  manual  up                     up
```

The following is the EIGRP configuration FutureTech placed on RnD1 to start with.

```
RnD1(config)#router eigrp 65000
RnD1 (config-router)#network 10.1.1.0
RnD1 (config-router)#network 10.1.0.0
RnD1 (config-router)#network 10.0.0.0
```

A network statement was entered for each of the networks that existed on an interface for RnD1. What will the configuration look like when you look in the running configuration? Let's look.

```
RnD1#sh running-config
Building configuration . . .
Current configuration : 779 bytes
!
version 12.4
```

```
service timestamps debug datetime msec
service timestamps log datetime msec
no service password-encryption
!
hostname Router1
[output cut]
router eigrp 65000
network 10.0.0.0
auto-summary
```

Controlling Interfaces Placed in the Routing Process

Why is there only one network command listed in the configuration? Well, it is because I configured it that way. The network command that I used is a classful network configuration command, so the router automatically puts only the classful network into the configuration. That isn't the worst part of this situation. Since I used that classful command, all the interfaces that fall into that network range have been placed into the EIGRP routing process. All of the interfaces being placed into the process means that that the router will discover neighbors and exchange routing updates on all those interfaces. That isn't always bad, if you want all the interfaces to belong to the routing process. But if there is even one interface that you don't want included, then it could be a problem. For instance, if one of the interfaces is connected to a service provider, you wouldn't want that interface to share routing updates with the service provider router.

So, let's take a look at how you can use the network command to control which interfaces are placed into the routing process. Here is the configuration I used to specifically add each interface to the process.

```
RnD1 (config)#router eigrp 65000
RnD1 (config-router)#network 10.0.0.4 0.0.0.3
RnD1 (config-router)#network 10.1.0.0 0.0.0.3
RnD1 (config-router)#network 10.1.1.0 0.0.0.255
RnD1 (config-router)#no auto-summary
```

You can now see that I added each of the interfaces networks individually and included a wildcard mask in the configuration. This allows only the interfaces with the networks specified in the commands to be placed in the routing process.

I am going to move on and configure the rest of the network so it is ready when you need it for the rest of the exercises in chapter. The two core devices are the multilayer switches that were described in the test network (Core1 and Core2). In my test network, they are 3560 series switches. Each of the other four RnD routers are true 2811 routers.

Alert

At this point you may be getting an alert on your RnD1. You will if you have a test network set up just like mine and there are no configurations on your switches. The alert may look something like this.

```
IP-EIGRP(Default-IP-Routing-Table:65000): Neighbor 10.0.0.6 not on common subnet
for FastEthernet0/1
IP-EIGRP(Default-IP-Routing-Table:65000): Neighbor 10.1.0.1 not on common subnet
for FastEthernet0/0
```

The reason for this alert is that you have two interfaces on the router with different IP addresses that are communicating to one another and the router knows the interfaces should not be communicating.

How are they communicating? Well, at this point fa0/0 of RnD1 is connected to Core1 and fa0/1 is connected to Core2. On the switch side, all of the interfaces are in the default VLAN 1 and the switches have created a default trunk between each other for the traffic to pass across. That is how.

Now I need to show you how to fix this issue. Go onto the switches and make each of the interfaces that connect to the routers a routed port. Let's take a look at that configuration on Core1 (Switch1).

```
Core1(config)#interface range fa0/1 - 2
Core1(config-if-range)#no switchport
```

That is all it takes. Now each of those ports is a routed port that can have an IP address configured on it, and you should have seen the alerts stop on your router as well. I only made the two ports routed ports so that we can use the other interfaces between each pair of routers in the switch block.

Since you are already on the Core1 switch, go ahead and configure the IP addresses on each of the interfaces. Routed ports on a switch are configured just as if they were routed ports on a router. Just like this:

```
Core1(config)#interface fa0/1
Core1(config-if)#ip address 10.0.0.5 255.255.255.252
Core1(config-if)#no shut
Core1(config-if)#interface fa0/2
Core1(config-if)#ip address 10.0.0.9 255.255.255.252
Core1(config-if)#no shut
```

Configuring EIGRP on a Switch

Let's finish configuring the rest of the things that are needed on Core1. You have to turn on routing; don't forget routing isn't enabled by default on a switch. The interface that connects to Core2 (fa0/20) needs to be configured, as well. Then EIGRP routing for AS 65000 needs to be enabled using the specific network and wildcard mask combinations. Use the no auto-summary command to tell the router not to automatically summarize the network routes at the classful boundaries. In order to take full advantage of the classless features and see all of the subnets in the routing table, the no auto-summary command is required.

```
Core1(config-if)#interface fa0/20
Core1(config-if)#no switchport
Core1(config-if)#ip address 10.0.0.1 255.255.255.252
Core1(config-if)#no shut
Core1(config)#ip routing
Core1(config)#router eigrp 65000
Core1(config-router)#network 10.0.0.0 255.255.255.252
Core1(config-router)#network 10.0.0.4 255.255.255.252
Core1(config-router)#network 10.0.0.8 255.255.255.252
Core1(config-router)#no auto-summary
```

Make sure that there aren't any other ports that go between the core devices that might create trunks and pass traffic that you don't want passed. Put port fa0/3 and port fa0/4 into their own VLAN. I have you do this so that Router3 and Router4 (on their fa0/0 ports) are only connected to each other and nothing else.

```
Core1(config)#int range fa0/3 - 4
Core1(config-if-range)#switchport
Core1(config-if-range)#switchport access vlan 3
% Access VLAN does not exist. Creating vlan 3
```

Configuring the Rest of the Network

Now I want you configure Core2 (Switch2). The configuration is going to be very similar but with different IP addresses and networks. So, first configure the interfaces by making them routed ports and placing IP addresses on each interface.

```
Core2(config)#interface range fa0/3 - 4
Core2(config-if-range)#no switchport
Core2(config)#interface fa0/3
Core2(config-if)#ip address 10.0.0.13 255.255.255.252
Core2(config-if)#no shut
Core2(config-if)#int fa0/4
```

```
Core2(config-if)#ip add 10.0.0.17 255.255.255.252
Core2(config-if)#no shut
Core2(config-if)#interface fa0/20
Core2(config-if)#no switchport
Core2(config-if)#ip address 10.0.0.2 255.255.255.252
Core2(config-if)#no shut
```

Next, configure EIGRP for AS 65000, and don't forget the no auto-summary command.

```
Core2(config)#router eigrp 65000
Core2(config-router)#network 10.0.0.0 0.0.0.3
Core2(config-router)#network 10.0.0.12 0.0.0.3
Core2(config-router)#network 10.0.0.16 255.255.255.252
Core1(config-router)#no auto-summary
```

The last thing that you need to do is put the two interfaces that connect Router3 and Router4 into a different VLAN. I used VLAN 2 in my example.

```
Core2(config)#interface range fa0/1 - 2
Core2(config-if-range)#switchport access vlan 2
% Access VLAN does not exist. Creating vlan 2
```

Now I want you to configure the other three routers, Router2, Router3, and Router4. Here are the configurations that I used for my three routers. The configurations in the listing that follows go right down the line in numeric order, RnD2 to RnD4.

```
RnD2(config)#interface fa0/0
RnD2(config-if)#ip address 10.0.0.10 255.255.255.252
RnD2(config-if)#no shut
RnD2(config)#interface fa0/1
RnD2(config-if)#ip address 10.1.0.2 255.255.255.252
RnD2(config-if)#no shut
RnD2(config-if)#interface 100
RnD2(config-if)#ip address 10.1.2.1 255.255.255.0
RnD2(config-if)#no shut
RnD2(config-router)#no auto
RnD2(config-router)#network 10.0.0.8 0.0.0.3
RnD2(config-router)#network 10.1.0.0 0.0.0.3
RnD2(config-router)#network 10.1.2.0 0.0.0.255
RnD2(config-router)#no auto-summary
RnD3(config)#interface fa0/1
RnD3(config-if)#ip address 10.0.0.14 255.255.255.252
RnD3(config-if)#no shut
RnD3(config-if)#interface fa0/0
```

```
RnD3(config-if)#ip address 10.2.0.1 255.255.255.252
RnD3(config-if)#no shut
RnD3(config-if)#interface l00
RnD3(config-if)#ip address 10.2.1.1 255.255.255.0
RnD3(config-if)#no shut
RnD3(config)#router eigrp 65000
RnD3(config-router)#network 10.0.0.12 0.0.0.3
RnD3(config-router)#network 10.2.0.0 0.0.0.3
RnD3(config-router)#network 10.2.1.0 0.0.0.255
RnD3(config-router)#no auto-summary
RnD4(config)#interface fa0/1
RnD4(config-if)#ip address 10.0.0.18 255.255.255.252
RnD4(config-if)#no shut
RnD4(config-if)#interface fa0/0
RnD4(config-if)#ip address 10.2.0.2 255.255.255.252
RnD4(config-if)#no shut
RnD4(config-if)#interface l00
RnD4(config-if)#ip address 10.2.2.1 255.255.255.0
RnD4(config-if)#no shut
RnD4(config)#router eigrp 65000
RnD4(config-router)#network 10.2.0.0 0.0.0.3
RnD4(config-router)#network 10.0.0.18 0.0.0.3
RnD4(config-router)#network 10.2.2.0 0.0.0.255
RnD4(config-router)#no auto-summary
```

You can see from the routing table of RnD4 that all 11 networks that I configured are now known by RnD4. You can even see that for network 10.0.0.12/30, RnD4 has two known paths and they have the same metric. This means that RnD4 is equal-cost load balancing over both paths.

```
RnD4#sh ip route
Codes: C - connected, S - static, R - RIP, M - mobile, B - BGP
D - EIGRP, EX - EIGRP external, O - OSPF, IA - OSPF inter area
N1 - OSPF NSSA external type 1, N2 - OSPF NSSA external type 2
E1 - OSPF external type 1, E2 - OSPF external type 2
i - IS-IS, su - IS-IS summary, L1 - IS-IS level-1, L2 - IS-IS level-2
ia - IS-IS inter area, * - candidate default, U - per-user static route
o - ODR, P - periodic downloaded static route
Gateway of last resort is not set
10.0.0.0/8 is variably subnetted, 11 subnets, 2 masks
D 10.0.0.8/30 [90/33280] via 10.0.0.17, 00:00:38, FastEthernet0/1
D 10.0.0.12/30 [90/30720] via 10.2.0.1, 00:00:38, FastEthernet0/0
```

```
      [90/30720] via 10.0.0.17, 00:00:38, FastEthernet0/1
C  10.2.0.0/30 is directly connected, FastEthernet0/0
D  10.2.1.0/24 [90/156160] via 10.2.0.1, 00:00:38, FastEthernet0/0
D  10.1.2.0/24 [90/161280] via 10.0.0.17, 00:00:38, FastEthernet0/1
C  10.2.2.0/24 is directly connected, Loopback0
D  10.1.1.0/24 [90/161280] via 10.0.0.17, 00:00:39, FastEthernet0/1
D  10.0.0.0/30 [90/30720] via 10.0.0.17, 00:00:39, FastEthernet0/1
D  10.1.0.0/30 [90/35840] via 10.0.0.17, 00:00:39, FastEthernet0/1
D  10.0.0.4/30 [90/33280] via 10.0.0.17, 00:00:39, FastEthernet0/1
C  10.0.0.16/30 is directly connected, FastEthernet0/1
```

Improving EIGRP Operations

EIGRP has a few features available that can make its operation more efficient and secure in your network. One of the first things I want to cover is the ability to change the EIGRP metric calculation to fine-tune the paths that data takes across the network. You will see that it can be quite a challenge, though, to modify the metric; so caution must be used to not make any change that isn't well planned out and implemented uniformly.

Next, I go over manual route summarization and stub routers. Both of these features help EIGRP limit the scope or distance to which queries can be sent on the network. Both features can also help the CPU load on a router by limiting the number of network updates that have to be sent between routers.

Finally, I cover two additional features that help conserve and optimize the bandwidth used on various links in the network. Those features are load balancing and WAN link optimizations.

Changing the EIGRP Metric

EIGRP uses the same composite metric as IGRP to determine the best path, except that the EIGRP metric is multiplied by 256. The metric can be based on five criteria, but EIGRP uses only two of these criteria by default:

Bandwidth   The smallest bandwidth between source and destination

Delay   The cumulative interface delay along the path

The following criteria can be used, but are not recommended, because they typically result in frequent recalculation of the topology table:

Reliability   This value represents the worst reliability between source and destination, based on keepalives.

Loading   This value represents the worst load on a link between source and destination, computed based on the packet rate and the configured bandwidth of the interface.

MTU   This criterion represents the smallest maximum transmittable unit (MTU) in the path. MTU is included in the EIGRP routing update but is not actually used in the metric calculation.

How EIGRP Calculates Metrics

EIGRP calculates the metric by adding the weighted values of different variables of the link to the network in question. The default constant weight values are K1 = K3 = 1 and K2 = K4 = K5 = 0.

In EIGRP metric calculations, when K5 is 0 (the default), variables (bandwidth, bandwidth divided by load, and delay) are weighted with the constants K1, K2, and K3. The following is the formula used:

Metric = (K1 × bandwidth) + [(K2 × bandwidth) ÷ (256 − load)] + (K3 × delay)

If these K values are equal to their defaults, the formula becomes the following:

Metric = (1 × bandwidth) + [(0 × bandwidth) ÷ (256 − load)] + (1 × delay)

Metric = bandwidth + delay

If K5 is not equal to 0, the following additional operation is performed:

Metric = metric × [K5 ÷ (reliability + K4)]

Avoiding Unexpected Results

K values are carried in EIGRP hello packets. All of the K values must match between routers for updates to be exchanged. Any mismatched K values could make a neighbor reset. (Only K1 and K3 are used, by default, in metric compilation.) These K values should be modified only after careful planning; changing these values can prevent your network from converging and is generally not recommended.

You should also understand that the format of the delay and bandwidth values used for EIGRP metric calculations differs from those displayed by the show interface command. The EIGRP delay value is the sum of the delays in the path, in tens of microseconds, multiplied by 256. The show interface command displays the delay in microseconds. The EIGRP bandwidth is calculated using the minimum bandwidth link along the path, in kilobits per second. The value 10^7 is divided by this value, and then the result is multiplied by 256.

Default Routing

The EIGRP default route can be created with the ip default-network *network-number* command. If you configure one of your routers with this command, the router considers the network listed in the command as the gateway of last resort and the router will announce the network to other routers.

When you specify a network using ip default-network network-number, the router it is configured on must be able to reach the network before it will advertise the route as a candidate default route to other EIGRP routers. The network specified by this command must also be passed to other EIGRP routers so that those routers can use this network as their default network and set the gateway of last resort to this default network. This requirement means that the network must either be an EIGRP-derived network in the routing table or be generated using a static route that has been redistributed into EIGRP.

Multiple default networks can be configured; each of the downstream routers will use the configured EIGRP metric to determine the best default route. This works just as it would if the router were determining a route for any other network.

For example, in Figure 5.5, RnDEdge is directly attached to external network 192.168.10.0/24. RnDEdge is configured with the 192.168.10.0 network as a candidate default network using the `ip default-network 192.168.10.0` command.

FIGURE 5.5   Default-Network Command

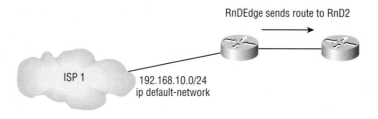

This network is passed to RnD2 because RnDEdge has the route configured in a `network` command under the EIGRP process. The routing table for RnDEdge will not have the gateway of last resort set. This is because the `ip default-network` command does not make the route better for RnDEdge as it is directly connected. On RnD2, the route would be learned through EIGRP and listed as 192.168.10.0; the network is flagged as a candidate default network—this is indicated with an asterisk (*) in the routing table. RnD2 also sets the gateway of last resort to the IP address of RnDEdge because that is how to reach the default network of 192.168.10.0.

Help! I Can't Remove this Default Network.

When you configure using the `ip default-network` command, a static route (the `ip route` command) is generated in the router configuration. You won't be told about this by the Cisco IOS software, as it does not display a message. You will only see an entry appear as a static route in the routing table on the router on which you configured the `ip default-network` command. This can be a source of confusion when you want to remove the default network. The configuration command must be removed with the `no ip route` command.

Now, EIGRP and Interior Gateway Routing Protocol (IGRP) behave differently from routing information protocol (RIP) when you use the `ip route 0.0.0.0 0.0.0.0` command. For example, EIGRP does not redistribute the 0.0.0.0 0.0.0.0 default route by default. However, if the `network 0.0.0.0` command is added to the EIGRP configuration, it redistributes a default route as a result of the `ip route 0.0.0.0 0.0.0.0` **interface** command (but not as a result of the `ip route 0.0.0.0 0.0.0.0` **address** or `ip default-network` command).

Summary Routes

Some EIGRP features, such as automatically summarizing routes at major network boundaries, are characteristics of distance vector operation. Traditionally, distance vector protocols did not exchange subnet masks with their routing updates. Therefore, these classful routing protocols could not assume or know what the mask was for a network that was not directly connected. The classful routing protocols would summarize their routes at major classful network boundaries. This creates smaller routing tables on the routers, and smaller routing tables mean the routing update process is less bandwidth intensive.

A drawback of distance vector protocols is their inability to configure a summary route that has an arbitrary bit boundary within a major network. Typically, this is desirable because summarizing routes creates smaller routing tables. Using an arbitrary bit boundary is the same as saying you are aggregating or making a new summary address. When you make a new summary address, you put a specified number of smaller routes into a single larger route.

With EIGRP you can disable automatic summarization and create one or more summary routes within the network on any bit boundary. You have to remember something when using an EIGRP summary route: The summary route is obviously acting as the single indicating route for multiple routes, which exist on the router's interfaces. For the summary route to be maintained in the routing table, at least one of the specific subnets that the summary identifies must be in the routing table. If all of the subnets are lost from the routing table, then the summary route will also be removed from the routing table. When you create a summary route, its metric is the lowest metric of the specific routes contained in the summary route.

To be effective when you configure manual summarization, the blocks of contiguous addresses (subnets) must all exist or come together at a common router or single point in the network where the summary route can be advertised from.

Determining the Maximum Subnets in a Summary Route

The number of subnets that you can represent in your summary route is found using the difference in the number of bits between the subnet mask of the networks being summarized and the summary mask itself. The formula is 2^n, where n equals the difference in the number of bits between the summary and subnet mask. This formula defines the maximum number of subnets can be represented by a single summary route. Let me give you an example. If the summary mask contains three fewer bits than the subnet mask, then eight subnets ($2^3 = 8$) can be aggregated into the one summary advertised route.

I will take that example a little further. You might have a network 172.16.0.0 and it is divided into /24 subnets. Let's then say that you wanted to summarize a block of eight of those networks. The range of subnets that you want to summarize spans the eight networks from 172.16.16.0/24 through 172.16.23.0/24. The summarization block or mask would be 172.16.16.0/21, the difference between the /24 networks and the /21 summarizations is three bits; therefore, $2^3 = 8$ subnets are aggregated.

Specifying the IP and Summary Mask

When configuring a summary route, you need to specify the IP address of the summary route and the summary mask. This is what I just did for you in the last example. I found the range of subnets to be summarized and then found the network address and mask that would identify that range. Luckily for us, the Cisco IOS software built into EIGRP on a router handles many of the details that surround proper implementation, including details about metrics, loop prevention, and removal of the summary route from the routing table if none of the more specific routes are valid.

Disabling Automatic Summarization

Automatic summarization is enabled by default for EIGRP. This means that EIGRP automatically summarizes routes at the classful network boundary. You may not always want automatic summarization. For example, if you have discontiguous networks, you need to disable automatic summarization to minimize router confusion and ensure that all of the subnets are in each router's routing table. Disabling automatic summarization is a straightforward process. You only have to use the no auto-summary command, which is under the EIGRP router configuration mode.

An EIGRP router does not perform an automatic summarization of networks in which it does not participate.

Manually Creating a Summary Route

You can use the ip summary-address eigrp interface command to manually create a summary route. This manual summary can be created with any bit length that is needed at that point in the network; this type of configuration is sometimes referred to as an arbitrary bit boundary. Again, the caveat to the creation of a manual summary route must be adhered to; there must be a more specific route in the routing table within the address block that you are summarizing. Table 5.1 describes the ip summary-address eigrp parameters.

TABLE 5.1   ip summary-address eigrp Command Options

Parameter	Description
as-number	EIGRP autonomous system (AS) number
Address	The IP address advertised as the summary address; this address does not need to be aligned on Class A, B, or C boundaries
Mask	The IP mask used to create the summary address
admin-distance	(Optional) Administrative distance; a value from 0 to 255

Controlling Query Propagation

There is one major thing left to discuss before we leave summarization. That is the ability to help control the propagation of queries in the network. The Cisco IOS software does this by automatically setting summary routes to interface nu110 in the routing table for automatically summarized routes. This also helps to prevent routing loops. For the same reason, Cisco IOS software also creates a summary route to interface nu110 when manual summarization is configured.

For example, I used the summary address 172.16.16.0/21. If one of those networks were to go down, then when the summarizing router receives a packet destined for the now down subnet that is part of the summarized range, the packet will still match the summary route based on the longest match. The packet will then be forwarded to the nu110 interface. When a packet is routed to the null interface, it is being dropped. Null interface routing is also called black hole routing for the same reason—whatever goes in or routed in never comes out. This action prevents the router from forwarding the packet to a default route and possibly creating a routing loop.

Having a summary route also means that if there is no other route to that destination network (meaning there is no feasible successor) then a query does not have to be sent out. A query doesn't have to be sent because the route that is actually being sent out (the summary route) didn't go down or change.

Stub Routers

It is common to use stub routing in hub-and-spoke network topologies. You can also use stub routing to again limit the query scope of the network. In a hub-and-spoke topology, having a full routing table on the spoke router serves no real functional purpose. This is because the only path to the rest of the corporate network and the Internet is always through the hub router. If the spoke router were to have a full routing table, the amount of memory required would significantly be increased. You can also implement route summarization and route filtering to conserve bandwidth and memory requirements on the spoke routers.

Typically, the connection from a hub router to a spoke router has significantly less bandwidth than a connection at the network core; attempting to use the connection to a remote router as a transit path typically results in excessive congestion. When a hub router sends traffic, it should not use a spoke router for its transit path. The EIGRP stub routing feature restricts the remote router from advertising the hub router routes back to other hub routers. Using the EIGRP stub routing feature improves network stability, reduces resource utilization, and simplifies stub router configuration.

The EIGRP stub feature was first introduced in Cisco IOS Software Release 12.0(7)T. You only have to configure the spoke routers as stubs. The stub router then sends a special peer information packet to all neighboring routers to report its status as a stub router. Any neighbor that receives a packet informing it of the stub status no longer queries the stub router for any routes. Instead, the hub router that is connected to the stub router will answer the query on behalf of the stub router. The stub routing feature does not prevent routes from being advertised to the remote router. This feature of not querying the stub routers is again one of the features you can use to limit the query scope of the network and avoid stuck-in-active (SIA) situations.

The EIGRP stub routing feature also simplifies the configuration and maintenance of hub-and-spoke networks. When stub routing is enabled in dual-homed remote configurations, you do not have to configure filtering on remote routers to prevent them from appearing as transit paths to the hub routers.

EIGRP stub routing should only be used on stub routers. A stub router is defined as a router connected back to the core of the network and through which core transit traffic should not flow. A stub router should only have hub routers for EIGRP neighbors; not setting up your network with this restriction in mind may cause less than desirable results. The savings in bandwidth that you wanted will no longer be realized.

To configure a router as an EIGRP stub, use the eigrp stub command. A router configured as a stub with this command shares information about connected and summary routes with all neighboring routers by default.

Table 5.2 describes the parameters of the eigrp stub command.

TABLE 5.2 Stub Router Options

Parameter	Description
receive-only	The *receive-only* keyword restricts the router from sharing any of its routes with any other router within an EIGRP autonomous system (AS). This keyword does not permit any other option to be specified, because it prevents any type of route from being sent. The three other optional keywords (connected, static, and summary) cannot be used with the receive-only keyword. Use this option if there is a single interface on the router.
connected	The connected keyword permits the EIGRP stub routing feature to send connected routes. If a network command does not include the connected routes, it might be necessary to redistribute connected routes with the redistribute connected command under the EIGRP process. This option is enabled by default and is the most widely practical stub option.
static	The static keyword permits the EIGRP stub routing feature to send static routes. Redistributing static routes with the redistribute static command is still necessary.
summary	The summary keyword permits the EIGRP stub routing feature to send summary routes. Summary routes can be created manually with the ip summary-address command or automatically at a major network border router with the auto-summary command enabled. This option is enabled by default.

The parameters of this command can be used in any combination, with the exception of the receive-only keyword. If one of these keywords, except receive-only, is used individually, then the connected and summary routes are not sent automatically.

The EIGRP stub routing feature does not automatically enable route summarization on the hub router. In most cases, you or the network administrator should configure route summarization on the hub routers.

If a true stub network is required, the hub router can be configured to send a default route to the spoke routers. This approach is the most simple and conserves the most bandwidth and memory on the spoke routers.

> Although EIGRP is a classless routing protocol, it has classful behavior by default, such as having automatic summarization on by default. When you configure the hub router to send a default route to the remote router, ensure that the ip classless command is issued on the remote router. By default, the ip classless command is enabled in all Cisco IOS images that support the EIGRP stub routing feature.

The EIGRP stub routing feature allows a network administrator to prevent sending queries to the spoke router under any condition. It is highly recommended that you use both EIGRP route summarization and EIGRP stub features to provide the best scalability.

Without the stub feature, a hub router will send a query to the spoke routers if a route is lost somewhere in the network. If there is a communication problem over the WAN link between the hub router and the spoke router, replies may not be received for all queries (this is known as being SIA), and the network may become unstable.

Load Balancing

Load balancing is the ability of a router to distribute traffic over multiple network ports going to a given destination address. Load balancing increases the use of network segments and increases effective network bandwidth.

Equal-Cost Load Balancing

Equal-cost load balancing is the ability of a router to distribute traffic over multiple ports that have or are the same metric to the destination address.

For IP, Cisco IOS software applies load balancing between a maximum of four equal-cost paths by default. With the maximum-path router configuration command, up to six equally good routes can be kept in the routing table. (Setting the maximum-path option to 1 disables load balancing.)

> In older Cisco IOS versions, you could only load balance over a total of six paths. However, in newer IOS versions that maximum has been increased to 16. The default number of paths configured for use is still set at four, but can be changed with the maximum-path command.

When a packet is process-switched, load balancing over equal-cost paths occurs on a per-packet basis. When packets are fast-switched, load balancing over equal-cost paths occurs on a per-destination basis. If you are testing your load-balancing configuration, don't ping to or from routers with the fast-switching interfaces. This is because packets that are locally generated by the router are process-switched rather than fast-switched and might produce confusing results.

Unequal-Cost Load Balancing

EIGRP can also balance traffic across multiple routes that have different metrics, a process called unequal-cost load balancing. The degree to which EIGRP performs load balancing is controlled with the variance command. By default this value is set to 1, which means that no unequal-cost load balancing will occur.

A value from 1 to 128 can be used for load balancing in the variance command. The default is 1, which indicates equal-cost load balancing. The variance value is simply described as a multiplier. The value defines the range of metric values that are accepted for load balancing by the EIGRP process. For example, I have a router that has three possible paths to a destination network. My best path route has an FD of 5000. If I configure the variance command to a value of 3, then the routing process would look at the other routes in the topology table, and use the new varied metric of 15000 to determine whether there are any additional routes to put in the routing table for use. If the FD of either of the other routes is between 5001 and 14999, then they should be placed in the routing table. Now I said "they should be," so you might be asking "what is the exception now?" In order for a route to be used in the unequal-cost load balancing process, it must be a feasible successor. Recall, a feasible successor router passes a route that has a lower AD than the FD of the successor or best route.

Let's take a look at what I mean by that.

 Real World Scenario

Unequal-Cost Load Balancing

In Figure 5.6, I have a sample network that one of my other network administrators has been working with to learn new ways to configure a network setup for some engineers. FutureTech's R&D engineers need multiple paths in the network, each with different speeds so that they can test a new security system that they are working on. This setup is perfect for me to show you how unequal-cost load balancing works. Unequal-cost load balancing is also useful in situations where you have multiple WAN links and you want to use all of the paths even though they are not the same speed. From the diagram, you can see that RnDA has three paths to get to RnDC, which is connected to network A. Network A is the destination network where RnDA is going to send packets. RnDA must decide which and how many paths it can use to the destination. Table 5.3 shows you a summary of the topology table information for each of the routes to network A.

FIGURE 5.6   Unequal-Cost Load Balancing

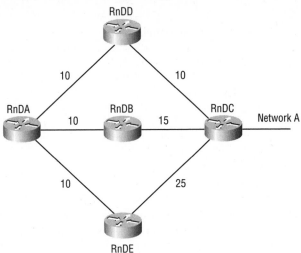

TABLE 5.3   Topology Summary for RouterA

Destination	Feasible Distance	Advertised Distance	Neighbor Router
Network A	35	15	RnDB
Network A	20	10	RnDD
Network A	35	25	RnDE

You can see from the diagram and the table that the path through RnDD is the best path. By default, that would be the only path used because it has the best FD and there isn't another path with the same metric. However, if I configure variance on RnDA to a value of 2, then there could be an unequal-cost path that could be used. Let's figure out if that is the case. When I change the variance to 2, the new FD for the best path is 40. The router always keeps track of the real FD and won't pick another path to replace the real successor. It only adds an additional path.

With the new FD, then, is there an additional path that is less than that number (40)? Yes! You can see that both of the other routes fall below the new FD.

So are all three paths placed into the routing table? That is a perfect question. The answer is no! Only an unequal-cost path that is a feasible successor can be used for load balancing.

Are either of the other routes feasible successors? Yes! You see that the path through RnDA's neighbor RnDB is a feasible successor. RnDB advertised a route where the AD is less than the FD of the successor, since 15 is less than 20. RnDA will now place the original route through RnDD and the new route through RnDB into the routing table.

Using EIGRP over WANs

EIGRP operates efficiently in WAN environments. It is scalable on both point-to-point links and on point-to-point and multipoint non-broadcast multi-access (NBMA) links. It was the goal of EIGRP designers to have a much simpler and straightforward configuration for WAN links than other routing protocols do. So, for instance, OSPF requires special configurations depending on the topology of the WAN circuits. This doesn't mean, however, that there aren't a few things for you to understand and know how to configure in order to really make your network and WAN connections function well.

There are inherent differences in the characteristics of WAN links and how they operate. For this reason, the default EIGRP configuration may not be the best option or setup for all WAN links. You are gaining a solid understanding of EIGRP operation; you will also have to have knowledge of your WAN connections and link speeds. Once you have an understanding of the upcoming WAN configurations, you will be able to set up and maintain an efficient, reliable, and scalable network over WANs.

By default, EIGRP gets to use up to 50 percent of the bandwidth of an interface or subinterface. EIGRP uses the configured bandwidth of the link set by the bandwidth command, or the default bandwidth of the link (T1 speed on all serial links) if none is configured, when calculating how much bandwidth to use. This percentage can be changed on a per-interface basis by using the ip bandwidth-percent eigrp *as-number percent* interface configuration command. In this command, *as-number* is the AS number, and *percent* is the percentage of the configured bandwidth that EIGRP can use. You can configure the percentage to be greater than 100 percent. This can be useful if the configured bandwidth is set artificially low for routing-policy reasons.

Cisco IOS software assumes that point-to-point frame relay subinterfaces (like all serial interfaces) operate at full T1 link speed. In many real world implementations, however, only fractional T1 speeds (speeds lower than 1.544 Mbps) are used, often as low as 56 or 64 Kbps. This can be easily taken care of by configuring these subinterfaces with the bandwidth command and setting the bandwidth to match the contracted committed information rate (CIR) of the permanent virtual circuit (PVC). This configuration though is only that simple in the case of point-to-point links where each subinterface can be configured for a given circuit.

When configuring multipoint interfaces, especially for frame relay (but also for ATM and integrated service digital network primary-rate ISDN PRI), it is important to understand that all neighbors share the bandwidth equally. This means that EIGRP will use the bandwidth command on the physical interface and divide that value by the number of frame relay neighbors connected on that physical interface to calculate the bandwidth that each of the neighbors has to use. The EIGRP configuration should then reflect the correct percentage of the actual available bandwidth on the line.

When configuring multipoint interfaces, configure the bandwidth to represent the minimum CIR multiplied by the number of circuits. By using this configuration, you will not fully use the higher-speed circuits, but it makes sure that the circuits with the lowest CIR are not completely consumed. If the topology has a small number of very low-speed circuits, these interfaces are typically defined as point to point so that their bandwidth can be set to match the provisioned CIR.

Let's take a look at what I mean with the multipoint configuration.

 Real World Scenario

Connecting to Remote Sites

You are a new WAN engineer for FutureTech and you are located in the headquarters building. Five remote sites are connected to the headquarters site through point-to-multipoint frame relay connections. These sites transfer data to and from the headquarters site. (Now, these bandwidth values that are not typical of real bandwidth values that you might purchase from a service provider but, for the sake of simplicity, I am going to use them anyway.)

The headquarters site has a CIR of 1,000 Kbps; four of the sites have a CIR of 200 Kbps; while the fifth site has a CIR of 100 Kbps, as shown in Figure 5.7. The headquarters site will automatically allocate the bandwidth to be used by EIGRP. It does this by taking the interface bandwidth and dividing it by the number of sites that are connected. In this case, each site would be assumed to have 200 Kbps. EIGRP, then, believes that it can use 50 percent of that bandwidth for routing data. In this case, each site could get up to 100 Kbps of routing data. That is fine for all of the sites except the one site whose CIR only has 100 Kbps.

FIGURE 5.7   Point-to-Multipoint WAN Routing

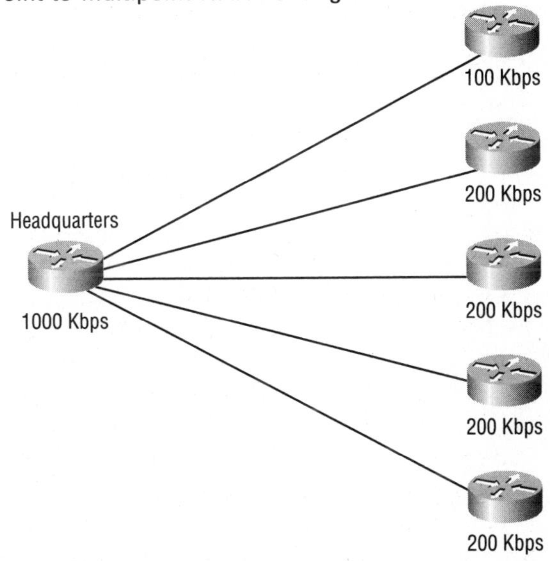

Headquarters

1000 Kbps

100 Kbps

200 Kbps

200 Kbps

200 Kbps

200 Kbps

The best fix for this situation is to reconfigure the site with the low CIR into a point-to-point site and allow the other sites to remain point to multipoint. If this is not possible for some reason, then the only thing to fix the amount of routing data that would come to that site is to change it for all of the sites. You must do this by changing the configured bandwidth at the HQ site. This will affect the amount of routing data that is sent to all of the sites. You must calculate this new bandwidth value by taking the site with the lowest CIR and multiplying it by the number of sites. You are basically reverse engineering the calculation that EIGRP will do on the interface anyway. In this case, the new bandwidth will need to be 100 Kbps × 5 = 500 Kbps. This is not the optimal configuration because you are now limiting the amount of routing traffic that can be sent to the other sites.

I also want to take you though a point-to-point configuration. The network setup will be basically the same as the last example, but will have different bandwidths. This example shows you the difference in how you will configure the network if the topology is different.

 **Real World Scenario**

Point-to-Point Connections

The headquarters site has a CIR of 250 Kbps to the ISP and each of the five branch sites has a CIR of 100 Kbps. Take a look at Figure 5.8. It shows you the network that I am talking about.

FIGURE 5.8   Point-to-Point WAN Routing

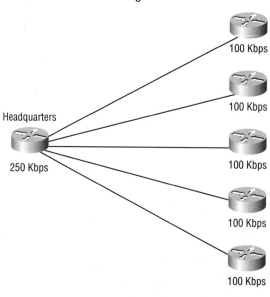

Before we even get to the routing portion of this example, let's look at the first thing that would have probably been done in this situation. If the CIR bandwidths were to be configured on the interfaces, in this case you would end up with an aggregation problem. If each of the sites were to send their maximum 100 Kbps to the HQ site at the same time, the HQ side of the connection would be overloaded. For this reason, the bandwidth at the remote site would be set artificially low to 50 Kbps.

Now with this setting, EIGRP would think that it could use 50 percent of that value, which is 25 Kbps and that could create a problem for EIGRP's making sure that all of its traffic is getting passed. This is how you end up with your routing issue.

As I described earlier, the `ip bandwidth-percent eigrp` *as-number percent* command specifies the allowed maximum percentage of the bandwidth on an interface that EIGRP can use. In this point-to-point topology, all of the virtual circuits are treated equally; the interfaces and subinterface were configured with a bandwidth that is lower than it should be. The EIGRP use percentage can then be raised to 200 percent of the specified bandwidth in an attempt to ensure that EIGRP packets are delivered through the frame relay network. This additional configuration allows the EIGRP packets to receive 50 Kbps of the provisioned 100 Kbps on each circuit. This configuration restores the 50-50 ratio that was altered when the bandwidth was set to an artificially low value.

Verifying and Troubleshooting

It is now time to look at the commands you can use to gather data about how EIGRP is running, and (hopefully not too often) use them to help in troubleshooting when there is a problem.

show ip eigrp neighbors

The EIGRP IP neighbor table can be displayed with the `show ip eigrp neighbors` command, as shown in the output from RnD1.

```
RnD1#show ip eigrp neighbors
IP-EIGRP neighbors for process 65000
H Address Interface Hold Uptime SRTT RTO Q Seq
sec) (ms) Cnt Num
1 10.1.0.2 Fa0/1 10 1d00h 1 200 0 32
0 10.0.0.5 Fa0/0 13 1d00h 49 294 0 69
```

Table 5.4 describes the key elements from the output.

TABLE 5.4 `show ip eigrp neighbors`

Column	Description
H (handle)	A number used internally by the Cisco IOS software to track a neighbor.
Address	The network-layer address of the neighbor.
Interface	The interface on this router through which the neighbor can be reached.
Hold Time	The maximum time, in seconds, that the router waits to hear from the neighbor without receiving anything from a neighbor before considering the link unavailable. Originally, the expected packet was a hello packet, but in current Cisco IOS software releases, any EIGRP packets received after the first hello from that neighbor resets the timer.
Uptime	The elapsed time, in hours, minutes, and seconds, since the local router first heard from this neighbor.
Smoothed round-trip time (SRTT)	The average number of milliseconds it takes for an EIGRP packet to be sent to this neighbor and for the local router to receive an acknowledgment of that packet. This timer is used to determine the retransmit interval, also known as the retransmission timeout (RTO).
RTO	The amount of time, in milliseconds, that the router waits for an acknowledgment before retransmitting a reliable packet from the retransmission queue to a neighbor.
Queue count	The number of packets waiting in the queue to be sent out. If this value is constantly higher than 0, a congestion problem might exist. A value of 0 indicates that no EIGRP packets are in the queue.
Seq Num	The sequence number of the last update, query, or reply packet that was received from this neighbor.

show ip eigrp topology

Another command used to verify EIGRP operations is the `show ip eigrp topology` command. For example, the output illustrates that Router1 has an ID of 10.0.0.6 and is in AS 65000—the EIGRP ID is the highest IP address on an active interface for this router.

```
RnD1#show ip eigrp topology
IP-EIGRP Topology Table for AS(65000)/ID(10.0.0.6)
```

```
Codes: P - Passive, A - Active, U - Update, Q - Query, R - Reply,
r - reply Status, s - sia Status
P 10.0.0.8/30, 2 successors, FD is 30720
via 10.0.0.5 (30720/28160), FastEthernet0/0
via 10.1.0.2 (30720/28160), FastEthernet0/1
P 10.0.0.12/30, 1 successors, FD is 33280
via 10.0.0.5 (33280/30720), FastEthernet0/0
P 10.2.0.0/30, 1 successors, FD is 35840
via 10.0.0.5 (35840/33280), FastEthernet0/0
P 10.2.1.0/24, 1 successors, FD is 161280
via 10.0.0.5 (161280/158720), FastEthernet0/0
P 10.1.2.0/24, 1 successors, FD is 156160
via 10.1.0.2 (156160/128256), FastEthernet0/1
P 10.2.2.0/24, 1 successors, FD is 161280
via 10.0.0.5 (161280/158720), FastEthernet0/0
P 10.0.0.0/30, 1 successors, FD is 30720
via 10.0.0.5 (30720/28160), FastEthernet0/0
P 10.1.1.0/24, 1 successors, FD is 128256
via Connected, Loopback0
P 10.1.0.0/30, 1 successors, FD is 28160
Codes: P - Passive, A - Active, U - Update, Q - Query, R - Reply,
r - reply Status, s - sia Status
via Connected, FastEthernet0/1
P 10.0.0.4/30, 1 successors, FD is 28160
via Connected, FastEthernet0/0
P 10.0.0.16/30, 1 successors, FD is 33280
via 10.0.0.5 (33280/30720), FastEthernet0/0
```

As shown in the output, this command output lists the networks known by this router through the EIGRP routing process. The codes in the command output are described in Table 5.5.

TABLE 5.5   `show ip eigrp topology`

Code	Description
Passive (P)	This network is available, and installation can occur in the routing table. Passive is the correct state for a stable network.
Active (A)	This network is currently unavailable, and installation cannot occur in the routing table. Being active means that there are outstanding queries for this network.

TABLE 5.5   show ip eigrp topology *(continued)*

Code	Description
Update (U)	This code applies if a network is being updated (placed in an update packet). This code also applies if the router is waiting for an acknowledgment for this update packet.
Query (Q):	This code applies if there is an outstanding query packet for this network other than being in the active state. This code also applies if the router is waiting for an acknowledgment for a query packet.
Reply (R) status	This code applies if the router is generating a reply for this network or is waiting for an acknowledgment for the reply packet.
Stuck-in-active (SIA) status	This code signifies an EIGRP convergence problem for the network with which it is associated.

The number of successors available for a route is indicated in the command output. In this example, all networks have one successor. If there were equal-cost paths to the same network, a maximum of six paths would be shown. The number of successors corresponds to the number of best routes with equal cost.

For each network, the FD is displayed, followed by the next hop address, which is followed by a field similar to (30720/28160), such as in the first entry of the output. The first number in this field is the FD for that network through this next hop router, and the second number is the AD from the next hop router to the destination network.

show ip route

To verify that the router recognizes EIGRP routes for any neighbors, use the show ip route eigrp command, as shown in the output below. The output also shows the show ip route command, which displays the full IP routing table, including the EIGRP routes.

```
RnD1#show ip route eigrp
10.0.0.0/8 is variably subnetted, 11 subnets, 2 masks
D 10.0.0.8/30 [90/30720] via 10.1.0.2, 1d00h, FastEthernet0/1
[90/30720] via 10.0.0.5, 1d00h, FastEthernet0/0
D 10.0.0.12/30 [90/33280] via 10.0.0.5, 23:26:05, FastEthernet0/0
D 10.2.0.0/30 [90/35840] via 10.0.0.5, 23:23:58, FastEthernet0/0
D 10.2.1.0/24 [90/161280] via 10.0.0.5, 23:22:57, FastEthernet0/0
D 10.1.2.0/24 [90/156160] via 10.1.0.2, 1d00h, FastEthernet0/1
D 10.2.2.0/24 [90/161280] via 10.0.0.5, 23:19:07, FastEthernet0/0
D 10.0.0.0/30 [90/30720] via 10.0.0.5, 1d00h, FastEthernet0/0
```

```
D 10.0.0.16/30 [90/33280] via 10.0.0.5, 23:21:43, FastEthernet0/0
RnD1#show ip route
Codes: C - connected, S - static, R - RIP, M - mobile, B - BGP
D - EIGRP, EX - EIGRP external, O - OSPF, IA - OSPF inter area
N1 - OSPF NSSA external type 1, N2 - OSPF NSSA external type 2
E1 - OSPF external type 1, E2 - OSPF external type 2
i - IS-IS, su - IS-IS summary, L1 - IS-IS level-1, L2 - IS-IS level-2
ia - IS-IS inter area, * - candidate default, U - per-user static route
o - ODR, P - periodic downloaded static route
Gateway of last resort is not set
10.0.0.0/8 is variably subnetted, 11 subnets, 2 masks
D 10.0.0.8/30 [90/30720] via 10.1.0.2, 1d00h, FastEthernet0/1
[90/30720] via 10.0.0.5, 1d00h, FastEthernet0/0
D 10.0.0.12/30 [90/33280] via 10.0.0.5, 23:26:13, FastEthernet0/0
D 10.2.0.0/30 [90/35840] via 10.0.0.5, 23:24:07, FastEthernet0/0
D 10.2.1.0/24 [90/161280] via 10.0.0.5, 23:23:06, FastEthernet0/0
D 10.1.2.0/24 [90/156160] via 10.1.0.2, 1d00h, FastEthernet0/1
D 10.2.2.0/24 [90/161280] via 10.0.0.5, 23:19:17, FastEthernet0/0
C 10.1.1.0/24 is directly connected, Loopback0
D 10.0.0.0/30 [90/30720] via 10.0.0.5, 1d00h, FastEthernet0/0
C 10.1.0.0/30 is directly connected, FastEthernet0/1
C 10.0.0.4/30 is directly connected, FastEthernet0/0
D 10.0.0.16/30 [90/33280] via 10.0.0.5, 23:21:53, FastEthernet0/0
```

EIGRP supports several route types: internal, external, and summary. EIGRP routes are identified with a D in the left column; any external EIGRP routes (from outside of this autonomous system) would be identified with a D EX.

After the network number, there is a field that looks similar to [90/30720]. The first number, 90 in this case, is the administrative distance. The second number is the EIGRP metric. Recall that the default EIGRP metric is the least-cost bandwidth plus the accumulated delays. The EIGRP metric for a network is the same as its feasible distance (FD) in the EIGRP topology table. Both are used to select the best path when a router learns two or more routes from different routing sources. For example, consider that this router also uses RIP, and RIP has a route to network 10.0.0.12 that is three hops away. Without the administrative distance, the router cannot compare the three hops of RIP to an EIGRP metric of 33280. The router does not know the bandwidth associated with hops, and EIGRP does not use hop count as a metric.

To correct this problem, Cisco established an administrative distance value for each routing protocol, the lower the value, the more strongly preferred the route is. By default, EIGRP internal routes have an administrative distance of 90, and RIP has an administrative distance of 120. Because EIGRP has a metric based on bandwidth and delays, it is preferred over the RIP hop count. As a result, in this example, the EIGRP route is installed in the routing table.

The next field, via 10.1.0.2 in this example, identifies the address of the next hop router to which this router passes the packets for the destination network 10.0.0.8/30. The next hop address in the routing table is the same as the successor in the EIGRP topology table.

Each route also has a time associated with it: the length of time, perhaps days or months, since EIGRP last advertised this network to this router. EIGRP does not refresh routes periodically; it resends the routing information only when neighbor adjacencies change. You may see this represented a little differently, depending on the length of time that the route has been in the table. From the output, you can see there is 1d00h. This means the route has been up for 1 day and 0 hours. You might also see 23:26:13, which means the route has been up for 23 hours, 26 minutes, and 13 seconds. The next field in the output is the interface, FastEthernet0/1 in this case, from which packets for 10.0.0.8/30 are sent.

Notice that the routing table includes routes, to nu110, for the advertised routes. Cisco IOS software automatically puts these routes in the table; they are called summary routes. Nu110 is a directly connected, software-only interface. The use of the nu110 interface prevents the router from trying to forward traffic to other routers in search of a more precise, longer match. For example, if the router from Figure 5.4 receives a packet to an unknown subnet that is part of the summarized range, the packet matches the summary route based on the longest match. The packet is forwarded to the nu110 interface (in other words, it is dropped, or sent to the bit bucket), which prevents the router from forwarding the packet to a default route and possibly creating a routing loop.

show ip protocols

The show ip protocols command gives information about any and all dynamic routing protocols running on the router.

```
RnD1#show ip protocols
Routing Protocol is "eigrp 65000"
Outgoing update filter list for all interfaces is not set
Incoming update filter list for all interfaces is not set
Default networks flagged in outgoing updates
Default networks accepted from incoming updates
EIGRP metric weight K1=1, K2=0, K3=1, K4=0, K5=0
EIGRP maximum hopcount 100
EIGRP maximum metric variance 1
Redistributing: eigrp 65000
EIGRP NSF-aware route hold timer is 240s
Automatic network summarization is not in effect
Maximum path: 4
Routing for Networks:
10.0.0.4/30
10.1.0.0/30
10.1.1.0/24
```

```
Routing Information Sources:
Gateway Distance Last Update
10.1.0.2 90 23:19:26
10.0.0.5 90 23:19:26
Distance: internal 90 external 170
```

As shown in the output, when EIGRP is running, the `show ip protocols` command output displays any routing filtering occurring on EIGRP outbound or inbound updates. It also identifies whether EIGRP is generating a default network or receiving a default network in EIGRP updates.

The command output provides information about additional default settings for EIGRP, such as default K values, hop count, and variance.

 Because the routers must have identical K values for EIGRP to establish an adjacency, the `show ip protocols` command helps to determine the current K value setting before an adjacency is attempted.

This sample output also indicates that automatic summarization is enabled (this is the default) and that the router is allowed to load balance over a maximum of four paths. (Cisco IOS software allows configuration of up to six paths for equal-cost load balancing, using the `maximum-path` command.)

The networks for which the router is routing are also displayed. As shown in the figure, the format of the output varies, depending on the use of the wildcard mask in the `network` command. If a wildcard mask is used, the network address is displayed with a prefix length. If a wildcard mask is not used, the Class A, B, or C major network is displayed.

The routing information sources portion of this command output identifies all other routers that have an EIGRP neighbor relationship with this router. The `show ip eigrp neighbors` command provides a detailed display of EIGRP neighbors.

The `show ip protocols` command output also provides the two administrative distances. First, an administrative distance of 90 applies to networks from other routers inside the AS; these are considered internal networks. Second, an administrative distance of 170 applies to networks introduced to EIGRP for this AS through redistribution; these are called external networks.

show ip eigrp interfaces

The `show ip eigrp interfaces` command displays information about interfaces configured for EIGRP.

```
Router1#show ip eigrp interfaces
IP-EIGRP interfaces for process 65000
Xmit Queue Mean Pacing Time Multicast Pending
Interface Peers Un/Reliable SRTT Un/Reliable Flow Timer Routes
Fa0/0 1 0/0 49 0/1 248 0
```

```
Fa0/1 1 0/0 1 0/1 50 0
L00 0 0/0 0 0/1 0 0
```

Table 5.6 describes the key elements from the output.

TABLE 5.6   `show ip eigrp interfaces`

Column	Description
Interface	Interface over which EIGRP is configured
Peers	Number of directly connected EIGRP neighbors
Xmit Queue Un/Reliable	Number of packets remaining in the unreliable and reliable transmit queues
Mean SRTT	Mean SRTT interval, in milliseconds
Pacing Time Un/Reliable	Pacing time used to determine when EIGRP packets should be sent out of the interface (unreliable and reliable packets)
Multicast Flow Timer	Maximum number of seconds in which the router will send multicast EIGRP packets
Pending Routes	Number of routes in the packets in the transmit queue waiting to be sent

show ip eigrp traffic

The `show ip eigrp traffic` command displays statistics about each of the types of messages that are sent and the number of them that have been sent and received.

```
Router1#show ip eigrp traffic
IP-EIGRP Traffic Statistics for AS 65000
Hellos sent/received: 81853/65407
Updates sent/received: 30/31
Queries sent/received: 2/6
Replies sent/received: 6/2
Acks sent/received: 33/30
Input queue high water mark 2, 0 drops
SIA-Queries sent/received: 0/0
SIA-Replies sent/received: 0/0
Hello Process ID: 164
PDM Process ID: 162
```

Summary

I have covered quite a few things in this chapter. You saw the Cisco-proprietary routing protocol EIGRP. EIGRP is an advanced distance vector protocol. I described many of the terms that are essential to full understanding of how EIGRP operates.

I showed you the tables and information stored in them that EIGRP uses to build the routing table and provide a router with the information it needs to forward traffic. I also gave you the breakdown of what values EIGRP uses for its composite metric. You can change those values but you have to be careful doing it!

I then went through the configuration of EIGRP and through the advanced features of EIGRP. There you learned how to limit the query scope with summarization and stub routers. I also showed you how to configure unequal-cost load balancing with the `variance` command. The last of the advanced features was how to configure routing over different kinds of WAN setups.

Finally, I showed you the commands to allow you to verify and troubleshoot the operation of EIGRP. There is a command to let you see all the information from each of the three tables—all of which are very valuable to you.

In the next chapter, you finally get to see how to route out of the AS and communicate with the ISP. Chapter 6 covers how and why you will be using BGP in an enterprise network.

Review Questions

1. What algorithm does EIGRP use to provide a loop-free network and fast convergence?
    A. Bellman Ford
    B. Dijkstra
    C. DUAL
    D. Shortest path first

2. What two values by default are used by EIGRP for its composite metric?
    A. Load
    B. Bandwidth
    C. MTU
    D. Delay

3. EIGRP uses multicast for the hello protocol to establish neighbor relationships?
    A. True
    B. False

4. What best describes a feasible successor?
    A. Primary route
    B. Shortest route
    C. Backup route
    D. Default route

5. What transport layer protocol does EIGRP use for its messages?
    A. UDP
    B. TCP
    C. RTP
    D. ICMP

6. What command allows EIGRP to perform classless summarization? (Choose two.)
    A. `router eigrp`
    B. `network`
    C. `no auto-summary`
    D. `ip subnet-zero`

7. What protocol is considered an advanced distance vector protocol?

    A. IS-IS

    B. OSPF

    C. EIGRP

    D. RIPv1

8. What command does EIGRP use to create a manual summary address on an interface?

    A. `summary-address`

    B. `ip summary-address eigrp AS# network mask`

    C. `aggregate-address`

    D. `area range`

9. What feature allows EIGRP to limit its query scope?

    A. Network

    B. Default route

    C. Stub router

    D. Neighbor

10. What feature allows EIGRP to perform unequal-cost load balancing across multiple paths?

    A. Variance

    B. Debug

    C. Stub

    D. Summarization

Answers to Review Questions

1. C. The Diffused Update ALgorithm (DUAL) is the algorithm that EIGRP uses.

2. B and D. The values used for the metric are bandwidth and delay.

3. A. True. EIGRP uses multicast for the hello protocol.

4. C. A feasible successor is best described as a backup route that can automatically replace the successor when lost.

5. C. RTP is the transport layer protocol used.

6. C. The `no auto-summary` command is used to allow for classless routes.

7. C. EIGRP is the protocol that is considered to be an advanced distance vector protocol.

8. B. The `ip summary-address eigrp AS# network mask` command is used to create a manual summary route.

9. C. The stub router feature allows EIGRP to limit its query scope.

10. A. The variance feature allows EIGRP to perform unequal-cost load balancing.

Chapter

6

Link State Routing Protocols

IN THIS CHAPTER, YOU WILL LEARN HOW TO DO THE FOLLOWING:

✓ Explain the functions and operation of link state routing protocols

✓ Explain the functions and operations of OSPF and multi-area OSPF

✓ Configure OSPF and multiarea OSPF routing, including stub, totally stubby, and NSSA

✓ Verify or troubleshoot OSPF and multiarea OSPF routing configurations

✓ Describe the features and benefits of integrated IS-IS

✓ Configure and verify integrated IS-IS

This chapter is a link state festival. I start with some basic open shortest path first (OSPF) discussion and configuration that reviews some of what you learned in CCNA studies. I then move into the advanced features of OSPF. You will learn about message types, router relationships and communication, multiarea OSPF, and how OSPF areas pass routing information back and forth. You will also gain an understanding of all the stub area types can be used in OSPF. Once done with OSPF I take you through the basics of IS-IS, including the benefits and drawbacks of using it. Additionally, I cover the routing levels, router interaction, and how IS-IS compares to OSPF in use and function.

For up-to-the-minute updates on this chapter, check out www.sybex.com/ go/CiscoProGuidetoInternetworking or www.lammle.com.

Introduction to Link State Protocols

Open shortest path first (OSPF) is extremely versatile. It is one of the most widely used open standard IP routing protocols today. Open standard means that any vendor can use the protocol, and most vendors do provide some level of support for open standard protocols. Both enterprise and service provider networks use, and benefit from, OSPF.

IS-IS is the other link state protocol; it is an OSI standard protocol. IS-IS is widely used in service provider networks. I discuss IS-IS later in this chapter.

I describe link state routing protocols and discuss the primary characteristics of the OSPF routing protocol, including the OSPF hierarchical structure, link state adjacencies, shortest path first (SPF) calculations, and how OSPF verifies that its links are still in an active state. I finish the chapter with information about IS-IS.

Link State Protocol Improvements

Distance vector routing protocols have limitations that prevent them from being used in all situations. You will recall some of the limitations in distance vector protocols:

- Hop count limits the size of the network.

- Broadcasting the entire routing table uses a lot of bandwidth.

- Limited knowledge of the network slows convergence and inhibits speedy routing decisions.
- Classful protocols don't allow the use of VLSM, discontiguous networks, or manual summarization.

These limitations forced the need to create and develop a better breed of protocols. The product of that work was link state routing protocols. Link state routing protocols have the following characteristics and benefits:

- Have no hop count limit.
- Respond quickly to network changes.
- Send triggered updates when a network change occurs.
- Send periodic updates, known as link state refresh, at long intervals, such as every 30 minutes.
- Classless protocols allow for the use of VLSM, discontiguous networks, and manual summarization.

OSPF

As with any new protocol or feature, a bunch of new terms and acronyms can make learning difficult. This is why when I teach a class of new students I start with good study techniques. One of the first things that I suggest is to make a vocabulary list or flash cards. Because there are so many terms in OSPF, I am giving you a couple of lists of OSPF terms in Table 6.1 and Table 6.2.

TABLE 6.1 OSPF Terms

Term	Description
Link	In OSPF, a link is considered an interface. Everything in OSPF is configured and thought about from the interface level.
State	State is defined by the physical condition of the interface. All updates and information are sent out based on this condition.
Neighbor	An OSPF neighbor router is a router that is connected to the same physical medium as the local router. Hello messages can be exchanged between these routers.
Adjacent Router	An OSPF adjacent router can share routing updates with the local router. Each router must send a Hello message back and forth to establish bidirectional communication and allow an adjacency to be formed.

TABLE 6.1 OSPF Terms *(continued)*

Term	Description
Area	An area is a collection of OSPF routers that share the same link state database. The area boundary serves as the limit for how far routing data will be propagated through the network.
Area Designation	Area designations are seen most of the time as a single truncated number, such as 0 or 1. However, this area ID is actually formatted like a 32-bit IPv4 address. For example area 0, the backbone area, is actually area 0.0.0.0. You can use this format to your advantage by identifying the area with the address space that is represented within it. For instance, if you have a switch block where all of the subnets within it were summarized to 10.1.1.0, you can give the area for this switch block an area ID of 10.1.1.0.
Backbone Area	Every OSPF network must have a backbone area. In OSPF, the backbone area must be designated as area 0. This backbone area is often called a transit area because, in a well-designed network, traffic typically just passes across this area. Almost all of the traffic passes across this network because, in a multiarea network, all other areas must be directly connected to the backbone area. This basically creates a two-layer hierarchy in the routing network. As I tell you more about update types you will understand that almost all updates types are allowed in the backbone area, as well as standard areas.
Standard Area	A standard area is usually used as a populated area, which means that there are subnets with hosts and end stations on them. This type of area will typically be used for the subnets located in a switch block or branch office. This type of area can be designated as anything other than area 0.
Stub Area	There are a handful of different kinds of stub areas that meet a variety of needs or uses. Regardless of the type of stub area, the primary goal is to reduce the size of the routing table.

The next few terms (router names) are ways to describe a router by its location or purpose in the network. They are not settings that are configured, but they provide a way for you and other engineers communicate and to describe and reference a specific router. A router in an OSPF system will often be identified by more than one of these names. For example, a backbone router is often an area border router as well. That will make more sense here in just a couple of paragraphs. Table 6.2 provides a listing of the router names and a description of the location within the system.

TABLE 6.2   OSPF Router Terms

Term	Description
Backbone Router	A router that has at least one interface located in the backbone area.
Area Border Router (ABR)	A router that connects multiple areas (in the same routing domain or AS) together to share routing information. It is defined as having at least one interface in more than one area. Manual summarization for an area is typically done on this router.
Autonomous System Boundary Router (ASBR)	A router that connects the local OSPF routing domain to another routing domain or protocol. It is defined as having at least one interface in separate routing domains. Some types of stub areas do not allow an ASBR.
Internal Router	A router that has all of its interfaces in the same area.
Router Identity (RID)	The identifier used to distinguish between routers. This determination might be used for an instance between routers on the same broadcast network. All of the routers on the broadcast segment would compare RID values to see which router will be the designated router (DR) and control the routing updates for the network.
Designated Router (DR)	A router that is elected for each broadcast or non-broadcast multi-access (NBMA) network. DRs limit the number of update messages that have to be transmitted by controlling the number of adjacent routers on the network.
Backup Designated Router (BDR)	As its name implies, this is the backup for the DR. The BDR has the same goal as the DR, but it will only take the job when the DR goes down. There is no preempting in OSPF, so even if a new router were to come online on the network that had a better RID it would not take over for the DR until it were to go down.

OSPF Tables

OSPF stores and updates information in tables, in a way that is very similar to EIGRP. In fact, EIGRP really took the idea from link state protocols. OSPF has very similar tables; they are the neighbor table, the link state database (topology table), and the routing table. Table 6.3 describes each of the OSPF tables.

TABLE 6.3   OSPF Table Descriptions

Table	Description
Neighbor Table	Stores a list of all the directly connected routers to the local router. It will show you the state of each router the local router has with it. The neighbor table is populated through the use of Hello packets.
Link State Database (LSDB)	Sometimes known as the topology table, but that is a bleed over from the term used with EIGRP. The LSDB stores all the network information for the internetwork or area in which the router is located. If there is only one area, then the router knows about the entire internetwork. If there are multiple areas in the AS, then each router knows about all of the routers and networks for that area.
	This information is all of the raw data for those routers and networks. There is no calculated data transmitted from one neighbor router to another. The routing information is propagated from router to router in link state update (LSU) packets and within those packets are different kinds of link state advertisements (LSA). I discuss the different types of LSAs and their uses in a bit.
Routing Table	Holds all of the best routes to each destination network. The shortest path first algorithm (derived from the Dijkstra algorithm) runs on all of the data is the LSDB and finds the best path for each destination.

OSPF Packet Types

OSPF uses five different packet types or message types to communicate its information between routers. All five OSPF packets are encapsulated directly into an IP payload. OSPF packets don't use TCP or UDP. However, OSPF does require reliable packet transmission. Since TCP is not used, OSPF has defined its own acknowledgment system using a specifically defined acknowledgment packet (OSPF packet type 5). I discuss each of the types of packets.

In the IP header of all OSPF packets, a protocol identifier of 89 is used and defines the packet as an OSPF packet. Each of the OSPF packets begins with the same header format. Table 6.4 lists the header fields.

TABLE 6.4   OSPF IP Header Fields

Field	Description
Version number	For OSPF version 2
Type	Differentiates the five OSPF packet types
Packet length	Length of OSPF packet in bytes

TABLE 6.4 OSPF IP Header Fields *(continued)*

Field	Description
Router ID	Defines which router is the source of the packet
Area ID	Defines the area where the packet originated
Checksum	Used for packet-header error detection to ensure that the OSPF packet was not corrupted during transmission
Authentication type	An option in OSPF that describes either no authentication, cleartext passwords, or encrypted Message Digest 5 (MD5) formats for router authentication
Authentication	Used in authentication scheme
Data (for hello packet)	Includes a list of known neighbors
Data (for database descriptor DBD packet)	Contains a summary of the link state database (LSDB), which includes all known router IDs and their last sequence number, among a number of other fields
Data (for LSR packet)	Contains the type of LSU needed and the router ID that has the needed LSU
Data (for LSU packet)	Contains the full link state advertisement (LSA) entries; multiple LSA entries can fit in one OSPF update packet
Data (for LSAck packet)	Is empty

All five packet types are used in the normal operation of OSPF. Table 6.5 contains descriptions of each type of packet.

TABLE 6.5 OSPF Packet Types

Type (number)	Packet Name	Description
1	Hello	Discovers neighbors and builds adjacencies between each router
2	DBD	Checks for database synchronization between routers

TABLE 6.5   OSPF Packet Types *(continued)*

Type (number)	Packet Name	Description
3	LSR	Requests specific link state records from router to router
4	LSU	Sends specifically requested link state records; records are sent as link state advertisements (LSA)
5	LSAck	Acknowledges the other packet types

Link State Advertisements (LSA)

There are many different types of link state advertisements (LSAs) and each of them has their specific uses. Table 6.6 describes the most common LSA types.

TABLE 6.6   LSA Types

Type (number)	Name	Description
1	Router link advertisements	Generated by each router for each area it belongs to. Flooded to a single area only.
2	Network link advertisements	Generated by designated routers describing the set of routers attached to a particular network. Flooded to the area that contains the network.
3	Summary link advertisements	Generated by ABRs describing inter-area routes. Describes routes to networks and is used for summarization.
4	Summary link advertisements	Generated by ABRs describing inter-area routes. Describes routes to the ASBR.
5	Links external to the autonomous system (AS)	Generated by the ASBR and describes links external to the autonomous system (AS). Flooded to all areas except stub areas.
6	Multicast	Specialized LSAs that are used in multicast OSPF applications.

TABLE 6.6   LSA Types *(continued)*

Type (number)	Name	Description
7	NSSA external routes	NSSA external routes generated by ASBR. Only flooded to the NSSA. The ABR converts LSA type 7 into LSA type 5 before flooding them into the backbone (area 0).
8	BGP	Specialized LSA that is used in internetworking OSPF and Border Gateway Protocol (BGP).
9	The opaque LSAs, types 9, 10, and 11, are designated for upgrades to OSPF for application-specific purposes. For example, OSPF-TE has traffic engineering extensions to be used by RSVP-TE in Multi-protocol Label Switching (MPLS). Opaque LSAs are used to flood link color and bandwidth information. Standard LSDB flooding mechanisms are used for distribution of opaque LSAs.	Denotes a link-local scope. Type-9 Opaque LSAs are not flooded beyond the local subnetwork.
10		Denotes an area-local scope. Type-10 Opaque LSAs are not flooded beyond the borders of their associated area.
11		Denotes that the LSA is flooded throughout the Autonomous System (AS). The flooding scope of type-11 LSAs are equivalent to the flooding scope of AS-external (type-5) LSAs. Specifically type-11 Opaque LSAs are 1. Flooded throughout all transit areas 2. Not flooded into stub areas from the backbone 3. Not originated by routers into their connected stub areas As with type-5 LSAs, if a type-11 Opaque LSA is received in a stub area from a neighboring router within the stub area the LSA is rejected.

OSPF Operation

Routers running the OSPF routing protocol must first establish neighbor adjacencies with its neighbor routers. Routers go through the neighbor adjacency process by exchanging Hello packets with neighboring routers. The following is an overview, to get the discussion going about OSPF operation; I describe each part of the process in much more detail as you move through this section.

1. The first thing that must happen is neighbor discovery.

    A router sends and receives Hello packets to and from its neighboring routers. The destination address that is typically used is a multicast address. The routers exchange Hello packets and must adhere to some protocol-specific parameters. For OSPF, those parameters are checking whether the neighbor is in the same AS and area. Routers can consider the neighbor up when this exchange is complete.

2. For a broadcast network like Ethernet, a DR/BDR election will occur so that all the other routers can form adjacencies with the DR routers.

3. Once two routers establish their neighbor adjacency using Hello packets, the next step is to synchronize their LSDBs.

    This is accomplished by exchanging LSAs and acknowledging the receipt of all LSAs from adjacent routers. The two neighbor routers then recognize that they have synchronized their LSDBs with each other.

    For OSPF, the routers are now in full adjacency state with each other. If necessary, the routers forward any new LSAs to other neighboring routers, ensuring complete synchronization of link state information inside the area.

4. Once all of the routers LSDB have been updated and are synchronized, the Dijkstra algorithm is run against the data. The best route for each of the destination networks will be placed into the routing table.

5. If there is any change to the network, such as a network or router being added or removed, then a new LSA must be made and propagated throughout the network to update all routers of the change.

Neighbor Discovery

OSPF bases its operation and functions from the interface (link) level. There must be at least one configured and active interface in order to start an OSPF process on a router. Once the process is started and the interface is placed into the OSPF process, generally done with the network command, then the router can begin to communicate to other routers. Every interface that participates in OSPF process will use the IP multicast address 224.0.0.5 to send Hello packets. The interval in which the Hellos are sent depends on the link type, but the Hellos are sent periodically based on the Hello interval. Table 6.7 describes the information contained in a Hello packet.

 If a DR and BDR have been selected for the network, any router added to the network will establish adjacencies with the DR and BDR only. I discuss the DR election process a little later in this chapter.

TABLE 6.7 Hello Packets

Field	Description
Router ID	The router ID is a 32-bit number that uniquely identifies the router. The highest IP address on an active interface is chosen by default, unless a loopback interface or the router-ID command is configured. For example, the IP address 192.168.15.1 would be chosen over 192.168.1.1.
	This identification is important and is the basis for establishing neighbor relationships and coordinating LSU exchanges. Also, note that the router ID breaks ties during the designated router (DR) and backup designated router (BDR) selection processes when the OSPF priority values are equal.
Hello and dead intervals	The Hello interval specifies the frequency, in seconds, at which a router sends out Hello packets. Ten seconds is the default on a multi-access networks.
	The dead interval is the time, in seconds, that a router waits to hear from a neighbor before declaring the neighboring router dead or out of communication. The dead interval is four times the Hello interval by default.
	These timers must be the same for neighboring routers; if they are not the same then an adjacency will not be formed.
Neighbors	The neighbors field lists the adjacent routers that have established bidirectional communication. This bidirectional communication is confirmed when the local router recognizes or sees itself listed in the neighbors field of a Hello packet sent from the neighbor router.
Area ID	To communicate, two routers must share a common segment and their interfaces must belong to the same OSPF area on that segment. They must also share the same subnet and mask.
	Routers with the same Area ID will all have the same link state information.
Router priority	The router priority is an 8-bit number that indicates the priority of a router. Priority is used when selecting a DR and BDR.
DR and BDR IP addresses	This field contains the IP addresses of the DR and BDR for the specific network, if they are known.
Authentication password	If router authentication is enabled, the routers must exchange this password.
	Authentication is not required, but if it is enabled, all peer routers must have the same password.
Stub area flag	A stub area is a special area. Two routers must agree on the stub area flag in the Hello packets. Designating a stub area is a technique that reduces routing updates by replacing them with a default route.

🌐 Real World Scenario

Bringing Up a New Manufacturing Line

The Bangalore plant is expanding and adding a whole new building and a significant amount of staff. The addition is happening so that an assembly and test line can be established for the new Super Widget XT line of devices. All of the new machines and people, including the supervisor, assemblers, and test tech workstations, will have to be hooked into the network. The small plant in Bangalore produced only a few product lines. Now with this expansion, the size of the plant (and the network) will quadruple.

The existing network runs RIP; it has been that way since the plant was acquired. Because the network is going to be so much larger, FutureTech has decided to configure and run OSPF at the plant. You would like to run the same routing protocol as the Dallas headquarters (EIGRP), but many of the routers in the plant are not Cisco and cost prohibits upgrading all of them at this time. So, the plant will run OSPF until all of the old devices can be upgraded. The upgrades are scheduled over the next 18–24 months. FutureTech will then evaluate cutting the network over to EIGRP.

You have been assigned to set up four routers so that you can begin to test out OSPF at the plant. Begin with these and explore the Hello or discovery process.

When routers running an OSPF process come up, an exchange process using the Hello protocol is the first thing that must happen. The exchange process is illustrated in the following steps and in Figure 6.1:

1.   BangRtr1 is enabled on the LAN and is in a down state because it has not exchanged information with any other router. It begins by sending a Hello packet through each of its interfaces participating in OSPF, even though it does not know the identity of the DR or of any other routers. The Hello packet is sent out using the multicast address 224.0.0.5.

2.   All directly connected routers (BangRtr2, BangRtr3, and BangRtr4 in the example) running OSPF receive the Hello packet from BangRtr1 and add BangRtr1 to their list of neighbors. This state is the initial state (init).

3.   BangRtr2, BangRtr3, and BangRtr4, which received the Hello packet, send a unicast reply Hello packet to BangRtr1 with their corresponding information. The neighbor field in the Hello packet includes all neighboring routers and BangRtr1.

4.   When BangRtr1 receives these Hello packets, it adds all the routers that had its router ID in their Hello packets to its own neighbor relationship database. This state is referred to as the two-way state. At this point, all routers that have each other in their neighbor lists have established bidirectional communication.

5. If the link type is a broadcast network, generally a LAN link like Ethernet, then a DR and BDR must first be selected. The DR forms bidirectional adjacencies with all other routers on the LAN link. This process must occur before the routers can begin exchanging link state information. I go through this full process of the DR election in the section, "Designated Router (DR) Elections."

6. Periodically (every 10 seconds by default on broadcast networks), the routers within a network exchange Hello packets to ensure that communication is still working. The Hello updates include the DR, BDR, and the list of routers whose Hello packets have been received by the router. Remember that received means that the receiving router recognizes its name as one of the entries in the received Hello packet.

FIGURE 6.1 Initial Hello Exchange

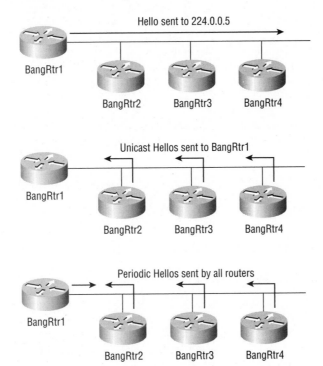

BangRtr4Router Identity (RID)

Before I move into the next major step, which is building the link state database (LSDB), I have to go over a couple of other things. I briefly described the fact that OSPF routers, when connected to a multi-access network, will elect a designated router and a backup designated router. I discuss why they are elected in the next section, but for now I have to tell you about router identities (RID). It is very important to understand what an RID is before you attempt to understand how the DR election process works.

Every OSPF router must determine for itself what its RID will be. Now by default, as soon as you enable the OSPF process on a router, the router will select its RID. The RID is actually a 32-bit number, and it is written just like an IP address. In fact, it is almost always an IP address that is assigned to the router. The RID can be determined in three ways for a router. The process that follows show what a router will do to determine its RID.

1. If the `router-id` command has been configured, then the number assigned using that command will be used first as the RID.

2. If the `router-id` command is not configured but there is a logical interface enabled on the router (there is a loopback interface), then the IP address on that interface will be used as the RID. If there is more than one loopback interface, then the highest IP address among all the loopbacks will be used.

3. If the `router-id` command is not configured and there is no loopback interface configured, then the router will use the highest IP address from an active physical interface.

There is a little trick to how this works though. If you don't configure these things in the proper order, you may not see the output that you expect. Let me explain.

If you enable the OSPF process on a router and don't enable the `router-id` command first or have a loopback interface configured, then the router immediately sets the RID to the highest active interface IP address. This is okay; you can still set the RID with the `router-id` command or configure a loopback interface, but if you configure one of those things after the router has set the RID, the router will not automatically change over to that new RID value that you want.

Never fear—there is a way to do this. You have to restart that OSPF process or reload the entire router. Typically, it will be much less intrusive to restart the OSPF process, especially since you are probably still configuring the protocol on the router. Also, it is more than possible that another process or feature running on the router would prevent you from reloading the entire router.

Designated Router (DR) Elections

In multi-access environments, every router has the ability to communicate directly with every other router. This arrangement is good for having available paths through the network and possible routes to use. However, when you examine the Hello process, if updates were allowed to go unchecked in that same environment, there would be a considerably higher amount of traffic generated. Many of the advantages of link state would be lost. Let's look at an example of what I mean.

1. Let's say BangRtr1 has an update to send out. It will send it to all of its adjacent routers. In this case is will go to BangRtr2, BangRtr3, and BangRtr4.

2. When BangRtr2 receives the update, it will, in turn, send the update to all of its adjacent routers.

3. When BangRtr3 receives the update, it will, in turn, send the update to all of its adjacent routers.

4. When BangRtr4 receives the update, it will, in turn, send the update to all of its adjacent routers.

5. Now, replies have to be sent by each router to every other router acknowledging each of the updates.

 Real World Scenario

Pre-cutover Testing in Bangalore

Before you cut over everything in the Bangalore plant, you have been asked to test the new equipment, make sure that all of the devices are talking, and make sure that you understand the interaction between the routers. You have four routers to work with. BangRtr1 will be your core router and the other three will be the distribution layer routers. As you go through the DR election process within this setup, you can accomplish two things: you can test the equipment and make sure you understand the elections.

Think about the core of the network and all of the distribution layer routers connecting to the core. In Figure 6.2, you can see the four routers running OSPF. BangRtr1 is the core layer router, and BangRtr2, BangRtr3, and BangRtr4 are distribution layer routers connecting to that portion of the network. All four of the routers are connected via a Gigabit Ethernet network that is a broadcast medium. Unless you do something, nothing in the network to control or limit the routers will become adjacent and, therefore, no control over how many updates will be sent or to which routers.

FIGURE 6.2   Sending an Update with no DR

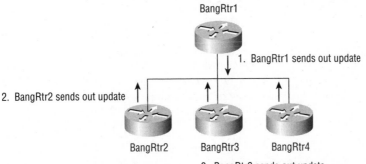

You can see that a huge number of updates are sent, just because one little update needed to be propagated. This should almost remind you of the broadcast method that distance vector protocols use. Not very efficient!

Now, let's look at this process after a DR has been elected. I'll skip the details—BangRtr3 has been elected as the DR and BangRtr4 had been elected as the BDR. With a DR and BDR on the network, all of the other routers (in this case it is only Routers A and B, but it could be any number of additional routers) will only create adjacencies with the DR. Each of the other routers does form an adjacency with the BDR, but this is for backup purposes only. As long as the DR does its job, the BDR will remain silent and only update itself. Let's look at this process step by step. You can see how the process works in Figure 6.3.

FIGURE 6.3   Sending an Update with a DR

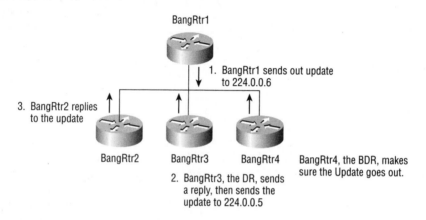

1. BangRtr1 again has an update to send out. BangRtr1 is only adjacent with the DR and BDR. To ensure that only they get the update and to make the process more efficient, the DR and BDR are listening for updates on a separate multicast address 224.0.0.6. So, BangRtr1 sends its update to the address of 224.0.0.6 and only the DR and BDR get the update.

2. The DR would then reply to BangRtr1 that it received the update.

3. It is now the job of the DR to send out the update to all of its adjacent routers. In this case, that is all of the other routers that are on the network since all the other routers are only adjacent with the DR routers. The DR is now going to send out the update using the multicast address 224.0.0.5. All of the other routers will be listening on this address even the DR and BDR. This allows the BDR to make sure that the DR is doing its job.

4. All of the other routers (in this case just BangRtr2) would reply to the DR that they have the update.

Now that you understand why the DR and BDR are in place, I need to tell you how they are put into place. Really, it comes down to how the election process occurs. In the last section, I told you how each of the routers in an OSPF network found their RID. That could, and in most networks would, be important for this process.

When OSPF routers come up on a broadcast network, just like the one in the last example, they have a DR election. During the Hello process, each of the routers sends a Hello and replies to Hellos so that two-way communication is established. Once communication is established, each of the routers inspects the Hello packets of their neighboring routers. The first look is at the priority field of each router. The priority is the first value that will be used to determine which routers will be the DR and the BDR. The router with the highest priority will become the DR and the router with the second highest priority will be the BDR.

Now, the gotcha to this step is that by default the priority is the same for every router—a default value of 1. If you want to set the DR and BDR, meaning that you want to decide which routers on your network will take those roles, then you would have to manually set the priority values. You can do it this way, but it is a manual process that requires you to set the priority value on each router. The drawback to doing this is that all of the work in setting the priority value does nothing else for you. The priority value is only used for this one process.

Why is that a big deal? Well, because the recommended way to set which router will be the DR is still a manual one, but using another value will be useful for other things.

So, "what is this other way?" you ask.

Set a loopback address on each or your routers!

I know. I can hear you saying, "Huh?"

You are going to configure a loopback interface on each of your routers because you are going to determine the RID that way.

The RID is used as the tiebreaker for the DR election when all the routers have the same priority value. By default, all the routers are going to have the same priority. After the priority value, then each router compares all of the RID values for every other router. The router with the highest RID will be the DR and the router with the second highest RID will be the BDR.

I want to take you through a quick example to illustrate this process. Remember each router is going to determine its own RID. If you have a loopback configured on each router and no `router-id` command, then the loopback address is going to be the RID.

Look at Figure 6.4. You can see I have used the same network from previous examples, but now there are Lo0 interfaces defined.

FIGURE 6.4   Determining the DR with Loopbacks

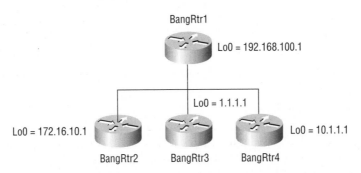

Now, assuming that all other values have been left as the default, which one of the routers is going to be the DR? Which router is going to be the BDR? When the comparison is done, the election process simply looks at each number, not the class of address or anything else, just the number. For this example, you don't have to go past the first octet in the addresses. There is a 1, 10, 172, and 192. In this case, BangRtr1 with a 192 will become the DR, and BangRtr2 with a 172 will become the BDR.

I want to make a couple of things clear here—things that often I hear people get messed up. When you are finding the DR, the election process always looks at the priority first. So, if you have your loopbacks all set up but someone has gone in and raised the priority on one of the routers, the router with the highest priority will become the DR. The process never looks at the RID. The other thing to remember is the order of finding the RID. Often, people want to mix the process of finding the RID and finding the DR. I have seen people thinking all sorts of things, such as trying to use the physical addresses that are on the broadcast network itself or not looking at the loopback. Just follow each process separately and in the correct order and you will get it.

One other thing of note about the DR and BDR election process. Once the election has occurred and the DR is set, there is no preempting. Once the election is done, if you go in and try to raise the priority or reset a loopback address, the election will not rerun. The only way to get a new DR is to bring the elected DR down and make the other routers think it failed. Now, if you only bring down the DR, the BDR automatically takes its place and a new BDR is elected. So, if you don't want either the current DR and BDR to be in those positions, then you have to bring them both down.

The Link State Database

Just to recap the process up to this point. You know that neighbor OSPF routers must recognize each other on the network before they can share information because OSPF routing depends on the status of the link between two routers. I discussed this process and the fact that it is done using the Hello protocol. The Hello protocol establishes and maintains neighbor relationships by ensuring bidirectional (two-way) communication between neighbors. Bidirectional communication occurs when a router recognizes itself listed in the Hello packet received from a neighbor. That information is stored and updated in the neighbor table.

Creating an LSDB

After the DR and BDR have been selected (if they are to be), the routers are considered to be in the exstart state. They are ready to discover the link state information about the internetwork and create their link state databases (LSDBs). The process used by the routers to discover the routing information is called the exchange protocol. This process moves the routers to a full state of communication, where *full* describes the fact that each router has all of the routes for the routing area.

The first step in this process is for the DR and BDR to establish adjacencies with each of the other routers. Once all of the routers are in a full state, they do not have to go through the exchange protocol unless there is a change to routing information.

1. In the exstart state, the DR and BDR establish adjacencies with each router in the net-work. During this process, a master-slave relationship is created between each router and its adjacent DR and BDR. The router with the higher RID acts as the master during the exchange process.

> In a relationship between two routers where there is a DR, the DR is going to always win the master-slave relationship. It won the role of DR because it had the highest RID on the network. In situations where there is no DR, which on non-broadcast media is default, there is still a master-slave rela-tionship formed.

2. The master and slave routers exchange one or more DBD packets. The routers are in the exchange state.

The DBD packets contain information about the LSA entry headers. This is a representa-tion of the information that is in the LSDB for that router. These entries are not the actual routing data, but a description of that data. The listing is known to that router and can represent a link or a network. Each LSA entry header includes this information:

- Link state type
- Address of the advertising router
- Cost of the link
- Sequence number

The sequence number is used to figure out how old the link state information is.

Processing DBD Information

When a router receives a DBD, it must process the information. Here is a basic run down of that process:

1. The receiving router must acknowledge receiving the DBD by using the LSAck packet.
2. It compares the information it received with the information it has. If the DBD has a newer link state entry than the router currently holds, then the router must request the data by sending an LSR to the router with the newer link state entry. The process of sending LSRs is called the loading state.
3. The router with the newer link state entry then sends back the complete information about the requested entry in an LSU packet. Again, when the router receives an LSU, it sends an LSAck.
4. Finally, the receiving router can add the new link state entries to its LSDB, which brings it up to date.
5. When all LSRs have a response and are updated for a given router, the adjacent routers are considered synchronized and in a full state.

The routers must be in a full state before they can route traffic. At this point all the routers in the area should have identical LSDBs.

Change Process

In an OSPF network, or any link state routing environment for that matter, it is extremely important for the LSDBs for all routers to be synchronized (meaning they are up to date and the same). If a change to the link state occurs, the routers notify every other router using a flooding process. LSUs are the mechanism used for flooding LSAs.

I described the basic update process in the DR election discussion. You will see the flooding process steps for a multi-access network are basically the same.

1. When any router notices a change to that link state, it must multicast an LSU packet that includes the updated LSA entry to all OSPF DRs and BDRs. It does this by sending the LSU to 224.0.0.6. A single LSU packet can contain many individual LSAs.

2. The DR acknowledges receipt of the change and floods the LSU to all the other routers on its network using the OSPF multicast address 224.0.0.5. After receiving the LSU, each router responds to the DR with an LSAck. To make the flooding procedure reliable, each LSA must be acknowledged separately.

3. If a router is connected to other networks, it floods the LSU to those networks as well by forwarding the LSU to the DR of the multi-access network (or to the adjacent router if it is in a point-to-point network). The DR on that network, in turn, multicasts the LSU to the other routers on that network.

4. The router updates its LSDB using the LSU that includes the changed LSA. It then computes the route using the shortest path first (SPF) algorithm against the updated database. After the SPF delay, the process updates the routing table as necessary.

When each router receives the LSU, it does the following:

1. If the LSA does not already exist, the router adds the entry to its LSDB, sends a link state acknowledgment (LSAck) back, floods the information to other routers, runs SPF, and updates its routing table.

2. If the entry already exists and the received LSA has the same sequence number, the router ignores the LSA entry.

3. If the entry already exists but the LSA includes newer information (it has a higher sequence number), the router adds the entry to its LSDB, sends an LSAck back, floods the information to other routers, runs SPF, and updates its routing table.

4. If the entry already exists but the LSA includes older information, it sends an LSU to the sender with its newer information.

OSPF simplifies the synchronization issue by requiring only adjacent routers to remain synchronized.

Keeping the LSBD Current

Each LSA entry has its own aging timer, which is carried in the link state age field. The default timer value for OSPF is 30 minutes (expressed in seconds in the link state age field).

When an LSA entry reaches its age value, the router that originated the entry sends the LSA in an LSU. The LSA will have a higher sequence number; this allows the routers to verify that the link is still active. An LSU can again hold more than one LSA. Using this

LSA validation process saves on bandwidth compared to distance vector routers. As I said before, link state protocols don't have to send their entire routing table at short intervals.

These summaries of individual link state entries (not the complete link state entry) are sent every 30 minutes to ensure LSDB is up to date. Each link state entry has a timer to determine when the LSA refresh update must be sent. Every link state entry additionally has a maximum age or lifetime of 60 minutes. If an entry is not refreshed within this 60-minute window, it will be removed from the LSDB.

I want to explain to you now a little more detail about how what values are used to keep the LSDB current. A router uses a combination of these things to help maintain the database:

- Link state sequence numbers
- Maximum age (maxage)
- Refresh timers

With these values, OSPF can maintain a database of only the most recent link state records.

The first value in the list is the link state sequence number field. It is in the LSA header and is 32 bits in length. The value itself begins with the leftmost bit set, so the first valid sequence number is 0x80000001. This value is really like any other sequence or revision number, the higher the number, the more times it has been changed and the newer the information is.

To further ensure the accuracy of the database, OSPF floods (refreshes) each LSA every 30 minutes; this ensures the entry is up to date and that the 60 minute maxage timer is not reached. Every time a record is flooded, the sequence number is incremented by one. An LSA record will reset its maximum age when it receives a new LSA update. Again, an LSA cannot stay in the database longer than the maximum age of one hour without being refreshed.

An LSA can stay in the database in almost indefinitely, as long it is being refreshed every 30 minutes. There is one exception. Eventually, the sequence number will reach its maximum value and have to wrap around to the starting sequence number. When this occurs, the existing LSA will be prematurely aged out. That means that the maxage timer will be immediately set to one hour and the LSA flushed. The LSA will then begin all over again with its sequence number at 0x80000001.

The Routing Table

You have now learned that OSPF only generates and sends routing updates when there is a change in the network topology. When a link changes state, the device that detected the change creates a link state advertisement (LSA) for that link.

The LSA propagates to all neighboring devices usually using the multicast address 224.0.0.5. Every router takes a copy of the LSA, updates its link state database (LSDB), and forwards the LSA to all neighboring devices within its network or area. The flooding of the LSA ensures that all routers have their databases updated before modifying the routing table.

The LSDB is used to calculate the best paths through the network. Link state routers find the best paths to a destination network by running Dijkstra's algorithm, also known as SPF, against the data in the LSDB to build the SPF tree. The best path to each destination is then pulled from the SPF tree and placed in the routing table as a route.

I have explained already that link state routing protocols collect routing information from all other routers in the network or area. It is important to understand that each router has its own copy of all the data. Each router then independently calculates its best paths to all destinations in the network using Dijkstra's algorithm. Remember, this is different from distance vector protocols that use precomputed information from a neighbor router.

Incorrect information from any one source router is less likely to cause a problem, because each router maintains its own view of the network. For consistent routing decisions to be made by all the routers in the network, each router must keep a record of the following information.

Its Immediate Neighbor Routers   If the router loses contact with a neighboring router, within a few seconds, it will invalidate all paths through that router and recalculate its paths through the network.

All the Other Routers in the Network or Area and Their Attached Networks   The router recognizes other routers and networks through LSAs.

The Best Paths to Each Destination   Each router independently calculates best paths to each destination in the network using Dijkstra's algorithm. The best paths are then offered to the routing table or forwarding database.

OSPF Cost

By default, OSPF calculates the OSPF metric for an interface according to the inverse bandwidth of the interface. By default on Cisco routers the cost is calculated using the formula (100 Mbps) / (bandwidth in Mbps). To give you an example:

64-kbps link = 100,000,000/64,000 = 1,562 for a metric

T1 link = 100,000,000/1,544,000 = 64 for a metric

However, the cost is calculated based on a maximum bandwidth of 100 Mbps. This would give you a cost of 1; like this:

100Mbps link = 100,000,000/100,000,000 = 1 for a metric

Typically, you will be using the bandwidth of the interface to determine OSPF cost, so you always want to remember to use the `bandwidth value` interface command. If this is not accurately set to the bandwidth of the interface (in kbps) then you can have an incorrect cost value.

To override the default cost, manually define the cost using the `ip ospf cost interface-cost` command set on a per-interface basis. The cost value is an integer from 1 to 65,535. The lower the number, the better and more strongly preferred the link.

If you have faster interfaces such as Gigabit or 10Gigabit, you may want to modify the cost of 1 to a higher bandwidth. If interfaces that are faster than 100Mbps are being used, you should use the `auto-cost reference-bandwidth` *ref-bw* command on all routers in the network to ensure accurate route calculations. The *ref-bw* is a reference bandwidth in megabits per second and ranges from 1 to 4,294,967.

OSPF Features and Benefits

I now go through some of the drawbacks, benefits, and additional features of OSPF. It is important to understand when and when not to use OSPF. Also, I will go over some of the features that didn't fit well into the previous discussion of how OSPF operates.

OSPF Drawbacks

The operation of OSPF has two main drawbacks that you have to consider. The amount of memory resources that are needed to maintain all of the tables represents the first drawback to link state protocols and OSPF. The topology table is the exact same for all OSPF routers in an area and it holds the full amount of information for every router and link in the area. Each router has a full picture of the network topology because of this, but it comes at a price in terms of the amount of memory and processing it takes to maintain all of that information.

The second drawback, and I am sure that you are starting to see this, is the number of options and configurations that can be accomplished in OSPF. I know that I haven't gone over all of the configuration commands yet, but you can see the large number of variables in the protocol.

OSPF Benefits

Using a link state routing protocols has some major benefits, as well. A protocol like OSPF has the ability to scale to huge networks and bring them down to a manageable size. The network can be organized into logical sections, known as areas. The areas within an OSPF network have benefits of their own. Also, the amount of routing data or overhead for an OSPF network is significantly reduced over a distance vector protocol.

I said that an OSPF network can scale to huge networks. This can, in some cases, only be limited by the number of routers that are to communicate with each other. And as I said, one of the drawbacks to OSPF is the amount of memory and processing that is required. This is especially true with a large number of routers. This drawback, however, is combated with the second benefit that I mentioned, which is the logical breakdown of the network into areas. The optimal number of routers per area varies based on factors such as network stability, but in the *Designing Large-Scale IP Internetworks* document, Cisco recommends that there generally be no more than 50 routers per area. That is still a large number of routers for most networks, but many networks are much bigger than that. This is the reason that the routers are assigned areas.

Link state routing protocols can additionally reduce the overhead of the Dijkstra calculations by partitioning the network into areas. The number of routers and LSAs that flood can be limited to the smaller areas. This, in turn, means that the LSDB for an area is much smaller. Ultimately, this allows the Dijkstra calculations to be less intrusive and take much less time. Link state routing protocols utilize a two-layer area hierarchy to connect and control the topology of these areas. I discuss the hierarchy of the areas and how they relate to one another in the coming sections. For now though, here is the basic idea of what the areas are.

Transit Area   An OSPF area whose primary function is the fast and efficient movement of IP packets. Transit areas interconnect with other OSPF area types. Generally, end users are not found within a transit area. OSPF area 0, also known as the backbone area, is by definition a transit area.

Regular Area   An OSPF area whose primary function is to connect users and resources. Usually, regular areas are set up along functional or geographical groupings. By default, a regular area does not allow traffic from another area to use its links to reach other areas. All traffic from other areas must cross a transit area, such as area 0. An area that does not allow traffic to pass through it is known as a regular area, or non-backbone area, and can have a number of subtypes, including standard areas, stub areas, totally stubby areas, and not-so-stubby areas (NSSAs).

OSPF Hierarchy

If you have more than one area in your network, then OSPF requires a two-layer area hierarchy. The underlying physical connections in the network must also map to the two-layer tier design. It must be this way because all of the non-backbone areas must attach directly to area 0. Area 0, which is also called the backbone area, is the core of the design and often the core layer of the network is designated as area 0. The core of the network has all of the physical connections from the switch blocks. In most cases, each of these switch blocks make a perfect representation of a single OSPF area, thereby maintaining the OSPF rule that all other areas must directly connect to area 0. Take a look at Figure 6.5; you can see the basic structure.

FIGURE 6.5   Widget Line OSPF Area Structure

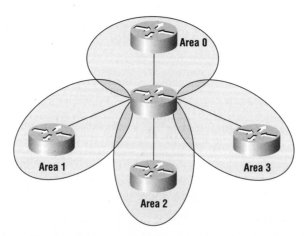

Real World Scenario

Area Design for the Bangalore Plant

In order to keep this very large expansion manageable, the network design calls for you break up the OSPF network into multiple areas. The existing network (the offices, managers, servers and voice/video devices) are assigned to area 0. The old product lines, in the existing manufacturing building, are assigned to area 1. The two new buildings will house the Widget XT product assembly lines and the product test/quality assurance areas. Each of these buildings will be assigned its own area. Test and quality assurance will be assigned area 2 and the production building will be assigned area 3. Figure 6.5 shows the network design.

In Figure 6.5, notice that links between area 1 routers and area 2 or 3 routers are not allowed. Each of the separate areas must connect to area 0, which is a transit area. Traffic that must pass from area 1 to area 2 will transit through area 0 to reach its destination.

All inter-area traffic must pass through the backbone area, area 0.

As I discussed earlier, in link state routing protocols every router keeps a copy of the LSDB, and that link state database is the same and has all the information for the network. The more OSPF routers in a network, the larger the LSDB will be and this kind of design will not scale to large network sizes.

The area structure is therefore a compromise. Routers inside a single area maintain all the detailed information about the routers and links within that area. Only general or summary information about routers and links in other areas is maintained.

When a router or link fails, that information is flooded along adjacencies only to the routers in the local area. Routers outside the area do not receive this information. By maintaining a hierarchical structure and limiting the number of routers in an area, an OSPF autonomous system (AS) can scale to very large sizes.

OSPF Link Types

OSPF defines three types of networks, each of these types of networks can have specific configurations and different operation depending on how the network allows for communication. Here is a basic definition for each type of network as is required for OSPF.

Point-to-Point   A network that connects a single pair of routers.

Broadcast   A multi-access broadcast network, such as an Ethernet network. This type of network can connect any number of routers above just two.

Non-broadcast Multi-access   A network type that connects more than two routers but does not have any broadcast capability. The most common examples of non-broadcast multi-access (NBMA) networks are frame relay, ATM, and X.25. There are five modes of OSPF operation available for NBMA networks.

Let's look at each of the different network types and their operation. I'll start off with point-to-point networks and work through the other two.

Point-to-Point

A point-to-point (PP) network connects a single pair of routers. A T1 serial line or most kinds of dedicated serial connections configured with point-to-point protocol (PPP) or High-Level Data Link Control (HDLC) Layer 2 protocols is an example of a point-to-point network.

On point-to-point networks, the router dynamically finds and creates its neighbor relationship with the other router by multicasting its Hello packets to the all OSPF routers through multicast address 224.0.0.5. On point-to-point networks, neighboring routers become adjacent whenever they can communicate directly. No designated router (DR) or backup designated router (BDR) election is performed because there can be only two routers on a point-to-point link, so there is no need for a DR or BDR. The default OSPF Hello and dead intervals on point-to-point links are 10 seconds and 40 seconds, respectively.

Broadcast

An OSPF router on a multi-access broadcast network, such as Ethernet, FastEthernet, and Gigabit Ethernet networks, forms an adjacency with its DR and BDR. Adjacent routers have identical link state databases (LSDBs). The shared media segment is the basis for an adjacency. The network that supports FutureTech manufacturing line is an example. When routers first come up on the segment, they perform the Hello process and then elect the DR and BDR. The other routers then attempt to form adjacencies with the DR and BDR. The routers on the segment must elect a DR and a BDR to represent the multi-access broadcast network.

Non-broadcast Multi-access

In a NBMA network, normally a single interface connects multiple sites over the same network, but the non-broadcast type of network can prevent proper connectivity. **NBMA networks** support two or more routers, but without the ability to send broadcast traffic. Say for example, if the NBMA topology is not fully meshed, then a broadcast or multicast sent by one router will not reach all the other routers. Frame relay, ATM, and X.25 are examples of NBMA networks.

To allow for broadcast or multicast traffic on an NBMA network, a router must replicate the broadcast or multicast traffic and send it separately over every permanent virtual circuit (PVC) to all destination routers. The problem with this setup is that it is processor (CPU time) and bandwidth intensive.

The default OSPF Hello and dead intervals on NBMA interfaces are 30 seconds and 120 seconds, respectively.

OSPF is built such that the NBMA environment should function similar to other broadcast media. The problem with that is NBMA clouds are very often built as hub-and-spoke topologies, using PVCs or switched virtual circuits (SVCs). If you have a hub-and-spoke topology, the NBMA network is a partial mesh; so the physical topology doesn't give the multi-access capability that OSPF needs.

The DR election can be a problem in NBMA topologies, mostly in terms of the configuration required. The DR and BDR must have full physical connectivity with all routers in the NBMA network. The DR and BDR also need to have a list of all the other routers so that they can establish adjacencies. Since OSPF can't automatically build adjacencies (meaning the dynamic neighbor discovery process) with neighboring routers, you may have to do some manual configuration to help out the process.

By the standard in RFC 2328, OSPF can run one of the following two modes in a NBMA topology.

Non-broadcast   Non-broadcast mode simulates the operation of OSPF in broadcast networks. Neighbors must be manually configured and DR and BDR election is required. This configuration is typically used with fully meshed networks.

Point-to-Multipoint   The point-to-multipoint mode treats the non-broadcast network as a collection of point-to-point links. In this environment, the routers automatically identify their neighboring routers but do not elect a DR and BDR. This configuration is typically used with partially meshed networks.

The difference between non-broadcast and point-to-multipoint modes changes how the Hello protocol and flooding process work over a non-broadcast network. The good thing about point-to-multipoint mode is less manual configuration for you, and the good thing about non-broadcast mode is there is less traffic creating overhead for your network.

On top of the two modes that are defined by the open standard of OSPF, Cisco has also included, for your configuration pleasure, three additional modes. These three extra modes are:

- Point-to-multipoint non-broadcast
- Broadcast
- Point-to-point

The configuration for any of these modes is completed on the interface that is connected to the given network. The command to configure a given mode is `ip ospf network <parameter>`. Table 6.8 gives a breakdown of each of the possible parameters that can be configured and a brief description for each mode. The table helps me remember what things have to be done for each mode.

TABLE 6.8   NBMA Network Mode Parameters

Parameter	Description
non-broadcast	One IP subnet
	Neighbors must be manually configured
	DR and BDR elected
	DR and BDR need to have full connectivity with all other routers
	Typically used in a full-mesh or a partial-mesh topology

TABLE 6.8   NBMA Network Mode Parameters *(continued)*

Parameter	Description
point-to-multipoint	One IP subnet
	Uses multicast OSPF Hello packet to automatically discover the neighbors
	DR and BDR not required—router sends additional LSAs with more information about neighboring routers
	Typically used in partial-mesh or star topology
point-to-multipoint non-broadcast	If multicast and broadcast are not enabled on the virtual circuits, the RFC-compliant point-to-multipoint mode cannot be used because the router cannot dynamically discover its neighboring routers using Hello multicast packets; this Cisco mode should be used instead
	Neighbors must be manually configured
	DR and BDR election is not required
broadcast	Makes the WAN interface appear to be a LAN
	One IP subnet
	Uses multicast OSPF Hello packet to automatically discover the neighbors
	DR and BDR elected
	Requires a full-mesh or a partial-mesh topology
point-to-point	Different IP subnet on each subinterface
	No DR or BDR election
	Used when only two routers need to form an adjacency on a pair of interfaces
	Interfaces can be either LAN or WAN

Stub Type Areas

Within the OSPF standard, there have been several special-case area types defined as stub areas, totally stubby areas, and not-so-stubby areas (NSSAs). With the exception of the totally stubby area, these special purpose areas are defined in the open standard of OSPF. Totally stubby areas were been defined by Cisco and are, therefore, proprietary (meaning you have to have a Cisco router to use this area type).

The main purpose of these types of stub areas is ultimately to reduce the size of the routing table and the amount of traffic being flooded. Here are the benefits:

- Reduced amount of flooding
- Reduced link state database (LSDB) size
- Reduced routing table size

Simply explained, this is accomplished by injecting default routes into an area, and not allowing external and summary link state advertisements (LSAs) to be flooded in.

Stub Areas

Now, you have to understand what it is about stub areas that makes them different. You know why to use them; you want to reduce the size of the routing table. To accomplish that, stub areas do not accept any external routes, known as type-5 LSAs. All OSPF routers inside the stub area, including ABRs and internal routers, must be configured as stub routers before they can become neighbors and exchange routing information.

A stub area has a single exit point or, if there are multiple exits, one or more ABRs inject a default route into the stub area. However, when there is more than one exit point, then you can end up with suboptimal routing paths. With multiple exits, when routing data to other areas or autonomous systems, the data could take a path that is not the best to reach the destination. You can end up routing data out an exit at a point that is farther from the destination than other exits.

The other things that must be met in order to be a stub area are:

- There is no ASBR inside the stub area.

- The area is not the backbone area, area 0.

- The area cannot be used as transit area for virtual links, nor have virtual links configured at all.

 Real World Scenario

Branch Office Stub Areas

Think about all of the branch offices in the FutureTech network. If you were to use the OSPF routing protocol for the entire company it wouldn't be necessary for the branch office routers to have all of the headquarter networks in their routing tables. If the routers in the branch office don't know where a given destination is, the only place they can send the data is back to the backbone area or the core of the network at HQ. To save traffic and overhead, these are perfect stub area applications.

Every router in the stub area must be configured as being in the stub area for them to create adjacencies and pass LSAs. The command to accomplish that is area *area-id* stub, under the OSPF routing configuration mode. The *area-id* option is the area number assigned to the stub area. Take a look at Figure 6.6 and you can see what I am talking about with the area structure and which routers have to be configured.

FIGURE 6.6 Stub Area

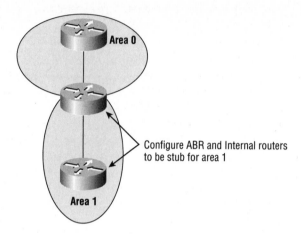

Configure ABR and Internal routers
to be stub for area 1

Area 0

Area 1

Totally Stubby Areas

The totally stubby area is a Cisco-proprietary feature that reduces the number of routes in the routing table even more. A totally stubby area is much like a stub area in that it blocks external type-5 LSAs, but also blocks summary type-3 and type-4 LSAs (inter-area routes) from coming into the area. Blocking all of these types of routes means that a totally stubby area only has intra-area routes and the default route of 0.0.0.0 in the routing table. Similar to a stub areas, totally stubby areas have the same rules for their use but have a slightly different way of being configured.

Like a stub area, a totally stubby area has a single exit point or, if there are multiple exits, one or more ABRs inject a default route into the stub area. However, if there is more than one exit point, then you could end up with suboptimal routing paths. This means that with multiple exits, when routing data to other areas or autonomous systems, that the data could take a path that is not the best to reach the destination. You could end up routing data out an exit at a point that is farther from the destination than other exits.

Here are the other rules for use in a totally stubby area:

- All internal OSPF routers inside the totally stubby area must be configured as stub area routers. This allows the routers from vendors other than Cisco within the area.

- Since this is a proprietary configuration, the ABRs must be Cisco routers and must be configured as totally stubby routers. The ABRs prevent the entrance of the external and summary routes into the area.

- There is no ASBR inside the totally stubby area.

- The area is not the backbone area, area 0.

- The area cannot be used as transit area for virtual links.

- The area cannot have virtual links configured at all.

Just as with the stub area, a totally stubby area can easily be used for branch offices and parts of the network where there are limited paths coming and going. With this type of configuration, you can further reduce the size of the routing tables for these routers and prevent a lot of flooded routing traffic.

Every internal router in the totally stubby area must be configured as being a stub area router; this will again allow them to create adjacencies and pass LSAs. The command to accomplish that is still `area area-id stub`, under the OSPF routing configuration mode. The *area-id* option is the area number that is the stub area. The ABR in this case must be configured with the `area area-id stub no-summary` command. This is the command to tell the ABR that the area is a totally stubby area and to no allow external and summary routes in. The `no-summary` option should hopefully make sense as that is what is being added to the functionality of this area "no summary" routes are now allowed in. Take a look at Figure 6.7 and you can see what I am talking about with the area structure and which routers have to be configured.

FIGURE 6.7 Totally Stubby Area

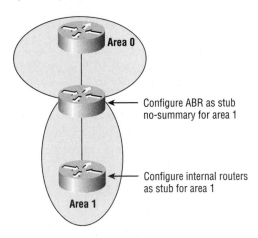

Configure ABR as stub no-summary for area 1

Configure internal routers as stub for area 1

Not So Stubby Area

The OSPF not-so-stubby area (NSSA) is a nonproprietary addition that allows the injection of specific external routes into the stub area. When I say specific, I mean that within an NSSA you can now have an ASBR. I know this sounds a bit confusing, but most of the same rules that were in a stub area are still in place here. The ABR that connects the NSSA to area 0 does not allow external routes to enter the NSSA. So, if there are any ASBRs anywhere else in the network, their routes will not be allowed into the NSSA.

Real World Scenario

Adding a New Office

FutureTech has acquired a small competitor, TechnoRama, located in the same building as the New York office, a large branch office. The New York office is currently configured as a stub area and connected back to the Dallas headquarters, where area 0 is located. You are assigned to make sure that this new part of the company (the company that was just bought) has its network attached to the network right away. The new part of the network will continue to run RIP because of many of the systems that are in the network.

So, adding to the problem, Finance has decided to become a pain and tell you how to make this all connect together. The budget requires that the branch routers remain stub routers because they can't handle the processing load and there are no funds budgeted to upgrade them. Of course, there is no way they are going to pay for a new WAN link for the new part of the office. That means you have to attach this new office (running RIP) into the New York office (which has to be a stub area) and make it work.

Take a look at Figure 6.8. The branch office network is area 1 and the core of the FutureTech network is area 0. The newly acquired company is shown by the RIP routing domain.

FIGURE 6.8   NSSA

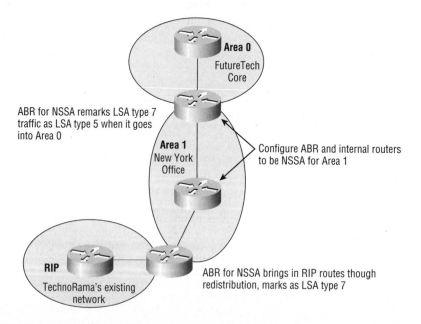

Now you have to connect the New York stub area to a completely separate network with a different routing protocol. This means you have to redistribute and have an ASBR, but you know that you can't have an ASBR in a stub area. Imagine yourself as the first person to ever have this problem. What are you going to do? Being the outstanding engineer that you are, come up with the idea to make a new type of area. In order to do this, you are going to have to identify the routing updates differently. You don't want to change all of the existing code that says external routes are type-5 LSAs, and you don't want to change the fact the stub areas won't accept type-5 LSAs.

So you say, "Why not create a new type of LSA?"

You call it a type-7 LSA. A type-7 LSA is still an external route, but it is an external route from the ASBR that you are putting into the stub area. You identify this new type of area as a not-so-stubby area, which can have an ASBR. That ASBR brings type-7 LSAs into the area as external routes. You don't want to change the code for all of the other routers, so you will have the ABR that goes into area 0 change those type-7 LSAs back into type-5 LSAs—and the rest of the network is none the wiser.

The creation of the NSSA network may not have happened exactly like that, but I am sure that it was an entertaining reason nonetheless. To recap all of the NSSA information: All OSPF routers inside the NSSA, including ABRs and internal routers, must be configured as NSSA routers before they can become neighbors and exchange routing information.

Like a stub area, an NSSA has a single exit point or, if there are multiple exits, one or more ABRs inject a default route into the stub area. However, if there is more than one exit point, then you could end up with suboptimal routing paths. This means that with multiple exits, when routing data to other areas or autonomous systems, that the data could take a path that is not the best to reach the destination. You could end up routing data out an exit at a point that is farther from the destination than other exits.

Here are a few more rules for an NSSA:

- The area is not the backbone area, area 0.
- The area cannot be used as transit area for virtual links, nor have virtual links configured at all.
- There is an ASBR allowed in a NSSA.
- Redistribution into an NSSA creates a special type of LSA known as type 7.
- Type-7 LSAs can exist only in an NSSA.
- An NSSA ASBR generates the type-7 LSA and an NSSA ABR translates it into a type-5 LSA that is then propagated into the OSPF domain.

The type-7 LSA is described in the routing table as an O N2 or O N1 (N means NSSA). N1 means that the metric is calculated like external type 1 (E1). An E1 route has the additional cost of the links added to its cost as the route passes through the OSPF routed network. N2 means that the metric is calculated like external type 2 (E2); an E2 does not have the internal or additional cost of the OSPF links added to its cost as it passes through the OSPF network. The default is O N2.

Configuring OSPF

Now I want to take you through the configurations for OSPF. I start off with the basics just like always. You will turn on the routing process and configure the network statements for the interfaces. Then, I discuss the other configurations required.

 Real World Scenario

Configuring the Bangalore Test Network

Let's go back and look at the Bangalore plant OSPF upgrade again. Figure 6.9 shows the layout for this network. The two routers labeled BangRtr1 and BangRtr2 (I may call them core routers for short) will make up the backbone area, area 0. Even though this is just a test, you want to configure the routers so that you can eventually move them to their real physical location in the complex. Remember that area 0 is located in the main building; this is where the offices and managers are located. The four routers labeled RnD1 through RnD4 will go into the test/quality assurance building when you are done with all of testing. So, set them up as if they were already located in different buildings to test the links and all of the features that you need to implement for this site.

FIGURE 6.9   FutureTech OSPF Network

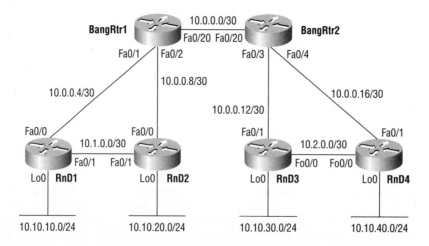

Let's start with the core routers. I want to enable OSPF on each of the interfaces.

- The interfaces between the switches will be in area 0.
- The interfaces going to RnD1 and RnD2 will be in area 1.
- The interfaces going to RnD3 and RnD4 will be in area 2.

The command to enable OSPF on a router is `router ospf process-id`, where the *process-id* is a number assigned to identify the instance of OSPF being enabled on the router. The *process-id* is locally significant to the router and doesn't have to be the same for all of your routers. For your own sanity, I highly recommend making it the same. It will make your configurations and your life much easier.

Multiple OSPF Processes

While it is possible to enable more than one instance of OSPF on a router, it is not recommended. Remember that multiple processes on the router will not be able to communicate.

The second thing, then, is enabling the interfaces for OSPF; the command to accomplish this is the `network network-id bit-mask area area-id`. Where the *network-id* is the network or IP address of the interface network, and the *bit-mask* is the reverse mask that gives you the number of significant bits. For this configuration, it is possible to enable the interface by using the network, subnet, or IP address of the interface. You can identify which one you are using with the *bit-mask* option. It is generally recommended to use the most specific one, the interface IP address. I suggest using the IP address for the interface, as well.

```
BangRtr1(config)#router ospf 1
BangRtr1(config-router)#network 10.0.0.1 0.0.0.0 area 0
BangRtr1(config-router)#network 10.0.0.5 0.0.0.0 area 1
BangRtr1(config-router)#network 10.0.0.9 0.0.0.0 area 1


BangRtr2(config)#router ospf 1
BangRtr2(config-router)#network 10.0.0.2 0.0.0.0 area 0
BangRtr2(config-router)#network 10.0.0.13 0.0.0.0 area 2
BangRtr2(config-router)#network 10.0.0.17 0.0.0.0 area 2
```

I now want to do the same thing for each of the RnD routers. Notice, I had you put the interfaces on the core switches into area 1 and area 2 that connect to these routers because you want to think about how these connections might physically be laid out. If the connections to the RnD routers were WAN links and you had configured the core interfaces to be in area 0; then the interfaces on each of the RnD routers would have to be in area 0. That would mean that all of the routing traffic for area 0 would be flooded across the WAN link to the RnD routers for nothing. This is the configuration for each of the RnD routers.

```
RnD1(config)#router ospf 1
RnD1(config-router)#network 10.0.0.6 0.0.0.0 area 1
RnD1(config-router)#network 10.1.0.1 0.0.0.0 area 1
RnD1(config-router)#network 10.1.1.1 0.0.0.0 area 1

RnD2(config)#router ospf 1
RnD2(config-router)#network 10.0.0.10 0.0.0.0 area 1
RnD2(config-router)#network 10.1.0.2 0.0.0.0 area 1
RnD2(config-router)#network 10.1.2.1 0.0.0.0 area 1

RnD 3(config)#router ospf 1
RnD3(config-router)#network 10.2.0.1 0.0.0.0 area 2
RnD3(config-router)#network 10.0.0.14 0.0.0.0 area 2
RnD3(config-router)#network 10.2.1.1 0.0.0.0 area 2

RnD4(config)#router ospf 1
RnD4(config-router)#network 10.2.0.2 0.0.0.0 area 2
RnD4(config-router)#network 10.2.0.2 0.0.0.0 area 2
RnD4(config-router)#network 10.0.0.18 0.0.0.0 area 2
```

Now, if I was going to make area 1 a stub area; then I would have to configure the ABR and the internal routers as stub routers. I use the area 1 stub command on BangRtr1 and RnD1 and RnD2. It looks like this:

```
BangRtr1(config)#router ospf 1
BangRtr1(config-router)#area 1 stub

RnD1(config)#router ospf 1
RnD1(config-router)# area 1 stub

RnD2(config)#router ospf 1
RnD2(config-router)# area 1 stub
```

If you wanted to make area 2 into a totally stubby area, then you have to configure the ABR as a totally stubby area and the internal routers (RnD 3 and 4) are configured as stub routers. The command for a totally stubby area is area 2 stub no-summary. This is what that looks like.

```
BangRtr2(config)#router ospf 1
BangRtr2(config-router)#area 2 stub no-summary
```

```
RnD3(config)#router ospf 1
RnD3(config-router)# area 2 stub

RnD4(config)#router ospf 1
RnD4(config-router)# area 2 stub
```

Now let's say you were going to make area 2 into a NSSA instead. Remember, you have to configure the ABR and the internal routers all to be a NSSA. The command for a NSSA is area 2 nssa. Again, it looks like this:

```
BangRtr2(config)#router ospf 1
BangRtr2(config-router)#area 2 nsaa

RnD3(config)#router ospf 1
RnD3(config-router)# area 2 nssa

RnD4(config)#router ospf 1
RnD4(config-router)# area 2 nssa
```

Verifying OSPF

Now, you will want to verify your configuration. You want to look at all of the tables (neighbor, LSDB, and routing). Then, you will look at the interface and other routing information you can get from OSPF. First of all, let's look at the table information.

Here is a look at the neighbor table.

```
BangRtr1#sh ip ospf neighbor

Neighbor ID  Pri  State     Dead Time  Address      Interface
10.0.0.17     1   FULL/BDR  00:00:36   10.0.0.2     FastEthernet0/20
10.1.2.1      1   FULL/BDR  00:00:33   10.0.0.10    FastEthernet0/2
10.1.1.1      1   FULL/BDR  00:00:35   10.0.0.6     FastEthernet0/1
```

Here is a look at the LSDB table.

```
BangRtr1#sh ip ospf database

        OSPF Router with ID (10.0.0.9) (Process ID 1)

            Router Link States (Area 0)
```

Link ID	ADV Router	Age	Seq#	Checksum	Link count
10.0.0.9	10.0.0.9	268	0x80000004	0x0048AA	1
10.0.0.17	10.0.0.17	154	0x80000003	0x00D70B	1

Net Link States (Area 0)

Link ID	ADV Router	Age	Seq#	Checksum
10.0.0.1	10.0.0.9	268	0x80000002	0x006C83

Summary Net Link States (Area 0)

Link ID	ADV Router	Age	Seq#	Checksum
10.0.0.4	10.0.0.9	268	0x80000002	0x0044D8
10.0.0.8	10.0.0.9	269	0x80000002	0x001CFC
10.0.0.12	10.0.0.17	154	0x80000002	0x00C349
10.0.0.16	10.0.0.17	154	0x80000002	0x009B6D
10.1.0.0	10.0.0.9	21	0x80000002	0x006AB4
10.1.1.1	10.0.0.9	21	0x80000002	0x0067B2
10.1.2.1	10.0.0.9	21	0x80000002	0x005CBC
10.2.0.0	10.0.0.17	1781	0x80000001	0x0030E6
10.2.1.1	10.0.0.17	1759	0x80000001	0x002DE4
10.2.2.1	10.0.0.17	1643	0x80000001	0x0022EE

Router Link States (Area 1)

Link ID	ADV Router	Age	Seq#	Checksum	Link count
10.0.0.9	10.0.0.9	24	0x80000005	0x0010A3	2
10.1.1.1	10.1.1.1	56	0x80000005	0x00723D	3
10.1.2.1	10.1.2.1	1874	0x80000005	0x00A4FE	3

Net Link States (Area 1)

Link ID	ADV Router	Age	Seq#	Checksum
10.0.0.5	10.0.0.9	25	0x80000002	0x007C7D
10.0.0.9	10.0.0.9	25	0x80000002	0x006193
10.1.0.1	10.1.1.1	56	0x80000002	0x008780

Summary Net Link States (Area 1)

Link ID	ADV Router	Age	Seq#	Checksum
10.0.0.0	10.0.0.9	273	0x80000002	0x006CB4

```
10.0.0.12       10.0.0.9       273      0x80000002 0x00FD16
10.0.0.16       10.0.0.9       275      0x80000002 0x00D53A
10.2.0.0        10.0.0.9       1783     0x80000001 0x006AB3
10.2.1.1        10.0.0.9       1760     0x80000001 0x0067B1
10.2.2.1        10.0.0.9       1644     0x80000001 0x005CBB
```

Here is a look at the routing table.

```
BangRtr1#sh ip route
Codes: C - connected, S - static, R - RIP, M - mobile, B - BGP
       D - EIGRP, EX - EIGRP external, O - OSPF, IA - OSPF inter area
       N1 - OSPF NSSA external type 1, N2 - OSPF NSSA external type 2
       E1 - OSPF external type 1, E2 - OSPF external type 2
       i - IS-IS, su - IS-IS summary, L1 - IS-IS level-1, L2 - IS-IS level-2
       ia - IS-IS inter area, * - candidate default, U - per-user static route
       o - ODR, P - periodic downloaded static route

Gateway of last resort is not set

     10.0.0.0/8 is variably subnetted, 11 subnets, 2 masks
C       10.0.0.8/30 is directly connected, FastEthernet0/2
O IA    10.0.0.12/30 [110/2] via 10.0.0.2, 00:31:20, FastEthernet0/20
O IA    10.2.1.1/32 [110/3] via 10.0.0.2, 00:29:31, FastEthernet0/20
O IA    10.2.0.0/30 [110/3] via 10.0.0.2, 00:29:54, FastEthernet0/20
O       10.1.2.1/32 [110/2] via 10.0.0.10, 00:31:20, FastEthernet0/2
C       10.0.0.0/30 is directly connected, FastEthernet0/20
O IA    10.2.2.1/32 [110/3] via 10.0.0.2, 00:27:35, FastEthernet0/20
O       10.1.1.1/32 [110/2] via 10.0.0.6, 00:31:21, FastEthernet0/1
O       10.1.0.0/30 [110/2] via 10.0.0.10, 00:31:21, FastEthernet0/2
                    [110/2] via 10.0.0.6, 00:31:21, FastEthernet0/1
C       10.0.0.4/30 is directly connected, FastEthernet0/1
O IA    10.0.0.16/30 [110/2] via 10.0.0.2, 00:31:21, FastEthernet0/20
```

Here is the show ip ospf interface output.

```
BangRtr1#sh ip ospf interface
FastEthernet0/20 is up, line protocol is up (connected)
  Internet Address 10.0.0.1/30, Area 0
  Process ID 1, Router ID 10.0.0.9, Network Type BROADCAST, Cost: 1
  Transmit Delay is 1 sec, State DR, Priority 1
  Designated Router (ID) 10.0.0.9, Interface address 10.0.0.1
```

```
  Backup Designated router (ID) 10.0.0.17, Interface address 10.0.0.2
  Timer intervals configured, Hello 10, Dead 40, Wait 40, Retransmit 5
    oob-resync timeout 40
    Hello due in 00:00:08
  Supports Link-local Signaling (LLS)
  Index 1/1, flood queue length 0
  Next 0x0(0)/0x0(0)
  Last flood scan length is 2, maximum is 3
  Last flood scan time is 0 msec, maximum is 0 msec
  Neighbor Count is 1, Adjacent neighbor count is 1
    Adjacent with neighbor 10.0.0.17   (Backup Designated Router)
  Suppress hello for 0 neighbor(s)
FastEthernet0/2 is up, line protocol is up (connected)
  Internet Address 10.0.0.9/30, Area 1
  Process ID 1, Router ID 10.0.0.9, Network Type BROADCAST, Cost: 1
  Transmit Delay is 1 sec, State DR, Priority 1
  Designated Router (ID) 10.0.0.9, Interface address 10.0.0.9
  Backup Designated router (ID) 10.1.2.1, Interface address 10.0.0.10
  Timer intervals configured, Hello 10, Dead 40, Wait 40, Retransmit 5
    oob-resync timeout 40
    Hello due in 00:00:08
  Supports Link-local Signaling (LLS)
  Index 2/3, flood queue length 0
  Next 0x0(0)/0x0(0)
  Last flood scan length is 2, maximum is 2
  Last flood scan time is 0 msec, maximum is 0 msec
  Neighbor Count is 1, Adjacent neighbor count is 1
    Adjacent with neighbor 10.1.2.1   (Backup Designated Router)
  Suppress hello for 0 neighbor(s)
FastEthernet0/1 is up, line protocol is up (connected)
  Internet Address 10.0.0.5/30, Area 1
  Process ID 1, Router ID 10.0.0.9, Network Type BROADCAST, Cost: 1
  Transmit Delay is 1 sec, State DR, Priority 1
  Designated Router (ID) 10.0.0.9, Interface address 10.0.0.5
  Backup Designated router (ID) 10.1.1.1, Interface address 10.0.0.6
  Timer intervals configured, Hello 10, Dead 40, Wait 40, Retransmit 5
    oob-resync timeout 40
    Hello due in 00:00:02
  Supports Link-local Signaling (LLS)
  Index 1/2, flood queue length 0
  Next 0x0(0)/0x0(0)
```

```
Last flood scan length is 2, maximum is 2
Last flood scan time is 0 msec, maximum is 8 msec
Neighbor Count is 1, Adjacent neighbor count is 1
  Adjacent with neighbor 10.1.1.1  (Backup Designated Router)
Suppress hello for 0 neighbor(s)
```

Here is the show ip ospf statistics output.

BangRtr1#sh ip ospf statistics

```
              OSPF Router with ID (10.0.0.9) (Process ID 1)

  Area 0: SPF algorithm executed 5 times

  Area 1: SPF algorithm executed 10 times

  Summary OSPF SPF statistic

  SPF calculation time
  Delta T   Intra D-Intra Summ   D-Summ  Ext    D-Ext   Total   Reason
  00:34:47  0     0       0      0       0      0       0       R, N,
  00:33:53  0     0       0      0       0      0       0       R,
  00:33:43  0     0       0      0       0      0       0       R,
  00:32:24  0     0       0      0       0      0       0       R, N,
  00:32:14  0     0       0      0       0      0       0       R, N,
  00:32:04  0     0       0      0       0      0       0       R,
  00:31:54  0     0       0      0       0      0       0       R,
  00:30:23  0     0       0      0       0      0       0       X
  00:30:01  0     0       0      0       0      0       0       X
  00:28:05  0     0       0      0       0      0       0       X

  RIB manipulation time during SPF (in msec):
  Delta T    RIB Update    RIB Delete
  00:34:58   0             0
  00:34:04   0             0
  00:33:54   0             0
  00:32:36   0             0
  00:32:26   0             0
  00:32:16   0             0
  00:32:06   0             0
```

```
00:30:34    0              0
00:30:12    0              0
00:28:16    0              0
```

Here is the show ip ospf traffic output.

BangRtr1#sh ip ospf traffic

```
OSPF statistics:
  Rcvd: 698 total, 0 checksum errors
        637 hello, 7 database desc, 3 link state req
        26 link state updates, 25 link state acks

  Sent: 755 total
        688 hello, 10 database desc, 1 link state req
        39 link state updates, 18 link state acks



          OSPF Router with ID (10.0.0.9) (Process ID 1)

OSPF queues statistic for process ID 1:

  OSPF Hello queue size 0, no limit, drops 0, max size 2
  OSPF Router queue size 0, limit 200, drops 0, max size 2



Interface statistics:


    Interface FastEthernet0/20

OSPF packets received/sent
     Invalid  Hellos  DB-des  LS-req  LS-upd  LS-ack  Total
Rx:  0        225     2       1       9       6       243
Tx:  0        231     3       0       9       8       251

OSPF header errors
  Length 0, Checksum 0, Version 0, Bad Source 0,
  No Virtual Link 0, Area Mismatch 0, No Sham Link 0,
  Self Originated 0, Duplicate ID 0, Hello 0,
```

MTU Mismatch 0, Nbr Ignored 0, LLS 0,
Authentication 0,

OSPF LSA errors
   Type 0, Length 0, Data 0, Checksum 0,

   Interface FastEthernet0/2

OSPF packets received/sent

	Invalid	Hellos	DB-des	LS-req	LS-upd	LS-ack	Total
Rx:	0	199	3	1	8	8	219
Tx:	0	229	4	1	14	5	253

OSPF header errors
   Length 0, Checksum 0, Version 0, Bad Source 0,
   No Virtual Link 0, Area Mismatch 0, No Sham Link 0,
   Self Originated 0, Duplicate ID 0, Hello 0,
   MTU Mismatch 0, Nbr Ignored 0, LLS 0,
   Authentication 0,

OSPF LSA errors
   Type 0, Length 0, Data 0, Checksum 0,

   Interface FastEthernet0/1

OSPF packets received/sent

	Invalid	Hellos	DB-des	LS-req	LS-upd	LS-ack	Total
Rx:	0	213	2	1	9	11	236
Tx:	0	229	3	0	16	5	253

OSPF header errors
   Length 0, Checksum 0, Version 0, Bad Source 0,
   No Virtual Link 0, Area Mismatch 0, No Sham Link 0,
   Self Originated 0, Duplicate ID 0, Hello 0,
   MTU Mismatch 0, Nbr Ignored 0, LLS 0,
   Authentication 0,

OSPF LSA errors
   Type 0, Length 0, Data 0, Checksum 0,

```
Summary traffic statistics for process ID 1:

  Rcvd: 698 total, 0 errors
        637 hello, 7 database desc, 3 link state req
        26 link state upds, 25 link state acks, 0 invalid
  Sent: 757 total
        689 hello, 10 database desc, 1 link state req
        39 link state upds, 18 link state acks, 0 invalid
```

Integrated IS-IS

You will often find that books written about IS-IS are written as a comparison to OSPF. This happened over time because OSPF was typically chosen as a more widely supported native IP protocol. Currently, it is more difficult to find information and expertise on IS-IS than on OSPF. With that being said, many of the largest internetworks in place today use IS-IS.

IS-IS is most commonly used by ISPs. IS-IS makes a great routing protocol for large internetworks because it is simple and stable. IS-IS is the primary protocol for use in networks that support Open Systems Interconnection (OSI) protocols.

If you go back and look at the history of link state routing protocols, the development of IS-IS actually started before OSPF. In the beginning of the Internet, the U.S. government required support for OSI protocols in addition to IP. That requirement was obviously removed later, but IS-IS still meets the requirements to carry both protocol suites.

One thing that I want you to understand is that IS-IS is primarily used by service providers. Now that doesn't mean that no private companies use IS-IS, but there aren't that many. Quite a few network engineers out there know IS-IS very well and swear by it, or they have taken the time to learn it and now swear by it. Many networks that exist today still use IS-IS because it has good support for things like MPLS. There are other ways to handle that; I prefer to use BGP instead. I am not recommending or saying that you have to use BGP, but it is something that you should explore if you are in a position where IS-IS might be an option.

 Real World Scenario

Using IS-IS in FutureTech

The Mexican manufacturing plant is running IS-IS. It is running IS-IS because it was a separate device manufacturing company before purchase by FutureTech. I show you the operation of IS-IS so that you can continue to operate this network, but know that next year FutureTech plans to swap that plant over to running EIGRP, like the corporate office does. The network has three areas, and uses area addresses of 49.000x (with the x being 1, 2, or 3 to correspond to each of the areas in place).

IS-IS Features

IS-IS is the dynamic link state routing protocol. Originally, IS-IS routed for the OSI protocol stack and then for IP as well. IS-IS operates very similarly to OSPF. IS-IS uses areas to break the routing domain into smaller pieces. IS-IS routers establish adjacencies using Hello protocol and exchange link state information, using link state packets (LSPs), throughout an area to build the LSDB.

Each router then runs Dijkstra's SPF algorithm against its LSDB to pick the best paths. A minimal amount of information is communicated between areas, which reduces the burden on routers supporting the protocol.

IS-IS routing takes place at two levels within an AS: Level 1 and Level 2. There are actually four levels of routing within the OSI standards, but Cisco only supports two levels. I am going to cover the levels of routing in the coming section, "Levels of Routing."

IS and ES

In OSI standard protocols, an IS is a router and an ES is a host system.

Cisco routers don't support the ES-IS protocol, but I have to talk about the process for a second because the whole Hello neighbor adjacency process is tied to it. In OSI terms, an ES is capable of communicating to the ISs through the use of ES-IS. The ESs send a Hello packet called an End System Hello (ESH). This establishes communication with the ISs. In return, the IS can send back an Intermediate System Hello (ISH) to tell the ESs where they are. Since you are using IS-IS only to carry IP routes on an IP network and probably won't have OSI hosts, you won't use that part. IP has its own protocols for handling this traffic such as ICMP, ARP, and DHCP.

However, the part that you will use is the IS-IS Hello (IIH), which allows the IS to communicate to other ISs and form adjacencies. Even if you are using IS-IS to support IP only, the ISs will use Connectionless Network Service (CLNS) to send the routing data and form adjacencies with IIHs.

Understanding IS-IS Addressing

In IS-IS, the CLNS addresses that are used by routers are called Network Service Access Point (NSAP) addresses. Unlike IP addresses, NSAP addresses apply to an entire system and not to individual interfaces. There are a variety of NSAP address formats.

NSAP addresses identify the router and are used by the link state packets (LSPs) to build the topology table and the underlying routing tree. Because of this, the NSAP addresses must be present for IS-IS to function properly, even if it is only being used to route IP. NSAP addresses contain more information than an IP address; they contain the OSI address of the device and the link to the higher-layer process. If you think about the NSAP address in terms of IP, it is similar to combining an IP address with the upper-layer protocol—all in the IP header.

NSAP addresses contain a maximum of 20 bytes. The high-order bits identify the inter-area structure and the low-order bits identify unique systems within an area.

You can look at Figure 6.10 and see the format of a NSAP address as Cisco implements them. The address can be broken into three fields:

- Area address

- System ID

- Network selector (NSEL)

Cisco routers routing CLNS use addressing that conforms to the ISO 10589 standard. The ISO NSAP address consists of quite a few different fields. I take you through each of them.

FIGURE 6.10   Cisco Implemented IS-IS Address

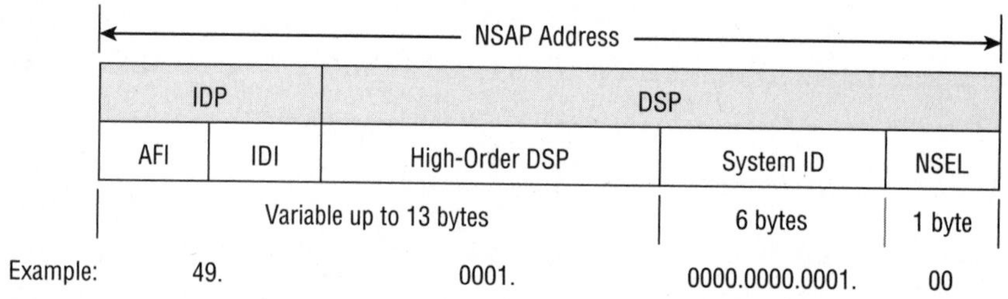

	NSAP Address			
IDP		DSP		
AFI	IDI	High-Order DSP	System ID	NSEL
Variable up to 13 bytes			6 bytes	1 byte

Example: 49.   0001.   0000.0000.0001.   00

Initial Domain Part (IDP)   The IDP corresponds roughly to an IP classful major network. The IDP is made up of two subcomponents the AFI and the IDI.

Authority and Format Identifier (AFI)   The AFI byte specifies the format of the address and the authority that assigned that address. Table 6.9 shows you a few of the values that the AFI can take on.

TABLE 6.9   AFI Values

AFI Value	Address Description
39	ISO Data Country Code (DCC)
45	E.164
47	ISO 6523 International Code Designator (ICD)
49	Locally administered (private)

The AFI value 49 is used for private addresses. Think about them like RFC 1918 addresses for IP. IS-IS routes these addresses like any other addresses, but you should not advertise these addresses to other CLNS networks because other companies that use the 49 address could have used different numbering. This could cause a great deal of confusion.

Initial Domain Identifier (IDI)   The IDI identifies a subdomain under the AFI. For example, the IDI of 47.0005 was given to the civilian departments of the U.S. government. The IDI of 47.0006 was given to the U.S. Department of Defense.

Domain-Specific Part (DSP)   The DSP gives part of the routing information needed within an IS-IS routing domain. The DSP is made up of three parts, the high-order domain-specific part (HO-DSP), the system ID, and the NSEL.

High-Order Domain-Specific Part (HO-DSP)   The HO-DSP subdivides the domain into areas. Think of the HO-DSP as similar to an IP subnet.

System ID   The system ID identifies an individual OSI device. In OSI, a device has an address just like a device did in DECnet (when DECnet was used, which it isn't used any more this protocol is old and made by Digiatal Equipment Company), while in IP each interface has an address.

NSEL   The NSEL identifies a process on the device and corresponds roughly to a port or socket in IP. The NSEL is not used in routing decisions.

Using IS-IS Addresses

The simplest NSAP address that you can use for your IS-IS routing protocol consists of these parts.

- Area address
- System ID
- NSEL

Area Address   This part of the address must be 1 byte in length and is made up of two parts: the AFI and the area ID. The area address is sometimes called a prefix. Area ID and area address are typically used as one in the same terms.

System ID   On a Cisco router, the system ID can be a maximum of 6 bytes per the U.S. Government OSI Profile (GOSIP). It is recommended to make the system ID unique across the entire routing domain. However, it is only required that it be unique within an area where it will be used for routing. When you are setting the system ID, the MAC address from one of the devices interfaces is typically used. You could also use an IP address from the device as the system ID; just pad the rest of the digits with zeros.

NSEL   The NSEL is always set to 0 to describe a router. When the NSAP has NSEL field set to 0, the address is called a Network Entity Title (NET). The NET is used by the router to identify itself in a protocol data unit (PDU). An example of a PDU that you have already learned about is an LSP.

Levels of Routing

As I mentioned earlier, the OSI standards have four levels of routing. Cisco only supports the two levels of routing that the IS-IS protocol is responsible for—the Level 1 and 2 routing areas. Level 0 routing is accomplished using the ES-IS protocol, and Level 3 routing is done by the Inter-domain Routing Protocol (IDRP).

Level 0 OSI routing begins with ES-IS, when the ESs discover the nearest IS by listening to ISH packets. When an ES needs to send a packet to another ES, it sends the packet to an IS on an attached network. This process is known as Level 0 routing.

Level 1 Level 1 routing occurs within an IS-IS area. It recognizes the location of the end systems (ESs) and ISs and then builds a routing table to reach each system. All devices in a Level 1 routing area have the same area address. Routing within an area is accomplished by looking at the locally significant address portion (known as the system ID) and choosing the lowest-cost path. An IS can send a redirect message to the source and tell it there is a more direct path.

Level 2 Level 2 routers learn the locations of Level 1 routing areas and build an inter-area routing table. All ISs in a Level 2 routing area use the destination area address to route traffic using the lowest-cost path.

Level 3 In OSI terms, if you need to route between separate domains, you use Level 3 routing. Level 3 routing performs a function similar to border gateway protocol (BGP) inter-domain routing used for IP (I will cover BGP in Chapter 7, "Exterior Gateway Protocols"). Level 3 routing passes traffic between different autonomous systems, which might have different routing logic and so might not have metrics that can be directly compared. Level 3 OSI routing is not implemented on Cisco routers. It is specified as being accomplished through the Inter-domain Routing Protocol (IDRP).

Types of Routers

In order for IS-IS to support the two levels of routing, it has defined three types of routers. I just described for you the routing levels and how the data is passed between different systems and areas. These are the different router classifications that pass the traffic for you.

Level 1 A Level 1 router only learns about paths that are located within the area it is connected to (intra-area).

Level 2 A Level 2 router only learns about the paths that exist between areas (inter-area).

Level 1–2 A Level 1–2 router learns about the paths both within the area it is located in and the paths between the areas. Level 1–2 routers are equivalent to ABRs in OSPF.

IS-IS Compared to OSPF

OSPF has more in common with IS-IS than they are different. Just to get you started, here are the basics of what both protocols do and support.

- Both are open-standard link state routing protocols.
- Both support VLSM.
- Similar mechanisms maintain the LSDB.

- Both use the SPF algorithm, with similar update, decision, and flooding processes.
- Both are successful in the largest and most demanding ISP deployments.
- Both converge quickly after changes.

The history between the protocols is long and full of some good ol' mudslinging. The two protocols were developed around the same time. The two groups who developed them, Digital Equipment Corporation (DEC) for IS-IS and the U.S. Department of Defense (DOD) for OSPF, were conflicted about how the protocols were made and who did a better job.

In the late 1980s, both protocols were published, but the Internet Engineering Task Force (IETF) gave an unofficial endorsement to OSPF, which eventually made it more popular. However, in the early to mid-1990s, many ISPs still chose IS-IS because they felt it was more mature and it supported both IP and CLNS.

Protocol Differences

While the two protocols differ, they are not huge differences.

Backbone Areas   The concept of the backbone area is different in IS-IS. In IS-IS, the backbone area is the collection of all the Level 2 and Level 1–2 routers and the paths between them. All the areas in IS-IS and the backbone must be contiguous.

Area Boundaries   Another difference in how IS-IS is implemented compared to OSPF is the boundary of an area. In IS-IS, the area boundary is on a link between routers; in OSPF, the ABR is the boundary. IS-IS routers belong to only one area. The routers must determine which area they are in, compare the neighbor router's address, and then make relationships based on their area. Routers form a Level 1 relationship if their neighbors are in the same area and a Level 2 relationship if they are in a different area. Only a Level 1–2 router can have both types of neighbor relationships.

Update Exchange   OSPF creates a significantly higher number of LSAs (route updates) than IS-IS does. IS-IS updates are put together into one larger link state packet (LSP). The more update packets there are, the more routing must be done by the routers further taking more resources. Since IS-IS has fewer LSPs, it can have more routers in an area (over 1,000) which means you could say it is more scalable than OSPF.

Efficiency   The process that IS-IS uses to add and remove routing data is more efficient that OSPF. It uses the NET address, which is already summarized.

If you look at the default timers of the two protocols, the IS-IS will detect a change faster than OSPF, which means the IS-IS will converge faster. Also with that change if there are many adjacent routers, processing on the router comes into play. IS-IS is less CPU intensive than OSPF, which means convergence could happen that much faster.

Protocol Changes   Changes in the OSPF protocol are more difficult because it requires the creation of new LSA types. IS-IS is easier to extend because a change to the type, length, value (TLV) mechanism only needs to be changed. This TLV field is also called a tuple, and it is responsible for encoding all of the routing updates for IS-IS. Extending IS-IS simply requires a new type code for the same update packets.

Area Types   OSPF includes more area types, which provide more functions for controlling routing data. OSPF includes standard areas, stub areas, and NSSA.

Metrics   OSPF has a scaled metric. That means that based on the bandwidth of a link the metric will be scaled. In IS-IS every link has a metric of 10 and you must manually change it to show preference of a link.

Vendor Support   OSPF is supported by more vendors.

Engineers and Information   Far more engineers have an in depth knowledge of OSPF than use IS-IS.

It is also much easier to find data and examples on the use and operation of OSPF than it is for IS-IS.

Configuring IS-IS

Now I am going to go through the configuration process of IS-IS with you. Look at Figure 6.11. It is a basic diagram of the Mexico City manufacturing switch block. There are three areas in the network that are running IS-IS.

FIGURE 6.11   IS-IS in Mexico City

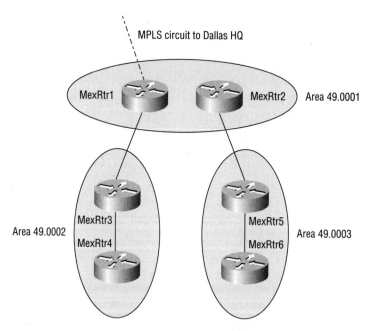

Start with the basic command set to get IS-IS running on a router. The first command simply starts the IS-IS protocol. The only option is the area tag, which is just like the process

ID in OSPF. It is locally significant and would only keep multiple instances of IS-IS on the local router separate. If you don't use the option here, the router will default it to 0.

```
MexRtr1(config)#router isis [area tag]
```

The next command is the net command. This command puts the NSAP address onto the router. Because this is a router, the NSAP address is called a NET address.

```
MexRtr1(config-router)#net network-entity-title
```

Because IS-IS does not run IP, it must be enabled on each of the interfaces. This is similar to telling the routing protocol to advertise the network from the interface. So, with that thought, you must put this command even on stub interfaces and loopback interfaces if you want the network to be advertised. The command also enables the interface to use CLNS to communicate to other routers.

```
MexRtr1(config-if)#ip router isis [area tag]
```

On a Cisco router, every router defaults to being a Level 1–2 router. If you want to change the level, the command is:

```
MexRtr1(config-router)#is-type [level-1 | level-1-2 | level-2-only]
```

The is-type command changes the level of the router globally from the default of Level 1–2. If you only want to change the level for a specific circuit or interface, then you can change the level on an individual interface.

```
MexRtr1(config-if)#isis circuit-type [level-1 | level-1-2 | level-2-only]
```

You will generally have to change the metric for an IS-IS router because the default metric of 10 is used on every interface. Here, you can change the metric per interface or on a global basis. The first command changes the metric just on an interface.

```
MexRtr1(config-if)#isis metric metric [delay-metric | expense-metric | error-metric] [level-1 | level-2]
```

This command will change the metric on a global basis.

```
MexRtr1(config-router)#metric default-value [level-1 | level-2]
```

Summary

You have done it, completed another successful implementation for your network. You have had to go through quite a few things in this chapter. I described the all communications that occur in OSPF, including the Hello process, DR election, updating the LSDB, and propagating changes in the network.

You learned how to configure OSPF in single and multiple area environments. You looked at different types of stub areas and learned the special features and limitations of each one. I then took you through the configuration of OSPF and how to verify the operation.

Then you turned your attention to IS-IS. The objectives for IS-IS are small in scope, but the fundamentals of its operation are similar to OSPF. I compared OSPF and IS-IS, showed you how the routing levels and addressing work in IS-IS, and then covered the router types and configurations.

Review Questions

1. What type of message in OSPF provides for neighbor discovery and populated the neighbor table?

    A. Update

    B. Hello

    C. Acknowledgment

    D. Discovery

2. What number does the backbone area of OSPF have to be?

    A. 0

    B. 1

    C. 2

    D. 3

3. What is the name of a router that connects multiple OSPF areas together?

    A. ASBR

    B. Internal

    C. Backbone

    D. ABR

4. What type of LSA is used by an ASBR when redistributing routes into OSPF in a standard area?

    A. Router (type 1)

    B. Network (type 2)

    C. External (type 5)

    D. External (type 7)

5. What type of stub area allows the inclusion of an ASBR in the area?

    A. Stub

    B. Totally stub

    C. NSSA

    D. Not quite stubby

6. More than one process of OSPF can be enabled a single router.

    A. True

    B. False

    C. Not sure

    D. All of the above

7. IS-IS is based on what protocol for its transport?

   A. CLNS

   B. DEC

   C. Banyan Vines

   D. IP

8. Cisco supports how many levels of routing with IS-IS?

   A. 1

   B. 2

   C. 3

   D. 4

9. IS-IS uses what address prefix to specify a private area?

   A. 35

   B. 39

   C. 47

   D. 49

10. IS-IS uses less processing power than OSPF does.

   A. True

   B. False

   C. Not sure

   D. All of the above

Answers to Review Questions

1. B. Hello messages are used to provide neighbor discovery and populate the neighbor table.

2. A. Backbone area must be 0.

3. D. In OSPF, the router that connects areas together is called the ABR

4. C. The ASBR uses LSA type 5.

5. C. An NSSA allows the inclusion of an ASBR.

6. A. More than one process may be enabled; however, they will not route to each other without redistribution

7. A. IS-IS uses the OSI protocol CLNS.

8. B. Cisco only supports two levels of routing (Levels 1 and 2) even though IS-IS has four total levels of routing.

9. D. IS-IS has the prefix of 49 specified for private areas.

10. A. IS-IS uses less processing power because it sends few updates.

Chapter

7

Exterior Gateway Protocols

IN THIS CHAPTER, YOU WILL LEARN HOW TO DO THE FOLLOWING:

✓ Describe the functions and operations of BGP

✓ Configure or verify BGP operation in a nontransit AS

✓ Configure BGP path selection including, local preference, AS-path, weight, or MED attributes

Border gateway protocol (BGP) is the only exterior gateway routing protocol allowed on the Internet today. BGPv4, to be exact, is the current version of the protocol. In this section, I explain the operation of BGP, as well as how and why BGP is used. BGP provides routing between autonomous systems (AS). It provides a way for ISPs and enterprise networks to be connected and have reachability. BGP is a path vector protocol; this means that it finds a path and a direction to a destination AS.

 For up to the minute updates on this chapter, check out www.sybex.com/go/CiscoProGuidetoInternetworking or www.lammle.com.

BGP Operations

The Internet is simply a huge web of interconnected autonomous systems. They are interconnected to provide communication between all of them. Without BGP to provide routing between these autonomous systems you would have no Internet to surf.

⊕ Real World Scenario

FutureTech's Internet Connections

You are in charge of FutureTech's large enterprise network and need to connect that network to the Internet. You are going to connect the enterprise through multiple ISPs for redundancy. If the network only needed a single connection to one ISP, then you could use a simple default route. However, since you need to have multiple connections to multiple ISPs, using BGP is the appropriate solution. BGP is perfect in this situation because it allows for the manipulation of the attributes (in BGP, attributes are used instead of metric values, we will discuss this in much more detail), using metrics and policy based routing lets you can select the optimal path for your data. Not all of FutureTech's sites will connect to the Internet using BGP. Only the headquarters and large offices will connect to the Internet with BGP. Many of the smaller offices may have an Internet connection primarily for sending data, not for being known as a FutureTech office. Those smaller offices connected to the rest of the enterprise using WAN links and VPNs (I discuss WANs and VPNs in later chapters). The Dallas office as well as the New York, London, and Brussels offices will be connected to the Internet using BGP.

I take you through some of the requirements of BGP so that as you move through the chapter you can build on the need for these connections.

All of the routing protocols that you have learned about so far have been interior protocols. To understand BGP, you must understand the ways in which it is different from the other protocols. You already learned about the two categories that routing protocols fall into: interior or exterior:

IGP   An IGP is a routing protocol that exchanges routing information within an AS. RIP, IGRP, OSPF, IS-IS, and EIGRP are examples of IGPs.

EGP   An EGP is a routing protocol that exchanges routing information between different autonomous systems. BGP is an example of an EGP.

When Not to Use BGP

For all of the interior protocols I covered thus far, I told you about their uses and what their strengths are. You got information that allows you can select the best protocol for your application. For the interior protocols, it was always a matter of which one is the best. But for exterior protocols, there are applications where you should not to use it at all.

You should not use BGP at all:

- If you have a single connection to a single ISP
- If you don't have powerful enough routers to run BGP
- If you don't have staff with a knowledge of how BGP works

When to Use BGP

Now, there are obviously reasons to use BGP, as well. They are pretty much the opposite of the reasons to not use BGP. The first one is the easiest to decide on. If you have multiple Internet connections going out and need to control where and how the traffic is being sent, then the best way to do that is with BGP. The other reasons for using BGP can be more complex to decide on. In some cases, they are just harder for people's egos to accept. Ask yourself these questions when determining to use BGP.

- Do you have the equipment to support it?
- Do you have the staff to support it?
- Does your AS appear to other autonomous systems to have a single coherent interior routing plan and present a consistent picture of reachable destinations?

Determining whether your equipment can support BPG can depend a little bit on how you are going to set up BGP. You can set up BGP so that you only get a partial routing table. This option only places routes in your table that belong to the ISP or ISPs that you are actually connecting to. You could also include a full routing table with all of the routes that are on the Internet. I have seen many conflicting counts as to how many routes there really are for the Internet, but the most common and reliable numbers that I know are between 170,000 and

200,000 routes on a router that has all of the routes for the Internet. That is a significant number of routes, and that many routes will take a lot of memory and processing to maintain. You are going to need a pretty beefy device to handle that kind of traffic.

Having the people on board to run BGP is the most subjective of all. Staff must be capable of running BGP and not screwing it up. This is hard to quantify. Of course, no one is going to say they aren't capable of doing something, and that is where the problems begin. This is often compared to the chicken and the egg problem. You shouldn't let anyone work with BGP that doesn't have experience doing so, and the people who don't have experience always ask how they can get experience if you don't let them. Hopefully, you will have a few people that have some experience and can teach others how to operate BGP.

Here is one other thing to think about when you are considering running BGP. Autonomous systems often use more than one IGP inside for routing, potentially with several sets of metrics. From the BGP point of view (and this is important for every system that might be connecting to yours), the most important thing for your AS is that it appears to other autonomous systems to have a single coherent interior routing plan and presents a consistent picture of reachable destinations. All parts of an AS must connect to each other.

Ways to Connect a Network

When your AS has more than one connection to the Internet, your network is multihoming. BPG gives you a way to control traffic in and out of your network and permits more the one connection for reliability. Two typical reasons for multihoming are:

- To increase the reliability of the connection to the Internet. If one connection fails, the other connection remains available.

- To increase the performance of the connection. Better paths can be used to certain destinations.

The benefits of BGP are most easily seen when you have an AS that has multiple BGP connections to either a single AS or multiple autonomous systems. Having multiple connections allows your network to have redundant connections to the Internet so that if a single path becomes unavailable, connectivity can still be maintained.

Your network can be multihomed to either a single ISP or to multiple ISPs. A drawback to having all of your connections to a single ISP is that connectivity problems in or to that single ISP can cause your AS to lose connectivity to the Internet. By having connections to multiple ISPs, you gain the following benefits:

- Redundancy with the multiple connections

- Not tied into the routing policy of a single ISP

- More paths to the same networks for better policy manipulation

Once you decide to implement multihoming with BGP, there are three common ways:

1. Each ISP passes only a default route to the AS and that default route is passed to the internal routers.

2. Each ISP passes only a default route and provider-owned specific routes to the AS. These routes may be passed to internal routers, or all internal routers in the transit path can run BGP and pass these routes between them.

3. Each ISP passes all routes to the AS. All internal routers in the transit path run BGP and pass these routes between them.

Default Route from ISP

The first multihoming option is to receive only a default route from each ISP. This configuration requires the fewest resources on the devices within the AS. It is also slightly easier for the administrators because a default route is used to reach any external destinations. The AS sends all its routes to the ISPs, which process and pass them on to other autonomous systems. So, all of your local networks will be known outside of your AS, but you will not know any external routes inside of your AS.

If a router in the AS learns about multiple default routes, the local interior routing protocol (IGP, whatever you have running) installs the best default route in the routing table. For each local router, it will take the default route with the least-cost IGP metric. This IGP default route routes packets destined to the external networks to an edge router of the AS that is running BGP with the ISPs. The edge router uses the BGP default route to reach all external networks. The route that inbound packets take to reach the AS is decided outside the AS (within the ISPs and other autonomous systems).

To better understand, let's look at how ISPs are connected together and organized. A bunch of regional ISPs service smaller areas and towns so that people and businesses can get Internet connections. The regional ISPs then have multiple connections to national or international ISPs. The regional ISPs do not use BGP for path manipulation; however, they require the ability to add new customers, as well as the networks of the customers. This can be very important if the new customer owns its address space. If the regional ISP does not use BGP, then each time that regional ISP adds a new set of networks, the customers must wait until the national ISPs add these networks to their BGP process and place static routes pointing at the regional ISP. By running BGP with the national or international ISPs, the regional ISP needs to add only the new networks of the customers to its BGP process. These new networks automatically propagate across the Internet with minimal delay.

A customer that chooses to receive default routes from all providers must understand the limitations of this option:

- Path manipulation cannot be performed because only a single route is being received from each ISP.

- Bandwidth manipulation is extremely difficult and can be accomplished only by manipulating the IGP metric of the default route.

- Diverting some of the traffic from one exit point to another is challenging because all destinations are using the same default route for path selection.

Default Route and Partial Route Table

In the second design option for multihoming, all ISPs pass default routes and select specific routes to the AS.

You can run BGP with an ISP if you want a partial routing table. Generally, you will receive the networks that the ISP and its other customers own; the AS you are connected to will send you its routes. The enterprise can also receive the routes from any other AS, if you choose to have additional routes and the ISP will provide that service.

Major ISPs are assigned between 2,000 and 10,000 classless interdomain routing (CIDR) blocks of IP addresses from the Internet Assigned Numbers Authority (IANA); they reassign these addresses to their customers. If the ISP passes this information to a customer that wants only a partial BGP routing table, the customer can redistribute these routes into its IGP. This can be the major benefit because the internal routers of the customer (the routers not running BGP) can then receive these routes via redistribution. They can then use those routes to find the nearest exit point, based on the best metric of specific networks instead of taking the nearest exit point based on the default route. Acquiring a partial BGP table from each provider is beneficial because path selection will be more predictable than when using a default route. It just takes more resources on your devices and you have to manage the additional routing load.

Full Route Table

In the third multihoming option, all ISPs pass all routes to the AS, and BGP is run on at least all of the routers in the transit path through your AS. This option allows the internal routers of the AS to take the path to the best ISP for each route. This type of configuration requires a lot of resources within the AS because it must process all the external routes. The AS sends all its routes to the ISPs, which process the routes and pass them to other autonomous systems. This has the best route response and path selection but again has the most overhead and is the most work for you.

Path Vectors

Internal routing protocols announce a list of networks and the metrics to get to each network. One of things that I love about BGP is that its routers exchange network reachability information, called path vectors. Path vectors are made up of attributes. The path vector information includes a list of the full path of BGP AS numbers (hop by hop, called the AS-path) necessary to reach a destination network and the networks that are reachable at the end of the path. That is one of the biggest differences you have to learn or remember about BGP. BGP does not tell you how to get to a specific network, like the IGPs you learned about. BGP simply tells you how to get to an AS. The information BGP carries about the AS are the network prefixes that are in the AS. So, if you compare this to an IGP, the IGP gives you the destination network in the route. When you get information from BGP, it gives you a destination AS and then tells you what networks are in that AS.

Other attributes include the IP address to get to the next AS (the next-hop attribute) and an indication of how the networks at the end of the path were introduced into BGP (the origin code attribute). The AS path information is useful to construct a graph of loop-free autonomous systems and is used to identify routing policies so that restrictions on routing behavior can be enforced based on the AS path.

BGP allows routing-policy decisions at the AS level to be enforced. These policies can be implemented for all networks owned by an AS, for a certain CIDR block of network numbers (prefixes), or for individual networks or subnetworks.

BGP specifies that a BGP router can advertise to neighboring autonomous systems only those routes that it uses itself. This rule reflects the hop-by-hop routing paradigm that the Internet uses. The hop-by-hop routing paradigm does not support all possible policies. For example, BGP does not enable one AS to send traffic to a neighboring AS intending that the traffic take a different route from that taken by traffic that originates in that neighboring AS. In other words, you cannot tell a neighboring AS to route traffic differently than you would route the traffic, but you can tell your traffic how to get to a neighboring AS. BGP can support any policy that conforms to the hop-by-hop routing paradigm.

BGP Transmissions

None of the other routing protocols that I have told you about use TCP for a transport protocol. However, BGP does use TCP as its transport protocol, which provides connection-oriented reliable delivery. BGP assumes that its communication is reliable; therefore, it does not have to implement separate retransmission or error recovery mechanisms like OSPF does. BGP uses TCP port 179. Two routers running BGP form a TCP connection with each another and exchange messages to open and confirm the connection parameters. Once those two BGP routers have established this session, they are called peer routers or neighbors.

After the connection is made, BGP peers exchange full routing tables. However, because the connection is reliable, BGP peers subsequently send only changes (incremental or triggered updates) after that. Reliable links do not require periodic routing updates; therefore, routers use triggered updates instead. BGP sends keepalive messages, similar to the hello messages sent by OSPF, IS-IS, and EIGRP.

The TCP Advantage

BGP is the only IP routing protocol that uses TCP as its transport layer protocol. OSPF, IGRP, and EIGRP reside directly above the IP layer, and RIP version 1 (RIPv1) and RIP version 2 (RIPv2) use User Datagram Protocol (UDP) for their transport layer.

OSPF and EIGRP have their own internal processes to ensure that update packets are explicitly acknowledged. A downside of these protocols is they use a one-for-one window. If OSPF or EIGRP have more than one packet to send, a second packet cannot be sent until the router receives an acknowledgment for the first update packet. This process would be very inefficient and cause unacceptable latency if thousands of update packets had to be exchanged, especially over a slow link. OSPF and EIGRP would not normally have thousands of update packets to send. EIGRP, for example, can carry about 100 network entries in one EIGRP update packet. This means if a router sent 100 EIGRP update packets, it would be sending to as many as 10,000 networks. Most companies don't have 10,000 subnets in their internetwork, but the potential is there.

BGP, on the other hand, has more than 170,000 networks (and growing) on the Internet to advertise and it uses TCP to handle the acknowledgment function. TCP uses a dynamic window, which allows 65,576 bytes to be outstanding before it stops and waits for an acknowledgment. For example, if 1,000-byte packets are being sent, BGP would stop and wait for an acknowledgment only when 65 packets had not been acknowledged, when using the maximum window size.

TCP is designed to use a sliding window, where the receiver will acknowledge at the halfway point of the sending window. This method allows any TCP application, such as BGP, to continue to stream packets without having to stop and wait, as OSPF or EIGRP would require.

BGP Tables

BGP keeps its own tables to store BGP information that it receives from and sends to other routers, including a neighbor table, a BGP table (also called a forwarding database or topology database), and an IP routing table.

For BGP to establish an adjacency, you must configure it explicitly for each neighbor. BGP forms a TCP relationship with each of the configured neighbors and keeps track of the state of these relationships by periodically sending a BGP/TCP keepalive message. By default, BGP sends BGP/TCP keepalives every 60 seconds.

After establishing an adjacency, the neighbors exchange the BGP routes that are in their IP routing table. Each router collects these routes from each neighbor that successfully establishes an adjacency and then places them in its BGP forwarding database. All routes that have been learned from each neighbor are placed into the BGP forwarding database. The best routes for each network are selected from the BGP forwarding database using the BGP route selection process and then offered to the IP routing table.

Each router compares the offered BGP routes to any other possible paths to those networks, and the best route, based on administrative distance, is installed in the IP routing table.

EBGP routes (BGP routes learned from an external AS) have an administrative distance of 20. IBGP routes (BGP routes learned from within the AS) have an administrative distance of 200.

BGP Messages

The four BGP message types are:

- Open
- Keepalive
- Update
- Notification

After a TCP connection is established, the first message sent by each side is an open message. If the open message is acceptable, the side that receives the message sends a keepalive message confirming the open message. After the receiving side confirms the open message and establishes the BGP connection, the BGP peers can exchange any update, keepalive, and notification messages.

BGP peers initially exchange their full BGP routing tables. Incremental updates are sent only after topology changes in the network. BGP peers send keepalive messages to ensure that the connection between the BGP peers still exists; they send notification packets in response to errors or special conditions.

Table 7.1 contains more details about the different types of BGP messages.

TABLE 7.1 BGP Messages

Message Type	Content	Comments
Open message	Version number	The suggested version number. The highest common version that both routers support is used. Most BGP implementations today use BGP4.
	AS number	The AS number of the local router. The peer router verifies this information. If it is not the AS number that is expected, the BGP session is torn down.
	Hold time	Maximum number of seconds that can elapse between the successive keepalive and update messages from the sender. On receipt of an open message, the router calculates the value of the hold timer by using whichever is smaller: its configured hold time or the hold time that was received in the open message.
	BGP router ID	This 32-bit field indicates the BGP ID of the sender. The BGP ID is an IP address that is assigned to that router, and it is determined at startup. The BGP router ID is chosen in the same way that the OSPF router ID is chosen: it is the highest active IP address on the router unless a loopback interface with an IP address exists. In this case, the router ID is the highest loopback IP address. The router ID can also be statically configured.

TABLE 7.1   BGP Messages *(continued)*

Message Type	Content	Comments
	Optional parameters	These parameters are type, length, and value (TLV)-encoded. An example of an optional parameter is session authentication.
Keepalive message	BGP keepalive messages are exchanged between BGP peers often enough to keep the hold timer from expiring.	If the negotiated hold-time interval is 0, then periodic keepalive messages are not sent. A keepalive message consists of only a message header.
Update message	A BGP update message has information on one path only; multiple paths require multiple update messages.	All the attributes in the update message refer to that path, and the networks are those that can be reached through it. An update message can include withdrawn route, path attribute, and network-layer reachability fields.
	Withdrawn routes	This list displays IP address prefixes for routes that are withdrawn from service, if any.
	Path attributes	These attributes include the AS path, origin, local preference, and so on (as described later in this module). Each path attribute includes the attribute TLV. The attribute type consists of the attribute flags, followed by the attribute type code.
	Network-layer reachability information	This field contains a list of IP address prefixes that are reachable by this path.
Notification message	A BGP notification message is sent when an error condition is detected; the BGP connection is closed immediately after this is sent.	Notification messages include an error code, an error subcode, and data that are related to the error.

Types of BGP Connections

BGP can be used two different ways, internally or externally. The nice thing is BGP is configured the same way, regardless of the type you use. When BGP is running between routers in different autonomous systems, it is called external BGP (EBGP). When BGP is running between routers in the same AS, it is called internal BGP (IBGP). BGP allows the path that packets take to be manipulated by the AS. It is important to understand this works to avoid creating problems for your AS as you run BGP. There isn't a router anywhere that can handle being connected or communicating with every router that runs BGP. If you tried to connect to all of them, you would be connecting to the thousands of routers that run BGP and are connected to the Internet, with more than 21,000 autonomous systems. Let's take a look.

BGP Speaker   A BGP router forms a direct neighbor relationship with a limited number of other BGP routers. Through these BGP neighbors, a BGP router learns of the paths through the Internet to reach any advertised network. Any router that runs BGP is known as a BGP speaker.

BGP Peer   The term *BGP peer* has a specific meaning: a BGP speaker that is configured to form a neighbor relationship with another BGP speaker for the purpose of directly exchanging BGP routing information with each other. A BGP speaker has a limited number of BGP neighbors with which it peers and forms a TCP-based relationship.

BGP Neighbor   BGP peers are also known as BGP neighbors and can be either internal or external to the AS. A BGP peer must be configured with a BGP neighbor command. The administrator instructs the BGP speaker to establish a relationship with the address listed in the neighbor command and to exchange the BGP routing updates with that neighbor.

EBGP Neighbor   You will recall that when BGP is running between routers in different autonomous systems, it is called EBGP. By default, routers running EBGP are directly connected to each other.

An EBGP neighbor is a router outside this AS; an IGP is not run between the EBGP neighbors. For two routers to exchange BGP routing updates, the TCP-reliable transport layer on each side must successfully pass the TCP three-way handshake before the BGP session can be established. Therefore, the IP address used in the BGP neighbor command must be reachable without using an IGP, which can be accomplished by pointing at an address that is reachable through a directly connected network or by using static routes to that IP address. Generally, the neighbor address that is used is the address on a directly connected network.

IBGP Neighbor   Recall that BGP that runs between routers within the same AS is called IBGP. IBGP runs within an AS to exchange BGP information so that all BGP speakers have the same BGP routing information about outside autonomous systems.

Routers running IBGP do not have to be directly connected to each other as long as they can reach each other so that TCP handshaking can be performed to set up the BGP neighbor relationships. The IBGP neighbor can be reached by a directly connected network, static routes, or by the internal routing protocol. Because multiple paths generally exist within an AS to reach the other IBGP routers, a loopback address is generally used in the BGP `neighbor` command to establish the IBGP sessions.

IBGP in a Transit AS

BGP was originally intended to run along the borders of an AS with the routers in the middle of the AS ignorant of the details of BGP (hence the name *border* gateway protocol). A transit AS, such as the one in Figure 7.1, is an AS that routes traffic from one external AS to another external AS. Typically, transit autonomous systems are Internet service providers (ISPs). All routers in a transit AS must have complete knowledge of external routes. Theoretically, one way to achieve this goal is to redistribute BGP routes into an IGP at the edge routers. However, this approach has problems.

 Real World Scenario

Oops . . . FutureTech Shouldn't Be Doing This

You have just discovered that the FutureTech AS is acting as a transit AS. In Figure 7.1, you can see that AS 65043 is the FutureTech network. FutureTech is peered with two ISPs. The ISPs are represented as AS 65081 and AS 64076. FutureTech's being a transit AS means that it is letting the two ISPs pass data back and forth between the ISP's networks. This type of arrangement could be set up if the FutureTech network could handle the traffic load. However, the ISPs would have to compensate FutureTech for allowing them to pass data across its AS. This is the exact type of arrangement that ISPs make between one another. The connections and agreements between ISPs allowing data to be passed back and forth is the actual backbone of the Internet; without these connections we would have no Internet. Not very often though does a private company have this sort of agreement with ISPs. In this case, you've discovered that FutureTech does not have an agreement and is not being compensated. The last network engineer that set the peering up did it wrong. You've just found something else you are going to have to fix.

Because the current Internet routing table is very large, redistributing all the BGP routes into an IGP is not a scalable method for the interior routers within an AS to learn about the external networks. The best method you can use to carry the BGP routes across the AS is to run IBGP on the routers within the AS.

IBGP in a Nontransit AS

A nontransit AS, such as an organization that is multihoming with two ISPs, does not pass routes between the ISPs. However, the BGP routers within the AS still require knowledge of all BGP routes passed to the AS to make proper routing decisions.

FIGURE 7.1   Transit AS

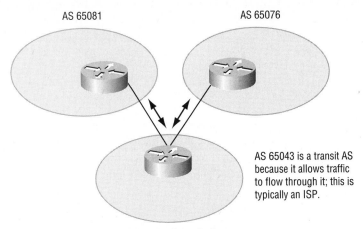

AS 65081

AS 65076

AS 65043 is a transit AS
because it allows traffic
to flow through it; this is
typically an ISP.

AS 65043—FutureTech

BGP does not work in the same manner as IGPs. Because the designers of BGP could not guarantee that an AS would run BGP on all routers, a method had to be developed to ensure that IBGP speakers could pass updates to one another while ensuring that no routing loops would exist.

To avoid routing loops within an AS, BGP specifies that routes learned through IBGP are never propagated to other IBGP peers.

Recall that the `neighbor` command enables BGP updates between BGP speakers. By default, each BGP speaker is assumed to have a neighbor statement for all other IBGP speakers in the AS, which is known as full mesh IBGP. Look at Figure 7.2, you can see this type of network as well.

 Real World Scenario

The Nontransit AS Fix

Now you have reconfigured to the nontransit AS that FutureTech's devices should be. In the nontransit AS, FutureTech has connections to multiple ISPs. Those ISPs provide redundancy and load balancing capabilities. In Figure 7.2, you can see that FutureTech is again AS 65043, but now traffic is not allowed to pass between the ISP networks using FutureTech as a path. If the two ISPs need to pass data between one another, they must have their own connection and agreement to do so.

If the sending IBGP neighbor is not fully meshed with each IBGP router, the routers that are not peering with this router will have different IP routing tables from the routers that are peering with it. The inconsistent routing tables can cause routing loops or routing black holes, because the default assumption by all routers running BGP within an AS is that each BGP router is exchanging IBGP information directly with all other BGP routers in the AS.

FIGURE 7.2   Nontransit AS

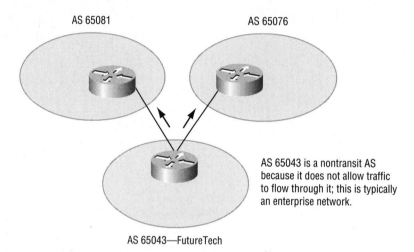

AS 65081

AS 65076

AS 65043 is a nontransit AS because it does not allow traffic to flow through it; this is typically an enterprise network.

AS 65043—FutureTech

If all IBGP neighbors are fully meshed, when a change is received from an external AS, the BGP router for the local AS is responsible for informing all other IBGP neighbors of the change. IBGP neighbors that receive this update do not send it to any other IBGP neighbor, because they assume that the sending IBGP neighbor is fully meshed with all other IBGP speakers and has sent each IBGP neighbor the update.

IBGP Full and Partial Mesh

The top portion of Figure 7.3 shows IBGP update behavior in a partially meshed neighbor environment.

 **Real World Scenario**

Making Sure All Your Routers Are Up To Date

Even in a network the size of FutureTech's, not all of the routers will learn or know about every network that exists outside of the FutureTech AS. There are far too many networks to know, and not all of the routers you use will be able to handle that load. However, the routers that connect FutureTech to the ISPs must be able to communicate and share the BGP routing information. For this reason, you set up IBGP between the routers that connect to the ISP routers. Figure 7.3 shows how you've set up the routers in the Dallas office. There is a rule for how IBGP routers can share updates; the routers must all be fully meshed. This rule prevents loops and also prevents a break in the path through the AS.

FIGURE 7.3   Partial Mesh vs. Full Mesh

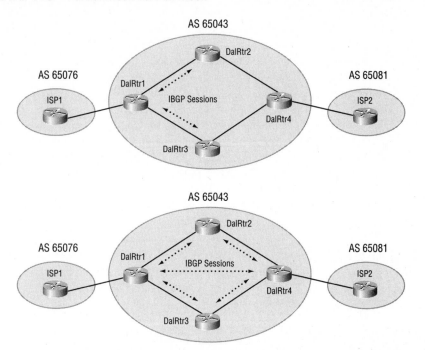

DalRtr1 receives a BGP update from ISP1. DalRtr1 has two IBGP neighbors, DalRtr2 and DalRtr3, but does not have an IBGP neighbor relationship with DalRtr4. DalRtr2 and DalRtr3 learn about any networks that were added or withdrawn behind DalRtr1. Even if DalRtr2 and DalRtr3 have IBGP neighbor sessions with DalRtr4, they assume that the AS is fully meshed for IBGP and do not replicate the update and send it to DalRtr4.

Sending an IBGP update to DalRtr4 is the responsibility of DalRtr1 because it is the router with firsthand knowledge of the networks in and beyond AS 65076. DalRtr4 does not learn of any networks through DalRtr1 and will not use DalRtr1 to reach any networks in AS 65076 or other autonomous systems behind AS 65076.

In the lower portion of Figure 7.3, IBGP is fully meshed. When DalRtr1 receives an update from ISP1, it updates all three of its IBGP peers, DalRtr2, DalRtr3, and DalRtr4. The IGP is used to route the TCP segment containing the BGP update from DalRtr1 to DalRtr4 as the routers are not directly connected. The update is sent once to each neighbor and not duplicated by any other IBGP neighbor, which reduces unnecessary traffic. In fully meshed IBGP, each router assumes that every other internal router has a neighbor statement that points to each IBGP neighbor.

Now the path through the FutureTech AS is complete from one side to the other.

TCP and Full Mesh

TCP was selected as the transport layer for BGP because TCP can move a large volume of data reliably. With the very large full Internet routing table changing constantly, using TCP for windowing and reliability was determined to be the best solution, as opposed to developing a BGP one-for-one windowing capability like OSPF or EIGRP.

TCP sessions cannot be multicast or broadcast because TCP has to ensure the delivery of packets to each recipient. Because TCP cannot use broadcasting, BGP cannot use it either.

Since each IBGP router needs to send routes to all the other IBGP neighbors in the same AS (so that they all have a complete picture of the routes sent to the AS) and they cannot use broadcast, they must use fully meshed BGP (TCP) sessions.

When all routers running BGP in an AS are fully meshed and have the same database as a result of a consistent routing policy, they can apply the same path selection formula. The path selection results will therefore be uniform across the AS. Uniform path selection across the AS means no routing loops and a consistent policy for exiting and entering the AS.

BGP Attributes

As I talked about earlier, BGP routers send BGP update messages about destination networks to other BGP routers. The BGP update messages contain one or more routes and a set of BGP metrics attached to the routes. The BGP metrics again are called path attributes.

Concept: Path Attributes

An attribute can be either well known or optional, mandatory or discretionary, and transitive or nontransitive. An attribute may also be partial. Only optional transitive attributes can be marked as partial.

The path attributes fall into the following four categories:

- Well-known mandatory

- Well-known discretionary

- Optional transitive

- Optional nontransitive

Every router that has BGP implemented must recognize a well-known attribute and propagate it to the other BGP neighbor routers. Well-known attributes are either mandatory or discretionary. A well-known mandatory attribute must be present in all BGP updates. A well-known discretionary attribute does not have to be present in all BGP updates.

Attributes that are not well known are called optional. BGP routers do not have to support an optional attribute. Optional attributes are either transitive or nontransitive. You have to remember the implementation rules of optional attributes:

- BGP routers that implement the optional attribute may propagate it to the other BGP neighbors, based on its meaning.

- BGP routers that do not implement an optional transitive attribute should pass it to other BGP routers untouched and mark the attribute as partial.

- BGP routers that do not implement an optional nontransitive attribute must delete the attribute and must not pass it to other BGP routers.

TABLE 7.2 BGP Path Attribute Categories

Category	Path Attribute
Well-known mandatory attributes	Autonomous system (AS) path
	Next-hop
	Origin
Well-known discretionary attributes	Local preference
	Atomic aggregate
Optional transitive attribute	Aggregator
Optional nontransitive attribute	Multi-exit discriminator (MED)

Weight

The weight attribute is a Cisco-proprietary attribute that defines the path selection process. The weight is configured locally on a router and is not propagated to any other routers. This attribute is specifically used for cases when you have one router configured with multiple exit points out of an AS. You will see this differs from the local preference attribute (next attribute I define), which is used when you have two or more routers that are providing multiple exit points.

The weight can have a value from 0 to 65535. Paths that the router originates have a weight of 32768 by default, and other paths have a weight of 0 by default. Routes with a higher weight are preferred when multiple routes exist to the same destination. Take a look at Figure 7.4; you can see the type of situation that I am referring to.

🌐 Real World Scenario

Path Selection Using Weight

You're back working at the Dallas office again. The guys in the Dallas office get to be your guinea pigs for all of these things. Say you have two paths out of the Dallas office. You want one of them to be used as the primary link when sending data to a given set of destinations and the other path to be the backup. You modify the weight value so that the path you want to be the primary would have a higher weight than the other path. Right now, you just modify the weight value. Hang on to that little nugget of information. Later in the chapter, when you look at the route maps, you may decide to use the route maps to modify the attributes.

FIGURE 7.4   Weight Attribute

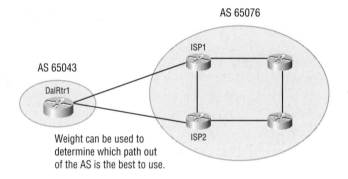

Weight can be used to
determine which path out
of the AS is the best to use.

Local Preference

Local preference is a well-known discretionary attribute, meaning that it will be in all implementations of BGP. This attribute provides an indication to routers in the AS (in case where there are multiple routers with paths out of the AS, unlike the weight attribute) about which path is preferred to exit the AS. A path with a higher local preference is preferred.

The local preference is an attribute that is configured on a router and exchanged among routers within the same AS only. For a Cisco router, the default value for local preference is 100. Compare Figure 7.5 with Figure 7.4; you can see how local preference differs from weight.

Path Selection Using Local Preference

Still in the Dallas office, but now you learn about a destination network in AS 65045 from two different autonomous systems. Here you decide to use local preference to set your preferred routing. In Figure 7.5, you can see that FutureTech is connected with two ISPs. Since you learned about the network from both of the ISPs, you consider modifying the local preference to pick which ISP you want to send the data through to reach the destination in AS 65045.

You ask yourself, "Why would I pick one ISP over the other?" Great question, and the answer can vary. Consider your local conditions; most often one ISP has a better connection or one of the ISPs links is cheaper and you will want to use it more often.

FIGURE 7.5   Local Preference Attribute

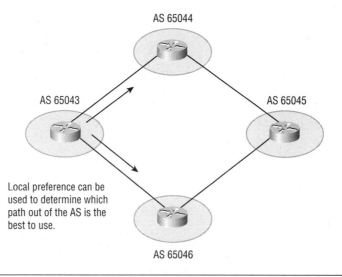

AS 65044

AS 65043   AS 65045

Local preference can be
used to determine which
path out of the AS is the
best to use.

AS 65046

Origin

The origin attribute defines the origin of the path information. The origin attribute can be one of the three values listed in Table 7.3.

TABLE 7.3   Origin Attribute BGP Values

Value	Definition
IGP	The route came from inside the originating AS. You will typically see this type of result when the network command is used to advertise the route via BGP. An origin of IGP is indicated with an "i" in the BGP table.
EGP	This type of route was learned via EGP. This type is displayed with an "e" in the BGP table. EGP is considered a historical routing protocol and is not supported on the Internet because it performs only classful routing and does not support classless interdomain routing (CIDR).
Incomplete	The origin of the route is unknown or has been learned by some other means. This value usually results when a route is redistributed into BGP. An incomplete origin is indicated with a question mark (?) in the BGP table.

AS-Path

The AS-path attribute is a well-known mandatory attribute. Whenever a route update passes through an AS, the AS number is prepended (added to the front of the AS list in the attribute field) to that update when it is advertised to the next external border gateway protocol (EBGP) neighbor. The AS-path attribute is actually the list of AS numbers that a route has traversed to reach a destination, with the number of the AS that originated the route at the end of the list. Figure 7.6, shows you an example of what I mean.

FIGURE 7.6   AS-Path Attribute

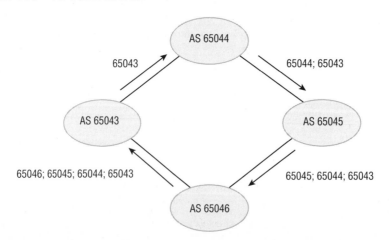

This attribute has two very important features that it performs. The first, in no particular order, is to provide a type hop count for autonomous systems. This can provide BGP with a way of determining distance in the number of systems that are traversed to get to a destination. The second feature that is provided by the AS-path attribute is loop avoidance. Because each of the systems that an update passed through adds its AS number to the list, an AS will know if the update passes through a second time because its number will already be present.

Multi-Exit Discriminator

The multi-exit discriminator (MED) attribute, also called the metric, is an optional non-transitive attribute.

The MED is an indication to EBGP neighbors about the preferred path into an AS. The MED attribute is a dynamic way to influence another AS about which path it should choose to reach a certain route when multiple entry points into an AS exist. A lower metric is preferred. Figure 7.7 shows you an example of this type of setup.

 Real World Scenario

Using the MED Attribute

You've been assigned to work in the Dallas and the New York offices. The two offices are connected with the FutureTech AS by a MPLS WAN connection. Both offices also have Internet connections out to the same ISP. It is common to learn the same destination routes from the ISP through both of the Internet connections. However, the New York office often sends a bunch of data to a partner company also located in New York. The ISP has a better path to this partner company from its NY location. There is no reason for FutureTech's NY office to send its data across the WAN to Dallas, where the data would be sent to the ISP only to be carried back to NY in the ISP's AS. Even though it's not commonly used, for this case you set up MED to be used by the ISP routers. When the ISP advertises the routes for the partner company, the update coming from the ISP-NY1 router now has a higher MED value than the route coming from the ISP-Da11 router. The New York office will now see the route through ISP-NY1 as the better route out of the FutureTech network to the partner company.

FIGURE 7.7 MED Attribute

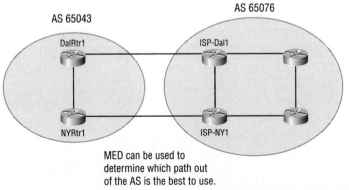

MED can be used to determine which path out of the AS is the best to use.

Unlike local preference, the MED is exchanged between autonomous systems. The MED is sent to EBGP peers; those routers propagate the MED within their AS, and the routers within the AS use the MED but do not pass it on to the next AS. When the same update is passed on to another AS, the metric is set back to the default of 0.

MED influences inbound traffic to an AS, and local preference influences outbound traffic from an AS.

By default, a router compares the MED attribute only for paths from neighbors in the same AS.

Next-hop

The BGP next-hop attribute is a well-known mandatory attribute that indicates the next-hop IP address that is to be used to reach a destination.

BGP routes AS by AS, not router by router. The next-hop address of a network from another AS will be an IP address of the entry point of the next AS along the path to that destination network.

Choosing a Path

Multiple paths may exist to reach a given network. As paths for the network are evaluated, those determined not to be the best path are eliminated from the selection criteria but kept in the BGP forwarding table (which can be displayed using the `show ip bgp` command) in case the best path becomes inaccessible.

BGP is not designed to perform load balancing; paths are chosen because of policy, not based on bandwidth. The BGP selection process eliminates any multiple paths until a single best path is left.

The best path is submitted to the routing table manager process and is evaluated against any other routing protocols that can also reach that network. The route from the source with the lowest administrative distance is installed in the routing table.

The decision process is based on the attributes described earlier.

After BGP receives updates about different destinations from different autonomous systems, it decides the best path to choose to reach a specific destination. BGP chooses only a single best path to reach a destination.

The decision process is based on the BGP attributes. When faced with multiple routes to the same destination, BGP chooses the best route for routing traffic toward the destination. BGP considers only (synchronized) routes with no AS loops and a valid next hop. The following process summarizes how BGP chooses the best route on a Cisco router:

1. Prefer the route with the highest weight. (Recall that the weight is proprietary to Cisco and is local to the router only.)

2. If multiple routes have the same weight, prefer the route with the highest local preference. (Recall that the local preference is used within an AS.)

3. If multiple routes have the same local preference, prefer the route that the local router originated. A locally originated route has a next hop of 0.0.0.0 in the BGP table.

4. If none of the routes were locally originated, prefer the route with the shortest AS path.

5. If the AS path length is the same, prefer the lowest origin code:

IGP < EGP < incomplete

6. If all origin codes are the same, prefer the path with the lowest MED. (Recall that the MED is exchanged between autonomous systems.)

7. The MED comparison is made only if the neighboring AS is the same for all routes considered, unless the `bgp always-compare-med` command is enabled.

8. If the routes have the same MED, prefer external paths (EBGP) to internal paths (IBGP).

9. If synchronization is disabled and only internal paths remain, prefer the path through the closest IGP neighbor. This step means that the router will prefer the shortest internal path within the AS to reach the destination (the shortest path to the BGP next hop).

10. For EBGP paths, select the oldest route to minimize the effect of routes going up and down (flapping).

11. Prefer the route with the lowest neighbor BGP router ID value.

12. If the BGP router IDs are the same, prefer the router with the lowest neighbor IP address.

Only the best path is entered in the routing table and propagated to the BGP neighbors of the router.

 Real World Scenario

Seven Paths

For example, suppose there are seven paths to reach network 10.0.0.0 from the London office. All of the paths are learned by the edge router in London. The edge router must use the path selection process to choose which path is the best.

All paths have no AS loops and have valid next-hop addresses, so all seven paths proceed to Step 1, which examines the weight of the paths.

All seven paths have a weight of 0, so they all proceed to Step 2, which examines the local preference of the paths. Four of the paths have a local preference of 200, and the other three have local preferences of 100, 100, and 150.

The four with a local preference of 200 will continue the evaluation process to the next step. The other three will still be in the BGP forwarding table but are currently disqualified as the best path.

BGP will continue the evaluation process until only a single best path remains. The single best path that remains will be submitted to the IP routing table as the best BGP path.

Route Maps

Route maps are similar to access control lists (ACL), but they give you much more flexibility and power for editing. In many ways, they work like an ACL but route maps are more complex. I like to think of them as more powerful rather than more complex, because complex makes them sound scary—and they shouldn't be. True, they are more involved to configure, but that is usually due to the fact that you are familiar with ACLs. They are similar to a scripting language in that they use if-then logic.

A route map statement is comparable to a statement in an ACL, but in a route map they are numbered for easier editing. It is like the numbering you have in a named or sequenced ACL. You can add or remove lines in the map easily with the numbered statements. Route maps offer top-down processing and, when a match occurs, further processing of statements stops. To make keeping track of the route maps less complicated, they are all named; you don't have to keep track of number ranges (and what they mean) as you must in ACLs.

In an ACL the statement, the entire statement is included in the one line. With a route map, when you create a statement, it will includes other lines, the match and set lines. These additional lines are what provide the flexibility and power. You can match (or specify) much more than just a source or destination IP address in a route map. The set command allows you to not only permit or deny something but to modify actions. You will get a look at many of these options in just a minute.

First, let's see where and for what purpose you can use route maps. You saw in Chapter 4 that a route map can be used for redistribution. Using a route map in redistribution allows you the control to select through the matching process exactly which routes to allow and not allow.

Route maps also can be used to set and control BGP routing policy. BGP attributes can be changed with route maps. Route maps can control which updates and information are exchanged between BGP peers or neighbors.

Concept: Using a Route Map to Manipulate Attributes

Remember earlier in the chapter I mentioned that I would bring up modifying BGP attributes with a route map. Now you will see through the use of a route map you can match specific destination networks that are learned from other autonomous systems and then set different attribute values. I have used the words *match* and *set* specifically in this case. In the coming section when you configure a route map, you will see those are the commands that are used; the match and set commands.

The last application of route maps that you will learn about is one called policy-based routing (PBR). This is a very cool feature where you can match traffic based on many things such as source address, destination address, protocol type, or application. When you have traffic that matches one of these things, you can use the set command to define an interface or next-hop address to which you want the traffic sent to. This really means that you can select traffic and have it sent differently that it might have been sent by the routing table or process.

Configuring a Route Map

Let's take a look at some of these commands so that we can start to put the pieces together. The `route-map` command looks like this:

`route-map map-tag [permit | deny] [sequence-number]`

The `map-tag` parameter specifies the name of the route map; all of the statements within a route map include this name to tie them together as a single route map. The name is similar to the ACL number that is used to identify all of the statements that make up an ACL.

The `permit` or `deny` parameters determine whether the route map will evoke the specified action in the `set` command. A packet that is permitted by a route map statement may be allowed to go through the redistribution process, or to be routed to a different neighbor; it depends on the purpose of the route map. A packet that is denied by the route map or doesn't match any statements (which means it matches the implicit deny at the end of the list) will not be routed with any policy-based routing decision or to be redistributed depending on the use of the route map. In the case of PBR, maps that are put in place to route specific types of traffic differently send traffic via a special routing process when a match is found. Traffic that doesn't match the map is sent back to the routing table for normal routing. So in a route map, a `deny` setting doesn't always mean that the traffic will be dropped, like it does with an access list.

The last parameter in the command is the *sequence number*. The sequence number is used to keep track of the statements and make editing them easier. You can specify a statement by number and remove it. You add a new statement between two existing statements. For this reason, the statements are normally identified using sequence numbers that upcount by 10. The first statement would be sequence number 10, the second 20, and so on. If you do not specify a sequence number in the command line, the default numbering up count by 10.

Once you have entered the `route-map` command, you will be placed into a route map configuration mode. In route map configuration mode, you can configure the `match` and `set` commands for the statement. Those commands are simply `match` {*conditions*} and `set` {*actions*}. Table 7.4 and Table 7.5 list some of the `match` and `set` parameters that can be used to configure a route map. Not all of them can be used for every map. Some are for redistribution, while others are specifically for use with BGP.

TABLE 7.4   Match Command Parameters for Route Maps

Command	Description
`match community`	Matches a BGP community
`match interface`	Matches any routes that have the next-hop out of one of the interfaces specified
`match ip address`	Matches any routes that have a destination network number address that is permitted by a standard or extended ACL

TABLE 7.4   Match Command Parameters for Route Maps *(continued)*

Command	Description
match ip next-hop	Matches any routes that have a next-hop router address that is passed by one of the ACLs specified
match ip route-source	Matches routes that have been advertised by routers and access servers at the address that is specified by the ACLs
match length	Matches based on the Layer 3 length of a packet
match metric	Matches routes with the metric specified
match route-type	Matches routes of the specified type
match tag	Matches tag of a route

TABLE 4.5   Set Command Parameters for Route Maps

Command	Description
set as-path	Modifies an AS-path for BGP routes
set automatic-tag	Computes automatically the tag value
set community	Sets the BGP communities attribute
set default interface	Indicates where to output packets that pass a match clause of a route map for policy routing and have no explicit route to the destination
set interface	Indicates where to output packets that pass a match clause of a route map for policy routing
set ip default next-hop	Indicates where to output packets that pass a match clause of a route map for policy routing and for which Cisco IOS software has no explicit route to a destination
set ip next-hop	Indicates where to output packets that pass a match clause of a route map for policy routing
set level	Indicates where to import routes for IS-IS and OSPF
set local-preference	Specifies a BGP local preference value

TABLE 4.5 Set Command Parameters for Route Maps *(continued)*

Command	Description
set metric	Sets the metric value for a routing protocol
set metric-type	Sets the metric type for the destination routing protocol
set tag	Sets tag value for destination routing protocol
set weight	Specifies the BGP weight value

Creating Match Statements

A single route map statement can have more than one match or set command used in it. A single match statement can have more than one condition used within it. Let's take a look at a hypothetical route map that we might use to perform policy-based routing. For this example, it isn't important where we are going to implement it, just how we can write the statements.

```
RouterA(config)#route-map test permit 10
RouterA(config-route-map)#match ip address D  E  F
RouterA(config-route-map)#match ip address G  H  I
```

You can see in the example, two match lines are under route map statement 10. Now in the first match statement, I used the letters *D,* E and *F* to represent potential IP addresses that are to be matched. When you have more than one match condition in the same line, each condition is looked at individually. An OR function is used to determine the match. So, during the processing of the statement this first match line would be looked at and the subject IP address would be compared. Does the IP address match *D* OR *E* OR *F*? If any one of them is a match, then this line would be considered a match. If this were the only match line, then processing would stop and the set command would be looked at. Because there is a second match line in our example, the comparison must go on.

When there is more than one match command, the lines are used in conjunction with each other. A logical AND is used between the lines. In the example, one of the conditions from the first match line would have had to match to trigger processing of the second line.

Let's say that the IP address matched IP address *E*. So now the second match line comes into play. The comparison now requires that the address match E AND *G* OR *H* OR *I*. For a route map statement to match, then something from this second line must match. The result might be that E AND *G* match. In that case, the statement would have a match, and we could move on to the set portion of the statement. If our IP address only matched something in the first line and nothing in the second line, then there is not match and processing would continue to the next statement, if there was one.

Creating Set Statements

The set lines in a statement work exactly the same way. You can have more than one set line and a logical AND would be applied to the lines. If there is more than one condition on a single line, then a logical OR is applied to the conditions. To continue with the example of policy based routing, I've added a set statement.

```
RouterA(config)#route-map test permit 10
RouterA(config-route-map)#match ip address D  E  F
RouterA(config-route-map)#match ip address G  H  I
RouterA(config-route-map)#set serial0 serial1
```

Now with this set statement in place, when a packet comes through and matches a condition from each one of the match lines, processing continues down to the set statement. The set line then controls which interface will be used to send the traffic. With the set statement, I configured, the traffic will be sent out Serial0. If for some reason Serial0 is down and cannot be used, then the traffic will be sent out Serial1.

Implementing a Route Map

The last thing that you need to know is how to implement a route map—how to tie the map to an interface or redistribution process. Let's look at implementing the route map that I created above. When I created the map, I wanted to implement policy-based routing and control the flow of data. To do that, the route map has to be placed where data is coming in. You guessed it, the map must be placed on an interface. So to put a route map named test on an interface, you would:

```
RouterA(config)#route-map test permit 10
RouterA(config-route-map)#match ip address D  E  F
RouterA(config-route-map)#match ip address G  H  I
RouterA(config-route-map)#set serial0 serial1
RouterA(config-route-map)#interface fa0/0
RouterA(config-if)#ip policy route-map test
```

Configuring BGP

Now, I want to take you through the configuration steps of enabling BGP and setting up connections to neighbors. Some of the configuration for BGP is very much like other routing protocols. You have to enable the protocol with the router command, and add subnets to the process with the network command.

Basic Setup

Let's start off with enabling the routing process. Use the `router bgp` *autonomous-system* command to start the configuration on the router and to add subsequent subcommands to the routing process in router mode. This command identifies the local autonomous system (AS) in which this router belongs. You have to tell the router about the AS so it can determine whether the BGP neighbors that you configure next are IBGP or EBGP neighbors.

The `router` command does not activate the routing protocol; a neighbor command must be entered to activate the process. Only one process of BGP can be configured on a single router.

Neighbor Establishment

You will use the `neighbor` *ip-address* `remote-as` *autonomous-system* command to activate a BGP session for both external and internal neighboring routers. The *ip-address* portion of the command is the IP address of the neighbor you wish to peer with. In the case of making an EBGP connection, the address should be a directly connected IP address of the neighbor. This is because there is no routing (IGP) that occurs between the devices. It is possible to use a static route to make the routers reach one another, but a directly connected network and IP address is recommended.

The IP address for an IBGP connection can be a directly connected interface but does not have to be. This is because there is typically an IGP routing protocol running that will allow the TCP traffic from one BGP router to reach the other. The *autonomous-system* number after the `remote-as` command designates what AS the peer router belongs to. If the AS number is the neighbor command is different than the AS number in the `router bgp` command, then the local router knows the neighbor connection will be an EBGP connection. If the AS number from the two commands are the same, then the router knows that the connection will be an IBGP connection.

Administratively Shutting down a Neighbor

If you are going to implement a major policy change to a neighboring router and you change multiple parameters, you should always administratively shut down the neighboring router before you implement the changes. Then, once the changes are made, bring back up the neighboring router. This will prevent the route or the neighbor from flapping and creating instability in the BGP process. When you need to shut down a neighbor, use the `neighbor` *ip-address* `shutdown` command. When you are finished and ready to reenable the neighbor, use the `no neighbor` *ip-address* `shutdown` command to bring back up the BGP neighbor.

Source and Destination IP Address Assignment

Remember that BGP uses a TCP session to maintain its relationship with neighbors. The TCP session is only established if the IP addresses that the router sees in the packets are the same as those you have configured in the neighbor statements. It has to work like this: The BGP neighbor statement that you configure tells the router the destination IP address for each packet being sent to a neighbor. The router then must decide which IP address will be used as the source IP address in the BGP packet.

During the creation of a BGP packet for a neighbor, the router must check the routing table for the destination network to reach the specific neighbor. In the routing table, the outbound interface for the destination network is listed, as indicated by routing table that interfaces IP address is used as the source IP of the BGP packet.

Now when the router on the other end receives the packet from this new neighbor, the source IP address in the packet is compared to the neighbor statements that you have configured. The IP address must match the address in a corresponding neighbor statement. If there is a match in a neighbor statement, then the session will be created and a relationship formed. If no match is found in the neighbor statements, then the routers will not become BGP peers because the session will not be established.

So now I want you to look at Figure 7.8, where you can see that there are four routers in AS 65043. I want to show you what you can do to prevent session establishment problems in this AS. Problems normally occur when you are connecting internal routers for IBGP sessions. If there is more than one path for the routers to take inside the AS, as there is in this example network, you can end up with traffic sourced from the wrong interface.

 **Real World Scenario**

Establishing a BGP Peer

Again, in the Dallas office you are getting the same four routers to talk, but you start to experience problems. For some reason, some of the routers lose their peering sessions.

DalRtr1 is attempting to connect to DalRtr2. You have put neighbor statements on each of the routers so that they can start the session. If DalRtr1 sends a packet to DalRtr2 and sends it out of its 10.1.1.1 interface, but I have put a neighbor statement on DalRtr2 telling it that DalRtr1 should be the 10.1.0.1 router. Then DalRtr2 will reject the packet because it doesn't have a 10.1.1.1 router in its neighbor list. Moving the packets the other way could have the same affect. If DalRtr2 were to send a packet out of its 10.2.1.1 interface, that IP would be the source address. But if you have configured DalRtr1 with a neighbor statement that says 10.2.0.1 should be DalRtr2, then it would reject the packet.

The best way to prevent this from happing is to use a loopback interface. If you place a loopback interface on each of the routers, then each router can always be known by its loopback interface. To make sure that a router always sends its BGP updates with the loopback IP as the source, though, you are going to have to use the update-source command.

Update-source

The BGP router must know that it is communicating with the router that it is configured to talk to. You can ensure this happens by using a loopback address in the neighbor statement. Each of the routers can be configured with a loopback interface; this may already be done if you are using one for the IGP that is running within the AS. Using the loopback address in the neighbor statement is easy enough; you just have to configure it with that address. But making the router use that address as the source address for all its packets is what takes an additional configuration. You can accomplish this using the *update-source* option with the `neighbor` command.

FIGURE 7.8   BGP Session Establishment

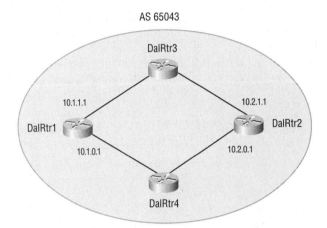

The *update-source* configuration is typically used only for IBGP connections. This is because by default EBGP connections must be directly connected. The time to live (TTL) of all EBGP packets is 1. A loopback interface is not directly connected as the packet must pass through the physical interface and be routed to the loopback.

The default TTL of 1 was set up because internal routing information is not exchanged between the external peers; the router must point to a directly connected address for a specific external neighbor.

EBGP-multihop

As I said, a loopback interface is never directly connected. Therefore, if you want to use a loopback interface instead of the directly connected interface address, you must add an additional configuration. There must be a static route that points to the physical address of the directly connected network (the next-hop address). The static route will get the traffic to the neighbor router but will not allow BGP to accept the packet, as the TTL is still set to the default of 1. In order for this configuration to work, you have to use the `neighbor` *ip-address* `ebgp-multihop` [*ttl*] router configuration command.

Using this configuration lets the router start and set up BGP connections to external routers that do not reside on directly connected networks. This command increases the default of one hop for EBGP peers by changing the default TTL to a value greater than 1. It allows routes to be sent to the EBGP loopback address with a hop value greater than 1. Unless you specify a TTL value that is different in the command, it will default to a value of 255; you can see that there is an option at the end of the command to set this value but it is not required. This configuration command can be especially valuable if there are redundant or multiple paths between EBGP neighbors.

Next-Hop Issues

The BGP protocol is very different from IGPs; BGP is an AS-to-AS routing protocol, not a network-to-network protocol. BGP is an external routing protocol that learns and passes routes about paths to other autonomous systems and the networks that those other autonomous systems own. BGP is a hop-by-hop routing protocol similar to an IGP, but unlike an IGP, the default next-hop is the next AS. This means that even an IBGP neighbor router that learns about a network outside of its autonomous system will see the same next-hop address because the next-hop address is not changed by default when an edge router learns a route through EBGP and then passes it to an IBGP neighbor. This, however, could be a problem for the IBGP router, if the router doesn't know how to reach that next-hop address.

In order to overcome the problem of an IBGP router being unable to reach the next-hop address, you have yet another configuration that you can add to the mix. The `neighbor next-hop-self` command forces a BGP router to use its own IP address as the next-hop address for each network that it advertises to its IBGP neighbor. This overrides the default action of letting the protocol choose the next-hop address to use.

Peer Groups

You can see here that there could potentially be a lot of commands that must be configured for each of the neighbors you set up on a router, especially when it comes to IBGP neighbors that may need a couple of extra commands so that they can reach all of the other routers and another AS. Peer groups are here to save your tired typing fingers and to help save from potential misconfigurations. Using peer group configuration can lower the overhead on your routers and prevent the same update from having to be made for all of the neighbor routers.

To get the ball rolling, you have to enter the `neighbor` *peer-group-name* `peer-group` command; this command creates the peer group. The `neighbor` *ip-address* `peer-group` *peer-group-name* command then links the address of a neighbor to the peer group; rather than linking the neighbor just to an AS or configuring it with one specific command. The next commands you must enter are the individual commands that you would have configured for each of the neighbor routers, but instead of typing out them all for each of the neighbors, you one configure them once and you link them to the peer group.

 Real World Scenario

Configuration Made Easier

In a network the size of FutureTech, you might have dozens of routers that are all running IBGP. The use of the peer group configuration can save you time, number of entries in the configuration, and the possibility of making errors during configuration.

You can see in Figure 7.9, that there are four routers in the 65043 AS. For DalRtr1, each of the other three routers will be IBGP neighbors, and the configurations for each of the routers will be the same. You can see in the following outputs that even with just three routers for peers the configuration is shorter and easier. Imagine how much easier your life is going to be when I tell you to do this with 50 routers!

Let's take a look at an example, in Figure 7.9.

FIGURE 7.9   Peer Groups

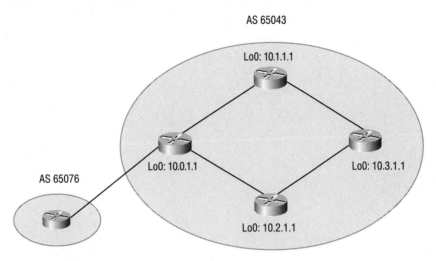

Look at the following outputs. The first section of configuration shows you all of the commands that would be needed it a peer group was not used. The second group of commands shows you the configuration using a peer group configuration.

```
DalRtr1(config)#router bgp 65043
DalRtr1(config-router)#neighbor 10.1.1.1 remote-as 65043
DalRtr1(config-router)#neighbor 10.1.1.1 update-source Loopback 0
DalRtr1(config-router)#neighbor 10.1.1.1 next-hop-self
DalRtr1(config-router)#neighbor 10.1.1.1  distribute-list 10 out
DalRtr1(config-router)#neighbor 10.2.1.1 remote-as 65043
DalRtr1(config-router)#neighbor 10.2.1.1 update-source Loopback 0
DalRtr1(config-router)#neighbor 10.2.1.1 next-hop-self
DalRtr1(config-router)#neighbor 10.2.1.1 distribute-list 10 out
DalRtr1(config-router)#neighbor 10.3.1.1 remote-as 65043
DalRtr1(config-router)#neighbor 10.3.1.1 update-source Loopback 0
DalRtr1(config-router)#neighbor 10.3.1.1 next-hop-self
DalRtr1(config-router)#neighbor 10.3.1.1 distribute-list 10 out
```

Here is the configuration using a peer group.

```
DalRtr1(config)#router bgp 65043
DalRtr1(config-router)#neighbor futuretech peer-group
DalRtr1(config-router)#neighbor futuretech remote-as 65043
DalRtr1(config-router)#neighbor futuretech update-source Loopback 0
DalRtr1(config-router)#neighbor futuretech next-hop-self
```

```
DalRtr1(config-router)#neighbor futuretech distribute-list 10 out
DalRtr1(config-router)#neighbor 10.1.1.1  peer-group futuretech
DalRtr1(config-router)#neighbor 10.2.1.1  peer-group futuretech
DalRtr1(config-router)#neighbor 10.3.1.1  peer-group futuretech
```

Network

Now I want to help you explore the network command. This command operates much differently in BGP than it does in an IGP. In an IGP, the network command would enable the interface in the protocol. This, in turn, would allow the routing protocol to advertise the network. In BGP, the network command only tells the router what network or prefix to advertise, it has nothing to do with enabling interfaces. BGP doesn't care about interfaces, as it using whatever interface it must to establish its session.

The only purpose of the network command is to notify BGP which network to advertise. The entire command looks like this network network-number [*mask network-mask*] [*route-map map-tag*].

If you use the command without the mask option, it will announce only the classful network number. There is a requirement though; at least one subnet of the specified major network must be present in the IP routing table. BGP will only start announcing the classful network as a BGP route when there is a route in the routing table.

However, if you do use the *network-mask* option, then there must be an exact match to the network (both address and mask) in the routing table. BGP checks to see whether the network can be reached before it will be advertised. If you specify a network to be advertised by BGP and it will not be placed in the routing table either by an IGP or from being directly connected, then you will have to add it to the routing table with a static route. If you will want to advertise a network with a different mask than what is in the table quite often, a static route can be added that routes the network to nu110.

Example Configuration

Now I want to go through an entire scenario. There will be connections to multiple ISPs and the use of BGP is going to be required for the network. The topology that I will use for this example is shown in Figure 7.10.

The first thing that you'll want to do is to establish the connection between these two EBGP neighbors. On the CE1 router, the configuration will require you to start the BGP process and then activate it with a neighbor command. It will look like this.

```
CE1(config)#router bgp 65043
CE1(config-router)#neighbor 192.168.1.2 remote-as 65076
```

For the ISP router, there is a similar set of commands to get the process started. Here is each of those.

```
PE1(config)#router bgp 65076
PE1(config-router)#neighbor 192.168.1.1 remote-as 65043
```

🌐 Real World Scenario

FutureTech IBGP/EBGP Setup

You have been assigned to connect three routers in the Dallas office using IBGP and the CE1 router to an ISP using EBGP. You can see in Figure 7.10 that there is a connection out to an ISP, which is represented by AS 65076. The FutureTech AS number is 65043. The edge router in the FutureTech AS is called CE1; the CE stands for customer edge. The ISP's router is PE1, where the PE stands for provider edge.

FIGURE 7.10   BGP Example

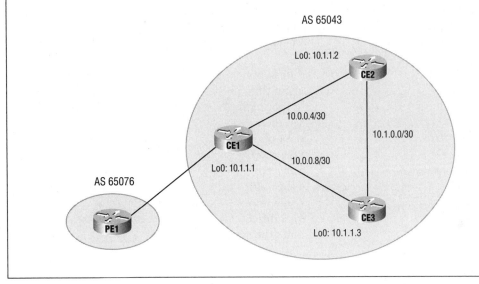

Now to get each of the routers within AS 65043 started, use a peer-group configuration. Remember this is for IBGP connections within the same AS.

```
CE1(config-router)#router bgp 65043
CE1(config-router)#neighbor futuretech peer-group
CE1(config-router)#neighbor futuretech remote-as 65043
CE1(config-router)#neighbor futuretech update-source loopback 0
CE1(config-router)#neighbor futuretech next-hop-self
CE1(config-router)#neighbor 10.1.1.2 peer-group futuretech
CE1(config-router)#neighbor 10.1.1.3 peer-group futuretech
CE2(config-router)#router bgp 65043
CE2(config-router)#neighbor futuretech peer-group
CE2(config-router)#neighbor futuretech remote-as 65043
CE2(config-router)#neighbor futuretech update-source loopback 0
```

```
CE2(config-router)#neighbor 10.1.1.3 peer-group futuretech
CE2(config-router)#neighbor 10.1.1.1 peer-group futuretech
CE3(config-router)#router bgp 65043
CE3(config-router)#neighbor futuretech peer-group
CE3(config-router)#neighbor futuretech remote-as 65043
CE3(config-router)#neighbor futuretech update-source loopback 0
CE3(config-router)#neighbor 10.1.1.1 peer-group futuretech
CE3(config-router)#neighbor 10.1.1.2 peer-group futuretech
```

Now you will have to advertise the network prefixes to each of the opposite autonomous systems. Start by advertising the 10.0.0.0 network to the 65076 AS from the CE1 router. Remember, if you use the mask option in the network command, then there must be an exact matching route in the routing table. I didn't have you set up a route in the table that matches 10.0.0.0/8, so let's forgo using the mask option.

```
CE1(config-router)#router bgp 65043
CE1(config-router)#network 10.0.0.0
```

You still have a problem at this point. If you look in the routing table of the PE1 router, it has received no network. Take a look at this cut output from the running-config of the CE1 router and see if you can tell what the problem might be.

```
!
router bgp 65043
no synchronization
bgp log-neighbor-changes
network 10.0.0.0
neighbor futuretech peer-group
neighbor futuretech remote-as 65043
neighbor futuretech update-source Loopback0
neighbor futuretech next-hop-self
neighbor 10.1.1.2 peer-group futuretech
neighbor 10.1.1.3 peer-group futuretech
neighbor 192.168.1.2 remote-as 65076
no auto-summary
!
```

If you say that it is because no auto-summary was turned on by default, then you are right. If you turn off no auto-summary at this point, then the route would be advertised to the PE1 router. Chances are that you don't want to turn on auto-summary, though. So, your option (if this is the prefix that you want to advertise) is to use the mask option and put a static route in the routing table. Making that change would look like this.

```
CE1(config-router)#router bgp 65043
CE1(config-router)#no network 10.0.0.0
```

```
CE1(config-router)#network 10.0.0.0 mask 255.0.0.0
CE1(config)#ip route 10.0.0.0 255.0.0.0 null0
```

Now you should have a route in the routing table of PE1, and all of your routers should be happy.

Verifying BGP

Now let me show you some of the show commands for BGP that are useful for making sure that your routers are communicating properly and all of the traffic is being exchanged.

First, look at the show ip bgp command. Here is the output from the CE1 router you just configured.

```
CE1#show ip bgp
BGP table version is 6, local router ID is 10.0.0.9
Status codes: s suppressed, d damped, h history, * valid, > best, i - internal,
r RIB-failure, S Stale
Origin codes: i - IGP, e - EGP, ? - incomplete
Network          Next Hop          Metric LocPrf Weight Path
*> 10.0.0.0        0.0.0.0                0           32768 i
*> 172.16.10.0/24  192.168.1.2            0           0 65076 i
*> 172.16.20.0/24  192.168.1.2            0           0 65076 i
```

The status codes are shown at the beginning of each line of output, and the origin codes are shown at the end of each line. In this output, there is an asterisk (*) in most of the entries in the first column. This means that the next-hop address is valid. The next-hop address is not always the router that is directly connected to this router. Other status codes that you might see in the first column are listed in Table 7.5.

TABLE 7.5   BGP Route Status Codes

Code	Description
s	Suppressed indicates that the specified routes have been suppressed (usually because routes have been summarized and only the summary route is being sent)
d	Dampening indicates that the route is being dampened (penalized) for going up and down too often. Although the route might be up right now, it is not advertised until the penalty has expired.
h	History indicates that the route is unavailable and is probably down; historic information about the route exists, but a best route does not exist.

TABLE 7.5 BGP Route Status Codes *(continued)*

Code	Description
r	Routing information base (RIB) failure indicates that the route was not installed in the RIB. The reason that the route is not installed can be displayed using the show ip bgp rib-failure command.
S	Stale indicates that the route is stale (this symbol is used in the nonstop forwarding-aware router).

The second column shows ">" when BGP has selected the path as the best path to a network.

The third column is either blank or shows i. If it is blank, BGP learned that route from an external peer. An i indicates that an IBGP neighbor advertised this path to the router.

The fourth column lists the networks that the router learned.

The Next Hop column lists all the next-hop addresses for each route. This column may contain the entry 0.0.0.0, which signifies that this router is the originator of the route.

The three columns to the left of the Path column list three BGP path attributes that are associated with the path: metric (multi-exit discriminator [MED]), local preference, and weight.

The column with the Path header may contain a sequence of autonomous systems in the path. From left to right, the first AS listed is the adjacent AS that this network was learned from. The last number (the rightmost AS number) is the originating AS of this network. The AS numbers between these two represent the exact path that a packet takes back to the originating AS. If the path column is blank, the route is from the current AS.

The last column signifies how this route was entered into BGP on the original router. If the last column contains an i, the originating router probably used a network statement to introduce this network into BGP.

If the character is an e, the originating router learned this network from EGP, which is the historical predecessor to BGP. A question mark (?) signifies that BGP cannot absolutely verify the availability of this network because it is redistributed from an IGP into BGP.

The next command that I want you to take look at is the show ip bgp summary command. Again, I show you the output code from the CE1 router you just configured.

```
CE1#show ip bgp summary
BGP router identifier 10.0.0.9, local AS number 65043
BGP table version is 6, main routing table version 6
3 network entries using 351 bytes of memory
3 path entries using 156 bytes of memory
3/2 BGP path/bestpath attribute entries using 348 bytes of memory
1 BGP AS-PATH entries using 24 bytes of memory
0 BGP route-map cache entries using 0 bytes of memory
0 BGP filter-list cache entries using 0 bytes of memory
```

```
BGP using 879 total bytes of memory
BGP activity 4/1 prefixes, 4/1 paths, scan interval 60 secs
Neighbor       V AS MsgRcvd MsgSent TblVer  InQ OutQ Up/Down  State/PfxRcd
10.1.1.2       4 65043   52      51       6    0    0 00:48:03        0
10.1.1.3       4 65043   51      52       6    0    0 00:47:50        0
192.168.1.2    4 65076   73      73       6    0    0 01:10:15        2
```

The show ip bgp summary command is one way to verify the neighbor relationship. The code above shows you the output from this command. Some of the details of this command output are listed in Table 7.6.

TABLE 7.6 show ip bgp summary Command Details

Item	Description
BGP router ID	IP address that all other BGP speakers recognize as representing this router
BGP table version	Increases in increments when the BGP table changes
Main routing table version	Last version of the BGP database that was injected into the main routing table
Neighbor	The IP address that is used in the neighbor statement with which this router has a relationship
Version (V)	The version of BGP that this router is running with the listed neighbor
AS	The AS number of the listed neighbor
Messages received (MsgRcvd)	The number of BGP messages that have been received from this neighbor
Messages sent (MsgSent)	The number of BGP messages sent to this neighbor
Table version (TblVer)	BGP table version
In queue (InQ)	The number of messages waiting to be processed from this neighbor
Out queue (OutQ)	The number of messages queued and waiting to be sent to this neighbor; TCP flow control prevents this router from overwhelming a neighbor with too much data at one time.
large update.Up/Down	The length of time that this neighbor has been in the current BGP state (established, active, or idle)

TABLE 7.6   show ip bgp summary Command Details *(continued)*

Item	Description
State [established, active, idle, open sent, open confirm, or idle (admin)]	The BGP state; you can set a neighbor to administratively shut down (admin state) by using the neighbor shutdown router configuration command.
Prefix received (PfxRcd)	When the session is in the established state, this value represents the number of BGP network entries received from the listed neighbor.

Summary

There were a lot of things to cover to get you through BGP. The first thing I talked about was whether you should even use BGP or not. BGP is the only routing protocol that I gave you reasons not to use it. Then, after you have decided that you are going to use BGP, I took you through the ways that you can connect your network to the Internet.

Next, I described for you the characteristics of BGP and what the decision-making process for the protocol is. I covered for you the many tables and messages that BGP creates and sends out. Once those messages are being sent out, you had to learn what kind of connections you could make full or partial mesh transit or nontransit.

After the connection types, you had to go through the exciting and numerous attribute types. Once you were aware of all the attributes that BGP uses, you had to know how and in what order BGP uses them. It wouldn't have been any fun if I didn't show you how you could modify the attributes and change all of the default rules for them. So I showed you how to use route maps.

Finally, I took you through the basic configuration commands to get BGP running and peering with other routers. The last of the commands were how to verify BGP and make sure it is actually running.

Review Questions

1. What is a partial route table?
   A. Router isn't done processing
   B. Receive only some routes from ISP
   C. Not done loading
   D. Router out of room

2. What transport layer protocol does BGP use?
   A. UDP
   B. RTP
   C. TCP
   D. ICMP

3. If you peer with a router in the AS, what type of connection is that?
   A. IBGP
   B. EBGP
   C. OBGP
   D. YBGP

4. Private companies are often set up as a transit AS.
   A. True
   B. False

5. ISPs are typically set up as a transit AS.
   A. True
   B. False

6. What company or organization made the weight attribute?
   A. IEEE
   B. Cisco
   C. IETF
   D. FCC

7. What feature can be used to modify an attribute?
   A. ACL
   B. Distribute list
   C. Route map
   D. Template

8. What address on a router can be used to ensure that a session will be established if there is more than one interface from which to send updates?

    A. Primary address

    B. Secondary address

    C. Master address

    D. Loopback address

9. What feature in BGP can help reduce the amount of configuration commands you have to use?

    A. Router groups

    B. BGP groups

    C. Peer groups

    D. Help groups

10. What is the purpose of the network command?

    A. Inject routes into BGP

    B. Remove routes from BGP

    C. Nothing

    D. Start the BGP process

Answers to Review Questions

1. B. A partial route table is when you only receive part of the Internet routing table.

2. C. BGP uses TCP because of the large amount of data that can be sent.

3. A. A peer in the same AS makes an internal BGP session.

4. B. False. A private company is rarely a transit AS.

5. A. True. An ISP is almost always a transit AS; that is what makes the Internet backbone.

6. B. Weight is a Cisco-proprietary attribute.

7. C. A route map can be used to modify an attribute's value.

8. D. A loopback address can be used so that a router is always known as the same address, regardless of exit interface.

9. C. A peer group can reduce the number of commands that have to be configured.

10. A. The network command injects routes into BGP to be passed on to peer routers.

Chapter

8

Multicast

IN THIS CHAPTER, YOU WILL LEARN HOW TO DO THE FOLLOWING:

✓ Describe IP multicast (e.g., Layer 3 to Layer 2 mapping, IGMP, etc.)

✓ Describe, configure, and verify IP multicast routing (i.e., PIM sparse-dense mode)

Many organizations today have increased their use of applications and programs that send large amounts of data to a whole group of users. Using multicast could enhance many of these applications or reduce the amount of data that is sent across a network. Many types of data can be more efficiently transmitted using multicast: audio and video used for meetings, collaboration, training, and company bulletins, and instant messaging applications that allow whole groups to communicate. In this chapter, you will get a look at how applications can be improved with multicast. Then, of course, I cover the protocols and functions that make multicast work. It wouldn't be a good discussion if I didn't include some of the configurations for setting this up on your network, so I do that too.

What Is Multicast?

Let's start with what multicast really is, before I get to the pros and cons of using it. You will learn about the different transmission types that can be used on a network, and the benefits and drawbacks of each. I also have to discuss the addressing ranges for multicast use. The class D range of IP addresses is split into different ranges of specific use. The discussion must also include the Layer 2 addressing for multicast. It is important you know how MAC addresses are determined from the IP address and what the outcome of that translation will be.

Transmission Types

Let's examine the different ways that data can be sent on a network. Each type has its own effects on the network, which can include bandwidth utilization and overhead on routers and switches. There are three different types of transmissions:

- Unicast
- Broadcast
- Multicast

Unicast Unicast transmission is known as one-to-one transmission. Unicast traffic is sent from one specific source to one specific destination. This is the standard type of data forwarding that you learned about in the routing chapters. If more than one host needs to receive the same traffic, then a separate copy of each packet is sent to each destination.

This can have a severe impact on bandwidth utilization for the network, because so many extra packets are being sent. It minimizes the amount of processing overhead on the end devices because they only process traffic addressed to them. It does, however, increase the load on the network devices because they are processing so many more packets, as shown in Figure 8.1.

FIGURE 8.1   Sending Unicast Traffic to Multiple Hosts

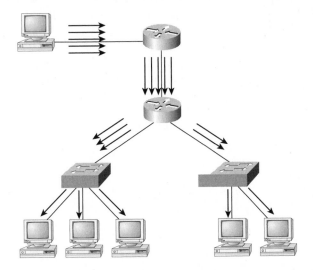

Broadcast   Broadcast transmission is known as a one-to-all transmission. A broadcast is a packet that is sent from one source host using the broadcast address; all hosts on the subnet must receive and process the packet. While this type of transmission can use less bandwidth than a unicast transmission when more than one host needs the traffic, it can have a severe impact on the processing overhead of all the hosts on the network, especially if not all the hosts need the traffic but must still process it.

Multicast   Multicast transmission is known as a one-to-many transmission. Multicast traditionally can be sent from one host to a specific group of destination hosts. Only a single copy of a packet can be sent on a single network. As the packet travels out toward the edge of the network, each Layer 3 device duplicates the packet down each network path that is required for packet delivery. This allows for efficient use of bandwidth and a minimum amount of processing for all devices. The network devices only have to send one copy of the data, and the end devices only have to process traffic that is destined for it, as shown in Figure 8.2.

There are several different types of multicast applications or models. The software installed on the host and clients will determine the particular implementation in your system and select an appropriate multicast mode for data transmission.

FIGURE 8.2   Sending Multicast Traffic to Multiple Hosts

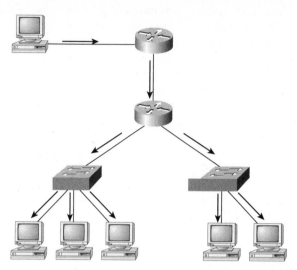

The two most common multicast models are one to many and many to many. In the one-to-many model, a single host sends to two or more receivers. This model is perfect for audio and video distribution, media that is being pushed out, monitoring systems, and announcement systems. If the receivers of the data need to send feedback to the sender, then the model changes to a many-to-one or many-to-many model. In the more common many-to-many model, the traffic can be sent from a source or a receiver. In some cases, a host can be both a sender and a receiver and two or more receivers can act as senders. The downside of implementing multicast like this is the increased complexity of the multicast application because receiving traffic from multiple sources introduces its own challenge. The benefit, however, of this type of multicast is that it provides a basis for a whole new breed of applications to be built and use this type of data flow. Applications for collaboration, concurrent processing, and media that can be widely distributed and provide an interactive experience.

Multicast Pros and Cons

Let's take a look at a few more things that make multicast a great possibility on your network. There are great positives about using multicast on the network.

Efficiency over Unicast   Available network bandwidth is utilized more efficiently because multiple copies of data are replaced with a single transmission.

Optimized Processing   Fewer copies of the data require far less forwarding of packets and processing for devices.

Distributed Applications   Multipoint applications are not effective or really possible with unicast as demand, usage, and the amount of traffic grows. This is due to the fact the unicast transmission cannot scale. The number of copies of data that must be sent grows linearly with the number of hosts that need the traffic.

Multicast gives you the possibility for a whole new breed of applications that aren't possible or efficient with unicast. Unfortunately, multicast does have its faults or problems too. Let's talk about the cons of using multicast to transmit data.

Most multicast applications use the Layer 4 protocol, User Datagram Protocol (UDP). This foundation can create some undesirable outcomes, effects similar to unicast TCP applications. UDP's best-effort delivery can result in the occasional dropped packet. A lot of realtime multicast applications that operate this way (for example, video and audio) may be affected by these losses. There is also no way to request retransmission of lost data at the application layer. The applications only act like realtime; they are "almost realtime" applications. Realtime is not feasible with UDP.

A period of heavy drops or data loss can play havoc on voice applications. Jittery, unintelligible speech or voice that can render a conversation or stream intolerable when the drop rate gets too high. Moderate to heavy drops in video are better tolerated; the human eye won't pickup all of the flaws. Drops might appear as an unusual spot or blip in the picture. Video applications that use compression can have an entirely different outcome. Compression algorithms may be severely affected by drops causing the video picture to become jerky, jittery, or freeze for a few seconds while the decompression algorithm catches up.

Let's cover the cons.

Lack of Congestion Control   Without congestion control, an overall network degradation can occur as the use of UDP-based multicast applications grow.

Duplicate Packets   Duplicate packets can occur occasionally and are generated as multicast network topologies change. Applications must be designed to expect duplicate packets once in a while and must be designed to handle it.

Out-of-Sequence Delivery Packets   Applications must also deal with sequence issues that occur during network topology changes or other network changes that affect the flow of multicast traffic.

No Reliability Mechanisms for UDP   Reliability issues must be addressed and mechanisms designed into the multicast applications if they require reliable data transfer.

Eavesdropping and Security Issues   The issue of restricting multicast traffic to only a selected group of receivers. When the traffic is placed onto the network, it is destined for a specific group but this doesn't mean that an attacker couldn't just begin listening to all the multicast traffic. This can be a big problem for some applications, such as financial data, where security and reliability is a must.

Multicast Addressing

Multicast IP addresses use the class D address space and are identified by the three high-order bits being set to 1s (1110). Therefore, the multicast IP address range is 224.0.0.0–239.255.255.255.

The multicast IP address space is separated into the following address groups as defined in RFC 3171.

TABLE 8.1 Multicast Address Space Groups

Address Range	Prefix	Description
224.0.0.0–224.0.0.255	(224.0.0/24)	Local Network Control Block
224.0.1.0–224.0.1.255	(224.0.1/24)	Internetwork Control Block
224.0.2.0–224.0.255.0		AD-HOC Block
224.1.0.0–224.1.255.255	(224.1/16)	ST Multicast Groups
224.2.0.0–224.2.255.255	(224.2/16)	SDP/SAP Block
224.252.0.0–224.255.255.252		DIS Transient Block
225.0.0.0–231.255.255.255		RESERVED
232.0.0.0–232.255.255.255	(232/8)	Source Specific Multicast Block
233.0.0.0–233.255.255.255	(233/8)	GLOP Block
234.0.0.0–238.255.255.255		RESERVED
239.0.0.0–239.255.255.255	(239/8)	Administratively Scoped Block

There are three general groups of multicast address groups that are used for reference. Those groups include:

- Local scope addresses
- Global scope addresses
- Administratively scoped addresses

Local scope addresses run from 224.0.0.0 through 224.0.0.255 and are reserved by Internet Assigned Numbers Authority (IANA) for network protocol use. Multicasts in this range are never forwarded off the local link or network, no matter what the time to live (TTL) is (and usually the TTL is set to 1). Table 8.2 lists examples of local multicast addresses.

TABLE 8.2 Local Multicast Addresses

Address	Description
224.0.0.1	All hosts
224.0.0.2	All multicast routers

TABLE 8.2   Local Multicast Addresses *(continued)*

Address	Description
224.0.0.4	All Distance Vector Multicast Routing Protocol (DVMRP) routers
224.0.0.5	All open shortest path first protocol (OSPF) routers
224.0.0.6	All OSPF designated routers (DRs)
224.0.0.9	All Routing Information Protocol version 2 (RIPv2) routers
224.0.0.10	All Enhanced Interior Gateway Routing protocol (EIGRP) routers

Global scope addresses run from 224.0.1.0 through 238.255.255.255 and are allocated dynamically throughout the Internet. For example, the 224.2.X.X range is used in multicast backbone (Mbone) applications. Mbone is a collection of Internet routers that support IP multicasting. The Mbone is used as a virtual network (multicast channel) on which various public and private audio and video programs are sent. The Mbone network was started by the Internet Engineering Task Force (IETF) in an effort to multicast audio and video meetings.

Administratively scoped addresses run from 239.0.0.0 through 239.255.255.255. They are reserved for use inside private domains. The administratively scoped multicast address space is divided into the following scopes per IANA:

- Site-local scope (239.255.0.0/16, with 239.252.0.0/16, 239.253.0.0/16, and 239.254.0.0/16 also reserved)

- Organization-local scope (239.192.0.0 to 239.251.255.255)

Now that we have pretty fully explored the Layer 3 addressing for multicast, it is time to look at the Layer 2 addressing. A multicast MAC address is determined by mapping part of the IP address into the MAC address. The translation between IP multicast and MAC address is done by mapping the low-order 23 bits of the IP (Layer 3) multicast address into the low-order 23 bits of the IEEE (Layer 2) MAC address. You can tell that the MAC address is a multicast frame because the low-order bit (0x01) in the first octet tells you that the frame is a multicast frame. The 0x01005e prefix (vendor code also known as OUI) has been reserved for use in mapping Layer 3 IP multicast addresses into Layer 2 MAC addresses.

You know there are 23 bits mapped into the MAC because the first 24 bits of the MAC address are 0x01005e, and the 25th bit must be a zero. So, the last 23 bits of the MAC come from the last 23 bits of the IP address. Think about the multicast IP for a second; there are 28 bits of unique address space in the address, a total of 32 bits minus the first 4 bits (1110) which indicate it is a class D prefix. So, you are left with 28 bits. With the last 23 bits of the IP address mapped into the MAC, it then leaves us with five bits that are not used or otherwise accounted for. If you calculate the number of IP addresses that can be made with those 5 bits, you get $2^5 = 32$. That tells you there is a 32 address discrepancy between the Layer 3 addresses and the Layer 2 addresses. Therefore, you must keep in mind that there are 32 IP or Layer 3 addresses that can potentially map to a single Layer 2 multicast address. Take a look at Figure 8.3; it shows the process of mapping a multicast IP address into a multicast MAC.

FIGURE 8.3   Multicast IP Mapping to Multicast MAC

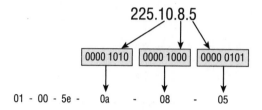

Let's think about the mapping going the other way. What if you only knew the MAC address of a multicast frame that just came to a host. Put yourself in the host's position. You receive a frame, it has a MAC address of 01-00-5e-08-00-01, and you know that it is a MAC address because of the vendor code. Now, you have to figure out whether you need to process the frame. It has the multicast IP address of the group that you are a part of, but from the MAC address you only know that this frame could be for one of 32 different IP addresses. Look at Table 8.2; all the IP multicast addresses map to the same Layer 2 multicast of 01-00-5e-08-00-01. So, the host must look further into the packet header to see if the group IP address is really the group that it wants traffic from.

TABLE 8.2   Multicast IPs That Map to MAC, 01005e080001

IP's Where 9th bit is 0	IP's Where 9th bit is 128
224.8.0.1	224.136.0.1
225.8.0.1	225.136.0.1
226.8.0.1	226.136.0.1
227.8.0.1	227.136.0.1
228.8.0.1	228.136.0.1
229.8.0.1	229.136.0.1
230.8.0.1	230.136.0.1
231.8.0.1	231.136.0.1
232.8.0.1	232.136.0.1
233.8.0.1	233.136.0.1

TABLE 8.2   Multicast IPs That Map to MAC, 01005e080001 *(continued)*

IP's Where 9th bit is 0	IP's Where 9th bit is 128
234.8.0.1	234.136.0.1
235.8.0.1	235.136.0.1
236.8.0.1	236.136.0.1
237.8.0.1	237.136.0.1
238.8.0.1	238.136.0.1
239.8.0.1	239.136.0.1

Multicast Protocols

You've learned some of the reasons that multicast transmissions are good to use on the network. I have also taken care of the addressing woes of multicast. Now, let's go through the protocols that make multicast work. I start with Internet Group Multicast Protocol (IGMP), a host-to-router protocol. After that I go through a couple of protocols that allow a switch to make better forwarding decisions for multicast frames. Cisco Group Management Protocol and IGMP snooping. Finally, I will cover protocol-independent multicast, a router-to-router protocol that allows the routing of multicast traffic through the network.

Internet Group Management Protocol (IGMP)

Internet Group Management Protocol (IGMP) is a host-to-router protocol used to enable hosts to join a multicast group if they want to receive a specific flow of traffic. With the original, IGMP version 1, routers send a periodic membership query to the multicast address 224.0.0.1. Hosts then send membership reports to the group multicast address they want to join. One down side of version 1 is that hosts silently leave the multicast group, not notifying the router that they no longer wish to receive the traffic.

Since limitations that were found in IGMPv1, IGMP version 2 was developed. Most of the changes between IGMPv1 and IGMPv2 addressed the issues of leave and join latencies, as well as ambiguities in the original protocol specification.

Here are some of the important changes made when the protocol moved from IGMP version 1 to IGMP version 2:

Group-Specific Queries   Group specific queries were added in IGMPv2; they allow the router to query a single group for membership instead of requiring queries to go to all groups. This optimized the way a router discovers whether any members are left in a particular group without asking all groups to report. The difference between the group-specific query and the membership query is that a membership query is multicast to the all-hosts (224.0.0.1) address. A group-specific query, to group 224.1.1.1, for example, is a multicast to that specific group multicast address.

Leave Group Message   A leave group message allows hosts to tell the router that they are leaving the group. This message reduces the amount of time for a specific group on the segment to know when the last member leaves a group.

Querier Election Mechanism   This mechanism, like many things in the network world, allows you to have a backup or redundant configuration. You can have more than one router on the segment and the router with the highest IP address will become the designated querier.

Query-Interval Response Time   The query-interval response time was added to control the bursting and timeliness of reports. This time is set inside the queries to tell the members how much time they have to respond to a query with a report. IGMPv2 is backward-compatible with IGMPv1.

IGMPv3 is a proposed standard. It allows the hosts to specify a particular source from which it would like to receive traffic on a given multicast group, and thus provides more efficient routing. IGMPv3 includes a list that it uses for source filtering; source filtering gives a host the ability to report its wish to receive packets from only a specific source addresses or allow all but a specific source address. This is sometimes referred to as the "include or exclude" list. The information can be used by multicast routing protocols to avoid sending multicast packets from specific sources to networks where there are no hosts that want to receive them.

Cisco Group Management Protocol (CGMP)

Now, let me show you the effect of multicast traffic on other network devices, namely the switches that are responsible for the delivery of the traffic to the end hosts. By default, Layer 2 switches treat multicast traffic like it has an unknown MAC address or a broadcast frame that causes the frame to be flooded out every port within a VLAN. This treatment is acceptable for traffic that is actually unknown or broadcasts, but, as I discussed before, IP multicast hosts can join and be interested in specific multicast groups. So on your Layer 2 switches, all of the multicast traffic is forwarded out of all ports, which means you have tons of wasted bandwidth both for the segments and on the end hosts.

On a Cisco Catalyst switch, you can prevent some of this. It isn't the most desirable way, though; it requires that the administrator configure the switch manually and statically associate a multicast MAC address with the switch ports the traffic should be delivered out of. For example, an administrator could configure ports 1 through 4 so that only ports 1 through 4 will receive the multicast traffic that is sent to a multicast group. As with other protocols that we have talked about, the manual way is not scalable and for sure not much fun. IP multicast hosts dynamically join and leave groups, using IGMP to tell the router to send traffic. Dynamically configuring the switches would be way easier and more efficient in the long run.

So, the first of these more automatic ways to give your switch better forwarding information is Cisco Group Management Protocol (CGMP). CGMP is the most common, at least for Cisco switches, multicast forwarding protocol; it was designed by Cisco.

You can think of CGMP as creating a type of client/server relationship, where the router would be considered a CGMP server and the switch takes on the client role. Protocol processes run on both devices. The router takes in the IGMP messages, translates the messages into CGMP commands and sends them to the switch for processing. In the switch, they are used to populate the Layer 2 forwarding tables with the multicast entries needed to forward multicast traffic out to the ports that requested it.

The whole idea here is that the IP multicast router sees all IGMP packets and takes in all that information. When it has done that, it can tell the switch when specific hosts on specific ports join or leave multicast groups. Routers communicate to the switches using well-known CGMP multicast MAC addresses. This is how they send the CGMP command packets to the switch. The switch can then use those commands to set up the forwarding table.

So, for example, when the router receives an IGMP message packet, it creates a CGMP packet that contains the request type (join or leave), the Layer 2 multicast MAC addresses, and the actual MAC address of the client. That packet is then sent to the well-known CGMP multicast MAC address, 0x0100.0cdd.dddd. All Cisco switches running CGMP listen to this address. The CGMP control message is then processed by the switch, and the proper entries are created in the switch content-addressable memory (CAM) table. Once the entries are in the table, then the switch forwards the multicast traffic for a group to only the hosts that requested it.

IGMP Snooping

The second multicast switching solution is IGMP snooping. With this process running, switches become IGMP aware in a way. They can listen in on the IGMP conversations between hosts and routers. As the name sort of tells you, this is an extra process the switch runs, which can have an adverse effect of the processing overhead.

The IGMP snooping process requires the CPU in each switch to listen for, identify, and intercept a copy of all IGMP packets traveling between the routers and end hosts. The process collects:

- IGMP membership reports
- IGMP leaves

If you are not careful about how you configure IGMP snooping, a switch may have to collect every single Layer 2 multicast packet so that it can figure out which ones are IGMP packets. This can have a significant, in some cases huge, impact on switch performance. To effectively implement IGMP snooping, proper design may need a Layer 3 switch with ASICs to avoid the overhead. Of course, that can make the cost of the switch be a little bit more, because a Layer 3 switch can take the load and have the processing capability. This is really making your switches become Layer 3 aware, but it can help to avoid the performance problems and overhead that IGMP snooping will create.

Protocol Independent Multicast (PIM)

It is now time to look at multicast routing. There are a few different routing protocols out there that can be used, but I give you look at Protocol Independent Multicast (PIM) because it is really the only one that Cisco supports on its routers. Before I get too far into that though, I discuss the basics of how multicast paths are created. I show you what the topologies are going to look like. In multicast, the paths are called trees. You can have shortest path trees (SPT) and shared trees. After that, you will get a look at the way the PIM makes use of these trees and what you have to do to make them work.

Multicast routing is a little different from unicast routing. When you route unicast traffic, you always know the source and destination hosts when the traffic is sent. Packets are only going to a single destination. Multicast traffic can have numerous destinations and is totally dependent on the number of hosts that need to receive the traffic. Multicast paths must be loop free, just as unicast paths are, but since the traffic can be traveling on multiple networks at the same time, a different method must be used to ensure that no loops are made. The method is called reverse path forwarding (RPF). RPF has to check every single multicast packet that it receives to make sure that it is traveling in the correct direction. Packets must be traveling away from the root of the tree, always in the direction of the hosts who need the traffic.

When a packet is received at the router, the source address must be determined. This is the opposite of unicast routing, which is concerned with the destination. The path back to the source must be verified to ensure that the receiving interface is the interface that has the best path back to the source. If the interface is not in the best path from the source, then it is assumed that the traffic is from a looped path or was sent from a different place. In either case, the packet is dropped. The actual multicast distribution trees tell us the path from the source to the receivers or destinations; only traffic flowing over that path is accepted.

There are two types of multicast distribution trees:

- Source rooted trees, also called shortest path trees (SPTs)
- Shared trees

With a shortest path tree, a separate tree is built from each source down to where each and every member of its group is located. Because the source-rooted tree takes a direct, or the shortest, path from source to its receivers, it is also called an SPT.

In a shared tree situation, the creation of the forwarding paths relies on a centrally located router called a rendezvous point (RP). The RP serves as a go-between for the multicast sources and destinations. Sources start out by sending their multicast traffic to the RP router, the RP then forwards data down through a shared tree, ultimately to all the members of the group. A shared tree is less efficient than an SPT where the data flow is concerned, but it is less demanding on routers (memory, CPU). The inefficiency is due to the fact that paths between the source and receivers are not necessarily the shortest path.

Multicast routing protocols generally fall into two different categories: dense mode and sparse mode.

Dense Mode Protocols   Dense mode protocols assume that the network has been built for a lot of multicast traffic and flood the packets to all parts of the network. After they have completely flooded the network, a prune process trims back the flows in places where there are no receivers. You will see this flood-and-prune mechanism run periodically.

Sparse Mode Protocols   Sparse mode protocols use an explicit join mechanism. Using explicit tree join message information from the IGMP process, these protocols build distribution trees based on demand. The join messages are sent by the routers that have directly connected receivers.

Take a look at Figure 8.4; it shows a SPT that goes from source 1 down to host 1 and host 2. The path between the source and receivers is the lowest cost path as determined by a routing protocol.

FIGURE 8.4   Building a SPT

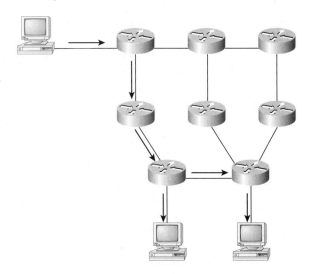

Packets are forwarded through the SPT using the source and group address pair. Because of this the routes are written like with this notation (S, G) (pronounced "S comma G"), where S is the IP address of the source and G is the multicast group address. The multicast route entries appear in the multicast tables and look like this:

- (S, G): A particular source, S, sends to a particular group, G. These entries typically reflect an SPT, but may also appear on a shared tree.

- (*, G): Any source (*) sending to the particular group G. These entries usually indicate a shared tree, but are also created (in Cisco routers) for any existing (S, G) entry.

SPT entries can use more router memory because there is an entry for each sender and group. However the traffic is sent over the best path to each receiver, this can minimize extra delay in the packet getting to the host.

Shared distribution tree entries take up less router memory, but you don't always get the best paths from a source to receivers; this can then introduce extra delay in the packet delivery.

PIM dense mode (PIM-DM) starts out flooding multicast traffic to all parts of the network. In the example in Figure 8.5, multicast traffic being sent by source 1 is flooded throughout the entire network. As each router receives the multicast traffic, it verifies that the interface is the RPF interface (the interface in the direction of the source). If the interface is the RPF interface, then it can forward the multicast traffic out to all of its PIM-DM neighbors.

FIGURE 8.5   Flooding in PIM Dense Mode

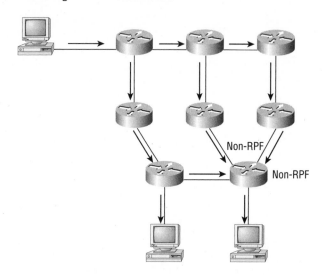

Some traffic will be received on a non-RPF interface and will be dropped. Packets being received here are normal for the beginning of the flood, but they are corrected by the pruning mechanism. Prune messages are only sent on RPF interfaces when the router has hosts that want the multicast traffic from that source. There is one thing that you must take into consideration. All the prune messages expire in 3 minutes. When they do, the multicast traffic is flooded again to all of the routers. This flood-and-prune process is normal and must be considered when a network is designed to use PIM-DM.

PIM-SM (PIM sparse mode) is described in RFC 2362. As with PIM-DM, PIM-SM is also independent of underlying unicast protocols. PIM-SM uses shared distribution trees, but you can also use it with a SPT. Like I said before, sparse mode is based on the host requesting the traffic. Therefore, traffic is forwarded only to the parts of the network that need it.

PIM-SM uses an RP to coordinate forwarding of multicast traffic from a source to receivers. I always use the analogy of a real estate agent. The source of the traffic is like a person who wants to sell their house; they are going to list the house with the agent (in multicast that is the RP). Group members then join the shared tree using their local designated router (DR); this is the buyer's real estate agent. The buyer's agent brings them to the seller's agent (the RP) and the shared tree is built. This way it is always rooted at the RP.

PIM-SM is appropriate for wide-scale deployment for both densely and sparsely populated groups in the enterprise network. It is the optimal choice for all production networks, regardless of size and membership density.

There have been some upgrades made to PIM, which include bidirectional PIM mode and source-specific multicast (SSM).Bidirectional PIM mode was made for many-to-many applications. SSM is a variant of PIM-SM that builds only source-specific SPTs and does not need an active RP for source-specific groups (address range 232/8).

In Figure 8.6, notice the receiver attached to a router at the bottom of the tree; this also called a leaf router. The leaf router has joined multicast group X and knows the IP address of the RP because you have to configure the RP on every single router. It sends a (*, G) join message for Group X toward the RP. This message travels hop by hop toward the RP, building a path of the shared tree that goes from the RP to the leaf router that is directly connected to the receiver. Now it is possible for the traffic from Group X to be forwarded down the shared tree to the receiver.

FIGURE 8.6   Sparse Mode Path Selection

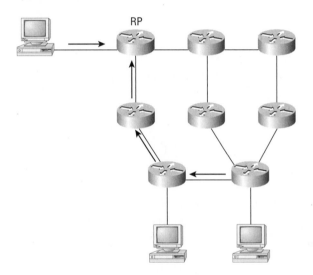

Cisco offers a proprietary combination of PIM sparse-dense mode. It supports the automatic selection of RPs for each multicast group. PIM sparse-dense mode is the recommended by Cisco as the go-to mode for IP multicast because PIM-DM does not scale well and requires heavy router resources and PIM-SM offers limited RP configuration options. The combination mode allows the automatic shift to a mode. If no RP is found for a multicast group and you don't have one manually configured, then PIM sparse-dense mode operates in dense mode. Because it goes to dense mode, you should have auto RP discovery turned on with PIM sparse-dense mode.

Multicast Operation and Configuration

So, let's take a look at this process. I discussed quite a few pieces, now let's make sure they all fit together. You have to start out with a multicast source. There has to be some traffic or data that a user can sign up for or request to receive. The sign up or request process can be accomplished by clicking on a link the user received in email or picking a selection from a multicast application loaded on their host machine. The application must be updated somehow about the available data or sessions; the content usually maps to one or more IP multicast groups.

These are several possibilities for applications to learn about the sessions:

- The application may join a well-known predefined group, to which announcements about available sessions are made.

- Some type of directory services is available, and the application may contact the appropriate directory server. There are Session Directory (sd) applications that can act like a guide, displaying multicast content. The application runs on a host machine and displays available content to end users. The directory application uses either Session Description Protocol (SDP) or Session Announcement Protocol (SAP) to learn about the content.

- The application might be launched from a web page with the available content sessions listed as URLs or perhaps email messages are used to notify users of new content.

 Real World Scenario

Improving Corporate Announcements and Policy Changes

The significant growth of FutureTech, both in the number of offices and the number of employees, has made communicating policy changes and announcements from executives difficult to disperse. To help solve this problem, you will test a new video distribution system that utilizes multicast traffic for distributing the announcement and training videos. FutureTech has purchased a system that includes a cluster of servers where the content will be held. They have been placed in the Dallas datacenter. This server cluster will serve as the multicast source where the traffic will start. The client side of the software has been deployed to the workstations of all the users in the Dallas office. I want you to make sure that the system is working and all multicast routing issues are worked out before the system is rolled out to the rest of the company.

With the software on each of the user's computers they will get reminders and updates when there is new content on the system for them to view. When a user clicks one of the announcements in the application, the application generates an IGMP message for the multicast group that the content belongs to. The IGMP message goes to the local router. Once the local router receives the message, the router can use PIM to request across the network to receive the content. The local router then makes a CGMP message for the switch so that only the proper port or ports will forward the traffic.

If the network is using dense mode, the router will send the request to the traffic source. It will send the request to the RP, if sparse mode is being used.

Once the path from the source or the RP has been made down to the leaf router, the traffic can begin to flow through the new branch and ultimately get to the new host.

Now, you can take a look at some of the commands that are required to make this process happen. A few basic steps have to be completed in order to make multicast operate on a network. The first is to enable multicast routing. The second is to enable PIM. Finally, the third is to set the RPs.

The first step, then, is to enable multicast routing; it is not enabled on Cisco routers by default. To do this, use the following command to in global configuration mode:

DalRtr1(config)#`ip multicast-routing`

The second step is to enable PIM on interfaces; this automatically starts IGMP. PIM is enabled on the interface, so study your network and figure out which router interfaces should support PIM. Once you figure that out, activate PIM in interface-configuration mode. PIM runs in three modes: sparse, dense, and sparse-dense.

DalRtr1(config-if)#`ip pim {`*dense-mode* `|` *sparse-dense-mode* `|` *sparse-mode*`}`

You can also set the PIM version; use the following interface-configuration command.

DalRtr1(config-if)# `ip pim version {`*1* `|` *2*`}`

The final step is to configure RPs. You have to manually configure the RP on every router—even the RP itself. Use the following global configuration command:

Router(config)# `ip pim rp-address ip-address [`*access-list*`] [`*override*`]`

You can also use Auto-RP to dynamically determine the RP. With Auto-RP, some routers to be voluntold to be RPs (voluntold is the military way of saying that you were told that you volunteered for something, that is the case here since you configure the router to volunteer). Other routers need to advertise the RPs.

Auto-RP can then find a centrally located router to perform the job of mapping agent. The mapping agent is going to hear about the potential RPs; they make themselves known over the Cisco-RP-Announce multicast address 224.0.1.39. The mapping agent then puts together the list of which routers are the RPs for each group and sends the list to client routers on 224.0.1.40. To define a router as a mapping agent, use the following global configuration command:

DalRtr1(config)# `ip pim send-rp-discovery scope ttl`

Configure a router as a candidate RP with the following global configuration command:

DalRtr1(config)# `ip pim send-rp-announce type mod/num scope ttl [`*group-list access- list*`] [`*interval seconds*`]`

Verify Multicast

Now, I take you through a few of the commands that allow you to see and verify the multicast configuration on a router. My discussion includes the multicast routing table, interface information, and RP information.

The command to show a multicast routing table is:

DalRtr1#**show ip mroute** [*group-address*] [*summary*] [*count*][*active kpbs*]

Here is a sample of the output from a routing table.

```
DalRtr1#show ip mroute
IP Multicast Routing Table
Flags: D - Dense, S - Sparse, C - Connected, L - Local, P - Pruned
       R - RP-bit set, F - Register flag, T - SPT-bit set, J - Join SPT
Timers: Uptime/Expires
Interface state: Interface, Next-Hop, State/Mode

(*, 225.225.125.25), 00:01:10/00:01:32, RP 10.10.10.1, flags: SPF
  Incoming interface: Tunnel35, RPF nbr 10.10.20.2, Mroute
  Outgoing interface list: Null

(10.1.1.1/32, 225.225.125.25), 00:01:10/00:00:59, flags: PFT
  Incoming interface: Ethernet0, RPF nbr 0.0.0.0, Registering
  Outgoing interface list: Null
```

You can use the show ip pim interface command to verify settings on interfaces. Once you enter the command, you can see:

- IP address on the interface
- Interface type—the PIM version (either 1 or 2)
- PIM mode (Dense, Sparse, or Sparse-Dense)
- Number of neighbors
- Query timer
- Router that is the designated querier

```
DalRtr1#show ip pim interface
```

Address	Interface	Version/Mode	Nbr Count	Query Intvl	DR
10.10.10.1	Ethernet0	v2/S	1	30	10.10.10.10

The show ip pim neighbor command gives a list of neighbors.

```
DalRtr1#show ip pim neighbor
PIM Neighbor Table
```

Neighbor Address	Interface	Uptime	Expires	Ver	Mode
192.168.0.10	Ethernet0	00:01:37	00:01:05	v2	Sparse

When you use the `show ip pim rp` command, you can display the RPs for your multicast groups:

```
DalRtr1#show ip pim rp
Group: 225.225.125.25, RP: 10.10.10.1, uptime 00:00:30, expires never
```

Now you know some of the basic commands that can be used to verify and check your configurations.

Summary

You and I have discussed and fought through lots of topics in this chapter. You learned about the different ways that traffic can be transmitted on a network, and the benefits and drawbacks of each. Then I took you through the multicast addressing range. You saw how the whole range of addresses is broken up into smaller groups that are used for specific types of transmissions. Then, just as important was the translation of the multicast IP address to the multicast MAC address. During that process, you saw that there was a little problem in determining the IP address from the MAC.

After the addressing section, came the breakdown of the multicast protocols that are used across the network. We started out with IGMP, going through each of the three versions. Again, IGMP is used to allow the hosts to request traffic for a given group. Then, came the two protocols that you can use to limit the flooding of multicast traffic in your switched networks. The first open protocol was IGMP snooping, which allows the switch to listen in on all of the IGMP join messages so that it can learn which hosts want the traffic. Its counterpart that is fed information from the router, thus preventing the overhead, is CGMP. CGMP works in conjunction with the router to learn which ports should be used to forward the traffic.

The last protocol that you looked at was PIM. You saw that PIM has three modes of operation. Those modes can take advantage of the tree-like topologies that are available with multicast routing. The three modes are dense, sparse, and sparse-dense. The two tree structures were source rooted and shared. Each of the tree structures had pros and cons. The shared tree structure required the additional configuration of an RP.

You then looked at the multicast process as a whole and finished by learning some of the commands that you can use to verify and check the configurations.

Review Questions

1. How many streams of data would multicast have to send to reach 10 host machines?

   A. 1

   B. 2

   C. 5

   D. 10

2. How is multicast better than unicast when sending the same data to multiple clients?

   A. Uses more bandwidth

   B. Sends the data twice

   C. Uses less bandwidth

   D. Sends the data multiple times

3. What protocol allows communication between hosts and the local router for multicast?

   A. CGMP

   B. PIM

   C. MOSPF

   D. IGMP

4. What Cisco-proprietary protocol allows the router to tell a switch what ports to forward multicast traffic out?

   A. CGMP

   B. PIM

   C. MOSPF

   D. IGMP

5. What transport layer protocol is used for multicast traffic typically?

   A. TCP

   B. RTP

   C. UDP

   D. ICMP

6. What is the multicast address range from 224.0.0.0–24.0.0.255 called?

   A. Local scope addresses

   B. Global scope addresses

   C. Administratively scoped addresses

   D. Reserved

7. What is the multicast reserved OUI portion of a MAC address?

   A. 00-01-05

   B. 00-01-5e

   C. 01-00-05

   D. 01-00-5e

8. How many multicast IP addresses can be made from a single multicast MAC address?

   A. 1

   B. 8

   C. 16

   D. 32

9. What is the open standard solution for a switch to determine where a multicast host is located?

   A. CGMP

   B. PIM

   C. IGMP

   D. IGMP snooping

10. What extension did Cisco add to the PIM protocol?

   A. PIM-SM

   B. PIM-DM

   C. PIM extra-dense mode

   D. PIM sparse-dense mode

Answers to Review Questions

1. A. A multicast source only has to send one stream of data.

2. C. Multicast uses less bandwidth by only sending the data once.

3. D. IGMP allows the router and the hosts to communicate.

4. A. CGMP is the Cisco protocol that allows the router to tell the switch where hosts are located for multicast traffic.

5. C. Multicast uses UDP to carry traffic.

6. A. The range is local scoped and can only be used on a single network segment.

7. D. The reserved multicast MAC address OUI is 01-00-5e.

8. D. From one MAC address 32 IP addresses can be made.

9. D. IGMP snooping can be used by most switches to determine where hosts are located that have requested multicast traffic.

10. D. Cisco added the PIM sparse-dense mode of operation to PIM.

Chapter

9

Internet Protocol Version 6 (IPv6)

IN THIS CHAPTER, YOU WILL LEARN HOW TO DO THE FOLLOWING:

- ✓ Describe IPv6 addressing operations

- ✓ Describe IPv6 interoperation with IPv4

- ✓ Describe, configure, and verify OSPF routing with IPv6 addressing

In this chapter, I give you the nuts and bolts of Internet Protocol version 6 (IPv6). IPv6, often called the next-generation Internet protocol, was originally created to fix the inevitable address exhaustion of IPv4. IPv6 also brought greater efficiency and more functionality than its predecessor, IPv4. With the IPv6, the header and address structure was completely overhauled and many features that were add-ons or afterthoughts in IPv4 are now standard. IPv6 is well equipped to handle the demands of the Internet for years to come.

For up to the minute updates on this chapter, check out www.sybex.com/go/CiscoProGuidetoInternetworking or www.lammle.com.

Operating Internet Protocol Version 6

The number of people and devices that connect to networks increases daily. This is a terrific thing; we find new and exciting ways to communicate with more people all the time. The major problem with all this communication was that IPv4 is running out of addresses. IPv4 only has about 4.3 billion addresses available and not all of those can be used. Only about 250 million of those addresses can be assigned to devices. Sure, the use of CIDR and NAT helped to extend the time, but it is going to happen. Consider that there are about 6.5 billion people in the world today. It is estimated that just over 10 percent of that population is connected to the Internet. Under IPv4, there wasn't enough address space for every person to connect even a single computer. And what about all the other types of devices like phones, PDAs, appliances, and TVs that can have an IP address. I have more than one computer; I am sure you do, too. Now, add in the laptops, game consoles, routers, switches, and other devices we all use every day! We had to do something or we would run out of addresses. That is where IPv6 comes in.

In order to begin setting up this test network, I go through the way the addresses are determined and the basic functions of IPv6.

🌐 **Real World Scenario**

Implementing IPv6 in FutureTech

You can't implement IPv6 all in one day. Every system has to have its address changed and the routing set up, not to mention that all of the operating systems and devices on the network that have to support the changeover. Additionally, all of the applications and software that you use have to support the new protocol suite.

To start this process for FutureTech, you are going to set up part of the research and development network to use IPv6. This will allow all of the applications and devices to be tested.

The Benefits of IPv6

What is the big deal with IPv6? Is it worth it to upgrade? Of course, there are always people with the old resistance to change syndrome, but the answer is "Yes!"

Not only does IPv6 provide a lot of addresses (3.4×10^{38}; that is a bunch!), but many other features are built into this version that make the upgrade worth the effort. Later, in the section called "Interoperating IPv6 and IPv4," I talk about some of the transition types for moving from version 4 to version 6. The ability to migrate from one version to the next, without having to upgrade every bit of hardware and software in your network at one time is a huge benefit. Today's networks and the Internet have many requirements that were not considered necessary when IPv4 was created. To meet those requirements, add-ons were created, which can make implementation difficult as they are not applied by a standard. IPv6 has, by default and mandatory implementation, included many of those features. One such feature is IPSec for end-to-end security. Another is mobility, which allows a device to roam from one network to another without dropping connections.

Some of the biggest benefits that apply to every network are the efficiency features. To start off, the header in an IPv6 packet removed half of fields and aligned the fields to 64 bits, which allows processing and lookups to occur faster. Much of the information in the IPv4 header that was taken out in IPv6 can still be provided in optional extension headers that follow the basic header fields.

The number of addresses available significantly increased. Well, this increase in the number of addresses had to come from somewhere right? The number of addresses and some other benefits came from a larger address space. This means the address is bigger, four times bigger! An IPv6 address is 128 bits in length. I break down what the address looks like in the section called "Interoperating IPv6 and IPv4." The bigger address space allows more levels of hierarchy inside the address space, as well as flexible address architecture. It also allows for efficient and scalable routing because the addresses can be aggregated more effectively.

IPv6 also allows multiple addresses for hosts and networks. This is especially important for enterprises that need high availability. The new version of IP now includes a broader use of multicast communication, which will increase efficiency of networks because the communications can be more specific. In IPv4, the use of broadcasts was prevalent; this caused many problems and the worst is a broadcast storm. A broadcast storm involves uncontrolled forwarding of broadcast traffic, which can bring an entire network down and use all the bandwidth. Another significant problem with broadcast traffic is the interruption of every device on the network each time broadcast traffic is received. When a broadcast is sent, every device must stop and respond to the traffic, even if the traffic is not for that host. Now, in IPv6, the broadcasts have been removed, replaced by multicast traffic instead.

There are two other types of communication: unicast, which is the same as in IPv4, and a new type called anycast. Anycast is communication that allows an address to be placed on more than one device. When traffic is sent to that address, it is routed to the nearest host with that common address. I tell you more about these types of communication in the section called "Address Types."

IPv6 Addressing

It is equally important that you understand the structure and uses of IPv6 addressing. I have already said that the IPv6 address is much larger (128 bits). Because of this and the new ways the addresses can be used, it will be more complex to manage. But not to worry, I break down the basics: what the address looks like, how you can write it, and what many of the common uses are. Before you know it, this will be as easy as counting sheep!

So let's take a look. What does an IPv6 address look like? Here is an example in Figure 9.1.

FIGURE 9.1   Sample IPv6 Address

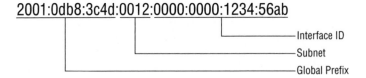

You can see the address is much larger, but what else is different? Well, it has eight groups of numbers instead of four. The groups are separated by colons instead of periods and—hey, wait a second—there are letters in that address! Yes, the address is expressed in hexadecimal, just like a MAC address. So, an IPv6 address could be said to have eight 16-bit, hexadecimal, colon-delimited blocks. That is a mouthful and you haven't even tried to say the address out loud yet.

Making HTTP Connections to IPv6 Devices

One other thing of note I want to mention to you for when you set up your test network to play with IPv6. (I know all of you are going to do that.) When you use a web browser to make an HTTP connection to an IPv6 device, you must type the address into the browser with brackets around the literal address. You have to do this because the colon is already used by the browser so that you can specify a port number. If you don't enclose the address, the browser will have no way to identify the information. An example of this might be:

`http://[2001:0db8:3c4d:0012:0000:0000:1234:56ab]/default.html`

Now, obviously, you can always use names to specify a destination, but there will always be times that you will need to type in the address number.

Shortened Expressions

Now, a few things that will help you write these monster addresses. You can abbreviate the addresses somewhat, but there are a couple of rules for doing so.

You can drop any leading zeros from each of the individual blocks. So, the address

`2001:0db8:3c4d:0012:0000:0000:1234:56ab`

would look like this:

`2001:db8:3c4d:12:0:0:1234:56ab`

That is better, at least you don't have to write all of those extra zeros. But, what about whole blocks that don't have anything in them except zeros? Well, I would like to get rid of all of those, as well. Here is a little rule though; you can replace one or more all zero blocks from an address with double colons. To replace more than one block, the all zero blocks must be contiguous. And, you can only make one replacement per address. So, you can remove two blocks of zeros in

`2001:db8:3c4d:12:0:0:1234:56ab`

and replace them with double colons, like this:

`2001:db8:3c4d:12::1234:56ab`

Now, if your address had four blocks of zeros, but the four blocks were separated, you could not replace them all. Take a look at this address:

`2001:0000:0000:0012:0000:0000:1234:56ab`

The best shortened version you could get would be:

2001::12:0:0:1234:56ab

But, 2001::12::1234:56ab would not be a valid address. Remember, you can only have one set of double colons. If you removed sets of zeros that were not contiguous and put more than one set of double colons into the address, then the device looking at the address would have no way to know how to put those zeros back in when it came time to actually deliver packets. The router would look at the multiple double colons, know from the address length that four zero blocks need to be inserted, but do I place two blocks into the first double colons, and two into the second set? Do I place three blocks into the first set and one block into the second set?" So on and so on, there is no way for the device to know.

Address Types

In IPv4, there are the familiar unicast, broadcast, and multicast addresses, which roughly defines who (or at least how many other devices) you are talking to. In IPv6, there are unicast, multicast, and anycast addresses. Broadcast addressing is gone, as it is very inefficient. Let's look at what each of these types of addressing or communication does for you.

Unicast   Packets addressed to a unicast address are delivered to a single interface. For load balancing, multiple interfaces can use the same address. There are a few types of unicast addresses.

Global Unicast   Global unicast addresses are typically publicly routable addresses, just like a regular publicly routable address in IPv4.

Link-local   Link-local addresses are like private addresses in IPv4; they are not meant to be routed. Think of them as being used to throw a temporary LAN together for meetings or a small LAN that is not going to be routed but needs to share and access files and services locally.

Unique-local   Unique-local addresses are meant for nonrouting purposes like link-local, but they are almost globally unique so it is unlikely they will have an address overlap. Unique local addresses were designed as a replacement for site-local addresses.

Site-local   IPv4 site-local addresses were designed to do almost exactly what IPv4 private addresses do, allow communication throughout a site while being routable to multiple local networks. Site-local addresses were deprecated as of September 2004.

Multicast   Packets addressed to a multicast address are delivered to all interfaces identified by the multicast address, same as in IPv4. Multicast addresses are also called one-to-many addresses. In IPv6, multicast addresses always start with the first 8 bits being all 1s, FF.

The second octet contains the lifetime flag and the scope of the address. There doesn't have to be a time to live (TTL) for the address any more because with IPv6 it is defined in the address. The first 4 bits of the second octet defines the lifetime and is either a 0 for a permanent address or a 1 for a temporary multicast address. The last 4 bits of the second octet defines the scope of the address. Table 9.1 lists the values and what each means.

TABLE 9.1   Multicast Address Scope Indicators

Value	Scope
1	Interface or loopback transmission
2	Local link
3	Local subnet
4	Admin-local, administratively configured
5	Site
8	Organization, multiple sites
E	Global

Anycast   Anycast addresses identify multiple interfaces and are similar to multicast. However, the anycast packet is only delivered to one address, the first one it finds defined in the terms of routing distance. Anycast addresses can also be called one to one of many.

Special Addresses

There are a few addresses and address ranges worth mentioning and remembering because you will eventually use them. Table 9.2 lists some special or otherwise reserved for use addresses.

TABLE 9.2   IPv6 Special Addresses

Address	Description
0:0:0:0:0:0:0:0, ::	With IPv4 it was 0.0.0.0. Typically the source address of a host when you are using stateful configuration
0:0:0:0:0:0:0:1, ::1	With IPv4 it was 127.0.0.1. It is still defined as the loopback address.
0:0:0:0:0:0:192.168.100.1	In a mixed IPv6/IPv4 network, an IPv4 address could be written like this.
2000::/3	Global unicast address range
FC00::/7	Unique-local unicast range

TABLE 9.2   IPv6 Special Addresses *(continued)*

Address	Description
FE80::/10	Link-local unicast range
FF00::/8	Multicast range
3FFF:FFFF::/32	Reserved for examples and documentation
2001:0DB8::/32	Reserved for examples and documentation
2002::/16	6 to 4 transition system, the system which allows IPv6 packets to be transmitted over an IPv4 network without the need to configure explicit tunnels; see "Interoperating IPv6 and IPv4"

Using IPv6 in an Internetwork

I take you through some of the finer points of IPv6; I want you to see at how a host can be addressed and how a host can find other hosts and resources on a network. I help you explore a device's ability to automatically address itself, called stateless autoconfiguration, and then the other type of autoconfiguration, known as stateful. Stateful autoconfiguration uses a DHCP server and is very similar to what you might be used to with IPv4 configuration. I also want you to take a closer look at what ICMP and multicast do for you on a IPv6 network.

Autoconfiguration

Autoconfiguration is an extremely useful solution for allowing devices on a network to address themselves with a link-local unicast address. Autoconfiguration occurs by learning the prefix information from the router and then appending the device's own interface address as the interface ID. Where does it get the interface ID? Well, you know that every device on Ethernet networks has a physical MAC address. The MAC address is used as the interface ID. I know you are now asking yourself, "The interface ID in the IPv6 address is 64 bits in length and a MAC address is only 48 bits. Where did the extra 16 bits come from?" The MAC address is padded in the middle with FFFE. For example, the IPv6 address of a device with a MAC address of 0060.d673.1987 would look like this after padding 0260.d6FF.FE73.1987. Take a look at Figure 9.2, so that you can see where the padding is coming from.

Where did the 2 in the beginning of the address come from, right? Well, part of the process of padding (called modified eui-64 formatting) changes a bit to specify whether the address is locally unique or globally unique. The seventh bit in the address is the bit used.

- A bit value of 1 = globally unique
- A bit value of 0 = locally unique

FIGURE 9.2   Creating the Host Portion of the Address

0060.d673.1987	MAC address
ff.fe	Padding
0060.d6 ↓ 73.1987	Split MAC address
0260.d6ff.fe73.1987	Host portion of IPv6 address

So, in this example, is the address global or locally unique? If you said that it is a globally unique address, you would be correct!

For the most part, autoconfiguration is going to save you time in addressing your host machines, because they communicate with the router for this process. To begin the process, the host requests prefix information (similar to the network portion of an IPv4 address) to configure its interface. It sends a router solicitation (RS) request asking the router to send the prefix information. The RS is sent as a multicast to the all routers multicast address. The actual information being sent is a type of ICMP message. Like everything in networking, the ICMP message includes an identifying number. The RS message is ICMP type 133. Next, the router answers with the required prefix information. This is accomplished with a router advertisement (RA). An RA message is also a multicast packet, sent to the all-nodes multicast address and is ICMP type 134. RA messages are sent on a periodic basis, but to prevent a host from having to wait until the next scheduled RA, the host sends the RS for an immediate response. You can see the exchange of messages in Figure 9.3.

FIGURE 9.3   RS and RA Messages

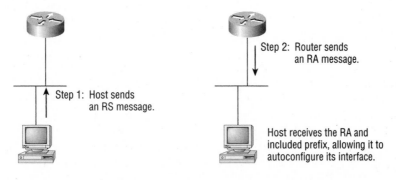

Step 1: Host sends an RS message.

Step 2: Router sends an RA message.

Host receives the RA and included prefix, allowing it to autoconfigure its interface.

This process is called stateless autoconfiguration because it doesn't contact or connect and receive any further information for other device. I talk about Stateful autoconfiguration next with DHCPv6.

In order to enable IPv6 on a router, use the ipv6 unicast-routing global configuration command.

```
DalRnDRtr1(config)#ipv6 unicast-routing
```

By default, IPv6 traffic forwarding is disabled so this command enables IPv6 traffic forwarding. By default, IPv6 is disabled on all interfaces, therefore, you must go to each interface where you want to run IPv6 and enable it. There are a few ways to enable an interface for IPv6. It can be easily done by adding an address to the interface. Use the interface configuration command ipv6 address <ipv6prefix>/<prefix-length> [eui-64].

```
DalRnDRtr1(config-if)#ipv6 address 2001:db8:3c4d:1:0260.d6FF.FE73.1987/64
```

The entire 128-bit global IPv6 address can be specified, or you can use the eui-64 option. Remember the eui-64 format allows the device to pad its MAC address to create the interface ID.

```
DalRnDRtr1(config-if)#ipv6 address 2001:db8:3c4d:1::/64 eui-64
```

You could also enable the interface and let an automatic link-local address be applied. Remember, if you only have a link-local address, you will only be able to communicate on that subnet. To do this, use the ipv6 enable interface configuration command:

```
DalRnDRtr1(config-if)#ipv6 enable
```

You have to configure one of these options on each of the interfaces that you want to run and forward IPv6 traffic on.

Dynamic Host Configuration Protocol for IPv6

Dynamic Host Configuration Protocol for IPv6 (DHCPv6) is much like it was in IPv4, but now, obviously, it supports the new addressing. DHCP still provides a couple of other things for us that autoconfiguration does not. With autoconfiguration there is no mention of DNS servers, domain names, or many of the other things that DHCP has always provided. This is why DHCP will still probably be used in most cases with v6. In IPv4 when the client booted, it sent a broadcast, a DHCP discover message, looking for a server to give it the required information. With IPv6, the RS and RA process happens first. If there is a DHCPv6 server on the network, the RA that is returned to the client will tell it if DHCP is available for use. If there is no router found, it sends a DHCP solicit message. The solicit message is a multicast message sent to ff02::1:2, which is the all-DHCP agents (servers and relays).

There is some support for DHCPv6 in the Cisco IOS, but the Cisco IOS only supports a stateless DHCP server. There is no address management for the pool, and the only options that you can configure in the pool are DNS server, domain name, and SIP servers. This means that you will need to have some other server to support giving out the other required information and to better manage address assignment.

Real World Scenario

Comparing Addressing Types

Think about the hosts in the research and development (RnD) network that you are converting over to use IPv6. Take a look at Figure 9.4; you can see two of the subnets that the RnD people use for design and to control new products that are in development.

FIGURE 9.4   RnD System Setup

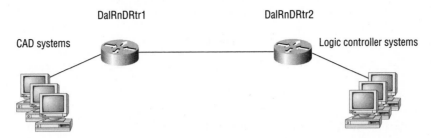

If you use autoconfiguration to address your subnets, each of the clients and devices on a subnet will get an address, but the address is a link-local address. That means that the CAD systems the RnD guys have on one subnet will be able to talk, but the logic controller systems would not be able to communicate with CAD systems. Autoconfiguration is very useful for getting basic connectivity to systems, but not for complete connectivity.

If you use DHCP, just as in IPv4, each system gets an address and all of the options that you want to set for the scope. This is the only way that a system, whether it's the CAD or logic controller system, would get the addresses for DNS, WINS, or whatever other services you might have running on the network that they need. Once the systems have received DHCP address information they can communicate off of the local subnet and out to the Internet if you are allowing them to do so.

Here is the configuration for the stateless DHCP server in the router IOS.

```
DalRnDRtr1(config)#ipv6 dhcp pool ?
WORD  DHCP pool name
DalRnDRtr1(config)#ipv6 dhcp pool test
DalRnDRtr1(config-dhcp)#?
IPv6 DHCP configuration commands:
default          Set a command to its defaults
dns-server       DNS servers
```

```
domain-name        Domain name to complete unqualified host names
exit               Exit from DHCPv6 configuration mode
no                 Negate a command or set its defaults
prefix-delegation  IPv6 prefix delegation
sip                SIP Servers options
DalRnDRtr1(config-dhcp)#dns-server ?
Hostname or X:X:X:X::X  Server's name or IPv6 address
DalRnDRtr1(config-dhcp)#domain-name ?
WORD  A domain name
DalRnDRtr1(config-dhcp)#domain-name lammle.com
DalRnDRtr1(config-dhcp)#prefix-delegation ?
X:X:X:X::X/<0-128>  IPv6  x:x::y/<z>
aaa                 Acquire prefix from AAA
pool                IPv6 prefix pool
DalRnDRtr1(config-dhcp)#prefix-delegation pool ?
WORD  IPv6 prefix pool
DalRnDRtr1(config-dhcp)#prefix-delegation pool test ?
lifetime  Configure prefix lifetimes
<cr>
DalRnDRtr1(config-dhcp)#prefix-delegation pool test lifetime ?
<60-4294967295>  Valid lifetime (seconds)
at                 Expire prefix at a specific time/date
infinite           Infinite valid lifetime
DalRnDRtr1(config-dhcp)#prefix-delegation pool test lifetime 3600 ?
<60-4294967295>  Preferred lifetime (seconds)
infinite           Infinite preferred lifetime
DalRnDRtr1(config-dhcp)#prefix-delegation pool test lifetime 3600 3600 ?
<cr>
DalRnDRtr1(config-dhcp)#prefix-delegation pool test lifetime 3600 3600
```

Now that you have the pool set, you just have to assign it to the server. That is done like this.

```
DalRnDRtr1(config)#int fa 0/0
DalRnDRtr1(config-if)#ipv6 dhcp server ?
WORD  Name of IPv6 DHCP pool
DalRnDRtr1(config-if)#ipv6 dhcp server test
DalRnDRtr1(config-if)#
```

You now have a fully configured DHCPv6 server applied to out an interface that will service the hosts from the subnet.

Internet Control Message Protocol for IPv6

IPv4 used Internet Control Message Protocol (ICMP) for many things; it provided error messages, such as destination unreachable, and troubleshooting functionality, such as ping and traceroute. ICMP for IPv6 (ICMPv6) still does those things for us, but unlike its predecessor the v6 flavor is not implemented as a separate Layer 4 protocol. ICMPv6 has been incorporated into IPv6 and information is carried in an extension header, appended to the basic IPv6 header information. Some of the most useful functions include:

- Packet fragmentation prevention
- Neighbor discovery
- Multicast listener discovery

Packet Fragmentation Prevention   ICMPv6 prevents packet fragmentation a process called path maximum transmission unit (MTU) discovery (PMTU-D). The source node of a connection sends a packet that is equal to the MTU size of its local link MTU. As this packet traverses the path toward the destination, any link that has an MTU smaller than the size of the current packet forces the intermediate router to send a packet too big message back to the source. The packet too big message tells the source the maximum size of the restrictive link, which allows the source to send a new packet at the new, smaller size.

The PMTU-D process continues until the destination is reached, with new, smaller packets sent as necessary. When the destination is reached, the source will have the new path MTU. Now when the rest of the data packets are transmitted, there will be no fragmenting of the packets.

Neighbor Discovery   ICMPv6 now takes over the task of finding the address of other devices on the local link, a task that the IPv4 address resolution protocol (ARP) used to perform. Now called neighbor discovery, the process is accomplished using the multicast address known as the solicited node address. All hosts join this multicast group when they connect to the network.

With the ARP process, when a host needed to know another host's MAC address, an ARP was broadcast containing the unknown hosts IP address. That unknown host would then send back its MAC address. Since, there is no broadcast in IPv6 the multicast neighbor discovery process was created. Now in IPv6, a discover message is sent out, and the unknown host will reply with its MAC address. The multicast request looks like this FF02:0:0:0:0:1:FF/104 and is called the solicited node address. The sender adds part of the IPv6 address (the rightmost 24 bits) of the unknown host's address to the end of the multicast address. When the address is queried, the corresponding host sends back its Layer 2 address. A device can use this process to find routers and keep track of other neighbor devices on the network. When I talked about RA and RS messages earlier in this chapter and told you that they were using multicast traffic to request and send address information, that too was a function of ICMPv6—specifically neighbor discovery.

Multicast Listener Discovery   In IPv4, the protocol IGMP was used to allow a host device to tell its local router that is was joining a multicast group and would like to receive the traffic for that group. This IGMP function as been incorporated into ICMPv6, as well; the process is called multicast listener discovery.

IPv6 Routing Protocols

Most of the routing protocols I've told you about have been upgraded for use in IPv6 networks. Many of these functions and configurations that you have already learned will be almost the same in IPv6. But, there are no broadcasts in IPv6 so any protocols that used entirely broadcast traffic are now out of luck; not that it is a bad thing since you didn't want to use them on your IPv4 networks! The IPv6 routing protocols got new names and a facelift.

- RIP next generation (RIPng)
- EIGRPv6
- OSPFv3

RIPng

RIP has worked very well on smaller networks for a long time and, for that reason, it is still around for IPv6. The primary features of RIPng are the same as they were in RIPv2. It is still a distance vector protocol, has a max hop count of 15, uses split horizon, poison reverse, and other loop avoidance mechanisms, and now uses UDP port 521. It still uses multicast to send its updates, but because we are now using IPv6 for transport the address is FF02::9. That is actually kind of nice, since the RIPv2 the multicast address was 224.0.0.9. The address still ends in 9, but now it is in the new IPv6 multicast range. Most of the routing protocols kept this similarity.

There are, of course, differences in the new version. As you know, in order to send data, routers store the address of the neighbor route for a given destination network. In RIPng, routers keep track of this next-hop address using a link-local address, not a global address.

Enabling RIPng

Probably one of the biggest changes with RIPng (and all of the IPv6 routing protocols for that matter) is the fact that you configure or enable the advertisement of a network from interface configuration mode, instead of using a network command from the router configuration mode. In the case of RIPng if you enable it directly on an interface, without going to router configuration mode and starting a RIPng process, a new RIPng process will be started for you. It will look something like this.

```
DalRnDRtr1(config-if)#ipv6 rip 1 enable
```

The one (1) in this command is a tag that identifies the process of RIPng that is running. Now like I said, this will start a process of RIPng and you will not have to go to router configuration mode. However, if you need to go to router configuration mode to configure some other function such as redistribution, then you still can. It will look like this on your router.

```
DalRnDRtr1(config)#ipv6 router rip 1
DalRnDRtr1(config-rtr)#
```

Remember RIPng will function much like RIP; the biggest difference is instead of using the network command you enable the interface to route the connected network.

EIGRPv6

Of course, we still have EIGRP. It already used protocol-dependent modules, so it was a simple matter to add a new module for the IPv6 protocol. Most of the features that EIGRP provided are still available in EIGRPv6.

- EIGRPv6 is still an Advance Distance Vector Protocol with some link state features.
- The neighbor discovery process using hellos still occurs.
- EIGRPv6 still provides reliable communication with reliable transport protocol.
- EIGRPv6 provides loop-free fast convergence using the Diffused Update ALgorithm (DUAL).
- Hello packets and updates are sent using multicast transmission, and like RIPng.
- The EIGRPv6 multicast address stayed very near the same; the IPv4 address 224.0.0.10 is now FF02::A (A = 10 in hexadecimal notation)

Enabling EIGRPv6

There are then the differences in the two versions of EIGRP. Most notably, just as with RIPng, the network and interface to be advertised must be enabled from the interface configuration mode. In EIGRPv6, the router configuration mode must still be used to enable the routing protocol. That is most of all because the routing process must be literally turned on, like an interface with the no shutdown command. The configuration for EIGRPv6 is going to look like this.

```
DalRnDRtr1(config)#ipv6 router eigrp 10
```

The 10 in this case is the autonomous system number.

```
DalRnDRtr1(config-rtr)#no shutdown
DalRnDRtr1(config-if)#ipv6 eigrp 10
```

Other options can be configured in the router configuration mode such as redistribution.

OSPFv3

We can round out the protocol list with OSPFv3. That is not a typo; it really is v3. OSPF for IPv4 was actually OSPFv2, so when it was updated for IPv6, it became OSPFv3. So don't get confused with the version numbers. The foundation of OSPF remains the same with this new version; it is still a link state routing protocol that divides an entire internetwork or autonomous system into areas, creating a hierarchy. But a few of the things that I talked about in Chapter 4, "Routing Concepts and Distance Vector Routing Protocols," are slightly different.

In OSPFv2, the router ID was determined with one of IP addresses assigned to the router (or an ID you assigned). In version 3, you must assign the router ID. The RID, area ID, and link state ID are still 32-bit values, but are not found using the IP address anymore because IPv6 addresses are 128 bits. Changes in the way these values are assigned along with the removal of the IP address information from the OSPF packet headers makes the new version of OSPF capable of being routed over almost any network layer protocol. Adjacencies and next-hop attributes now use link-local addresses. OSPF v3 still uses multicast traffic to send its updates and acknowledgements the addresses are now FF02::5 for OSPF routers and FF02::6 for OSPF designated routers. These are the replacements for 224.0.0.5 and 224.0.0.6 respectively.

OSPFv2 gave you the ability to assign the specific networks and interfaces that would be included in the OSPF process. Assignments were configured using the router configuration process. Now, like the other IPv6 routing protocols, the interfaces and therefore the networks attached to them are configured on the interface.

Enabling OSPFv3

The configuration for OSPFv3 is going to look like this.

```
DalRnDRtr1(config)#ipv6 router osfp 10
DalRnDRtr1(config-rtr)#router-id 1.1.1.1
```

Other configurations, such as summarization and redistribution, can be accomplished from router configuration mode. This configuration isn't required if you configure OSPFv3 from the interface. When the interface configuration is completed, this router configuration process is added automatically. The interface configuration looks like this.

```
DalRnDRtr1(config-if)#ipv6 ospf 10 area 0.0.0.0
```

When you configure OSPFv3 on an interface, the interface is placed into the routing process. All of the IP addresses that are configured on that interface are thereby placed into the process. You can't configure a specific address or prevent an address from being placed into the process.

Interoperating IPv6 with IPv4

So, now you know how IPv6 works and how to configure it to work on your networks. But what is the cost of doing this and how much work is really going to take?

Those are good questions. In terms of cost, it depends on the infrastructure that you currently have. If you have to upgrade all of your routers and switches so that they are IPv6 compliant, that could be a good chunk of change. And that doesn't even touch on server and computer operating systems (OS) costs or the cost of the work that will have to done to make applications compliant. But never fear. Many OSs and network devices have been IPv6 compliant for a few years now. You just haven't been using the features until now. The other question though, about the amount of work and time, could still be a hang up. It is going to take time to get all of your systems moved over and make sure that things work correctly. Let me introduce you to three of the primary migration strategies made to allow for a slower, phased-in integration. Dual stacking allows a device to have both an IPv4 and an IPv6 protocol stack running. Implementing IPv6 using dual stacking allows you to handle both existing IPv4 communications and newer IPv6 communications. The 6t04 tunneling approach is very useful if you have an all IPv6 network that must communicate over an IPv4 network to reach another IPv6 network. The third type of migration strategy is called network address translation–protocol translation (NAT-PT). It is not typical NAT that is translating public to private addresses. NAT-PT translates IPv6 addresses to IPv4 addresses.

Dual Stacking

Dual stacking is the most common migration strategy. It allows the devices to communicate using either IPv4 or IPv6. This technique allows for one-by-one upgrade of applications and devices on the network. As more and more things on the network are upgraded, more of you communication will occur over IPv6. Eventually all devices and software will be upgraded and the IPv4 protocol stacks can be removed. The configuration of dual stacking on a Cisco router is very easy; it requires nothing more than enabling IPv6 forwarding and applying an address to the interfaces which are already configured with IPv4.

 Real World Scenario

Getting RnD Data out of the RnD Network

You are still working with the RnD subnets. The R&D department still needs to send data out to the rest of the network and to the Internet. However, since the rest of the network is not converted over to IPv6, the RnD data is going to need to be converted so that all of the IPv4 devices on the rest of the network will know how to handle the data. The easiest method of accomplishing this task is by using a dual stacked router. Any of you who have had more than one network protocol running on your network are familiar with this term. I used to do it when I had IP and IPX running on the same network. Whatever router is on the border of the IPv6 and IPv4 networks will have addresses from each protocol. This allows the router to act as a translator between the two protocol types.

It will look something like this.

```
DalRnDRtr1(config)#ipv6 unicast-routing
DalRnDRtr1(config)#interface fastethernet 0/0
DalRnDRtr1(config-if)#ipv6 address 2001:db8:3c4d:1::/64 eui-64
DalRnDRtr1(config-if)#ip address 192.168.255.1 255.255.255.0
```

Tunneling

Tunneling is super useful for carrying IPv6 data over a network that is still IPv4. You can implement this solution in the network a couple of ways: manual tunnel and the automatic 6t04 tunnel.

In some cases, you will have IPv6 subnets or portions of your network that are all IPv6, and those networks will have to communicate with each other. Traffic may need to pass over a WAN or some other network that you do not control. So how do you fix this problem? By creating a tunnel that will carry the IPv6 traffic across the IPv4 network for you. Now creating a tunnel is not that hard and isn't difficult to understand. It is really taking the IPv6 packet that would normally being traveling across the network, grabbing it up, and placing an IPv4 header on the front of it.

 **Real World Scenario**

Carrying IPv6 Traffic across the Network

The IPv6 testing is progressing very well and the RnD department have been working out many of the bugs that are in the software and applications. The RnD department folks want to take the testing to the next level. It is required that the RnD systems in the London office run IPv6 and be able to communicate to the systems that are already IPv6 in Dallas. What you end up with are two islands of IPv6 networks. To keep the overhead down and so that there is no lose of information, you are going to connect the two networks using tunneling. Tunneling allows the native IPv6 packet to remain the same. When the border of the IPv4 network is reached, the IPv6 packets will be encapsulated with and IPv4 header. The IPv4 header allows the data to be carried across the rest of the FutureTech IPv4 network. Once the data reaches the IPv6 network in London, the encapsulation is removed and the IPv6 hosts read the packet as if nothing happened to it.

Take a look at Figure 9.5; it shows that exact scenario.

FIGURE 9.5   Tunneling

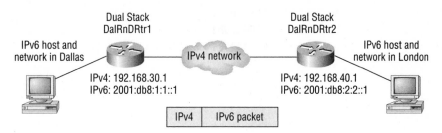

In order to make this happen, you are going to use couple of dual-stacked routers. You just have to add a little configuration to place a tunnel between the routers. Tunnels are very simple; you simply tell each router where the tunnel starts and where it ends. Use the information from the Figure 9.5 and configure the tunnel on each router.

```
DalRnDRtr1(config)#int tunnel 0
DalRnDRtr1(config-if)#ipv6 address 2001:db8:1:1::1/64
DalRnDRtr1(config-if)#tunnel source 192.168.30.1
DalRnDRtr1(config-if)#tunnel destination 192.168.40.1
DalRnDRtr1(config-if)#tunnel mode ipv6ip
LonRnDRtr2(config)#int tunnel 0
LonRnDRtr2(config-if)#ipv6 address 2001:db8:2:2::1/64
LonRnDRtr2(config-if)#tunnel source 192.168.40.1
LonRnDRtr2(config-if)#tunnel destination 192.168.30.1
LonRnDRtr2(config-if)#tunnel mode ipv6ip
```

The London and Dallas IPv6 networks can now communicate over the IPv4 network. Remember, this is not meant to be a permanent configuration; the end goal is to have an all IPv6 network end to end.

The second tunneling method is 6t04 tunneling. This method automatically creates a connection between IPv6 networks that are separated by a IPv4 network. The 6t04 tunneling method creates an IPv6 prefix for each of the IPv6 networks. This can make the deployment of IPv6 much faster because the addresses don't have to obtained from Internet service providers (ISPs) or registries.

The 6t04 tunneling method requires that the edge routers be updated with a special code or IOS, but all other IPv6 hosts and routers inside the 6t04 site aren't required to implement any new features or code to support 6t04. Each 6t04 site receives a /48 prefix, which is made up with two parts 0x2002 and the hexadecimal IPv4 address of the edge router.

⊕ Real World Scenario

Dynamic Tunnel Creation

Once the testing is complete between Dallas and London, there will be other sites that need to be added to the IPv6 network. The tunneling method I have shown you works well, but it is manual and doesn't allow for the rest of the network to change. The 6t04 tunneling method is dynamic and allows tunnels to be created whenever there is a destination to send traffic to. Let me give you an example.

The IPv4 address of the edge router is 192.168.10.1. It is the edge router on the IPv4 network; behind it is the IPv6 network. The router will automatically make the prefix for its IPv6 network, it would be 2002:c0a8:0a01::/48. The part of the prefix, c0a80a01 is created directly from the IPv4 address and is nothing more than the hexadecimal representation of 192.168.10.1. The IPv6 network can substitute any IP address in the space after the first 16-bit section (0x2002). The 2002 prefix has been specifically set aside for use in 6t04 tunneling.

So when an IPv6 packet reaches a router interface with a destination address in the range of 2002::/16, the 6t04 edge router extracts the IPv4 address that is embedded in the 2002:: destination address. That edge router then encapsulates the IPv6 packet into an IPv4 packet. The destination of the packet will be the IPv4 address that was pulled out of IPv6 destination address.

That new IPv4 destination address represents the address of the 6t04 edge router at the other end of the tunnel. Behind that router is the destination 6t04 site. The destination edge router removes the IPv6 packet from the IPv4 packet, finally forwarding the original IPv6 packet to its real destination IPv6 host.

One other thing that maybe noteworthy, if the IPv4 network that you are traversing has a NAT translation point, it will break the tunnel encapsulation that you created. NAT over the years has had many upgrades that allow it to handle specific protocols and dynamic connections. Without one of these upgrades, NAT breaks most connections. Since this transition strategy is not in most NAT implementations, connections often are broken. There is a way around this problem, it is called Teredo. Teredo allows all tunnel traffic to be placed in UDP packets. UDP packets do not have the problem of being broken like other protocols do. With Teredo in place, the packets will be able to slip by NAT without problems.

NAT-PT

You may have heard that IPv6 does not have any NAT in it. You are correct. IPv6 itself does not have a NAT implementation. The transition strategy is NAT protocol translation (NAT-PT). NAT-PT should be used as a last resort for making IPv4-only and IPv6-only hosts communicate. Much like NAT for IPv4, there are a couple of ways that you can implement it.

- Static NAT-PT provides a one-to-one mapping of a single IPv4 address to a single IPv6 address. (Remind you of static NAT?)
- Dynamic NAT-PT uses a pool of IPv4 addresses to provide a one to one mapping with an IPv6 address. (Sound kind of familiar?)
- Network Address Port Translation–Protocol Translation (NAPT-PT) provides a many-to-one mapping of multiple IPv6 addresses to a single IPv4 address and a port number.

As you can see, NAT is not being used to translate a public and private IPv6 address as it did in IPv4, but instead between the two address types (IPv4 and IPv6). Again, NAT-PT should be used as an absolute last resort. In most cases, a tunneling approach will work much better and without the headache of this configuration and system overhead.

Summary

IPv6 has many new things for you to learn and challenges to face in the future. Just when you were starting to get comfortable with IPv4, here I am telling you that there is a whole new protocol suite to learn. I started with the reasons why a new protocol suite is needed. While there are many compelling reasons to swap, ultimately your decision to change is going to come down to money or the fact that you just can't put any more hosts on the network. Even then, I don't know if some people will want to change.

The new addressing structures are exciting for me. I like that fact that I don't have to subnet anymore. The logic in the new address range is great because not as many addresses are wasted and there will be plenty of addresses for years to come. The autoconfiguration that is possible in IPv6 is great, too; now you can put new hosts on the network and they can start to communicate right away.

Some of the new ways to communicate are going to bring great benefits for the applications of tomorrow. You don't have to worry about broadcasts wasting bandwidth, and think of the possibilities that you have with the anycast address.

It is only fitting that I took the routing protocols that you know and work so well and showed you how to upgrade them to work with this new protocol suite. You saw that the way you configure them is going to make your administrative tasks much easier.

Finally, everyone knows that the migration to IPv6 is not going to happen overnight or all at once. So I showed you a few ways that you can slowly migrate and allow the old IPv4 devices and those that are converted to IPv6 communicate together. They may not be great solutions for the long run, but the end goal is to have an all IPv6 network anyway.

Review Questions

1. Why is IPv6 becoming necessary for networks today?

   A. Not enough devices

   B. Almost out of IPv4 addresses

   C. Too many addresses

   D. Just to upgrade

2. How many bits are in an IPv6 address?

   A. 32

   B. 64

   C. 96

   D. 128

3. How many sets of double colons can be used in an IPv6 address?

   A. 1

   B. 2

   C. 3

   D. 4

4. What is a required feature in all implementations of IPv6?

   A. Wireless

   B. No frames

   C. IPSec

   D. Broadcasting

5. What new type of transmission is included in IPv6?

   A. Unicast

   B. Multicast

   C. Broadcast

   D. Anycast

6. What is the first octet of an IPv6 multicast address?

   A. AA

   B. BB

   C. DD

   D. FF

7. During autoconfiguration a router sends out what type of message?

   A. RS

   B. RD

   C. RA

   D. RF

8. It is not possible to route IPv4 and IPv6 traffic at the same time.

   A. True

   B. False

9. What is the simplest and most common type of migration?

   A. Dual stacking

   B. Tunneling

   C. 6t04 tunneling

   D. NAT-PT

10. What type of tunneling provides dynamic tunnel creation for IPv6 networks?

   A. Tunneling

   B. 6t04 tunneling

   C. IPSec

   D. PPTP

Answers to Review Questions

1. B. The world is almost out of IPv4 addresses; IPv6 is the chosen solution to the problem.

2. D. There are 128 bits in an IPv6 address, expressed in hexadecimal.

3. A. Only one set of double colons can be used, or a device will not know where to place the fields back into the address.

4. C. IPSec and mobile IP must be included in all implementation of IPv6.

5. D. Anycast is used now in IPv6, and broadcasts have been removed.

6. D. The first 8 bits (octet) of a multicast address is FF.

7. C. A router sends out a router advertisement (RA) message to the clients.

8. B. False. It is possible for IPv4 and IPv6 to be routed at the same time on the same network.

9. A. Dual stacking is the most common and easiest to implement type of migration.

10. B. You can create 6t04 tunnels dynamically for use between IPv6 sites.

Chapter

10

Redundancy Protocols

IN THIS CHAPTER, YOU WILL LEARN HOW TO DO THE FOLLOWING:

- ✓ Explain the functions and operations of gateway redundancy protocols, including HSRP, VRRP, and GLBP

- ✓ Configure HSRP, VRRP, and GLBP

- ✓ Verify high availability configurations

In this chapter, I show you how to provide redundancy and load-balancing features to your network using just your routers. You don't always need to buy some overpriced load-balancing device. I show you how to configure and use HSRP and VRRP. You will see that while they are very similar in function, they operate slightly differently. Finally, I show you how to configure and use GLBP. GLBP allows you to use up to four routers in a true load-balancing solution.

For up-to-the-minute updates on this chapter, check out www.sybex.com/ go/CiscoProGuidetoInternetworking or www.lammle.com.

Client Redundancy Issues

How can you configure a client to send data off its subnet when its default gateway router has gone down? Typically, the answer is you can't. Most host operating systems don't allow you to change data routing. Sure, if a host's default gateway router goes down, the rest of the network will converge, but the network doesn't share that information with the hosts. Take a look at Figure 10.1; you can see what I am talking about. There are actually two routers available to forward data for the local subnet, but the hosts only know about one of them. They learn of this router when you give them the default gateway.

FIGURE 10.1   Default Gateway

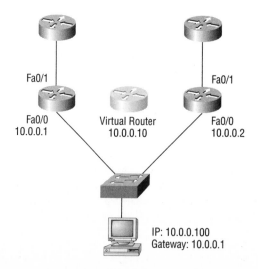

I am sure that you are asking, "Is there another way to use the other router?" The answer is complicated. There is feature that is enabled by default on Cisco routers called Proxy Address Resolution Protocol (Proxy ARP). Proxy ARP enables hosts, which have no knowledge of routing options, to obtain the MAC address of a gateway router that can forward packets off of the local subnet for them.

You can see how this happens in Figure 10.2. If a proxy ARP enabled router receives an ARP request for an IP address that it knows is not on the same subnet as the requesting host, it responds with an ARP reply packet to the host. The router will give its own local MAC address (the MAC address of its interface on the host's subnet) as the destination MAC address for the IP address that the host wishes to be resolved. After receiving the destination MAC address, the host will send all the packets to the router, not knowing that what it sees as the destination host is really a router. The router then forwards the packets toward the intended host; this process may have to be repeated along the path to the host.

FIGURE 10.2   Proxy ARP

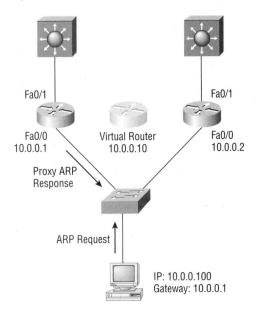

With proxy ARP, the host device sends traffic as if the destination device were located on its own network segment. If the router that responded to the ARP request fails, the source host continues to send packets for that destination to the same MAC address, but since that is to a failed router, the packets will be discarded.

After the timeout period on the host, the proxy ARP MAC address ages out of the ARP cache. The host can then make a new ARP request for the destination and get the address of another proxy ARP router. However, the host cannot send packets off of its subnet during the failover time. Not a perfect situation, there has to be a better way right? That is where redundancy protocols come to the rescue.

Introducing Redundancy Protocols

Redundancy protocols work by giving you a way to configure more than one router to appear as one single router. This makes client configuration and communication easier because you can configure a single default gateway and the host machine can use its standard protocols to talk.

How does a redundancy protocol accomplish this? The protocols that I am going to describe for you do this basically by presenting a virtual router to all of the clients. The virtual router has its own IP and MAC addresses. The IP address is the address that is configured on each of the host machines as the default gateway. The virtual MAC address is the address that will be returned when an ARP request is sent by a host. The hosts don't know or care which physical router is actually forwarding the traffic.

It is then the responsibility of the redundancy protocol to decide which physical router will actively forward traffic and which one will be placed in standby in case the active router fails. Even if the active router fails, the swap over to the standby router will be transparent to the hosts because the virtual router (which is really just the virtual IP and MAC addresses) are picked up by the standby router.

In the sections that follow, I discuss the following redundancy protocols.

- Hot Standby Router Protocol (HSRP)
- Virtual Router Redundancy Protocol (VRRP)
- Gateway Load Balancing Protocol (GLBP)

Hot Standby Router Protocol   HSRP provides a redundant, but not a load-balanced, gateway for hosts on a local subnet. HSRP is a Cisco-proprietary protocol that allows you to configure two routers into a standby group that shares an IP address and MAC address and provides a default gateway. When the IP and MAC addresses are independent from the routers' physical addresses, they can swap control of the address in the event that the current forwarding (active) router should fail.

Virtual Router Redundancy Protocol   VRRP also provides a redundant, but not a load-balanced, gateway for hosts on a local subnet. VRRP is an open standard protocol that functions almost identically to HSRP. Later in this chapter, I discuss the small differences that exist between the protocols.

Gateway Load Balancing Protocol   GLBP not only provides a redundant gateway, but is a true load-balancing solution for routers in a forwarding group. GLBP allow a maximum of four routers in each forwarding group. By default, the active router directs the traffic from hosts to each successive router in the group using a round-robin algorithm. The hosts are directed to send their traffic toward a specific router by being given the MAC address of the next router in line to be used.

Hot Standby Router Protocol

The first protocol I want to go over is HSRP. This is a Cisco-proprietary protocol that can be run on most, but not all, Cisco router and multilayer switch models. HSRP defines a standby group each of the standby groups that you define include:

- Active router
- Standby router
- Virtual router
- Any other routers that maybe attached to the subnet

The standby group will always have two routers that are participating in the group. The primary players in the group are the one active router and one standby router that communicate to each other using multicast Hello messages. The Hello messages provide all of the required communication for the routers. The Hellos contain the information required to accomplish the election that decides the active and standby router positions. They also hold the key to the failover process. If the standby router stops receiving Hello packets from the active router, then it takes over the active router role.

HSRP Timers

Before I go further into the roles that each of the routers can have in an HSRP group, I want to define the HSRP timers. The timers are very important in the operation of HSRP because they ensure communication between the routers and, if something goes wrong, allow the standby router to take over. The HSRP timers include:

- Hello timer
- Hold timer
- Active timer
- Standby timer

Hello Timer   The Hello timer is defined as the interval at which each of the routers sends out its Hello messages. The default interval for the Hello timer is 3 seconds. The Hello messages identify the state that each router is in. The state defines the role and actions each of the routers will take in the group. This timer can be changed, but it used to be thought that lowering the Hello value would place an unnecessary load on the routers. That isn't true with most of the routers today; in fact, you will see later in the chapter that it is possible for you to configure the timers in milliseconds. This allows the failover time to be much less than one second. However, increasing the value will make the standby router wait for a longer period before it takes over when the active router fails or can't communicate.

Hold Timer   The hold timer specifies the interval the standby router uses to determine whether the active router is offline or out of communication. By default, the hold timer is 10 seconds, roughly three times the Hello timer. If one timer is changed for some reason, it is recommended that this multiplier be used to adjust the other timers. By setting the hold timer at three times the Hello timer, you ensure that the standby router doesn't take over the active role every time there is a short break in communication.

Active Timer   The active timer is used to monitor the state of the active router. The timer resets each time a router in the standby group receives a Hello packet from the active router. This timer expires based on the hold time value that is set in the corresponding field of the HSRP hello message.

Standby Timer   The standby timer is used to monitor the state of the standby router. The timer resets any time a router in the standby group receives a Hello packet from the standby router. This timer expires based on the hold time value that is set in the respective hello packet.

Group Roles

Each of the routers in the standby group has a specific function and role to fulfill. The three main roles are the virtual router, active router, and standby router. Other routers may also be included in the group.

Virtual Router   The virtual router, by its very name, is not a physical entity. It really just defines the process that is held by one of the physical routers. The physical router that communicates as the virtual router is the current active router. The virtual router is nothing more than a separate IP address and MAC address that packets are sent toward.

Active Router   The active router is the physical router that receives data and routes it on toward the destinations. This router, in addition to accepting data sent to its own physical MAC address, accepts all the data sent to the MAC address of the virtual router. Not only will the active router take care of processing the data that is being forwarded, but any ARP requests that are sent out for the virtual routers IP address will be answered by the active router as well.

Standby Router   The standby router is the backup to the active router. Its job is to monitor the status of the HSRP group and quickly take the over packet-forwarding responsibility if the active router fails or loses communication. Both the active and standby routers transmit Hello messages to inform all other routers in the group of their role and status.

Other Routers   An HSRP group can have additional routers that are members of the group but are not taking a primary role of active or standby state. These routers constantly listen to the Hello messages sent by the active and standby routers. They make sure that an active and standby router exists for the HSRP group that they belong to. These other routers will forward data that is specifically addressed to their own IP addresses, but they will never forward data addressed to the virtual router unless elected to the active or standby state. These routers send "speak" messages based on the Hello interval. Speak messages allow other routers to know their position in an election.

Virtual MAC Address

A virtual router in a HSRP group has a virtual IP address and a virtual MAC address. Where does the virtual MAC come from, though? The virtual IP address isn't that hard to figure out; it just as to be a unique IP address on the same subnet as the hosts. But MAC addresses are a little different, right? Or are they?

Typically, people know that a TCP/IP host has a MAC address and most people today think that you can't change them, which is partly true. Most network interface controllers (NICs) today won't let you change the MAC address. It hasn't always been that way, on old NICs you set dip switches to set the MAC address. Why is that important? Well, nothing in the standard requires that a host have only one MAC address. You know that from multicast transmissions. Well, with HSRP you are going to create a totally new, made-up MAC address as well.

The HSRP MAC address you create is different from multicast MAC address though. You don't have to worry about translating it from the IP address. The HSRP MAC address only has one variable piece in the address. The first 24 bits still identify the vendor who manufactured the device (the organization identifier). The next 16 bits tell you that the MAC address is a well known HSRP MAC address. Finally, the last 8 bits of the address are the hexadecimal representation of the HSRP group number.

I want to show you what I mean. Here is an example of what a HSRP MAC address would look like.

    0000.0c07.ac0a

- The first 24 bits (0000.0c) are the vendor ID of the address; in the case of HSRP being a Cisco protocol the ID is assigned to Cisco.
- The next 16 bits (07.ac) are the well-known HSRP ID; this part of the address was assigned by Cisco in the protocol so you always recognize that the address is for use with HSRP.
- The last 8 bits (0a), which are the only variable bits, represent the HSRP group number that you assign. In this case, the group number is 10; the group number is converted to hexadecimal when it is placed in the MAC address where it becomes the 0a that you see.

You can see this MAC address added to the ARO cache of every router in the HSRP group. There will be the translation from the IP address to the MAC address and the interface that it is located on.

HSRP States

A router in an HSRP group can be in one of these states: initial, learn, listen, speak, standby, or active. Table 10.1 lists each of the states and provides a description.

TABLE 10.1 HSRP STATES

State	Description
Initial	The state at the start. The initial state indicates that HSRP does not run. This state is entered following a configuration change or when an interface first comes up.
Learn	The router is neither in the active or standby state, nor does it have enough information to attempt to claim the active or standby role.
Listen	The router knows the virtual IP address, but the router is neither the active router nor the standby router. It listens for Hello messages from those routers.
Speak	The router sends periodic Hello messages and actively participates in the election of the active or standby router. A router cannot enter speak state unless the router has the virtual IP address.
Standby	The router is a candidate to become the next active router and sends periodic Hello messages. With the exclusion of transient conditions, there is, at most, one router in the group in standby state.
Active	The router currently forwards packets that are sent to the group virtual MAC address. The router sends periodic hello messages. With the exclusion of transient conditions, there must be, at the most, one router in the active state in the group.

When a router is in one of these states, it performs the actions required for that state. Not all HSRP routers in the group will transition through all states. For example, if there were three routers in the HSRP group, the router that is not the standby or active router will remain in the listen state.

All routers begin in the initial state. This is the starting state and indicates that HSRP is not running. This state is entered following a configuration change, such as when HSRP is disabled on an interface, or when an HSRP-enabled interface is first brought up, and when the no shutdown command is issued. The purpose of the listen state is to determine if active or standby routers have been elected for the group. In the speak state, the routers actively participate in the election of the active router, standby router, or both. Each router uses the three HSRP timers. The timers monitor the intervals between Hello messages. When a timer, expires, the router transitions to a new HSRP state.

HSRP Group Communication and Configuration

Now, I want to go through the configuration steps for an HSRP group. I go through each step in the process as the routers communicate and transition through the states until an active and standby router is elected and running.

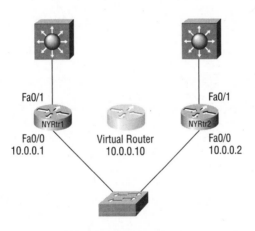

🌐 Real World Scenario

Ensuring Communications with the Dallas HQ

Since communications between the various internal departments, field offices, and the Dallas headquarters are vital, many of the switch blocks for the FutureTech network use two distribution layer routers (or multilayer switches in many cases). Access layer devices, then, are where hosts and traffic would be located and coming from.

FutureTech uses routers as the distribution layer devices and switches as the access layer devices. You will see later exactly why they did this, but for now, it is because they have multiple subnets or VLANs behind the routers in the switch block. Figure 10.3 shows the connections between the accounting offices in the Dallas headquarters and the New York office.

FIGURE 10.3   HSRP Router Setup

Dallas Headquarters Clients

Fa0/1   Fa0/1

NYRtr1   NYRtr2

Fa0/0   Virtual Router   Fa0/0
10.0.0.1   10.0.0.10   10.0.0.2

New York Headquarters Clients

Let's take a look at how the New York setup would be configured and the states through which the routers will transition as each router's role in the group is determined.

The first step in the configuration process is to start the HSRP process. At the minimum, you have to configure each of the routers to tell it the group number and the virtual IP address for the group. If you don't assign the group number in the command, the default group number, zero (0), will be assigned. The command for this configuration is standby *group number* ip *ip address*.

So, configure each of the routers using the standby command and an IP address. The command line entry would look like this.

```
NYRtr1(config-if)#standby 10 ip 10.0.0.10
```

Next, the routers transition through the HSRP states. Here's what happens during each one.

Each router starts out in the disabled state and moves into the init state. Once the router enters the init state, you know that the router is now enabled for HSRP. You can see these state changes if you turn on debug standby before you enable HSRP on the interface.

The following debug output is from NYRtr1 upon enabling HSRP on only the NYRtr1 router. The first line shows the time stamp added by the debug; I removed the time stamp from the rest of the debug output lines so that the output would fit on the page and be easier to read in this book. When you try this on your test network, you will see a time stamp on each line.

```
*Sep 28 21:22:51.890: HSRP: Fa0/0 API 10.0.0.10 is not an HSRP address
*HSRP: Fa0/0 Grp 10 Disabled -> Init
*HSRP: Fa0/0 Grp 10 Redundancy "hsrp-Fa0/0-10" state Disabled -> Init
*HSRP: Fa0/0 Interface up
*HSRP: Fa0/0 Starting minimum interface delay (1 secs)
*HSRP: Fa0/0 Interface min delay expired
*HSRP: Fa0/0 Grp 10 Init: a/HSRP enabled
*HSRP: Fa0/0 Grp 10 Init -> Listen
```

Consider that debug code output. You can see that the HSRP process was initially disabled, then the HSRP state moved from disabled to init to enabled as the interface was placed into the HSRP process. During that process, the interface was brought up and enabled; this is really telling you that the interface was enabled in the redundancy process. At this point, NYRtr1 is just listening on the network for any other routers sending HSRP Hellos. NYRtr1 hasn't sent anything yet. Take a look at what happens next. (Once again, I've removed the time stamps to make the code easier to read.)

```
*HSRP: Fa0/0 Redirect adv out, Passive, active 0 passive 1
*HSRP: Fa0/0 Grp 10 Redundancy "hsrp-Fa0/0-10" state Init -> Backup
*HSRP: Fa0/0 Grp 10 Listen: c/Active timer expired (unknown)
*HSRP: Fa0/0 Grp 10 Listen -> Speak
*HSRP: Fa0/0 Grp 10 Redundancy "hsrp-Fa0/0-10" state Backup -> Speak
*HSRP: Fa0/0 Grp 10 Hello  out 10.0.0.1 Speak    pri 100 vIP 10.0.0.10
*HSRP: Fa0/0 Grp 10 Hello  out 10.0.0.1 Speak    pri 100 vIP 10.0.0.10
```

Notice that the router moved from the listen state into the speak state. In the speak, state NYRtr1 sends out Hello messages announcing the information it knows and how it is configured to any other HSRP routers. You can see the Hello message that was sent by NYRtr1 in Figure 10.4.

FIGURE 10.4   NYRtr1 Sending a Speak Hello

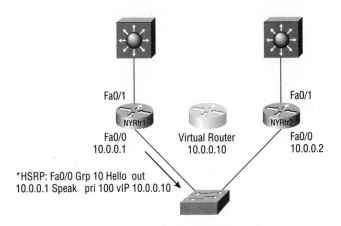

Dallas Headquarters Clients

So, what did that Hello message tell the rest of the network? Table 10. 2 lists and describes each piece of information that a Hello message contains, working from the left, where you see the asterisk, to the right where you'll find the virtual IP address for the group.

TABLE 10.2   HSRP Hello Message Elements

Item	Description
*Time stamp	Date and time information for each step in the process is generally displayed here. It has been removed in the illustration for ease of reading.
HSRP tag	This indicates that the Hello is an HSRP message.
Interface ID	The Interface ID indicates that the interface that is enabled for HSRP.
Group number	Sends the HSRP group number that is configured on the interface.
Hello tag	This tag tells other devices that this is a Hello message.
Direction tag	This tag tells other device the message direction. Out indicates that the message is being sent out from the interface identified in the Interface ID. In indicates that message was received by the sending device.
Real IP address	This is the IP address that is configured on the physical interface of the sending router.

TABLE 10.2 HSRP Hello Message Elements *(continued)*

Item	Description
Message type	The message type tag identifies the message type and the state of the sending router. Message types include: Active Listen Preempt Speak Standby
Priority	The priority field is made up of two parts. The pri part indicates that this is the priority field. The 100 is the priority value that was set on the router; the default value is 100 and you can configure it from 1 to 255. The higher the value the better. The priority value is the first value used to decide which router will be the active router and the standby router. If the priority value ends in a tie, then the real IP address of the router breaks the tie.
Virtual IP address	This is the virtual IP address for the HSRP group.

The elements included in Hello messages have changed over time. If you work with older routers, you might see Hello messages that include the `hellotime` and `holdtime` parameter values, or other elements that are not currently included.

Once the HSRP Hello message has been sent, the router begins the process of determining its role in the group. Take a look at the next debug output code.

```
*HSRP: Fa0/0 Grp 10 Speak: d/Standby timer expired (unknown)
*HSRP: Fa0/0 Grp 10 Standby router is local
*HSRP: Fa0/0 Grp 10 Speak -> Standby
*HSRP-5-STATECHANGE: FastEthernet0/0 Grp 10 state Speak -> Standby
*HSRP: Fa0/0 Grp 10 Redundancy "hsrp-Fa0/0-10" state Speak -> Standby
*HSRP: Fa0/0 Grp 10 Hello  out 10.0.0.1 Standby pri 100 vIP 10.0.0.10
```

After the standby timer expires, you see the router transition from speak to standby state. This tells other routers that NYRtr1 has not heard from and doesn't see any other routers that are better suited to become the standby router. NYRtr1 takes on the role of standby router. Now you can see in Figure 10.5 the standby Hello message sent by NYRtr1.

FIGURE 10.5   NYRtr1 Sending a Standby Hello

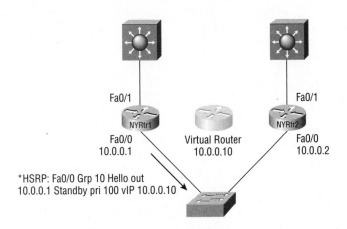

After taking on the standby role, the router begins looking to elect an active router. Take a look at the next debug output code.

```
*HSRP: Fa0/0 Grp 10 Standby: c/Active timer expired (unknown)
*HSRP: Fa0/0 Grp 10 Active router is local
```

Now the active timer has expired and the router has not heard another router that is better suited to be elected the active router; the router transitions from standby to active.

```
*HSRP: Fa0/0 Grp 10 Standby router is unknown, was local
*HSRP: Fa0/0 Grp 10 Standby -> Active
*HSRP-5-STATECHANGE: FastEthernet0/0 Grp 10 state Standby -> Active
*HSRP: Fa0/0 Redirect adv out, Active, active 1 passive 0
*HSRP: Fa0/0 Grp 10 Redundancy "hsrp-Fa0/0-10" state Standby -> Active
*HSRP: Fa0/0 Grp 10 Hello  out 10.0.0.1 Active  pri 100 vIP 10.0.0.10
```

You can see the steps in transitioning to the active state, and finally the last line of the output is the first Hello sent announcing itself as the active router. You can see the first active Hello message in Figure 10.6.

Now I want to show you the interaction of both routers when you enable HSRP on NYRtr2. Use the standby command on NYRtr2's interface to enable the process, add it to the HSRP group, and assign an IP address.

```
NYRtr2(config-if)#standby 10 ip 10.0.0.10
```

FIGURE 10.6   NYRtr1 Sending an Active Hello

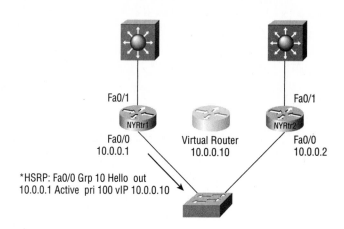

Dallas Headquarters Clients

Fa0/1   Fa0/1

NYRtr1   NYRtr2

Fa0/0   Virtual Router   Fa0/0
10.0.0.1   10.0.0.10   10.0.0.2

*HSRP: Fa0/0 Grp 10 Hello out
10.0.0.1 Active pri 100 vIP 10.0.0.10

New York Headquarters Clients

Now you are again going to see the debug output from the debug standby command. This time I show the output from NYRtr2's console. You can see that I left the time stamp in the first line of code again; this way you can see what it looks like. For all of the other lines in the output, I removed the time stamp so it will be easier to concentrate on the code itself.

```
*Sep 29 21:46:58.714: HSRP: Fa0/0 Grp 10 Disabled -> Init
*HSRP: Fa0/0 Grp 10 Redundancy "hsrp-Fa0/0-10" state Disabled -> Init
*HSRP: Fa0/0 Interface up
*HSRP: Fa0/0 Starting minimum interface delay (1 secs)
*HSRP: Fa0/0 Interface min delay expired
*HSRP: Fa0/0 Grp 10 Init: a/HSRP enabled
*HSRP: Fa0/0 Grp 10 Init -> Listen
```

From that last output, you can see that the HSRP process was enabled and moved from the disabled state into the init state. After the process is enabled, then the interface is recognized by the HSRP process as up and ready for use. NYRtr2 is now enabled in the redundancy process. At this point, NYRtr2 is just listening on the network for other routers that are sending HSRP Hellos; nothing has sent out by NYRtr2 yet. Take a look at what happens next.

```
*HSRP: Fa0/0 Redirect adv out, Passive, active 0 passive 1
*HSRP: Fa0/0 Grp 10 Redundancy "hsrp-Fa0/0-10" state Init -> Backup
*HSRP: Fa0/0 Grp 10 Hello  in  10.0.0.1 Active  pri 100 vIP 10.0.0.10
*HSRP: Fa0/0 Grp 10 Active router is 10.0.0.1
```

Notice that before any of the HSRP timers expire, R2 receives a Hello message from NYRtr1. The message includes the information that NYRtr1 is the active router, and provides NYRtr1's ID and IP address along with the virtual IP address is recognized as the same one that NYRtr2 was configured with. Having received the active router's Hello, NYRtr2 turns its attention to determining the existence of a standby router. Take a look at what happens next.

```
*HSRP: Fa0/0 Redirect adv out, Passive, active 0 passive 1
*HSRP: Fa0/0 Grp 10 Hello  in  10.0.0.1 Active  pri 100 vIP 10.0.0.10
*HSRP: Fa0/0 Grp 10 Hello  in  10.0.0.1 Active  pri 100 vIP 10.0.0.10
*HSRP: Fa0/0 Grp 10 Hello  in  10.0.0.1 Active  pri 100 vIP 10.0.0.10
*HSRP: Fa0/0 Grp 10 Listen: d/Standby timer expired (unknown)
*HSRP: Fa0/0 Grp 10 Listen -> Speak
*HSRP: Fa0/0 Grp 10 Redundancy "hsrp-Fa0/0-10" state Backup -> Speak
```

Once the standby timer expires, and no standby router has been identified, the router moves from the listen state into the speak state. Notice, too, that NYRtr2 continued to receive Hello messages from NYRtr1 confirming that NYRtr1, the active router, is communicating. In the speak state, NYRtr2 sends out Hello messages announcing to any other HSRP routers the information it knows and how it is configured. You can see the Hello messages that are being sent out by NYRtr2 in Figure 10.7.

FIGURE 10.7   NYRtr2 Sending a Speak Hello

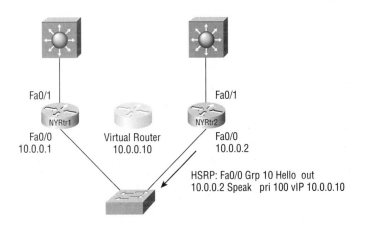

Dallas Headquarters Clients

Fa0/1

Fa0/1

NYRtr1

NYRtr2

Fa0/0
10.0.0.1

Virtual Router
10.0.0.10

Fa0/0
10.0.0.2

HSRP: Fa0/0 Grp 10 Hello out
10.0.0.2 Speak pri 100 vIP 10.0.0.10

New York Headquarters Clients

```
*HSRP: Fa0/0 Grp 10 Hello  out 10.0.0.2 Speak   pri 100 vIP 10.0.0.10
*HSRP: Fa0/0 Grp 10 Hello  in  10.0.0.1 Active  pri 100 vIP 10.0.0.10
```

```
*HSRP: Fa0/0 Grp 10 Hello  out 10.0.0.2 Speak   pri 100 vIP 10.0.0.10
*HSRP: Fa0/0 Grp 10 Hello  in  10.0.0.1 Active  pri 100 vIP 10.0.0.10
*HSRP: Fa0/0 Grp 10 Hello  out 10.0.0.2 Speak   pri 100 vIP 10.0.0.10
*HSRP: Fa0/0 Grp 10 Hello  in  10.0.0.1 Active  pri 100 vIP 10.0.0.10
*HSRP: Fa0/0 Grp 10 Hello  out 10.0.0.2 Speak   pri 100 vIP 10.0.0.10
*HSRP: Fa0/0 Grp 10 Speak: d/Standby timer expired (unknown)
*HSRP: Fa0/0 Grp 10 Standby router is local
*HSRP: Fa0/0 Grp 10 Speak -> Standby
*HSRP-5-STATECHANGE: FastEthernet0/0 Grp 10 state Speak -> Standby
*HSRP: Fa0/0 Grp 10 Redundancy "hsrp-Fa0/0-10" state Speak -> Standby
```

You can see in this section of code that NYRtr1 continues to send out active Hellos and NYRtr2 sends out speak Hellos. After the expiration of the standby timer, NYRtr2, seeing no other routers better suited to becoming the standby router, transitions to the standby state. You can see these Hellos in Figure 10.8.

FIGURE 10.8   Hello Interaction

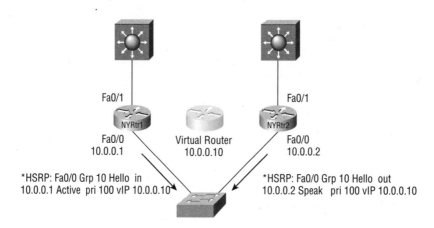

Dallas Headquarters Clients

New York Headquarters Clients

```
*HSRP: Fa0/0 Grp 10 Hello  out 10.0.0.2 Standby pri 100 vIP 10.0.0.10
*HSRP: Fa0/0 Grp 10 Hello  in  10.0.0.1 Active  pri 100 vIP 10.0.0.10
```

You can see with the continued Hello messages that NYRtr2 stays in the standby state and NYRtr1 stays in the active state. Is this how it should be?

Take a look at the priority of both routers. Both of routers were configured with the default (100) priority value. So, what's considered next, when all the routers carry the same priority configuration? Yes, the physical IP address is the tiebreaker. So, based on the IP addresses, which router should be the active router? If you said that NYRtr2 should be the active router because it has a higher IP address, you would normally be right. However, you will see in the next section that until you add an additional configuration that won't happen. Why? Because NYRtr1 was online first and elected itself as the active router before NYRtr2 was brought online.

Improving HSRP Operations

A few configuration changes can be made to HSRP so that it operation becomes much more efficient. You can add configurations for:

- Standby priority
- Preempt
- Timer values
- Interface tracking

I go through each of these and show you how it can improve your setup.

Standby Priority

Each standby group has its own active and standby routers. Network administrators can assign a priority value to each router in a standby group, allowing the administrator to control the order in which active routers for that group are selected.

To set the priority value of a router, enter this command in interface configuration mode: `standby group-number priority priority-value`. The default value for each router is 100. You can configure an interface with a value that ranges from 1 to 255, the higher the priority value the better. During the election process, the router with the highest priority in an HSRP group becomes the active router. In the case of a tie, the router with the highest IP address becomes the active router. To reinstate the default standby priority value, enter the `no standby priority` command.

Now, continuing on with the example from the previous section. I left off telling you the even though NYRtr1 has a lower IP address than NYRtr2 does; it is still the active router. That is because when NYRtr1 first came up and HSRP was enabled, there was no other router on the network, so it elected itself the active router.

Now, knowing that you can manually modify the priority on one of the routers, you ask, "Can't you basically set which router you want to be the active one by altering the priority?" Try the command `standby 10 priority 120` on NYRtr2. This should make NYRtr2 become the Active router, right? But, did it become active router? No? Why not?

Well, for the same reason it didn't become the active router when it came up on the network with a higher IP address. The addition of a router with a higher the IP address or a higher priority will not force an election. An active router, once elected, remains the forwarding router until it fails, is removed from service, or an election is forced. You will see in the next section how to force an election so that a router with a better priority or IP address can be elected as the active router.

Standby Preempt

The standby router automatically assumes the active router role whenever the active router fails or is removed from service. This new active router remains the forwarding router until it fails, is removed from service, or an election is forced—even when a former active router regains service in the network. Standby preempt is the mechanism by which an election can be forced.

The former active router can be configured to resume the forwarding router role by preempting a router with a lower priority. To enable a router to resume the forwarding router role, enter this command in interface configuration mode `standby [group-number] preempt [[delay] [minimum delay] [sync delay]`. You are essentially forcing the HSRP group to go through another election; this in both cases will let the other router take over as the active router.

When the `standby preempt` command is issued, the interface changes to the appropriate state. To remove the interface from preemptive status, enter the `no standby group preempt` command.

Now, place the standby preempt command on the NYRtr2 interface and see what happens. Did NYRtr2 become the active router?

Once the preempt command is configured, then any change in status for the group becomes a catalyst that will force the state to change. For you to see what I mean, I did just that. I waited to change the priority until after I configured the preempt command. This way you can see the messages in the debug output that forced the change.

Here is what that looks like. Just as before, I removed the time stamp from the beginning of the lines of code. Look at Figure 10.9; it shows the priorities on the two routers and the resultant Hello messages.

FIGURE 10.9 Router Priorities

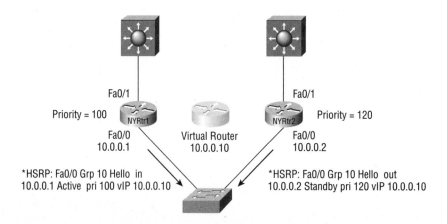

```
R2(config-if)#standby 10 preempt
R2(config-if)#standby 10 priority 120
```

```
*HSRP: Fa0/0 Redirect adv out, Passive, active 0 passive 1
*HSRP: Fa0/0 Grp 10 Hello  in  10.0.0.1 Active  pri 100 vIP 10.0.0.10
*HSRP: Fa0/0 Grp 10 Priority 100 -> 120
```

At this point, you can see that the priority change has taken effect. NYRtr1 is still the active router. But watch what happens next.

```
*HSRP: Fa0/0 Grp 10 Hello  out 10.0.0.2 Standby pri 120 vIP 10.0.0.10
*HSRP: Fa0/0 Grp 10 Hello  in  10.0.0.1 Active  pri 100 vIP 10.0.0.10
*HSRP: Fa0/0 Grp 10 Standby: h/Hello rcvd from lower pri Active router
(100/10.0.0.1)
```

Now NYRtr3 has received a Hello from a router (NYRtr1) and detects that the current active router has a lower priority. Being configured with the preempt command, NYRtr2 knows that it must take over the active role.

```
*HSRP: Fa0/0 Grp 10 Active router is local, was 10.0.0.1
*HSRP: Fa0/0 Grp 10 Standby router is unknown, was local
*HSRP: Fa0/0 Redirect adv out, Active, active 1 passive 2
*HSRP: Fa0/0 Grp 10 Coup   out 10.0.0.2 Standby pri 120 vIP 10.0.0.10
*HSRP: Fa0/0 Grp 10 Standby -> Active
*HSRP-5-STATECHANGE: FastEthernet0/0 Grp 10 state Standby -> Active
*HSRP: Fa0/0 Redirect adv out, Active, active 1 passive 1
*HSRP: Fa0/0 Grp 10 Redundancy "hsrp-Fa0/0-10" state Standby -> Active
*HSRP: Fa0/0 Grp 10 Hello  out 10.0.0.2 Active  pri 120 vIP 10.0.0.10
*HSRP: Fa0/0 REDIRECT adv in, Passive, active 0, passive 1, from 10.0.0.1
```

Through this section of code lines you can see the states change for the NYRtr2 and it takes over as the active router for the HSRP group 10.

```
*HSRP: Fa0/0 Grp 10 Hello  in  10.0.0.1 Speak   pri 100 vIP 10.0.0.10
*HSRP: Fa0/0 Grp 10 Hello  out 10.0.0.2 Active  pri 120 vIP 10.0.0.10
*HSRP: Fa0/0 Grp 10 Hello  in  10.0.0.1 Speak   pri 100 vIP 10.0.0.10
*HSRP: Fa0/0 Grp 10 Redundancy group hsrp-Fa0/0-10 state Active -> Active
```

Finally, the hellos from each of the two routers reflect that NYRtr2 is the active router and NYRtr1 is the standby router. If you wanted NYRtr1 to be the active router for this group, you could reverse the priority values between the routers.

Remember, this function was implemented so that when the active router fails and the standby router takes over, the original router can take back over when it recovers. So, in this case, once NYRtr2 becomes the active router, it becomes the forwarding router. If NYRtr2 were to fail and NYRtr1 took over, what would happen when NYRtr2 comes back online now that preempt is in place? NYRtr2 would take back over when it comes back. Perfect!

Timer Modification

An HSRP-enabled router sends Hello messages to indicate that the router is running and is capable of becoming either the active or the standby router. The hellotime parameter value specifies the interval between the Hello messages that a router sends. The holdtime parameter value indicates the amount of time that the current hello message is considered valid. The standby timer includes an msec parameter to allow for subsecond failovers. The hellotime, holdtime, and msec parameters are all configurable.

Lowering the hello timer results in increased traffic for hello messages and should be used cautiously.

If an active router sends a hello message, receiving routers consider that hello message to be valid for one holdtime. The holdtime value should be at least three times the value of the hellotime. The holdtime value must be greater than the value of the hellotime.

By default, HSRP hellotime is 3 seconds and holdtime is 10 seconds, which means that failover time could be as much as 10 seconds for clients to start communicating with the new default gateway. In some cases, this interval may be excessive for application support. To configure the time between hello messages and the time before other group routers declare the active or standby router to be nonfunctioning, enter this command in interface configuration mode standby *group-number* timers [msec] *hellotime holdtime*.

Interface Tracking

In some situations, the status of an interface directly affects which router needs to become the active router. This is particularly true because each of the routers in an HSRP group has a different path to resources within the campus network. Interface tracking enables the priority of a standby group router to be automatically adjusted, based on availability of the interfaces of that router. When a tracked interface becomes unavailable, the HSRP priority of the router is decreased. When properly configured, the HSRP tracking feature ensures that a router with an unavailable key interface will relinquish the active router role.

 Real World Scenario

Keep Those Paychecks Coming!

Just as I described for you earlier it is vitally important that the connection from the New York office to the Dallas office be up and available. To ensure that a failure of the WAN link does not bring down the connection, you will explore the configuration for tracking the WAN interfaces on the HSRP routers.

Routers NYRtr1 and NYRtr2 reside on the edge of the MPLS lines that connect New York back to the central accounting offices in the FutureTech Dallas headquarters. Each of these routers supports a Fast Ethernet link to the distribution devices in Dallas on the routers Fa0/1 interfaces. NYRtr2 has the higher priority and is the active forwarding router for standby group 10. NYRtr1 is the standby router for that group. NYRtr1 and NYRtr2 exchange hello messages through their Fa0/0 interfaces. Figure 10.10 shows the setup.

Let's look at what happens when the Fast Ethernet link between the active router (NYRtr2) in the standby group and the other building experiences a failure (the Fa0/1 line going to the Dallas distribution block). Before HSRP was enabled, NYRtr2 would have detected the failed link and sent an Internet Control Message Protocol (ICMP) redirect to NYRtr1. However, when HSRP was enabled, ICMP redirects were disabled. Therefore, neither NYRtr2 nor the virtual router sends an ICMP redirect.

To compound the problem, even though the Fa0/1 interface on NYRtr2 is no longer functional, NYRtr2 still sends Hello messages out interface Fa0/0, indicating that NYRtr2 is still the active router. Packets sent to the virtual router for forwarding to the distribution cannot be routed; they are simply dropped. You have been asked to implement interface tracking on the Fa0/0 interface on NYRtr2, track the Fa0/1 interface, and keep communications flowing. You use the command NYRtr2(config-if)#**standby 10 track fa 0/1 25.**

FIGURE 10.10   Interface Tracking Setup

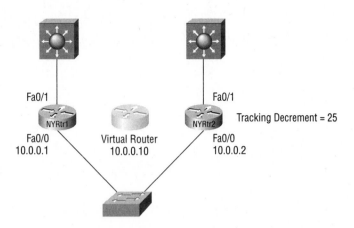

Dallas Headquarters Clients

Fa0/1

Fa0/1

NYRtr1

NYRtr2

Tracking Decrement = 25

Fa0/0
10.0.0.1

Virtual Router
10.0.0.10

Fa0/0
10.0.0.2

New York Headquarters Clients

In this example, the Fa0/0 interface on NYRtr2 tracks the Fa0/1 interface. If the link between the Fa0/1 interface and the Dallas headquarters were to fail, the router automatically decrements the priority on that interface the transmitted Hello messages out interface Fa0/0 will then have a lower priority. NYRtr1 then assumes the active router role when Hello messages are detected with a lower priority.

To disable interface tracking, enter the no standby group track command.

The command to configure HSRP tracking on a multilayer switch is the same as on the external router, except that the interface type can be identified as a switch virtual interface (vlan followed by the *vlan number* assigned to that interface) or by a physical interface.

Multiple tracking statements may be applied to an interface. For example, this may be useful if the currently active HSRP interface will relinquish its status only on the failure of two (or more) tracked interfaces.

Let's enable tracking on your test network and look at what happens when an interface is being tracked and it goes down. Again, I'm using the debug command and have removed most of the time stamps from the commands. In the interest of brevity, I also have removed some of the extra hello messages that pass between the devices. To see the interfaces I am talking about, look at Figure 10.10.

```
NYRTR2(config-if)#standby 10 track fa 0/1 25


*HSRP: Fa0/0 Grp 10 Hello  out 10.0.0.2 Active  pri 120 vIP 10.0.0.10
*HSRP: Fa0/0 Grp 10 Hello  in  10.0.0.1 Standby pri 100 vIP 10.0.0.1025
*HSRP: Fa0/0 Grp 10 Track "FastEthernet0/1" create interface object
*Sep 13 13:59:34.698: HSRP: Fa0/0 Grp 10 Track 1 add, decrement 25
*Sep 13 13:59:34.698: HSRP: Fa0/0 Grp 10 Track 1 Start tracking
*Sep 13 13:59:34.698: HSRP: Fa0/0 Grp 10 Track 1 link id 1
*HSRP: Fa0/0 Grp 10 Hello  in  10.0.0.1 Standby pri 100 vIP 10.0.0.10
*HSRP: Fa0/0 Grp 10 Hello  out 10.0.0.2 Active  pri 120 vIP 10.0.0.10
```

You can see that after I place the tracking command on the interface that it was included in the HSRP process. Notice NYRtr2 is still the active router with a priority of 120. Now, shut down the Fa0/1 interface that is being tracked on the test network. Use the commands:

```
NYRTR2(config-if)#int fa0/1
NYRTR2(config-if)#shut
```

Look at Figure 10.11; you can see what the network will look like with the interface having failed (in this case just shutdown).

Now, take a look at the debug output code to see what happened.

```
*HSRP: Fa0/0 Grp 10 Hello  out 10.0.0.2 Active  pri 120 vIP 10.0.0.10
*HSRP: Fa0/0 Grp 10 Hello  in  10.0.0.1 Standby pri 100 vIP 10.0.0.10
*HSRP: Fa0/0 Grp 10 Track 1 object changed, state Up -> Down
```

```
*HSRP: Fa0/0 Grp 10 Priority 120 -> 95
*HSRP: Fa0/0 Grp 10 Hello  in  10.0.0.1 Standby pri 100 vIP 10.0.0.10
*Sep 13 13:59:52.130: %LINK-5-CHANGED: Interface FastEthernet0/1, changed state
to administratively down
*HSRP: Fa0/0 Grp 10 Hello  out 10.0.0.2 Active  pri 95 vIP 10.0.0.10
*Oct 13 13:59:53.130: %LINEPROTO-5-UPDOWN: Line protocol on Interface
FastEthernet0/1, changed state to down
*HSRP: Fa0/0 Grp 10 Hello  in  10.0.0.1 Standby pri 100 vIP 10.0.0.10
*HSRP: Fa0/0 Grp 10 Hello  out 10.0.0.2 Active  pri 95 vIP 10.0.0.10
```

FIGURE 10.11   Interface Failure

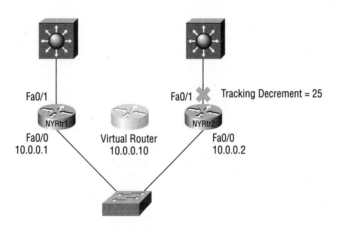

Dallas Headquarters Clients

New York Headquarters Clients

You can see at this point that the interface has gone down, and the priority for NYRtr2 has been decremented to 95 with the loss. The Hellos continue to be transmitted and no change in state has occurred.

```
*HSRP: Fa0/0 Grp 10 Hello  in  10.0.0.1 Standby pri 100 vIP 10.0.0.10
*HSRP: Fa0/0 Grp 10 Hello  out 10.0.0.2 Active  pri 95 vIP 10.0.0.10
*HSRP: Fa0/0 Grp 10 Hello  out 10.0.0.2 Active  pri 95 vIP 10.0.0.10
*HSRP: Fa0/0 Grp 10 Hello  in  10.0.0.1 Standby pri 100 vIP 10.0.0.10
*HSRP: Fa0/0 Grp 10 Hello  out 10.0.0.2 Active  pri 95 vIP 10.0.0.10
*HSRP: Fa0/0 Grp 10 Hello  in  10.0.0.1 Standby pri 100 vIP 10.0.0.10
*Sep 13 14:00:16.154: HSRP: Fa0/0 REDIRECT adv in, Passive, active 0, passive 1,
from 10.0.0.1
*HSRP: Fa0/0 Grp 10 Hello  out 10.0.0.2 Active  pri 95 vIP 10.0.0.10
```

```
*HSRP: Fa0/0 Grp 10 Hello  in  10.0.0.1 Standby pri 100 vIP 10.0.0.10
*HSRP: Fa0/0 Grp 10 Ignoring Coup (100/10.0.0.1 < 120/10.0.0.2)
```

At this point still nothing has occurred. There has been no state change and NYRtr1 has not taken over. Why is that?

If you said, "Because NYRtr1 is not configured to take over and needs to have the preempt command configured on it," then you are correct! Use the following commands to enable preempt on NYRtr1 and watch the debug output to see what happens now.

```
NYRTR1(config)#int fa0/0
NYRTR1(config-if)#standby 10 preempt
```

```
*HSRP: Fa0/0 API arp proto filter, 0000.0c07.ac0a is active vMAC for grp 10 -
filter
*HSRP: Fa0/0 REDIRECT adv in, Active, active 1, passive 1, from 10.0.0.1
*HSRP: Fa0/0 Grp 10 Hello  in  10.0.0.1 Active  pri 100 vIP 10.0.0.10
*HSRP: Fa0/0 Grp 10 Active router is 10.0.0.1, was local
*HSRP: Fa0/0 Grp 10 Standby router is unknown, was 10.0.0.1
*HSRP: Fa0/0 Grp 10 Active: g/Hello rcvd from higher pri Active router
(100/10.0.0.1)
*HSRP: Fa0/0 Grp 10 Active -> Speak
*HSRP-5-STATECHANGE: FastEthernet0/0 Grp 10 state Active -> Speak
```

Now you can see that the MAC address has been added to the ARP cache and there has been a preempt message. NYRtr1 has sent a preempt Hello with a higher priority than that of NYRtr2 and forced an election. NYRtr2 has changed states from active to speak. NYRtr2 must go through the election and make sure that there isn't another router that is better suited for the standby role.

```
*HSRP: Fa0/0 Redirect adv out, Passive, active 0 passive 1
*HSRP: Fa0/0 Grp 10 Redundancy "hsrp-Fa0/0-10" state Active -> Speak
*HSRP: Fa0/0 Grp 10 Resign out 10.0.0.2 Speak   pri 95 vIP 10.0.0.10
*HSRP: Fa0/0 API MAC address update
*HSRP: Fa0/0 Grp 10 Hello  out 10.0.0.2 Speak   pri 95 vIP 10.0.0.10
*HSRP: Fa0/0 Grp 10 Coup   in  10.0.0.1 Active  pri 100 vIP 10.0.0.10
*HSRP: Fa0/0 Grp 10 Hello  in  10.0.0.1 Active  pri 100 vIP 10.0.0.10
*HSRP: Fa0/0 Grp 10 Hello  out 10.0.0.2 Speak   pri 95 vIP 10.0.0.10
*HSRP: Fa0/0 Grp 10 Speak: d/Standby timer expired (unknown)
*HSRP: Fa0/0 Grp 10 Standby router is local
*HSRP: Fa0/0 Grp 10 Speak -> Standby
*HSRP-5-STATECHANGE: FastEthernet0/0 Grp 10 state Speak -> Standby
*HSRP: Fa0/0 Grp 10 Redundancy "hsrp-Fa0/0-10" state Speak -> Standby
```

Now NYRtr2 has gone through the election process and is in standby state again; because there were no other routers to take that spot. Notice there are still Hellos being sent that indicate the new priority values.

```
*HSRP: Fa0/0 Grp 10 Hello  out 10.0.0.2 Standby pri 95 vIP 10.0.0.10
*HSRP: Fa0/0 Grp 10 Hello  in  10.0.0.1 Active  pri 100 vIP 10.0.0.10
*HSRP: Fa0/0 Grp 10 Hello  out 10.0.0.2 Standby pri 95 vIP 10.0.0.10
*HSRP: Fa0/0 Grp 10 Hello  in  10.0.0.1 Active  pri 100 vIP 10.0.0.10
*HSRP: Fa0/0 Grp 10 Hello  out 10.0.0.2 Standby pri 95 vIP 10.0.0.10
```

If I go back and reenable the interface on NYRtr2, what do you think will happen? Take a look and let's see.

```
NYRTR2(config-if)# int fa 0/1
NYRTR2(config-if)#no shut
```

```
*HSRP: Fa0/0 Grp 10 Hello  in  10.0.0.1 Active  pri 100 vIP 10.0.0.10
*HSRP: Fa0/0 Grp 10 Hello  out 10.0.0.2 Standby pri 95 vIP 10.0.0.10
*HSRP: Fa0/0 Grp 10 Hello  in  10.0.0.1 Active  pri 100 vIP 10.0.0.10
*HSRP: Fa0/0 Redirect adv out, Passive, active 0 passive 1
*HSRP: Fa0/0 Grp 10 Hello  out 10.0.0.2 Standby pri 95 vIP 10.0.0.10
*HSRP: Fa0/0 Grp 10 Hello  in  10.0.0.1 Active  pri 100 vIP 10.0.0.10
*HSRP: Fa0/0 Grp 10 Hello  out 10.0.0.2 Standby pri 95 vIP 10.0.0.10
*HSRP: Fa0/0 Grp 10 Hello  in  10.0.0.1 Active  pri 100 vIP 10.0.0.10
*HSRP: Fa0/0 Grp 10 Hello  out 10.0.0.2 Standby pri 95 vIP 10.0.0.10
*Sep 13 14:01:04.546: %LINK-3-UPDOWN: Interface FastEthernet0/1, changed state
to up
*HSRP: Fa0/0 Grp 10 Track 1 object changed, state Down -> Up
*Sep 13 14:01:04.546: HSRP: Fa0/0 Grp 10 Priority 95 -> 120
```

You can see the interface came back up and the priority for NYRtr2 has been set back to its normal 120.

```
*HSRP: Fa0/0 Grp 10 Hello  in  10.0.0.1 Active  pri 100 vIP 10.0.0.10
*HSRP: Fa0/0 Grp 10 Standby: h/Hello rcvd from lower pri Active router
(100/10.0.0.1)
*HSRP: Fa0/0 Grp 10 Active router is local, was 10.0.0.1
*HSRP: Fa0/0 Grp 10 Standby router is unknown, was local
*HSRP: Fa0/0 Redirect adv out, Active, active 1 passive 2
*HSRP: Fa0/0 Grp 10 Coup   out 10.0.0.2 Standby pri 120 vIP 10.0.0.10
*HSRP: Fa0/0 Grp 10 Standby -> Active
*HSRP-5-STATECHANGE: FastEthernet0/0 Grp 10 state Standby -> Active
```

Now that the priority for NYRtr2 has been returned to its configured value of 120, it has taken back over the active role in the group. Notice right now the standby router is unknown.

```
*HSRP: Fa0/0 Redirect adv out, Active, active 1 passive 1
*HSRP: Fa0/0 Grp 10 Redundancy "hsrp-Fa0/0-10" state Standby -> Active
*HSRP: Fa0/0 Grp 10 Hello  out 10.0.0.2 Active  pri 120 vIP 10.0.0.10
*HSRP: Fa0/0 REDIRECT adv in, Passive, active 0, passive 1, from 10.0.0.1
*HSRP: Fa0/0 Grp 10 Hello  in  10.0.0.1 Speak   pri 100 vIP 10.0.0.10
*Sep 13 14:01:05.546: %LINEPROTO-5-UPDOWN: Line protocol on Interface
FastEthernet0/1, changed state to up
*HSRP: Fa0/0 Grp 10 Hello  out 10.0.0.2 Active  pri 120 vIP 10.0.0.10
*HSRP: Fa0/0 Grp 10 Hello  in  10.0.0.1 Speak   pri 100 vIP 10.0.0.10
*HSRP: Fa0/0 Grp 10 Redundancy group hsrp-Fa0/0-10 state Active -> Active
```

Finally, NYRtr2 is back to being the active router. You can see that NYRtr1 is in the speak state making sure that it isn't being beat by another router. NYRtr1 will be again elected as the standby router, and everything will stay that way until there is another failure.

Virtual Router Redundancy Protocol

Like HSRP, virtual router redundancy protocol (VRRP) allows a group of routers to form a single virtual router. In an HSRP or VRRP group, one router is elected to handle all requests sent to the virtual IP address. With HSRP, this is the active router. An HSRP group has one active router, at least one standby router, and perhaps many listening routers. A VRRP group has one master router and one or more backup routers. It is the open standard implementation of HSRP.

VRRP and HSRP Comparison

The LAN workstations are then configured with the address of the virtual router as their default gateway. VRRP differs from HSRP in these ways:

- VRRP is an IEEE standard (RFC 2338) for router redundancy; HSRP is a Cisco-proprietary protocol.
- The virtual router, representing a group of routers, is known as a VRRP group.
- The active router is referred to as the master virtual router.
- The master virtual router may have the same IP address as the virtual router group.
- Multiple routers can function as backup routers.
- VRRP is supported on Ethernet, Fast Ethernet, and Gigabit Ethernet interfaces, as well as on Multi-protocol Label Switching (MPLS) virtual private networks (VPNs) and VLANs.

Real World Scenario

Keeping Traffic Flowing

The oldest of the remote offices, the Portland office has a mixed bag of vendors for its network hardware, so HSRP cannot be used to keep traffic flowing. Thank goodness, VRRP is available to keep communications open between the accounting offices in the Portland offices and those in the Dallas headquarters. Just as important as the New York office, which sends the paychecks, Portland has an accounting office. The Portland office is responsible for bringing the money in from distributors and clients of the company. I am sure that you can guess, FutureTech wants the money to come in faster than it wants it to go out. So, the connections here are just as important.

The Portland office has three routers, PortRtr1, PortRtr2 and PortRtr3, which are members of the VRRP group that keeps traffic (and money) flowing. The IP address of the virtual router is the same as that of the LAN interface of PortRtr1 (10.0.0.1). PortRtr1 is responsible for forwarding packets sent to this IP address. Figure 10.12 shows the setup.

FIGURE 10.12   VRRP Group Setup

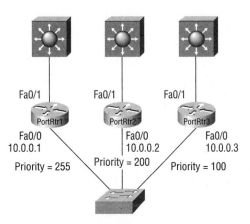

The clients are given a gateway address of 10.0.0.1. PortRrt2 and R3 are backup routers. If the master router fails, the backup router with the highest priority becomes the master router. When PortRtr1 recovers, it resumes the role of master router automatically; there is no need for additional preempt configuration.

VRRP Redundancy Characteristics

VRRP has some unique characteristics.

- VRRP provides redundancy for the real IP address of a router or for a virtual IP address shared among the VRRP group members.

- If a real IP address is used, the router with that address becomes the master.

- If a virtual IP address is used, the master is the router with the highest priority.

- A VRRP group has one master router and one or more backup routers.

- The master router uses VRRP messages to inform group members that it is the master.

- VRRP allows load sharing across more than one virtual router.

 Real World Scenario

Facilitating Faster Data Transfer

The marketing collateral files are prepared in the Portland office; print contracts and file transfers to individual print houses are let from the Dallas purchasing office. The files are huge; the traffic is heavy, particularly during quarterly campaign releases. Using VRRP, file transfer is reliable, but to facilitate faster transfers, you have been asked to set up dual virtual routers in a load-balancing VRRP solution. Figure 10.13 shows you the LAN topology specified by the network administrator. VRRP is configured so that PortRtr1 and PortRtr2 share the load of being the default gateway for the Portland clients. PortRtr1 and PortRtr2 act as backup virtual routers to one another should either one fail.

FIGURE 10.13   VRRP Load-Balancing Setup

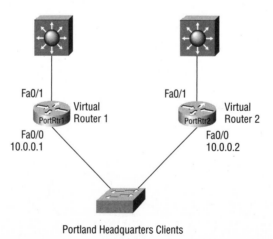

To accommodate the traffic, two virtual router groups are configured. For virtual router 1, PortRtr1 is the owner of IP address 10.0.0.1 and is therefore the master virtual router for clients configured with that default gateway address. PortRtr2 is the backup virtual router to PortRtr1.

For virtual router 2, PortRtr2 is the owner of IP address 10.0.0.2 and is the master virtual router for clients configured with the default gateway IP address 10.0.0.2. PortRtr1 is the backup virtual router to PortRtr2.

Given that the IP address of the VRRP group is that of a physical interface on one of the group members, the router owning that address will be the master in the group. Its priority is set to 255. Backup router priority values can range from 1 to 254; the default value is 100. The priority value zero has special meaning, indicating that the current master has stopped participating in VRRP. This setting is used to trigger backup routers to quickly transition to the master without having to wait for the current master to time out.

With VRRP, only the master sends advertisements. (Basically, the advertisements perform a function similar to an HSRP Hello.) The master sends the advertisement on multicast 224.0.0.18 protocol number 112 at a default interval of 1 second.

VRRP Timers

The dynamic failover, when the active (master) becomes unavailable, uses three timers within VRRP:

- Advertisement interval
- Master down interval
- Skew time

Advertisement Interval　　The advertisement interval is the time interval between advertisements (in seconds). The default interval is 1 second.

Master Down Interval　　The master down interval is the time interval for backup to declare the master down (in seconds). The default equals:

　　3 × advertisement interval + skew time

Skew time　　The skew time is measured in milliseconds. It is used to ensure that the backup router with the highest priority becomes the new master. Skew time is calculated using the following equation.

　　256 − priority / 256

VRRP Transition

I want to describe specifically the steps involved in transferring the master role to another VRRP router during a failover from the master router. Figure 10.12 shows the setup.

1. PortRtr1, currently the master, sends advertisements by default every 1 second. PortRtr1 is the only device sending advertisements.

2. PortRtr1 fails. Advertisements stop.

3. PortRtr2 and R3 stop receiving advertisements and wait for their respective master down interval to expire before transitioning to the master state. By default, the master down interval is 3 seconds plus the skew time.

4. Because the skew time is inversely proportional to priority, the master down interval of PortRtr2 is less than that of R3.

   The skew time for PortRtr2 equals (256 – 200) / 256, which is approximately equal to 0.2 seconds, so PortRtr2 has a master down interval of approximately 3.2 seconds.

   The skew time for R3 equals (256 – 100) / 256, which is approximately equal to 0.6 seconds, so R3 has a master down interval of approximately 3.6 seconds.

5. PortRtr2 transitions to the master state after 3.2 seconds and starts sending advertisements.

6. R3 receives the advertisement from the new master, so it resets its master down interval and remains in the backup state.

When a VRRP master is shut down properly, it sends an advertisement with a priority of 0. This priority setting then triggers the backup router to take over more quickly by waiting only the skew time instead of the full master down interval. Therefore, in the previous example, Router PortRtr2 would have waited only 0.2 seconds to transition to the master state.

Configuring VRRP

Table 10.3 lists the VRRP commands most often used when configuring VRRP and provides a description of each.

TABLE 10.3   VRRP Commands

Command	Description
vrrp *group-number* ip *virtual-gateway-addr*	Adds the interface as a member of the virtual group identified with the IP virtual address.

TABLE 10.3 VRRP Commands *(continued)*

Command	Description
vrrp *group-number* priority *priority_value*	Sets the priority of this router. Highest value will win election as active router. Default is 100. If routers have the same VRRP priority, the gateway with the highest real IP address is elected to the master virtual router role.
vrrp *group-number* timers advertise *timer-value*	Master router configures this parameter to advertise value to the other group members. Others configure timers learned to accept.
vrrp *group-number* timers learn	Configures nonmaster members to learn timer values from master.

Gateway Load Balancing Protocol

Although HSRP and VRRP provide gateway resiliency, the upstream bandwidth of the standby members of the redundancy group is not used while the devices are in standby mode. Only the active routers in HSRP and VRRP groups forward traffic for the virtual MAC. Resources associated with the standby router are not fully utilized. Some load balancing can be accomplished with these protocols through the creation of multiple groups and through the assignment of multiple default gateways, but these configurations create an administrative burden.

Cisco designed a proprietary load-balancing protocol, Gateway Load Balancing Protocol (GLBP), to allow automatic selection and simultaneous use of multiple available gateways in addition to automatic failover between those gateways. Multiple routers share the load of frames that, from a client perspective, are sent to a single default gateway address. With GLBP, resources can be fully utilized without the administrative burden of configuring multiple groups and managing multiple default gateway configurations, as is required with HSRP and VRRP.

GLBP Functions

GLBP essentially provides clients with:

- An active virtual gateway (AVG)
- An active virtual forwarder (AVF)

It also allows members of the group to communicate with each other through Hello messages sent every 3 seconds to the multicast address 224.0.0.102, User Datagram Protocol (UDP) port 3222.

GLBP AVG   Members of a GLBP group elect one gateway to be the AVG for that group. Other group members provide backup for the AVG in the event that the AVG becomes unavailable. The AVG assigns a virtual MAC address to each member of the GLBP group.

GLBP AVF   Each gateway assumes responsibility for forwarding packets that are sent to the virtual MAC address assigned to that gateway by the AVG. These gateways are known as AVFs for their virtual MAC address.

GLBP Features

GLBP provides upstream load sharing by utilizing the redundant uplinks simultaneously. It uses link capacity efficiently, thus providing peak-load traffic coverage. By making use of multiple available paths upstream from the routers or Layer 3 switches running GLBP, output queues may also be reduced. GLBP supports:

- Load sharing
- Multiple virtual routers
- Preemption
- Efficient resource utilization

Load Sharing   You can configure GLBP in such a way that traffic from LAN clients can be shared by multiple routers, thereby sharing the traffic load more equitably among available routers.

Multiple Virtual Routers   GLBP supports up to 1,024 virtual routers (GLBP groups) on each physical interface of a router and up to four virtual forwarders per group.

Preemption   The redundancy scheme of GLBP enables you to preempt an AVG with a higher priority backup virtual gateway that has become available. Forwarder preemption works in a similar way, except that forwarder preemption uses weighting instead of priority and is enabled by default.

Efficient Resource Utilization   GLBP makes it possible for any router in a group to serve as a backup, which eliminates the need for a dedicated backup router because all available routers can support network traffic.

You'll remember that only a single path is used with HSRP or VRRP, while other resources are idle, unless multiple groups and gateways are configured. That single path may encounter higher output queue rates during peak times, which leads to lower performance from higher jitter rates. The impact of jitter is lessened and over performance is increased with GLBP because more upstream bandwidth is available and additional upstream paths are used.

GLBP allows automatic selection and simultaneous use of all available gateways in the group. The members of a GLBP group elect one gateway to be the AVG for that group. Other members of the group provide backup for the AVG if it becomes unavailable. The

AVG assigns a virtual MAC address to each member of the GLBP group. All routers become AVFs for frames addressed to that virtual MAC address. As clients send address resolution protocol (ARP) requests for the address of the default gateway, the AVG sends these virtual MAC addresses in the ARP replies. A GLBP group can have up to four group members.

GLBP supports several operational modes for load balancing traffic across multiple default routers servicing the same default gateway IP address, including the following:

- Weighted load-balancing algorithm
- Host-dependent load-balancing algorithm
- Round-robin load-balancing algorithm

Weighted Load-Balancing Algorithm   The amount of load directed to a router is dependent upon the weighting value advertised by that router.

Host-Dependent Load-Balancing Algorithm   A host is guaranteed to use the same virtual MAC address as long as that virtual MAC address is participating in the GLBP group.

Round-Robin Load-Balancing Algorithm   As clients send ARP requests to resolve the MAC address of the default gateway, the reply to each client contains the MAC address of the next available router in round-robin fashion. All routers' MAC addresses take turns being included in address resolution replies for the default gateway IP address.

GLBP automatically manages the virtual MAC address assignment, determines who handles the forwarding, and ensures that each station has a forwarding path in the event of failures to gateways or tracked interfaces. If failures occur, the load-balancing ratio is adjusted among the remaining AVFs so that resources are used in the most efficient way.

GLBP Per-Host Traffic Balancing

The following steps describe how GLBP balances traffic using the round-robin algorithm.

1. When a client sends an ARP message for the gateway IP address, the AVG returns the virtual MAC address of one of the AVFs.

2. When a second client sends an ARP message, the AVG returns the next virtual MAC address from the list.

Having each resolved a different MAC address for the default gateway, each client will send their routed traffic to separate routers, although they both have the same default gateway address configured. Each GLBP router is an AVF for the virtual MAC address to which it has been assigned.

Real World Scenario

Plan to Change Over the Portland Office

When last you updated the Portland office network, you created two VRRP groups so that there could be some load balancing. Unfortunately, HSRP and VRRP don't truly load balance; you either have to send different subnets to different routers or break up the hosts into different groups with different default gateways.

If you configure GLBP in the Portland office, you will get real load balancing done by the routers in a single group and the hosts can all have the same default gateway. The only catch is that all the routers running GLBP must be Cisco routers because it is proprietary.

FIGURE 10.14   GLBP Operation

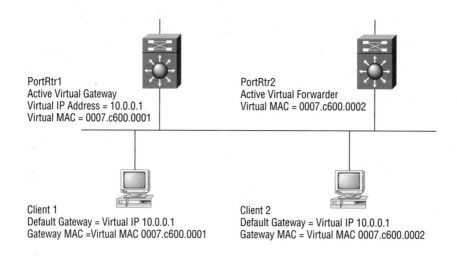

MPLS WANs to Dallas

PortRtr1
Active Virtual Gateway
Virtual IP Address = 10.0.0.1
Virtual MAC = 0007.c600.0001

PortRtr2
Active Virtual Forwarder
Virtual MAC = 0007.c600.0002

Client 1
Default Gateway = Virtual IP 10.0.0.1
Gateway MAC =Virtual MAC 0007.c600.0001

Client 2
Default Gateway = Virtual IP 10.0.0.1
Gateway MAC = Virtual MAC 0007.c600.0002

Portland Client Network

Like HSRP, GLBP can be configured to track interfaces. Take a look at Figure 10.14. If the WAN link from router PortRtr1 is lost, GLBP detects the failure because interface tracking is configured on PortRtr1. The job of forwarding packets for virtual MAC address 0007.c600.0001 will be taken over by the secondary virtual forwarder for the MAC, router PortRtr2. Therefore, the client sees no disruption of service nor does the client need to resolve a new MAC address for the default gateway.

Configuring GLBP

Table 10.2 lists the GLBP commands most commonly used to configure a GLBP group and provides a description of each.

TABLE 10.2   GLBP Commands

Command	Description
glbp *group-number* ip *virtual-gateway-addr*	Adds the interface as a member of the virtual group identified with the IP virtual address.
glbp *group-number* priority *priority_value*	Sets the priority of this router. Highest value wins election as active router. Default is 100. If routers have the same GLBP priority, the gateway with the highest real IP address will become the AVG.
glbp *group-number* timers *hello-value holdtime-value*	Adjusts the hello timer and hold timer in seconds. Place the argument *msec* before the values to enter subsecond values.

Summary

Now you can implement and configure three different redundancy protocols. HSRP and VRRP, you learned, are very close to being the same. VRRP is the open standard can be used on any vendor's equipment. HSRP is proprietary and has a couple of features and configurations not available in VRRP; remember the preempt and interface tracking features.

GLBP is also a Cisco-proprietary protocol. It can provide true load balancing for all of your clients, even if they are in the same subnet.

Review Questions

1. What protocol allows a router to answer for a host when it ARPs for a host that is not on the local subnet?

    A. HSRP

    B. VRRP

    C. Proxy ARP

    D. Server ARP

2. How many routers can participate in a HSRP group and be assigned a role?

    A. 1

    B. 2

    C. 3

    D. 4

3. What is the default priority setting on an HSRP router?

    A. 25

    B. 50

    C. 100

    D. 125

4. When the active router stops sending Hellos to the standby router, the standby router will take over.

    A. True

    B. False

5. What command must be configured on a router to enable it take the active role back after it has failed and the role shifted to the standby router?

    A. tracking

    B. preempt

    C. timers

    D. active

6. Is it possible for a VRRP router to use its real IP for the virtual router's IP?

    A. Yes

    B. No

    C. Only in the Cisco version

    D. Only on the weekend

7. You can configure the preempt feature on a VRRP router.

    A. True

    B. False

8. In a GLBP network, how many routers can be configured into one group?

    A. 2

    B. 3

    C. 4

    D. 8

9. You have to configure the host machines with different default gateways in order to use GLBP.

    A. True

    B. False

10. You can configure interface tracking on a GLBP router interface.

    A. True

    B. False

Answers to Review Questions

1. C. The feature is Proxy ARP.

2. B. Two routers in an HSRP group can actively have a role.

3. C. The default priority for an HSRP router is 100.

4. A. True. The standby router's job is to take over when there is a failure.

5. B. The `preempt` command must be configured before a router can automatically take back the active router role.

6. A. Yes. In VRRP, the real IP address of a router can be used.

7. B. False. On a VRRP router, the preempt command does not have to be configured. When the router that failed comes back online it will take back over.

8. C. Four routers can be placed into a GLBP group

9. B. False. The benefit of GLBP is that is does load balancing and doesn't require different host configurations

10. A. True. GLBP can use the interface tracking function.

Chapter 11

WAN and Teleworker Connections

IN THIS CHAPTER, YOU WILL LEARN HOW TO DO THE FOLLOWING:

- ✓ Describe cable (HFC) technologies

- ✓ Describe xDSL technologies

- ✓ Configure ADSL (PPPoE or PPPoA)

- ✓ Verify basic teleworker configurations

- ✓ Describe the components and operation of Frame-Mode MPLS

- ✓ Configure and verify Frame-Mode MPLS

In this chapter, I cover the most common types of connections for users and companies to connect their homes and offices. You will see how the small office/home office (SOHO) is becoming a natural extension to the corporate office. Because of this extension, your network must also extend and provide all of the normal network service and reliability. For the SOHO connections, I specifically cover DSL and broadband cable technologies. For corporate WAN connections, I cover basic frame mode MPLS.

For up to the minute updates on this chapter, check out www.sybex.com/go/CiscoProGuidetoInternetworking or www.lammle.com

Introduction to the Campus Edge

Now that you have learned much of the technology and many of the functions of the Enterprise Campus module, it is time to look at the edge of the network. You learned about the protocols and functions necessary to build switch blocks and connect them with redundant and deterministic paths. You worked your way up the TCP/IP stack, filling in the pieces that build the Enterprise Campus module. You learned about the switching technologies that connect all of the end devices to the network, and the routing protocols that connect all of the subnets. You even entered the campus edge when you learned how to get Internet connectivity into the enterprise using BGP.

To really work in the enterprise edge, you'll need to understand a couple more subcomponents:

- Enterprise branch
- WAN
- Teleworker

The subcomponents are covered in no particular order. Add these to the Internet connection piece that you learned about in the Chapter 7, "Exterior Routing Protocols" (the BGP chapter), and you'll be ready to go.

Enterprise Branch

The Enterprise Branch is built much like the Enterprise Campus. It contains switch blocks and the functions that make them resilient and redundant. Just as with the infrastructure built into the campus, the branch will be constructed to support businesses applications and services, including mission-critical data, voice, and video applications. Through the branch, these applications and services can be extended from the campus to any number of remote locations.

In the coming sections of this chapter, I am going to show you some of the ways branch locations, as well as smaller locations and even individuals, can be connected to the campus. The enterprise teleworker connection can be used for small office/home office (SOHO) connections. The two technologies I will discuss in depth are digital subscriber line (DSL) and broadband cable connections.

Digital Subscriber Line   DSL connections fall into a category typically known as high-speed commercial connections. DSL is popular because it is provided by most phone companies and is available in a large and every growing area. DSL is also convenient because it is carried over standard telephone lines which most everyone has running into their house anyway.

Broadband Cable   Broadband cable also falls into the high-speed commercial connection category. Broadband cable became very popular because it often offers higher bandwidths than other connections in its category including DSL. Cable got a bad name for a while when DSL providers tried to tell everyone that a DSL connection isn't shared and cable is shared. While this is true—cable is shared—DSL isn't the perfect point-to-point non-shared connection it was marketed to be. I will explain more as you go along through the chapter.

The Enterprise WAN can connect any size office and provide a full assortment of services over a single IP network. Remote connection options for the Enterprise WAN include:

- Private WAN Layer 2 technologies
- Service provider MPLS-based IP virtual private networks (VPNs)
- Site-to-site and remote-access with IPSec VPNs

Private WAN Layer 2 Technologies   Traditional private WAN Layer 2 technologies, such as frame relay, Asynchronous Transfer Mode (ATM), and leased lines, provide connections where the security of the connection depends on the service provider. Strong encryption with IPSec VPNs should be used to strengthen security.

Service Provider MPLS-Based IP VPNs   Service provider Multi-Protocol Label Switching (MPLS)-based IP VPNs offer flexible, scalable, any-to-any connectivity. The security level of the connections without additional IPSec deployment is almost the same as with traditional private WAN Layer 2 technologies.

Site-to-Site and Remote-Access with IPSec VPNs   Site-to-site and remote-access with IPSec VPNs over the public Internet offer connection security at a low cost.

At the end of the chapter, I introduce you to the functions of Frame Mode MPLS connections, but you'll have to wait for Chapter 12, "Virtual Private Networks," for a full exploration of IPSec and encapsulation methods.

Enterprise Teleworker

The enterprise teleworker solution aims to provide an always-on, secure, centrally managed connection. This is typically provided to create a link from a user's home back to the corporate network. Business and corporate IT departments want to achieve specific goals and meet specific requirements with these connections. Those often include:

- Continuity of operations despite inclement weather, commuter issues, manmade and natural disasters, and so forth

- Increased responsiveness across geographical, functional, business, and decision-making boundaries

- Secure, reliable, manageable employee access to critical network assets and confidential information

- Cost-effective access to data, voice, video, and realtime applications

- Increased employee productivity, satisfaction, and retention

Teleworkers, just like traditional on-site workers, require a diverse set of applications such as email, web-based applications, mission-critical applications, realtime collaboration, voice, video, and video conferencing. Some of these applications require high-bandwidth and for sure the combination of them will. With that in mind, the first factor to consider in a remote connectivity solution is the remote worker's access network technology and bandwidth available with that connection. Two options for providing the bandwidth needed include residential broadband cable and DSL. The dial-up modem connection of the past is not sufficient for teleworkers because of its low bandwidth.

The second consideration is to maintain the infrastructure services and security options of the corporate network, such as:

- IPSec VPN

- Security

- Authentication

- QoS

- Management

IPSec VPN   IPSec VPN establishes a secure tunnel over the existing broadband connection between the teleworker remote sites and the central site. Site-to-site VPNs are used to achieve an always-on, transparent VPN connection. Remote access VPNs are used to provide an on-demand, secured connection.

Security   Maintaining security safeguards the corporate network and prevents unguarded backdoors. You will want to consider security measures that deploy firewall, intrusion prevention, and URL filtering services. Depending on the enterprise corporate secure policy, split tunneling may be used to share the broadband connection between secured corporate access and unsecured Internet access at the same time.

Authentication   Authentication defines access to resources by deploying the identity-based network services using authentication, authorization, and accounting (AAA) servers, 802.1x port-based access control, Cisco Security, and Trust Agents.

QoS   QoS addresses application availability and behavior. QoS mechanisms prioritize the traffic, optimize the use of WAN bandwidth, address the difference in uplink and downlink speeds of the broadband connection, and achieve adequate performance for applications sensitive to delay and jitter.

Management   Management addresses the complex balance between support and loss of corporate control. In highly managed systems, corporate IT centrally manages and supports the teleworker connection, provides equipment for use by the teleworker, then transparently configures and pushes security and other policies to the remote devices. Tools can be used to implement performance and fault management and to monitor service-level agreements (SLAs).

Early teleworker solutions had limitations. The level of access was inferior to access at the corporate office. Early solutions could not deploy and support advanced applications, such as voice, video, and video conferencing. QoS was not available for efficient delivery and prioritization of traffic. Security was in the hands of the end user; IT departments had no control. Connection configuration, management, and support could not be centrally controlled. The business-ready teleworker solutions available today overcomes the weak points of the traditional teleworker (dial-up type) solution.

Cable Technologies

Before I get into how cable technologies work, it is important for you to understand some of the basic terminology. As an added bonus, once you understand these terms, you have a basic understanding of where the cable systems came from and how they operate.

Cable Terms

The following terms are commonly used to describe cable technology.

Broadband   Broadband is used to describe a method of data transmission where multiple pieces of data are sent simultaneously to increase the effective rate of transmission. In cable systems, the term *broadband* refers to the ability to frequency-division multiplex (FDM) many signals in a wide radio frequency (RF) bandwidth over a hybrid fiber-coaxial (HFC) network and the capability to handle vast amounts of information.

Community Antenna Television (CATV)   The original meaning of the term *CATV* changed over the years; today the term simply refers to cable TV.

Coaxial Cable   The primary medium used to build cable TV systems. Coaxial cable is used to transport RF signals and has certain physical properties that define the attenuation of the signal, including cable diameter, dielectric construction, ambient temperature, and operating frequency.

Tap   A tap divides the input signal RF power to support multiple outputs. Typically, the cable operators deploy taps with 2, 4, or 8 ports or subscriber drop connections.

Amplifier   Amplifiers magnify an input signal and produce a significantly larger output signal.

Hybrid Fiber-Coax (HFC)   A mixed optical-coaxial network where optical fiber replaces some or all of the trunk portion of the cable network.

Downstream   Downstream refers to the direction of the transmission of the RF signal (TV channels, data). Downstream runs from source (headend) to the destination (subscribers). Downstream is also called the forward path.

Upstream   Upstream transmissions of RF signal travel from subscribers to the headend. Upstream is also called a return or reverse path.

Cable Standards

Commonly used standards in cable systems include:

- National Television Standards Committee (NTSC)
- Phase Alternating Line (PAL)
- Sequential Couleur avec Mémoiré (SECAM).

NTSC   NTSC is a North American TV technical standard for analog TV system. The standard was created in 1941 and is named after the National Television System Committee formed in 1940. The standard uses a 6 MHz modulated signal.

PAL   PAL is a color encoding system used in broadcast television systems in most of Europe, Asia, Africa, Australia, Brazil, and Argentina. The PAL version uses 6 MHz, 7 MHz, or 8 MHz modulated signal. The color difference signals an alternate phase at the horizontal line rate.

SECAM   SECAM is an analog color TV system used in France and certain Eastern European countries and uses an 8 MHz modulated signal.

Concept: DTV and HDTV

Digital television (DTV) is an advanced broadcasting technology that allows you to view a greater number of channels and with better picture and sound quality. DTV also offers multiple programming choices, called multicasting and interactive capabilities. DTV is the umbrella term encompassing high-definition television (HDTV) and several other applications, including standard definition television, datacasting, multicasting, and interactivity.

All analog transmission of broadcast television ended in 2009. All TV subscribers must have a digital tuner in their TV or have an analog to digital converter box.

For more information on DTV and HDTV the Federal Communications Commission (FCC) has a great website at www.dtv.gov.

Cable Components

The cable system is composed of these major components:

- Antenna site
- Headend
- Transportation network
- Distribution network
- Subscriber drop

Antenna Site   An antenna site is a location chosen for optimum reception of over-the-air, satellite, and sometimes point-to-point signals. The main receiving antennas and satellite dishes are located at the antenna site.

Headend   Headend is a master facility where signals are received, processed, formatted, and distributed over to the cable network—the transportation and distribution network. The headend facility is usually unmanned, under security fencing, and is somewhat similar to a telephone company central office (CO).

Transportation Network   The transportation network is used to link a remote antenna site to a headend or a remote headend to the distribution network. The transportation network can be microwave, coaxial supertrunk, or fiber optic.

Distribution Network   In a classic tree-and-branch cable system, the distribution network is composed of trunk and feeder cables. The trunk is the backbone that distributes signals throughout the community service area to the feeder. It typically uses 0.750 inch (19 mm) diameter coaxial cable. The feeder branches emanate from a trunk and reach all of the subscribers in the service area via coaxial cables. The feeder cable is usually a 0.500 inch (13 mm) diameter coaxial cable.

In mixed fiber and coaxial cabling (the HFC architecture), optical fiber replaces some or all of the traditional trunks and carries TV signals and other data services. A web of fiber trunk cables connects the headend (or hub) to the nodes where optical-to-RF signal conversion is performed. Feeder cables originate from the node carrying RF signals to the subscribers. The effective service area of a distribution network segment (feeder segment) ranges from 100 to as many as 2,000 subscribers.

Subscriber Drop   A subscriber drop connects the subscriber to the cable services. The subscriber drop is a connection between the feeder part of distribution network and the subscriber terminal device, such as a TV set, VCR, high definition TV (HDTV) set-top box, or cable modem. A subscriber drop is composed of coaxial cabling (usually 59-series or 6-series coaxial cable), grounding and attachment hardware, passive devices, and a terminal device.

DOCSIS

Data Over Cable Service Interface Specification (DOCSIS) is an international standard developed by CableLabs, a nonprofit research and development consortium for cable-related technologies. CableLabs certifies cable equipment vendor devices, such as cable modems (CMs) and cable modem termination system (CMTS), through testing and, if compliant, grants DOCSIS certified or qualified status.

DOCSIS defines the communications and operation support interface requirements for a data over cable system and permits the addition of high-speed data transfer to an existing CATV system. Cable operators employ DOCSIS to provide Internet access over their existing HFC infrastructure.

DOCSIS specifies the Open System Interconnection (OSI) Layers 1 and 2 requirements on both the physical and MAC layer.

Physical Layer   On the physical layer, DOCSIS specifies the channel widths that cable operators can use for data signals. DOCSIS also specifies the modulation techniques that can be used to allow the RF signal to convey digital data.

MAC Layer   At the MAC layer, DOCSIS defines acceptable deterministic access methods— Time Division Multiple Access (TDMA) or Synchronous Code Division Multiple Access (S-CDMA).

Since frequency allocation band plans differ between North American and European cable systems, both DOCSIS and an adapted Euro-DOCSIS exist. The main differences account for differing channel bandwidths. European cable channels conform to PAL-based standards and are 7 MHz and 8 MHz wide, whereas the North American cable channels conform to NTSC standard, which specifies 6 MHz-wide cable channels. The wider channels in Euro-DOCSIS architectures permit more bandwidth to be allocated to the downstream data path.

Using Radio Waves for Data

Electromagnetic spectrum encompasses a broad range of electromagnetic frequencies, as shown in Figure 11.1. Frequency is the rate at which current (or voltage) cycles occur—the number of "waves" per second. Wavelength is the speed of propagation of the electromagnetic signal divided by its frequency in cycles per second. A portion of the electromagnetic spectrum between approximately 5 MHz and 1 GHz is known as radio waves, generally called RF.

FIGURE 11.1   RF Spectrum

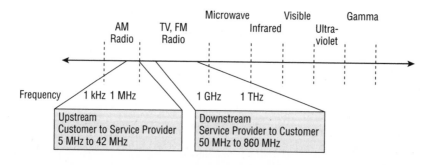

When you tune a radio or television to find a radio station or TV channel, you tune the radio or TV to a particular electromagnetic frequency within the RF spectrum. A broadband transmission sends multiple streams of data essentially at the same time. So, the cable that is connected into your TV carries all of the channels that you could watch coming into it at the same time. When you change the channel on your TV, you are really adjusting the tuner inside the TV; once the tuner is adjusted, it begins processing the data coming over a specific frequency.

This process isn't used just for TV, though. The cable TV industry uses the RF portion of the electromagnetic spectrum. Within the cable, those frequencies are used to carry not just the TV channels but data as well. At the subscriber end (home or work), equipment such as your TV, VCR, or HDTV set-top box tunes to those frequencies so you can view the TV channel and, if the terminating device is a cable modem, to provide high-speed Internet access.

The cable network transmits signals in either direction at the same time. For this to work, different frequencies carry each stream of data.

- Downstream frequencies are in the 50 MHz to 860 MHz range.

- Upstream transmissions, the reverse path from the subscriber to the cable operator, are in the 5 MHz to 42 MHz range.

The downstream frequency range is subdivided into even smaller channels, as defined by the frequency plan (6 MHz for DOCSIS, 7 MHz and 8 MHz for Euro-DOCSIS). Between the upstream and downstream frequency ranges, a guard band provides separation between channels. The guard band is maintained by the cutoff characteristics in the high-pass/low-pass filtering process that restricts transmission frequencies. The filtering process is used to make sure that signals do not spill into the adjacent spectrum.

In the over-the-air TV broadcast environment, two frequency ranges are defined:

- Very High Frequency (VHF) range covers TV channels 2 through 13, 30 MHz to 300 MHz

- Ultra High Frequency (UHF) range covers TV channels 14 through 83, 300 MHZ to 3000 MHz.

The cable industry defines the cable TV spectrum for the downstream path as listed in Table 11.1.

TABLE 11.1   Cable TV Spectrum Downstream Path Plan

Band	Use	Frequency Range (MHz)
Sub CATV	T7–T13	7–58
Low band	VHF TV channels 2–6	54–88
Mid band	UHF TV channels 95–99	91–120
	UHF TV channels 14–22	121–174

TABLE 11.1   Cable TV Spectrum Downstream Path Plan *(continued)*

Band	Use	Frequency Range (MHz)
High band	VHF TV channels 7–13	175–216
Super band	CATV channels 23–36	216–300
Hyper band	CATV channels 37–62	300–456
Ultra band	CATV channels 63–158	457–1002

There is no frequency plan for the upstream path. The cable operator can monitor the upstream frequency band and place the upstream data signals into clean areas where there is no interference from noise or other signals. The area between 5 and 15 MHz is usually noisy and is unusable.

Original Cable Systems

How many of you remember rabbit ears, the antennae that sat on top of the TV years ago? When over-the-air via radio waves was the only method of transmission, antennae were required. Originally, CATV was created to solve the problem of poor over-the-air TV reception. These cable systems used a type of coaxial cable—a center conductor surrounded by insulation and then a grounded shield of braided wire. The shield was designed to minimize electrical and RF interference.

These original CATV systems were composed of a shared antenna (replaced later with a satellite dish) placed in some high location. Multiple subscribers then connected their TVs via coaxial cable. The first CATV networks were one way and included various amplifiers in cascade to compensate for the signal loss over the coaxial cable in series. Taps coupled the video signal from the main trunks to subscriber homes via drop cables. A common problem with these cascaded networks was loss of signal and the amplification of noise. When the signal was amplified so that it would reach the end of the network, any noise in the transmission was also amplified causing more degradation in the signal.

The CATV system provided television via RF signals transmitted within a sealed coaxial cable line to ensure that consumers obtain cable service with the same TV sets they were using to receive over-the-air broadcasts. The system consisted of the headend, the trunk, the neighborhood node, the distribution cables, and the subscriber drop cables. Take a look at Figure 11.2, you can see what the original cable systems looked like from a logical standpoint.

Benefits of Using the Cable System

The cable system architecture was really all about a cost-effective solution for service providers in heavily populated areas who could use a cascading broadcast architecture to reach their subscribers. But improvements and advances over the years enabled service providers to provide many new services. The cable systems can now be upgraded to support telephony, high-speed data, and analog and digital video services. This allows integration of all the services and the collocation of equipment (telephone switches and cable modem termination systems).

FIGURE 11.2   Original Cable System

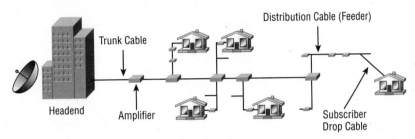

A high-speed cable data connection presents a cost-effective solution for accessing the Internet, not only for teleworkers, but for small and medium-size businesses. High-speed cable Internet access enables:

- VPN connectivity to corporate intranets
- SOHO capabilities for work-at-home employees
- Interactive television
- Public switched telephone network (PSTN)-quality voice and fax calls over the managed IP networks

Fiber Benefits

A simple but important problem to note with all cable systems is signal loss. The signal from the antenna is attenuated when traveling along the cable. In order to boost the signal along the path, service providers must add amplifiers. Amplifiers may have to be inserted in that path as much as every 2,000 feet (600 meters). This ensures that when the RF signal reaches you (or any subscriber), it will be received with enough power and clarity to receive all the channels (50 to 860 MHz) required to support analog TV, digital TV, and digital data cable modem services. Using coaxial cable over a 20-mile service length, a provider could have to add as many as 52 amplifiers. Unfortunately, the amplifier has limitations, as does any repeater device. The biggest issue is the introduction of noise and distortion. In addition, since the original cable implementation is serial, if there is a single amplifier failure, service is disrupted.

When fiber optics were added, the number of cable amplifiers required throughout the cable plant was reduced. As added benefits over regular coaxial cable, the new cables:

- Require less space and are thinner, lighter weight, and easier to handle
- Introduce virtually no noise into the run
- Lose much less signal

- Provide immunity from external influences, such as thunder or RF interference
- Increase the unamplified cable run from 600 m to 5 km to 40 km

Fiber is used for trunk cables and carries downstream traffic from the headend to the neighborhood node at a signal strength above 50 decibel (dB).

HFC Architecture

The HFC architecture is the major upgrade to original cable systems. It defines a network architecture that incorporates using both optical fibers and coaxial cable to create a broadband network. Upgrading a cable plant to HFC architecture gives the provider the ability to deploy a data network over the HFC system and offer high-speed Internet services. The system also allows more subscribers on the network. (They make more money and hopefully you get better service.) The cable network is also segmented into smaller service areas with fewer end users on each segment; thus, after each optical node typically five or fewer amplifiers are cascaded. This means a better connection with less noise and less congestion.

Figure 11.3 is a diagram of a typical HFC architecture.

FIGURE 11.3   HFC Architecture

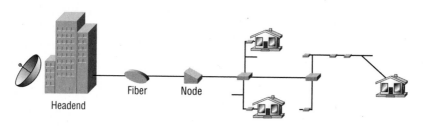

Cable network uses different RF frequencies than over-the-air transmissions. Downstream traffic is carried in the 50 to 860 MHz range. Each downstream data channel is a 6 MHz channel. Upstream traffic is carried in the 5 to 42 MHz range, also in 6 MHz (less for asymmetric cable connections) channels. Both upstream and downstream traffic are carried over the TV channel frequencies.

Data over Cable

Additional equipment is required to put data on the cable system. To put upstream and downstream data on the network, digital modem signals must be sent and received. This is accomplished using:

- A cable modem (CM) on the subscriber end
- A cable modem termination system (CMTS) at the cable operator's headend

At the headend, the CMTS communicates with the cable modems that are physically located in customer homes. In addition to the CMTS at the headend, providers also must maintain other computer systems to support required databases and services to provide Internet services to all the cable customers.

In newer HFC networks, typically 500 to 2,000 active data subscribers are connected to a single cable network segment; these customers share the upstream and downstream bandwidth of that segment. Figure 11.4 shows the components of an HFC high-speed data network.

FIGURE 11.4   Cable System High-Speed Data Architecture

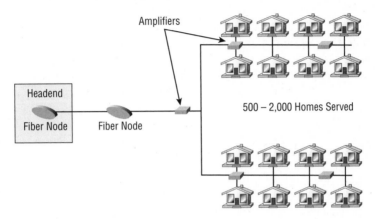

The actual bandwidth for Internet service data over a CATV line can be up to about 27 Mbps on the download path to the subscriber, with about 2.5 Mbps of bandwidth on the upload path. Depending on the cable network architecture, cable operator provisioning practices, and traffic load, an individual subscriber can typically get an access speed from 256 kbps to 6 Mbps.

In cases when high usage causes congestion, a cable operator has the flexibility to add additional bandwidth for data services. This is achieved by allocating an additional TV channel for high-speed data, thus doubling the downstream bandwidth available to subscribers. Another option to increase the amount of bandwidth available to subscribers is to reduce the number of subscribers that are served by each network segment. To do that, the cable network is further subdivided by laying the fiber-optic connections deeper into the neighborhoods.

Downstream Data Transfers

Let's look at the devices and functions that occur in during downstream data transfers.

1. At the local headend, signals are received through satellite dishes, antennas, analog and digital video servers, local programming, and other headends. This is where the distribution of the TV signals begins. The signals are sent to the customers via the distribution network.

2. The CMTS modulates the digital data into an RF signal.

3. The RF signals are combined onto a coaxial cable and then passed to the fiber transmitter.

4. The fiber transmitter performs RF to light (optical) signal conversion.

5. The fiber transmitter then sends the signals to a fiber node located somewhere in the town or neighborhood.

6. At the fiber node, a second conversion back from light (optical) to RF signal is performed.

7. The RF signal is passed via the coaxial network composed of amplifiers, taps, and drops.

8. At the subscriber end, an RF splitter divides the combined RF signal into its video and data components. The data is passed to the cable modem.

9. The cable modem, tuned to the data RF signal channels, demodulates the data RF signal back into the digital data.

10. Data passes to the computer or data network over an Ethernet connection.

Upstream Data Transfers

Now, let me show you what happens to data traveling the opposite direction, upstream toward the service provider.

1. You are now starting at the customer end. The cable modem takes the digital data from the computer over an Ethernet connection and modulates the data to an RF signal.

2. The cable modem then transmits the signal, at the negotiated RF and power level.

3. The coaxial network carries the signal through amplifiers, taps, and drops.

4. When the signal reaches the fiber node, the first conversion from RF signal to light (optical) is performed.

5. The fiber node now becomes the transmitter and sends the signals to the headend fiber node, the former fiber transmitter.

6. The headend fiber node performs the second conversion, light (optical) to RF, passes the signal to the CMTS.

7. The CMTS, tuned to the data RF channels, demodulates the data RF signal back to digital data and routes it to the Internet.

As a result of this process, the bandwidth available to a subscriber can vary based on how many subscribers use the service at the same time. The cable operator can resolve the issue by adding RF channels or splitting the service area into multiple smaller areas. There is also a risk of privacy loss. This can be addressed at the cable modem using encryption and other privacy features specified in the DOCSIS standard.

Provisioning a Cable Modem

The process of provisioning the cable modem is composed of several steps in order for the cable modem to operate with a host system for Internet services. The process is extremely important for you to know. This is often the only information you will have if you are on the customer end. Knowing the steps and possibly what indicators there are on the modem could be your only way to see what is wrong with a connection. The provisioning process steps in the initialization and registration are defined by the DOCSIS.

The headend, where CMTS is located, must have operational provisioning servers, such as DHCP and TFTP servers. The cable modems are designed and coded to undertake these steps:

1. Set up downstream transmissions.

   When the cable modem is powered up, it scans and locks the downstream path for the appropriate RF data channel (frequency) for the physical and data link layers to be established.

2. Set up upstream transmissions.

   The cable modem listens to the management messages received through downstream path. The messages include the information on how, where, and when to communicate in the upstream path, and are used to establish the upstream physical and data link layers.

3. Establish Layer 1 and 2 connections.

   The cable modem communicates with CMTS to establish physical and data link layers.

4. Obtain an IP address.

   After establishing Layer 1 and Layer 2 connectivity with the CMTS, the cable modem requests IP configuration parameters information (IP address, default gateway, and TFTP server) from the DHCP server.

5. Get the DOCSIS configuration.

   Next, the cable modem requests a DOCSIS configuration file from the TFTP server. A DOCSIS configuration file is an American Standard Code for Information Interchange (ASCII) file created by special DOCSIS editors and includes settings, such as downstream channel identification, class of service (CoS) settings, baseline privacy settings, general operational settings, network management information, and vendor specific settings.

6. Register QoS with CMTS.

   The cable modem registers, negotiates, and ensures QoS settings with the CMTS.

7. Initialize the IP network.

   When the cable modem initialization and registration is complete, the PC-based network initialization is performed—the PC requests its own IP configuration parameters from the DHCP server.

   If multiple PC connections behind the cable modem are required, a router can be used. A common scenario is for the router to obtain a public IP address from the DHCP server of the cable provider. The home router also performs Network Address Translation (NAT) and Port Address Translation (PAT) and serves as a DHCP server for the PCs connected behind the router.

DSL Technologies

If you think about the history of the Internet in terms of customer connections, most end users started out with a dial-up connection. If you are like me, you went through about four or five different modems as the speeds increased over the years. The speed topped out, though, and dial-up just wasn't enough to handle all of the applications and data that everyone wanted to access. Years ago, Bell Labs determined that voice conversation only required a small bandwidth, from 300 Hz to 3 kHz, and allocated only that bandwidth to plain old telephone systems (POTS). So, that is all the bandwidth that is available when you have a dial-up connection; that is the reason for the slow-speed connection.

A considerable amount of bandwidth exists on the line above 3 kHz, but for years that bandwidth between 3 kHz and 1 MHz went unused. Phone companies seeking increased offerings for their customers researched different ways to carry more data over the infrastructure already in place. That research and advances in technology led to digital subscriber line (DSL) and use of the additional bandwidth from 3 kHz up to 1 MHz. High-speed data services could now be delivered over ordinary copper lines

The most common implementation of DSL is asymmetric digital subscriber line (ADSL), which uses a frequency range of approximately 20 kHz to 1 MHz. Other implementations include:

- Synchronous digital subscriber line (SDSL)
- ISDN digital subscriber line (IDSL)
- High-bit-rate digital subscriber line (HDSL)
- Very-high-bit-rate digital subscriber line (VDSL)
- Rate adaptive digital subscriber line (RADSL)
- G.991.2 single-pair high-speed digital subscriber line (G.SHDSL)

With this technology, providers could deliver the high-bandwidth data rates to customers with relatively small changes to the existing telephone company infrastructure.

Figure 11.5 depicts the phone line spectrum and shows where the phone connection and the some of the DSL technologies reside. Notice that IDSL and SDSL bandwidths overlap POTS and ADSL, so while POTS and ADSL transmissions can coexist on the same wire, POTS and IDSL or SDSL cannot.

FIGURE 11.5   Phone Line Spectrum

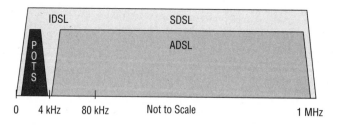

DSL, however, is not a complete end-to-end solution. It is really a physical layer transmission technology like dial, cable, or wireless. DSL connections are deployed in what is called the last mile of a local telephone network or local loop. The term *last mile* is a term that has been used quite a bit in the last few years with broadband connections. It basically means the same thing as local loop, and defines the physical connection from the customer to the first aggregation device of the provider network.

So, a DSL connection is set up between a pair of modems on either end of a copper wire that runs between the customer premises equipment (CPE) and the Digital Subscriber Line Access Multiplexer (DSLAM). A DSLAM is the device located at the provider's central office (CO) that concentrates connections from multiple DSL subscribers. Once the connection is aggregated, the service provider uses some other kind of transport for carrying the data to and from their point of presence (POP), the service provider's connection to the Internet.

DSL Categories

DSL transmissions, like CATV transmissions, can be categorized in terms of direction.

- Downstream transmissions travel from the CO toward the subscriber.
- Upstream transmissions travel from the subscriber toward the CO.

The DSL types can also be grouped by taking into account downstream and upstream speed:

Symmetrical DSL   Symmetrical DSL transmissions are used for communication between the source and destination nodes. Upstream and downstream speeds are equal.

Asymmetrical DSL   Asymmetrical DSL transmissions are used for the communication between two ends of a network. The downstream speed is typically higher than upstream.

DSL Characteristics

The term *xDSL* is used to describe quite a few variations of DSL, including ADSL, HDSL, RADSL, SDSL, IDSL, G.SHDSL, and VDSL.

The different kinds of DSL are often called flavors by technicians. Some DSL flavors, like ADSL and VDSL, do not use the voice frequency band, which allows the phone line to carry both data and voice signals at the same time. Other flavors, SDSL and IDSL, occupy the entire frequency range of the line and can carry only data.

Another term often used when describing the characteristics of broadband connections is always on. If you compare always-on connections to typical WAN connections, always on would be similar to a leased line or packet switched connection; the circuit is always up and a device can immediately transmit data without having to first establish the circuit.

The data rate that DSL service can provide depends on the distance between the subscriber and the CO. The shorter the distance, the higher data rate can be achieved. If you were close enough to a CO offering DSL service, you might be able to receive data at rates of up to 6.1 Mbps out of a theoretical 8.448 Mbps on an ADSL connection.

When discussing the DSL variants, the properties described in Table 11.2 are compared.

TABLE 11.2   DSL Properties

Property	Description
Nature	Nature of DSL is the relation between downstream and upstream speeds. Synchronous DSL has the same speeds in both directions, while asynchronous DSL has different downstream and upstream speeds.
Maximum data rate	Defines the maximum speed that can be deployed with certain type of DSL.
Line coding technology	Describes the technique used to represent digital signals to be transported over copper twisted pair so that the receiver can interpret them accurately.
Data and voice support	Depending on the usage of available frequency spectrum, certain DSL types support data and voice simultaneously, while others do not.
Maximum distance	Describes the maximum distance a certain type of DSL connection can span.

Types of DSL

DSL types include ADSL, VDSL, IDSL, SDSL, HDSL, and Multirate Symmetrical High-Speed Digital Subscriber Line (G.SHDSL).

ADSL   ADSL is designed to deliver more bandwidth downstream than upstream, and supports data and voice simultaneously over an existing copper lines. ADSL is meant to service residential customers where usually more bandwidth is required for the downstream transmissions to accommodate applications such as downloading music, movies, playing online games, surfing the Internet, or receiving email with large attachments. The downstream rate ranges from 256 kbps to 8 Mbps, while upstream speed can reach 1 Mbps. ADSL offers greater distance reachability, but speed is degraded as the distance increases. The maximum distance is limited to approximately 18,000 feet (5.46 km). ADSL2 and ADSL2+ are enhancements to basic ADSL and provide a downstream bandwidth of up to 24 Mbps and an upstream bandwidth of up to 1.5 Mbps.

RADSL   A RADSL refers to ADSL service with a data transmission rate that can be adapted to the local loop line conditions.

VDSL   VDSL can provide symmetrical or asymmetrical services. The downstream bandwidth ranges from 13 to 52 Mbps. Like ADSL, VDSL also supports data and voice over a single copper line. The Cisco Long Reach Ethernet (LRE) solution is based on Ethernet over VDSL. VDSL offers the highest operational speed but has the shortest achievable distance. For VDSL to support the maximum speed of 52 Mbps the subscriber has to be very close to the CO—a range of 1,000 feet (300 meters). The maximum operational distance is 4,500 feet (1.37 km).

IDSL   IDSL transmits data digitally (rather than via analog) on a regular twisted pair copper telephone line, across existing ISDN lines. IDSL delivers up to 144 kbps symmetrical bandwidth derived from the two bearer channels (2B) plus the signaling channel (D) (B = 64 kbps, D = 16 kbps); it is essentially a leased-line, basic rate ISDN (BRI) service with no D channel. IDSL does not support voice and can only carry data. Because it is always on, IDSL has an advantage over ISDN. The maximum operating distance of IDSL is limited to 18,000 feet (5.46 km). An IDSL line can be configured for a speed of 64 kbps, 128 kbps, or 144 kbps. The line coding mechanism used is two binary, one quaternary (2B1Q), which allows transparent operation through an ISDN U interface.

SDSL   SDSL delivers 768 kbps both downstream and upstream over a single copper twisted pair. SDSL technology is proprietary, nonstandardized, and can only carry data. The symmetrical nature of SDSL makes it ideal for commercial use where end users often must send and receive large amounts of data. These users run network applications, send and receive email messages with large attachments, upload data to corporate servers, and update web pages. The use of a single twisted pair limits the operating range of SDSL to about 22,000 feet (6.7 km).

HDSL   HDSL delivers 1.544 or 2.048 Mbps of symmetrical bandwidth over two copper twisted pairs. Service providers use HDSL as a substitute for T1 and E1 leased lines. Only data can be carried via HDSL. The operating range of HDSL is limited to approximately 12,000 feet (3.7 km).

G.SHDSL   Cisco describes the G.SHDSL acronym as Multirate Symmetrical High-Speed Digital Subscriber Line. G.SHDSL offers symmetrical data rates from 192 kbps to 2.3 Mbps. G.SHDSL is standardized and developed by the International Telecommunication Union (ITU) to address the worldwide SDSL market. The maximum operational distance supported by G.SHDSL is about 28,000 feet (8.5 km); this offers a greater reach over other deployed DSL technologies.

Speed vs. Distance Limitations

The DSL types are limited by distance and speed. Achievable speed is inversely proportional to distance—longer distance in the local loop means lower maximum speed that a particular DSL connection supports. The maximum speed that can be achieved by certain DSL connections is also influenced by various factors in the local loop that attenuate or distort the signal, as described in Table 11.3.

TABLE 11.3   Factors That Impede DSL Transmissions

Factor	Description
Signal attenuation	Attenuation causes signal loss over distance and is determined with the distance between subscriber and CO. The signal that travels along the medium is attenuated. The longer the distance the more attenuation and, thus, lower speeds are achievable.
Bridge tap	A bridge tap is an extra telephone wire with an unterminated cable end that is connected to the local loop. An unterminated tap introduces noise and reflections, and can radiate power that reduces signal strength and consequently speed. DSL providers should remove bridge taps before installing a DSL connection.
Load coil	Provisioning loading coils was a standard procedure for improving POTS voice quality on longer local loops. It is also called conditioning the loop. A loading coil is a wrap of wire placed at specific intervals along the local loop to extend the local loop distance. The coil creates a low-frequency band pass filter that cuts off (blocks) the DSL frequencies. For the DSL to operate, load coils must be removed from the loop.
Wire gauge	Wire gauge is the thickness of the wire used in the local loop. For higher speeds, thicker wire is needed.
Impedance mismatch	The impedance mismatch in the local loop causes echo, which results in noise. The impedance mismatch is caused by the changes in wire gauge, wire splices, or by corrosion.
Crosstalk	Crosstalk is the interference between the two wires in a bundle caused by electrical energy.
AM radio interference	AM radio frequencies can interfere with the DSL signal causing speed reduction. The interference is especially a problem with in-house wiring where untwisted or poorly twisted wiring exists.

Issues with DSL

If you're going to work with DSL, keep these three things in mind:

- The maximum data rate describes the maximum achievable downstream and upstream bandwidth with the shortest operational distance (distance between the subscriber and the CO).

- The maximum operational reach is the maximum achievable distance with the lowest operational data rate.

- Bandwidth and distance are inversely related.

When you experience problems with your xDSL operations, check the following:

1. Check for the presence of load coils in the system. Load coils must be removed from the line for xDSL to operate.

2. Verify impedance matching. Throughput is reduced when impedance mismatches are present (for example, different wire gauges are used in the line).

3. Check for the presence of open bridge taps. Bridge taps also reduce the achievable throughput.

4. Monitor the lines for crosstalk. Crosstalk from other lines and wiring will degrade the throughput.

5. Monitor the lines for external interference. External interference, like AM radio interference, results in unpredictable xDSL performance.

ADSL in Detail

ADSL is characterized by asymmetric data rates, with higher data rates for downstream transmissions and lower data rates for upstream. ADSL can coexist with POTS over the same twisted-pair telephone line. Depending on the ADSL flavor, three information channels can exist over the same wiring:

- POTS channel for analog voice
- Variable-speed duplex channel
- High-speed downstream channel

In these systems, customers can use the phone line and the ADSL connection simultaneously without adverse effects on either service.

The distance between the end user and the CO provides an approximate technological guideline for line speeds. Downstream, ADSL can support speeds up to just over 8 Mbps. The upstream speed can be up to roughly 1 Mbps. The maximum upstream rate can be provided at distances of up to 18,000 feet (5,486 m) over one-wire pair without repeaters on an optimized loop. The technical maximum downstream speed can be achieved at distances up to 12,000 feet (3,658 m) using standard 0.6 mm (24-gauge) wire on an optimal loop.

 Real World Scenario

But I Want DSL

Distance has always been a limiting factor with DSL. I can remember when it first came out and none of the enhancements that exist today were available. Nevertheless, I wanted DSL. People in my building who lived in apartments on the second floor or lower could get DSL but, those who lived on the third floor or higher couldn't get service. I was on the sixth floor, too far from the switch. I couldn't get the service. Angry!

ADSL was standardized in 2004. The newer variants, ADSL2 and ADSL2+, offer improvements. ADSL2 (ITU G.992.3/4) provides higher downstream rates of up to 12 Mbps for spans of less than 8,000 feet (2.5 km). ADSL2+ (ITU G.992.5) provides up to 24 Mbps for spans of less than 5,000 feet (1.5 km).

ADSL Equipment

The ADSL services are deployed between two ADSL modems, one at the subscriber end and one at the CO. The CPE ADSL modem is known as an ADSL terminal unit-remote (ATU-R). The CO modem is called an ADSL terminal unit-central office (ATU-C). At the CO, a special device called a DSLAM, which basically contains multiple ATU-Cs, is often used.

Benefits of ADSL

Again, probably the biggest benefit of ADSL is the ability to provide data and voice services on the same line. When analog voice is integrated with ADSL, a filter or splitter isolates the ADSL modem from the POTS channel. This guarantees uninterrupted phone service—even if there is a failure on the ADSL connection. Not only do both services use the same wire but the customer can use the phone line and the ADSL connection at the same time without adverse effects on either service, provided the filters or splitters are in place. The whole idea (and the service) would be much less attractive if this weren't the case. If they didn't work at the same time, you would have that dial-up modem limitation again.

Let's take a closer look at why and how voice is separated from data. ADSL offloads the data (modem) traffic from the voice switch and keeps analog POTS separate from data. By separating the voice and data traffic, you are provided with a fail-safe emergency-call service. This is especially important when you think about your phone connection as a public safety connection; you want to be able to call for emergency services any time you need them. Once the two channels are split, a data channel is established between the CPE modem and the CO DSLAM and a separate voice channel is established between the telephone and the voice switch at the CO.

POTS splitters are used to separate the DSL traffic from the POTS traffic. The POTS splitter is a passive device; one end connects to the wall jack, the other two connect to the CPE modem and a telephone. In the event of a power failure, the voice traffic is still carried to the voice switch in the CO. Splitters can be installed at the customer location but are almost always used in the CO. Microfilters can also used to separate the traffic for POTS only connections. A microfilter is a passive low-pass filter; one end connects to the telephone and the other end connects to the telephone wall jack.

The local loop terminates at the customer location at the demarcation point (DEMARC) on a device called the network interface device (NID). At the DEMARC, the point where the phone line enters the customer premise, a device called a splitter is attached to the phone line itself. The splitter separates the phone line traffic; one branch feeds the original house telephone wiring for the phone, and the other branch connects to the ADSL modem. In addition, the splitter acts as a low-pass filter, allowing only the 0–4 kHz frequencies to pass to or from the phone. Since installing the POTS splitter at the NID requires that a technician go to the customer site to set up the ADSL service, most installations today use microfilters. At the CO, the POTS splitter separates the incoming voice traffic, which goes to the voice switch, and the data traffic, which goes to the DSLAM.

Modulating ADSL

There are two basic types of modulation techniques associated with ADSL: a single-carrier Carrierless Amplitude and Phase (CAP), which is proprietary and multicarrier standardized Discrete Multitone (DMT).

CAP Modulation   CAP is an early and fairly easily implemented modulation method used in many of the early installations of ADSL. CAP modulation operates in such a way that it creates three separate channels on the wire by dividing the signals into three distinct bands, as described in Table 11.4. The three channels are widely separated to minimize the possibility of interference between the channels on one line and between the signals on different lines. A single-carrier notation means that only one frequency band is used to carry either an upstream or downstream channel.

TABLE 11.4   CAP Modulation Bands

Band	Frequency Range	Description
Voice channel	0–4 kHz	POTS voice traffic
Upstream channel	25–160 kHz	Upstream data traffic
Downstream channel	240–1.5 MHz	Downstream data traffic
		The actual width of the downstream channel (the upper frequency) varies and depends on a number of conditions, such as line length or line noise.

DMT Modulation   DMT modulation is standardized with the American National Standards Institute (ANSI) and ITU—ITU 992.1 (G.dmt), ITU 992.2 (G.lite), and ANSI T1.413 Issue 2. DMT is the prevailing modulation technique used in modern ADSL deployments. As with CAP, the DMT modulation technique divides the signals on the wire into separate channels. The main difference is that DMT does not use only two fairly wide channels for upstream and downstream data traffic. With DMT, the frequency band is divided into 256 separate 4-kHz-wide channels. Channels 6 to 38 are duplex and used for both upstream and downstream data traffic, channels 39 and onward are used only for downstream data traffic. To compensate for noise on a certain channel, the system constantly monitors each channel. With channel quality decreasing, the system adjusts the number of bits per channel or if the quality is too impaired, the signal is shifted to another channel. This system constantly shifts signals among different channels, searching for the best channels for transmission and reception.

Implementing DMT modulation is more complex in comparison to CAP modulation since it uses a large number of channels. On the other hand, DMT modulation offers more flexibility when traversing lines of differing quality.

Concept: G.lite

G.lite is a less complex version of the DMT standard. G.lite uses only half the subchannels (128) and is thus also known as half-rate DMT. The lower number of channels also determines a lower maximum downstream speed of 1.5 Mbps and a maximum upstream speed of 640 kbps.

Placing Data on ADSL

Let's look specifically at how data is carried from the DSL modem at the customer location, through service provider network, to the Internet. Remember, DSL is really just a high-speed Layer 1 transmission technology that works over copper wires. Here is the breakdown of where and how the data is sent across the network. I use the OSI layers to describe each of the steps in the process.

1. The DSL Layer 1 connection from the CPE is terminated at the DSLAM.

2. The DSLAM terminates the ADSL connections, and then switches the traffic over an ATM network to an aggregation router. The data link layer protocol that is usually used over DSL is ATM. A DSLAM is basically an ATM switch containing DSL interface cards (ATU-Cs).

3. The aggregation router is the Layer 3 device where an IP connection from a customer terminates.

The actual IP packets have to be encapsulated in some way to be carried over the ATM and DSL physical connections. There are three typical approaches to encapsulating the packets:

- RFC 1483/2684 Bridged
- PPP over Ethernet (PPPoE)
- PPP over ATM (PPPoA)

RFC 1483 Bridging

RFC 1483 bridging was the first round of the implementation process. The ADSL modem (CPE) simply bridges the Ethernet frame from the customer PC to the aggregation router where Integrated Routing and Bridging (IRB) is used to provide connectivity to the IP network (probably the Internet) beyond. RFC 1483 bridging has security and scalability issues. These issues made using it unpopular for deploying as a full architecture. PPPoE and PPPoA are more scalable and provide added authentication, making them more secure if more complex to implement.

PPP over Ethernet

RFC 1483 bridging is not scalable because the service provider could not control the number of clients that are connected to the network. Basically, they didn't want to support a bunch of nonpaying clients. Here is where the security part comes in to play; there is no way to authenticate a user if their data is allowed to just pass onto the network. PPP over Ethernet (PPPoE) was developed to resolve the security and authentication issues.

So, with PPPoE, the CPE still bridges Ethernet frames from the end user PC to the provider's aggregation router over ATM. Only now, the Ethernet frame carries a PPP frame inside it. The benefit to using PPP is the inclusion of an authentication mechanism and a way to control the session establishment.

The PPP session is established between the customer device and the aggregation router. The customer device must have PPPoE client support. Either an end user computer with PPPoE client software or a CPE router configured as a PPPoE client can be the PPPoE client. The CPE configuration varies based on whether the setup includes a modem or not. In Figure 11.6, I show you the three possible configurations. The figure also shows you the network from the CPE device to the service provider. The network connections from the DSLAM through the service provider network are often fiber optic trunks. In the figure, you can see this as an optical carrier 3 (OC3) connection.

FIGURE 11.6   PPPoE Client Configurations

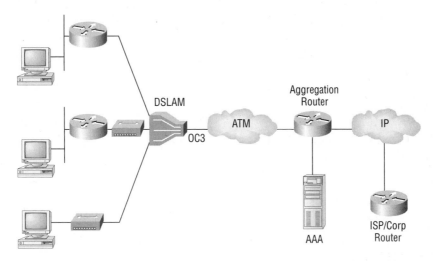

In the PPPoE architecture, the PPPoE client connects to the ADSL service. The PPPoE client first encapsulates the end user data into a PPP frame, and then the PPP frame is further encapsulated inside an Ethernet frame. The IP address allocation process for the PPPoE client is same as PPP in dial mode.

1.   The PPPoE client and the PPPoE server enter into IP Control Protocol (IPCP) negotiation to allocate the IP address.

2.   Either Password Authentication Protocol (PAP) or Challenge Handshake Authentication Protocol (CHAP) is used to authenticate the client.

The aggregation router can use either a local database or a RADIUS (authentication, authorization, and accounting—AAA) server to authenticate users.

The PPPoE client functionality is available as a software PPPoE client application on the end user PC. This way PPPoE provides the ability to connect a host over a simple bridging CPE to an aggregation router. In this model, a host uses its own PPP stack and the user is presented with a familiar user interface (using the PPPoE client software) similar to establishing a dial-up connection. Unlike PPPoA, access control, billing, and type of service can be controlled on a per-user, rather than a per-site, basis.

Three options are available for deploying PPPoE with DSL. They vary in terms of the equipment used, DSL termination, and the means for making PPPoE functionality available.

Router with Internal Modem and PPPoE Client   A router with an internal modem and an internally configured PPPoE client terminates DSL line and establishes PPPoE session. Use this option when supporting PPPoE client software is undesirable. The router can be a DHCP server that deploys Network Address Translation (NAT) and Port Address Translation (PAT) to connect multiple users behind the service provider using a single ADSL connection and a single PPP username and password.

External Modem and Router with PPPoE Client   An external modem terminates DSL line and a router with an internally configured PPPoE client establishes PPPoE session. A router can act as a DHCP server and provide NAT and PAT functionality

External Modem with End User PC and PPPoE Client Software   An external modem is used to terminate DSL line. An end user PC with PPPoE client software establishes a PPPoE session.

Establishing a PPPoE Session

PPP usually works over a point-to-point connection only. For PPP over an Ethernet multi-access environment, additional enhancements were needed. PPPoE has two distinct stages:

- Discovery stage
- PPP session stage

When a PPPoE client initiates a PPPoE session, it must first perform discovery to determine which PPPoE server can meet the client request. Then, the host must identify the Ethernet MAC address of the peer and establish a PPPoE session ID. Although PPP defines a peer-to-peer relationship, discovery is inherently a client-server relationship. In the discovery process, the PPPoE client discovers an aggregation router (the PPPoE server). Depending on the network topology, more than one PPPoE server might be available to the PPPoE client. The discovery stage allows the PPPoE client to discover all PPPoE servers and then select one. The process is the same whether the PPPoE client is configured on a router or installed as software on an end user computer.

Here is the discovery stage process:

1. The PPPoE client broadcasts a PPPoE Active Discovery Initiation (PADI) packet containing an indication of the service type required. The destination MAC address for the packet is set to broadcast.

2. The PPPoE server (aggregation router) sends a PPPoE Active Discovery Offer (PADO) packet describing the service it can offer. The destination MAC address is the unicast address of the client (end-user computer or router).

3. The PPPoE client sends a unicast PPPoE Active Discovery Request (PADR) packet to the PPPoE server.

4. The PPPoE server sends a unicast PPPoE Active Discovery Session-Confirmation (PADS) packet to the client.

When discovery is completed successfully, both the PPPoE client and the selected PPPoE server have the information they need to build their point-to-point connection over the Ethernet. After the PPPoE session begins, PPP uses the normal Link Control Protocol (LCP) and Network Control Program (NCP) for the IPCP process.

At any time after a session has been established, a PPPoE Active Discovery Terminate (PADT) packet can be sent to terminate the session. Either the PPPoE client or the PPPoE server can terminate the session.

Negotiating an MRU

As specified in RFC 2516, the maximum receive unit (MRU) option must not be negotiated to a size larger than 1,492 bytes. Remember that Ethernet has a maximum payload size of 1,500 octets. The PPPoE header uses 6 octets and the PPP protocol ID is 2 octets, so the PPP maximum transmission unit (MTU) must not be greater than1,492 bytes (1,500 – 8 = 1,492 bytes).

PPP over ATM

Unlike RFC 1483 bridging and PPPoE, where the CPE is set up as a bridge, bridging the Ethernet frames from the end user's computer to the aggregator router, PPPoA is a routed solution.

With PPPoA, the CPE routes the packets from the end user's computer over ATM to an aggregation router. The PPP session is established between the CPE and the aggregation router. Unlike PPPoE, PPPoA does not require host-based (PPPoE client) software. The aggregation router terminates the PPP session from the CPE. The CPE can be configured as a DHCP server and use NAT and PAT to support multiple hosts connected via Ethernet behind the CPE.

With PPPoA, a PPP session is established between the CPE and the aggregation router, as follows.

1. The CPE device is configured with a PPP username and password for authentication to the aggregation router.

2. The aggregation router uses either a local database or a RADIUS (AAA) server to authenticate users. The PPPoA session authentication can be based on PAP or CHAP.

3. After the PPP username and password have been authenticated, IPCP negotiation takes place and an IP address is assigned to the CPE.

4. After the IP address has been assigned, a host route is established both on the CPE and the aggregation router. The aggregation router must assign only one IP address to the CPE.

Configuring the CPE as a PPPoE Client

Let's look at the way you configure a customer router behind a DSL modem. Figure 11.7 shows a sample network. This type of configuration was popular a few years ago. Many consumer routers (such as the Linksys router) still can be configured for PPPoE.

 Real World Scenario

Setting Up a SOHO Network for FutureTech's Star Programmer

Sarah can make a computer do things that make most folk's head spin. She's friendly, easy-going and, in 10 years at FutureTech, she's never missed a deadline. When Sarah developed severe allergies to the industrial cleaners used in the Dallas headquarters, she offered to resign. Rather than lose her skills, you have been asked set up a SOHO network for her. You will, of course, be using a full enterprise grade Cisco ISR router that will allow you to connect and manage the network from the corporate office. The router will allow you to connect the multiple computers and provide all of the services Sarah needs to work from home.

FIGURE 11.7 Router as PPPoE Client with DSL Modem

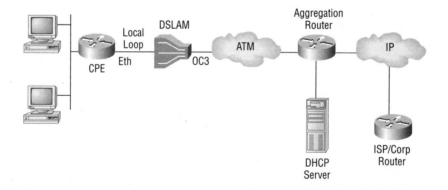

Using PPP over Ethernet (PPPoE) DSL configuration steps in addition to the dial-on-demand routing (DDR) derived commands, here is the process:

1. Configure the outside Ethernet interface with a PPPoE client configuration.
2. Create and configure the dialer interface for PPPoE with a negotiated IP address and a maximum transmission unit (MTU) size of 1,492.
3. Configure Port Address Translation (PAT) to allow the sharing of the dynamic public IP address of the dialer interface.
4. Configure the router as a DHCP server for the end user PCs behind it.
5. Configure a static default route.

Prior to Cisco IOS software Release 12.2(13)T, you had to configure a PPPoE Virtual Private Dialup Network (VPDN) group before you could begin the process described above. The VPDN group was only required for PPPoE, not for PPPoA.

Configuring the Outside Ethernet Interface

Because the SOHO configuration is behind a DSL modem, you need to configure two Ethernet interfaces on the router. The outside interface will act as the client for the PPP sessions. The inside interface will be configured with network services (DHCP and NAT) to provide the inside hosts with connectivity.

The first step in the process then is to configure the outside interface, in my example that is Fast Ethernet 0/1 (Fa0/1). I go through again step by step each of the configurations.

```
RmtWrkRtr1(config)#interface fa 0/1
RmtWrkRtr1(config-if)#pppoe enable
```

The interface command moves you to the correct Ethernet interface (in this case *Fa0/1*). The pppoe enable command enables PPPoE on the interface.

```
RmtWrkRtr1(config-if)#pppoe-client dial-pool-number 1
```

The pppoe-client command binds the interface to the dialer pool, which will ultimately bind the dialer interface together with the physical interface. This establishes the encapsulation for being a PPPoE client.

Configuring the Dialer Interface

```
RmtWrkRtr1(config)#interface dialer 1
```

The interface dialer command creates the virtual dialer interface. In this case, I have created interface *1*. (I could have used zero or some other number.)

This command comes from the days of demand-dial routing. Engineers had to find ways to make connections to different places with different configurations using the same hardware (usually the same physical interface). The problem with a setup like that was, if you put the configuration required to make a specific connection on the physical interface, then you couldn't automatically swap the connection to different configurations without going on the interface and changing the settings. Dialer interfaces were created to solve the problem.

A dialer interface provides a virtual interface that you can configure for a specific connection. The virtual dialer interface is then associated with a dialer pool, which just holds and makes resources available. The resources in this case are the physical interfaces.

Concept: Dialer List

A dialer list contains information that allows DDR to identify interesting traffic based on a specific call or destination and provide routing to the correct dialer interface based on available physical resources.

Many people experienced with DDR configurations wonder how dialer lists affect DSL. They don't. Since DSL is always on, there is no need for a list to specify interesting traffic for a specific call or destination.

When there is traffic to be sent, it is routed to the appropriate dialer interface. Once the dialer interface has traffic to send, the dialer pool binds the dialer interface to a physical interface where the configurations from the virtual interface would be temporarily used on the physical interface. Once the data is sent, the binding is removed and no configuration is left on the physical interface. When another dialer interface has data to send, its configuration would in turn be bound the physical interface and the traffic sent with that configuration.

```
RmtWrkRtr1(config-if)#encapsulation ppp
```

If you've worked with networks at all, you've used the encapsulation command. In this case, you will use the command to change the encapsulation on the interface to *ppp*.

```
RmtWrkRtr1(config-if)#ip address negotiated
```

The ip address command is a familiar command, as well. The *negotiated* option tells the interface to get an IP address from another device. In this case, the IP address will be negotiated through PPP, specifically IPCP.

```
RmtWrkRtr1(config-if)#no cdp enable
```

The no cdp enable command is an optional command, but it is a recommended security configuration. You won't want to send unnecessary traffic out to the service provider or valuable CDP data out to the Internet.

```
RmtWrkRtr1(config-if)#dialer pool 1
```

The `dialer pool` command associates the dialer interface to the proper dialer pool. Again, the dialer pool is the virtual entity that binds the dialer interface to the physical interface.

```
RmtWrkRtr1(config-if)#ip mtu 1492
```

The `ip mtu` command reduces the maximum size of the frame that can leave the interface. This is necessary because you are encapsulating a PPP frame into another frame type (in this case another Ethernet frame). You must reduce the size to 1492 because the PPPoE header and the PPP encapsulation require 8 bytes.

There is an alternative way to configure the MTU. I'll tell you about that later in this chapter.

```
RmtWrkRtr1(config-if)#ppp authentication chap callin
```

The `ppp authentication` command enables authentication for the connection.

The *chap* option specifies the use of authentication using CHAP; the other option is PAP. Remember, PAP has serious security issues, does not encrypt or hash the password text, and only authenticates the session at the beginning. PAP is vulnerable to man-in-the-middle attacks.

The *callin* option restricts the access server and only allows a session to be authenticated if the remote device being configured (this router in this configuration) initiates the call.

Effective CHAP passwords contain at least eight characters and include a mix of uppercase, lowercase, numerals, and special characters. I don't know what the maximum number of characters is, but I've had a router accept over 30 characters, including symbols and punctuation marks!

```
RmtWrkRtr1(config-if)#ppp chap password a;Cd12#4
```

Configuring NAT Overload (PAT)

Port address translation by any other name...you get the idea. Cisco dubbed PAT "NAT Overload." Begin by specifying the interesting source traffic.

```
RmtWrkRtr1(config)#access-list 110 permit ip 192.168.10.0 0.0.0.255 any
```

In NAT (and many other) configurations, the `access-list` command is used to specify interesting traffic, traffic that is to be sent through the NAT process and translated. Next, enable PAT.

```
RmtWrkRtr1(config)#ip nat inside source list 110 interface dialer 1 overload
```

The `ip nat` command enables the use of NAT for dynamic translation of one set of addresses into another set of addresses. Typically, it's used for private-to-public address translation.

The *inside source* option gives the NAT process the direction of translation. In this case, the source traffic will be coming from the interface configured with the `ip nat inside` command.

The `list list-number` option attaches an already configured `access-list` to the process and identifies authorized source traffic.

The `overload` option specifies that PAT should used to modify the transport layer port numbers so that each host session can be uniquely identified.

Once NAT is enabled on an interface, you can configure that interface. Use the `interface` command to move between interfaces and then use `nat inside` and `nat outside` to specify the inside and outside interfaces.

`RmtWrkRtr1(config)#interface fa0/0`

The `interface` command simply moves you to the configuration mode for the specified interface.

`RmtWrkRtr1(config-if)#ip nat inside`

The `ip nat inside` command tells the NAT process which interface is the inside interface. This is used by the `ip nat` command to specify the direction of translation.

`RmtWrkRtr1(config-if)#interface dialer 1`

Again, the `interface` command moves you to the specified interface.

`RmtWrkRtr1(config-if)#ip nat outside`

The `ip nat outside` command tells the NAT process which interface is the outside interface. Just like the `ip nat inside` command told the process which interface was the inside interface. This is used by the `ip nat` command to specify the direction of translation.

Configuring an Inside Ethernet Interface as a DHCP Server

Using the IOS, you can configure any router to be a fully functioning DHCP server. The router can then assign and manage IP addresses for DHCP clients. This is done by creating and assigning options to DHCP pools. More configurations are available (boottp options, DNS or WINS servers, DHCP relay, and the like), but those are beyond the scope of this book. For now, let's just get your DHCP server configured. Begin by creating a new DHCP pool.

`RmtWrkRtr1(config)#ip dhcp pool RmtWrk_dhcp`

The `ip dhcp pool` command creates a new DHCP pool where the options can be configured and a database of the addresses be maintained. RmtWrk_dhcp is the name that I assigned to this new pool.

`RmtWrkRtr1(dhcp-config)#import all`

The `import all` command allows this instance of DHCP to pull options from another centrally configured DHCP server. It is a great enhancement to the DHCP server process.

For example, with `import all` in place, you can update the options DNS and WINS in one place and all your pools will be updated.

In this specific example, `import all` allows the new server to pull the options from DHCP server connected to the outside interface you specified earlier. Now you don't have to configure the options yourself. If the service provider changes the configuration on the server connected to your outside interface, your servers will be updated automatically.

```
RmtWrkRtr1(dhcp-config)#network 192.168.10.0 255.255.255.0
```

The `network` command allows you to set the set the subnet (range of addresses) that will be available to be assigned to individual clients.

```
RmtWrkRtr1(dhcp-config)#default-router 192.168.10.1
```

The `default-router` command notifies DHCP of the address assigned to the interface you wish clients to use as the default gateway. This allows the clients to direct their traffic toward the router.

```
RmtWrkRtr1(config)#ip dhcp excluded-address 192.168.10.1
```

The `ip dhcp excluded-address` command tells the router which IP addresses not to give out to clients. Be sure to exclude the router's own address and any other addresses that you statically configured. This prevents IP conflicts.

Configure Static Default Route

```
RmtWrkRtr1(config)#ip route 0.0.0.0 0.0.0.0 dialer 1
```

This `ip route` command functions like any other default static route. In this case, you are just telling the router that all of the traffic needs to go toward the outbound interface to the service provider. This prevents your router from having to know any routing information for external networks.

Entire PPPoE Configuration

The entire configuration would look like this as a sample.

```
host RmtWrkRtr1
!
ip dhcp pool RmtWrk_dhcp
import all
network 192.168.10.0 255.255.255.0
default-router 192.168.10.1
!
ip dhcp excluded-address 192.168.10.1
!
interface fa0/0
```

```
ip address 192.168.10.1 255.255.255.0
ip nat inside
!
interface fa0/1
no ip address
pppoe enable
pppoe-client dial-pool-number 1
!
interface dialer 1
ip address negotiated
encapsulation ppp
no cdp enable
dialer pool 1
ip mtu 1492
ip nat outside
ppp authentication chap callin
ppp chap password abcd1234
!
access-list 110 permit ip 192.168.10.0 0.0.0.255 any
ip nat inside source list 110 interface dialer 1 overload
!
ip route 0.0.0.0 0.0.0.0 dialer 1
```

Configuring the CPE with PPPoE and an ATM Interface

It is also possible to configure the customer router to act as a PPPoE client, but not have
a DSL modem. You can use PPPoE to bridge through an ATM interface and onto the network. This would mean that the phone line would connect right into the customer router.
To accomplish this, the router must have an ATM 0 interface; the RJ-11 jack allows you to
plug the phone line directly into the CPE. Now, in this configuration, the router is still a
PPPoE client and still bridges the local packets onto the provider network.

The biggest difference between this configuration and a configuration that uses Ethernet
inside and out is that outside interface is an ATM interface. So, let's take a look at the configurations you'll need set on the ATM interface now. The current Cisco documentation recommends using a very simple ATM outside interface configuration, as follows.

```
RmtWrkRtr1(config)#interface atm 0
RmtWrkRtr1(config-if)#dsl operating-mode auto
RmtWrkRtr1(config-if)#pvc 8/35
RmtWrkRtr1(config-if)#pppoe-client dial-pool-number 1
```

The inside configuration is the same as the PPPoE configuration I described for you above. Seems simple enough, doesn't it? But I can't tell you how many very discouraged people have called me to ask advice when they couldn't get the ATM interface up using that minimum configuration.

Here is another configuration I've found useful when configuring PPPoE with an ATM interface. And this one works!

```
RmtWrkRtr1(config)#interface atm 0
RmtWrkRtr1(config-if)#bundle-enable
RmtWrkRtr1(config-if)#dsl operating-mode auto
RmtWrkRtr1(config-if)#interface atm0.1 point-to-point
RmtWrkRtr1(config-if)#no ip directed-broadcast
RmtWrkRtr1(config-if)#no atm ilmi-keepalive
RmtWrkRtr1(config-if)#pvc 0/35
RmtWrkRtr1(config-if)#pppoe-client dial-pool-number 1
```

Notice that, in these PPPoE over ATM configurations, I used two different permanent virtual circuit (PVC) number sets to indicate the virtual path/virtual circuit (vpi/vci). The two that you saw in the code listings are the two that service providers generally use . Make sure you verify the PVC settings your provider is using.

Configuring the CPE as a PPPoA Client

With PPPoA, a CPE device encapsulates the PPP session for transport across the network to the DSLAM. PPPoA is often used in SOHO and branch office environments. It can provide more flexibility for a home office than the average PPPoE deployment because the customer LAN behind the CPE is under the complete control of the customer. The customer router acts like a router as opposed to a bridge for PPPoE. You can see what I mean in Figure 11.8.

FIGURE 11.8   PPPoA Router Setup

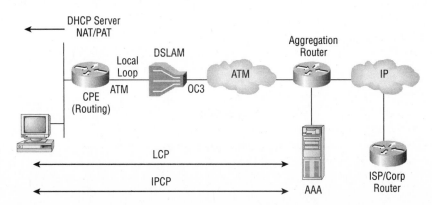

When you configure PPPoA, a logical interface known as a virtual access interface associates each PPP connection with an ATM virtual circuit (VC). You create this logical interface by configuring either an ATM permanent VC (PVC) or switched VC (SVC). The configuration is similar to the one you created for the PPPoE connection with an ATM interface. The difference is that this configuration encapsulates each PPP connection in a separate PVC or SVC, allowing each PPP connection to terminate at the router ATM interface, just as if received from a typical PPP serial interface.

Concept: Virtual Interface Templates

If you need to configure multiple VCs, I recommend that you create a virtual interface template (virtual template). With a virtual template in place, the virtual access interface for each VC obtains its configuration from the template as it is created. Virtual templates are great time savers and help prevent misconfigurations. For more information about creating virtual templates, see http://www.cisco.com.

Now I am going to show you the configuration steps for configuring the ATM interface for PPPoA. As you begin, only difference between this configuration and the PPPoE over ATM configuration is that now you will use the PVC mode.

```
RmtWrkRtr1(config)#interface atm 0
RmtWrkRtr1(config-if)#dsl operating-mode auto
RmtWrkRtr1(config-if)#pvc vpi/vci
```

Notice now you are in the ATM VC mode. From ATM VC mode you can configure the virtual interface for the ATM connection. First, set the encapsulation command. For DSL using PPPoA, the encapsulation is AAL5 in MUX mode. The other option, ppp dialer, sets the interface to receive PPP frames.

```
RmtWrkRtr1(config-atm-vc)#encapsulation aal5mux ppp dialer
```

Now, assign the interface to an appropriate dialer pool. For this exercise, I have made it a member of dialer pool 1.

```
RmtWrkRtr1(config-atm-vc)#dialer pool-member 1
```

Here is a sample of what the entire configuration would look like.

```
host RmtWrkRtr1
!
ip dhcp pool RmtWrk_dhcp
import all
network 192.168.10.0 255.255.255.0
```

```
default-router 192.168.10.1
!
ip dhcp excluded-address 192.168.10.1
!
interface ATM 0
no ip address
dsl operating-mode auto
pvc 8/35
encapsulation aa15mux ppp dialer
dialer pool-member 1
!
interface fa0/0
ip address 192.168.10.1 255.255.255.0
ip nat inside
!
interface dialer 1
ip address negotiated
encapsulation ppp
no cdp enable
dialer pool 1
ip nat outside
ppp authentication chap callin
ppp chap password abcd1234
!
access-list 110 permit ip 192.168.10.0 0.0.0.255 any
ip nat inside source list 110 interface dialer 1 overload
!
ip route 0.0.0.0 0.0.0.0 dialer 1
```

Once you have configured the router for PPPoA, the PPP subsystem starts and the router attempts to send a PPP configure request to the remote peer. If the peer does not respond, the router periodically goes into a listen state and waits for a configuration request from the peer. After a timeout, the router again attempts to reach the remote router by sending configuration requests.

The virtual access interface remains associated with a VC as long as the VC is configured. If you remove the configuration of the VC, the virtual access interface is marked as deleted. If you shut down the associated ATM interface, you will also cause the virtual access interface to be marked as down, and you will bring down the PPP connection. If you set a keepalive timer for the virtual template on the interface, the virtual access interface uses the PPP echo mechanism to verify the existence of the remote peer.

Minimizing Dropped Packets

Now, you'll remember that you configured the MTU on the dialer to account for the space needed for additional PPPoE encapsulation. But, it is still possible that client traffic could be dropped—even after you configured the MTU.

When a host initiates a TCP session with a destination device, it negotiates the IP segment size by using the Maximum Segment Size (MSS) option field in the TCP SYN packet. The value of the MSS Field is determined by the maximum transmission unit (MTU) configuration on the host. The default MSS value for a PC is 1,500 bytes.

The PPPoE standard supports an MTU of only 1,492 bytes. The disparity between the host and PPPoE MTU size can cause the router between the host and the server to drop 1,500-byte packets and terminate TCP sessions over the PPPoE network. Even if the path MTU (which detects the correct MTU across the path) is enabled on the host, sessions may be dropped because system administrators sometimes disable the Internet Control Message Protocol (ICMP) error messages that must be relayed from the host in order for path MTU to work.

You can configure the ip tcp adjust-mss command and help prevent TCP sessions from being dropped by adjusting the MSS value of the TCP SYN packets. This command can only be used in IOS versions 12.2(4) and later. If you have an IOS earlier than that, try using the ip adjust-mss command. If that doesn't work, upgrade your IOS or change up the router.

The ip tcp adjust-mss command is effective only for TCP connections passing through the router.

In most cases, the optimum value for the *max-segment-size* argument is 1,452 bytes. This value plus the 20-byte IP header, the 20-byte TCP header, and the 8-byte PPPoE header add up to a 1,500-byte packet that matches the MTU size for the Ethernet link.

If you are configuring the ip mtu command on the same interface as the ip tcp adjust-mss command, it is recommend that you use the following commands and values:

```
RmtWrkRtr1(config-if)#ip tcp adjust-mss 1452
RmtWrkRtr1(config-if)#ip mtu 1492
```

If that still doesn't work, you could try to change the MTU size on your host PC machines. (Some client machines do not allow you to change this value.) This would have to be done on every PC. Here are the steps for changing the MTU for a Windows 2000 or Windows XP PC. There is a tool you can download to help you change the registry values.

Complete these steps to change the MTU size.

1. Download the latest version of the Dr. TCP utility from http://www.dslreports.com/drtcp.

2. Refresh your browser page to ensure the page is current.

3. Run the Dr. TCP utility.

4. From the menu choose your Ethernet adapter.

5.   Type **1492** in the MTU field.

6.   Click Apply in order to save the change, and then click Exit.

7.   Reboot the PPPoE PC client.

The registry change is saved when the procedure finishes, so you need to run the utility only once per client.

Enterprise WAN

When you start to think about connecting your remote sites, you need to consider the different topologies that can be used. The best topology is a full mesh topology because it provides optimal routing. The full mesh topology provides a dedicated virtual circuit between any two customer edge (CE) routers in the network. The biggest problem with the full mesh solution is that with a large number of virtual links expense can get very high.

For a less expensive solution, customers may choose to use a partial mesh topology or a hub-and-spoke topology. The problem then becomes routing; it is no longer optimal. The partial mesh topology reduces the number of virtual circuits; usually this minimum number is just enough to provide optimal transport between major sites.

The hub-and-spoke topology provides the most drastic reduction of virtual circuits; it is usually defines by having many sites (spokes) connected only to the central site (or sites) or hub (or hubs), with no direct connectivity between the spokes. To prevent single points of failure, the hub-and-spoke topology is sometimes extended to a redundant hub-and-spoke topology.

Multi-protocol Label Switching Virtual Private Network (MPLS VPN) topology provides optimal routing between sites and customers need only one connection to the MPLS VPN service provider. From the service provider's point of view, MPLS gives the most flexibility and enables the providers to offer more services to their customers.

MPLS

On a traditional IP network, routing lookups are performed at every router a packet passes through. Each router in the network makes an independent decision when forwarding packets.

MPLS helps reduce the number of routing lookups and can forward based on criteria other than the default destination network. This capability eliminates the need to run a particular routing protocol on all the devices. To accomplish this, MPLS imposes labels; each packet gets an additional header. The labels are simply numbers that are used to make forwarding decisions. They are assigned on the edge of the MPLS of the network, and forwarding within the MPLS network is based on solely labels.

Labels usually correspond to a path to Layer 3 destination addresses; this is the equivalent of an IP destination in standard routing. Labels can be stacked to include other information, such as:

- A Layer 3 VPN destination (MPLS VPN)
- A Layer 2 circuit
- An outgoing interface on the egress router, Any Transport over MPLS (AToM)
- Quality of Service (QoS)
- A source address

MPLS was designed to support forwarding of other network layer protocols, not just TCP/IP. Label switching within the network is performed the same regardless of the Layer 3 protocol. In larger networks, the result of MPLS labeling is that only the edge routers perform a routing lookup. All the core routers forward packets based on the labels, which makes forwarding the packets through the service provider network faster.

Switching Types

MPLS is, at heart, a switching process. The whole idea was to have the performance of a switching process (very fast simple lookup), but the forwarding sophistication of a routing process (forwarding based on something other than just the next hop). In order to help you truly understand what MPLS does, let's look at the different switching types that have been supported by Cisco routers over the years.

- Process switching
- Cache switching
- Cisco Express Forwarding (CEF)

Process Switching

The first, oldest and slowest switching mechanism available in Cisco routers is process switching. Process switching must perform a destination lookup in the routing table (possibly a recursive lookup) and build a new Layer 2 frame header for every single packet. It is very slow and is normally not used.

Cache Switching

Due to the fact that process switching has such slow performance, another solution was needed. The Cisco IOS supports several switching mechanisms that use a cache; the cache stores the most recently routed destinations. The cache uses a faster searching mechanism and stores the entire Layer 2 frame header to improve the encapsulation performance. If the destination for the first packet in a session isn't in the fast-switching cache, then it is process switched and an entry is created in the cache. The subsequent packets are switched at the interface, using interrupt code and the cache to improve performance. Dubbed "route one, switch many," the first packet is routed through the router's central processor and the routing table; the remaining packets in the session are switched in hardware using the cache.

Take a look at what happens when a packet must be forwarded using process switching. Then I'll show you the steps for Cisco Express Forwarding (CEF).

When a routing update (whatever the routing protocol) is received and processed, an entry is created in the routing table, if the route is selected as the best route. When the first packet that is traveling toward this destination arrives, the router tries to find the destination in the fast-switching cache. Of course, it's not there yet, so the packet must be switched through the process-switching mechanism.

1. A recursive lookup is performed to find the outgoing interface.

2. If the Layer 2 address is not found in the ARP cache an Address Resolution Protocol (ARP) request is triggered. For example, if the destination device is in network 192.168.10.0/24, the next-hop to reach that network according to the routing protocol is 1.1.1.1, and to reach network 1.1.1.0/24, the outgoing interface is Fast Ethernet 0/0.

3. The entry is placed in the fast-switching cache, so that the following packets don't have to be process switched.

From then on, all of the packets going to that destination are fast-switched using the cache entry. The fast-switched process looks like this:

1. The switching occurs in the interrupt code; the packet is processed immediately.

2. Fast destination lookup is performed (no recursive lookup).

3. The encapsulation uses a pregenerated Layer 2 header that contains the destination and Layer 2 source (MAC) address. No ARP request or ARP cache lookup is necessary.

Cisco Express Forwarding

The latest and preferred Cisco IOS switching mechanism is CEF, which incorporates the best of the previous switching mechanisms:

- Per-packet load balancing (previously supported only by process switching)

- Per-source or per-destination load balancing

- Fast destination lookup

- Many other features not supported by other switching mechanisms.

The CEF cache, or Forwarding Information Base (FIB) table, is essentially a replacement for the standard routing table. The FIB table is a complete IP switching table, which holds the same information as the IP routing table. When you think about this table, think of it just like the routing table; it has the same authority.

The generation of entries in the FIB table is not packet triggered but change triggered. Whenever something changes in the IP routing table, that change is automatically reflected in the FIB table. This gives a major benefit that all of the updates and destinations are in the FIB table.

Because the FIB contains the complete IP switching table, the router makes definitive forwarding decisions based on that information. Whenever a router receives a packet that should be CEF switched, but the destination is not in the FIB, the packet is dropped. The FIB can drop packets if there is no entry just as with the routing table.

The FIB table is different from other fast-switching caches in that it does not contain information about the outgoing interface and the corresponding Layer 2 header. That information is stored in a separate table, the adjacency table. The FIB table is, more or less, a copy of the ARP cache, but instead of holding only destination MAC addresses, it holds the Layer 2 headers.

Router Architecture

In order for MPLS to support multiple protocols, the classic router architecture was separated into two components:

- Control plane
- Data plane

Control Plane   The control plane takes care of the routing information exchange and the label exchange between adjacent devices.

Data Plane   The data plane takes care of forwarding based on either destination addresses or labels; this is also known as the forwarding plane.

Figure 11.9 shows you a logical diagram of how these components fit together in a router.

FIGURE 11.9   Router Architecture

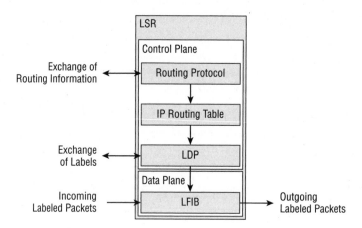

Control Plane

All of the different routing protocols you've studied so far, including OSPF, IIGRP, EIGRP, IS-IS, RIP, and BGP, can be used as the basis for the MPLS forwarding domain.

The control plane also holds label-swapping protocols for MPLS, such as:

- Label Distribution Protocol (LDP)
- Tag Distribution Protocol (TDP)
- BGP (used by MPLS VPN)

Resource Reservation Protocol (RSVP) is used by MPLS Traffic Engineering (MPLS TE) to reserve resources (bandwidth) in the network. I describe how the label exchange process works in detail a little later in this chapter.

Data Plane

The data plane, however, is a simple label-based forwarding engine that is independent of the type of routing protocol or label exchange protocol. In this situation, the label-swapping process is very similar to the more familiar routing process. You will remember that the process of routing a packet through a router doesn't hinge on the routing protocol that is running. The router must already have all the routing information in the table so that a packet can be forwarded.

Forwarding a packet using labels is the same; the label information must already be in the table in order the packet to be forwarded as a labeled packet. The Label Forwarding Information Base (LFIB) table is used to store the label information that the forwarding engine uses to forward packets. The LFIB table is populated by the label exchange protocol (LDP, BGP, and/or RSVP) used.

There's a huge difference that you must remember, though; the LFIB typically does not have the authority to drop packets. If there is not a next hop label in the LFIB table then the packet will be forwarded as a normal IP packet using the FIB table. Again, remember the FIB table is a more efficient copy of the routing table, and it does have the authority to drop packets.

Using Labels in MPLS

One of the great design ideas behind MPLS made it compatible with virtually any media (cable type) and Layer 2 encapsulation. Most Layer 2 encapsulations are frame based (such as with Ethernet), and MPLS simply shoves (imposes) a 32-bit label between the Layer 2 and Layer 3 headers. This label, often called the Layer 2 HF header, specifically describes the operation of frame mode MPLS. Figure 11.10 shows the placement of the header between the normal Layer 2 and 3 headers.

ATM is a special case because the technology requires a fixed-length cell (cell is similar in idea to a frame). Since the cell is fixed, a label cannot be inserted into it. MPLS uses the VPI/VCI fields in the ATM header as a label. You call this cell mode MPLS.

An MPLS label is composed of four separate fields and has a total size of 32 bits. The four fields the label (in order of appearance) are described in Table 11.5 and shown in Figure 11.11.

TABLE 11.5 MPLS Label Fields

Field	Size (bits)	Description
Label	20	The 20-bit label field is the actual label. Values 0 to 15 are reserved for specific MPLS functions.
EXP	3	The 3-bit EXP field is used by Cisco to define a class of service (CoS) (IP precedence).

TABLE 11.5   MPLS Label Fields *(continued)*

Field	Size (bits)	Description
Bottom-of-stack (S)	1	When set (1), the S bit indicates that this label is the last label in the packet, the bottom of the stack. Remember that MPLS allows multiple labels to be inserted.
TTL	8	The 8-bit TTL field serves the same purpose as the TTL field in the IP header.

FIGURE 11.10   MPLS Label Placement

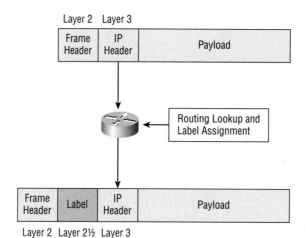

FIGURE 11.11   Label Fields

The MPLS label does not carry any information about the Layer 3 protocol in the packet. A new protocol ID (PID) is used for every MPLS-enabled Layer 3 protocol. This is because the device reading the frame coming in uses the PID to know which protocol is being used and to determine what kind of data follows the frame header. Since an MPLS header comes before the IP header, it has to be indentified that way.

Table 11.6 lists the typical Ethertype values that are used to identify Layer 3 protocols in most Layer 2 encapsulations.

TABLE 11.6   MPLS PID Values

Protocol	PID Value	Description
Unlabeled IP unicast	0x0800	Identifies the frame payload as a classic unicast IP packet.
Labeled IP unicast	0x8847	Identifies that the frame payload is a unicast IP packet with at least one label preceding the IP header. The bottom-of-stack bit indicates when the IP header actually starts.
Labeled IP multicast	0x8848	Identifies that the frame payload is a multicast IP packet with at least one label preceding the IP header. The bottom-of-stack bit indicates when the IP header actually starts.

Most of the time, only one label is assigned to a packet. However, as I mentioned before, there are some scenarios in which more than one label is used. Multiple labels are commonly used in conjunction with:

- MPLS VPNs
- MPLS TE
- MPLS VPNs combined with MPLS TE

MPLS VPNs   Multi-protocol BGP (MP-BGP) is used to propagate a second label that identifies the VPN in addition to the one that is propagated by LDP to identify the path.

MPLS TE   MPLS TE uses RSVP to establish Label Switched Path (LSP) tunnels. RSVP propagates labels that are used to identify the tunnel LSP in addition to the one that is propagated by LDP to identify the underlying LSP.

MPLS VPNs Combined with MPLS TE   Three or more labels are used to identify the VPN, tunnel LSP, and the underlying LSP.

Figure 11.12 shows an example of a stacked MPLS label.

FIGURE 11.12   Stacked MPLS Label

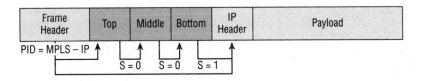

Concept: LSR and Edge LSR

Before I get much further into how MPLS works, I want to introduce you to another couple of terms.

- Label Switch Router (LSR)

- Edge LSR

An LSR is a device that forwards packets primarily based on labels. Routers that have all interfaces enabled for MPLS are called LSRs because they mostly forward labeled packets. The primary function of an LSR is to forward labeled packets. Therefore, every LSR needs a Layer 3 routing protocol (for example, OSPF, EIGRP, or IS-IS) and a label distribution protocol (for example, LDP).

An edge LSR is a device that primarily labels outgoing packets or removes labels from incoming packets. Routers that have some interfaces that are not enabled for MPLS are usually at the edge of an MPLS domain—autonomous system (AS). These routers also forward packets based on IP destination addresses and label them only if the outgoing interface is enabled for MPLS.

Label Allocation and Distribution

The steps that follow outline the process for unicast IP routing and MPLS label allocation and distribution.

1. Individual LSRs independently learn network routing information using standard or vendor-specific IGP, such as OSPF, IS-IS, or EIGRP.

2. Each LSR generates local labels. One locally unique label is assigned to each IP destination found in the routing table. The local labels are stored in the LIB table.

3. Each LSR then propagates the local labels to adjacent routers. These labels might be used as next-hop labels. They are stored in the FIB and LFIB tables to enable label switching.

4. Every LSR builds its LIB, LFIB, and FIB data tables based on received labels.

Building the Routing and FIB Tables

I am going to take you through a practical example of how labels are generated and distributed between all of the routers in a MPLS network. First, these data tables contain the label information:

Label Information Base   The LIB, in the control plane, is the table used by Label Distribution Protocol (LDP) where an IP prefix is assigned a locally significant label that is mapped to a next-hop label that has been learned from a downstream neighbor.

Label Forwarding Information Base   The LFIB, in the data plane, is the table used to forward labeled packets. Local labels, previously advertised to upstream (upstream means toward the destination) neighbors, are mapped to next-hop labels, previously received from downstream (downstream then means the opposite toward the source of the traffic) neighbors.

Forwarding Information Base   The FIB, in the data plane, is the table used to forward unlabeled IP packets. A forwarded packet is labeled if a next-hop label is available for a specific destination IP network. Otherwise, a forwarded packet is not labeled.

Not all enterprises would use something like MPLS within its network. Given the size of the FutureTech network, MPLS could be used in the core to provide the extra efficiency. However, the more likely setup is in the service provider network that the company is connected to. In either case, at least for this basic example, the MPLS setup would work the same.

In Figure 11.13, you can see that four routers, named R1 through R4, are serving as the MPLS network. R1 and R4 are edge LSRs; R2 and R3 are internal LSRs.

FIGURE 11.13   A Basic MPLS Network

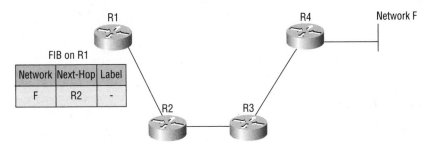

To begin, all of the routers exchange updates and build their routing tables. Now, as far as MPLS is concerned, it doesn't matter what routing protocol they are running. The routing protocol is running and all of the routers have up-to-date routing tables.

The next step is to enable CEF so that the FIB table will be built. The command to globally enable CEF on a router is `ip cef` from the global configuration mode. On many of the newer router platforms this is done for you by default, but you should verify that it is done using `show ip cef`. At this point, the FIB table is built.

Building the LIB Table

The next thing that must be done is to enable MPLS so that labels can be created for each of the destination networks. All Cisco routers should have MPLS functionality enabled by default. If for some reason MPLS is not enabled on your router, use the command `mpls ip` from global configuration mode.

You then need to enable MPLS on each of the individual interfaces that you want in the MPLS network. The command is actually the same for the interface as is was for the router in global mode. From interface configuration mode, use `mpls ip`. The LIB tables will now be built for each of the routers and local labels assigned to each of the destination networks. Each router assigns its own label to every destination network. Since the label is locally unique, it will only be of value to the local router and a specific, directly connected neighbor; the label is only good in one direction to that specific neighbor.

If you look at Figure 11.14, you can see now I have added the table examples for the one destination network, Network F. You can see the LIB was used to map the label to the IP prefix of a network.

FIGURE 11.14 Building the LIB Tables

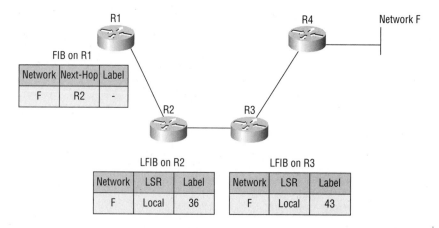

With MPLS enabled, you can now select a Label Distribution Protocol (LDP). You have two options for a LDP; you can choose to run LDP or Tag Distribution Protocol (TDP). TDP is a Cisco-proprietary protocol. To select TDP, you have to use `mpls label protocol tdp` command, globally or per interface.

> The default MPLS label distribution protocol changed from TDP to LDP in 12.4 versions of the IOS. If no protocol is explicitly configured by the `mpls label protocol` command, LDP is the default label distribution protocol. LDP configuration commands are saved using the `mpls ip` form of the command rather than the `tag-switching` form. Previously, commands were saved using the `tag-switching` form of the command, for backward compatibility.

Building the LFIB Table

Now that the LIB tables are built for each of the routers, it is the label distribution protocol's responsibility to exchange each local router's labels with their neighbor routers. Look at Figure 11.15; you can see the LFIB table for R2. R2's LFIB has the local label for network F, but has an untagged forwarding action. The untagged status means that R2 has not received a label for network F from its neighbor R3. Until R2 receives a label from R3, packets destined for network F will be forwarded as IP packets.

FIGURE 11.15   LFIB with an Untagged Value

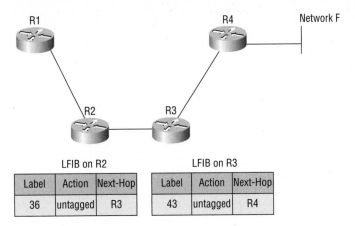

Label	Action	Next-Hop
36	untagged	R3

LFIB on R2

Label	Action	Next-Hop
43	untagged	R4

LFIB on R3

Once the LDP has exchanged R3's label between the routers, R2's LFIB updates and it can now forward data as labeled packets. You can see the update that was sent from R3 to R2 using LDP in Figure 11.16.

FIGURE 11.16   LDP Label Update

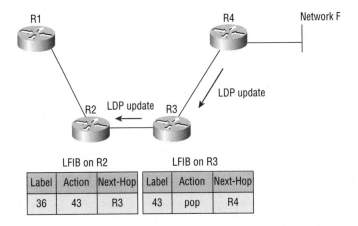

Label	Action	Next-Hop
36	43	R3

LFIB on R2

Label	Action	Next-Hop
43	pop	R4

LFIB on R3

Now, let's look at how a packet would traverse the network from R1 to R4. Just how will it be forwarded? Take a look at Figure 11.17; it shows the information in each router's tables.

Client to R1 to R2   When a packet comes into R1 destined for the MPLS network, R1 will look up the destination network in its FIB table. Since R1 received a label from R2, the destination network is there with a label that allows the data to be forward with a label. R1 will then forward the packet labeled as 36, the label it received from R2.

FIGURE 11.17 Forwarding a Packet through MPLS

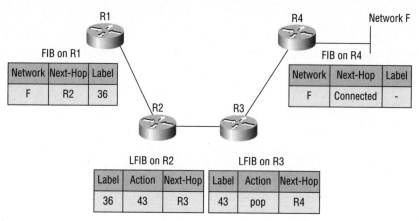

R2 to R3 When R2 receives the labeled packet, it knows to perform its lookup in the LFIB table. The LFIB on R2 tells it to forward the packet labeled as 43, the label R2 learned from R3.

R3 to R4 When the labeled packet reaches R3, it looks up the label in its LFIB table where it finds a pop label. The pop label tells R3 to remove the label and forward the packet as an IP packet. R3's LFIB contains the IP forwarding information. Now, when the packet reaches R4, R4 looks the IP address up in its FIB table and forwards the packet to the connected network F.

Concept: PHP

How did R3 get a pop label? What did it do? R3's LFIB had a pop label because that is the label that R4 sent it. R4 used a feature called Penultimate Hop Popping (PHP). By having R3 remove the label and forward just an IP packet, you prevent R4 from having to perform two lookups. If R3 had forwarded a labeled packet, R4 would have done a lookup in the LFIB found that it had no label to swap (the network is attached). R4 would then have to do a separate lookup in the FIB table to forward the IP packet properly. With PHP, you eliminated the need for R4 to have to perform two lookups!

Summary

I know that chapter was long—and to think, you only had to go through a few of dozens of possible remote and WAN connections that are available to you. I started you off taking you through broadband cable connections. I showed you the frequency ranges that are used and how the service providers break up and use that bandwidth. Then, you learned how the topology of cable networks has changed to provide a better and higher bandwidth service to customers.

Next, you learned that there are more flavors of DSL than one person should possibly have to endure. I explained why and how the data channels were added to your phone line, and which devices are required to make the connections happen. You learned which devices and corrections have to be made in the phone company's network to support data channels. The last thing I showed you in the DSL section was how to configure you CPE device for whichever type of DSL connection you may have. I covered PPPoE, the most common type, and explained that the placement of that configuration depends on the location of the PPP client and whether the customer has a DSL modem or not.

The final section in the chapter covered basic MPLS. You reviewed some basic switching and routing functions that are required for MPLS operation. Then I described problems that MPLS solves and how this is accomplished through the use of labels. I showed you the label components and how to stack them to create so that MPLS VPNs. Then I took you through the configuration of MPLS and showed how each of the tables are built and updated so that proper label forwarding occurs throughout the network.

Review Questions

1. What benefit does using a broadband cable connection give a remote teleworker over dial-up?

    A. Slower speed

    B. More bandwidth

    C. No benefit

    D. Not on all the time

2. What does the term *HFC* stand for?

    A. Hope for cable

    B. High frame corruption

    C. Hybrid fiber cable

    D. Half frequency connection

3. What cable standard is used in North America?

    A. NTSC

    B. PAL

    C. SECAM

    D. DSL

4. How wide is the data channel used by cable providers?

    A. 5 MHz

    B. 6 MHz

    C. 7 Mhz

    D. 8 MHz

5. What is the most common flavor of DSL?

    A. ADSL

    B. HDSL

    C. VDSL

    D. SDSL

6. What flavor of DSL is commonly used as a replacement for standard leased T1 lines?

    A. ADSL

    B. HDSL

    C. VDSL

    D. SDSL

7. What is the most common type of DSL implementation and encapsulation?

A. PPP

B. Bridging

C. PPPoE

D. PPPoA

8. Where is the MPLS label placed in a frame?

A. Layer 1½

B. Layer 2½

C. Layer 3½

D. Layer 4½

9. What is the EXP field in a MPLS label used for?

A. Future use

B. Label tag ID

C. QoS bits

D. Label number in stack

10. What does PHP prevent?

A. Triple lookups

B. Double lookups

C. Single lookups

D. All lookups

Answers to Review Questions

1. B. Broadband cable gives the user more bandwidth.

2. C. HFC stands for hybrid fiber coax.

3. A. The NTSC standard is used in North America.

4. B. The channel is 6 MHz wide.

5. A. The most common flavor is ADSL.

6. B. HDSL is commonly used for T1 replacement.

7. C. PPPoE is the most common type used.

8. B. The MPLS label is placed between the Layer 2 and 3 headers, making it the Layer 2½ header.

9. C. The EXP field is used to carry QoS bits.

10. B. PHP prevents the last router from having to do a double lookup, one for the label and a second for the IP destination.

Chapter

12

Virtual Private Networks

IN THIS CHAPTER, YOU WILL LEARN HOW TO DO THE FOLLOWING:

- ✓ Explain the functions and operation of virtual private networks

- ✓ Describe the components and operations of IPsec VPNs and GRE tunnels

- ✓ Configure a site-to-site IPsec VPN/GRE tunnel with SDM (i.e., pre-shared key)

- ✓ Verify IPsec/GRE tunnel configurations (i.e., IOS CLI configurations)

- ✓ Describe and configure Cisco Easy VPN solutions using SDM

In this chapter, I introduce you to virtual private networks (VPNs) and to Cisco Easy VPN. I use the graphical tool, Cisco Security Device Manager, to configure a site-to-site VPN and a GRE tunnel. I also show you what a VPN configuration looks like from a command line perspective. And last, I show you troubleshooting tips and information.

For up-to-the-minute updates on this chapter, check out www.sybex.com/go/CiscoProGuidetoInternetworking or www.lammle.com.

Introduction to Virtual Private Networks

Virtual private network (VPN) is a term that is used frequently, but has different meanings, depending on who you talk to and the context of your discussion. Let's define what I mean here when I discuss VPNs. When I say VPN, I am talking about a method for connecting two disparate networks, generally over the Internet. Also, for the purposes of discussion, I also assume that the sessions will be encrypted sessions. IPsec is the standard that you will be using in this chapter. IPsec stands for IP Security and is based on a series of requests for comments (RFCs) that were first issued during the mid-to-late 1990s. The information gathered has been continually updated and is very much in use today. In most applications, this protocol works hand in hand with Generic Routing Encapsulation (GRE) to overcome some of the limitations of each protocol experiences on its own. But more about that later.

 Real World Scenario

Securely Connecting to Remote Offices and B2B Partners

In this chapter, you will use Cisco Security Device Manager to set up a site-to-site VPN tunnel and a GRE tunnel. FutureTech maintains MPLS networks, with remote routers on each side. They also maintain some VPN connections, since they have Internet connections, as well. You will implement the VPN connection to Dubai for the purposes of sending sensitive sales data from Dubai to headquarters.

IPsec

Today's IPsec is largely derived from the 1998 RFC 2401, which outlines an IPv4 implementation of IP Security. While a number of RFCs make up the suite as it is implemented, the following list is generally used. This is not meant to be an exhaustive list, but those that are typically used.

- Authentication Header (AH)

- Encapsulating Security Protocol (ESP)

- Internet Key Exchange (IKE)

- Internet Security Association and Key Management Protocol (ISAKMP)

- Hash Message Authentication Code (HMAC)

- Secure Hash Algorithm (SHA-1)

- Message Digest 5 (MD5)

- Triple Data Encryption Standard (3DES)

- Advanced Encryption Standard (AES)

Entire books could be written on IPsec—and have—so I'll just try to convey a few of the most important topics. For starters, let's talk about where the primary IPsec protocols live. By primary, I mean Authentication Header (AH) and Encapsulating Security Payload (ESP). If you look at the IP header diagram shown in Figure 12.1, you can see the highlighted protocol field. This is typically where you might see ICMP or TCP.

FIGURE 12.1   IP Header

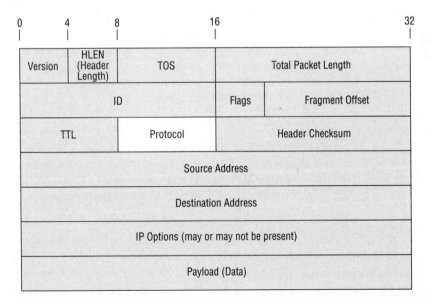

But there are other options for this field and that's where IPsec fits in. The more common IP types are listed in Table 12.1.

TABLE 12.1   Common IP Types

Designation	Type
ICMP	Protocol Type 1
TCP	Protocol Type 6
UDP	Protocol Type 17
ESP	Protocol Type 50
AH	Protocol Type 51

Let me give you a bit of background on the last two, ESP and AH, because they are the essence of IPsec.

Authentication Headers   The IP Authentication Header (AH) protocol is used to provide integrity and data origin authentication for IP datagrams in addition to optional, anti-replay capability. The anti-replay protection is only available if the receiver has the ability to perform a check on the sequence number (which was incremented by the sender). The authentication header provides an authentication for those fields in the IP header that don't typically change. For example, the AH would not know what the time-to-live (TTL) field would be when it arrives at the destination; therefore, that field would not be protected.

While there is still value in using the AH, there is a limitation of what can be done. The AH can be used by itself, or in conjunction with ESP, which we will talk about next.

Encapsulating Security Payloads   ESP can perform the same function as the AH, with the differences being in the fields that can be protected. Specifically, using ESP in tunnel mode can fully protect the entire IP header.

The Encapsulating Security Payload (ESP) is unique in that it is designed to work with both IPv4 and IPv6. As mentioned earlier, it may be used in tandem with AH or deployed in a stand-alone fashion. ESP is largely used in stand-alone mode in today's IPsec VPN tunnels. The reason is that ESP can provide multiple services with just a single protocol.

ESP can provide confidentiality using data encryption, authentication via a hash function, and a form of anti-replay capability.

ESP provides two methods of operation, tunnel mode and transport mode. Remember that I said that AH had some limitations? One of the ways that limitation is overcome with ESP is using tunnel mode. In tunnel mode, the ESP header is placed just before a completely encapsulated (encrypted) IP header. In transport mode, however, the ESP header is inserted after the IP header and before any upper layer protocol header. These modes are described in more detail later in this chapter.

Although you can select encryption (confidentiality) without authentication, this leaves the service open to certain vulnerabilities that would otherwise be closed if authentication were selected. This is the reason that most ESP implementations make use of both services.

 Real World Scenario

A GRE Tunnel for Voice Traffic

GRE tunnels can also be used when you need to connect offices, but not necessarily in a secure fashion. Voice traffic for users who work away from the office commonly needs this type of connection. Take a look at Figure 12.2. Here, FutureTech R&D engineers from the Dallas office, on router RND1, are connected to sales support staff in the New York office, on router MKT2. Now, let's configure the GRE tunnel to show how their voice traffic can tunnel across the MPLS cloud.

To configure a GRE tunnel on the source and destination routers and connect R&D to sales support, the tasks are:

1. Create a tunnel interface.

2. Assign an IP address to the tunnel interface.

3. Configure source and destination tunnel IP addresses.

4. Configure the tunnel as GRE mode.

5. Bring up the tunnel.

FIGURE 12.2 FutureTech GRE Tunnel

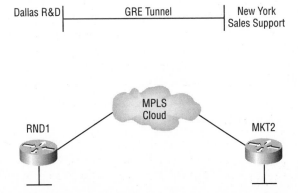

Generic Routing Encapsulation (GRE)

Generic Routing Encapsulation (GRE) is a way to tunnel IP traffic through another network. Invented by Cisco, it later became a standard.

So, why am I discussing it here and what is the relevance with respect to VPNs? GRE was once used as a way to connect like networks over a dissimilar network or series of networks. In the same fashion as a VPN tunnel, a GRE tunnel can also be used across the Internet to connect networks.

So, why not just use GRE tunnels instead of VPNs? GRE tunnels are not secure. That's why an encrypted tunnel, such as VPN, is more prevalently used.

Okay, so you're still wondering why I am telling you about them. Today, GRE tunnels can be used in conjunction with IPsec VPNs to carry routing protocols that cannot be natively carried over an IPsec VPN tunnel. This is the primary reason that you would want to do both.

Configuring a GRE Tunnel

So, let's get started! I want to take you through the configurations for setting up a GRE tunnel. First, you create a tunnel interface. It's similar to creating any other virtual interface, such as a loopback interface. Enter global configuration mode and perform the following configuration entry:

```
RND1(config)# interface tunnel 0
```

Once you have a new Tunnel 0 interface, enter interface configuration mode (on the new tunnel interface) and configure an IP address, just like any other interface.

```
RND1(config-if)#ip address 10.0.0.1 255.255.255.0
```

Go ahead and issue a no shutdown command so that the interface is ready for use. At this point, you might take notice that the state of the interface is in an up-down state. Note the following abbreviated output of a show ip interface brief command.

```
Tunnel0 10.0.1.1 YES manual up down
```

Next, you need to designate what the source and destination addresses will be. Again, under the Tunnel 0 interface, here is how you configure the source address.

```
RND1#configure terminal
RND1(config)#interface tunnel0
RND1(config-if)#tunnel source 10.0.0.1
```

It might seem redundant, but basically you need to tell the interface that it is the source address. While you are here, do the destination address as well. Here's how.

```
RND1(config-if)#tunnel destination 10.0.1.1
```

Last, you need to specify that you want the tunnel to be a GRE tunnel.

```
RND1(config-if)#tunnel mode gre
```

Of course, all of the commands you have used here need to be duplicated on the other side of the tunnel on MKT2.

At this point, your interface should have come up and you should be able to ping through from one end to the other.

VPN Operation

Now you know about the components of IPsec and types of VPNs, so let's jump into how it all works. First, I discuss generic operation and then get more specifically into how it works in the Cisco environment.

Obviously, you've read about a lot of different technology, but in order to make this a little more palatable, I can generically describe IPsec in just a few tasks. So let's summarize what those tasks involve. Assuming you have an existing configuration:

1. An IPsec process is started when traffic that is defined as interesting matches an existing policy.

   The interesting traffic is usually defined in terms of a source IP host or network and a destination IP host or network. This begins the IKE process.

2. IKE Phase 1 is initiated.

   What happens here is that the peers are authenticated and the IKE Security Associations (SAs) are negotiated. This, in turn, prepares for Phase 2 by setting up a secure channel. Phase 1 has two distinct modes that it uses: main mode and aggressive mode. The primary difference is that aggressive mode is faster. However, that speed comes with a cost. Aggressive mode is less secure because it uses only half of the key exchanges that main mode requires and some of those exchanges reveal information in cleartext.

3. In Phase 2, IPsec SAs are negotiated.

   At this point, you are able to transfer data. As long as data keeps flowing, the VPN will stay up.

When a Tunnel Goes Down

One of two things is usually the cause when a tunnel goes down. Either the SA is deleted or it times out because it has reached a previously configured timeout threshold.

Cisco-Specific Operation

Remember that I discussed interesting traffic in the first step for bringing up a VPN tunnel. Let's examine that from a Cisco perspective. If you have a Cisco router, you would have defined a specific access list that would determine source and destination traffic and would match a specific policy. When you defined the crypto map policy, you assigned the access list. Here's an example of what that access list might look like.

```
access-list 100 permit ip 192.168.23.0 0.0.0.255 192.168.24.0 0.0.0.255
```

And here's the entry in the crypto map that applies that access list.

```
match address 100
```

So, let's move on to IKE Phase 1.

IKE Phase 1

Remember that I said the purpose of IKE Phase 1 is to authenticate the IPsecIPsec peers and to set up a secure channel between the peers to enable IKE exchanges. The IKE parameters used are part of a policy. An example policy is shown below:

```
crypto isakmp policy 1
encr 3des
authentication pre-share
group 2
```

IKE Phase 2

During Phase 2, you have a protected IKE SA to use to negotiate an IPsec SA using parameters that were provided in the configuration. Those configuration parameters are listed next:

```
crypto ipsec transform-set ESP-3DES-SHA esp-3des esp-sha-hmac
crypto map SDM_CMAP_1 1 ipsec-isakmp
description Tunnel t010.100.1.1
set peer 10.100.1.1
set transform-set ESP-3DES-SHA
match address 100
```

Summing It Up

I've already talked about matching the access list, which gives you the interesting traffic. The only thing left is to send and receive data and to tear down the tunnel when finished (timeout).

So let's summarize the activity using Figure 12.3.

Configuring Site-to-Site VPN

Site-to-site VPN configuration is easily accomplished using the Cisco Security Device Manager (SDM). Once I show you how easy it is, you will get a look at configuring site-to-site VPN from a command line perspective as well.

FIGURE 12.3   Cisco IPsec

Does traffic match interesting traffic defined by Access-List?

↓

Have IPsec SAs been established?

↓

If IPsec is established, encrypt traffic based on policy and transmit.

↓

If IKE SA is not established, check for IKE policies and proceed with negotiation.

↓

If IKE SA is established, negotiation of the IPSsec SA is carried out as specified in policy,
then packet is encrypted and transmitted.

SDM Configuration

The SDM really makes things easy as far as doing the configuration, but there are many things to consider when you use SDM solely. So let's jump in and get started.

SDM Home

Figure 12.4 shows the Home screen. The Home screen opens whenever you bring up the SDM. If you've never used the SDM before, notice that you have a toolbar across the top for the operation you're going to perform and then within each menu item, you have choices along the left side of the screen. Looking at the About Your Router tab, you can see the type of router you're working with. In this case, a Cisco 2811 router is being used. On the Configuration Overview tab, you will find the number of interfaces on the router and their types, as well as which interfaces are actually configured. On this tab, you can also get information about the state of the firewall policies, VPNs, routing, intrusion prevention, interfaces and connections, and the like.

The SDM Configure Tool

Now, let me introduce the Configure tool. When you click the Configure button, you will notice the Tasks pane appears on the left side of the screen. Obviously, you want to choose VPN button. Once the VPN task is selected, you see the screen shown in Figure 12.5. Notice the way the configuration tasks are broken down by technologies.

The Site-to-Site VPN Wizard

Since you are going to build an IPsec site-to-site VPN, then choose Site to Site VPN from the task tree, as shown in Figure 12.6. As you can see in Figure 12.6, this leads you to a wizard that gives you a couple of options for the type of site-to-site VPN you'd like to build.

FIGURE 12.4 Cisco Router and Security Device Manager Home

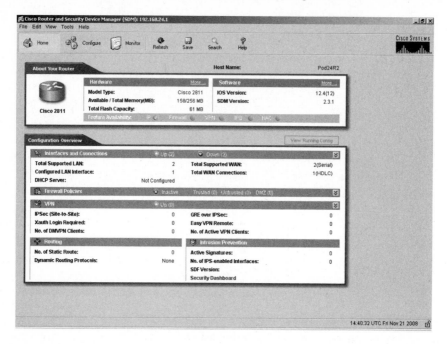

FIGURE 12.5 Cisco Router and Security Device Manager Configure VPN Task

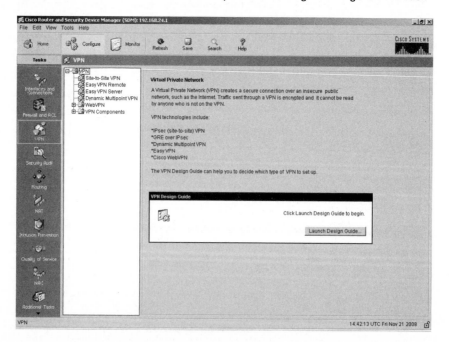

FIGURE 12.6   Cisco Router and Security Device Manager Create Site to Site VPN Tab

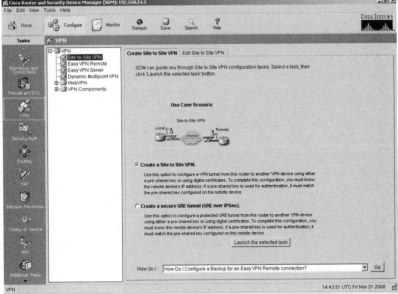

Choosing the Site to Site VPN task from the task tree takes you to the screen shown in Figure 12.7. Quick setup is the default option. Quick setup works well for this application, so go ahead and choose it. When you want to manually configure all the options yourself, choose Step by step wizard. From this screen, you can also view the default settings.

FIGURE 12.7   Cisco Router and Security Device Manager VPN Wizard

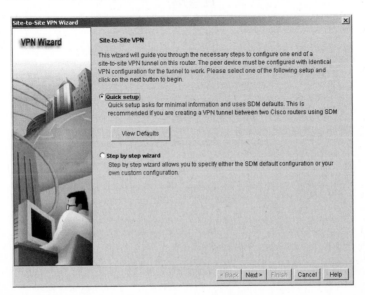

Selecting the Next button takes you to the screen shown in Figure 12.8, where you have a number of choices. Table 12.2 describes the options.

TABLE 12.2 VPN Connection Information Options

Option	Setting
Interface Selection	You can select which interface you want to you to terminate your VPN tunnel. The drop-down menu is limited to those interfaces that are configured and in an "up" status.
Peer Identity	This option selects the peer type and this is where you enter the remote peer IP address.
Authentication	This option is where you select either pre-shared key or digital certificate. For this exercise, select pre-shared key.
Traffic to Encrypt	Select the interface you will use to originate VPN traffic and which host/network will be passing through the VPN tunnel.

FIGURE 12.8 Cisco Router and Security Device Manager VPN Wizard Connection Information

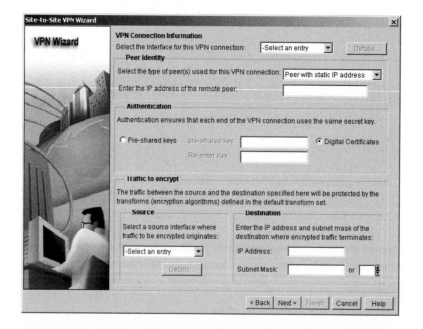

Figure 12.9 shows the choices I made. Notice that I used the Seria10/0/1 interface as the local peer. This interface is the entry point into the MPLS cloud. The local Ethernet port, FastEthernet0/0, is the point at which I chose to encrypt traffic locally destined for the remote network.

FIGURE 12.9 Cisco Router and Security Device Manager VPN Wizard Connection Information

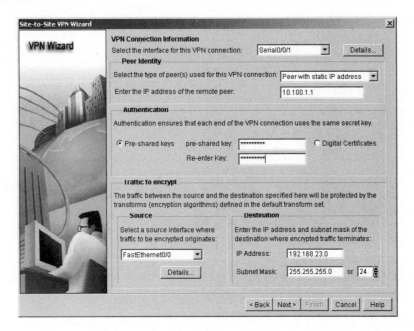

Now that you've entered your connection information, click the Next button and take a moment to review the summary page shown in Figure 12.10. Previously, I did not show you a screenshot of the default policies and settings, but if I had, you would see something similar to Figure 12.10.

When you click the Finish button, SDM sends the finished configuration to the router. The information you entered through the wizard equates to 26 commands for the router, as you can see in Figure 12.11.

And that's the configuration using SDM. Depending on your situation, you may have to configure a remote router as the other end of this VPN tunnel. But many times, the other end of the VPN tunnel is a business partner where you have no control over the configuration. That's why I show you some troubleshooting later on—to see some of the issues that come up when you deal with that kind of situation. In the next section, you explore what those same commands look like in Cisco IOS command line on the router.

FIGURE 12.10 Cisco Router and Security Device Manager VPN Wizard Summary of the Configuration

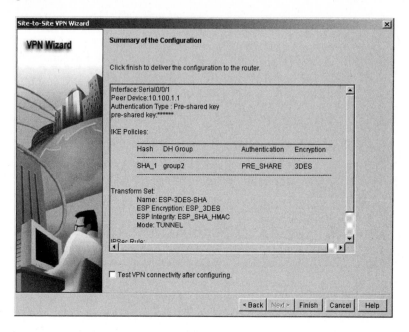

FIGURE 12.11 Cisco Router and Security Device Manager VPN Wizard Connection Information

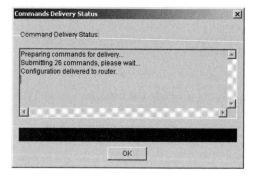

Verify and Troubleshoot VPN

Now that you've configured a VPN using the SDM, let's have a look at what the configurations look like in IOS Command Line Interface (CLI). For the purposes of this exercise,

I show you one end of the VPN tunnel that I configured. First, let's look at the ISAKMP policy that is shown below.

```
crypto isakmp policy 1
encr 3des
authentication pre-share
group 2
```

First, you can see that the wizard has created a policy with the numeric identifier of 1. The identifier could be any number, but the first one configured through the SDM wizard will be numbered 1. Next, the wizard specified 3DES as the encryption type. This is the default and is what you'll see if you don't specify something else using the wizard. You chose a pre-shared key for authentication. Last, the wizard specified group 2. This indicates that Diffie-Hellman Group 2 is being used. Diffie-Hellman Group 2 is 1024 bits, as opposed to the default, which is Diffie-Hellman Group 1 and 768 bits.

Moving right along, the next piece of the configuration is where you specified the pre-shared key and the remote side peer that you need to match up to. The pre-shared key is starred out, both here and when you used SDM as well. Note that pre-shared keys must match on both ends of the tunnel.

```
crypto isakmp key ********* address 10.100.1.1
```

Now, look at is the transform-set. The transform-set is where the wizard designated the type of authentication and encryption you will be using. The transform-set can be named virtually anything, but in this case, SDM named it esp-3des-sha. esp-3des-sha is descriptive in that it tells us what is in the transform-set. If you are using one device to set up VPN IPsec tunnels with multiple other sites, it is not uncommon to have multiple transform-sets defined and sometimes defined by the site that uses them. Of course, you can use any naming scheme you like. As I mentioned, in this case the transform-set defines 3DES as the encryption scheme used and SHA-HMAC as the authentication used.

```
crypto ipsec transform-set ESP-3DES-SHA esp-3des esp-sha-hmac
```

Next, the wizard define the crypto map. The first line of the configuration defines the type of crypto tunnel and names it. The name shown below in the configuration is the name defined by the SDM. Notice the optional description field shown, where the SDM took the remote IP and wrote a somewhat useful description. Next, the peer remote IP address was set. Notice that if you don't take the default, you can be more creative as to how the description is used. For instance, if FutureTech was setting up a tunnel from the HQ to Chicago, then you might call it TunneltoChicago or something like that.

The next line is used to determine which transform-set was actually used. Bear in mind, you could have multiple tunnels on the same router and, therefore, potentially multiple transform-sets. Last, the wizard specified your interesting traffic (the traffic that is allowed to traverse the tunnel) via an existing access list. I show the access list in a bit. In the crypto map, the wizard used a match statement to specify the access list to use.

```
crypto map SDM_CMAP_1 1 ipsec-isakmp
description Tunnel to10.100.1.1
set peer 10.100.1.1
set transform-set ESP-3DES-SHA
match address 100
```

And now take a look at the access-list 100 that is used to show the local-to-remote traffic that can traverse the tunnel.

```
access-list 100 permit ip 192.168.23.0 0.0.0.255 192.168.24.0 0.0.0.255
```

But hold on a minute! Is there something missing? What about the tunnel endpoint—don't we have to specify where the crypto map is applied? Indeed we do. If you will recall in the crypto map above, it was named SDM_CMAP_1. The wizard used that name to apply the crypto map to the appropriate interface, which in this case is Serial0/0/1.

```
interface Serial0/0/1
ip address 10.100.1.2 255.255.255.0
clock rate 2000000
crypto map SDM_CMAP_1
```

Okay, now you have seen a couple of things that the SDM can do for you. SDM automates a good bit of the work involved in creating an IPsec VPN. But you may want to use command line in order to change the options that are available. The choice is up to you.

VPN Troubleshooting

As you might imagine, a number of issues can come up when trying to ascertain the trouble when a VPN doesn't work correctly. I cover a number of the commands used when troubleshooting.

Checking the Crypto Map

To verify the crypto map, use a show command. (You can also show the running configuration.) Looking at your RND1 router, issue the show crypto map command.

```
RND1#show crypto map
Crypto Map "SDM_CMAP_1" 1 ipsec-isakmp
Description: Tunnel to10.100.1.1
Peer = 10.100.1.1
Extended IP access list 100
access-list 100 permit ip 192.168.23.0 0.0.0.255 192.168.24.0 0.0.0.255
Current peer: 10.100.1.1
Security association lifetime: 4608000 kilobytes/3600 seconds
```

```
PFS (Y/N): N
Transform sets={
ESP-3DES-SHA,
}
Interfaces using crypto map SDM_CMAP_1:
Serial0/0/1
```

The result tells you everything about the crypto map that is contained in the running configuration.

Checking Security Associations

Now let's move on to some other show commands. When using the command line interface, one of the primary ways to see what is happening with the VPN tunnel is to look at the ISAKMP security associations or SAs. See the below output from issuing the show crypto isakmp sa command. Note the state of MM_NO_STATE. This is not the normal state of a functioning VPN tunnel. The normal state is QM_IDLE.

```
RND1#show  crypto  isakmp sa
dst             src             state           conn-id slot status
10.100.1.1      10.100.1.2      MM_NO_STATE           1     0 ACTIVE
```

So let's explore this particular issue in depth. The usual issues that cause an MM_NO_STATE message are that the pre-shared keys don't match or that the interesting traffic doesn't match on both sides.

Besides doing a comparison of configurations, you will find that debug commands are your best friend. So, let's take a look at the issue at hand and try to do some troubleshooting using the debug commands.

First, turn on the crypto ipsec and isakmp debugs.

```
RND1#debug crypto isakmp
Crypto ISAKMP debugging is on
RND1#debug crypto ipsec
Crypto IPSEC debugging is on
```

To verify which debugging you have turned on, issue the show debug command, as shown in the code that follows.

```
RND1#show debug
Cryptographic Subsystem:
Crypto ISAKMP debugging is on
Crypto IPSEC debugging is on
```

Now that you have verified that debugging turned on, let's get into some troubleshooting. I've noted that there is an MM_NO_STATE in the state field, so I will be looking for some debug output that will give me an idea of the cause of the problem.

Let's assume the SA has completely timed out and there's nothing displayed when you do a show crypto ipsec sa command.

Now, source a ping command from one end of the tunnel to the other and watch what is displayed from a debug perspective.

```
*Nov 4 01:11:52.127: ISAKMP: New peer created peer = 0x45CE4878 peer_handle = 0x80000002
*Nov 4 01:11:52.127: ISAKMP: Locking peer struct 0x45CE4878, IKE refcount 1 for isakmp_initiator
*Nov 4 01:11:52.127: ISAKMP: local port 500, remote port 500
*Nov 4 01:11:52.127: ISAKMP: set new node 0 to QM_IDLE
*Nov 4 01:11:52.127: insert sa successfully sa = 44FACE7C
*Nov 4 01:11:52.127: ISAKMP:(0:0:N/A:0):Can not start Aggressive mode, trying Main mode.
*Nov 4 01:11:52.127: ISAKMP:(0:0:N/A:0):found peer pre-shared key matching 10.100.1.2
*Nov 4 01:11:52.127: ISAKMP:(0:0:N/A:0): constructed NAT-T vendor-07 ID
*Nov 4 01:11:52.127: ISAKMP:(0:0:N/A:0): constructed NAT-T vendor-03 ID
*Nov 4 01:11:52.127: ISAKMP:(0:0:N/A:0): constructed NAT-T vendor-02 ID
*Nov 4 01:11:52.127: ISAKMP:(0:0:N/A:0):Input = IKE_MESG_FROM_IPSEC, IKE_SA_REQ_MM
*Nov 4 01:11:52.131: ISAKMP:(0:0:N/A:0):Old State = IKE_READY New State = IKE_I_MM1
*Nov 4 01:11:52.131: ISAKMP:(0:0:N/A:0): beginning Main Mode exchange
*Nov 4 01:11:52.131: ISAKMP:(0:0:N/A:0): sending packet to 10.100.1.2 my_port 500 peer_port 500 (I) MM_NO_STATE
*Nov 4 01:11:52.179: ISAKMP (0:0): received packet from 10.100.1.2 dport 500 sport 500 Global (I) MM_NO_STATE
*Nov 4 01.:11:52.183: ISAKMP:(0:0:N/A:0):Input = IKE_MESG_FROM_PEER, IKE_MM_EXCH
*Nov 4 01:11:52.183: ISAKMP:(0:0:N/A:0):Old State = IKE_I_MM1 New State = IKE_I_MM2
*Nov 4 01:11:52.183: ISAKMP:(0:0:N/A:0): processing SA payload. message ID = 0
*Nov 4 01:11:52.183: ISAKMP:(0:0:N/A:0): processing vendor id payload
*Nov 4 01:11:52.183: ISAKMP:(0:0:N/A:0): vendor ID seems Unity/DPD but major 245 mismatch
*Nov 4 01:11:52.183: ISAKMP (0:0): vendor ID is NAT-T v7
*Nov 4 01:11:52.183: ISAKMP:(0:0:N/A:0):found peer pre-shared key matching 10.100.1.2
*Nov 4 01:11:52.183: ISAKMP:(0:0:N/A:0): local preshared key found
*Nov 4 01:11:52.183: ISAKMP : Scanning profiles for xauth . . .
*Nov 4 01:11:52.183: ISAKMP:(0:0:N/A:0):Checking ISAKMP transform 1 against priority 1 policy
*Nov 4 01:11:52.183: ISAKMP: encryption 3DES-CBC
*Nov 4 01:11:52.183: ISAKMP: hash SHA
*Nov 4 01:11:52.183: ISAKMP: default group 2
*Nov 4 01:11:52.183: ISAKMP: auth pre-share
```

*Nov 4 01:11:52.183: ISAKMP: life type in seconds

*Nov 4 01:11:52.183: ISAKMP: life duration (VPI) of 0x0 0x1 0x51 0x80

*Nov 4 01:11:52.183: ISAKMP:(0:0:N/A:0):atts are acceptable. Next payload is 0

*Nov 4 01:11:52.223: ISAKMP:(0:1:SW:1): processing vendor id payload

*Nov 4 01:11:52.223: ISAKMP:(0:1:SW:1): vendor ID seems Unity/DPD but major 245 mismatch

*Nov 4 01:11:52.223: ISAKMP (0:134217729): vendor ID is NAT-T v7

*Nov 4 01:11:52.223: ISAKMP:(0:1:SW:1):Input = IKE_MESG_INTERNAL, IKE_PROCESS_MAIN_MODE

*Nov 4 01:11:52.223: ISAKMP:(0:1:SW:1):Old State = IKE_I_MM2 New State = IKE_I_MM2

*Nov 4 01:11:52.223: ISAKMP:(0:1:SW:1): sending packet to 10.100.1.2 my_port 50peer_port 500 (I) MM_SA_SETUP

*Nov 4 01:11:52.2.23: ISAKMP:(0:1:SW:1):Input = IKE_MESG_INTERNAL, IKE_PROCESS_COMPLETE

*Nov 4 01:11:52.223: ISAKMP:(0:1:SW:1):Old State = IKE_I_MM2 New State = IKE_I_MM3

*Nov 4 01:11:52.283: ISAKMP (0:134217729): received packet from 10.100.1.2 dport 500 sport 500 Global (I) MM_SA_SETUP

*Nov 4 01:11:52.283: ISAKMP:(0:1:SW:1):Input = IKE_MESG_FROM_PEER, IKE_MM_EXCH

*Nov 4 01:11:52.283: ISAKMP:(0:1:SW:1):Old State = IKE_I_MM3 New State = IKE_I_MM4

*Nov 4 01:11:52.283: ISAKMP:(0:1:SW:1): processing KE payload. message ID = 0

*Nov 4 01:11:52.327: ISAKMP:(0:1:SW:1): processing NONCE payload. message ID =0

*Nov 4 01:11:52.327: ISAKMP:(0:1:SW:1):found peer pre-shared key matching 10.100.1.2

*Nov 4 01:11:52.331: ISAKMP:(0:1:SW:1):SKEYID state generated

*Nov 4 01:11:52.331: ISAKMP:(0:1:SW:1): processing vendor id payload

*Nov 4 01:11:52.331: ISAKMP:(0:1:SW:1): vendor ID is Unity

*Nov 4 01:11:52.331: ISAKMP:(0:1:SW:1): processing vendor id payload

*Nov 4 01:11:52.331: ISAKMP:(0:1:SW:1): vendor ID is DPD

*Nov 4 01:11:52.331: ISAKMP:(0:1:SW:1): processing vendor id payload

*Nov 4 01:11:52.331: ISAKMP:(0:1:SW:1): speaking to another IOS box!

*Nov 4 01:11:52.331: ISAKMP:(0:1:SW:1):Input = IKE_MESG_INTERNAL, IKE_PROCESS_MAIN_MODE

*Nov 4 01:11:52.331: ISAKMP:(0:1:SW:1):Old State = IKE_I_MM4 New State = IKE_I_MM4

*Nov 4 01:11:52.331: ISAKMP:(0:1:SW:1):Send initial contact

*Nov 4 01:11:52.331: ISAKMP:(0:1:SW:1):SA is doing pre-shared key authentication using id type ID_IPV4_ADDR

*Nov 4 01:11:52.331: ISAKMP (0:134217729): ID payload

next-payload : 8

type : 1

address : 10.100.1.1

protocol : 17

port : 500

```
length : 12
*Nov 4 01:11:52.331: ISAKMP:(0:1:SW.:1):Total payload length: 12
*Nov 4 01:11:52.335: ISAKMP:(0:1:SW:1): sending packet to 10.100.1.2 my_port 500
peer_port 500 (I) MM_KEY_EXCH
*Nov 4 01:11:52.335: ISAKMP:(0:1:SW:1):Input = IKE_MESG_INTERNAL, IKE_PROCESS_
COMPLETE
*Nov 4 01:11:52.335: ISAKMP:(0:1:SW:1):Old State = IKE_I_MM4 New State = IKE_I_MM5
*Nov 4 01:11:52.339: ISAKMP (0:134217729): received packet from 10.100.1.2 dport
500 sport 500 Global (I) MM_KEY_EXCH
*Nov 4 01:11:52.339: ISAKMP (0:134217729): received packet from 10.100.1.2 dport
500 sport 500 Global (I) MM_KEY_EXCH
*Nov 4 01:11:52.339: ISAKMP (0:134217729): received packet from 10.100.1.2 dport
500 sport 500 Global (I) MM_KEY_EXCH
*Nov 4 01:11:52.343: ISAKMP (0:134217729): received packet from 10.100.1.2 dport
500 sport 500 Global (I) MM_KEY_EXCH
*Nov 4 01:11:52.343: ISAKMP (0:134217729): received packet from 10.100.1.2 dport
500 sport 500 Global (I) MM_KEY_EXCH
*Nov 4 01:11:52.343: ISAKMP: Info Notify message requeue retry counter exceeded
sa request from 10.100.1.2 to 10.100.1.1 . . .
Success rate is 0 percent (0/5)
RND1#
```

Okay, it certainly looks like a bunch of gobbledegook, doesn't it? I'm not going to go through it line by line, but let me point out a couple of key things. One, take a look at something that shows that at least part of the debug is displaying correct behavior and that is the line above that says atts are acceptable. If you look right above that line, you will see the IKE (Cisco calls this ISAKMP) configuration. But let's move toward the end of the debug output and look where the problems are. Note the MM_KEY_EXCH entry that repeats itself many times. Kind of looks familiar, doesn't it? This indicates that the key exchange failed.

Let's look at a different type of failure to see what changes. In this case, a fault condition had been configured that prevented the VPN from coming up. Again, issue a ping from one end of the tunnel and watch the debug output.

```
*Nov 4 03:17:42.355: IPSEC(sa_request): ,
(key eng. msg.) OUTBOUND local= 10.100.1.1, remote= 10.100.1.2,
local_proxy= 192.168.23.0/255.255.255.0/0/0 (type=4),
remote_proxy= 192.168.24.0/255.255.255.0/0/0 (type=4),
protocol= ESP, transform= esp-3des esp-sha-hmac (Tunnel),
lifedur= 3600s and 4608000kb,
spi= 0x5449DE2B(1414127147), conn_id= 0, keysize= 0, flags= 0x400A
*Nov 4 03:17:42.359: ISAKMP: received ke message (1/1)
*Nov 4 03:17:42.359: ISAKMP:(0:0:N/A:0): SA request profile is (NULL)
*Nov 4 03:17:42.359: ISAKMP: Created a peer struct for 10.100.1.2, peer port 50 0
```

```
*Nov 4 03:17:42.359: ISAKMP: New peer created peer = 0x45CECB28 peer_handle = 0
x80000006
*Nov 4 03:17:42.359: ISAKMP: Locking peer struct 0x45CECB28, IKE refcount 1 for
isakmp_initiator
*Nov 4 03:17:42.359: ISAKMP: local port 500, remote port 500
*Nov 4 03:17:42.359: ISAKMP: set new node 0 to QM_IDLE
*Nov 4 03:17:42.359: insert sa successfully sa = 44FACE7C
*Nov 4 03:17:42.359: ISAKMP:(0:0:N/A:0):Can not start Aggressive mode, trying
Main mode.
*Nov 4 03:17:42.359: ISAKMP:(0:0:N/A:0):found peer pre-shared key matching 10.1
00.1.2
*Nov 4 03:17:42.359: ISAKMP:(0:0:N/A:0): constructed NAT-T vendor-07 ID
*Nov 4 03:17:42.359: ISAKMP:(0:0:N/A:0): constructed NAT-T vendor-03 ID
*Nov 4 03:17:42.359: ISAKMP:(0:0:N/A:0): constructed NAT-T vendor-02 ID
*Nov 4 03:17:42.359: ISAKMP:(0:0:N/A:0):Input = IKE_MESG_FROM_IPSEC, IKE_SA_REQ_MM
*Nov 4 03:17:42.359: ISAKMP:(0:0:N/A:0):Old State = IKE_READY New State = IKE_I_MM1
*Nov 4 03:17:42.359: ISAKMP:(0:0:N/A:0): beginning Main Mode exchange
*Nov 4 03:17:42.359: ISAKMP:(0:0:N/A:0): sending packet to 10.100.1.2 my_port
500 peer_port 500 (I) MM_NO_STATE
*Nov 4 03:17:42.411: ISAKMP (0:0): received packet from 10.100.1.2 dport 500
sport 500 Global (I) MM_NO_STATE
*Nov 4 03.:17:42.411: ISAKMP:(0:0:N/A:0):Input = IKE_MESG_FROM_PEER, IKE_MM_EXCH
*Nov 4 03:17:42.411: ISAKMP:(0:0:N/A:0):Old State = IKE_I_MM1 New State = IKE_I_MM2
*Nov 4 03:17:42.411: ISAKMP:(0:0:N/A:0): processing SA payload. message ID = 0
*Nov 4 03:17:42.411: ISAKMP:(0:0:N/A:0): processing vendor id payload
*Nov 4 03:17:42.411: ISAKMP:(0:0:N/A:0): vendor ID seems Unity/DPD but major
245 mismatch
*Nov 4 03:17:42.411: ISAKMP (0:0): vendor ID is NAT-T v7
*Nov 4 03:17:42.411: ISAKMP:(0:0:N/A:0):found peer pre-shared key matching
10.100.1.2
*Nov 4 03:17:42.411: ISAKMP:(0:0:N/A:0): local preshared key found
*Nov 4 03:17:42.411: ISAKMP : Scanning profiles for xauth . . .
*Nov 4 03:17:42.411: ISAKMP:(0:0:N/A:0):Checking ISAKMP transform 1 against
priority 1 policy
*Nov 4 03:17:42.411: ISAKMP: encryption 3DES-CBC
*Nov 4 03:17:42.411: ISAKMP: hash SHA
*Nov 4 03:17:42.411: ISAKMP: default group 2
*Nov 4 03:17:42.411: ISAKMP: auth pre-share
*Nov 4 03:17:42.411: ISAKMP: life type in seconds
*Nov 4 03:17:42.411: ISAKMP: life duration (VPI) of 0x0 0x1 0x51 0x80
```

```
*Nov 4 03:17:42.415: ISAKMP:(0:0:N/A:0):atts are acceptable. Next payload is 0
*Nov 4 03:17:42.451: ISAKMP:(0:1:SW:1): processing vendor id payload
*Nov 4 03:17:42.451: ISAKMP:(0:1:SW:1): vendor ID seems Unity/DPD but major 245
mismatch
*Nov 4 03:17:42.451: ISAKMP (0:134217729): vendor ID is NAT-T v7
*Nov 4 03:17:42.451: ISAKMP:(0:1:SW:1):Input = IKE_MESG_INTERNAL, IKE_PROCESS_
MAIN_MODE
*Nov 4 03:17:42.451: ISAKMP:(0:1:SW:1):Old State = IKE_I_MM2 New State = IKE_I_MM2
*Nov 4 03:17:42.451: ISAKMP:(0:1:SW:1): sending packet to 10.100.1.2 my_port
500 peer_port 500 (I) MM_SA_SETUP
*Nov 4 03:17:42.4.55: ISAKMP:(0:1:SW:1):Input = IKE_MESG_INTERNAL, IKE_PROCESS_
COMPLETE
*Nov 4 03:17:42.455: ISAKMP:(0:1:SW:1):Old State = IKE_I_MM2 New State = IKE_I_MM3
*Nov 4 03:17:42.511: ISAKMP (0:134217729): received packet from 10.100.1.2
dport 500 sport 500 Global (I) MM_SA_SETUP
*Nov 4 03:17:42.511: ISAKMP:(0:1:SW:1):Input = IKE_MESG_FROM_PEER, IKE_MM_EXCH
*Nov 4 03:17:42.511: ISAKMP:(0:1:SW:1):Old State = IKE_I_MM3 New State = IKE_I_MM4
*Nov 4 03:17:42.511: ISAKMP:(0:1:SW:1): processing KE payload. message ID = 0
*Nov 4 03:17:42.555: ISAKMP:(0:1:SW:1): processing NONCE payload. message ID =
0
*Nov 4 03:17:42.559: ISAKMP:(0:1:SW:1):found peer pre-shared key matching 10.10
0.1.2
*Nov 4 03:17:42.559: ISAKMP:(0:1:SW:1):SKEYID state generated
*Nov 4 03:17:42.559: ISAKMP:(0:1:SW:1): processing vendor id payload
*Nov 4 03:17:42.559: ISAKMP:(0:1:SW:1): vendor ID is Unity
*Nov 4 03:17:42.559: ISAKMP:(0:1:SW:1): processing vendor id payload
*Nov 4 03:17:42.559: ISAKMP:(0:1:SW:1): vendor ID is DPD
*Nov 4 03:17:42.559: ISAKMP:(0:1:SW:1): processing vendor id payload
*Nov 4 03:17:42.559: ISAKMP:(0:1:SW:1): speaking to another IOS box!
*Nov 4 03:17:42.559: ISAKMP:(0:1:SW:1):Input = IKE_MESG_INTERNAL, IKE_PROCESS_
MAIN_MODE
*Nov 4 03:17:42.559: ISAKMP:(0:1:SW:1):Old State = IKE_I_MM4 New State = IKE_I_MM4
*Nov 4 03:17:42.559: ISAKMP:(0:1:SW:1):Send initial contact
*Nov 4 03:17:42.559: ISAKMP:(0:1:SW:1):SA is doing pre-shared key authentication
using id type ID_IPV4_ADDR
*Nov 4 03:17:42.559: ISAKMP (0:134217729): ID payload
next-payload : 8
type : 1
address : 10.100.1.1
protocol : 17
port : 500
```

length : 12

*Nov 4 03:17:42.559: ISAKMP:(0:1:SW.:1):Total payload length: 12

*Nov 4 03:17:42.563: ISAKMP:(0:1:SW:1): sending packet to 10.100.1.2 my_port
500 peer_port 500 (I) MM_KEY_EXCH

*Nov 4 03:17:42.563: ISAKMP:(0:1:SW:1):Input = IKE_MESG_INTERNAL, IKE_PROCESS_
COMPLETE

*Nov 4 03:17:42.563: ISAKMP:(0:1:SW:1):Old State = IKE_I_MM4 New State = IKE_I_MM5

*Nov 4 03:17:42.571: ISAKMP (0:134217729): received packet from 10.100.1.2
dport 500 sport 500 Global (I) MM_KEY_EXCH

*Nov 4 03:17:42.575: ISAKMP:(0:1:SW:1): processing ID payload. message ID = 0

*Nov 4 03:17:42.575: ISAKMP (0:134217729): ID payload

next-payload : 8

type : 1

address : 10.100.1.2

protocol : 17

port : 500

length : 12

*Nov 4 03:17:42.575: ISAKMP:(0:1:SW:1):: peer matches *none* of the profiles

*Nov 4 03:17:42.575: ISAKMP:(0:1:SW:1): processing HASH payload. message ID = 0

*Nov 4 03:17:42.575: ISAKMP:(0:1:SW:1):SA authentication status: authenticated

*Nov 4 03:17:42.575: ISAKMP:(0:1:SW:1):SA has been authenticated with 10.100.1.
2

*Nov 4 03:17:42.575: ISAKMP: Trying to insert a peer 10.100.1.1/10.100.1.2/500/
, and inserted successfully 45CECB28.

*Nov 4 03:17:42.575: ISAKMP:(0:1:SW:1):Input = IKE_MESG_FROM_PEER, IKE_MM_EXCH

*Nov 4 03:17:42.575: ISAKMP:(0:1:SW:1):Old State = IKE_I_MM5 New State = IKE_I_MM6

*Nov 4 03:17:42.575: ISAKMP:(0:1:SW:1):Input = IKE_MESG_INTERNAL, IKE_PROCESS_
MAIN_MODE

*Nov 4 03:17:42.575: ISAKMP:(0:1:SW:1):Old State = IKE_I_MM6 New State = IKE_I_MM6

*Nov 4 03:17:42.579: ISAKMP:(0:1:SW:1):Input = IKE_MESG_INTERNAL, IKE_PROCESS_
COMPLETE

*Nov 4 03:17:42.579: ISAKMP:(0:1:SW:1):Old State = IKE_I_MM6 New State = IKE_P1_
COMPLETE

*Nov 4 03:17:42.579: ISAKMP:(0:1:SW:1):beginning Quic.k Mode exchange, M-ID of
-1948338380

*Nov 4 03:17:42.579: ISAKMP:(0:1:SW:1): sending packet to 10.100.1.2 my_port
500 peer_port 500 (I) QM_IDLE

*Nov 4 03:17:42.579: ISAKMP:(0:1:SW:1):Node -1948338380, Input = IKE_MESG_
INTERNAL, IKE_INIT_QM

*Nov 4 03:17:42.579: ISAKMP:(0:1:SW:1):Old State = IKE_QM_READY New State = IKE_
QM_I_QM1

*Nov 4 03:17:42.583: ISAKMP:(0:1:SW:1):Input = IKE_MESG_INTERNAL, IKE_PHASE1_
COMPLETE

```
*Nov 4 03:17:42.583: ISAKMP:(0:1:SW:1):Old State = IKE_P1_COMPLETE New State =
IKE_P1_COMPLETE
*Nov 4 03:17:42.591: ISAKMP (0:134217729): received packet from 10.100.1.2
dport 500 sport 500 Global (I) QM_IDLE
*Nov 4 03:17:42.591: ISAKMP: set new node -614552533 to QM_IDLE
*Nov 4 03:17:42.591: ISAKMP:(0:1:SW:1): processing HASH payload. message ID = -
614552533
*Nov 4 03:17:42.591: ISAKMP:(0:1:SW:1): processing NOTIFY PROPOSAL_NOT_CHOSEN
protocol 3
spi 1414127147, message ID = -614552533, sa = 44FACE7C
*Nov 4 03:17:42.591: ISAKMP:(0:1:SW:1): deleting spi 1414127147 message ID =
-1948338380
*Nov 4 03:17:42.591: ISAKMP:(0:1:SW:1):deleting node -1948338380 error TRUE
reason "Delete Larval"
*Nov 4 03:17:42.591: ISAKMP:(0:1:SW:1):deleting node -614552533 error FALSE
reason "Informational (in) state 1"
*Nov 4 03:17:42.591: ISAKMP:(0:1:SW:1):Input = IKE_MESG_FROM_PEER, IKE_INFO_NOTIFY
*Nov 4 03:17:42.591: ISAKMP:(0:1:SW:1):Old State = IKE_P1_COMPLETE New State =
IKE_P1_COMPLETE
.

Success rate is 0 percent (0/5)
```

Once again, you see the atts are acceptable message, meaning that you matched an IKE policy. But a couple of things don't look right later on.

The first thing that looks wrong is peer matches *none* of the profiles line. Okay, you have an issue there. The other thing is a little later in the debug that says PROPSAL NOT CHOSEN. This would lead us to believe that something didn't match when an IPsec SA was set up. Often when you are setting up a VPN tunnel with a third party, you don't necessarily have access to the other side of the tunnel. Recognize the problem in the future when you run into it.

You have covered just a couple of the potential issues that could come up when troubleshooting a site-to-site VPN. There are many others to deal with. One of the best ways to help troubleshoot is to turn on debug, as I illustrated. If you see an error message that you aren't familiar with, check the Cisco Web site under Support and see if you can find out what that exact error message means. Set up a few of these tunnels and, over time, you will become very acquainted with specific issues.

Cisco Easy VPN

Because doing VPNs requires a great deal of coordination and expertise, Cisco saw the need for a method of reducing a good bit of the administrative burden in configuring VPNs. Enter Cisco Easy VPN.

Cisco Easy VPN has a number of benefits over manual configuration.

- Centralized control over security policy
- Reduced dependence on remote access equipment
- No need for client PC software installations
- VPN configurations held on central server
- Dynamic end user administration

Let's talk a little about the architecture of Cisco Easy VPN. It resembles a typical client-server application; however, the server in this case can be any number of network devices such as a Cisco IOS router, Cisco PIX or ASA firewall, or VPN Concentrator. The client can also be any of these devices, but also includes host workstations, such as those running Windows, MacOS X, and Linux, for remote access applications. The key is that the devices in question must support the Cisco Unity Client Protocol, which allows the majority of VPN administration to be defined on the Cisco Easy VPN server.

Three types of operations are supported with Cisco Easy VPN.

Client Mode   This is generally for remote access. NATs or Port Address Translations (PATs) are in use here and this is similar to the Cisco VPN client in terms of functionality.

Network Extension Mode   This configuration allows hosts at the remote end to have routable addresses within the network.

Network Extension Plus Mode   This is the same as network extension mode, except that an additional IP is configured as a loopback address. This IP can then be used for trouble-shooting or remote administration.

All three methods allow for split-tunneling, which means that users and devices can reach all resources on the local subnet, in addition to being able to access network resources on the other side of the VPN tunnel.

Configuring Cisco Easy VPN

Let's now use the SDM to configure a Cisco Easy VPN. Once again, in Figure 12.12, you see the familiar SDM Configure screen. In this case, you are going to configure the router as an Easy VPN Server.

Notice that, in order to configure an Easy VPN Server, you must have AAA enabled. For the purposes of this exercise, I have enabled AAA. I will tell you more about AAA in Chapter 13, "Device Security." So at this point, just be sure AAA is enabled and then click the Launch Easy VPN Server Wizard button to start the process.

The splash screen shown in Figure 12.13 gives you a summary of what you're going to be configuring in the upcoming screens. Take a moment to review it and then click the Next button.

Similar to what you did to configure a VPN tunnel, you must select the proper interface to use for this VPN. In this case, as shown in Figure 12.14, use the FastEthernet0/0 interface. Again, for Authentication, select Pre-Shared key and then click Next.

FIGURE 12.12   Cisco Router and Security Device Manager Create Easy VPN Server Tab

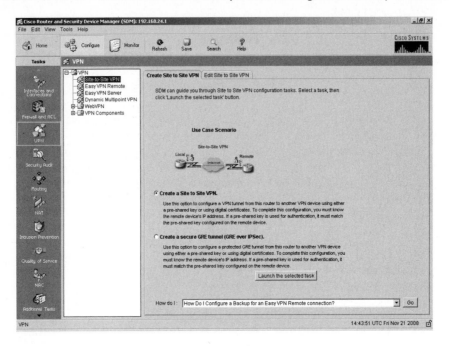

FIGURE 12.13   Cisco Router and Security Device Manager Create Easy VPN Server Wizard

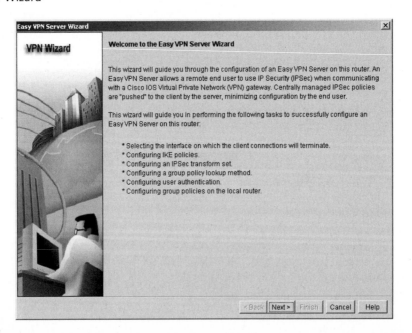

FIGURE 12.14   Cisco Router and Security Device Manager Create Easy VPN Server Interface and Authentication

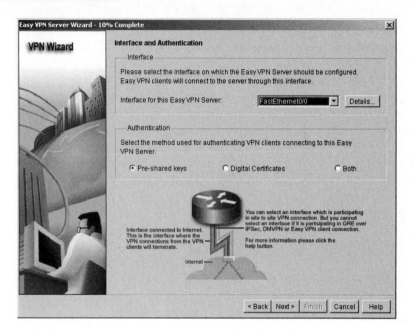

The next screen defines what you'd like to configure as far as IKE proposals. In this case, take the defaults: 3DES for encryption, SHA_1 as the hash, and pre-shared key as the type of authentication, as shown in Figure 12.15.

FIGURE 12.15   Cisco Router and Security Device Manager Create Easy VPN IKE Proposals

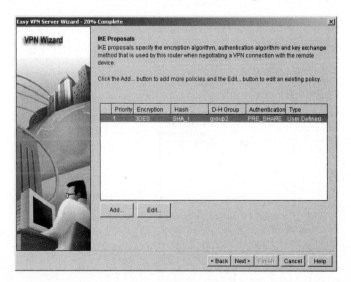

The next screen, shown in Figure 12.16, defines the Transform Set to be used. Just as when you configured a site-to-site VPN, select the default setting, which is `ESP-3DES` for encryption and `ESP-SHA-HMAC` for ESP Integrity.

You might be noticing a pattern here—the SDM makes it very easy to configure and the defaults mean that you don't even have to specify anything. Just choose and go.

FIGURE 12.16   Cisco Router and Security Device Manager Create Easy VPN Server Transform Set

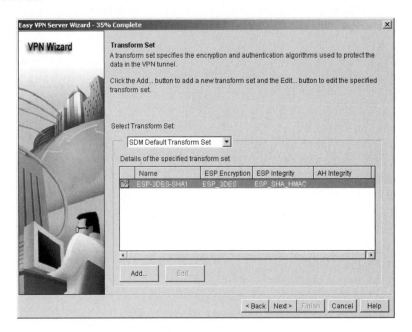

The next screen, shown in Figure 12.17, designates the group authorization and group policy choices. This might seem familiar to you, if you've every configured a VPN concentrator. All of these choices must be configured, if you are setting up a VPN concentrator for remote access. In similar fashion, you need to do the same here. Remember that you had to turn on AAA services in order to get to this option. Here you choose whether to make use of a local database on this server, use an existing or new RADIUS server, or use both services. RADIUS stands for Remote Authentication Dial-In User Service. It evolved from the early days of the Internet, when thousands of remote dial-in users were connecting. There had to be a database of users that could be used to authenticate each connection. RADIUS served that need. Today's RADIUS is built into some operating systems and can be stand-alone third-party services as well.

For the purposes of this exercise, select a local database, in order to keep this simple. Also, assume that you don't have an existing RADIUS server.

The Extended User Authentication or XAuth, is shown in Figure 12.18. For this exercise, you will need to select Local Only authentication.

FIGURE 12.17 Cisco Router and Security Device Manager Create Easy VPN Server Group Authorization and Group Policy Lookup

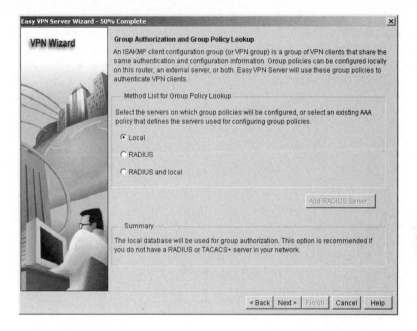

FIGURE 12.18 Cisco Router and Security Device Manager Create Easy VPN Server XAuth

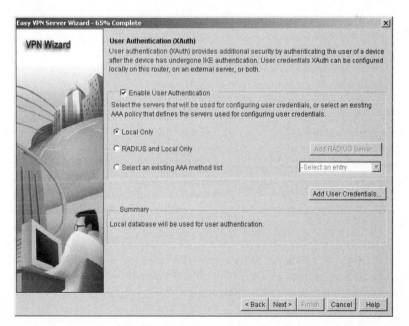

Group policies and group authorization settings are shown in Figure 12.19. Again, this is largely used for remote users. Add a placeholder default group policy by selecting the Add button.

FIGURE 12.19   Cisco Router and Security Device Manager Create Easy VPN Server Group Authorization and User Group Policies

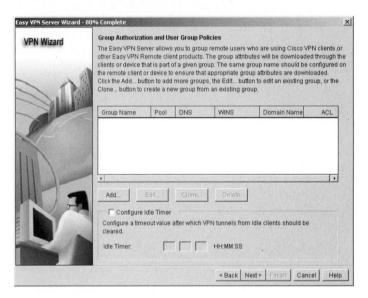

Once you click the Add button from the previous screen, you will see the screen shown in Figure 12.20. This screen has several tabs. The General tab gives you the opportunity to make pre-shared keys and IP DHCP pool assignments. These are the kind of assignments you need to make for VPN clients and other remote clients.

The DNS/WINS screen shown in Figure 12.21 is pretty self-explanatory. Here you can enter DNS and WINS servers that you would like to make available to remote users.

The Split Tunneling tab of the Group Policy creation page is shown in Figure 12.22. Split tunneling is important if you want to be able to access local resources at the same time you are accessing the remote resources. To enable split tunneling, click the check box and define the networks that you would like to be able to access locally.

Moving right along to the Client Settings tab, pictured in Figure 12.23, you can make policy settings specifically for a client. You can configure the backup servers to be used in the event the primary Easy VPN Server is unavailable. Next, if you enforce local firewalls on the client, then select that option. The two local firewall options that are supported are Zone Alarm and Black Ice.

Remember that you just had the option to configure split tunneling. Well, suppose you just wanted the local network that a remote user was on. There is a check box here on this screen that allows you to do just that, without configuring split tunneling explicitly. And the last option on this screen is Perfect Forward Secrecy. Only configure this if you have specified this at the server level.

FIGURE 12.20   Cisco Router and Security Device Manager Create Easy VPN Server Add Group Policy

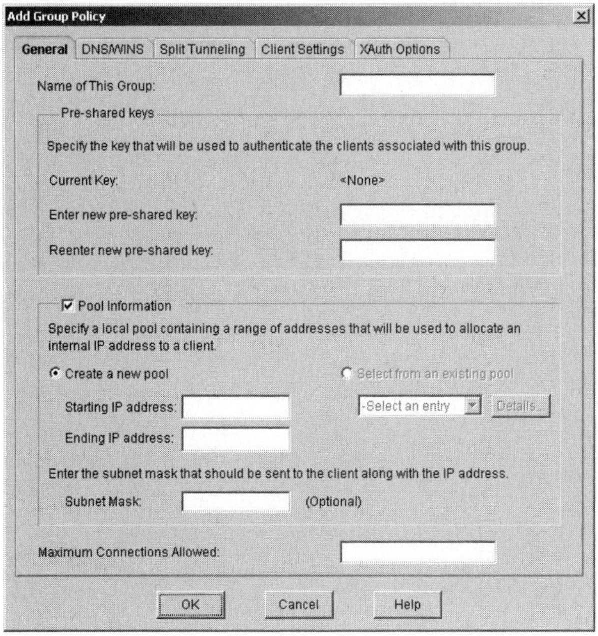

FIGURE 12.21   Cisco Router and Security Device Manager Create Easy VPN Server Add Group Policy DNS/WINS

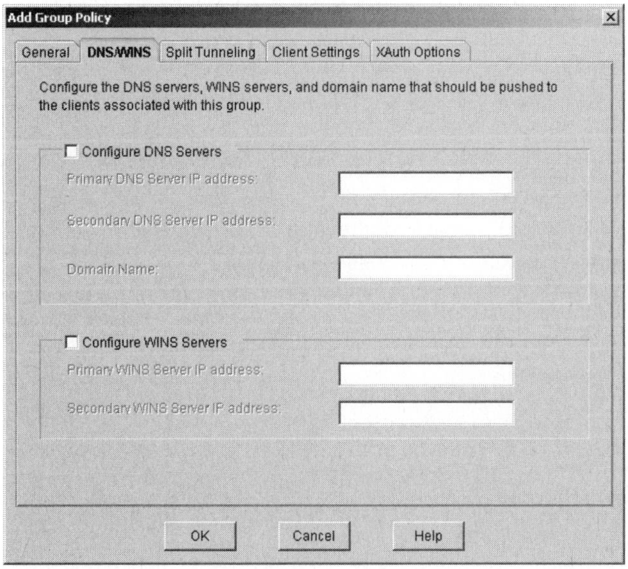

FIGURE 12.22   Cisco Router and Security Device Manager Create Easy VPN Server Add Group Policy Split Tunneling

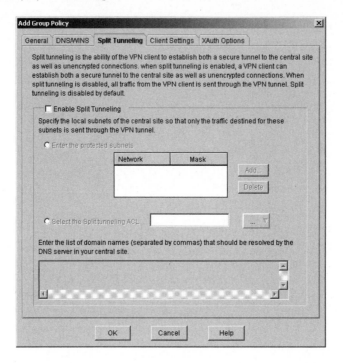

FIGURE 12.23   Cisco Router and Security Device Manager Create Easy VPN Server Add Group Policy Client Settings

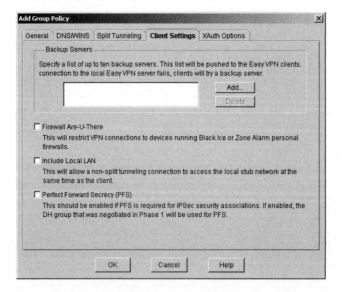

The last tab on the Group Policy screen is for XAuth Options, shown in Figure 12.24. The options here allow you to to lock users into certain groups and to save your password.

FIGURE 12.24 Cisco Router and Security Device Manager Create Easy VPN Server Add Group Policy XAuth Options

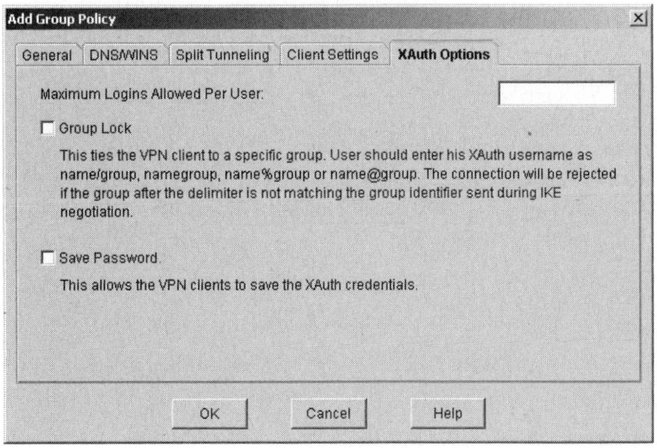

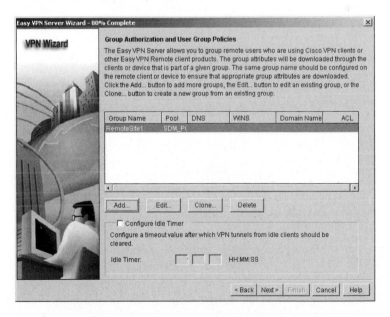

Take a look at Figure 12.25. Notice that you have added your group policy. It shows up in the policy window. Again, in this case, you have not specified any particular parameters for your policy.

FIGURE 12.25 Cisco Router and Security Device Manager Create Easy VPN Server Group Authorization and User Group Policies

And last, as before, a summary list of the configuration, as shown in Figure 12.26, is displayed. After completing the server portion, of course, you would have to do the remote devices as well, by going back to the beginning and choosing the tree selection Easy VPN Remote, instead of Easy VPN Server.

FIGURE 12.26   Cisco Router and Security Device Manager Create Easy VPN Server Configuration Summary

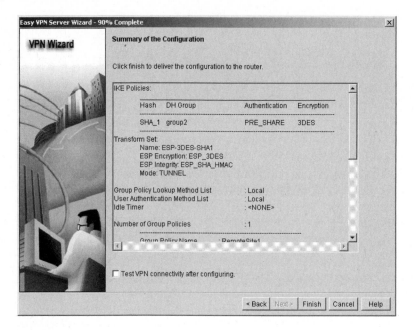

And once again, the wizard has delivered the commands to the router via SDM, as shown in Figure 12.27.

FIGURE 12.27   Cisco Router and Security Device Manager Create Easy VPN Server Commands Delivery Status

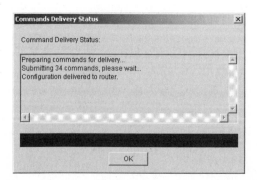

If you click the OK button from the delivery screen, you are taken back to the Easy VPN Server Edit tab shown in Figure 12.28. You can now see the Easy VPN Server that you have just configured. At this point, you have the option to add another one, edit the existing one, or delete it.

FIGURE 12.28   Cisco Router and Security Device Manager Create Easy VPN Server Edit Tab

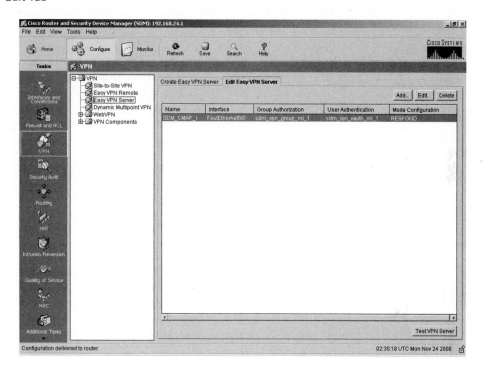

Redundant Connections and Equipment

VPNs are starting to become mission critical in today's business world. For that reason, it is important to cover a few of the techniques and technology used to keep those connections available at all times.

The concept of having redundant Internet Service Provider (ISP) connections is a design consideration that is important for a number of reasons. Generally, when you have more than one ISP connection to your network, you would use BGP (see Chapter 7, "Exterior Routing Protocols," for more information). Next, if you want to have VPN redundancy, this generally means having more than one network device available for this connectivity. You saw in the Easy VPN server configuration that you could configure multiple servers to give to the client. Depending on how large your network is and how diverse you want to be, you may want to have equipment in multiple geographical locations, as well as redundant equipment at your primary location.

Dead Peer Detection

The Dead Peer Detection (DPD) periodic message option is a feature that was first introduced in Cisco IOS version 12.3(7)T. It is a configurable option that allows routers to periodically send a Hello message to determine whether a peer is alive. This is an improvement over the default behavior, which only sends a Hello when it has traffic destined for the VPN tunnel. DPD can be useful when you have multiple Easy VPN servers configured and also when you are using GRE over an IPsec VPN to carry routing updates. Obviously, the quicker that a peer is marked dead, the more responsive the routing will be.

Redundant Routes

Last, while I am on the subject of routing, let's talk a bit about how redundant routes can be used in conjunction with VPN technology. If I configured a GRE over IPsec tunnel and gave it a lower administrative cost, then I could have a backup route available over VPN traversing the Internet without the cost of an additional circuit. There is also a floating static route that can also be used. A floating static route was previously used when doing Dial-on-Demand services such as ISDN. If we were not using a routing protocol such as EIGRP, a backup "floating static route" can be configured with a higher administrative distance, which would come into play if the original route was unavailable. Check back in Chapter 4, "Routing Concepts and Distance Vector Routing Protocols," for more details about configuring EIGRP and floating static routes. Additional information on these topics is available on Cisco's Web site in the Support section.

Summary

In this chapter, you learned about IPsec and used it to configure a VPN using the Cisco Security Device Manager. You also learned about and configured a GRE tunnel using SDM. Then, you dissected the VPN configuration in the command line and learned some troubleshooting techniques. And last, you used SDM to configure an Easy VPN server. Although there are many things to learn about VPNs, I covered the basic techniques and knowledge you need to get started with configuring your networks with VPN. Now, let's move on to device security.

Review Questions

1. Which IPsec protocol does both encryption and authentication?
    - **A.** AH
    - **B.** ESP
    - **C.** PPTP
    - **D.** GRE

2. What is the default encryption type when using SDM to configure an IPsec VPN tunnel?
    - **A.** DES
    - **B.** AES
    - **C.** 3DES
    - **D.** RSA

3. When an IPsec VPN tunnel is configured, how does the router determine what traffic is to traverse the VPN tunnel?
    - **A.** Policy map
    - **B.** Access list
    - **C.** Transform set
    - **D.** Tunnel list

4. If you were working in IOS command line and needed to check on the status of a VPN tunnel, what command would you enter?
    - **A.** `show interface`
    - **B.** `show access-list`
    - **C.** `show crypto isakamp`
    - **D.** `show crypto ipsec sa`

5. Once again, if you were working in IOS command line, in a single command, what could you do to determine the "interesting traffic" for a particular VPN tunnel?
    - **A.** `show interesting traffic`
    - **B.** `show access-list`
    - **C.** `show crypto map`
    - **D.** `show ip interface`

6. What is the "peer address" when discussing a VPN tunnel?
    - **A.** The remote device VPN endpoint
    - **B.** The interesting traffic
    - **C.** The local outside interface
    - **D.** The remote end loopback address

7. What is split tunneling?

    A. A dual tunnel to two locations

    B. The ability to access both local resources and those over the VPN

    C. The ability to only access remote locations

    D. None of the above

8. What is the advantage of Dead Peer Detection?

    A. Lower cost

    B. More bandwidth

    C. Faster convergence

    D. More security

9. You can only have one transform set to define the type of authentication and encryption.

    A. True

    B. False

10. Name one commonly used debug command when troubleshooting VPN connectivity.

    A. `debug ip`

    B. `debug crypto isakmp`

    C. `debug crypto ipsec`

    D. `debug vpn`

Answers to Review Questions

1. B. ESP (Encapsulating Security Payload). Remember that AH only does the authenticating and no encryption.

2. C. The default encryption type is 3DES—this is what SDM uses when you choose the default configuration.

3. B. An access list is used to define "interesting traffic," which is the traffic that is allowed to traverse the VPN tunnel.

4. D. The command you would enter is `show crypto ipsec sa`. This displays any IPsec Security Associations. You can also use this to determine some error conditions in order to do further troubleshooting.

5. C. The `show crypto map` command displays all components of the crypto map, including the access list that controls interesting traffic. Note: answer B could be used if you knew which access list was related to the crypto map.

6. A. The peer address is the remote endpoint of the VPN device that you are connecting to.

7. B. Split tunneling is the ability for a remote VPN client to be able to access resources across the VPN tunnel and also those on the local network.

8. C. Dead Peer Detection (DPD) is used to speed network convergence when you want any site that has gone down to be discovered as quickly as possible.

9. B. False. When defining VPN tunnels to different business partners and sites, it's often advantageous to have different transform sets to describe what parameters you are using with each partner.

10. B or C. The two used in the chapter that were described are the `debug crypto isakmp` and `debug crypto isakmp`.

Chapter 13

Device Security

IN THIS CHAPTER, YOU WILL LEARN HOW TO DO THE FOLLOWING:

✓ Describe, configure, and verify AutoSecure/One-Step Lockdown implementations (CLI and SDM)

✓ Describe, configure, and verify AAA for Cisco Routers

✓ Describe and configure IOS secure management features (SSH, SNMP, SYSLOG, NTP, Role-Based CLI, and the like)

This chapter covers security, primarily for your routing devices. Some of those features, such as securing management traffic, will carry over to other devices on your network. The majority of the chapter focuses on the built-in features that are available to secure routing devices. First, you learn some of the basic reasons to secure your devices and which services to secure. Then, you learn how to use AutoSecure to lock down CLI services. Finally, you get a look at two useful SDM wizards that allow you to lock down your routing devices: the Security Audit and One-Step Lockdown wizards.

Why Secure Your Devices?

I can't tell you how many people ask, "Which services and processes on a router should I turn off?" Table 13.1 contains a listing of the most vulnerable and most commonly attacked services and processes, and you should seriously consider disabling these. The listing is not complete by any means, but it is a great place to start your security audit.

TABLE 13.1   Vulnerable Items to Secure

Item	Comments
Open router interfaces	Limit unauthorized access to the router and the network by disabling unused, open router interfaces.
Bootp server	This service is enabled by default. This service is rarely required and should be disabled.
Cisco Discovery Protocol (CDP)	This service is enabled by default. If not required, this service should be disabled globally or on a per-interface basis.
Configuration auto-loading	This service is disabled by default. Auto-loading of configuration files from a network server should remain disabled when not in use by the router.
FTP server	This service is disabled by default. Because it allows access to certain files in the router Flash memory, this service should be disabled when it is not required.

TABLE 13.1　Vulnerable Items to Secure *(continued)*

Item	Comments
TFTP server	This service is disabled by default. This service should be disabled when it is not in use because it allows access to certain files in the router Flash memory.
Network Time Protocol (NTP) service	This service is disabled by default. Disable this service when it is not required.
Packet assembler and disassembler (PAD) service	This service is enabled by default. This service should be explicitly disabled when not in use.
TCP and User Datagram Protocol (UDP) Minor services	These services are enabled in Cisco IOS software releases prior to Cisco IOS software Release 11.3 and disabled in Cisco IOS software Releases 11.3 and later. Disable this service.
Maintenance Operation Protocol (MOP) service	This service is enabled on most Ethernet interfaces. Should be disabled when it is not in use.
Simple Network Management Protocol (SNMP)	This service is enabled by default. Disable this service when it is not required.
HTTP configuration and monitoring	The default setting for this service is Cisco device dependent. You should disable this service if it is not required. If this service is required, restrict access to the router HTTP service using access control lists (ACLs).
Domain Name System (DNS)	This client service is enabled by default. If the DNS lookup service is required, make sure that you set the DNS server address.
ICMP redirects	This service is enabled by default. This service should be disabled when not required.
IP source routing	This service is enabled by default. Disable this service when it is not required.
Finger service	This service is enabled by default. Disable this service when it is not required.
ICMP unreachable notifications	This service is enabled by default. This information can be used to map networks and should be disabled on interfaces to untrusted networks.
ICMP mask reply	This service is disabled by default. This information can be used to map the network, and this service should be disabled on interfaces to untrusted networks.

TABLE 13.1 Vulnerable Items to Secure *(continued)*

Item	Comments
IP identification service	This service is enabled by default. This data can be used by an attacker to gather information about your network, and this service should be disabled.
TCP keepalives	This service is disabled by default. Keepalives should be enabled globally to manage TCP connections and prevent certain DoS attacks.
Gratuitous ARP	This service is enabled by default. You should disable gratuitous ARPs on each router interface unless this service is otherwise needed.
Proxy ARP	This service is enabled by default. This service should be disabled unless the router is being used as a LAN bridge.
IP directed broadcast	This service is enabled in software releases prior to Cisco IOS software Release 12.0 and disabled in Cisco IOS software Releases 12.0 or later. This service should be disabled when not required.

The process of going through each of your routers and manually disabling all of these services would be a nightmare, not to mention how long and potentially error-prone the task could be. It would be easy for you to overlook some of the services that should be disabled. This means that you could be trying to do a lot of good work and still leave the network open to some kind of attack.

For this reason, a couple of great additions to the IOS will help you in automating the lockdown of your devices. The first one is the Command Line Interface (CLI) based feature called AutoSecure. The second is the Web-based (SDM) wizard that allows you to audit the current security setup or provide a one-step lockdown.

CLI-Based AutoSecure

The AutoSecure feature is fairly new and is available in IOS versions 12.3 and later. AutoSecure is a simple, single command that allows you to quickly and easily secure a device from potential threats. AutoSecure can help make your efforts efficient and consistent when securing your routers.

AutoSecure allows two modes of operation: interactive and noninteractive.

Interactive Mode Prompts you to choose the way you want to configure router services and other security-related features. In interactive mode, you have control over the router security-related features. The wizard asks you questions about what you would like to secure.

Noninteractive Mode   Configures your router's security-related features based on a set of Cisco defaults. It was designed for times when you need to quickly secure a router and can't sit and babysit the process. The noninteractive mode can be enabled by using the `no-interact` option.

Lockdown Items

The AutoSecure feature goes through each of the different planes on the router to systematically lock down and secure the whole system. Remember the term *planes* from my other discussions, such as with CEF? A router is broken down into functional planes to help manage and control where and what functions do. Following is a look at what the AutoSecure feature does in the different planes of a router.

Management Plane   The management plane includes management services, such as finger, pad, udp and tcp small servers, password encryption, tcp-keepalives, cdp, bootp, http, source routing, gratuitous arp, proxy-arp, icmp (redirects, mask-replies), directed broadcast, mop, and banner. It also includes the login functions, such as password security and failed login attempt actions, as well as the secure shell (SSH) access.

Forwarding Plane   The forwarding plane hardening consists of enabling Cisco Express Forwarding (CEF) and configuring ACLs for traffic filtering.

Here are some of the other things that will also be looked at for during the AutoSecure security and lock down feature:

- The firewall component allows you to activate the Cisco IOS Firewall inspection for common protocols and applications.

- Login functions include password configuration, and setting options for failed login attempts.

- NTP functionality sets up authenticated NTP connectivity.

- SSH feature configures a hostname and a domain name, if not configured already, and enables SSH access to the protected router.

- The TCP Intercept function enables the TCP intercept feature with default settings.

Rollback

Unfortunately, with all of the things that get secured, if you are not careful you could be locked out of your router or lose your configuration. Here are a few things that you should think about so this doesn't happen to you:

- IOS version 12.3(8)T added a roll-back feature for AutoSecure configuration.

- Roll-back enables a router to revert back to its pre-AutoSecure configuration state if the AutoSecure configuration fails.

- A pre-AutoSecure snapshot is saved into the router Flash memory as `pre_autosec.cfg` before AutoSecure applies the configuration to the router. You can use this saved file to recover initial router settings.

- To replace the current running configuration with the configuration file that has been saved by AutoSecure, use the `configure replace` command in privileged EXEC mode.
- Prior to Cisco IOS Release 12.3(8)T, rollback of the AutoSecure configuration was unavailable; this means you better save the running configuration before using AutoSecure.

Configuring AutoSecure

You start the AutoSecure process by using the `auto secure` command in privileged mode:

```
auto secure [management | forwarding] [no-interact | full] [ntp | login | ssh |
firewall | tcp-intercept]
```

AutoSecure uses this syntax to give you more control over the process. To secure all components and functions, choose the `full` option. To avoid configuration prompts, select the `no-interact` keyword. To limit the scope of hardening, use any of the remaining options described in Table 13.2.

TABLE 13.2   AutoSecure Options

Option	Description
management	Only the management plane will be secured.
forwarding	Only the forwarding plane will be secured.
no-interact	The user will not be prompted for any interactive configurations. No interactive dialog parameters will be configured, including usernames or passwords.
full	The user will be prompted for all interactive questions. This is the default.
ntp	Specifies the configuration of the Network Time Protocol (NTP) feature in the AutoSecure command-line interface (CLI).
login	Specifies the configuration of the Login feature in the AutoSecure CLI.
ssh	Specifies the configuration of the SSH feature in the AutoSecure CLI.
firewall	Specifies the configuration of the firewall feature in the AutoSecure CLI.
tcp-intercept	Specifies the configuration of the TCP-Intercept feature in the AutoSecure CLI.

AutoSecure configures all functions and services in the following order:

1. Identify outside interfaces.

2. Secure the management plane.

3. Create security banner.

4. Configure passwords, AAA, and SSH.

5. Secure the interface settings.

6. Secure the forwarding plane.

If you do not specify any options, AutoSecure defaults to the interactive mode and proceeds to secure the full scope of services and functions.

 Real World Scenario

Securing the Dubai Branch Office

The Dubai branch is a new expansion to the FutureTech Corporation. You have already built out most of the infrastructure for the location. The cabling and devices are in place. You have done a fabulous job with the design and layout of the switch blocks. Before you have the Internet connection brought into the office, you need to go through some security setup.

Now, you can secure all of your routers. You know about the many services and interfaces that should be secured on a router. However, Headquarters wants you to use the feature called AutoSecure; they believe this will make the process faster and more reliable.

The first time through, I use AutoSecure the way you would to configure every router in the network. Then, I show you how to use AutoSecure to secure a router that is at the edge or connected to the Internet. Nothing to fear—you need only answer a couple of questions.

Once you finish with the AutoSecure setup, you learn how to use two SDM wizards to accomplish nearly the same security configuration.

Later in the chapter you learn how you can control access to the network and devices using authentication, authorization, and accounting (AAA). With AAA configured on your routers, you can control network access from one central location.

Finally, you learn ways that you can secure management traffic on your network. You don't want an attacker getting a hold of that kind of data!

To begin, start AutoSecure and answer the following questions at the prompts:

- Is the router going to be connected to the Internet?

- How many interfaces are connected to the Internet?

- What are the names of the interfaces connected to the Internet?

```
Router>en
Router#auto secure
```

```
--- AutoSecure Configuration ---
*** AutoSecure configuration enhances the security of
the router, but it will not make it absolutely resistant
to all security attacks ***
AutoSecure will modify the configuration of your device.
All configuration changes will be shown. For a detailed
explanation of how the configuration changes enhance security
and any possible side effects, please refer to Cisco.com for
AutoSecure documentation.
At any prompt you may enter '?' for help.
Use ctrl-c to abort this session at any prompt.
Gathering information about the router for AutoSecure
Is this router connected to internet? [no]:
```

Because most routers in a network are not directly connected to the Internet, I answered no to the Internet question this time through.

Had I said yes, the process would have continued and asked me to specify the number of interfaces that would be connected and provide a name for each connection. Armed with that information, AutoSecure can configure access lists and the IOS Firewall. You can see that process in the output that follows:

```
Securing Management plane services . . .
Disabling service finger
Disabling service pad
Disabling udp & tcp small servers
Enabling service password encryption
Enabling service tcp-keepalives-in
Enabling service tcp-keepalives-out
Disabling the cdp protocol
Disabling the bootp server
Disabling the http server
Disabling the finger service
Disabling source routing
Disabling gratuitous arp
```

At this point, the AutoSecure process has disabled all of the unnecessary Management Plane services. The process then prompts you to set a banner. It even gives an example of what to put in the banner:

```
Here is a sample Security Banner to be shown
at every access to device. Modify it to suit your
enterprise requirements.
Authorized Access only
This system is the property of So-&-So-Enterprise.
```

```
UNAUTHORIZED ACCESS TO THIS DEVICE IS PROHIBITED.
You must have explicit permission to access this
device. All activities performed on this device
are logged. Any violations of access policy will result
in disciplinary action.
Enter the security banner {Put the banner between
k and k, where k is any character}:
# This is a test banner for FutureTech Inc #
```

This is an important point. There is said to have been a legal precedent set that would require administrators to not include the word "Welcome" in any banners. This makes would-be attackers feel welcome in the system, and they could get away with attacking the system. I have never found conclusive proof that this is true but, even if it is not, there is no reason to make someone feel welcome when they are not. It's just too bad I can't guard my device interfaces with a gun!

The process next prompts you to configure passwords and local AAA authentication to the device lines:

```
Enable secret is either not configured or
is the same as enable password
Enter the new enable secret:
Confirm the enable secret :
Enter the new enable password:
Choose a password that's different from secret
Enter the new enable password:
Confirm the enable password:
Configuration of local user database
Enter the username: Pat
Enter the password:
Confirm the password:
Configuring AAA local authentication
Configuring Console, Aux and VTY lines for
local authentication, exec-timeout, and transport
```

Next, you have an opportunity to secure against login attacks:

```
Securing device against Login Attacks
Configure the following parameters
Blocking Period when Login Attack detected: 60
Maximum Login failures with the device: 5
Maximum time period for crossing the failed login attempts: 30
```

When securing the device against login attacks, you specify the following:

- Duration of time in which login attempts are denied (also known as a quiet period, in seconds)

- Maximum number of failed login attempts that triggers the quiet period

- Duration of time in which the allowed number of failed login attempts must be made before the blocking period is triggered

When you're finished, AutoSecure prompts you to configure the SSH server. If you answer "yes," AutoSecure automatically configures the SSH timeout to 60 seconds and the number of SSH authentication retries to two. If the router does not already have a unique hostname, you will also be prompted to configure one.

If you configured a hostname for this router prior to starting AutoSecure, you will not be prompted to enter one here. However, if the router is still using the factory default hostname, Router, you will be prompted to enter a unique hostname, as shown in the output. This is important because SSH requires a unique hostname generate the key that will be used the secure the connections.

Notice that AutoSecure also prompted you to define the domain to which the router belongs. Like the hostname parameter, a domain name is important for SSH key generation.

```
Configure SSH server? [yes]:
Enter the hostname: DubRtr1
```

Enter the domain-name: **futuretech.com**. Notice now that AutoSecure automatically disabled the following services on all router interfaces:

- IP redirects

- IP proxy ARP

- IP unreachables

- IP directed-broadcast

- IP mask replies and mop on Ethernet interfaces

```
Configuring interface specific AutoSecure services
Disabling the following ip services on all interfaces:
no ip redirects
no ip proxy-arp
no ip unreachables
no ip directed-broadcast
no ip mask-reply
Disabling mop on Ethernet interfaces
Securing Forwarding plane services . . .
Enabling CEF (This might impact the memory requirements for your platform)
Enabling unicast rpf on all interfaces connected
to internet
```

The AutoSecure process then prompts you to enable the firewall feature. I didn't enable it for this go around, but here is what the output looks like if you had enabled it. I will show you an output where I selected the firewall feature a bit later:

```
Configure CBAC Firewall feature? [yes/no]: n
Tcp intercept feature is used prevent tcp syn attack
on the servers in the network. Create autosec_tcp_intercept_list
to form the list of servers to which the tcp traffic is to
be observed
Enable tcp intercept feature? [yes/no]: n
```

The next output shows the actual configuration that was applied to my routers by AutoSecure. I run through the sections of the output next.

```
This is the configuration generated:
no service finger
no service pad
no service udp-small-servers
no service tcp-small-servers
service password-encryption
service tcp-keepalives-in
service tcp-keepalives-out
no cdp run
no ip bootp server
no ip http server
no ip finger
no ip source-route
no ip gratuitous-arps
no ip identd
```

AutoSecure disables several router global services that are considered possible attack points and enables other services that help to protect the router:

```
banner motd ^C This is a test banner for FutureTech Inc ^C
security passwords min-length 6
security authentication failure rate 10 log
```

AutoSecure configures an authentication failure rate of 10. This allows a user 10 failed login attempts before the router sends an authentication failure event to the logger (router log or Syslog server). You are not asked to give a value for this; this is performed automatically by AutoSecure.

```
enable secret 5 $1$COvX$UzdRxlTIAWefBQZ6xjDDe/
enable password 7 050D131B345E4B1D1C061F43
username Pat password 7 00071C08085A05
```

```
aaa new-model
aaa authentication login local_auth local
line con 0
login authentication local_auth
exec-timeout 5 0
transport output telnet
line aux 0
login authentication local_auth
exec-timeout 10 0
transport output telnet
line vty 0 4
login authentication local_auth
transport input telnet
```

AutoSecure enables local AAA authentication, and configures the console 0, auxiliary 0, and vty lines 0 through 4 for local authentication, an EXEC timeout, and outgoing Telnet connections:

```
line tty 1
login authentication local_auth
exec-timeout 15 0
login block-for 60 attempts 5 within 30
hostname Router1
ip domain-name futuretech.com
crypto key generate rsa general-keys modulus 1024
ip ssh time-out 60
ip ssh authentication-retries 2
line vty 0 4
transport input ssh telnet
```

AutoSecure asked me to set the hostname and domain name. These are required for the key generation, which enables SSH access to the router. SSH optional settings are configured. AutoSecure configures VTY lines 0 through 4 to support both SSH and Telnet incoming connections. Note that Telnet was previously configured for the VTY lines. This step simply adds SSH to the list of possible incoming connection types.

```
service timestamps debug datetime msec localtime show-timezone
service timestamps log datetime msec localtime show-timezone
logging facility local2
logging trap debugging
service sequence-numbers
logging console critical
logging buffered
interface FastEthernet0/0
```

```
no ip redirects
no ip proxy-arp
no ip unreachables
no ip directed-broadcast
no ip mask-reply
no mop enabled
interface FastEthernet0/1
no ip redirects
no ip proxy-arp
no ip unreachables
no ip directed-broadcast
no ip mask-reply
no mop enabled
interface Serial0/0/0
no ip redirects
no ip proxy-arp
no ip unreachables
no ip directed-broadcast
no ip mask-reply
ip cef
access-list 100 permit udp any any eq bootpc
!
end
Apply this configuration to running-config? [yes]:
Applying the config generated to running-config
The name for the keys will be: Router1.futuretech.com
% The key modulus size is 1024 bits
% Generating 1024 bit RSA keys, keys will be non-exportable . . . [OK]
DubRtr1#
000045: *Oct 29 03:24:44.940 UTC: %AUTOSEC-1-MODIFIED: AutoSecure configuration
has been Modified on this device
```

As promised, I'll show you what the output sections look like if you answer yes at the Internet interface and the firewall prompts. First, here are the prompts that are presented when you let AutoSecure know that you have an interface facing the Internet:

```
Is this router connected to internet? [no]: y
Enter the number of interfaces facing the internet [1]: 1
Interface IP-Address OK? Method Status Protocol
FastEthernet0/0 1.1.1.1 YES manual up up
FastEthernet0/1 unassigned YES unset administratively down down
Serial0/0/0 unassigned YES unset administratively down down
Enter the interface name that is facing the internet: FastEthernet0/0
```

Here is the output from answering yes to the firewall question:

```
Configure CBAC Firewall feature? [yes/no]: y
```

There is no other output in the process, just the output of code that is put into the configuration. Here is that output:

```
ip inspect audit-trail
ip inspect dns-timeout 7
ip inspect tcp idle-time 14400
ip inspect udp idle-time 1800
ip inspect name autosec_inspect cuseeme timeout 3600
ip inspect name autosec_inspect ftp timeout 3600
ip inspect name autosec_inspect http timeout 3600
ip inspect name autosec_inspect rcmd timeout 3600
ip inspect name autosec_inspect realaudio timeout 3600
ip inspect name autosec_inspect smtp timeout 3600
ip inspect name autosec_inspect tftp timeout 30
ip inspect name autosec_inspect udp timeout 15
ip inspect name autosec_inspect tcp timeout 3600
ip access-list extended autosec_firewall_acl
permit udp any any eq bootpc
deny ip any any
interface FastEthernet0/0
ip inspect autosec_inspect out
ip access-group autosec_firewall_acl in
```

SDM-Based Security Audit Wizard

Cisco SDM contains a Security Audit Wizard that provides a comprehensive router security audit. Cisco SDM uses the Cisco Technical Assistance Center (TAC) and International Computer Security Association (ICSA) recommended security configurations as its basis for comparisons and default settings. The Security Audit Wizard checks the vulnerability of the router under its current configuration and provides a fast way to comply with basic security policies for routers.

Additionally, the second part of the SDM wizard can configure almost all of the configurations that you saw in AutoSecure. This is done using the One-Step Lockdown feature in the SDM.

The Cisco SDM security audit feature compares router configurations to a predefined checklist. (This is not a complete list of the checks performed.)

- Shuts down unneeded servers on the router
- Shuts down unneeded services on the router
- Applies a firewall to the outside interfaces

- Disables SNMP or enables it with hard-to-guess community strings
- Shuts down unused interfaces using the `no ip proxy-arp` command
- Forces passwords for the router console and vty lines
- Forces an enable secret password
- Enforces the use of ACLs

The Security Audit Wizard contains two modes:

Security Audit   Examines router configuration, then displays the Report Card window, which shows a list of possible security problems. You can choose which vulnerability you would like to lock down.

One-Step Lockdown   Initiates the automatic lockdown using recommended settings.

Let's go through the security audit mode, which is the first option you will see once in the security audit section of SDM.

SDM Security Audit

To use the SDM wizard, you must make an HTTP connection into your router and run SDM. I know that you have done this already, so at this point, open the SDM interface. The following steps start from the Home page.

Complete the following steps to perform a security audit:

1. Click the Configure button in the main toolbar, shown in Figure 13.1.

2. Click the Security Audit icon in the Tasks toolbar on the left.

3. You have two wizard buttons available; click the Perform Security Audit button.

FIGURE 13.1   SDM Home Page

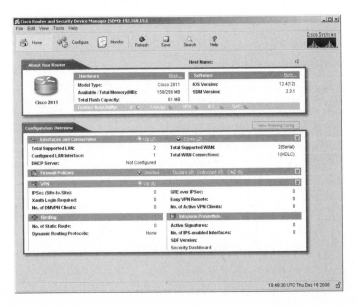

Choose the Configure button shown in Figure 13.1. The Interfaces and Connections dialog box, shown in Figure 13.2, will open.

FIGURE 13.2 SDM Configure Page

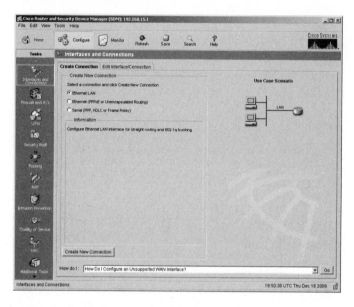

You have to choose the Security Audit button from the vertical toolbar. The Security Audit dialog box, shown in Figure 13.3, will open.

FIGURE 13.3 SDM Security Audit Page

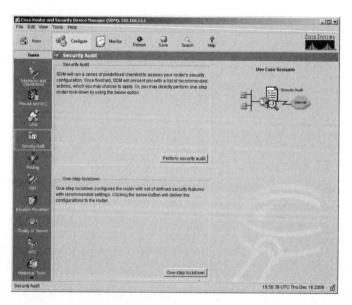

Click the Perform Security Audit button to start the wizard. When the wizard opens, you will see a screen similar to the one shown in Figure 13.4. It outlines the process the wizard will use to secure the router.

FIGURE 13.4   Security Audit Wizard Page

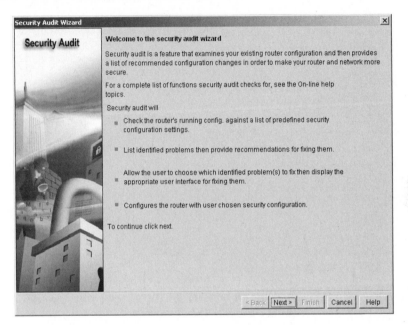

You can see that the wizard does quite a few things for you. First, it checks the router's configuration against the set of recommended settings. It then shows you a list of the all the security-related items it checked for and the current status of each of those items. The wizard also lets you choose to fix any items that it finds are unsecure or not in the recommended setting. Finally, it makes the changes that you chose to fix. Click Next to continue on to the Security Audit Interface Configuration dialog box, shown in Figure 13.5.

Here you have to choose which interfaces are trusted (inside) and which are untrusted (outside). The inside interfaces are typically the interfaces that don't face the Internet or are on the networks that you are trying to protect. The outside interfaces are the interfaces that are facing the Internet. You can choose any number of interfaces for either setting, whatever they actually are. Click Next to perform the audit. Figure 13.6 shows typical results.

Figure 13.6 shows you the audit page with a full list of the items that were checked during the audit. You can choose Save Report or Close. When you choose, the Fix It page, shown in Figure 13.7, opens.

This shows you the same list from the audit page, but now you have the opportunity to choose which things you want to fix.

If you click the Fix All button, the wizard will fix the items in the list. Additional windows will appear and you can configure settings where they are required, such as a password.

FIGURE 13.5   Wizard Interface Configuration

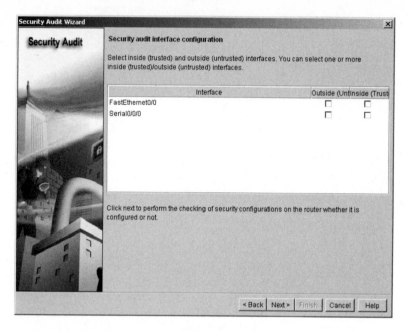

FIGURE 13.6   Security Audit Page

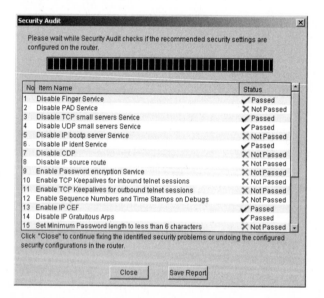

FIGURE 13.7   Fix It Page

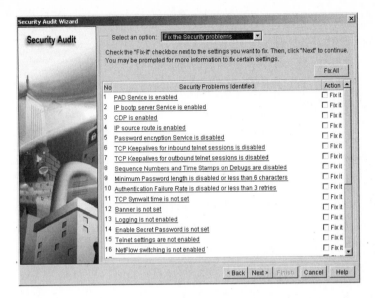

As an alternative, you can choose any number of individual items from the list for fixing. If you click the hyperlinks, you can get more information about what that selection does. Be careful not to lock yourself out of the router.

Click the Fix All button to see the steps that the wizard takes you through to fully secure your router. Figure 13.8 shows the first step.

FIGURE 13.8   Enable Secret and Login Banner

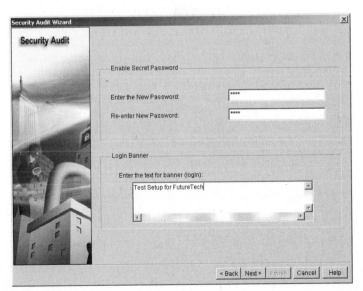

The first step the wizard guides you through adds an enable secret password. You can see this setting in Figure 13.8. This password should be a secure non-dictionary password that cannot be easily guessed. The use of uppercase and lowercase letters, numbers, and special characters will make the password even stronger.

The second configuration on this screen, in Figure 13.8, is a login banner. As I mentioned in the AutoSecure configuration, the banner should not be inviting or include the word "Welcome" in the text. Once you add the password and banner text, click Next to open the user configuration options shown in Figure 13.9.

FIGURE 13.9   User for Secure Access

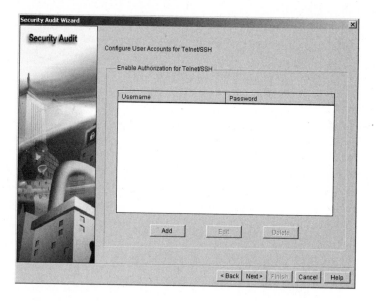

The user account can be used by an administrator to access the router via Telnet or SSH. For security and logging purposes, each user who can access a device should have a separate account. To add a new user to the local database, click the Add button. Figure 13.10 shows the Add Telnet/SSH Account dialog box.

FIGURE 13.10   Add User Screen

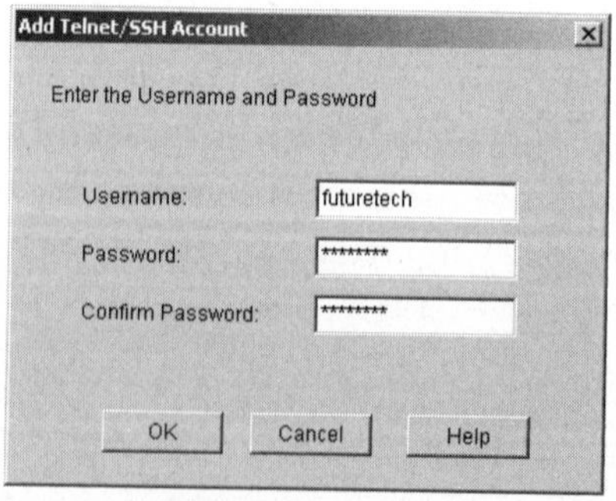

This dialog allows you to configure the options for a new user. The options are simply the username and password. When you are finished adding the user, click OK. The new user will be listed in the database, as shown in Figure 13.11.

FIGURE 13.11   User Added to Local Database

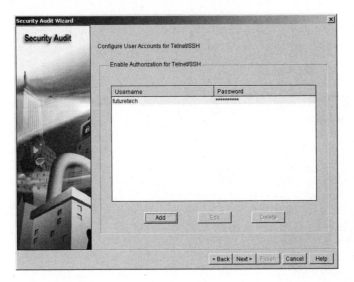

Now you can verify that the new user you just created is in fact present in the database. If you want to add more users to the database, select the Add button again and repeat the process until all of the users you need are in the database. When you are finished, click Next to move on to enabling logging, as shown in Figure 13.12.

FIGURE 13.12   Enable Logging

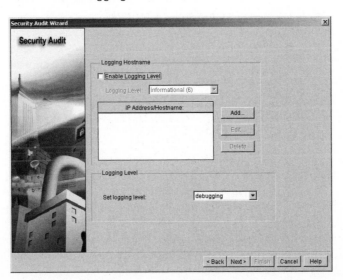

This screen shows you the options to set up logging for the router. By default the check box is selected to enable logging. I have unchecked it for this sample setup because I don't have a syslog server to send the data to. However, on your real production network you are going to have a place to send all of your logging data to. That is the first option on this page; you have to tell the router the IP address of the syslog server on your network so that the logging data can be sent there. The second option at the bottom of the screen allows you to set the logging level for the router. When you are finished, click Next to move on to the IOS firewall setup shown in Figure 13.13.

FIGURE 13.13 IOS Firewall Setup

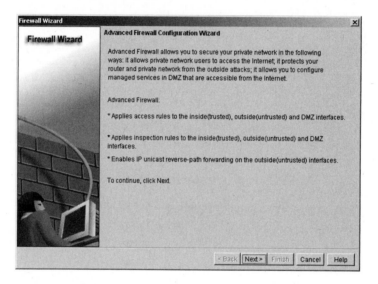

At this point, the Security Audit Wizard actually starts another wizard, the IOS Firewall Wizard. You are now in the Advanced Firewall Wizard. I'll just give you a brief rundown of the steps here for this process. Chapter 15, "Cisco IOS Firewall," explains in depth for you how the firewall feature works on a router.

This first step from the figure tells you what features and steps the firewall can do for you. Just click Next. You begin configuring on the next screen, shown in Figure 13.14.

The second screen of the Firewall Wizard lets you configure the trusted and untrusted interfaces of the firewall. At the bottom of the screen, note that you can configure a third interface for use as a DMZ. Again, you learn all about what this does in more detail in Chapter 15. Click Next to continue the configuration, as shown in Figure 13.15.

On this screen, you configure the security level of the firewall. Right in the middle of the screen there is a slide bar where you can set one of three levels of security. The yellowish box to the right of the slide bar gives you a basic description of what each level does.

You can also set your own security level by choosing the Use a Custom Application Security Policy radio button. For now, just click Next. Once you click Next, the wizard will configure the firewall and then display a summary of the steps that the wizard takes to configure the router. Figure 13.16 shows a typical output.

FIGURE 13.14   Firewall Interface Selection

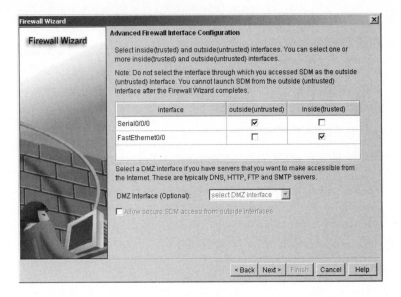

FIGURE 13.15   Firewall Security Level Selection

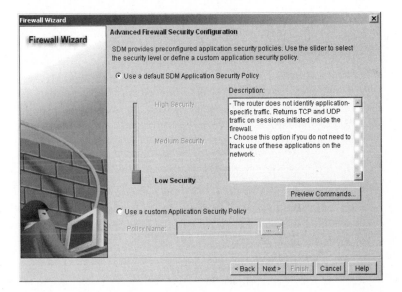

FIGURE 13.16 Firewall Configuration Summary

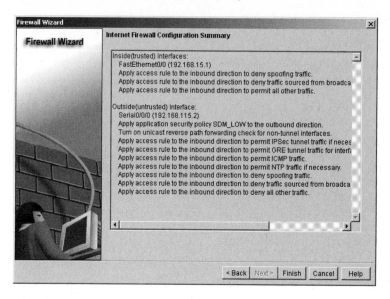

Click Back if you need to make changes. Click Finish to complete the configuration. Figure 13.17 shows the Summary page that appears when the wizard is finished.

FIGURE 13.17 Summary Page

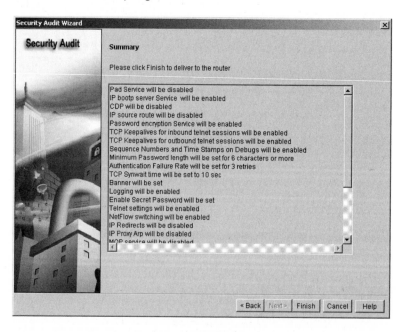

Make sure that you review everything. When you click Finish, all of the settings will be saved to the router.

One-Step Lockdown

Now, I want you to reload your router to get rid of all the configurations that are currently on it. Go back into the SDM Security Audit page, shown in Figure 13.3. Let's use the One-Step Lockdown Wizard. Click the One-Step Lockdown button. A warning, shown in Figure 13.18, will appear.

FIGURE 13.18 SDM Warning

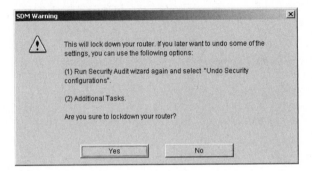

At this point, if you choose Yes, the wizard automatically goes through and sets up all of the recommended security settings. Go ahead and choose Yes. A verification dialog box, shown in Figure 13.19, will appear.

FIGURE 13.19 Verification Page

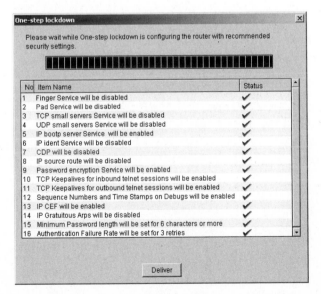

At this point the router has gone through all of the settings and provides you with a list of all the things it is going to add to your router. You can see the only option that you have is to deliver the commands to the router, so click Deliver. The delivery information box, shown in Figure 13.20, appears.

FIGURE 13.20   Delivery Screen

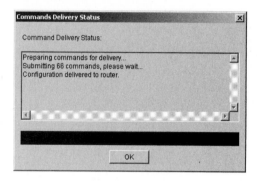

At this point the running configuration is getting all of the commands that the wizard added. It is usually about 65 or 66 commands when the router is blank. Here is a list of all the things that were checked and what the process did during the wizard:

- Disable Finger Service

- Disable PAD Service

- Disable TCP Small Servers Service

- Disable UDP Small Servers Service

- Disable IP Bootp Server Service

- Disable IP Identification Service

- Disable CDP

- Disable IP Source Route

- Enable Password Encryption Service

- Enable TCP Keepalives for Inbound Telnet Sessions

- Enable TCP Keepalives for Outbound Telnet Sessions

- Enable Sequence Numbers and Time Stamps on Debugs

- Enable IP CEF

- Disable IP Gratuitous ARPs

- Set Minimum Password Length to Less Than 6 Characters

- Set Authentication Failure Rate to Less Than 3 Retries

- Set TCP Synwait Time

- Set Banner
- Enable Logging
- Set Enable Secret Password
- Disable SNMP
- Set Scheduler Interval
- Set Scheduler Allocate
- Set Users
- Enable Telnet Settings
- Enable NetFlow Switching
- Disable IP Redirects
- Disable IP Proxy ARP
- Disable IP Directed Broadcast
- Disable MOP Service
- Disable IP Unreachables
- Disable IP Mask Reply
- Disable IP Unreachables on NULL Interface
- Enable Unicast RPF on Outside Interfaces
- Enable Firewall on All of the Outside Interfaces
- Set Access Class on HTTP Server Service
- Set Access Class on VTY Lines
- Enable SSH for Access to the Router

AAA

AAA stands for authentication, authorization, and accounting. The AAA feature, which is supported by almost every Cisco networking device currently on the market, allows for the centralized management of these features across the entire network. Here is a description of each of those three features.

Authentication   Authentication requires users and administrators to prove that they really are who they say they are. Authentication is established using a username and password, challenge and response, token cards, and other methods.

Authorization   After authenticating the user and administrator, authorization services decide which resources the user and administrator are allowed to access and which operations the user and administrator are allowed to perform.

Other typical authorization tasks are:

- Assigning parameters, such as IP addresses and access control lists (ACLs) to connected users
- Assigning privilege levels to users who run exec sessions
- Controlling the usage of specific exec commands

Accounting and Auditing   Accounting records what the user and administrator actually did, what they accessed, and how long they accessed it for accounting and auditing purposes. Accounting keeps track of how network resources are used.

AAA has two primary purposes:

1. Authenticating remote users attempting access to the enterprise network through a remote method such as dial-in or some kind of Internet connection
2. Authenticating administrators attempting to access a router's console port, aux port, or VTY ports

Cisco gives you three ways to implement AAA services for use with Cisco routers, network access servers (NASs), VPN concentrators, firewalls and switch equipment, as shown in Figure 13.21.

FIGURE 13.21   AAA Basic Setup and Use

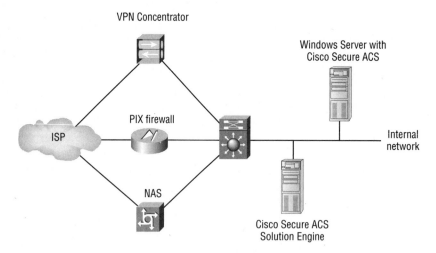

Think about how much work it would be for an administrator to maintain a separate database on each of the access devices coming in from the Internet. If the database was local, every time a user's password had to be reset or updated, you would have to update the local database on each of the other devices. Understand, too, that only a single ACS server need be used in a network. The following table shows you the different implementation options that you have.

🌐 Real World Scenario

AAA in Dubai

In FutureTech's Dubai branch office, multiple devices allow users to access the network remotely. A separate AAA server is normally used, such as one of the server type devices on the internal network. This type of AAA server is used so that there is a single place for all of the security and access requests to be sent, and a local database on each one of the access devices does not have to be maintained.

Table 13.3 lists the Cisco AAA services that are available.

TABLE 13.3   Cisco AAA Services

Service	Description
Self-contained AAA	AAA services are self-contained in the router itself; this is also called local authentication.
Cisco Secure ACS loaded on a Windows Server	AAA services on the router or device contact an external Cisco Secure Access Control Server (ACS) loaded on a Windows server for user and administrator authentication.
Cisco Secure ACS Solution Engine	AAA services on the router or NAS contact an external Cisco Secure ACS Solution Engine for user and administrator authentication.

The most widely used and supported types of AAA protocols are TACACS+ and RADIUS. TACACS+ replaces older versions of TACACS and XTACACS. TACACS+ and RADIUS have different features that make them best suited for different uses.

RADIUS is a standards-based protocol that was created by the Internet Engineering Task Force (IETF); TACACS+ is a proprietary Cisco Systems technology that encrypts data. Another key difference is that TACACS+ runs in TCP, whereas RADIUS operates in User Datagram Protocol (UDP).

TACACS+ provides many benefits for configuring Cisco devices to use AAA for management and terminal services. TACACS+ can control the authorization level of users, whereas RADIUS cannot. Also, because TACACS+ separates authentication and authorization, it is possible to use TACACS+ authorization and accounting while using another method of authentication such as Kerberos.

RADIUS

I want to start off showing you the authentication process with RADIUS protocol. Figure 13.22 shows you the step-by-step process of a client device trying to connect to the network.

 Real World Scenario

RADIUS in Dubai

The client device is accessing the Dubai internal network from a remote location. The router in the process is an edge access router on the Dubai branch office network. The server located on the internal network is running RADIUS for its AAA protocol.

FIGURE 13.22   Client Connecting with RADIUS

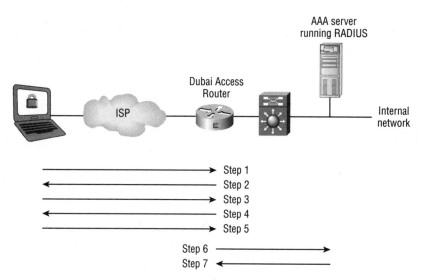

1. The client requests access.

2. The router prompts the client for a username.

3. The client provides the username to the router.

4. The router prompts the client for a password.

5. The client provides the password to the router.

6. The router forwards the information about the username and the password to the RADIUS server using an Access-Request datagram, which contains all the necessary AV-pairs.

7. If the user information is correct, the server responds with an Access-Accept data-gram. The Access-Accept message also contains authorization parameters in the form of AV-pairs, such as the IP address to be assigned, and so on.

If the user information is invalid, an Access-Reject message is returned and the router terminates the connection.

Table 13.4 lists the four RADIUS message types and provides a description for each.

TABLE 13.4   RADIUS Message Types

Message Type	Description
Access-Request	This message is sent by the router or other device and contains attribute-value pairs (AV-pairs) for the username, password (this is the only information that is encrypted by RADIUS), and additional information such as the router port.
Access-Challenge	This message can also be sent by the router for challenge-based authentication methods such as Challenge Handshake Authentication Protocol (CHAP), Microsoft CHAP (MS-CHAP), and Extensible Authentication Protocol Message Digest 5 (EAP-MD5).
Access-Accept	This message is sent by the RADIUS server and is the positive answer if the user information is valid.
Access-Reject	This message is sent by the RADIUS server and is the negative reply if the user information is invalid.

Contained within the message types are AV-pairs. The AV-pairs are the actual information that allows a network device to authenticate, authorize, and account for a host. Examples of commonly used RADIUS AV-pairs are:

- User-Name
- User-Password (the only encrypted entity in RADIUS)
- CHAP-Password
- NAS-IP-Address
- NAS-Port
- Service-Type
- Framed-IP-Address

Approximately 50 other AV-pairs are defined in the Internet Engineering Task Force (IETF) standard, and Cisco has added several vendor-specific attributes on the server-side.

 NOTE   Cisco IOS devices will, by default, always use Cisco AV-pairs but they can be configured to use only IETF attributes for standard compatibility.

The Cisco implementation of RADIUS is the RADIUS (IETF) standard plus IETF attribute 26. This attribute is the Vendor Specific Attribute (VSA) for Cisco. Only using this VSA can an authorization request specified in the TACACS+ specification be sent to an access device through RADIUS.

Limiting factors of RADIUS are:

- Security features; only the passwords are encrypted.

- Authorization can only be accomplished if done in conjunction with authentication.

Accounting information is sent within special RADIUS accounting messages.

TACACS+

TACACS+, the Cisco proprietary protocol, provides a lot more flexibility than the RADIUS protocol. A TACACS+ server can use an extended conversation with the client in order to get enough information for the user to be authenticated. You can configure the conversation to include other names or personal information that should be known, sort of like security questions when you are logging in to a bank Web site.

TACACS+ is the primary protocol for Cisco AAA implementations and is supported on IOS routers, switches, and the PIX/ASA firewalls.

TACACS+ uses TCP port 49 as a default transport layer. Normally, each AAA transaction uses a dedicated TCP connection. A single session can be established to ensure less server load and better detection of a break in communication. This session persists as long as the server or the network device is operational.

Figure 13.23 shows you the authentication process using the TACACS+ protocol. Similar to the example for RADIUS, now you have a client trying to access the Dubai branch office but the router will be communicating to an AAA server that is running TACACS+.

1. The client requests access.

2. The router requests a username prompt from the TACACS+ server.

3. The TACACS+ server provides a username prompt.

4. The router prompts the client.

5. The client provides the username.

6. The router forwards the username to the TACACS+ server.

7. The router requests the password prompt from the TACACS+ server.

8. The TACACS+ server provides a password prompt.

9. The router prompts the client for a password.

10. The client submits the password.

11. The router forwards the password to the TACACS+ server.

12. The TACACS+ server accepts or rejects the user.

FIGURE 13.23   Client Connecting with TACACS+

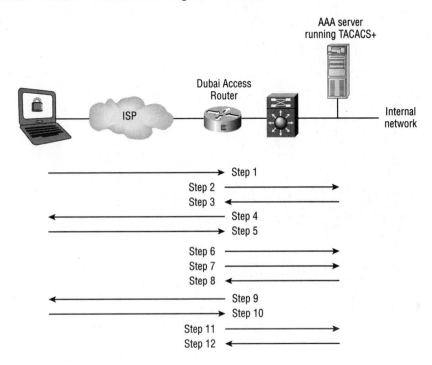

The router eventually receives one of the following responses from the TACACS+ server:

ACCEPT   The user is authenticated and service may begin. If the router is configured to require authorization, authorization will begin at this time.

REJECT   The user has failed to authenticate. The user may be denied further access, or will be prompted to retry the login sequence, depending on the TACACS+ daemon.

ERROR   An error occurred at some time during authentication. This can be either at the server or in the network connection between the server and the router. If an ERROR response is received, the router will typically try to use an alternative method to authenticate the user.

CONTINUE   The user is prompted for additional authentication information.

Following authentication, the user is also required to undergo an additional authorization phase, if authorization has been enabled on the router. Users must first successfully complete TACACS+ authentication before proceeding to TACACS+ authorization.

If TACACS+ authorization is required, the TACACS+ server is again contacted and it returns an ACCEPT or REJECT authorization response. If an ACCEPT response is returned, the response will contain data in the form of attributes that are used to direct the EXEC or NETWORK session for that user. This determines the services that the user can access. Services can include the following:

- Telnet
- rlogin
- PPP
- Serial Line Internet Protocol (SLIP)
- EXEC services
- Connection parameters, including the host or client IP address, ACL, and user timeouts

The authorization process with TACACS+ begins after the user has successfully authenticated. A per-user ACL and static route can be uploaded to the router. TACACS+ can be used for uploading a variety of other parameters to the router. The following messages are involved in the exchange:

1. The router issues an authorization request for network access to the TACACS+ server.
2. The TACACS+ server permits or denies access. If the access is permitted, authorization parameters are sent to the router to be applied to the user connection.

Another important aspect of authorization is the access control to services available to a user. Controlling access to configuration commands greatly simplifies the infrastructure security in large enterprise networks. Per-user permissions can easily be configured on the ACS, which simplifies the configuration on network devices and limits administrators depending on their role.

Examples of TACACS+ attributes frequently used for authentication and authorization are listed and described in Table 13.5.

TABLE 13.5   Frequently Used TACACS+ Attributes

Attribute	Description
ACL (EXEC authorization)	Contains an access-class number to be applied to a line
ADDR (SLIP, PPP/IP authorization)	Specifies the IP address of the remote host that should be assigned when using a SLIP or PPP/IP connection
CMD (EXEC)	The AV-pair is used for starting an authorization request for an EXEC command
Priv-lvl (EXEC authorization)	Specifies the current privilege level for command authorizations, a number from 0 to 15

TABLE 13.5   Frequently Used TACACS+ Attributes *(continued)*

Attribute	Description
Route (PPP/IP, SLIP authorization)	Specifies a route to be applied to an interface
InACL (PPP/IP, SLIP authorization)	Contains an inbound IP ACL for SLIP or PPP/IP connections
OutACL	Contains an outbound IP ACL for SLIP or PPP/IP
Addr-pool	Specifies the name of a local address pool from which to get the address of the remote host
Autocmd	Specifies a command to be automatically executed at EXEC startup

Many other attributes exist and accommodate most network applications, including dial-in solutions, proxy-authentication on firewalls, or command authorization for Cisco devices.

Configuring AAA

This section shows you the commands to configure each of the three functions of AAA. First are the global commands that must be configured regardless of the individual function you might configure on a particular device.

The aaa new-model command is required to enable all AAA functionality on a router or device. It will look like this on a router or switch:

```
DubRtr1(config)#aaa new-model
```

The next command tells the router or device where the AAA server is. Regardless of the type of AAA server (Cisco Secure ACS, Microsoft IAS, or other), you must tell the network device where on the network the server is. I'll go through the RADIUS commands first and then the TACACS+ commands.

Configuring Communications with a RADIUS Server

The command is radius-server *host X.X.X.X*, where the X's at the end of the command specify the IP address of the server:

```
DubRtr1(config)#radius-server host 1.1.1.1
```

The next command specifies the encryption key that is to be used when communicating with the RADIUS server. This key will also be configured on the RADIUS server itself.

The command is radius-server key *key*, where the *key* option at the end of the command specifies the actual key string that is used for encryption and must match the key set on the server:

```
DubRtr1(config)#radius-server key abcd1234
```

I want to point out a feature here that will help you with redundancy and security in your network. Like anything else in this world, you should have more than one of everything—an AAA server is no different. The only hitch is that if you use the two separate commands (the commands that told the router where the server is and what the key is) that I have shown you so far, and then you configure an additional server, the two servers would have to use the same key. This is because you can use the radius-server key command only once. To provide better security for your network and the servers themselves, you can configure a separate key for each of the servers. To accomplish this, use the following configuration instead of the two separate commands I already showed you. I'll configure two AAA servers so that you can see how this works.

```
DubRtr1(config)#radius-server host 1.1.1.1 key abcd1234
DubRtr1(config)#radius-server host 2.2.2.2 key wxyz5678
```

Configuring Communications with a TACACS+ Server

The commands for a TACACS+ server are very similar. You need to specify the different protocol type in the commands. The aaa new-model command must still be specified when configuring the TACACS+ protocol. When configuring a network device with the location of a TACACS+ server the command is tacacs-server host *X.X.X.X single-connection*. The Xs again are the IP address of the server. The single connection option again is a feature of TACACS+ using TCP connections between the network device and the server. If you specify the *single-connection* option, only one connection will be maintained between the two devices. This provides a much more efficient interface rather than establishing and tearing down a new connection for every request.

```
DubRtr1(config)#tacacs-server host 1.1.1.1 single-connection
```

You must also specify an encryption key for the TACACS+ server. You do this with the tacacs-server key *key* command:

```
DubRtr1(config)#tacacs-server key abcd1234
```

Again for the same reason as RADIUS, you can configure the *key* option with the tacacs-server host command. This allows you to configure more the one server and each of the servers utilize their own key for encryption.

```
DubRtr1(config)#tacacs-server host 1.1.1.1 key abcd1234
DubRtr1(config)#tacacs-server host 2.2.2.2 key wxyz5678
```

Authentication Process

The next thing that you have to enable is the authentication process. The commands are the same no matter whether you are using RADIUS or TACACS+. Just be sure you set the option correctly.

Authentication is done using the `aaa authentication login` command. This is often referred to as an authentication list, because it has the list of methods or places that the router is going to refer to for authentication. The whole command is `aaa authentication login [default | list-name] group [group-name | radius | tacacs+] [method2 method3 method4]`.

The first option is the type of list that you are going to create. Your options are *default* or a named *list-name*. If you use the `default` option, the list you are creating will automatically be applied to every interface and line that the device has. If you make a named *list-name*, that list must be applied individually to the interface or line where you want it used. You see how to apply a list coming up next.

If you configure more than one list, say, for example, a default list and a named list, the default list will be applied everywhere. However, if you apply the named list to one of the lines, say to the console line, the named list will override the use of the default list on that line.

The next set of options is the type of *group* that you are going to use. This will tell the router to use the TACACS+ or RADIUS servers that you already configured. If you use the option *group-name*, you will have to predefine a group of servers using the `aaa group server radius` or `aaa group server tacacs+` commands.

Finally, the last option or options will be any other methods for authentication. The methods will be used in the order that they are specified. An additional method will only be used if there is an error with the previous method, such as a timeout.

If the previous method returns a FAILED authentication, an additional method cannot be used, and authentication has failed. Table 13.6 is a general list of methods that can be configured.

TABLE 13.6 Authentication Methods

Method	Description
enable	Uses the enable password for authentication
group	Uses server-group
krb5	Uses Kerberos Version 5 for authentication
line	Uses the line password for authentication
local	Uses the local username and password database for authentication
local-case	Uses case-sensitive local username authentication
none	Uses no authentication

Here is what a couple of the authentication lists would look like:

DubRtr1(config)#**aaa authentication login default group tacacs+ local**
DubRtr1(config)#**aaa authentication login pats_list group tacacs+**

To apply a named list to a line you have to use the login authentication *list-name* command on the line. I am going to place my list on the console port of a router:

DubRtr1(config)#**line console 0**
DubRtr1(config-line)#**login authentication pats_list**

Authorization Process

The authorization process is configured basically as a list just as the authentication process was. It must be configured after the global AAA process has been enabled. The command to configure a device to authorize actions is aaa authorization [network | exec | commands *level* | config-commands | reverse-access] [default | list-name] [method2 method3 method4]. Table 13.7 provides a breakdown of the options that you can use in the command.

TABLE 13.7 aaa authorization Command Options

Option	Description
network	All network services, including Serial Line Internet Protocol (SLIP), PPP, and AppleTalk Remote Access Protocol (ARA Protocol)
exec	exec process
commands level	All EXEC commands at the specified level (0–15)
config-commands	For configuration mode commands
reverse-access	For reverse Telnet connections
if-authenticated	Allows the user to use the requested function if the user is authenticated
local	Uses the local database for authorization (with the username password or username secret commands)
none	Performs no authorization
group radius	Uses RADIUS for authorization
group tacacs+	Uses TACACS+ for authorization

Here is a sample of the command and how it can be used:

```
DubRtr1(config)#aaa authorization exec default group tacacs+ local
DubRtr1(config)#aaa authorization exec pats_list group tacacs+
```

Accounting Process

The accounting process is configured basically as a list just as the authentication and authorization processes were. It must be configured after the global AAA process has been enabled. The command to configure a device to account for connections is aaa accounting [commands *level* | connection | exec | network | system] [default | list-name] [start-stop | stop-only | wait_start]group [tacacs+ | radius]. Table 13.8 provides a breakdown of the options that you can use in the command.

TABLE 13.8   aaa accounting Command Options

Option	Description
commands level	Audits all commands at the specified privilege level (0–15).
Connection	Audits all outbound connections, such as Telnet and rlogin.
Exec	Audits the EXEC process.
Network	Audits all network service requests, such as SLIP, PPP, and ARAP.
System	Audits all system-level events, such as reload.
start-stop	Sends a start accounting notice at the beginning of a process and a stop accounting notice at the end of a process. The start accounting record is sent in the background. The requested user process begins regardless of whether the start accounting notice has been received by the accounting server.
stop-only	Sends a stop accounting notice at the end of the requested user process.
wait-start	As in start-stop, sends both a start and a stop accounting notice to the accounting server. With the wait-start keyword, the requested user service does not begin until the start accounting notice is acknowledged. A stop accounting notice is also sent.
group tacacs+ or radius	Uses TACACS+ for accounting, or enables RADIUS-style accounting.

Here is an example of the command and how it can be used:

```
DubRtr1(config)#aaa accounting exec default start-stop group tacacs+
DubRtr1(config)#aaa accounting exec pats_list start-stop group tacacs+
```

Securing Management Functions

Several network management protocols are available, including:

- Simple Network Management Protocol (SNMP)
- Syslog
- Trivial File Transfer Protocol (TFTP)
- Network Time Protocol (NTP)

SNMP

SNMP is a network management protocol that can be used to retrieve information from a network device (commonly referred to as read-only access) or to remotely configure parameters on the device (commonly referred to as read-write access). Both SNMP version 1 and version 2 use passwords (called community strings) within each message, as a very simple form of security. Unfortunately, SNMP v1/v2 devices send the community string in clear text along with the message. Therefore, SNMP v1/v2 messages may be intercepted by anyone with a packet sniffer located along the data path between the device and the management server. SNMP v3 overcomes these shortcomings by providing authentication and encryption to the message exchange.

These are recommendations for the correct use of SNMP tools:

- Configure SNMP with only read-only community strings.
- Set up access control on the device you wish to manage via SNMP to allow access by only the appropriate management hosts.
- Use SNMP version 3; this version provides secure access to devices through a combination of authenticating and encrypting management packets over the network.

Syslog

The Syslog protocol was designed to carry messages from a device that has been configured for logging to a Syslog server that collects that information. The messages are sent as clear text between the managed device and the management host. Syslog has no packet-level integrity checking to ensure that the packet contents have not been altered in transit. An attacker may alter syslog data in order to confuse a network administrator during an attack.

When possible, the following management practices are advised:

- Encrypt syslog traffic within an IPSec tunnel.

- Implement RFC 3704 filtering at the perimeter router when allowing syslog access from devices on the outside of a firewall.

- Implement ACLs on the firewall to allow syslog data from only the managed devices themselves to reach the management hosts.

- When possible, encrypt TFTP traffic within an IPSec tunnel to reduce the chance of interception.

TFTP

TFTP is used for transferring configuration or system files across the network. TFTP uses UDP for the data stream between the requesting host and the TFTP server. As with other management protocols that send data in clear text, the network administrator should recognize that the data within a TFTP session might be intercepted by anyone with a packet sniffer located along the data path between the device and the management server.

Where possible, TFTP traffic should be encrypted within an IPSec tunnel to reduce the chance of interception.

Securing TFTP data from the router can be accomplished with a transport layer IPSec tunnel. You have to be careful, though; not all operating systems where you might have the TFTP server located can provide this service. For that matter, not every version of IOS supports making an IPSec tunnel. Verify both things before you attempt to secure the traffic this way.

NTP

NTP is used to synchronize the clocks of various devices across a network. Synchronization of the clocks within a network is critical for digital certificates and for correct interpretation of events within syslog data. A secure method of providing clocking for the network allows network administrators to implement their own master clocks for private networks synchronized, via satellite or radio, to Coordinated Universal Time (UTC). If network administrators do not wish to implement their own master clocks because of cost or other reasons, clock sources are available for synchronization via the Internet.

The current version of NTP is version 4. The latest version defined by an RFC is version 3; version 3 is recommended from a security perspective.

An attacker could attempt a DoS attack on a network by sending bogus NTP data across the Internet in an attempt to change the clocks on network devices in such a manner that digital certificates are considered invalid. An attacker could also attempt to confuse a network administrator during an attack by disrupting the clocks on network devices. This scenario makes it difficult for the network administrator to determine the order of syslog events on multiple devices.

The following are recommendations to follow when using NTP:

- Implement your own master clock for private network synchronization.

- Use NTP version 3 or above because these versions support a cryptographic authentication mechanism between peers. NTP v3 is currently supported by most vendors, including Cisco. The latest version 4 is not defined by any RFC, and therefore is not widely supported.

- Use ACLs that specify which network devices are allowed to synchronize with other network devices.

Summary

Now you should be much more comfortable securing access to your network and devices such as routers. This chapter started off telling you about all of the services and items that could be attacked on the network.

You then learned a few new ways to confidently and thoroughly secure those services and interfaces that are left open on routers and network devices.

The first feature described was AutoSecure. AutoSecure provides a process to secure a router on the inside of your network or on the edge.

The next two features were the two wizard-based approaches in the SDM interface. The first is the Security Audit Wizard. The nice thing about this process is that you get to review the items the wizard believes are wrong with the router. Then, you can choose to fix them or leave them. The second wizard—the One-Step Lockdown Wizard—doesn't give you that option. You run the One-Step Lockdown Wizard and it does just that, locks down in one step.

You then went through the steps for configuring AAA on your network devices. This is a great feature because it allows you to centrally control access to your devices and the network.

Finally, you looked at how to secure access to all the management traffic that flows across your network. It is vitally important to keep that traffic from the wrong hands; it is much easier for attackers to take advantage of your network if they have access to your management traffic.

Review Questions

1. What CLI-based feature is built into a router for securing the device?
    A. Security Audit Wizard
    B. AutoSecure
    C. One-step lockdown
    D. Interface securer

2. What SDM-based feature allows you to secure your router and have control over what is being done?
    A. Security Audit Wizard
    B. AutoSecure
    C. One-step lockdown
    D. Interface securer

3. What individual controls do you have in the One-step lockdown feature?
    A. Per interface control
    B. Per service control
    C. Per step control
    D. None

4. You can use the AutoSecure feature to secure an edge router.
    A. True
    B. False

5. What additional wizard can be run within the Security Audit Wizard if you want to secure your connection to the Internet?
    A. PIX firewall
    B. Advanced IOS firewall
    C. Advanced IPS firewall
    D. No other wizard

6. What protocols can be used in the AAA service to the server? (Choose two.)
    A. Telnet
    B. RADIUS
    C. SSH
    D. TACACS+

7. TACACS+ uses what protocol to transport its data from the access device to the AAA server?

   A. UDP

   B. RTP

   C. TCP

   D. ICMP

8. Which of the following AAA protocols is an open standard defined by the IETF?

   A. RADIUS

   B. TACACS+

   C. TACACS

   D. SDEE

9. Which of the following management protocols should be secured on your network?

   A. Syslog

   B. NTP

   C. TFTP

   D. All of the above

10. What security method can be used to secure TFTP and syslog data as it traverses the network?

   A. Telnet

   B. Secure TFTP

   C. IPSec

   D. GRE tunneling

Answers to Review Questions

1. B. AutoSecure is the CLI-based security feature for locking down your routers.

2. A. The Security Audit Wizard allows you to control the services and steps that get locked down.

3. D. None, there are no steps that you can configure using the One-Step Lockdown Wizard.

4. A. True. The AutoSecure feature allows you to configure the IOS firewall and other service to secure an edge router.

5. C. The Advanced IOS firewall can be configured in the Security Audit Wizard.

6. B and D. The RADIUS and TACACS+ protocols can be used in the AAA service.

7. C. TACACS+ uses TCP to transport its data, whereas RADIUS uses UDP for transport.

8. A. RADIUS is an open standard that was developed by the IETF.

9. D. All of these management protocols should be secured on the network to prevent unauthorized access.

10. C. IPSec should be used to provide transport security of management traffic where it is possible.

Chapter

14

Switch Security

IN THIS CHAPTER, YOU WILL LEARN HOW TO DO THE FOLLOWING:

✓ Describe common Layer 2 network attacks (MAC flooding, rogue devices, VLAN hopping, DHCP spoofing, and more)

✓ Explain and configure Port Security, 802.1x, VACLs, Private VLANs, DHCP snooping, and DAI

Over time much of the IT industry's attention has been focused on security attacks from outside the boundaries of the organization and/or the upper layers of the OSI. Security for the network too often focuses just on edge devices and being able to filter traffic using Layer 3 and Layer 4 information. Usually devices will scan the headers, ports, and do some stateful packet inspection. Many things can be put into place for the issues surrounding Layer 3 and above, focused specifically on traffic making its way into the network from the Internet. Most people and administrators give little or no thought to access devices and Layer 2 communication. This chapter provides a solid foundation in Layer 2 security.

Introduction to Layer 2 Security

If you think about how networking equipment is configured when you buy it nowadays, you can very clearly see that far lower security settings are configured by default on equipment that is used inside your enterprise. External protection devices, such as firewalls, come almost completely secured. Only traffic that you specifically authorize and configure is allowed. Granted, for a long time, the primary thoughts about routers and switches has been that they are for internal communication, and provide an efficient (or fast as possible) delivery to enterprise traffic. With almost no security configuration, those devices are open targets for attack. Unfortunately, a Layer 2 network that is compromised can quickly lead to a large portion of the network being open for attack and very little knowledge of the attack may be known.

As mentioned in the previous chapter, ways exist to increase the level of security on Layer 2 devices. Just as policies for upper-layer security had to be created, policies must be created for Layer 2. Once a policy has been created, the appropriate features can be configured to protect the devices, and ultimately the network, against attacks.

Layer 2 attacks are typically launched by or from a device that is (or has been) physically connected to the enterprise network. Perhaps it was placed on the network with malicious intent, for the purpose of providing a means of attack. It could also be a device that you placed on the network, one that should be trusted, but has been taken over by an attacker. Unfortunately, in most cases you or devices on the network see the traffic coming from this device as being legitimate. These devices are often known simply as *rogue devices*. The next section describes in more detail what a rogue device is and what it does.

Rogue Devices

Rogue access comes in several forms. A user could plug in an unauthorized switch, which could allow other devices to connect to the network. With a switch, the damage to network data is more focused on what else might get plugged in. However, potential damage can result to the logical network configuration and setup, such as with STP. You can mitigate Spanning Tree Protocol (STP) attacks and changes by using Root Guard and Bridge Protocol Data Unit (BPDU) Guard configurations.

Root Guard is designed to provide a way to enforce the root bridge placement in the network. BPDU Guard is designed to allow network designers to keep the active network topology predictable, although BPDU Guard may seem unnecessary. Even though the administrator can set the bridge priority to zero, there is still no guarantee that it will be elected as the root bridge because there might be a bridge with priority zero and a lower bridge ID. BPDU Guard is best deployed toward user-facing ports to prevent rogue switch-network extensions by an attacker.

A potentially bigger problem would be the addition of a wireless access point (AP). Commercial APs have become inexpensive and readily available; it is easy for an employee to plug one into the enterprise LAN and make a wireless network without the IT department knowing or approving the addition. These rogue APs can be a serious breach of security because they can be attached to the network behind the firewall where protection from outside exists. Now even worse, employees do not typically enable any security on the rogue AP. It is easy for unauthorized users to use the access point to connect to the network, intercept traffic, hijack sessions, or access resources. An AP attached to the network maliciously can be an even bigger risk because it is intentionally hidden from physical and network views. Though this type of AP is much less common than employee-installed APs, these rogue access points create an unsecured wireless LAN connection that puts the entire wired network at risk. Malicious rogues?

Layer 2 Attacks

Attacks using or against Layer 2 devices can generally be categorized into:

- MAC layer attacks
- VLAN attacks
- Spoof attacks
- Attacks on switch devices

Table 14.1 lists some of the threats and outlines possible security solutions.

TABLE 14.1 Layer 2 Threats

Category	Threat	Possible Solution
MAC layer attacks	MAC address flooding Frames with unique, invalid source MAC addresses flood the switch, exhausting content-addressable memory (CAM) table space, disallowing new entries from valid hosts. Traffic to valid hosts is subsequently flooded out all ports.	Port Security, MAC address VLAN access maps.
VLAN attacks	VLAN hopping By altering the VLAN ID on packets encapsulated for trunking, an attacking device can send or receive packets on various VLANs, bypassing Layer 3 security measures.	Tighten up trunk configurations and the negotiation state of unused ports. Place unused ports in a common VLAN.
	Devices in same VLAN Devices may need protection from one another, even though they are on a common VLAN. This is especially true on service-provider segments that support devices from multiple customers.	Implement private VLANs (PVLANs).
Spoof attacks	DHCP starvation and DHCP spoofing An attacking device can exhaust the address space available to the DHCP servers for a period of time or establish itself as a DHCP server in man-in-the-middle attacks.	Use DHCP snooping.
	Spanning tree compromises Attacking device spoofs the root bridge in the STP topology. If successful, the network attacker can see a variety of frames.	Proactively configure the primary and backup root devices. Enable Root Guard.
	MAC spoofing Attacking device spoofs the MAC address of a valid host currently in the CAM table. Switch then forwards frames destined for the valid host to the attacking device.	Use DHCP snooping, Port Security.

TABLE 14.1   Layer 2 Threats *(continued)*

Category	Threat	Possible Solution
	Address Resolution Protocol (ARP) spoofing Attacking device crafts ARP replies intended for valid hosts. The attacking device's MAC address then becomes the destination address found in the Layer 2 frames sent by the valid network device.	Use dynamic ARP inspection, DHCP snooping, Port Security.
Switch Device Attacks	Cisco Discovery Protocol (CDP) manipulation Information sent through CDP is transmitted in clear text and unauthenticated, allowing it to be captured and divulge network topology information.	Disable CDP on all ports where it is not intentionally used.
	Secure Shell Protocol (SSH) and Telnet attacks Telnet packets can be read in clear text. SSH is an option but has security issues in version 1.	Use SSH version 2, use Telnet with vty ACLs.

MAC Layer Attacks

One of the most common Layer 2 switch attacks is MAC flooding; this causes a switch's content-addressable memory (CAM) table to overflow. Once the CAM table is full, the switch cannot learn new legitimate MAC addresses. This causes flooding of all data frames out all ports, even ones that should be properly forwarded. A MAC flooding attack can be done maliciously for the purpose of collecting traffic, which would not be possible unless the traffic is being flooded to all the ports.

A switch's CAM tables are limited in size; they can hold only a limited number of entries at one time. The number of entries that can be held by a switch depends on the model and capability of the switch. For example, tables in Cisco's standard access layer switches (such as the model 2950) can hold a maximum of 8192 entries. An attacker can flood a switch with a large number of frames that have source MAC addresses from an invalid range. If the attacker can get enough new entries into the table before the old ones expire, new valid entries can't be accepted into the table. When the table is full and traffic arrives on a switch port from a legitimate device, it will not be able to create a CAM table entry. The switch would then have to flood frames to that address out all ports rather than simply forward the frames to that specific host.

This has two adverse effects:

- Switch traffic is not forwarded efficiently and a significant amount of extra forwarding must be done.

- The attacker can be connected to any switch port and capture traffic that is normally only forwarded but is now being flooded.

Let's say, for example, that an attack occurs early in the morning before the start of a workday; the CAM table would already be full when the most of the users power on their computers. The frames received from those legitimate hosts would be unable to create CAM table entries as they power on. If this happens with most of the network devices, the number of MAC addresses for which traffic will be flooded will be high, and any switch port will carry flooded frames from a large number of devices.

What's even worse about this situation is that, if the flood of invalid CAM table entries happens only once, the switch will age out the older, invalid CAM entries. This will allow new, legitimate devices to create entries. If the traffic flooding stops it may never be detected, and the attacker could have captured a significant and unknown amount of data from the network and you'd never know it.

VLAN Attacks

On networks using trunking protocols, rogue traffic can create security vulnerabilities by hopping from one VLAN to another. VLAN hopping attacks are best mitigated by close control of trunk links. When you think about controlling trunk links, you should always remember the basics. Don't leave your switch ports in their default state. By default, almost all Cisco switch ports are in the dynamic desirable mode. This means that if an attacker could get a connection to your switch, they could send a DTP packet and potentially create a trunk link with the switch. If you are using an unsecure implementation of VTP, the attacker could easily learn all of the VLANs on your switch. With this connection and knowledge of the VLANs, it would be very easy for the attacker to gain access and capture data from any or all of your VLANs.

At a minimum, all switch ports should be configured as access ports. Even better is shutting down all unused ports. Many administrators don't like to do this because it is inconvenient to enable the ports when they need to be used. I always wonder how inconvenient those same administrators will find it when their network gets hacked!

A couple of other features can be enabled to help automate the process of protecting your switches and access to other devices. Private VLANs (PVLANs) can be configured to establish security regions within a single VLAN without subnetting. VLAN access control lists (VACLs) can be used to filter traffic within a VLAN.

Switch Spoofing

Basically, the scenario that I just described is your typical switch spoofing attack. The attacker configures a system (often a host or device that the attacker gained access to, if the attack is remote) to spoof itself as a switch. The attack can emulate or send fake Inter-Switch Link (ISL) or 802.1Q signaling along with dynamic trunking protocol (DTP) messages. This signaling attempts to create a trunk link to the switch.

A switch port that is configured in a dynamic DTP mode (which is the default) could negotiate to become a trunk link if and when it receives a DTP negotiation packet. Normally, the DTP packet would come from another switch that you trust and placed on the network. In this case it could be generated by an attacker's machine. Once the trunk link has been established it could then accept traffic destined for any VLAN supported on that trunk. The malicious device can then send packets to, or collect packets from, any VLAN carried by the negotiated trunk.

Let's take a look at how this process would work.

 Real World Scenario

The Case of the Unscrupulous Contractor

In Figure 14.1, you can see there is a switch with users connected; they are divided between three different VLANs. There is also an attacker machine attached to the switch. Can you tell which machine it is? No? Well, neither can the network administrator. The attacker could be:

- Someone who is trusted enough to be on the network anyway

- A guest in one of the buildings, using a port in a conference room or work room

- A remote attacker who has taken over a legitimate host that is on the network

This is not an all-inclusive list, but gives you some of the most common ways that access to the network is achieved. These attacks happened in the FutureTech Corporate office; the security holes have since been plugged.

FIGURE 14.1   Spoofing a Switch

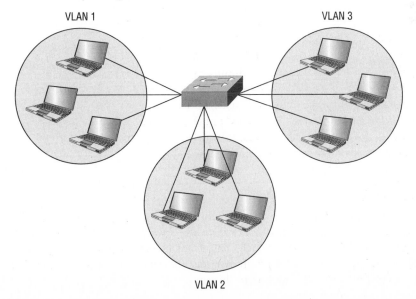

Steps in a Switch Spoofing Attack

1. It was a busy Monday morning, and everyone was hurrying around the office trying to get everything started for the week. While the employees were focused on other tasks, one of the contractors doing a job for the company slipped into a conference room unauthorized. All that the attacker needed was an open port that is connected to a switch. The attacker could have done two fairly easy things to gain access to the switch and most of the network.

2. The attacker forced the switch to make a trunk link. This was a small challenge, and FutureTech never did figure out how the attacker accomplished it, although they did narrow it to two approaches. Either way, it was possible because the switch ports were not configured correctly. The network administrator at the time thought it was too inconvenient to enable particular switch ports for meeting attendees.

    a. The contractor could have had software loaded on a laptop that would allow him to send trunk negotiation messages to the switch. There is software that will allow an attacker to send DTP frames to the switch and negotiate the switch port into a trunk link. Once this has occurred, the attacker could access most of the traffic from any VLAN that is allowed to traverse that trunk link. This, by default, would be all of the VLANs configured on the switch.

    b. The attacker could have used a small switch, easily carried in his bag. Cisco makes a wonderful line of little 8-port switches. They have all of the features and con-figuration ability of a full-size rack mount switch, but they are compact and don't have noisy running fans. A foul-intentioned person can easily use one; plug it into a switch port and allow that switch to connect. If the offending switch port in the conference room is not configured to prevent this type of connection, the attacker would gain access to a large portion of the network. This type of access is a little easier; if the port in the conference room is set up in the default mode, it will dynamically create a trunk with the attacker's switch. Even worse, because FutureTech used VTP on the network, and there was no password in the configura-tion, the attacker's switch would learn all of the VLANs as well.

3. Once the trunk link was formed with the switch, the attacker could easily tag traffic to send frames to whatever VLAN he chose. Because the attacker was not familiar with the network (he didn't know which VLANs are configured), he might have had to do some guessing at first to send frames onto the network. He could also have promiscuously listened to all of the traffic that came over the trunk link. Once traf-fic had been received, the attacker could see the tags on the traffic and know what VLANs exist.

4. Finally, the attacker was able to collect and send data to and from the network.

Double Tagging

Another method of VLAN hopping is for a device to generate frames that contain two 802.1Q headers. This causes the switch to forward the frames into a VLAN that would (and should) be inaccessible to an attacker under normal circumstances.

It is possible and useful to tag frames with more than one 802.1Q header. Double tagging is used legitimately by service providers. A service provider can offer the ability to make VLANs reachable between different sites in an enterprise. This is done by handing a trunk link off to the service provider, who will in turn "re-trunk" or place the customer's trunk link in their own trunk; this is typically called Q-in-Q tunneling. The trunk link is carried through the service provider's network using the outside header. Once the data gets to the edge of the provider's network, it will be passed back off to the customer's network, and the outside header will be removed. This leaves just the first header that identified the customer's VLAN; when the traffic gets back into the customer's network, the switches see it and handle it as though nothing happened to it.

The first switch to receive the double-tagged frame removes the first tag from the frame, and then forwards the frame out. It does this only because the first tag matches a trunk port native VLAN.

The switch forwards the frame, using the inner 802.1Q tag, out all the switch ports; this includes all trunk ports configured with the same native VLAN the network attacker connected into. When the frame reaches the second switch, that switch will forward the frame to the destination, based on the VLAN ID in the second 802.1Q header. If the trunk does not match the native VLAN of the attacker, the frame would be untagged and flooded to only the original VLAN.

This type of attack is the reason why it is recommended to place the native VLAN of trunk links into a parked VLAN. A parked VLAN is a VLAN that does not have any access ports. The native VLAN of an 802.1Q trunk link is the VLAN where the switch will forward any frames that are otherwise untagged. To protect from threats, you don't want to allow any untagged frames or frames with an undetermined destination. Any untagged frames that reach a switch will be placed into the native parked VLAN. Once in that parked VLAN, the frames will have no ports to be forwarded out of.

Spoofing Attacks

Dynamic Host Configuration Protocol (DHCP), Media Access Control (MAC), and Address Resolution Protocol (ARP) spoofing are all methods used to gain unauthorized access to a network or to redirect traffic for malicious purposes. DHCP snooping, Port Security, and dynamic ARP inspection (DAI) can be configured to guard against these threats.

DHCP Server Spoof Attack

An attacker can gain access to network traffic by spoofing responses that would be sent by a valid DHCP server. The device sending the DHCP-spoofed messages replies to clients that have made DHCP requests. The legitimate DHCP server will most likely reply as well but, if the spoofing device is on the same segment as the client or its reply is just received by the client first, the attacker's information will be used.

The attacker's DHCP reply offers the client an IP address and other applicable networking information that uses the attacker's information as the default gateway or Domain Name System (DNS) server. For example, let's say that the attacker is using the default gateway approach. After a client receives the bogus TCP/IP information from the rogue DHCP server, the client uses the attacker's address and will begin forwarding packets to the rogue device. The attacker can, in turn, send the packets to the real destination. This is known as a man-in-the-middle attack; it may go entirely undetected as an intruder intercepts the data flow through the network.

ARP Spoof Attack

For a host machine to find the MAC address of another host, it uses ARP. In ARP, the host sends out a broadcast to determine the MAC address of another host with an otherwise known IP address. The device that is assigned the specific IP address replies with its MAC address. The originating host caches the ARP response; it uses the MAC address to fill the destination address field in the Layer 2 frame header of packets sent to that IP address.

An attacker can take advantage of this process by spoofing an ARP reply from a legitimate device with a gratuitous ARP. The attacking device then appears as the destination host. The ARP reply from the attacker causes the sender to store the MAC address of the attacking system in its ARP cache. All packets destined for those IP addresses will be forwarded through the attacker system.

 Real World Scenario

An ARP Spoofing Attack

This sort of attack could happen almost anywhere if it is not properly guarded against. All it takes is an attacker getting enough control over a device on the network to configure it or put software on it; rogue devices will answer ARP requests to other devices. Unfortunately, this kind of attack can be perpetrated through the use of Trojan horses or worms that load software or leave backdoors into systems. You can do several things to ensure viruses don't get on the network, but if one does, you need to be aware of this sort of attack and what can be done on the Layer 2 level.

If you look at Figure 14.2, you can see that two hosts are connected on the same subnet through a switch to a router. R1 is the default gateway for the hosts on this subnet. The FT2 device is the host, which, thanks to that same lazy network administrator, was taken over by an attacker. This security hole has since been plugged. And guess where that network administrator works now—not at FutureTech.

FIGURE 14.2 ARP Spoofing Attack

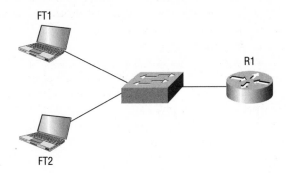

1. FT1, the host that has not been taken over, sends an ARP request looking for the MAC address of the R1. (R1 is the default gateway for the hosts on this subnet.)

2. R1 sends a reply to FT1 with its MAC and IP addresses. It would also update its own ARP cache with the information about FT1.

3. FT1 then binds R1's MAC address with its IP address in the local ARP cache of FT1.

4. FT2, the attacking host, then sends an ARP message that causes FT2's MAC address to be bound to R1's IP address.

5. FT1 then updates its ARP cache with this new information incorrectly binding FT2's MAC address and R1's IP address.

6. FT2 then sends an ARP message that causes FT2's MAC address to be bound to FT1's IP address.

7. R1 updates its local ARP cache with FT2's MAC address, now bound to FT1's IP address.

8. Once this has been completed, all of the normal traffic and packets from FT1 and R1 will be diverted through FT2's attacking machine.

Switch Device Attacks

This category of attacks on switches is not much different from similar attacks aimed at out-looking routers and Layer 3 devices. To protect your network from these attacks, you need to look at the management protocols and the ways that you access devices remotely. Because most of your switches aren't going to be facing the outside of the network, I'll just point out a couple of things.

First, even if the device is not facing the outside (as I already said, it doesn't matter if a device is on the outside or not—you need to be as secure as possible), you need to secure the communication that you use to access the device remotely. Telnet is a perfect example of a protocol that you don't want to use on the network. It is insecure and sends all of the data in clear text. You should aim to move all of your devices to using SSH. The process for configuring SSH on switches is the same as for routers.

The other protocol or type of communication that I want to talk about here is CDP. You will read in many places that you should turn it off where it is not required, and I urge you to do that. Just remember that there are going to be places that you have to leave it on, such as ports where a Cisco VOIP phone is connected. Later, in Chapter 17, "Voice," I will go over the specific reasons that you need to have CDP turned on for those ports. For now know that the phones and the switches talk so that they can agree on QoS settings and to become aware of each other.

Securing Layer 2

You can implement some techniques and features to mitigate the dangers of DHCP, MAC, and ARP spoofing. The following features can be configured to guard against these threats:

- DHCP snooping
- Port Security
- Dynamic ARP inspection (DAI)

Dangers from an attacker who hops VLANs and creates security vulnerabilities can be controlled through proper configuration of ports and trunks. The features that can be configured to aid in protecting against these threats include:

- Private VLANs (PVLANs)
- VLAN access control lists (VACLs)

Port Security

Port Security is a super useful and powerful feature supported on Cisco switches that restricts a switch port to a specific set or number of MAC addresses. By specifying the number of MAC addresses on a port, you can limit or control the devices that are connected to your switches and keep users from attaching a wireless access point and opening that security hole into the network. By statically specifying the MAC addresses allowed on a port, you can bar untrusted devices from connecting. With these measures in place, a would-be attacker will have a very tough time sniffing traffic, poisoning a switch's MAC table, ARP spoofing, or putting a rogue DHCP server on the network.

Port Security can learn the authorized MAC addresses dynamically or from your static configuration. If you limit the number of addresses but do not configure specific MAC addresses, the port will allow any MAC addresses to be learned dynamically until the maximum number of addresses is reached. Port Security acts like a bouncer at a popular night spot, allowing access on a first-come, first-served basis and cutting off access when the maximum capacity is reached. You can configure your switch ports to age out the dynamically learned address when a host disconnects.

Port Security can be used to mitigate spoof attacks by limiting access through each switch port to a single MAC address. This prevents intruders from using multiple MAC addresses over a short period of time but does not limit port access to a specific MAC address. The most restrictive Port Security implementation would specify the exact MAC address of the single device that is to gain access through each port. Implementing this level of security, however, requires considerable administrative overhead, because you would have to go to every single switch port on every switch and manually configure the authorized address.

The sticky learning Port Security feature (only available on some switch platforms) combines the features of dynamically learned and statically configured addresses. When this feature is configured on an interface, the interface converts dynamically learned addresses to sticky secure addresses. They are added to the running configuration, just as if they were configured using the `switchport port-security mac-address` command.

Port Security includes a sticky MAC address feature that can limit switch port access to a single, specific MAC address without the network administrator having to gather the MAC address of every legitimate device and manually associate it with a particular switch port. When sticky MAC addresses are used, the switch port converts dynamically learned MAC addresses to sticky MAC addresses and subsequently adds them to the running configuration as if they were static entries for a single MAC address allowed by Port Security. Sticky secure MAC addresses are added to the running configuration but do not become part of the startup configuration file unless the running configuration is copied to the startup configuration after addresses have been learned. If you do save the running configuration in the startup configuration, the secure addresses will not have to be relearned upon switch reboot, and this provides a higher level of network security.

The command that follows converts all dynamic port-security learned MAC addresses to sticky secure MAC addresses:

```
switchport port-security mac-address sticky
```

 The command that converts all dynamic port-security learned MAC addresses to sticky secure MAC addresses cannot be used on ports where a voice VLAN is configured.

Port Security Points of Interest

Here are a few points to remember about Port Security configurations:

- Port Security must be enabled on a port-by-port basis.
- By default, only one MAC address is allowed access through a given switch port when Port Security is enabled.
- Port Security doesn't have a specific restriction on a particular MAC address, just on the total number of addresses on that port.

- Learned addresses are not aged out by default but can be configured to do so after a specified time using the `switchport port-security aging value` command. The *value* option can be any number from 1 to 1024.

- Access to the switch port can be restricted to one or more specific MAC addresses.

- If the number of specific MAC addresses assigned is lower than the value set in the `port-security max` command, the remaining allowed addresses can be learned dynamically.

- If you specify a list of MAC addresses that is equal to the maximum number allowed, access is limited to that list of MAC addresses.

- By default, if the maximum number of connections is achieved and a new MAC address attempts to access the port, the switch must take one of these actions:

  1. Protect: Frames from the non-allowed address are dropped, but there is no log of the violation.

  2. Restrict: Frames from the non-allowed address are dropped, a log message is created, and a Simple Network Management Protocol (SNMP) trap is sent.

  3. Shut down: If any frames are seen from a non-allowed address, the interface is err-disabled, a log entry is made, an SNMP trap is sent, and manual intervention or err-disable recovery must be used to make the interface usable.

WARNING   Make sure you set the *value* parameter to a value of 2 when you have a port supporting a VoIP phone and computer. If the default value is used, a port-security violation will result.

AAA

Authentication, authorization, and accounting (AAA) network security services provide the primary framework through which access control is set up on a switch. AAA is an architectural framework for configuring a set of three independent security functions in a consistent manner. AAA provides a modular way of performing these services and operates the same way on Layer 2 devices as it did on Layer 3 devices. For a review of AAA, see Chapter 13, "Device Security."

802.1x

The IEEE 802.1x standard defines a port-based access control and authentication protocol that restricts unauthorized workstations from connecting to a LAN through publicly accessible switch ports. The authentication server authenticates each workstation that is connected to a switch port before making available any services offered by the switch or the LAN.

Until the workstation is authenticated, 802.1x access controls allow only Extensible Authentication Protocol over LAN (EAPOL) traffic through the port to which the workstation is connected. After authentication succeeds, normal traffic can pass through the port.

With 802.1x port-based authentication, the devices in the network have specific roles, as described in Table 14.2.

TABLE 14.2   802.1x Device Roles

Role	Description
Client	The device (workstation) that requests access to the LAN and switch services, and responds to requests from the switch. The workstation must be running 802.1x-compliant client software, such as the software client offered in the Microsoft Windows XP operating system. (The port that the client is attached to is the supplicant [client] in the IEEE 802.1x specification.)
Authentication server	Performs the actual authentication of the client. The authentication server validates the identity of the client and notifies the switch whether or not the client is authorized to access the LAN and switch services. Because the switch acts as the proxy, the authentication service is transparent to the client. The RADIUS security system with Extensible Authentication Protocol (EAP) extensions is the only supported authentication server.
Switch (also called the authenticator)	Controls physical access to the network based on the authentication status of the client. The switch acts as an intermediary (proxy) between the client (supplicant) and the authentication server, requesting identifying information from the client, verifying that information with the authentication server, and relaying a response to the client. The switch uses a RADIUS software agent, which is responsible for encapsulating and decapsulating the EAP frames and interacting with the authentication server.

The switch port state determines whether or not the client is granted access to the network. The port starts in the unauthorized state. While in this state, the port disallows all ingress and egress traffic except 802.1x protocol packets. When a client is successfully authenticated, the port transitions to the authorized state, allowing all traffic for the client to flow normally.

If the switch requests the client identity (authenticator initiation) and the client does not support 802.1x, the port remains in the unauthorized state, and the client is not granted access to the network.

In contrast, when an 802.1x-enabled client connects to a port and the client initiates the authentication process (supplicant initiation) by sending the EAPOL-start frame to a switch that is not running the 802.1x protocol, no response is received, and the client begins sending frames as if the port is in the authorized state.

You control the port authorization state by using the `dot1x port-control` interface configuration command and the keywords described in Table 14.3.

TABLE 14.3   dot1x Port Control Keywords

Keyword	Description
force-authorized	Disables 802.1x port-based authentication and causes the port to transition to the authorized state without any authentication exchange required. The port transmits and receives normal traffic without 802.1x-based authentication of the client. This is the default setting.
force-unauthorized	Causes the port to remain in the unauthorized state, ignoring all attempts by the client to authenticate. The switch cannot provide authentication services to the client through the interface.
auto	Enables 802.1x port-based authentication and causes the port to begin in the unauthorized state, allowing only EAPOL frames to be sent and received through the port. The authentication process begins when the link state of the port transitions from down to up (authenticator initiation) or when an EAPOL-start frame is received (supplicant initiation). The switch requests the identity of the client and begins relaying authentication messages between the client and the authentication server. The switch uniquely identifies each client attempting to access the network by using the client MAC address.

If the client is successfully authenticated (receives an "accept" frame from the authentication server), the port state changes to authorized, and all frames from the authenticated client are allowed through the port.

If the authentication fails, the port remains in the unauthorized state, but authentication can be retried. If the authentication server cannot be reached, the switch can retransmit the request. If no response is received from the server after the specified number of attempts, authentication fails, and network access is not granted.

When a client logs out, it sends an EAPOL-logout message, causing the switch port to transition to the unauthorized state.

The configuration of dot1x is very similar to that of the regular AAA authentication lists that you have already seen. The primary difference is that in the authentication list command you specify dot1x instead of login.

VACLs

Cisco Systems' multilayer switches support three types of ACLs:

- Router access control list (RACL)

- Port access control list (PACL)

- VLAN access control list (VACL)

Router Access Control Lists   RACLs are supported in the TCAM hardware on Cisco multilayer switches. In Cisco Catalyst switches, RACL can be applied to any routed interface, including a switch virtual interface (SVI) or Layer 3 routed port.

Port Access Control Lists   PACLs filter traffic at the port level. PACLs can be applied on a Layer 2 switch port, trunk port, or EtherChannel port.

VLAN Access Control Lists   VACLs are supported in software on Cisco multilayer switches.

Cisco Catalyst switches support four ACL lookups per packet: input and output security ACL and input and output quality of service (QoS) ACLs. The switches use two methods of performing a merge: order independent and order dependent. With an order-independent merge, ACLs are transformed from a series of order-dependent actions to a set of order-independent masks and patterns. The resulting access control entry (ACE) can be very large. The merge is processor and memory intensive.

Order-dependent merge is a recent improvement on some Catalyst switches in which ACLs retain their order-dependent aspect. The computation is much faster and is less processor-intensive.

RACLs are supported in hardware through IP standard ACLs and IP extended ACLs, with permit and deny actions. ACL processing is an intrinsic part of the packet forwarding process. ACL entries are programmed in hardware. Lookups occur in the pipeline, whether or not ACLs are configured. With RACLs, access list statistics and logging are not supported.

Private VLANs

Service providers often have devices from multiple clients, in addition to their own servers, on a single demilitarized zone (DMZ) segment or VLAN. As security issues proliferate, it becomes necessary to provide traffic isolation between devices, even though they may exist on the same Layer 3 segment and VLAN. Catalyst 6500/4500 switches implement private VLANs (PVLANs) to allow some switch ports to be shared and keep some switch ports isolated, even though all the ports exist on the same VLAN. The 2950 and 3550 switches support protected ports, which are functionally similar to PVLANs on a per-switch basis.

The traditional solution to address Internet service provider (ISP) requirements is to provide one VLAN per customer, with each VLAN having its own IP subnet. A Layer 3 device then provides interconnectivity between VLANs and Internet destinations.

Here are the challenges with this traditional solution:

- Supporting a separate VLAN per customer may require a high number of interfaces on service provider network devices.

- Spanning tree becomes more complicated with many VLAN iterations.

- Dividing network address space into many subnets wastes space and increases management complexity.

- Securing multiple ACL applications to maintain security on multiple VLANs results in increased management complexity.

PVLANs provide Layer 2 isolation between ports within the same VLAN. This isolation eliminates the need for a separate VLAN and IP subnet per customer.

A port in a PVLAN can be one of three types:

- Isolated
- Promiscuous
- Community

Isolated   An isolated port has complete Layer 2 separation from other ports within the same PVLAN, except for the promiscuous port. PVLANs block all traffic to isolated ports, except the traffic from promiscuous ports. Traffic received from an isolated port is forwarded to only promiscuous ports.

Promiscuous   A promiscuous port can communicate with all ports within the PVLAN, including the community and isolated ports. The default gateway for the segment would likely be hosted on a promiscuous port, given that all devices in the PVLAN will need to communicate with that port.

Community   Community ports communicate among themselves and with their promiscuous ports. These interfaces are isolated at Layer 2 from all other interfaces in other communities, or in isolated ports within their PVLAN.

Because trunks can support the VLANs carrying traffic between isolated, community, and promiscuous ports, isolated and community port traffic might enter or leave the switch through a trunk interface.

PVLAN ports are associated with a set of supporting VLANs that are used to create the PVLAN structure. A PVLAN uses VLANs in three ways:

- As a primary VLAN
- As an isolated VLAN
- As a community VLAN

Primary VLAN   A primary VLAN carries traffic from promiscuous ports to isolated, community, and other promiscuous ports in the same primary VLAN.

Isolated VLAN   An isolated VLAN carries traffic from isolated ports to a promiscuous port.

Community VLAN   A community VLAN carries traffic between community ports and to promiscuous ports. You can configure multiple community VLANs in a PVLAN.

Isolated and community VLANs are called secondary VLANs. You can extend PVLANs across multiple devices by trunking the primary, isolated, and community VLANs to other devices that support PVLANs.

A promiscuous port can service only one primary VLAN. A promiscuous port can service one isolated VLAN or many community VLANs.

With a promiscuous port, you can connect a wide range of devices as access points to a PVLAN. For example, you can connect a promiscuous port to the server port to connect an isolated VLAN or a number of community VLANs to the server.

You can use a load balancer to load-balance the servers present in the isolated or community VLANs, or you can use a promiscuous port to monitor or back up all the PVLAN servers from an administration workstation.

DHCP Snooping

DHCP snooping is a Cisco Catalyst feature that determines which switch ports can respond to DHCP requests. Ports are identified as trusted and untrusted. Trusted ports can source all DHCP messages, whereas untrusted ports can source requests only. Trusted ports host a DHCP server or can be an uplink toward the DHCP server. If a rogue device on an untrusted port attempts to send a DHCP response packet into the network, the port is shut down. This feature can be coupled with DHCP Option 82, in which switch information, such as the port ID of the DHCP request, can be inserted into the DHCP request packet.

Untrusted ports are those that are not explicitly configured as trusted. A DHCP binding table is built for untrusted ports. Each entry contains the client MAC address, IP address, lease time, binding type, VLAN number, and port ID recorded as clients make DHCP requests. The table is then used to filter subsequent DHCP traffic. From a DHCP snooping perspective, untrusted access ports should not send any DHCP server responses, such as DHCPOFFER, DHCPACK, or DHCPNAK.

The steps for configuring DHCP snooping are.

1. Configure global DHCP snooping.

2. Configure trusted ports.

3. Configure Option 82 insertion off (default enabled by step 2).

4. Configure rate limiting on untrusted ports.

5. Configure DHCP snooping for the selected VLANs.

IP Source Guard

IP Source Guard is similar to DHCP snooping. This feature can be enabled on a DHCP snooping untrusted Layer 2 port to prevent IP address spoofing. To start, all IP traffic on the port is blocked except for DHCP packets that are captured by the DHCP snooping process.

When a client receives a valid IP address from the DHCP server, or when a static IP source binding is configured by the user, a per-port and VLAN access control list (PVACL) is installed on the port.

This process restricts the client IP traffic to those source IP addresses configured in the binding; any IP traffic with a source IP address other than that in the IP source binding will be filtered out. This filtering limits a host's ability to attack the network by claiming a neighbor host's IP address.

If IP Source Guard is enabled on a trunk port with a large number of VLANs that have DHCP snooping enabled, you might run out of access control list (ACL) hardware resources, and some packets might be switched in software.

IP Source Guard supports only Layer 2 ports, including both access and trunk. For each untrusted Layer 2 port, two levels of IP traffic security filtering exist, as follows:

Source IP Address Filter   IP traffic is filtered based on its source IP address. Only IP traffic with a source IP address that matches the IP source binding entry is permitted.

An IP source address filter is changed when a new IP source entry binding is created or deleted on the port. The port PVACL will be recalculated and reapplied in the hardware to reflect the IP source binding change. By default, if the IP filter is enabled without any IP source binding on the port, a default PVACL that denies all IP traffic is installed on the port. Similarly, when the IP filter is disabled, any IP source filter PVACL will be removed from the interface.

Source IP and MAC Address Filter   IP traffic is filtered based on its source IP address in addition to its MAC address; only IP traffic with source IP and MAC addresses that match the IP source binding entry are permitted.

Dynamic ARP Inspection

To prevent ARP spoofing or poisoning, a switch must ensure that only valid ARP requests and responses are relayed. Dynamic ARP inspection (DAI) prevents these attacks by intercepting and validating all ARP requests and responses. Each intercepted ARP reply is verified for valid MAC-address-to-IP-address bindings before it is forwarded to a PC to update the ARP cache. ARP replies coming from invalid devices are dropped.

DAI determines the validity of an ARP packet based on a valid MAC-address-to-IP-address bindings database built by DHCP snooping. In addition, to handle hosts that use statically configured IP addresses, DAI can also validate ARP packets against user-configured ARP ACLs.

To ensure that only valid ARP requests and responses are relayed, DAI takes these actions:

- Forwards ARP packets received on a trusted interface without any checks
- Intercepts all ARP packets on untrusted ports
- Verifies that each intercepted packet has a valid IP-to-MAC address binding before forwarding packets that can update the local ARP cache
- Drops, logs, or drops and logs ARP packets with invalid IP-to-MAC address bindings

Configure all access switch ports as untrusted and all switch ports connected to other switches as trusted. In this case, all ARP packets entering the network would be from an upstream distribution or core switch, bypassing the security check and requiring no further validation.

DAI can also be used to rate-limit the ARP packets and then err-disable the interface if the rate is exceeded.

Summary

Now you can see that security can be applied to every level of a network. I showed you many of the common Layer 2 attacks and what you can do to help prevent them. This chapter covered MAC attacks, VLAN attacks, and spoofing attacks. You learned to use some of the features built into switches to mitigate these attacks.

It also covered Port Security, which allows you to control what MAC addresses and how many can be on a switch port, as well as VLAN access lists (access-maps), private VLANs, DHCP snooping, DAI, and IP Source Guard.

You also learned that some of the simplest things can help keep your network secure, such as securing access to your switches, and making sure basic port and trunk configurations don't make it easy for an attacker to get on the network.

Review Questions

1. A device that is attached to the network without authorization could potentially cause harm; what do you call this type of device?

   A. Free upgrade

   B. Switch

   C. Rogue device

   D. Manager's computer

2. MAC flooding attacks are accomplished by filling what table on a switch?

   A. ARP table

   B. MAC address table

   C. IP address table

   D. Name table

3. Double tagging is an example of what kind of attack?

   A. VLAN hopping

   B. Spoofing

   C. MAC address

   D. ARP caching

4. Placing an unauthorized DHCP server on the network is an example of what kind of attack?

   A. VLAN hopping

   B. Spoofing

   C. MAC address

   D. ARP caching

5. Disabling unused or unnecessary services is a poor security practice.

   A. True

   B. False

   C. Maybe

   D. Always

6. 802.1x helps to secure the network by authenticating what?

   A. Server

   B. Switch

   C. Router

   D. Host machine

7. AAA is a service that does nothing for the security of the network.

   A. True

   B. False

   C. Maybe

   D. On the weekend

8. In addition to their security functions Private VLANs can also save an ISP what?

   A. Nothing

   B. Number of devices

   C. Address space

   D. Things to configure

9. DHCP snooping helps to make sure that spare (backup) DHCP servers are not put on the network.

   A. True

   B. False

   C. Always

   D. On other people's network

10. Dynamic ARP inspection uses the information collected by what other feature?

   A. MAC table

   B. Spanning Tree

   C. DHCP snooping

   D. Port Security

Answers to Review Questions

1. C. A rogue device is a device unauthorized on the network.

2. B. The MAC address table when filled will cause traffic to flood out all ports.

3. A. Double tagging allows an attacker to appear like they are on the same VLAN, which lets traffic hop to a VLAN it shouldn't.

4. B. A rogue DHCP server can spoof IP addresses and make hosts send traffic to IPs where they shouldn't.

5. B. False, disabling unused services is always a good practice.

6. D. The host machine is authenticated in 802.1x.

7. B. False, AAA provide multiple layers of security by authenticating devices, controlling what those devices can do, and then keeping track of what they do.

8. C. The use of Private VLANs can save an ISP address space.

9. B. False, backup DHCP servers would be authorized servers, DHCP snooping makes sure rogue servers are not placed on the network.

10. C. DAI uses the table with IP-address-to-MAC-address mappings that are built by DHCP snooping.

Chapter

15

Cisco IOS Firewall

IN THIS CHAPTER, YOU WILL LEARN HOW TO DO THE FOLLOWING:

✓ Describe the functions and operations of Cisco IOS Firewall (stateful firewall, CBAC, and more)

✓ Configure a Cisco IOS Firewall with SDM

✓ Verify Cisco IOS SDM configurations with IOS CLI configurations

In this chapter, I introduce the Cisco IOS Firewall feature set and discuss its major functions. I walk through configuring the firewall with Cisco Security Device Manager (SDM), what those configurations look like in IOS command line, using SDM to monitor the firewall, and reviewing firewall commands.

Function of the Cisco IOS Firewall

Cisco IOS Firewall feature set provides a stateful security software component to the traditional IOS router software. It allows you to provide a firewall to a router environment, where a separate, hardware firewall is not feasible from either a cost or design perspective. The Cisco IOS Firewall feature set includes the following functions:

- Stateful packet inspection for true firewall function
- Authentication proxy to control access to resources
- Application inspection for protection of common protocols and applications
- Transparent firewall support
- Protection against Distributed Denial of Service (DDOS)
- Logging of transactions and support for audit and alerts

Here's an overview.

Authentication Proxy

Authentication proxy is a method by which you can restrict access to certain resources by requiring users to authenticate. This support is usually tied to sending authentication requests to servers elsewhere in the network. It commonly uses AAA services on the router to do so. AAA-supported servers include RADIUS and TACACS, as well as others. A typical application would grant outbound access to the Internet. Users who tried to access the Internet using a browser would be prompted for username and password in order to gain access. The username and password would be sent to the authentication server in order to determine whether the user has access to the resource requested.

Transparent Firewall

Transparent firewall is a new feature that was first introduced in IOS 12.3(7)T on limited platforms and is now in mainline release starting in 12.4(1). Transparent firewall can be used when you want to have a firewall in between network segments where introducing a Layer 3 firewall is impractical for whatever reason. Transparent firewall utilizes Layer 2 bridging and applies the IOS Firewall between those segments that are bridged.

Stateful Packet Inspection

Content-based Access Control (CBAC) was Cisco's first implementation of stateful packet inspection (SPI) based in IOS software. Prior to the introduction of CBAC, there was no stateful feature, just Layer 3 access control lists (ACLs). CBAC introduced a way to do more than just permit or deny, based on IP address or port usage. This functionality was introduced in IOS Version 11.2p and was the first time packets were inspected.

Concept: Content-Based Access Control

CBAC, also referred to as stateful packet inspection, is the core component in a stateful firewall. The inspection uses ACLs to determine traffic to filter but is augmented with the ability to monitor several attributes in TCP, UDP, and ICMP packets to ensure that traffic permitted is legitimate return traffic from connections originating on the inside or secure side of the firewall.

Content-Based Access Control

Let's talk a bit about how the process for CBAC and how it works. Figure 15.1 shows the basic components.

FIGURE 15.1   Cisco IOS CBAC Components

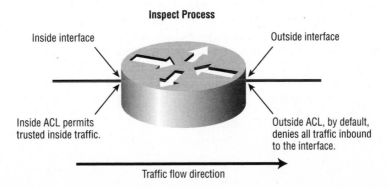

🌐 Real World Scenario

Surfing for Parts

FutureTech has a buyer in Brussels who is looking for hard-to-find parts for one of the European manufacturing facilities. She is scouring the Internet looking for a left-handed widget. CBAC is in place on the Internet connection. Let's examine what happens when a packet leaves the buyer's PC and heads out to the Internet.

The buyer opens her favorite browser, intending to search for that left-handed widget. She likes using Google to search. As soon as she types http://www.google.com and hits Enter, a packet leaves the PC headed toward the router and then the Internet. The packet will first be checked against an outgoing access list, inspected, and state information will be saved. Because the state information is saved, a temporary inbound access list is configured in order to allow that return traffic to come back from Google's servers. The packet is then allowed out at this point. On the return trip, the packet will be evaluated against the inbound access list. Because CBAC added the temporary inbound list, the packet is allowed back in. And that's a quick look at a CBAC scenario. The step-by-step process is outlined below.

1. Packet is sent from that inside workstation toward the Internet.

2. Packet is checked against outgoing access list.

3. Packet is inspected and state information is saved as a new state table entry.

4. State information is used to create a temporary access list that allows return traffic back in.

5. Packet is allowed out to the Internet.

6. Return traffic comes back to the outside interface.

7. Packet is checked against inbound access list.

8. Because the packet is part of the original outbound conversation and therefore matches inbound access list, the packet is allowed back to original host.

9. Packet is inspected again.

10. When the conversation is terminated or it times out, temporary access list is removed.

Figures 15.2 shows how TCP packets are handled; Figure 15.3 shows the process for UDP handling.

FIGURE 15.2   Cisco IOS Firewall TCP Handling

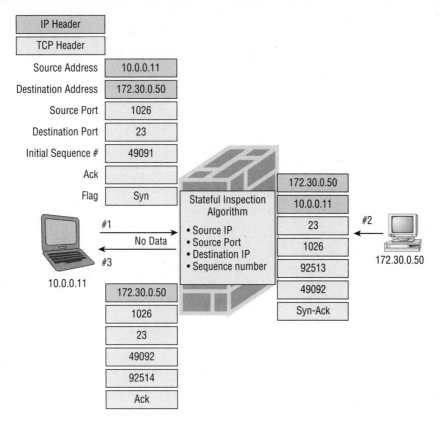

FIGURE 15.3   Cisco IOS Firewall UDP Handling

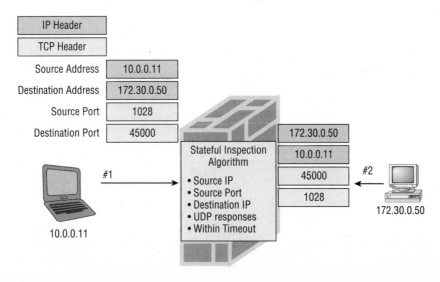

DDOS Protection

Distributed Denial of Service (DDOS) is a very real attack vector in today's Internet environment. DDOS attacks are used to deny resources for political purposes, extortion attempts, and just to show you it can be done. The attack is usually accomplished with botnets—hundreds and even thousands of disparate computers that have been taken over by malware and are under the control remotely of a command and control computer, usually run by hackers or criminal organizations.

 Real World Scenario

FutureTech under Attack

A competitor of FutureTech has rented a botnet from a Russian hacker. The competitor launches a Distributed Denial of Service during the time frame that the Brussels buyer was expecting bids into the website. Lucky for her that the IOS Firewall DDOS protections were configured before the attack started.

Cisco IOS Firewall feature set includes protections against DDOS attacks with some default settings that are activated when an inspection rule is applied. These monitor and regulate TCP SYN half-open connections.

Concept: Half-Open Connections

Whenever someone sends a packet to a service that is listening on a specific TCP port, a half-open connection can occur. Initially, a SYN packet is sent to the TCP port, which responds with a SYN-ACK. Because DDOS packets are generated artificially, there is no way to complete the TCP three-way handshake with an ACK or acknowledgment. The connection remains open because the firewall is expecting a completion that never happens. Generate enough of these and you start chewing up valuable resources on the firewall and legitimate connections cannot be made.

When the default inspect settings are in place, some finite thresholds are set for half-open connections. When these are met, you can send a reset or just kill the connection. Once the connection is reset or killed, another can take its place. We will look at this in more detail later in the chapter.

Configure Cisco IOS Firewall with SDM

You can configure an IOS Firewall using the Cisco Security Device Manager (SDM). You should be familiar with the basic operation of SDM now, after using it in previous chapters. However, you will use a different tab for this configuration. As in the past, click the Configure tab at the top of the screen. Next, click on the Firewall and ACL selection on the left side of the screen in the Taskbar as shown in Figure 15.4.

FIGURE 15.4   Cisco Router and Security Device Manager Firewall and ACL

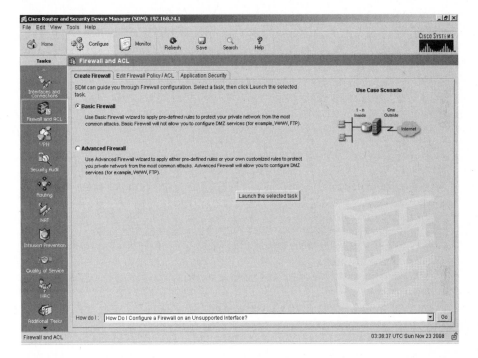

There are three tabs on this screen, but you will start with the first one (default), which is Create Firewall.

Basic Firewall

There are two options for creating a firewall using the SDM. The first and default selection is Basic Firewall. Basic Firewall is used when you don't have a demilitarized zone (DMZ) in place and are not offering services externally. The Basic Firewall uses predefined rules and provides basic protection against common attacks. A common use for this configuration would be a remote office that has a single Internet connection.

⊕ Real World Scenario

Protecting FutureTech's Small and Home Offices

Let's start with FutureTech's very small remote office in Pully, Switzerland. It's a three-person office that does a sales function for a small part of Europe. This office would not require an investment in a fixed hardware firewall. The budget for this type of office is for a small router with the IOS Firewall feature set. So that's where you come in. Time to do the configuration for a Basic Firewall, since this office is only connected to the Internet and has the aforementioned three people on the local LAN. Not a big complex network, but it requires the same level of security as headquarters. Let's jump in and configure a Basic Firewall using SDM that will allow work to get accomplished and allow Internet access, but still protect the resources on the local LAN. Figure 15.5 shows the Internet connection.

FIGURE 15.5   FutureTech Pully, Switzerland, Office Internet Connection

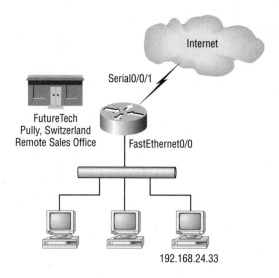

Take a look at Cisco's Use Case Scenario shown on the tab (Figure 15.4). This gives you a idea of what I was just describing. I come back to the Advanced Firewall configuration later on in the chapter.

The next screen presented by the wizard (shown in Figure 15.6) outlines exactly what will happen when you configure Basic Firewall. As you can see, default rules are applied both inbound and outbound, default inspection rules are deployed, and IP unicast reverse-path forwarding is enabled on the outside interface.

> ### Concept: IP Unicast Reverse-Path Forwarding
>
> Without getting into detail, IP unicast reverse-path forwarding is a method of having the router verify the reachability of the source IP address. This is important when trying to limit malicious traffic from entering your network. Many options are available with this feature, so be aware: if you use the default as the wizard does, the least restrictive functionality is enabled.

FIGURE 15.6   Cisco Router and Security Device Manager Basic Firewall Configuration Wizard

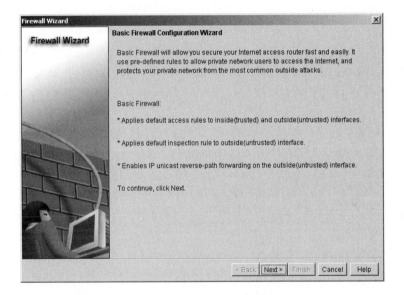

The next screen, shown in Figure 15.7, is the interface configuration screen. As would be expected, you have to select an outside or untrusted interface (usually facing the Internet) and an inside interface that is usually the inside and therefore trusted interface.

For the Pully firewall, the outside interface is Serial0/0/1, which goes to the Internet. The inside interface is FastEthernet0/0. Figure 15.8 shows selections.

Once you've selected the inside and outside interfaces, click Next to configure the firewall. Figure 15.9 shows what actions were taken on which interface.

I show you how this configures from a IOS command line perspective a little bit later in the chapter. For now, remember that all of these actions are canned, so to speak, and the only customization available in the Basic Firewall is the inside and outside interface selection. Later in the chapter, I show you other options that are available using SDM.

FIGURE 15.7 Cisco Router and Security Device Manager Basic Firewall Interface
Configuration

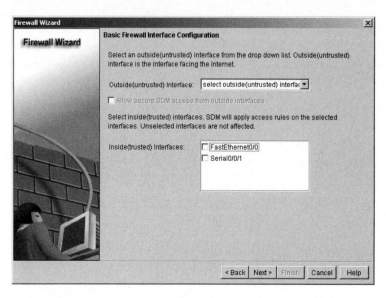

FIGURE 15.8 Cisco Router and Security Device Manager Basic Firewall Interface
Configuration

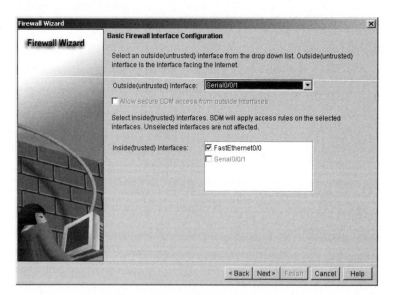

And, of course, I haven't forgotten about delivering the configuration to the router. Figure 15.10 shows the command delivery status message. By now this should be old hat. As you can see, 49 command entries were delivered to the router by the wizard.

FIGURE 15.9 Cisco Router and Security Device Manager Internet Firewall Configuration Summary

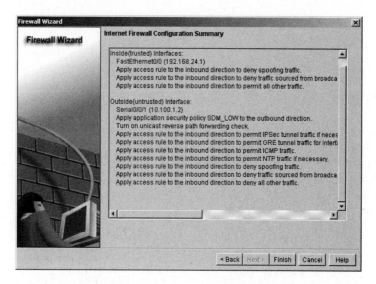

FIGURE 15.10 Cisco Router and Security Device Manager Command Delivery Status

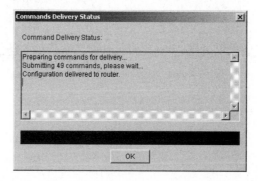

To complete the whole experience, take a look at Figure 15.11. If your screen looks like this, it's obvious that you successfully completed this configuration task.

Once the configuration is complete, you can see graphically which commands have been delivered to the router and which policies are in place on the Edit Firewall Policy/ACL tab. Figure 15.12 shows the Edit Firewall Policy/ACL tab. You now have the option to edit what was delivered, as needed. The default view shows you the rules as they apply to outbound packets.

FIGURE 15.11 Cisco Router and Security Device Manager Information

FIGURE 15.12 Cisco Router and Security Device Manager Edit Firewall Policy/ACL

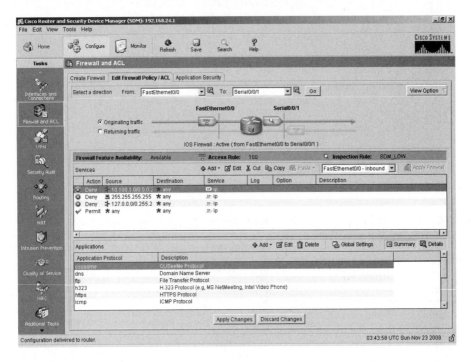

If you click on the drop-down list for the From direction, you can change the packet direction and look at the rules and policies that are applied to packets traveling from Seria10/0/1 to FastEthernet0/0, as shown below in Figure 15.13.

Click the Application Security tab to review application security policies that were put in place. The initial view, Figure 15.14, shows you what the SDM_LOW policy has set as far as inspection. The initial view puts you on the E-mail section, where you can see which applications will be inspected. (A checked box indicates that an inspection policy is in place for that application.) Each checked item is converted to a inspect statement in the command line. By default, esmtp, imap, and pop3 email applications are inspected. Inspection policies can be put in place for email, instant messaging, and peer-to-peer networks. URL, HTTP, and application/protocol filtering is also available. Click a task button to view the settings that were put in place by the wizard and edit the selections to fit your operations.

FIGURE 15.13   Cisco Router and Security Device Manager Edit Firewall Policy/ACL

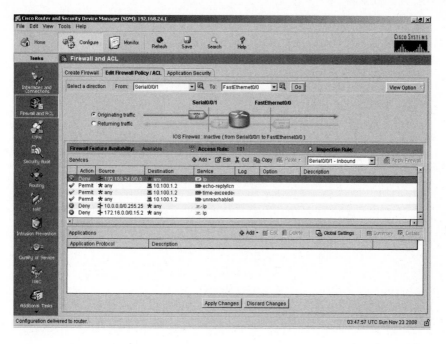

FIGURE 15.14   Cisco Router and Security Device Manager Application Security

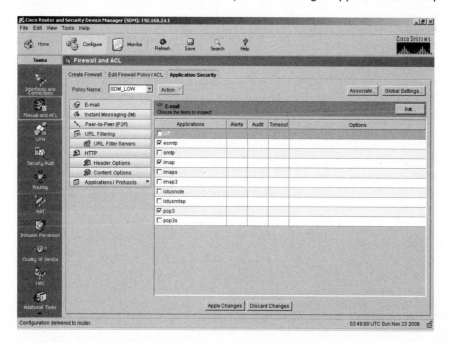

Advanced Firewall

So, now I am moving on to the Advanced Firewall configuration.

 **Real World Scenario**

FutureTech Remote Office

FutureTech's European purchasing agent works at a home office and has decided to offer up her own website for the purposes of collecting bid information. She has sent out requests for proposals (RFPs) for some parts and is asking that suppliers submit their bids via the website.

But, before FutureTech will allow her to offer a website, they require a DMZ segment on her firewall. Her router has an unused FastEthernet interface that would be perfect for the DMZ, as shown in Figure 15.15. You've already activated the interface and it is available for use. Now that an interface for the DMZ is available, you must set rules to allow access inbound from the Internet for HTTP, in this case. So let's jump right into the configuration of the Advanced Firewall.

FIGURE 15.15   European Purchasing Home Office Internet Connection

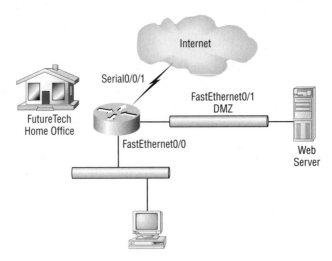

Go back to the Create Firewall tab. Select Advanced Firewall and then click the Launch the selected task button. Figure 15.16 shows the Create Firewall tab with Advanced Firewall selected.

FIGURE 15.16   Cisco Router and Security Device Manager Create Firewall

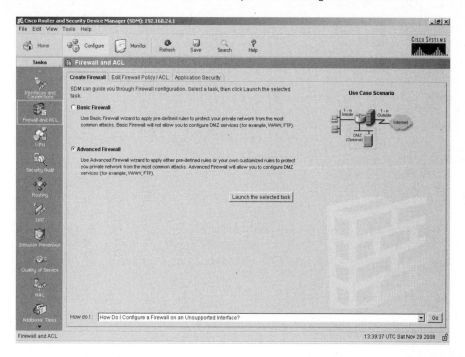

Again, as shown in Figure 15.17, the wizard gives you a summary of the tasks required to configure the firewall. Compared to the Basic Firewall wizard, the major difference is that Advanced Firewall offers the option to configure a DMZ interface. You would set up a DMZ when you have services exposed to the Internet, such as a publicly available web server or an externally available Outlook Web Access email server. You can also use a DMZ to separate network segments. For instance, marketing might not need access to finance and vice versa.

Click Next to move on to the Advanced Firewall Interface Configuration screen shown in Figure 15.18. Again, it's pretty much the same screen as before, with the notable addition of a DMZ interface selection. Choose the FastEthernet0/1 to serve as the DMZ interface, Seria10/0/1 for the outside interface, and FastEthernet0/0 for the inside interface.

Once you've made your selections, your screen should look like Figure 15.19. Notice that the new Ethernet interface, FastEthernet0/1, now shows up as the DMZ interface. As before, the Seria10/0/1 is the outside interface and FastEthernet0/0 the inside interface. Click Next to continue.

Your next step will be to set up your DMZ. Figure 15.20 shows the Advanced Firewall DMZ Services Configuration dialog box. A typical scenario might have SMTP, HTTP, and HTTPS services deployed in a DMZ. Click the Add button and move on to the creation of some services.

FIGURE 15.17   Cisco Router and Security Device Manager Advanced Firewall
Configuration Wizard

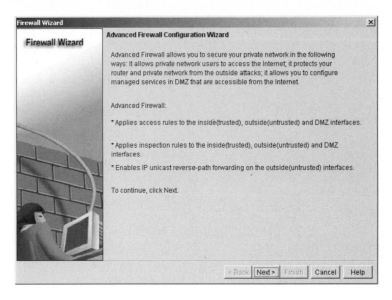

FIGURE 15.18   Cisco Router and Security Device Manager Advanced Firewall Interface
Configuration

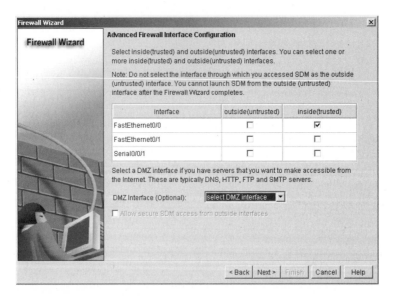

FIGURE 15.19   Cisco Router and Security Device Manager Advanced Firewall Interface Configuration

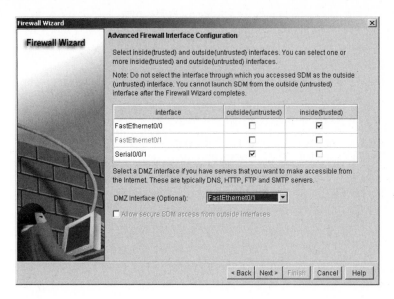

FIGURE 15.20   Cisco Router and Security Device Manager Advanced Firewall DMZ Service Configuration

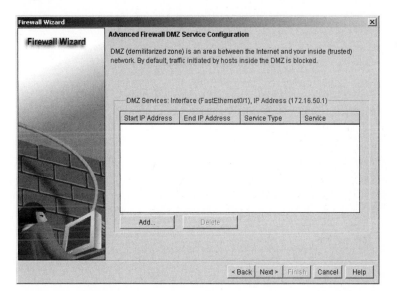

Figure 15.21 shows the DMZ Service Configuration dialog box. This is where you start to configure the host for the bid website. Then, you can select either TCP or UDP and the port number of the service. When you've finished, you can use this dialog box to configure another host. Simply choose Add again.

FIGURE 15.21   Cisco Router and Security Device Manager DMZ Service Configuration

If you click the button with the dots (next to the service box), it brings up the list of services shown in Figure 15.22.

FIGURE 15.22   Cisco Router and Security Device Manager Service

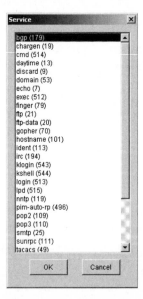

I have configured the web server, shown in Figure 15.23. If you have multiple servers to configure, you will have the opportunity to add more when you get back to the Service Configuration dialog box.

FIGURE 15.23   Cisco Router and Security Device Manager DMZ Service Configuration

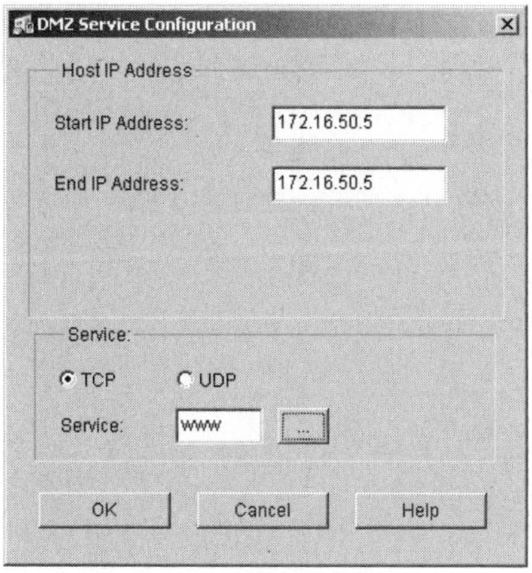

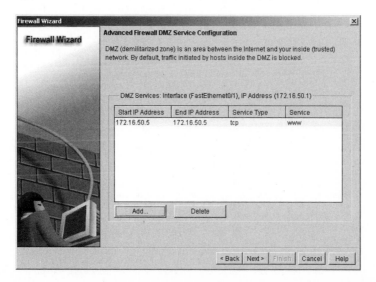

Figure 15.24 shows Advanced Firewall DMZ Service Configuration dialog box with the first service in place. As previously mentioned, you can click Add to configure as many more services as required. By the way, since it is not unusual to have more than one service on a server, the SDM allows you to configure more than one service. You simply configure each one individually.

FIGURE 15.24   Cisco Router and Security Device Manager Advanced Firewall DMZ Service Configuration

As with the Basic Firewall wizard, the Advanced Firewall wizard allows you to review the configuration commands that are going to be sent to the router. These are the inspect commands that are going to be delivered. Figure 15.25 shows the preview screen. When you've finished reviewing the inspect commands, click Close.

FIGURE 15.25 Cisco Router and Security Device Manager Preview SDM Security Configuration

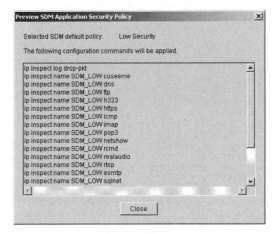

Now that you have configured the Application Security Policy, you can move on to the firewall configuration. Here you have the option to use a default security policy or a custom one that you have defined. For this exercise, let's move forward with a default LOW security policy, as shown in Figure 15.26.

FIGURE 15.26 Cisco Router and Security Device Manager Advanced Firewall Security Configuration

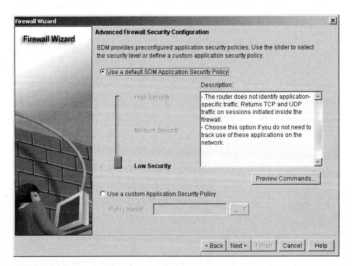

When you click Next, the wizard again, as shown in Figure 15.27, provides a summary of the commands that are going to be delivered to the router. Take particular notice that CBAC is going to be activated on the DMZ interface. This is because you configured a service that is to be inspected. Remember that there has to be an access list and an inspect policy; a policy by itself or an access list by itself is useless.

FIGURE 15.27   Cisco Router and Security Device Manager Internet Firewall Configuration Summary

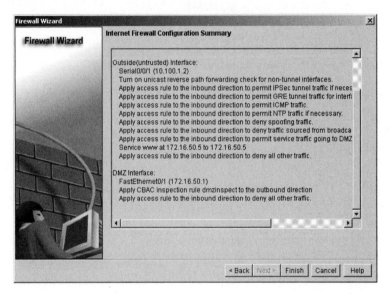

Next, as shown in Figure 15.28, you see the familiar delivery screen. Note the number of commands that are going to be delivered this time. The commands have gone up significantly in number, largely because the office now has a DMZ interface, and this makes the configuration more complex.

FIGURE 15.28   Cisco Router and Security Device Manager Commands Delivery Status

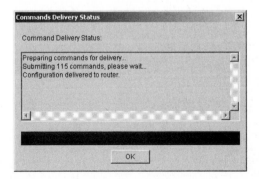

And finally, as shown in Figure 15.29, you are back to the Edit Firewall Policy/ACL tab. Here you can see all of the things that have been configured for the router. And, as before, you can review rules and policies for the reverse direction by clicking the appropriate buttons.

FIGURE 15.29   Cisco Router and Security Device Manager Edit Firewall Policy/ACL

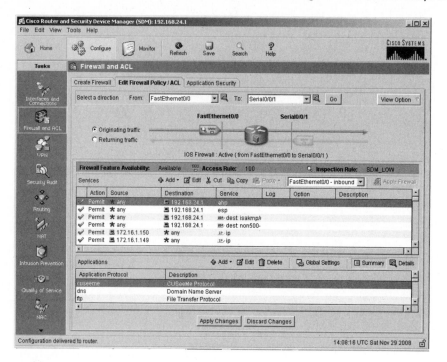

That completes your configuration with the Advanced Firewall wizard. I review the configuration with you from a command line perspective in the next section so you can get a more detailed look at what was sent to the router.

Verify Cisco IOS Firewall Configurations

Now that we have done the various configurations using the SDM, I show you what was configured from a command line perspective and discuss those configurations in a bit more detail.

Basic Firewall

Starting with the access list section, I take you through the configurations for Basic Firewall. As you will recall, the Basic Firewall didn't give you a lot of options for configuring things; it just put some defaults out there. Actually, the Basic Firewall wizard gave you no options. So, let's take a look at some snippets of the configuration using the command line interface.

Inspection

Let's have a look at the command line interface code that shows the inspection process that you configured for the Basic Firewall. Because the default preconfigured selection was used, the inspect name is SDM_LOW. The inspection policy that is put in place when you select the defaults is what Cisco has designated as the minimum inspection level policy.

```
ip inspect name SDM_LOW cuseeme
ip inspect name SDM_LOW dns
ip inspect name SDM_LOW ftp
ip inspect name SDM_LOW h323
ip inspect name SDM_LOW https
ip inspect name SDM_LOW icmp
ip inspect name SDM_LOW imap
ip inspect name SDM_LOW pop3
ip inspect name SDM_LOW netshow
ip inspect name SDM_LOW rcmd
ip inspect name SDM_LOW realaudio
ip inspect name SDM_LOW rtsp
ip inspect name SDM_LOW esmtp
ip inspect name SDM_LOW sqlnet
ip inspect name SDM_LOW streamworks
ip inspect name SDM_LOW tftp
ip inspect name SDM_LOW tcp
ip inspect name SDM_LOW udp
ip inspect name SDM_LOW vdolive
```

As you can see, the SDM_LOW is set up for those applications that might be used from inside the network to go out to the Internet.

HTTPS

Let's take a look at a common application that is used, HTTPS. To have an SSL session with a website on the Internet, an outgoing access list would have to exist. A temporary inbound access list would be installed for the duration of the session. This is provided as the CBAC function monitors the state of the connection.

```
interface FastEthernet0/0
description $FW_INSIDE$
ip address 192.168.24.1 255.255.255.0
ip access-group 100 in
duplex auto
speed auto
!
```

The Inside Interface and Outbound ACL

Moving right along, here is the interface FastEthernet0/0, which is designated as the inside interface for the firewall. The only command that is applied here is the access list inbound. The wizard applied that access list with the `ip access-group 100 in` statement.

```
interface FastEthernet0/0
 description $FW_INSIDE$
 ip address 192.168.24.1 255.255.255.0
 ip access-group 100 in
 duplex auto
 speed auto
!
```

The Outside Interface and Inbound ACL

Next, take a look at the outside interface for the firewall, Serial0/0/1. The wizard applied three commands to this interface. `access -list 101` was set in the inbound direction. Also, because this is an external-facing interface, this is where the `ip verify unicast reverse-path` command is placed. Remember that this command attempts to verify the path to avoid spoofing. And last, the inspect rule is applied to the outside or external-facing interface. The wizard implemented the default SDM_LOW rule set.

```
!
interface Serial0/0/1
description $FW_OUTSIDE$
ip address 10.100.1.2 255.255.255.0
ip access-group 101 in
ip verify unicast reverse-path
ip inspect SDM_LOW out
access-list 100 remark auto generated by SDM firewall configuration
access-list 100 remark SDM_ACL Category=1
access-list 100 deny ip 10.100.1.0 0.0.0.255 any
access-list 100 deny ip host 255.255.255.255 any
access-list 100 deny ip 127.0.0.0 0.255.255.255 any
access-list 100 permit ip any any
access-list 101 remark auto generated by SDM firewall configuration
access-list 101 remark SDM_ACL Category=1
access-list 101 deny ip 192.168.24.0 0.0.0.255 any
access-list 101 permit icmp any host 10.100.1.2 echo-reply
access-list 101 permit icmp any host 10.100.1.2 time-exceeded
access-list 101 permit icmp any host 10.100.1.2 unreachable
access-list 101 deny ip 10.0.0.0 0.255.255.255 any
access-list 101 deny ip 172.16.0.0 0.15.255.255 any
```

```
access-list 101 deny ip 192.168.0.0 0.0.255.255 any
access-list 101 deny ip 127.0.0.0 0.255.255.255 any
access-list 101 deny ip host 255.255.255.255 any
access-list 101 deny ip host 0.0.0.0 any
access-list 101 deny ip any any log
!
```

The Access Lists

Two access lists were applied to the interfaces. Let's start with access list 100, which was applied inbound to the FastEthernet0/0 interface. First, traffic that would be identified as from the Seria10/0/1 interface is denied access to prevent spoofing. Because the command is applied inbound to the interface, only spoofing traffic would ever be inbound here. This command is followed by a couple of antispoofing statements that disallow the Internet loopback space and an IANA-reserved block.

If you want to get into more detail on these special antispoofing addresses, check out RFC 3330 and RFC 3704.

Then, of course, the wizard allows all the rest of the legitimate traffic. The permit ip any any statement does just that. So much for the inside interface.

Now, take a look at the access list for the outside interface, access list 101. As with the previous access list, the first thing the wizard did was prevent traffic from the other interface's address space—again, this shouldn't happen. Next, because this is an external interface, the wizard allowed specific ICMP statements. The first one allows a ping reply. The next statement allows the firewall to respond with a time-exceeded message. This can be important in troubleshooting. And last, unreachable messages are allowed.

The next set of statements basically deny everything inbound. The first set denies RFC 1918 addresses inbound. The assumption here is that the RFC 1918 addresses are prohibited from being routed on the Internet. The Internet is connected on the outside interface.

You might run into some problems if you used the wizard to create an internal firewall and you used RFC 1918 addresses in your internal network. But don't get hung up on that right now.

Moving down to the last statement, you find a deny ip any any log statement. You might be asking yourself, "Why not just use the one line and be done with it?" The key here is that the keyword log is used on the end of the deny statement. Basically, that's saying that you aren't interested in any of the previous statements from a logging perspective, but you are interested in everything else. That essentially finishes off the configuration of the Basic Firewall. It's very basic, but makes it easy to implement the minimum for a router that isn't offering services to the Internet, but does have an interface on the Internet.

Putting It All Together

So, let's take this a step further and follow the path of a packet. We examine both directions that it might take in our scenario. Looking back at Figure 15.9, you can see that the rules, such that they are, have been applied in the outbound direction from FastEthernet0/0 to Serial 0/0/1.

 Real World Scenario

Downloads on the Down Low

The purchasing agent mentioned earlier has been searching for a new widget that is needed in the United States but is supposedly only manufactured somewhere in Europe. Her PC is a host on the inside interface of this network with an IP address of 192.168.24.33. The agent comes across a site that purports to be the central hub for finding widgets. But when she clicks the link, she doesn't find any widget information and the website launches a series of attempts to download Trojans to the purchasing agent's PC. But, because you have set up CBAC on the router, all the attempts are denied, because they were not part of the conversation originated by the purchasing agent's PC. CBAC saves the day! Let's look at what happened.

If we examine the rules that are applied, the incoming packets first faces three deny statements. These are the IP spoofing addresses that I discussed earlier. This means any packet or sender matching those rules would be denied from entering the router on interface FastEthernet0/0.

The next statement is a `permit any any` and since the packet didn't match any of the deny statements, it is allowed into the router. So any IP that exists on the FastEthernet0/0 interface will be allowed into the router so long as it doesn't match any of the deny rules you put in place.

Now let's look at the reverse direction. Take a look back at Figure 15.10 and you will see that the originating traffic is now coming in on the Seria10/0/1 interface. A packet faces a few more rules here. First and foremost is the rule denying any traffic from the 192.168.24.0 network. This is an antispoofing rule. Rules are processed in order, so the next three lines are permits that allow some types of ICMP traffic to the outside interface.

The next two lines deny any of the RFC 1918 address space, since it shouldn't appear on the Internet. And then some more antispoofing rules, followed by a `deny any any` statement. So, other than permitting the ICMP traffic to the outside interface, you haven't allowed any traffic into the router.

Advanced Firewall

Now, I want to take you through the Advanced Firewall configuration. I show you a snippet from the configuration that shows all of the relevant sections. Remember that the primary difference in the Basic and the Advanced Firewall configurations is the use of a DMZ interface.

Inspection

Here is an excerpt from the show running-configuration output showing all of the relevant sections pertaining to the firewall configuration.

```
ip inspect name SDM_LOW cuseeme
ip inspect name SDM_LOW dns
ip inspect name SDM_LOW ftp
ip inspect name SDM_LOW h323
ip inspect name SDM_LOW https
ip inspect name SDM_LOW icmp
ip inspect name SDM_LOW imap
ip inspect name SDM_LOW pop3
ip inspect name SDM_LOW netshow
ip inspect name SDM_LOW rcmd
ip inspect name SDM_LOW realaudio
ip inspect name SDM_LOW rtsp
ip inspect name SDM_LOW esmtp
ip inspect name SDM_LOW sqlnet
ip inspect name SDM_LOW streamworks
ip inspect name SDM_LOW tftp
ip inspect name SDM_LOW tcp
ip inspect name SDM_LOW udp
ip inspect name SDM_LOW vdolive
ip inspect name dmzinspect tcp
ip inspect name dmzinspect udp
```

Right away you will notice a slight difference in the inspect statements in that some inspection is occurring on that DMZ interface. Other than those last two statements that set up the DMZ inspections, the configuration is the same as you saw in the Basic Firewall.

The Inside Interface and Outbound ACL

```
interface FastEthernet0/0
description $FW_INSIDE$
ip address 192.168.24.1 255.255.255.0
ip access-group 100 in
ip inspect SDM_LOW in
duplex auto
speed auto
```

```
crypto map SDM_CMAP_1
!
```

Next, we have the same access list inbound on the inside interface. No change here except that now we have an ip inspect statement on this interface.

The DMZ Interface and ACLs

```
interface FastEthernet0/1
description $ETH-LAN$$FW_DMZ$
ip address 172.16.50.1 255.255.255.0
ip access-group 101 in
ip inspect dmzinspect out
duplex auto
speed auto
!
```

Here is a look at the DMZ interface. It looks similar to the outside interface on a Basic Firewall, but notice that we have the inspect statement in the outbound direction.

The Outside Interface and Inbound ACL

```
interface Serial0/0/1
description $FW_OUTSIDE$
ip address 10.100.1.2 255.255.255.0
ip access-group 102 in
ip verify unicast reverse-path
```

Taking a look at the outside interface, you can see a typical configuration with an access list and as before, a verify unicast reverse-path statement. So now, let's look at the actual access lists and see what is different here than the Basic Firewall.

```
!
ip local pool SDM_POOL_1 172.16.1.100 172.16.1.150
!
```

Okay, this line is here for a reason. Obviously, a local pool of addresses is defined. It is a holdover from a previous remote access VPN connection. So, why is it relevant? When you look at the access lists below, you will notice that the SDM took note of this and created an access list that reflects the addresses that are part of the pool. The wizard takes into account all local addresses, not just those assigned to a specific interface. For instance, if the remote VPN access was enabled, then those connecting would get a local address from the above pool. They would be treated just like someone connected on the local LAN.

```
!
access-list 100 remark auto generated by SDM firewall configuration
```

```
access-list 100 remark SDM_ACL Category=1
access-list 100 permit ahp any host 192.168.24.1
access-list 100 permit esp any host 192.168.24.1
access-list 100 permit udp any host 192.168.24.1 eq isakmp
access-list 100 permit udp any host 192.168.24.1 eq non500-isakmp
access-list 100 permit ip host 172.16.1.150 any
access-list 100 permit ip host 172.16.1.149 any
access-list 100 permit ip host 172.16.1.148 any
access-list 100 permit ip host 172.16.1.147 any
access-list 100 permit ip host 172.16.1.146 any
access-list 100 permit ip host 172.16.1.145 any
access-list 100 permit ip host 172.16.1.144 any
access-list 100 permit ip host 172.16.1.143 any
access-list 100 permit ip host 172.16.1.142 any
access-list 100 permit ip host 172.16.1.141 any
access-list 100 permit ip host 172.16.1.140 any
access-list 100 permit ip host 172.16.1.139 any
access-list 100 permit ip host 172.16.1.138 any
access-list 100 permit ip host 172.16.1.137 any
access-list 100 permit ip host 172.16.1.136 any
access-list 100 permit ip host 172.16.1.135 any
access-list 100 permit ip host 172.16.1.134 any
access-list 100 permit ip host 172.16.1.133 any
access-list 100 permit ip host 172.16.1.132 any
access-list 100 permit ip host 172.16.1.131 any
access-list 100 permit ip host 172.16.1.130 any
access-list 100 permit ip host 172.16.1.129 any
access-list 100 permit ip host 172.16.1.128 any
access-list 100 permit ip host 172.16.1.127 any
access-list 100 permit ip host 172.16.1.126 any
access-list 100 permit ip host 172.16.1.125 any
access-list 100 permit ip host 172.16.1.124 any
access-list 100 permit ip host 172.16.1.123 any
access-list 100 permit ip host 172.16.1.122 any
access-list 100 permit ip host 172.16.1.121 any
access-list 100 permit ip host 172.16.1.120 any
access-list 100 permit ip host 172.16.1.119 any
access-list 100 permit ip host 172.16.1.118 any
access-list 100 permit ip host 172.16.1.117 any
access-list 100 permit ip host 172.16.1.116 any
access-list 100 permit ip host 172.16.1.115 any
```

```
access-list 100 permit ip host 172.16.1.114 any
access-list 100 permit ip host 172.16.1.113 any
access-list 100 permit ip host 172.16.1.112 any
access-list 100 permit ip host 172.16.1.111 any
access-list 100 permit ip host 172.16.1.110 any
access-list 100 permit ip host 172.16.1.109 any
access-list 100 permit ip host 172.16.1.108 any
access-list 100 permit ip host 172.16.1.107 any
access-list 100 permit ip host 172.16.1.106 any
access-list 100 permit ip host 172.16.1.105 any
access-list 100 permit ip host 172.16.1.104 any
access-list 100 permit ip host 172.16.1.103 any
access-list 100 permit ip host 172.16.1.102 any
access-list 100 permit ip host 172.16.1.101 any
access-list 100 permit ip host 172.16.1.100 any
access-list 100 deny ip 10.100.1.0 0.0.0.255 any
access-list 100 deny ip 172.16.50.0 0.0.0.255 any
access-list 100 deny ip host 255.255.255.255 any
access-list 100 deny ip 127.0.0.0 0.255.255.255 any
access-list 100 permit ip any any
access-list 101 remark auto generated by SDM firewall configuration
access-list 101 remark SDM_ACL Category=1
access-list 101 deny ip any any log
access-list 102 remark auto generated by SDM firewall configuration
access-list 102 remark SDM_ACL Category=1
access-list 102 deny ip 172.16.50.0 0.0.0.255 any
access-list 102 deny ip 192.168.24.0 0.0.0.255 any
access-list 102 permit icmp any host 10.100.1.2 echo-reply
access-list 102 permit icmp any host 10.100.1.2 time-exceeded
access-list 102 permit icmp any host 10.100.1.2 unreachable
access-list 102 permit tcp any host 172.16.50.5 eq www
access-list 102 deny ip 10.0.0.0 0.255.255.255 any
```

Without going line by line, which I don't think is necessary, I want to point out the next to the last line, which is where the wizard configured the web server. Notice that the outside interface is allowing any host on the Internet to access the web server IP on port 80 or www. Other than that, it's pretty much the same configuration as a Basic Firewall, with the notable exception of the DMZ.

Summary

In this chapter, you learned about the Cisco IOS Firewall feature set and how it can be used. You also learned about and configured firewall features using the Cisco Security Device Manager, both the Basic Firewall and Advanced Firewall. You then learned about the configuration from a command line perspective and looked more closely at the options the firewall wizard used. The IOS Firewall feature set is a powerful tool to have available for any Internet-facing router.

Review Questions

1. Which function is not an IOS Firewall feature?
   - **A.** Antivirus
   - **B.** DDOS protection
   - **C.** Stateful packet inspection
   - **D.** Access lists

2. What is another name for CBAC?
   - **A.** Protection policy
   - **B.** Stateful packet inspection
   - **C.** Access control
   - **D.** None of the above

3. What is a command that is used to specify inspection?
   - **A.** `policy map`
   - **B.** `access-list`
   - **C.** `transform-set`
   - **D.** `tunnel-list`

4. If you configured an authentication proxy on your firewall, what type of server is supported as an authentication server?
   - **A.** RADIUS
   - **B.** TACACS
   - **C.** All of the above
   - **D.** None of the above

5. What is the primary difference between a Basic Firewall and an Advanced Firewall configuration?
   - **A.** A loopback interface
   - **B.** Stateful packet inspection
   - **C.** More access lists
   - **D.** DMZ interface configuration

6. The `ip unicast verify reverse-path` feature allows specific packets to traverse the firewall.
   - **A.** True
   - **B.** False

7. Which one of the following is not a Basic Firewall default inspect service?

    A. cuseeme

    B. realaudio

    C. rtmp

    D. https

8. Why would you log your deny statements on the firewall?

    A. To see who is trying to traverse your network

    B. Better security

    C. Increase performance

    D. Reduce log files

9. Access lists provide better protection than CBAC for inbound attacks from the Internet.

    A. True

    B. False

10. The transparent firewall takes advantage of which feature in order to provide this service?

    A. IP routing

    B. Virtual access lists

    C. Bridging

    D. Hot Standby Routing Protocol

Answers to Review Questions

1. A. Antivirus is not a feature of the IOS Firewall feature set.

2. B. Stateful packet inspection is another name for what CBAC does today.

3. B. An access list is used to activate CBAC.

4. C. All of the above. Both RADIUS and TACACS servers are supported.

5. D. The primary difference is there is a DMZ interface and the configuration of it.

6. B. False. The `ip unicast verify reverse-path` is an antispoofing feature that requires the verification of the reachability of the source address.

7. C. RTMP is not one of the services under the Basic Firewall inspect settings.

8. A. When you log your deny statements on the firewall, you can monitor those log messages to see who is trying to get into your network.

9. B. False. Access lists are actually part of the CBAC solution and prior to the implementation of CBAC, static access lists provided less protection than the current CBAC solution.

10. C. Bridging is used in the transparent firewall configuration because it might be used where there isn't a possibility to insert new IP ranges.

Chapter

16

Cisco IOS IPS

IN THIS CHAPTER, YOU WILL LEARN HOW TO DO THE FOLLOWING:

✓ Describe the functions and operations of IDS and IPS systems including IDS/IPS signatures, IPS alarms, and the like

✓ Configure Cisco IOS IPS using SDM

This chapter takes you through the exciting and ever-changing world of intrusion detection and intrusion prevention. It explains the difference between detection and prevention as it relates to network security, and also discusses the different scopes or places that you can implement to use this technology.

You also learn about the features a network sensor uses to detect and scan for malicious traffic, including the constantly updated signature database. Finally, this chapter shows you how to deploy one of these sensors in your network using the SDM.

For up-to-the-minute updates on this chapter, check out www.sybex.com/go/CiscoProGuidetoInternetworking or www.lammle.com.

Securing Networks with IDS and IPS

Intrusion Detection System (IDS) and Intrusion Prevention System (IPS) sensors protect your network from malicious traffic. The two systems are deployed differently and scan for malicious traffic in different ways. Each system has strengths and weaknesses when deployed separately, but when used together, IDS and IPS can provide a much richer and deeper level of security. The sections that follow show you each system individually, then bring them together and show you how they complement one another.

Basic Functions of the Intrusion Detection System (IDS)

IDS is typically characterized as a passive listening device. This label is given to these systems because traffic does not have to pass through the system; IDS sensors listen promiscuously to all traffic on the network.

The active response that the IDS can take is limited because it is essentially a passive device. You can configure the IDS to block malicious traffic using other network devices, but only after it has detected the traffic. The original malicious traffic has already passed through the network to its destination and could not be blocked. The other network devices (for example, security appliances like the Cisco PIX firewall, Cisco ASA firewall, or network routers) can be configured to respond to malicious traffic detection to prevent further intrusion. Subsequent traffic in the flow will be blocked by the security device. The IDS is also capable of sending a TCP reset to the end or source host and terminate any malicious

TCP connections if you enable the sensor to actively respond to threats. Based on your configuration and depending on a signature's severity level, action is taken. You can configure on a variety of signatures and actively or passively respond to the threat.

Real World Scenario

More Security for the Dubai Branch Office

The Dubai office has been under attack from some malicious attackers. They have been sending malicious traffic into the network causing porn to pop up instead of the corporate screen saver and a flood of Viagra ads in people's inboxes. In response, FutureTech wants to expand the security functions for that network. You have been asked to implement an IDS sensor for the network. Figure 16.1 shows the proposed location of the IDS in the Dubai office network.

FIGURE 16.1 IDS in the Dubai Office Network

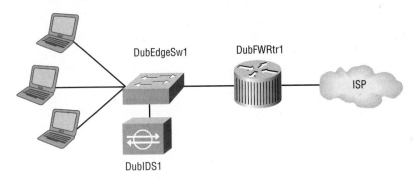

For traffic to reach the sensor, the switch, DubEdgeSw1, must send it there. When the IDS sensor detects malicious traffic, it sends an alert to the local IT monitoring station. Local IT personnel then configure the firewall to block further traffic from that source.

To recap, the functions that the IDS sensor can take when malicious traffic is detected are:

- Send an alert to a management station.
- Configure a network device to block traffic.
- Send TCP reset to the traffic source.

Basic Functions of the Intrusion Prevention System (IPS)

IPS is characterized as an active device. This is because the device is implemented as an inline sensor. The IPS requires the use of more than one interface, and all traffic must pass through the sensor. Network traffic enters through one interface and exits through another.

 Real World Scenario

Adding IPS to the Dubai Office Network

The Dubai office attacks have stepped up in severity and are actually introducing viruses into the network. Because of this, FutureTech has decided that you should add an IPS sensor in the network.

When the IPS sensor detects malicious traffic, it should not only send an alert to the local IT monitoring station, but also block the traffic before it enters the network. Once the sensor is in place, local IT personnel will continue to tune the IPS sensor to make the operation efficient. If any traffic should slip by the IPS sensor, an IDS sensor with more resources will analyze traffic in greater detail. You need to provide the local IT personnel with the tools they need to catch stray malicious traffic and help with their IPS sensor tuning efforts.

In Figure 16.2 you can see where the IPS (DubIPS1) and IDS (DubIDS1) sensors will be located inline. All traffic headed for the Dubai office network must pass through the IPS sensor and will be further analyzed by the IDS sensor.

FIGURE 16.2   IPS Located in the Dubai Office Network

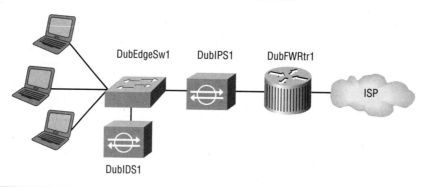

IPS is different from IDS. When the IPS detects malicious traffic, it can also send an alert to the management station. But, more importantly, it can immediately block the malicious traffic. The traffic is blocked by the IPS, not by another device, so the original and subsequent traffic are blocked proactively by the IPS. IPS prevents the attacks before the traffic enters the network.

The IPS is capable of responding in real time, before network security can be compromised. The most common action for many events is to send an alert and log the event to a syslog or Security Device Event Exchange (SDEE). You can configure the IPS to perform other actions, as appropriate for a given threat. IPS can drop the packet, reset the connection, block traffic from a specific source IP address, or block traffic for a specific connection.

Remember, IPS is more aggressive and capable of blocking the traffic before it enters the network.

Alarm   Send an alarm to a syslog server or a centralized management interface. This action is typically combined with other preventive actions.

Packet Drop   Drop the packet. This action is effective for all IP protocols and does not affect any legitimate user if the source IP address was spoofed.

Reset the Connection   IPS is capable of sending a TCP reset to the end or source host and terminate any malicious TCP connections. This action works only for TCP sessions.

Block Traffic   IPS can block traffic from the source IP address of the attacker for a specified amount of time. This action imposes a penalty on the attacker IP address and prevents traffic from that IP from entering the network. IPS can also block traffic on a connection for which the signature was seen for a specified amount of time. This action imposes a penalty on the attacker session.

Because network attack mechanisms are becoming more sophisticated, this proactive approach is required to protect against network viruses, worms, malicious applications, and vulnerability exploits.

Using IDS and IPS Together

When you think about having one or the other of these sensors on your network, think about the benefits you would get from having both. An IPS sensor is much like a firewall; it can block traffic that is malicious or threatening. It should only block traffic that is known to be a threat, though. IPS should not block legitimate traffic or you could suffer a disruption in legitimate connectivity and find that applications are unable to perform their tasks. In some cases, that could mean the company losing money—never a good thing for an IT person to have caused!

As you design and configure your IPS, you also have to think about the processing overhead and the latency that can be introduced into the traffic path if the IPS sensor is trying to scan for too many things as the traffic passes through. That basically means that you have to tune the IPS device so that it only scans for things that are known to be malicious. This can leave an open or grey area that is not totally being secured.

Enter the IDS sensor. The IDS device can be placed into the network so that it verifies or checks on the IPS device. The IPS must be tuned so that all of the good traffic is allowed into the network. Anything that may slip in under the radar could then be further scanned by the IDS device. The IDS device can scan for everything. You do not have to worry about IDS dropping something that is legitimate or taking too long and causing delay.

In addition to that, you can look at the data between the two devices and see what improvements you can make to the IPS setup, if the IDS device keeps finding a threat. It is a great way to stay on top of what is getting into or, even worse, being generated on your network.

Benefits and Drawbacks of IPS/IDS Sensors

A network-based monitoring system has the benefit of easily seeing attacks that are occurring across the entire network. Seeing the attacks against the entire network gives a clear indication of the extent to which the network is being attacked. Furthermore, because the monitoring system is only examining traffic from the network, it does not have to support every operating system that is used on the network.

On the drawbacks side, encryption of the network traffic stream can effectively blind the sensor. Reconstructing fragmented traffic can also be a difficult problem to solve. Possibly the biggest drawback to network-based monitoring is that, as networks become increasingly larger (with respect to bandwidth), it becomes more difficult to place the sensor at a single location in the network and successfully capture all the traffic. Eliminating this problem requires the use of more sensors throughout the network. However, multiple sensors increase costs.

Types of IDS and IPS Sensors

Intrusion sensors can be categorized into a few different types or groups based on the approach they use to identifying malicious traffic. The second criterion for grouping the sensors is by scope; this means how many systems or what part of the network the sensor is capable of protecting. Scope-based classification is covered next.

Sensor Scope

IDS and IPS sensors can be broken into two different scopes of use: network based and host based. You will generally see acronyms like NIDS, NIPS, HIDS, and HIPS for network-based or host-based IDS or IPS. This chapter focuses mostly on IPS sensors. IPS is the primary function built into the Cisco IOS for a router and IPS provides more functionality. A network-based device is placed on the network and is intended to protect many hosts. A host-based version is placed on a single system, generally as software, and protects that single host from attack.

Network Based (NIPS)

Network-based sensors examine packets and traffic that are traversing through the network for known signs of malicious activity. Because these systems are watching network traffic, any attack signatures detected may succeed or fail. It is usually difficult, if not impossible, for network-based monitoring systems to assess the success or failure of the actual attacks. They only indicate the presence of intrusive activity.

NIPS can detect malicious packets that are designed to be overlooked by the simplistic filtering rules of a firewall. NIPS are placed in the network to verify traffic (or at least the critical areas of traffic) in the network. NIPS is good at preventing lower-layer (meaning low layers in the OSI model) attacks but, unfortunately, it can't read or accurately evaluate encrypted traffic that passes through the sensor. A NIPS device for the most part only sees traffic at the time it is passing through (not as a flow or sequence of packets). This severely limits the device's ability to correlate traffic with its threat potential.

Host Based (HIPS)

A host-based sensor examines information at the local host or operating system. The HIPS has full access to the internals of the end station, and can relate incoming traffic to the activity on the end station to understand the context. Host-based sensors can be implemented to a couple of different complexity levels. HIPS can be more aggressive and complex when the system is configured to examine actual system calls, or the implementation can be much simpler, just examining system log files. In VPN environments, where encrypted traffic flows through the network, the HIPS is the only option to examine traffic in clear text.

Some host-based monitoring systems can halt attacks before they start, much less succeed, whereas others types of scanners only report what has already happened. Cisco offers a HIPS solution that consists of a software package for individual computers, whatever the operating system/hardware mix, called Cisco Secure Agents (CSA). The software can be deployed on hosts to protect them and reports their actions to a central management console. In Cisco's implementation, the central suite is called Cisco Secure Agent Management Center (CSAMC).

However, HIPS is usually made for a specific operating system (OS) and does not protect against attacks targeting the lower layers of the OSI model (Layers 1 through 3, generally). Another disadvantage is that an attacker could, with enough reconnaissance, detect that the host is still there, and possibly even figure out that the host has HIPS protecting it.

Malicious Traffic Identification Approaches

IDS and IPS sensors have a few different approaches they can use to scan for and identify offending traffic. Each of the approaches has benefits and drawbacks, but by using a mix of different approaches, you can get very good results. The approaches that can be used by the sensors include:

- Signature-based
- Policy-based
- Anomaly-based
- Honeypot

Signature-Based Approach

A signature is a coded definition of bit sequences and malicious content characteristics. The signature-based approach is simply pattern matching. The device (IPS or IDS) looks for a specific sequence of bits in a packet or content that is known to be malicious. A device using signature-based scanning requires the use of a signature database, which contains all the individual signatures used for data comparison. This type of approach is pretty easy to employ, but (and I am sure you can guess) it doesn't leave any room for dynamic learning.

Typically the system will only scan for a signature if a packet is associated with a particular service (a destination port is usually used). The scanner using a method like this reduces the amount of inspection and time it takes to process each packet. The inspection process can be made more stringent for systems that need to recognize traffic with protocols that do not use well-known ports. For applications such as Trojan horses and their associated traffic, identification can be almost impossible for a signature to properly classify because these applications move ports at will.

In the short period of time from when you implement the IPS sensor until you start to tune its operation, you will (I am sure) get a bunch of alerts for traffic and things that are not malicious. These are called false positives, and occur when a signature fires on traffic that is not malicious. After the system is tuned and adjusted to the specific network parameters, there will be fewer false alerts than with a policy-based approach.

Policy-Based Approach

A policy-based approach uses an algorithm to make decisions. For example, let's say that a sensor on the FutureTech network scans for port sweeps on all of the systems for a given subnet. A policy-based sensor has been implemented that detects a port sweep. The policy can be set to look for the presence of a unique port or set of ports that are being scanned on a particular machine. When a specific threshold of ports or packets probing the ports is reached, the policy would alarm. The policy could be further restricted or filtered to look for specific types of packets that are of interest. You can set the policy for multiple requirements as well—for example, that all the probe packets must originate from a single source. You have countless ways to configure the policy to look for traffic or scans.

Policy-based approaches require you to perform some tuning so that the security measures conform to your overall security policy for the network and your company. Also, you will want to make sure the sensor is checking for unauthorized patterns on the specific network it is monitoring. Policy-based approaches can be used to look for a very simple statistical event or complex relationships.

Anomaly-Based Approach

Anomaly-based signatures look for network traffic that is outside the definition of what is considered normal. The most difficult task that an administrator faces with this type of monitoring is to effectively define normal traffic.

Some scanning systems have hard-coded definitions of normal traffic patterns. Other systems are allowed learn what normal traffic behavior should be. In either case, it can be very difficult to maintain the definition of normal. You want to reduce, and hopefully eliminate, the chances of improperly classifying abnormal traffic as normal traffic.

Anomaly-based scanning can be much easier to implement in small networks where the number of variables to define is likely to be smaller. Using the anomaly-based approach in a large network with a huge number of traffic types, applications, changes, accesses, and variables to define can be a daunting task.

The two types of anomaly-based IDS and IPS are statistical and nonstatistical.

Statistical Anomaly Detection   A statistical anomaly-based system learns the profile of the monitored network (traffic patterns) from the network itself over a period of time. After that period, the system can detect when statistical properties of the network traffic deviate enough from the usual pattern, and when they do, the system triggers an alarm.

Nonstatistical Anomaly Detection A nonstatistical anomaly-based system has a predefined definition of known good behavior (usually coded by the vendor). An alarm triggers when an event outside the profile occurs. Examples of events that can be considered malicious by nonstatistical anomaly IPS or IDS systems include:

- A communication between two devices using the Internet Package Exchange (IPX) protocol in a network where only the TCP/IP protocol is to be used
- A routing protocol update that originated from a user device
- A broadcast storm or a network sweep
- An anomalous packet, such as a Christmas tree packet (in which all TCP flags are set)
- A TCP segment where the source and destination IP addresses are the same and the TCP source and destination ports are the same

Honeypot Approach

Honeypot systems are one of my favorite security devices to implement; a dummy server or host is used to attract attacks. One of the original ideas behind the honeypot approach was to distract attacks away from the real network devices. A honeypot system also gives you the ability to analyze incoming attacks and malicious traffic. This approach allows you to prepare for malicious traffic and attacks before they attack the real network.

When you implement a honeypot, you must dedicate a server that can be sacrificed and compromised. These systems should be placed out in a DMZ network or actually outside of your network boundary (outside the firewall). Once the system has been left out for attack, never trust the system back onto the internal trusted network because it may have been compromised without you noticing it.

Many operating systems have been modified to act specifically as a honeypot. These OSs give you the ability to have an inner system (the system that gets attacked) and also an outer system (used to monitor and watch what happens to the inner system).

Working with Signatures

This section takes a closer look at what a signature does. Signatures are the primary means for a sensor to identify traffic and take action on it. The actual process within an IPS sensor that matches traffic to a signature is called a microengine or a signature microengine (SME). A sensor has multiple microengines; each of the microengines is responsible for a group of signatures. The signatures are grouped by protocol or other characteristics that are similar. Table 16.1 provides a list of SMEs that are supported by the IOS IPS. The IOS version 12.4(11) T is the point at which a large upgrade to SME and signature versions happened. I explain more about this in the section titled "Signature Files."

TABLE 16.1   SMEs Supported by IOS IPS

SME before 12.4(11)T	SME after 12.4(11)T	Description
ATOMIC.IP	ATOMIC.IP	Provides simple Layer 3 IP alarms
ATOMIC.ICMP	ATOMIC.IP	Provides simple Internet Control Message Protocol (ICMP) alarms based on the following parameters: type, code, sequence, and ID
ATOMIC.IPOPTIONS	ATOMIC.IP	Provides simple alarms based on the decoding of Layer 3 options
ATOMIC.UDP	ATOMIC.IP	Provides simple User Datagram Protocol (UDP) packet alarms based on the following parameters: port, direction, and data length
ATOMIC.TCP	ATOMIC.IP	Provides simple TCP packet alarms based on the following parameters: port, destination, and flags
SERVICE.DNS	SERVICE.DNS	Analyzes the Domain Name System (DNS) service
SERVICE.RPC	SERVICE.RPC	Analyzes the remote-procedure call (RPC) service
SERVICE.SMTP	STATE	Inspects Simple Mail Transfer Protocol (SMTP)
SERVICE.HTTP	SERVICE.HTTP	Provides HTTP protocol decode-based string engine that includes anti-evasive URL de-obfuscation
SERVICE.FTP	SERVICE.FTP	Provides FTP service special decode alarms
STRING.TCP	STRING.TCP	Offers TCP regular expression–based pattern inspection engine services
STRING.UDP	STRING.UDP	Offers UDP regular expression–based pattern inspection engine services
STRING.ICMP	STRING.ICMP	Provides ICMP regular expression–based pattern inspection engine services
MULTI-STRING	MULTI-STRING	Supports flexible pattern matching and supports Trend Labs signatures
OTHER	OTHER	Provides internal engine to handle miscellaneous signatures

Signature Types

Generally, four categories of signatures are defined:

- Exploit signatures
- Connection signatures
- String signatures
- DoS signatures

Exploit Signatures   Because exploit signatures typically identify a traffic pattern unique to a specific exploit, each exploit variant may require its own signature. Attackers may be able to bypass detection by slightly modifying the attack payload. Therefore, it is often necessary to produce an exploit signature for each attack tool variant.

Connection Signatures   Connection signatures generate an alarm based on the conformity and validity of the network connections and protocols.

String Signatures   The string signature engines support regular expression pattern matching and alarm functionality.

DoS Signatures   DoS signatures contain behavior descriptions that are considered characteristic of a DoS attack.

To understand how traffic is scanned by the sensor and which components are used, you have to think about the microengines and signatures I just described. As traffic passes through the sensor, one or more sensor microengines are activated. Once activated, the microengine can inspect data. The sensor must decide which microengine to activate so the traffic can be scanned with the right signatures to determine whether the traffic is malicious. Microengine selection is based on:

- The network protocol of the traversing traffic
- The type of the operating system associated with a signature
- The session port
- Type of attack

Signature Files

The signatures that an IPS sensor uses are loaded into the system with a signature definition file (SDF). The SDFs must be downloaded from the Cisco website. You must have a login for the Software Download Center with a current support agreement on the device which requires the SDF in order to access and download the file. If you have all of that in place, you can download updated SDFs from the site and load them onto your router in flash. I talk about where and how you can load the files in the section titled "Configuring IOS IPS."

The SDFs are written based on the different versions of operating systems for the mainline IPS sensor platforms. The older versions of SDFs were written to the version 4 standard, and most of the new SDFs are written to the version 5 standard. The version 5 standard became available in IOS version 12.4(11)T. The newest version of IPS platform OS is version 6, but the files for the IOS router are not yet compatible with the version 6 standard.

For IPS sensor platforms like the Cisco IPS 4200 series, almost 2,000 signatures are available. For the IOS IPS, about 1,700 signatures are available. The total number of signatures available isn't as important as the number that your device can support. Cisco IOS IPS uses SDFs that contain signature descriptions for the most relevant attacks; these are updated by Cisco on a regular basis. The files can be downloaded from Cisco's site in different sizes, based on the amount of RAM your router has in typical default configurations. You can download the 128MB.sdf, which is called the basic signature set, or you can get the 256MB.sdf file, which is called the advanced signature set. With the default amount of RAM, an 1800 series router would use the 128MB.sdf and a 3800 series would use the 256MB.sdf.

Using Old SDFs

I want to make a quick, cautionary note about using old SDFs. If you are using an SDF with a name such as attack-drop.sdf, I recommend that you update the file. These files contain outdated signature files and won't provide necessary protection against newer attacks.

One last thing before I move on to IPS alarms. Prior to the IOS 12.4(11)T release, IOS IPS had 132 built-in signatures available. The built-in signatures are included in the image for backward compatibility. Starting in IOS release 12.4(11)T and later, no built-in (hard coded) signatures are available within the IOS.

IPS Alarms

An IPS sensor can react in real time when a signature is matched. This allows the sensor to act before network security has been compromised. The sensor can optionally log whatever happened with a syslog message or Security Device Event Exchange (SDEE).

Concept: IPS Reporting

An IPS can send alerts using syslog or SDEE. SDEE is recommended because it is the newer, more secure feature for sending the alert data. SDEE uses HTTPS to exchange the alerts with the IPS and a monitoring station.

When using IOS IPS on a router, SDEE is used to report events to the SDM. However, the SDM is limited by the fact that it can't do real-time monitoring or correlate the events from multiple sensors. To have these advanced features, you will have to deploy Cisco Security Monitoring, Analysis, and Response System (CS-MARS) or Cisco Works.

For those of you who have a smaller scale implementation of IPS or can't afford to use the MARS or Cisco Works solution, Cisco has an alternative. You can download the Cisco IPS Event Viewer (IEV) software. The download requires a CCO login and, to get signature updates, you must have a valid maintenance contract for each of the sensors you are using.

Like I said, you can configure IPS to choose a response to whatever the threats might be. Following are the response actions that the IPS can take when packets in a session match a signature.

Send an Alarm   IPS can send an alarm to a syslog server or a centralized management interface. This action is typically combined with other preventive actions.

Drop the Packet   This action is effective for all IP protocols and does not affect any legitimate user if the source IP address was spoofed.

Reset the Connection   This action works only for TCP sessions. The IPS can send a TCP RST message to the source and destination of the session. To do this, it spoofs the IP address of each device, making the source believe it is the destination and the destination believe it is the source.

Block the Traffic   The sensor has the ability to block traffic, either from a specific IP address or from a connection. Care should be taken when using the IP address option, because the attacker could be spoofing the IP address they are using. If the attacker is spoofing the IP address, you could inadvertently block a legitimate user's IP.

> **Source IP Address**   Blocking the source IP address of an attacker blocks the traffic for a specified amount of time. Again, you should be careful with this action; it does block the IP address but the IP address could be being spoofed. If an IP address is being spoofed, the attack could continue and enter the network disguised as a different source, because you only blocked the previous, spoofed IP.

> **Connection**   When you block a connection that a signature matched, that connection is only blocked for a specified amount of time. You can use this approach to deny the attacker's session and have less chance of being spoofed.

Configuring IOS IPS

It is now time to look at the configuration of IOS IPS. This section takes you through the configuration process using the SDM interface. The SDM gives you quite a few configuration capabilities for IOS IPS. You can configure every option through the IPS Edit menu.

SDM also uses the IPS Policies Wizard, which makes the deployment much faster on a new router. The wizard allows you to set interface and traffic flow, SDF location, and signature deployment. The wizard will also check and make sure the router has enough memory and resources before it actually configures the router. The IPS Policies Wizard configures IPS using default signature descriptions, as defined in the SDF files provided by Cisco or the built-in signatures included in Cisco IOS.

If you want to customize the signatures after the wizard deploys the default settings, you can use the IPS Edit menu available in SDM. Using the IPS Edit menu allows you to modify a signature parameter, as well as disable and delete a signature.

Start off by opening the SDM interface on a router with no configuration. The router needs an IP address on one of its interfaces so that you can get to the SDM, but other than that, leave it blank.

Figure 16.3 shows the SDM Home screen.

FIGURE 16.3   SDM Home Screen

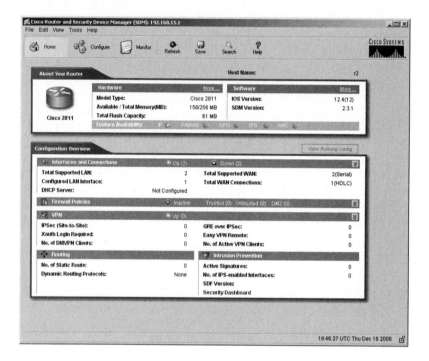

Next, click the Configure button in the main toolbar at the top of the screen. When the Configuration screen (shown in Figure 16.4) opens, the Interface and Connections button in the Tasks bar is selected.

Click the Intrusion Prevention button in the Tasks bar. When the Intrusion Prevention System (IPS) page opens, as shown in Figure 16.5, check to be sure that you are on the Create IPS tab. Notice the Launch IPS Rule Wizard button toward the bottom of the screen; click that button to start the wizard.

Figure 16.6 shows you a notification that should pop up if your router hasn't been otherwise configured. The wizard is going to enable SDEE for you so that the SDM can receive alerts from the IPS when something happens. Click OK to continue.

The Welcome screen, shown in Figure 16.7, goes over the basic configuration steps. You can see that you will have to choose the interface where the IPS rule is going to be set. Then you will determine the direction that traffic is going to flow in. Finally, you will specify the location of the SDF that the sensor is going to use for its signature database. Click Next to continue.

FIGURE 16.4   Default Configuration Screen

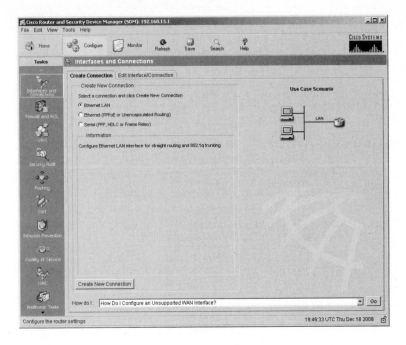

FIGURE 16.5   Default IPS Screen

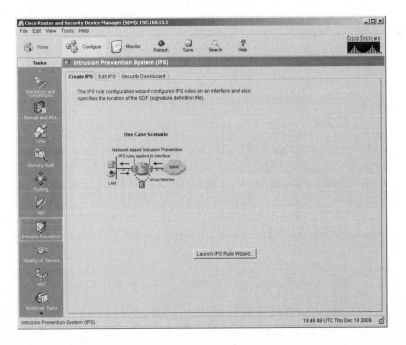

FIGURE 16.6 SDEE Enable Notification

FIGURE 16.7 IPS Wizard Welcome Screen

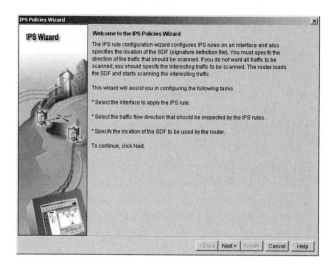

FIGURE 16.8 Select Interfaces Screen

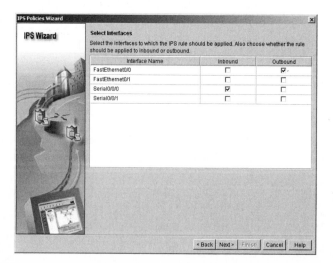

Click Next to continue.

When the SDF Locations page shown in Figure 16.9 opens, you will be able to set the location of the SDF for the router. By default most routers have an SDF loaded on them. As discussed before, the file that is loaded on the router is based on the capacity of your router. The router that I am working with has the 128MB.sdf.

Real World Scenario

Using the Wizard to Configure IPS for the Dubai Office Network

The first thing that you have to determine for the IPS setup is the interface where the rule is to be located and the direction the traffic should be flowing through the router. Figure 16.8 shows selections for the Internet connection for the Dubai office network.

The inbound interface is the interface that comes in from the Internet. The office has a T1 that comes in and provides that Internet connection. That T1 is connected to Serial 0/0/0 on the router so interface Serial 0/0/0 was selected as the inbound interface. The rule is also going to be applied to this interface. The wizard does that for you automatically.

In the Dubai office, the internal network is connected to the FastEthernet 0/0 interface so the FastEthernet 0/0 interface was selected as the outbound interface. (If you are configuring your test network, you can select the two interfaces that are appropriate for your setup.)

FIGURE 16.9 SDF Locations Screen

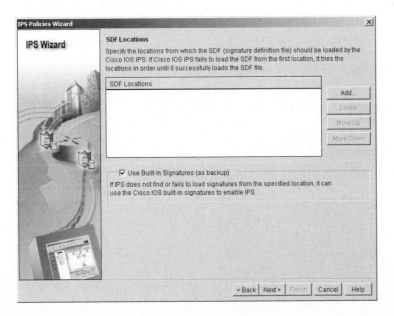

By default the Use Built-In Signatures (As Backup) check box is checked. As I mentioned earlier, it is not recommended to use these signatures on their own; they don't provide up-to-date threat signatures.

Click the Add button on the top right of the screen. The Add a Signature Location dialog box, shown in Figure 16.10, will allow you to specify a location of the SDF file for the wizard.

FIGURE 16.10   Add a Signature Location Dialog Box

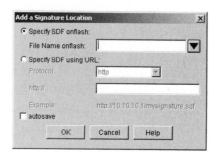

The Dubai office router has an SDF on the flash.

There should be an SDF on the flash on your router if you bought the router with the license for IPS services. If you are upgrading a router to an IOS that supports IPS or upgrading the SDM version to support IPS, there will be a default file in both of those upgrades. Otherwise you can purchase the appropriate software and load it onto your router. Flash is the recommended location for storing the file.

So, back to the Add a Signature Location dialog box. By default, the Specify SDF onflash radio button is selected. Click the drop-down arrow and if there is a file in flash, you can choose it from the list.

There could also be a file stored on an external server, such as an HTTP server. To use an SDF stored on an external server, click the Specify SDF Using URL radio button and then specify the protocol and location of the server and the file for the wizard.

When you are finished, check to be sure that Autosave is enabled (checked) and then click OK to continue to the next step.

If you look at Figure 16.11, you can see that the flash://128MB.sdf is now the SDF location specified for the Dubai office IPS. You can configure more than one file; simply click Add again and specify the next SDF location. Additional files are typically specified as a backup measure. The next file will be added to the bottom of the list. Once the configuration is in place, the router will try to load the files in order, top to bottom, until one loads. So, if you are putting more than one location in the list, make sure that each file is up-to-date and the file you want loaded is at the top of the list. When you have specified all the file locations you want, click Next to move on.

FIGURE 16.11   SDF Locations with File Added

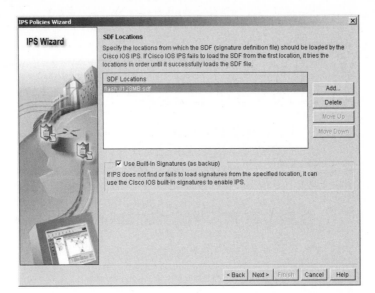

When the Summary page for the wizard opens, shown in Figure 16.12, you can review the settings that you have configured. You can see the rules that will be applied for setting the traffic flow direction, and the location of the SDF that you specified. Click Finish to apply the settings.

FIGURE 16.12   Wizard Summary Page

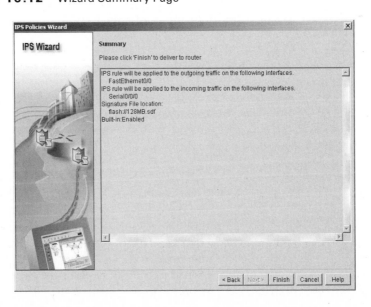

The Commands Delivery Status information box, shown in Figure 16.13, shows you the status of the commands that SDM is sending to the router. You can see that 12 commands are being sent to the Dubai router. Before sending the commands, the wizard verifies that the router has adequate resources for the configuration.

FIGURE 16.13   Commands Delivery Status

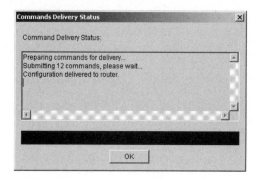

Once the configuration has been delivered to the router, click OK. After the wizard is complete, the Edit IPS tab on the Intrusion Prevention System (IPS) page opens, as shown in Figure 16.14. Make sure that you have the Edit IPS tab selected.

This screen contains three sections from which you can select and configure your settings. Right below the tabs you can see that there is a column of buttons. The first one is IPS Policies, which should be selected at this time. From this screen, you can see which interfaces have an inbound or outbound policy enabled. You can also disable or edit the policy using the buttons along the top of the screen.

Figure 16.15 shows the Global Setting page. To get to this screen, simply choose the Global Settings button on the left side of the screen. You can get quite a bit of information from this screen. You can change any of the options by choosing the Edit button on the top right of the screen. You can see if syslog and SDEE are enabled, and what the alert thresholds are.

The engine options are very useful. You can see what the default security stance of the IPS is; notice that Fail Closed is disabled. This means that if any of the SMEs don't operate, the IPS will allow traffic to pass without being scanned. If you want the IPS to drop traffic when it can't scan it, you must change the Fail Closed option to Enabled.

The CLI global command `ip ips fail closed` can be used to enable the Fail Closed option. If you want to disable the option, the no form of the command is used like this: no ip ips fail closed.

You will remember that I left the Use Built-in Signatures check box, checked, so the Use Built-in Signatures (As Backup) option is enabled. The default setting for the IPS is to drop traffic; you can see that with the Deny Action on IPS Interface option listed as Enabled.

FIGURE 16.14   IPS Policies Edit Screen

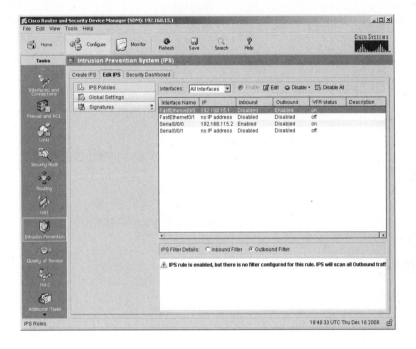

FIGURE 16.15   Global Settings Edit Screen

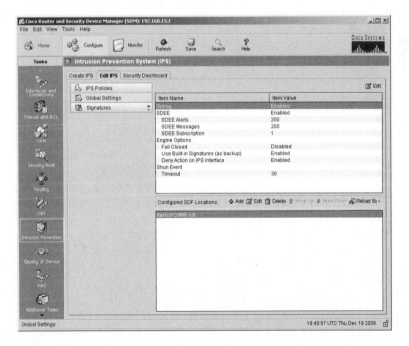

Finally, you can access the last of the three editing features on the Edit tab by clicking the Signatures button. Figure 16.16 shows the Signatures screen. You will most likely spend most of your time in this screen; this is where you can tune, enable, or disable signatures that are in the database. You can filter or look at just a specific group of signatures by selecting a folder from the drop-down list on the left side of the screen.

FIGURE 16.16   Signatures Edit Screen

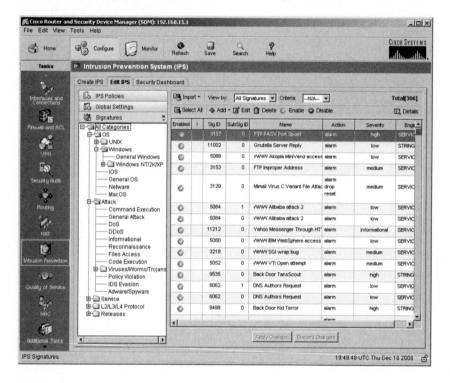

I am going to edit the Signature ID 3157, the FTP PASV Port Spoof, Signature, so that you can see what the screens for editing look like.

Figure 16.17 and Figure 16.18 show you the screen that you get when you choose a signature to edit (two figures are used because the screen is long). Figure 16.17 is the top of the screen; scroll down to see the rest of the editable options in Figure 16.18.

You can change many options, and the options vary from signature to signature, depending on what the signature is accomplishing. When you first open the Edit Signature dialog box, the option settings are grayed out and there is a square green icon next to each option; this indicates that the default settings are being used. If you click the icon, you can change the setting. Once you change the setting the icon changes a red diamond. If you want to put the setting back to the default, simply click the red diamond; the setting will go back to default and you will see and green square icon again.

FIGURE 16.17   Edit Signature Screen

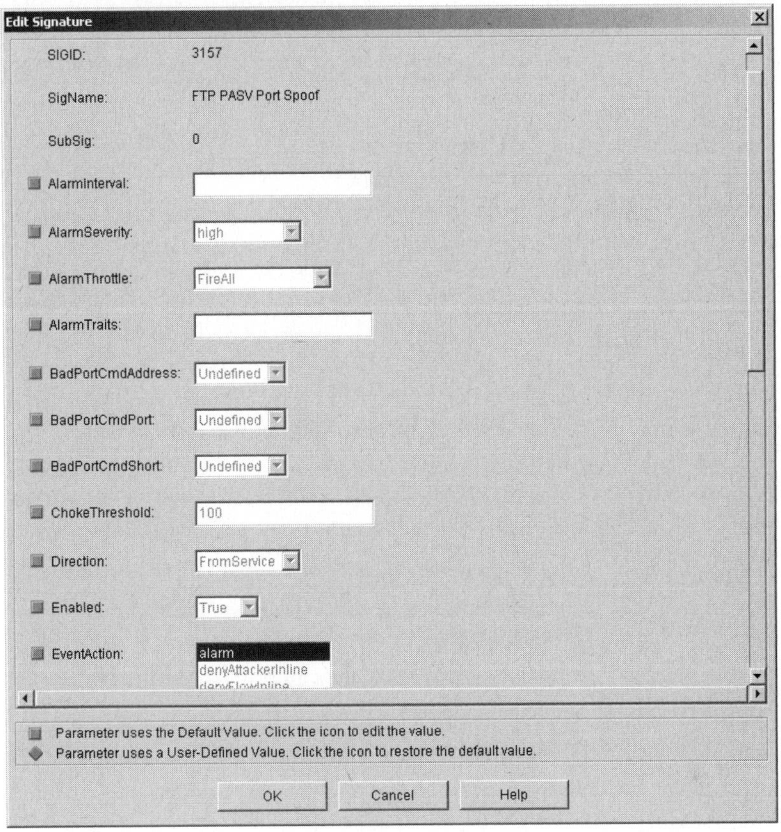

The final thing I want show you is the Security Dashboard. If you select the Security Dashboard tab from the Intrusion Prevention System (IPS) page, you will see the screen such as I have it in Figure 16.19. The Security Dashboard is useful for having a semi-automated way to keep up-to-date with the newest threats. It is a lot of work to stay up with every one of the newest threats and make sure that the appropriate signature is on your router; the Top Threats field on the Dashboard makes that process easier for you. Top Threats allows SDM to go out to Cisco's website and get the newest threat information. It then displays a list of those threats. You can see in the left column that the current SDF file running on this router doesn't have the signatures for these threats.

The Select Signature Definition File (SDF) field allows you to specify an SDF that has all of the signatures in it. You can download this file from Cisco and it will have a file name such as IOS-S252.zip. You tell SDM where this file is stored, and the SDM will go to that file and get the signatures that are needed for the new threats.

Once that is done, click the Deploy Signatures button and the new signatures will be added to the current signature database that is on the router.

FIGURE 16.18   Edit Signature Screen Continued

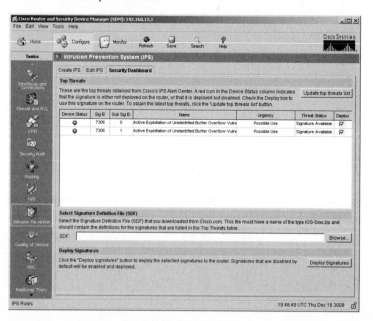

FIGURE 16.19   Security Dashboard

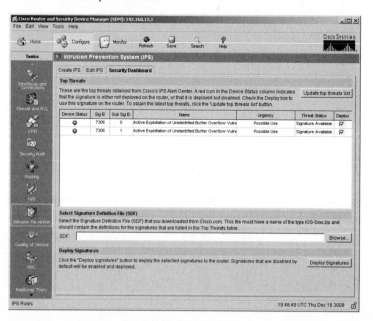

Summary

Well, you had to go through a lot once again, but you have one more technology mastered. This chapter showed you the differences between IDS and IPS. You learned that you can use both types of sensors in your network; in fact, they help each other do a better job. You saw the different implementation scopes that the sensors can use: host-based and network-based. Each of the scopes has particular types of threats that they are best at defending against, but again, using them together gives you a more secure, layered defense.

You learned about the different approaches that can be employed when a sensor is scanning traffic. You took a deeper look at signature-based scanning, and even got to see the components that make signatures really tick. Then, you were taken through the actions that a sensor can take when malicious traffic is detected.

Finally, you learned the process of configuring IPS on an IOS router. You used the SDM to perform the setup and learned how to edit and tune the sensor once it was set up.

Review Questions

1. Which type of sensor blocks traffic before it is allowed into the network?
   A. IDS
   B. HIDS
   C. IPS
   D. SDEE

2. Which type of sensor promiscuously listens to traffic as it enters the network?
   A. IDS
   B. HIPS
   C. IPS
   D. SDEE

3. Which scope of sensor is made for a specific computer operating system?
   A. HIPS
   B. NIDS
   C. NIPS
   D. SDEE

4. Which scope of sensor is best at blocking DoS attacks for the whole network segment?
   A. HIPS
   B. NIDS
   C. NIPS
   D. SDEE

5. What does a honeypot do for your network?
   A. Defend the network from attack.
   B. Get attacked so you can learn.
   C. Allow you to put up an SMTP relay.
   D. No purpose for the network.

6. What is the most common type of approach for scanning traffic?
   A. Honeypot
   B. Signature
   C. Policy
   D. Anomaly

7. Which component in the IPS matches the traffic to a signature?

   A. Signature microengine SME

   B. Subject matter expert SME

   C. Policy generator

   D. Policy engine

8. Which type of file is downloaded from Cisco and updated on the router to give you the newest signatures?

   A. Signatures

   B. Signature policy

   C. SFD

   D. SDF

9. The Cisco IOS IPS has a built-in set of signatures in the IOS.

   A. True

   B. False

10. An IPS sensor can block traffic as one of its actions.

   A. True

   B. False

Answers to Review Questions

1. C. An IPS sensor by definition and location in the network can block traffic entering the network.

2. A. An IDS's primary function is to scan the traffic and perform a deep inspection of its intent.

3. A. The host-based sensors like HIPS must be written for each OS that it is going to be used on.

4. C. Network-based sensors are best at defending the whole network segment and the only one that can block traffic is the IPS.

5. B. A honeypot is put into place so that you can learn what types of attacks are being run. This way you can learn from the attacks and better defend your network.

6. B. The most common type of scanning is with signatures.

7. A. A signature microengine SME is used to scan the traffic against a signature and determine if it matches.

8. D. The SDF is used to get the most up-to-date signatures and put them on your sensors; they must be downloaded from Cisco.

9. A. True. The IOS IPS has roughly 100 built-in signatures, but they shouldn't be used because they aren't up-to-date.

10. A. True. Only the IPS sensor can block traffic coming into the network.

Chapter

17

Voice

IN THIS CHAPTER, YOU WILL LEARN HOW TO DO THE FOLLOWING:

- ✓ Describe the characteristics of voice in the campus network

- ✓ Describe the functions of Voice VLANs and trust boundaries

- ✓ Configure and verify basic IP phone support (Voice VLAN, Trust, and CoS options)

- ✓ Describe the functions and operations of a VoIP network (packetization, bandwidth considerations, CAC, and so on)

- ✓ Describe and identify basic voice components in an enterprise network (gatekeepers, gateways, and so on)

In this chapter, you learn why the networking industry has been moving toward converged network infrastructures.

When I say converged, you need to think of combining traditional data traffic with voice and video traffic all on the same network infrastructure. The primary focus of this chapter is understanding the requirements for carrying voice traffic on the data network that you have been building. It is not my goal for this to be a complete look at every voice protocol and their detailed functions. (I could write a whole book on just voice protocols.) That being said, putting voice together with data offers many benefits. But doing so is not without its challenges.

You also learn about the characteristics and needs of voice traffic. In learning about voice, you learn about the additional configurations and devices needed on the network to support the combinations of different traffic.

For up-to-the-minute updates on this chapter, check out www.sybex.com/ go/CiscoProGuidetoInternetworking or www.lammle.com

Introduction to Voice Networks

I know some of you do not use voice often or at all. For that reason, I want to talk about a few basic voice functions before I dig too far into the chapter topics. Historically, enterprise phone systems all ran off of a private branch exchange (PBX). The PBX provided switching between the company's analog telephones. The switching connects the company's internal phones to each other when someone makes a call or sends the call out to the phone company if the call is not destined for a private number. Once a phone call is transmitted out of the company's system onto the phone company's network, usually called the public switched telephone network (PSTN), time-division multiplexing (TDM) is used to connect the callers. TDM allows multiple channels of data to be sent across the same line simultaneously. This is done by assigning time slots to each of the channels or phone calls. That way, each channel gets a slice of time and, from end-to-end, all the calls look like they are sent at the same time, even though they are time-sharing the line.

When you move to a digital system, a voice over IP (VoIP) phone system, the phones and data transmission are controlled by a call agent. Cisco's product for a call agent is Communication Manager; you probably know this as Call Manager. When you send voice traffic as packets over an IP network the phone call is controlled in a separate data stream from the actual voice traffic. The packets that contain the actual voice traffic (as opposed to the call control traffic) are called the bearer channel and are typically sent as real-time transport protocol (RTP) traffic. The control data stream is called the signaling data stream and is most commonly sent using the H.323 protocol, media gateway control protocol (MGCP), or session initiation protocol (SIP). This chapter covers the benefits to putting voice traffic onto the IP network and what protocols and configurations are required.

Converging Voice Traffic

Many companies have realized the benefits of putting their voice traffic onto their data network for some time. The consolidation of infrastructure can save time, money, manpower, and provide new services to end users. More specifically, the benefits include:

- Lower transmission costs
- Consolidated network infrastructure
- Shared bandwidth and equipment
- Increased features for user productivity
- Increased connectivity with other devices, including computers, wireless devices, PDAs, cable boxes, and household appliances

Costs of Transmission   A traditional phone circuit requires a 64-kbps channel for each call. Consolidating those circuits for transport across the network can take a huge amount of gear and work. Telephony calls transported over a packet network are statistically multiplexed, which means that the voice traffic is carried on the same network equipment and paths as data traffic. This obviously gives you and your company a huge savings; no need to buy two separate links, and because your voice traffic is being carried as data between your corporate sites, you don't incur the long-distance costs.

Consolidated Network Infrastructure   The discussion of the costs of transmitting your voice traffic can be expanded past just the links to carry it. With separate voice transmission you had two traffic connections to equip and maintain. When voice networks are brought onto the packet-switched network, you have a single integrated infrastructure.

Bandwidth and Equipment   Most data networks have more bandwidth than is required. If not, it is cheaper to add bandwidth to a data network than to a voice infrastructure. Telephony-based networks use a separate 64-kbps channel for each call. Packet-based networks share the bandwidth among multiple logical connections.

User Productivity and Features   IP phones can provide full, rich business applications. You can configure IP phones to do directory lookups and access databases for applications. For example, a retail store could let employees use the phone to look up information about an item in the inventory and enter orders. IP phones don't have to be just hardware devices or tied with a wire to the network. New technology allows you to provide software-based phones and wireless phones that offer mobility and location freedom to your users.

New Devices   Packet technology enables new levels of connectivity, levels that would not be possible on a time-division multiplexing (TDM) network. On an IP phone, network computers, wireless devices, household appliances, personal digital assistants (PDAs), and cable set-top boxes can all connect. Because these devices can directly communicate using the same network and applications, companies and service providers are able to provide many new services and a much larger amount of data to a growing population of customers.

Voice Components

A packet telephony solution isn't just for IP phones, though. Other devices are needed to properly route the traffic, control which phone gets the traffic, conference multiple phones, and provide access to application data. An IP phone network, depending on the features you implement, could include:

- Phones
- Gateways
- Multipoint control units (MCUs)
- Application servers
- Gatekeepers
- Call agents
- Video endpoints
- Digital signal processors (DSPs)
- Gateway interfaces
  - Foreign exchange stations (FXSs)
  - Foreign exchange offices (FXOs)
  - Earth and Magneto or ear and mouth (E&M)
  - Digital interfaces

Phones   Phones provide telephony features to users, allowing a means for users to talk and look up data. Phone devices include IP phones, software-based phones loaded as software on PCs, faxes, modems, and traditional analog phones.

Gateways   Gateways connect the packet telephony world with traditional telephony devices. Gateways are generally voice-enabled routers with voice ports. These ports allow the connection of analog or ISDN phones, faxes, circuit-based PBX systems, or public switched telephone network (PSTN) switches.

Multipoint Control Units (MCU)   MCU is required for conferences. If more than two parties are in a call, all the members of the conference send their media to the MCU. The MCU then routes the traffic so that all of the users get the voice transmission. If the users are using a different means of encoding their voice traffic, the MCU re-encodes the data. Voice encoding types are called *codecs*.

Application Servers   Application servers provide XML-based services to IP phones. Using these services and the applications that support them, IP phone users can access directories and databases.

Gatekeepers   Gatekeepers provide Call Admission Control (CAC), and translate telephone numbers or names to IP addresses for call routing in an H.323 network.

Call Agents   A call agent is the central device or system that controls most of your IP voice network. Cisco calls their call agent the Call Manager or the Communications Manager. Call agents provide call control, CAC, bandwidth control, and address translation services to IP phones and media gateway control protocol (MGCP) gateways.

Video Endpoints   Video endpoints provide video telephony features to users. As with audio-only calls, video calls need an MCU for conferences. For video conferences, the MCU has to be capable of mixing video and audio streams.

Digital Signal Processors   In an IP telephony network, some of the work that a gateway (or other) device does, like encoding and converting data, must be offloaded to a digital signal processors (DSPs). DSPs are used for converting analog voice signals into digital format and back. They also provide voice compression, transcoding (converting between codecs), and conferencing. DSPs are pieces of hardware; they look similar to a RAM chip. Some of the new routers, the ISRs, have slots built into the motherboard to accept DSPs. On older routers, though, they are typically located on voice modules that are installed in the router.

Gateway Interfaces   I talked about ports that a gateway can have installed to allow it to accept analog devices and connections from a PBX or PSTN. Following are the three analog ports and the digital port types.

   FXS   Often known as foreign exchange station, FXS is a port placed into a gateway to connect end units. Examples of analog end units are analog phones, fax machines, or answering machines. The port is typically just a standard RJ-11 phone jack.

   FXO   Often known as foreign exchange office, FXO is also a port installed into a gateway, but FXOs connect to other analog systems such as a PBX or PSTN. The port is also typically a standard RJ-11 phone jack.

   E&M   The origin of this term causes a bit of a debate among IT folk and engineers. Most people say that it comes from the term Earth and Magneto, but some call it ear and mouth. Either way, E&M provides signaling for analog trunks. These trunks connect two PBX type connections; for instance, two PBXs or a PBX and a PSTN switch.

   Digital Interfaces   In terms of the hardware, digital interfaces include T1, E1, and basic rate interfaces (BRI). BRI interfaces support ISDN phones. T1 and E1 interfaces can connect a PBX or PSTN to the gateway.

Two types of signaling are used with digital interfaces. The first is channel associated signaling (CAS). In CAS, the signaling bits that maintain the call are being carried in the same channel as the voice call. The other type of signaling is common channel signaling (CCS). In CCS, all of the signaling bits are carried in their own channel, and not separate from the voice traffic itself.

Making a Phone Call

I won't go through the process of exactly how every voice protocol works, but I will explain, in general, what happens when an IP voice call is made. This is important for you to understand the traffic and the connections that are made over the network. These are generic and always happen, regardless of the protocol.

The three basic phases of a phone call are call setup, call maintenance, and call teardown. Here is what happens in each of the phases.

Call Setup   The first step in call setup is to get the call-routing information so that the destination of the call can be found. This lookup also tries to get the bandwidth requirements for the call. If the bandwidth requirements are known, then call admission control (CAC) determines whether there is sufficient bandwidth for the call. If bandwidth is available, call setup generates a setup message and sends it to the destination. If bandwidth is not available, call setup notifies the source of the call by giving them a busy signal. Different call control protocols specify different messages for setup. But they all have to determine some basic information about the call, including the IP addresses of the source and destination devices, the UDP port numbers for the RTP streams, and the format used to digitize voice data.

Call Maintenance   Voice-enabled devices such as the gateways send information back and forth to determine the quality of a connection. If the quality is good, the call will continue. However, if the quality of the call deteriorates to a point at which it will be unclear or delayed, the call can be dropped. To perform this function, call maintenance keeps track of the call's packet count, packet loss, jitter, and delay through its duration.

Call Teardown   Call teardown lets the voice-enabled devices know to release the resources of a call. Once released, resources can be used for another call. This happens when either side of a call hangs up.

Call Control

The type of call control you implement in a voice network is often determined by the type of equipment that you can get for you network and the protocol that is used for signaling. The two types of call control are as follows.

- Distributed call control
- Centralized call control

I explain the call control process for each of the types and then describe the process of converting the voice signal from the analog signal that your speech creates into the digital bits that are carried by an IP packet. The conversion can be done either by an IP phone that itself directly puts the data into an IP packet, or by a voice gateway that converts the analog signal it receives from a traditional analog phone into the digital bits that will be carried in an IP packet. For the sake of this discussion, analog phones will be connected to voice gateways. The voice gateways are connected by an IP packet network.

🌐 Real World Scenario

Voice Upgrade for Bangalore Manufacturing

The Bangalore manufacturing plant has been on a legacy PBX phone system for quite a few years. The site, building, and related systems were in place when FutureTech purchased them a couple of years ago. You, as a member of the network engineering team, have been assigned to assess, test, and determine the best system and implementation for this site. You have been asked to look at a few possible scenarios.

Because FutureTech already has a large Cisco Communications system in place, the final solution will probably be a centralized implementation using the Cisco Communications Manager as a central call agent. But management wants you to go through a distributed solution as well, just to see how it would work and what the impact on the network might be.

Bangalore is a large site with 300 support staff that work in offices and help to maintain the plant. Each of the support people will have a phone located in the offices at their desk. More than a hundred phones are located on the manufacturing floor to allow the operators and engineers to communicate. One goal of the project is to allow access to inventory and other data stored on backend servers from the phones on the manufacturing floor.

A couple of test devices have been set up to evaluate various processes for providing voice traffic crossing the Bangalore network.

Distributed Call Control

In the distributed call control model, the phones are connected to voice gateways. The analog phones are connected into the routers with an FXS port that is installed in the router. Typically, signaling protocols such as H.323 and session initiation protocol (SIP) use a distributed call control model. In this model, the voice gateway controls all three steps in the call process, from setup to teardown. Figure 17.1 is the simplified diagram of voice traffic flow. Two voice gateways each have a phone connected to them. Between the gateways is the Bangalore IP network. Let's look at this process from the time one of the phones is picked up and a call is made to the other phone.

1. When BangVrtr1 detects a phone off the hook (often called a service request in voice terms), BangVrtr1 will play a dial tone for the phone.

2. As the caller on phone1 dials the destination extension, the digits are collected by BangVrtr1.

3. BangVrtr1 then looks up the dialed number in its local call routing table. To connect the call, the destination number must be in the call table or you will get that really annoying "can't make the call" sound. The destination for this call is the far gateway BangVrtr2.

4. Having found the destination in its local call routing table, BangVrtr1 initiates the call process by sending a call setup message to BangVrtr2.

5. When BangVrtr2 receives the setup message from BangVrtr1, BangVrtr2 must look up the number that was dialed in its local call routing table. Again, to connect the call, the number must be in the call table. The lookup finds that the number can be reached on a local voice (FXS) port installed in the router.

6. Having found the number in the local call routing table, BangVrtr2 then sends a ring voltage (and the call) out the local port.

FIGURE 17.1   Simplified Distributed Call Control Setup

When the receiving phone is picked up, the call is being established, and the call process goes into call maintenance. At the time the phone rings and the call is being established, no actual voice traffic has been sent. The only data sent across the network up to this point is signaling traffic. Once the call is established and a person begins to speak into the phone, voice traffic begins to be sent. Your speech, the actual voice traffic, is called *voice bearer traffic*. The voice bearer traffic must have higher priority than your network data traffic and is delay sensitive as it crosses the network.

The Busy Signal

You might be asking, "What if the line's busy?"

When a call is initiated, the call source router, BangVrtr1, never knows whether the destination router port is in use or ready to take a call. If the destination port is in use, BangVrtr2 sends BangVrtr1 a message and BangVrtr1 then gives its user a busy signal.

Centralized Call Control

The biggest difference between distributed and centralized call control is where the call lookup happens and what device controls where and when the voice traffic is going to flow. With the distributed model, each of the voice gateways has control of where and when it sends the call. In the centralized model, a central device, called the call agent, controls where and when a call is sent. Networks using the media gateway control protocol (MGCP) often use the centralized call control model. Figure 17.2 shows a simplified diagram of the voice traffic flow. You can see the only real difference is the inclusion of the call agent in the network. The steps that follow outline the process.

1. BangVrtr1 detects a phone off the hook, and informs the call agent.

2. The call agent directs BangVrtr1 to play a dial tone and collect the number dialed by the user.

3. BangVrtr1 sends the number to the call agent, one-by-one, as the digits are collected.

4. The call agent looks up the called number in its call routing table. For this call, the call agent finds that the phone number can be reached on BangVrtr2, which port it can be reached on, and that BangVrtr2 is under its control.

5. If the call routing table contains the called number, the port connection where number can be reached, and that connection is also controlled by this call agent, the call agent sends a message requesting that the call is passed to the port.

FIGURE 17.2   Centralized Call Control Setup

You can see that in centralized call control the call agent looks up and controls all aspects of the call signaling. The way that centralized call control separates the call setup and the voice bearer traffic is a big distinction you have to understand before you can move on past the call setup phase. At this point in the process, only call setup has happened, and if you are using a call agent only the call signaling traffic gets passed to the call agent. The call agent will not get traffic in the next phase when you start seeing actual voice traffic being sent. Voice bearer traffic is always sent along the best path between voice gateways.

Converting and Transmitting Voice

Once a call is set up, you can begin to send the voice traffic across the network. In order for the analog speech to be carried across a digital IP network, it must be converted into digital information. It is important to understand how the conversion process works so that you can tell whether the quality will be high enough and determine the bandwidth the call requires to cross the network.

You have to know whether the quality is high enough to allow the digital information to be converted back into an analog signal at the far end. If the quality isn't high enough to allow reconversion, the user at the destination won't hear your speech. Knowing the bandwidth is essential so that you know how much voice traffic the network can carry and you can ensure that the voice traffic is handled properly.

The process for converting an analog signal to digital includes:

- Sampling
- Quantizing
- Encoding
- Compressing

Sampling   When an analog signal is sampled, a measurement of the signal at periodic intervals is taken. The sampling rate (how often a sample is taken) affects the quality of the digital signal and the later conversion back to analog. The frequency range for a clear, high-quality phone is much smaller than the full range of audible sound for humans. For years the frequency range supported for phone calls has been between 300 Hz and 3300 Hz. The highest necessary frequency for voice support is 4000 Hz.

According to the Nyquist theorem, the sampling rate must be twice the highest frequency to maintain high-quality signal conversion. For this reason, the sampling rate of voice is 8000 samples per second, or once every 125 microseconds. The sampling makes a pulse amplitude modulation (PAM) signal, which is a plotted signal on the X and Y axis where the X axis represents time and the Y axis represents the voltage of the actual signal.

Quantizing   The second step in the process is to quantize the signal. For each sampling point, the height of the analog signal is read. The quantization process takes this reading based on predetermined step values. It happens that these step values rarely exactly match the actual signal. So, the actual value is rounded up or down to the nearest step value. The variation is called *quantization noise*.

Encoding   Each of the samples is then encoded into an 8-bit expression so it can be carried digitally in a packet. Each of the samples is broken down into 8 bits like this:

- One polarity bit indicates whether the signal is positive or negative.
- Three segment bits identify the logarithmically sized segment number (0–7).
- Four step bits identify the linear step within a segment.

Compression   Codecs compress the data so that the amount of information that is sent is lower. This is good for bandwidth, but too much compression can be bad for the quality of the call. A couple of example codecs that are supported by Cisco are G.711, which requires a 64 Kbps stream, and G.729, which requires an 8 Kbps stream. The Kbps stream requirements do not include any of the overhead for packet encapsulation.

Protocol Usage and Encapsulation Overhead

Voice traffic has slightly different needs than other data you place on the network. It can't be sent reliably with TCP traffic because a retransmitted packet would cause huge delays or be received out of order. Voice cannot handle either of those outcomes. If you look at the needs voice traffic does have, you will see that it requires time stamping, re-ordering, and multiplexing. Many of these things are accomplished by TCP, but voice traffic doesn't need to be reliable and you can't turn that off in TCP. The typical replacement protocol would be UDP, but UDP only supports one of the four voice requirements, re-ordering. Neither TCP nor UDP protocols will support voice on their own. So, what protocol will support the voice requirements? There is always RTP, and if you use RTP and UDP together you can support all three of the voice requirements.

The only thing you really have to think about now is the amount of overhead created by encapsulating the voice traffic. A large amount of overhead is added when you encapsulate voice traffic. If you add the IP, UDP, and RTP headers, you are adding a total of 40 bytes of information to each packet. A single voice packet typically contains 20 ms of voice data, 160 samples. With a G.711 codec that contains 8 bits per sample, that is 160 bytes of data. The G.729 codec uses code words to minimize the amount of data sent, so you only have 20 bytes of data for the same 160 samples.

Compare that amount of voice data to the amount of overhead and you will find that you are increasing the amount of data sent by 25 to 100 percent. This can have a huge impact when you send voice over a low bandwidth link, such as a WAN. To mitigate the impact, consider the codec that is used. It makes sense to use G.729 over WAN links because the amount of data sent is much smaller. Next, use RTP header compression (cRTP). Header compression can reduce the amount of header information that must be sent for each packet from 40 bytes down to 2 or 4 bytes. The RTP compression mechanism can remove all of the data that is the same from subsequent packets and only send information that is changing or necessary to rebuild the headers.

You must always be careful when using compression, though. It takes time and processing for the devices on each end of a link to compress (remove) and uncompress (replace) the data in each one of the packet headers. In some cases, this delay and processing can do more harm than good. If the delay is too long and the phone call sounds bad, the compression isn't doing you any good.

Introduction to QoS for Voice

You will need to understand a bit about Quality of Service (QoS) so that you can understand voice configurations and some of the terms required for working with switches and phones. The discussion of QoS in this chapter is not all inclusive; Chapter 18, "DiffServ Quality of Service (QoS)," provides the detail missing here.

QoS is the ability of an administrator to use control features to manage specified types of traffic that are sensitive to loss, delay, and delay variation (jitter). QoS allows preference or priority to be given to critical flows of data. Be cautious; when you give preference to some data, it is to the detriment of other data. Bandwidth is the most common resource that is in short supply. You can force a higher priority for voice traffic to ensure that it is forwarded, but other traffic will be held up or possibly dropped in the process. QoS tools do give you the ability to manage and predict service for a variety of networked applications and traffic types in a complex network.

Ultimately, implementing QoS on a Cisco network will provide many benefits, including:

- Better control over access to network resources
- Better response when traffic experiences latency, jitter, or packet loss
- Improved ability to ensure that mission-critical applications receive priority

Priority Access   QoS allows you to control which traffic is allowed to access resources like bandwidth, equipment, and WAN links.

Management   Network management indicators can notify you when specific traffic is experiencing latency, jitter, and packet loss, and then QoS tools can be used to adjust how that traffic is handled.

Coexistence of Applications   QoS technologies can ensure that mission-critical business applications receive priority access to network resources while providing adequate processing for applications that are not delay sensitive. Multimedia and voice applications tolerate little latency and require priority access to resources. Other traffic that is delay tolerant, such as Simple Mail Transfer Protocol (SMTP), HTTP, or FTP, can still be adequately serviced.

To provide this type of service on a network, the different kinds of traffic have to be separated somehow. This is done through a process called *classification*. Once the traffic is classified, you can mark the traffic so that the type of traffic can be easily identified and acted upon by a device or QoS policy further into the network.

Classification

Classification is the identification of specific traffic for use later in the network for prioritization or other control of the traffic. Classification can be accomplished using many different values from header information in the traffic itself to where the traffic came from or is going to. Table 17.1 lists the most common items used to identify traffic for classification by layer.

TABLE 17.1   Common Items Used to Identify Traffic for Classification

Layer	Item Used to Identify Traffic
Layer 2 information	MAC address
	Multiprotocol Label Switching (MPLS)
	ATM cell loss priority (CLP) bit
	Frame Relay discard eligible (DE) bit
	ingress interface
Layer 3 information	IP precedence
	DiffServ Code Point (DSCP)
	QoS group
	IP address
	ingress interface

TABLE 17.1   Common Items Used to Identify Traffic for Classification *(continued)*

Layer	Item Used to Identify Traffic
Layer 4 information	TCP or UDP ports ingress interface
Layer 7 information	Application signatures ingress interface

Marking

Once the traffic has been classified, you must mark the traffic to allow other devices in the network to handle the traffic the way you specify. Perhaps some traffic requires a higher priority so it is not delayed. Maybe it is vital that some traffic is not dropped. Different types of markings are used to identify traffic and how you want it handled.

Class of Service (CoS) markings are carried at Layer 2; CoS can be carried in a trunk header or in an MPLS label. The CoS value is 3 bits long; this means that you can have eight different markings from 0 to 7. The lowest value is 0 and is the default; all traffic by default is marked with a 0. The highest user-assignable CoS value is 5, a setting normally reserved for voice traffic. The 6 and 7 values are for system use and are generally applied to routing and management traffic.

Layer 3 headers include a field called the type of service (ToS) field. The ToS field contains 8 bits. The older marking standard only used the three most significant bits of the ToS field, the IP precedence bits. The three bits map directly to the Layer 2 CoS bits. Differentiated services codepoint (DSCP) is the new standard for marking at Layer 3. The DSCP marking uses the six highest-order bits from the ToS field. The DSCP marking can specify how a device should handle traffic for priority and drop probability.

Now that you've been introduced to the types of markings available, let's look at where the classification and marking process should happen in your network. If you think about how you have designed all of the pieces of the network, you know that as you go up from the access layer toward the core of the network, there is more and more aggregation of traffic and devices. A single access switch can have a mix of 20 to 40 hosts and phones on it. When you go up from there, a single distribution switch might have 10 to 20 access layer switches connected.

Thinking in terms of the overall design structure of your network, the closer to the core the traffic gets the more aggregation occurs. For this reason, it is recommended that traffic classification and marking happen as close to the edge of the network as possible. Use an edge device, such as a host or phone, in the access layer. This way a single device is only doing the processing for the smallest number of devices possible. The device that is closest to the edge of the network becomes your trust boundary. That device can mark traffic with markings that you can trust. That edge device is the last device that you can completely control. Here you can consistently mark traffic based on policies you set for the way traffic should be handled.

You almost never trust traffic that is marked on a user client machine. It is too easy for a user or attacker to load software that mismarks traffic.

Figure 17.3 illustrates what I mean when I say mark the traffic as close to the edge of the network as possible. The best place to mark traffic is on a trusted edge device such as a phone that you can set a policy on. The second place would be the access layer switch, and last would be the distribution layer switch or router. Again, the closer to the core you get the greater number of devices that are being aggregated and the higher the load will be on the device that is doing the classification.

FIGURE 17.3   Trust Boundary

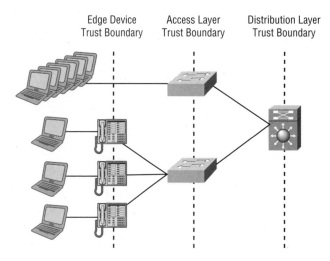

Configurations for Voice

It is time to take a look at how to configure your network devices to support voice traffic. You might remember that I mentioned in Chapter 2, "Switching," that I would come back to the configurations for voice traffic. I won't cover in detail here the creation of VLANs and how to set basic switchport commands. If you need a review of those things, refer back to Chapter 2. What I do cover are the commands for setting up a phone on a voice gateway (router). Figure 17.1 shows the basic setup that you learn to configure.

Switch Configuration

Most newer Cisco switches give you a feature called auxiliary VLAN. I look at auxiliary VLANs as rule breakers. In this case, a broken rule is a good thing and useful. Auxiliary

VLAN allows you to connect a phone and an end-user computer to the same switch port. Voice and data traffic are in different VLANs but there is no requirement for a trunk link. You get the functions of a trunk without configuring the port as one. The auxiliary VLAN feature allows you logically divide the network between the voice traffic and the data traffic even though you are not physically changing the network. You basically overlay the voice topology onto the data network.

With the auxiliary VLAN feature, phones are placed into their own VLANs without user interaction or continuous attention from an administrator. The VLAN assignments are seamlessly maintained, even if a user moves the phone to a new location.

The user simply plugs the phone into the switch and the switch automatically provides the phone with the necessary VLAN information. The switch and phone communicate this information through the Cisco Discovery Protocol (CDP). To implement this feature, your network must use Cisco phones and Cisco switches. Because phones are automatically placed into their own VLANs, you can preserve the existing IP topology for the data end stations. IP phones are fully compatible with DHCP, and can easily be assigned to different IP subnets using standards-based DHCP operation.

Finally, because of the logical separation you can more easily identify and troubleshoot network problems, and create and enforce QoS or security policies. Auxiliary VLAN makes the configuration on the switch ports much easier to do and simpler to understand.

 Real World Scenario

Switch Configuration for Bangalore

Back at the Bangalore office, it is time to go over the configurations that will be needed on the access layer switches so that they can properly handle voice traffic that comes in from connected phones.

First you will configure the voice VLAN, which is actually the auxiliary VLAN. Then you go through the process of configuring the CoS trust boundary between the switch and the phone. You will see that you can move the trust boundary to the phone or have it on the switch.

The setup for this scenario is such that it does not require you to have a physical phone to complete the configuration on your test network. However, if you have a phone that you can use for this setup, you will have the opportunity to see the switch find the phone with CDP and move the trust boundary to the phone from the switch.

So, let's enable the voice VLAN on the switch port and associate a VLAN ID:

```
BangSW1(config-if)#switchport voice vlan vlan-id
```

This is the only command that can be used to create and identify a voice VLAN. You may have created the VLAN with the global configuration command vlan, but the actual voice VLAN is not created until you apply the voice VLAN using the `switchport voice vlan` *vlan-id* command. If you remember from Chapter 2, "Switching," a VLAN can be created by simply putting a port into a VLAN, whether or not it already exists.

The next command sets the switch port as the trust boundary. With the switchport set to be the trust boundary, the switch will trust the CoS value of frames as they arrive at the switch port. This is useful for a port that is attached to a device that the switch can't talk to, something other than a Cisco phone.

```
BangSW1(config-if)#mls qos trust cos
```

You can add to the previous command and make the trust boundary conditional upon a Cisco IP phone being attached. If you attach a Cisco phone to a port with the following command, the phone and the switch will communicate using CDP and move the trust boundary out to the phone from the switchport. This can happen automatically only if you are using a Cisco phone capable of communicating with CDP.

```
BangSW1(config-if)#mls qos trust device cisco-phone
```

Optionally, you could use the next command to force the switchport to overwrite CoS values that enter the switch from an attached host machine. With this command, you can set the CoS value of frames coming from the host machine attached to the IP phone with a CoS value that you choose.

```
BangSW1(config-if)#switchport priority extend cos cos_value
```

The next couple of commands allow you look at the options you have configured on a switchport. This show command specifically will display voice parameters configured on the interface:

```
BangSW1#show interfaces interface-id switchport
```

The following show command will display QoS parameters configured on the interface:

```
BangSW1#show mls qos interface interface-id
```

Gateway Configuration

This section shows you the configuration for setting up for voice gateways in a distributed call control network. You can use this setup in smaller installations where you don't have many phones or maybe don't have the funding for a Communications Manager installation.

First, let's set up the IP address on the LAN interface of the gateway so that it can communicate across the IP network:

```
BangVrtr1(config)#interface FastEthernet 0/0
BangVrtr1(configj-if)#ip address 192.168.10.1 255.255.255.0
```

Real World Scenario

Gateway Configuration for Bangalore

Figure 17.4 gives you the basic information for this setup. Notice the IP addresses on the gateways. These IP addresses are going to be the destination addresses that are used when there is voice traffic that must go to a distance gateway. You will remember that FutureTech has decided to update the Bangalore manufacturing plant network so voice traffic can be carried over the network.

Let's take a look at how you would set it up in a distributed call control configuration. You may not end up using a setup like this in a real network, especially one the size of the Bangalore network, but you could use this in places that are smaller or where you need a small separate setup.

FIGURE 17.4   Distributed Call Control Configuration

From the diagram, you can see that there are two phones that you need to make sure can communicate to one another. Let's look at the configuration commands for BangVrtr1 first; this router has a local analog phone that you have to put into the call routing table. BangVrtr1 must also know about the phone on the far end of the network, so when the phone number is dialed it can be found and traffic sent toward the phone. Each of these phones will have a similar setup but configured as a different kind of dial peer.

The next thing that you have to do is tell the gateway where the local phone is located and what the phone number is for the port or phone. This setup is done with the dial-peer setup.

```
BangVrtr1(config)#dial-peer voice 1 pots
```

The dial-peer command is used from the global configuration mode and takes you into the dial-peer configuration mode. The *voice* option in the command is to set this dial-peer for voice. The number in this command is called the tag; it must be unique on the gateway, a different number for each of the dial-peers that you create. I used a *1* because this is the first dial-peer I've created on the gateway. The last option specifies the type of voice connection. In this case, because the phone is local on an analog port the type is *pots* (plain old telephone system).

```
BangVrtr1(config-dial-peer)#destination-pattern 1001
```

The second command is the `destination-pattern` command, which sets the phone number for this dial-peer. This number will be looked up locally to find the destination port and phone. For a dial-peer that is not local, it will be the number looked up to reference where the distant phone is located. Think about this like the internal 4-digit extension you might be used to in your own office.

`BangVrtr1(config-dial-peer)#`**`port 1/0/0`**

The third command tells the gateway the physical location of the phone. In this case, because the line is local the command points the gateway to a local port.

Next, you have to configure the remote phone line. Start by creating a second dial-peer. For this second dial-peer command, the voice option is the same but the tag will have to be incremented to a unique number. In my example I'll use 2. It makes sense to create the dial-peers in some sort of order, maybe something that corresponds to the numbers on the lines themselves. The last option is going to be different this time as well. The last dial-peer was local, so the option was *pots* for a local analog port. This second phone is remote and must cross the IP network, so use *voip*.

`BangVrtr1(config)#`**`dial-peer voice 2 voip`**

The destination-pattern is no different than it was the last time, but be sure you specify the correct extension number for the phone.

`BangVrtr1(config-dial-peer)#`**`destination-pattern 1002`**

The last command for this second dial-peer specifies the destination. For the local phone, it was a local port. Because this phone is remote and must cross the IP network, you have to specify the IP host address that should receive the IP packets that contain the voice traffic for the second phone. So you are telling your gateway which gateway on the network this destination phone is connected to. You do that with the `session target` command and specify the IP address of the remote gateway. In this case you have an IPv4 network, so that is the type of address that you use.

`BangVrtr1(config-dial-peer)#`**`session target ipv4:192.168.10.2`**

Now you have one side of this configuration completed. You still have to set up the gateway on the other end of the network (BangVrtr2). Let's go through and see what that is going to look like.

The first thing again you need to configure is the IP address on the LAN interface of the gateway. The remote gateway must have this to communicate on the IP network.

`BangVrtr2(config)#`**`interface FastEthernet 0/0`**
`BangVrtr2(configj-if)#`**`ip address 192.168.10.2 255.255.255.0`**

Next, you have to configure the dial-peer for the local phone. The `dial-peer` command is the same on this router as it was before. The *voice* option works the same as do the *pots* and *voip* options.

`BangVrtr2(config)#`**`dial-peer voice 1 pots`**

The `destination-pattern` command is the same; be sure that you set the correct phone number for the proper phone connection. Notice now the *1002* extension is the local dial-peer on this router.

```
BangVrtr2(config-dial-peer)#destination-pattern 1002
```

The dial-peer that I am setting first is the local dial-peer, so you have to set the local port it is located on.

```
BangVrtr2(config-dial-peer)#port 1/0/0
```

Next you have to configure the second dial-peer on this gateway. The only thing of note again is the tag option. Like I said it is used the same way, but remember, the tag number must be unique on the local gateway. I have used the same tag numbers on both of the gateways; this is okay because they are only of local significance.

```
BangVrtr2(config)#dial-peer voice 2 voip
BangVrtr2(config-dial-peer)#destination-pattern 1001
BangVrtr2(config-dial-peer)#session target ipv4:192.168.10.1
```

Now, if you have a couple of analog phones and a couple of FXS ports, you can set this up and try it for real. If you would like to go through the configuration on your test network, that's what you'll need—fair warning, FXS ports are expensive.

Summary

This chapter just scratched the surface of the world that is IP-based voice. It covered a good number of basic voice concepts. I hope this gets you going and makes you want to learn more.

I started out talking about the benefits of combining your voice and data networks. Next, I took you through the most common voice devices you will see on a network. I started with a phone and video end point and moved through the components, all the way to the device that controls them—the call agent. Then, I went through the types of interfaces that are used for voice. I showed you both analog and digital interfaces.

Once you'd been introduced to the devices and interfaces that connect everything together, I showed you how calls are set up and controlled. Remember that calls can be controlled centrally or in a distributed fashion. With that knowledge in hand, I took you through the process of converting the analog signal to a digital signal and then back again. Then I told you about some of the basic requirements for handling voice traffic on the network. Generally, QoS will be required.

Finally, I showed you how to configure a switch to accommodate voice traffic and some of the QoS configurations that you will use to prioritize and forward the traffic. Finally, I showed you how to configure a voice gateway (router) to provide distributed call control.

Review Questions

1. What reason is a benefit to putting your voice onto the IP network?
    A. Lower cost
    B. Higher cost
    C. Less bandwidth used
    D. Data separated

2. What device provides central control for call control?
    A. Gateway
    B. Call agent
    C. MCU
    D. DSP

3. What type of interface in a gateway allows you to connect an analog phone?
    A. E&M
    B. FXO
    C. FXS
    D. T1

4. What type of interface allows you to connect a gateway to a PBX?
    A. E&M
    B. FXO
    C. FXS
    D. T1

5. What device controls a call in the distributed call control setup?
    A. Call agent
    B. MCU
    C. Gateway
    D. Voice gateway

6. What is the first step in the process of converting an analog signal to a digital signal?
    A. Sampling
    B. Quantizing
    C. Encoding
    D. Compression

7. What can be done to data to reduce the amount of information being sent?

   A. Smashing

   B. Coding

   C. Compression

   D. Sampling

8. What does QoS do for your voice traffic?

   A. Priority

   B. Delay

   C. Jitter

   D. Slow down

9. What Layer 2 marking can be used to classify traffic?

   A. ToS

   B. DSCP

   C. IP precedence

   D. CoS

10. What device should be the trust boundary?

   A. Voice phone

   B. Distribution switch

   C. Core router

   D. WAN firewall

Answers to Review Questions

1. A. The cost is lowered having voice on your data network.

2. B. The call agent controls the call.

3. C. The FXS interface is used for an analog phone.

4. B. The FXO interface is used for a PBX.

5. C. The gateway controls the call.

6. A. Sampling is the first step.

7. C. Compression can be used to send less data.

8. A. QoS can provide priority for your voice traffic.

9. D. CoS is used at Layer 2 for marking.

10. A. The voice phone should be the first device, second is the access switch.

Chapter

18

DiffServ Quality of Service (QoS)

IN THIS CHAPTER, YOU WILL LEARN HOW TO DO THE FOLLOWING:

- ✓ Describe and configure NBAR for classification

- ✓ Explain congestion management and avoidance mechanisms, such as FIFO, PQ, WRR, and WRED

- ✓ Describe traffic policing and traffic shaping (traffic conditioners)

- ✓ Describe WAN link efficiency mechanisms, including payload and header compression

Quality of Service (QoS) is a framework of multiple protocols and mechanisms that allow you to control the flow and timing of traffic across your network. This chapter goes over the basics of QoS—what you need to know in order to make sure that your voice and video has priority forwarding and doesn't get dropped. Then of course, you will want to know how to guarantee other mission-critical types of traffic some bandwidth to send their traffic. I describe the functions and mechanisms, such as queuing, link conditioners, and congestion avoidance, which allow you to control your flows of traffic. Then, I tell you about the four different ways QoS can actually be configured. Finally, you learn how to create and write a QoS policy.

For up-to-the-minute updates on this chapter, check out www.sybex.com/go/CiscoProGuidetoInternetworking or www.lammle.com.

Introducing QoS

QoS can be a complex beast to understand and implement when you are first learning about it. Many different mechanisms allow you to manipulate how traffic will flow. This chapter covers the whole implementation process of QoS. You learn why QoS is needed and how it can help fix problems such as:

- Low bandwidth
- Delay (or variation of delay called jitter)
- Packet loss

After I discuss the problems, I show you the process of implementing QoS. You need to understand what to look for and how to break up traffic so that you can actually fix the problems. The tasks to accomplish these repairs are:

- Identify the traffic
- Classify the traffic
- Mark the traffic
- Create a policy

Many different functions and features are used to accomplish each of these tasks. Here are some the features that I discuss in more detail throughout the chapter.

Network Based Application Recognition (NBAR)   NBAR is used in identifying traffic. NBAR can be run on a Cisco router to provide traffic statistics. NBAR gives statistics on a per-interface basis and per direction for each type of protocol that is recognized.

Class of Service (CoS)   CoS is a type of traffic marking that can be used to identify specific classes of traffic. CoS is carried in the trunking protocol header of a Layer 2 frame.

IP Precedence   IP precedence is another type of traffic marking; it is carried in the Type of Service field of a Layer 3 IP packet. Like CoS, IP precedence specifies classes of traffic.

Differentiated Service Code Point (DSCP)   DSCP is another Layer 3 marking; it is carried in the same field as IP precedence, but the name of the field was changed to DSCP when the QoS standard was accepted. DSCP offers much more granularity in its markings and includes options for specifying other features, such as drop probability of the traffic.

Modular QoS CLI (MQC)   Once the traffic has been classified and marked, the next step is to create a policy to apply actions and other features that affect traffic flows. The most common and most versatile method of creating a QoS policy uses the MQC.

Queuing   Queuing is a mechanism added to the outbound hardware queue of a router interface. The queuing feature adds a software queue that provides multiple queues based on your classes of traffic. Depending on the type of queuing used, you can control which type and how much traffic gets forwarded at a time.

Traffic Conditioning   Traffic conditioning mechanisms provide you a way to drop or buffer traffic to help prevent or relieve congestion on network links. The most common types of conditioners are policing for dropping or remarking traffic and shaping for buffering or holding traffic.

Congestion Avoidance   Congestion avoidance mechanisms allow you to prevent congestion on an interface before it happens. When the queue or buffer for an interface becomes full due to heavy traffic, all of the traffic that won't fit is dropped. This is called *tail dropping*— traffic at the tail end of the queue gets dropped. To prevent tail dropping (which drops all traffic regardless of priority), avoidance mechanisms such as weighted random early detection (WRED) monitor the capacity of the interface queues. When the level reaches certain limits, the dropping mechanism begins to drop low-priority traffic to prevent tail dropping.

The Problems You Face

As described in Chapter 17, "Voice," many different types of traffic are being put onto IP data networks today. Each of these different types of traffic has different requirements for sending it across the network. For example, voice and video traffic are sensitive to delay and packet loss. That sensitivity must be balanced with the bandwidth available on the network. As I go through these issues, I describe what you can do about each of them.

QoS will be the framework for implementing the features to control and prevent the problems that arise with a converged network. As I go through each of the potential network problems I offer you recommendations for improving performance or preventing the problems. As the chapter progresses, you will see that some of the improvements help with more than just one problem. For that reason, sections are devoted to implementing the solutions.

Bandwidth

Bandwidth can be viewed in a couple of different places in the network. If you view bandwidth end-to-end on the network, the maximum bandwidth that you have available is the bandwidth of your slowest link. The slowest link is usually a WAN link. The other place is at other aggregation points, such as uplinks between switches or routers.

What does a lack of bandwidth cause, then? A lack of bandwidth can cause performance degradation on network applications; specifically time-sensitive applications such as voice or bandwidth-intensive applications such as video. Not just the converged traffic placed on the network is interrupted; services that are interactive, like terminal services and remote desktops, could be affected by low bandwidth and experience slow application responses.

Here are few solutions that can prevent degradation and improve performance:

- Increased bandwidth
- Prioritized traffic
- Compressed data

Increase Bandwidth   The best way to prevent degradation is to increase the bandwidth by upgrading the link speed with your service provider to a level that accommodates all the applications and users. Granted, this is usually the least popular solution, at least in the eyes of company bean counters. The process of increasing bandwidth is, of course, more expensive but it also takes time to implement.

Priority Forwarding   The next option is more directly related to using QoS. You can assign QoS classes to your traffic and then forward the traffic based on its importance. This type of forwarding is called priority forwarding and uses one of the most basic QoS mechanisms, queuing. The most common type of queuing is First-In-First-Out (FIFO). FIFO does not provide any priority treatment of traffic; it is the default on most interfaces. Other queuing types provide additional granularity; these allow you to forward voice and business-critical data with a higher priority. You can configure a policy so that these traffic types receive sufficient bandwidth to support their application requirements. Voice traffic should receive prioritized forwarding; the least important traffic should receive whatever unallocated bandwidth remains. Quite a few queuing mechanisms are available that provide bandwidth priority to specific classes of traffic. The types of queuing that I go through here are:

- Weighted fair queuing (WFQ)
- Class-based weighted fair queuing (CBWFQ)
- Low latency queuing (LLQ)
- Weighted round robin (WRR)

Compression   You can increase the efficiency of a link by compressing the payload of frames. Compression only virtually increases link bandwidth because either some of the data is removed or a code-text is used to represent a larger amount of data. Unfortunately, with compression you always have to think about the overhead created. Compression increases delay because of the time and processing power it takes to perform the compression. Using hardware compression can accelerate packet payload compression. The Stacker and Predictor algorithms are the two algorithms available in Cisco IOS software.

As an alternative to payload compression for link efficiency, you can also use header compression. Header compression can be very effective across links where most of the packets carry small amounts of data. In other words, the amount of data compared to the amount of header information is close to the same. If you go back to Chapter 17, I described voice packets that fit this example. The most common examples of header compression are TCP header compression and Real-Time Transport Protocol (RTP) header compression.

I have a quick distinction for the use of compression types. Payload compression is best used in end-to-end compression, whereas header compression is best used in hop-by-hop or across a single link.

 Real World Scenario

Bandwidth Problem for Purchasing

Bandwidth limitations could be a problem in literally hundreds of places in a network the size of FutureTech. All of the WAN links to branch offices and manufacturing plants could suffer from low bandwidth.

When FutureTech's manufacturing plants were swapped over to a new corporate purchasing/ordering system, a new application was installed and hosted in the Dallas headquarters' data center. (The systems that they had were local systems; each of the sites had different software and a different process for controlling their materials.) A corporate decision was made to unify the process and only one application would be used and control all of the purchasing.

Having the application in the Dallas data center meant that the manufacturing plants would be sending all of that data back and forth over their WAN links. After a short time of using the new system, users began to notice that at certain times during the day the new purchasing system would react very slowly. Most of the time, orders and requests would still go through, but it took much longer than at other times. The biggest issue was for the purchasing clerks. First thing in the morning they needed to get reports downloaded and vendor orders uploaded. Timing was important because they were trying to meet vendor schedules. Delays would cause the order to bump to the next day. The users noted that the slowdowns typically occurred in the morning, when everyone was getting to work, and then again around lunch time.

It is important to understand that QoS is not a solution for a link that is always over utilized. QoS mechanisms are best suited on links when specific or peak times of overutiliza-
tion and congestion—usually caused by improper use, like someone doing some online
shopping or dropping by the single's chat room during the work day—halts legitimate
traffic. For example, if you always need to send 15 Mbps of data across a link that is only
capable of passing 10 Mbps of data, you are always going to have 5 Mbps of data that is
not being sent. In this situation, the only thing that QoS would do for you is ensure that
the classes of traffic that you designate as high priority get passed and the traffic that is
low priority times out or gets dropped.

A network assessment showed that there was heavy, legitimate, purchasing traffic during
the morning, but at lunch (when users were logging onto the Internet, accessing personal
e-mail accounts, and the like) the congestion was more difficult to justify. Problems hadn't
been noted before because the link was not saturated all day long.

FutureTech's network team recommended implementing a QoS policy that would guarantee
bandwidth for the new purchasing application. This way, even during times when users are
accessing e-mail and generating traffic by surfing the Internet, the traffic for the purchasing
application would always be allowed through the WAN.

Delay

Delay comes from four different places:

- Processing delay
- Queuing delay
- Serialization delay
- Propagation delay

The average length of the queue, average length of packets in the queue, and the link
bandwidth can all introduce delay factors.

Processing Delay   Processing delay is the actual amount of time that it takes a router or
multilayer switch to move a packet from the interface it comes in on to the output queue
of the interface it will go out of. The length of the processing delay depends on CPU speed,
CPU utilization, the switching mode, the router architecture, and the features configured
on the input and output interfaces.

Queuing Delay   The queuing delay time can be determined by simply looking at how long
a packet has to sit in the output queue of a router's interface. Queuing delay can depend
on the number of packets in the queue and the size of those packets. The bandwidth of the
interface can also be a factor of queuing delay, as can any queuing mechanism configured
on the interface.

Serialization Delay   The serialization delay is the amount of time it takes to serialize the data and actually put a frame on the physical wire to be sent. The serialization delay is typically inversely proportionate to the link bandwidth.

Propagation Delay   The propagation delay is defined as the amount of time it takes for the packet to cross the link from one end to the other. The time usually depends on the type of media.

The overall effects of delay can be looked at in two different ways. First is the end-to-end delay, the total sum of all the types of delays from a source to a destination across the network. The end-to-end delay can have an effect on an application's quality, especially real-time traffic.

The second effect of delay can be more severe; it is known as jitter. Jitter is variation in delay. That means that packets from a traffic flow reach their destination with significantly different amounts of delay. Even in real-time traffic, a longer but constant end-to-end delay has less effect than a shorter but unpredictable delay.

Let's take a look at the things you can do to reduce the effects of delay and improve performance on your network.

Increase Bandwidth   You have to first make sure that the router being used is powerful enough to forward the required amount of traffic. The right router or device for the job will reduce or limit the amount of processing delay. If your network is experiencing delays, the best thing that you can do is to upgrade the link. Sometimes, this is the only thing that can solve the problem when there is not enough bandwidth. Having enough bandwidth will allow queues to be reduced so that packets do not wait as long before being transmitted. Higher bandwidth also reduces the serialization time; serialization is the direct representation of bandwidth.

Priority Forwarding   Queuing can be more cost-effective than upgrading the link. Priority queuing can reduce the delay for traffic that is delay sensitive. Remember though, forwarding some data with less delay will impact other traffic, but that traffic shouldn't be as delay sensitive.

In some cases, traffic may have to be reprioritized when entering or exiting a device. This often happens with traffic that enters into a network such as an ISP. ISPs reprioritize your data when they don't support as many classes of traffic as you may have set up. This can be detrimental if you don't have the ISP reprioritize the data into classes that preserve your data quality. This means that you may have to group similar classes of traffic, such as all the real-time traffic together, all the business-critical traffic together, and then all the bulk traffic together.

Compression   Compression can reduce the size of packets or headers, so it gives a virtual increase to the link bandwidth, but payload compression uses complex algorithms that add delay. If you are using payload compression to reduce delay, make sure that the time it takes to compress the payload does not exceed the time you save by sending the compressed packets. Compression is especially important to assess when you are thinking about delay.

Header compression is not as CPU-intensive as payload compression and is used with other mechanisms to reduce delay. Header compression is especially useful for voice packets that have as much header data as actual voice data. Transmission time can be significantly improved by reducing the amount of header data that must be sent.

 Real World Scenario

Morning Conference Call Delay Issue

Every morning the Engineering VP located in the Dallas headquarters has a conference call with the manufacturing branch directors and product line managers. The call includes having everyone not only communicate with voice on the phone but now with video end points as well. A good amount of data in the form of reports and data sheets is being sent back and forth, reporting critical information for the day. This is all at the same time all the other employees are coming to work, firing up their systems, and checking e-mail and voice mail. I described earlier that delay can occur in any number of places in the FutureTech network. Still, the most common is going to be on the WAN links and slower-speed connections in the network.

To efficiently and effectively pass voice/video, HTTP, and SMTP data from headquarters to the manufacturing locations, you will need to use several approaches. To reduce the delay for the time-sensitive traffic (the voice), the recommendation is to implement header compression (RTP compression in this case for voice) and a queuing mechanism (LLQ recommended for voice as well). The LLQ queuing mechanism will provide priority forwarding and minimal delay for the voice traffic. You can then assign an amount of guaranteed bandwidth for each of other types of traffic. The video traffic will especially need to have a guarantee so that it can be passed with little delay. The bean counters may not be happy with this part of the solution; you might need to upgrade the WAN link so that it can forward enough data without introducing a significant amount of delay. With the inclusion of so much new data the link will probably not support it all concurrently.

Packet Loss

Packet loss happens for several reasons, but only one is common in a network—tail dropping. Tail dropping happens when an output interface queue is full and it cannot accept an incoming packet. If a packet cannot be accepted by the interface queue, the packet is dropped. And it's called tail dropping because it's usually the tail-end of the information that's dropped.

Although not as common, packets can also be lost due to an input queue drop, an overrun, or because the router has run out of buffer space and cannot handle an incoming packet. Packets also can be dropped as the result of a frame error. A frame error could be generated by receipt of a frame with an incorrect CRC or a runt/giant frame.

You can, of course, do some things to help prevent packet loss. If you are experiencing packet loss due to some of the less common causes, you must make sure that the router or forwarding device is capable of handling the traffic load that you are placing on it. If the device is not capable, you may experience some of those uncommon packet losses. In a case where you do begin to experience input dropping or the like, you may have to upgrade the device where the problem is occurring. But if you are experiencing output drops, here are some things you can do to resolve the problem.

Increase Bandwidth   As always, you can increase the bandwidth on the link. This decreases the wait time on the output interface and thereby reduces the chances of congestion. When congestion is reduced, packet drops decrease as well.

Priority Forwarding   Configure the device to forward the most important traffic first. In Cisco devices, you can configure LLQ, which can guarantee an amount of bandwidth and ensure the priority traffic has the lowest chance of being dropped.

Congestion Avoidance   You can prevent congestion on the interface by dropping lower-priority packets before congestion occurs. Yes, I just said that; you are going to drop packets, but you are going to drop packets that aren't sensitive to drops. Voice and video connections will have poor quality if the packets from their streams are dropped. However, if you drop packets from flows like HTTP and FTP that will retransmit lost packets, you will not suffer any real quality issues.

The most often used congestion avoidance mechanism is called weighted random early detection (WRED). When used in conjunction with a queuing mechanism, WRED drops packets from low-priority classes of traffic and allows higher-priority traffic to pass through without being dropped.

Preparing to Implement QoS

Implementing QoS on your network is a three-phase process. Let's start off by identifying the phases and then go through each phase in more detail:

1. Complete a network assessment to identify traffic types and technical requirements of each type of traffic.

2. Divide all the types of traffic into different classes so that QoS requirements can be associated to each class of traffic.

3. Create QoS policies that meet the requirements of the classes of traffic that you have for you network.

This section focuses primarily on the first two phases. You learn how to identify traffic and divide it into classes for assignment of QoS policies. In the section called "Configuring QoS," I take you through the steps and commands to create and write QoS policies.

Time to Talk to the Bean Counters

Because the traffic demands have increased so much in the Mexico manufacturing plant, you have had to continually add more and more fixes to the configuration of the edge router that passes traffic onto the WAN link. However, the network administrators in Mexico are still seeing problems of high CPU utilization and dropped packets.

You will remember that the Mexican plant was part of a separate company purchased by FutureTech and much of the equipment is older and outdated. You have already implemented QoS so that the new purchasing application would have priority access. You upgraded the link so that it could support sending enough data for the new video and voice conference calls.

The last remaining issue that is causing the router to be overworked and drop packets is the fact that it just doesn't have enough horsepower to keep up with the load that is now required. Upgrading equipment can be a hard sell sometimes, but if you have the data to show that the device is overloaded and causing a degradation in network performance, the discussion can be easier. It is usually much easier if you can show the bean counters how much money is being lost in time wasted and resources expended because of this poorly performing device. If you can show a return on investment (ROI) to the bean counters, you can more easily get what you need.

Identifying Traffic

Traffic identification requires a couple of things. First, and often the best, is a good knowledge of the traffic and applications running on your network. This can be a difficult task in a large network, especially when the tasks of running and operating the network are broken across multiple teams of people, each responsible for a different set of tasks or applications. So, a thorough assessment of the network is normally required when beginning the identification process. Suites of software are available that can make the assessment process much easier and less time consuming for you. Unfortunately, most of the good network assessment software suites that I know of are very expensive. In a large network, though, where traffic conditions change rapidly, a suite of software can be almost required.

As you begin to gather data and assess traffic, you will want to consider the following items.

Problems for the End Users   From a user's perspective, what traffic is slow and has poor quality? Once you know that, you can then measure the traffic on the network during congested periods, and conduct CPU utilization assessment on each of the network devices. From the user's position in the network during busy periods of time, this will give you a way to determine where problems might be occurring.

Concept: NBAR

If you do not have access to an expensive suite of software (can't afford one), you can use a process, Network Based Application Recognition (NBAR), built into Cisco routers to help with gathering traffic statistics. One of the capabilities of NBAR is the ability give you traffic statistics. The output that follows gives you a peek at the capability:

```
Router# show ip nbar protocol-discovery interface FastEthernet 0/0
FastEthernet0/0
Input                   Output
Protocol        Packet Count           Packet Count
Byte Count      Byte Count
5 minute bit rate (bps) 5 minute bit rate (bps)
---------------------   ----------------------  --------------------
eigrp                   344673                 0
85666105                0
6000                    0
rsvp                    279538                 14644
674344251               875554
0                       0
http                    43479                  254314
765550                  235630
0                       0
```

I provide more detail about NBAR in the section titled "QoS Mechanisms" later in this chapter.

Business Requirements for Traffic   Determine the business goals, and figure out what the business requirements for each type of traffic are. This will help you define the number of traffic classes and allow you to determine the business requirements, which are not necessarily the same as the technical requirements, for each class of traffic.

Acceptable Service Levels for Traffic   Define the service levels required by different traffic classes in terms of response time and availability. This can help you answer questions such as: Can file transfers wait until the network is underutilized? What is the impact on business if a transaction is delayed by two or three seconds?

Classifying Traffic

After the majority of network traffic has been identified and measured, use the business requirements to perform the second phase tasks—define the traffic classes.

Classification is the process of identifying traffic and categorizing that traffic into different classes. Classification uses a traffic descriptor to categorize a packet within a specific group in order to define that packet. In most networks, you will use these traffic descriptors:

- Incoming interface
- IP precedence
- Differentiated Services Code Point (DSCP)
- Source or destination address
- Application

After the packet has been classified or identified, the packet is then accessible for Quality of Service (QoS) handling on the network.

Using classification, network administrators can partition network traffic into multiple Classes of Service (CoSs). When traffic descriptors are used to classify traffic, the source implicitly agrees to adhere to the contracted terms and the network promises QoS. Different QoS mechanisms, such as traffic shaping, traffic policing, and queuing techniques, use packet traffic descriptors to ensure adherence to that agreement. I cover shaping, policing, and queuing in more detail in the section titled "QoS Mechanisms" later in this chapter.

Typically, once the traffic has been broken into assigned classes, you then identify the CoS for each class of traffic with a marking. A marking (also called a coloring) is an identifier that can be used more efficiently by devices and QoS policies for applying the assigned level of service. I cover marking types in the section titled "QoS Mechanisms" later in this chapter.

After the applications with the most critical technical requirements have been identified, the remaining traffic classes are defined using business requirements. An enterprise network, such as FutureTech's, could define its traffic classes into five separate classes as listed in Table 18.1.

TABLE 18.1 FutureTech Network Traffic Classes

Class	Priority Comments
Voice	VoIP traffic has the highest priority.
Mission-critical	Small number of applications defined by the business as critical for the function of the company.
Transactional	Interactive traffic, transaction services, database access, preferred data services.
Best-effort	E-mail, HTTP, SMTP—these can be a hard sell down here by many non-technical people because so many managers and salespeople swear by this type of data, but remember it is not time sensitive or as drop sensitive as real-time traffic.
Scavenger	The unspecified traffic is considered as less than best-effort. Scavenger applications, such as BitTorrent, Kazaa, and other point-to-point applications, will be served by the lowest class.

Models for Implementing QoS

Three models exist for implementing Quality of Service (QoS) in a network:

- The best effort model
- Integrated Services model (IntServ)
- Differentiated Services model (DiffServ)

Best Effort Model

The Internet was designed for best-effort delivery of packets (no-guarantee). QoS is not applied to packets. This is appropriate if it is not important when or how packets arrive. This behavior is still predominant on the Internet today.

If QoS policies are not implemented, traffic is forwarded using the best effort model. All network packets are treated exactly the same—an emergency voice message is treated exactly like a digital photograph attached to an e-mail. Without QoS implemented, the network cannot distinguish between different types of packets and, as a result, cannot give higher priority traffic preferential treatment.

Benefits   The best effort model has nearly unlimited scalability. The only way to reach scalability limits is to reach bandwidth limits, in which case all traffic becomes equally affected. You do not need to employ special QoS mechanisms to use the best effort model. It is the easiest and quickest model to deploy.

Drawbacks   Nothing is guaranteed. Packets will arrive whenever they can, in any order possible, if they arrive at all. Packets are not given preferential treatment. Critical data is treated the same as casual e-mail.

IntServ Model

The IntServ architecture model was motivated by the needs of real-time applications, such as multimedia conferencing, remote video, visualization, and virtual reality. This model was designed to provide very high QoS to IP packets. Essentially, applications signal to the network that they require special QoS for a period of time and that bandwidth should be reserved. With IntServ, packet delivery is guaranteed. However, the use of IntServ can severely limit the scalability of a network. The bandwidth reserved for the specified period of time is not available to other applications until the reserved resources are released by the IntServ process that held them for the traffic flow.

The IntServ model provides a way to deliver end-to-end QoS that real-time applications require by explicitly managing network resources to provide QoS to specific user packet streams (flows). IntServ uses Resource Reservation Protocol (RSVP) and admission control mechanisms as key building blocks to establish and maintain QoS. This practice is similar to a concept known as *hard QoS*. With hard QoS, traffic characteristics, such as bandwidth, delay, and packet-loss rates, are guaranteed end-to-end. This guarantee ensures both predictable and guaranteed service levels for mission-critical applications.

IntServ uses RSVP to explicitly signal the QoS needs of traffic generated by an application along the devices in the end-to-end path through the network. If all network devices along the path can reserve the necessary bandwidth, the originating application can begin transmitting. In the event that the requested reservation fails along the path, the originating application cannot send any data.

Benefits   IntServ supports admission control that allows a network to reject or downgrade new RSVP sessions if one of the interfaces in the path has reached the limit (that is, all reservable bandwidth is booked).

RSVP signals QoS requests per individual flow. In the request, the authorized user (authorization object) and needed traffic policy (policy object) are sent. The network can then provide guarantees to these individual flows.

RSVP informs network devices of flow parameters (IP addresses and port numbers). Some applications use dynamic port numbers, like H.323-based applications, which can be difficult for network devices to recognize. NBAR is a mechanism that was introduced to support applications that use dynamic port numbers but do not use RSVP.

Drawbacks   RSVP continuously signals because of its stateful nature. Because RSVP has to track each flow, the flow-based approach does not scale to large implementations, such as the public Internet. A possible solution is to combine IntServ with elements from the DiffServ model to provide the needed scalability.

DiffServ Model

DiffServ was designed to overcome the limitations of both the best effort and IntServ models. DiffServ provides an almost guaranteed QoS, while still being cost-effective and scalable. It provides the greatest flexibility and scalability in implementing QoS in a network. Network devices recognize traffic classes and provide different levels of QoS to different traffic classes.

The DiffServ model is similar to a concept known as *soft QoS*. In soft QoS, QoS mechanisms are used without prior signaling. Additionally, QoS characteristics (for example, delay and bandwidth) are managed on a hop-by-hop basis by policies that are established independently at each intermediate device in the network. This action is also known as the Per-Hop Behavior (PHB) or Pointy Haired Boss, which is what I think of every time I see it. The soft QoS approach is not considered an end-to-end QoS strategy because end-to-end guarantees cannot be enforced. However, soft QoS is a more scalable approach to implementing QoS than hard QoS (from the IntServ model), because many (hundreds or potentially thousands) of applications can be mapped into a small set of classes upon which similar sets of QoS behaviors are implemented. Although QoS mechanisms in this approach are enforced and applied on a hop-by-hop basis, uniformly applying global meaning to each traffic class provides both flexibility and scalability.

With DiffServ, network traffic is divided into classes based on business requirements. Each of the classes can then be assigned a different level of service. As the packets traverse a network, each of the network devices identifies the packet class and services the packet according to that class. It is possible to choose many levels of service with DiffServ. For example, voice traffic from IP phones is usually given preferential treatment over all other application traffic, e-mail is generally given best effort service, and non-business traffic can either be given scavenger service or blocked entirely.

Benefits   DiffServ is highly scalable and provides several different levels of quality.

Drawbacks   No absolute guarantee of service quality can be made. This model requires that a set of complex mechanisms work in concert throughout the network.

QoS Mechanisms

This section takes you through what I typically refer to as the QoS mechanisms. By mechanisms, I am referring to all of the features and standards that you can use in your network and policies to control traffic and prevent congestion, delay, and packet loss. I take you through the different standards that you can use to mark or color traffic. Once you have the traffic marked, you can use those markings to queue the traffic. Once you have queued the traffic it can be forwarded based on the priority that you set. Finally, I cover some of the other features in traffic conditioning and congestion avoidance the can help you maintain traffic flow and help resolve bandwidth issues. Overall, I cover these areas of QoS features:

- Traffic marking
- Queuing
- Traffic conditioning
- Congestion avoidance

Traffic Marking

Traffic marking refers to the different ways to mark or color traffic. Marking is related to classification; it allows network devices to classify a packet or frame once at the network edge based on a specific traffic descriptor.

Traffic can be marked in multiple ways. Here are the ways in which it can be marked and where in the frame or packet the marking is used. I talk more about markings in the sections that follow.

Data Link Layer   Class of Service (CoS) is used in a Inter-Switch Link (ISL) or 802.1q trunk header. For an 802.1q header, the three priority bits are stored in the 802.1p field.

Multiprotocol Label Switching (MPLS) uses the experimental (EXP) field to carry the three priority bits.

Frame Relay marks priority using the DE bit that is carried in a Frame Relay header.

Network Layer   IP precedence is the older of the two Layer 3 standards. IP precedence uses only the three high-order bits of the eight bits available in the Type of Service (ToS) field of the IP header.

Differentiated Service Code Point (DSCP) primarily utilizes the six higher-order bits in the ToS field to mark priority. The three high-order bits map to the IP precedence bits for backward compatibility; the remaining three bits are used for drop probability.

Class of Service (CoS)

The specifications for the CoS 3-bit field are defined by the IEEE 802.1p standard. These bits can be used to mark packets as belonging to a specific CoS. The CoS marking uses the three 802.1p user priority bits and allows a Layer 2 Ethernet frame to be marked with eight different levels of priority (values 0–7). Three bits allow for eight levels of classification, allowing a direct correspondence with IPv4 IP precedence ToS values. One disadvantage of using CoS markings is that frames lose their CoS markings when transiting a non-802.1q link, which carries the 802.1p field in the trunk header. Therefore, a more ubiquitous, permanent marking should be used for network transit. This is typically accomplished by translating a CoS marking into another marker or simply using a different marking mechanism.

Table 18.2 lists the eight different classes of service. Notice that CoS 6 and 7 are reserved for management traffic and routing data. These levels are generally not defined by the user.

TABLE 18.2   Classes of Service

CoS	Use or Application
7	Reserved for management traffic and routing data
6	Reserved for management traffic and routing data
5	Voice bearer
4	Video
3	Call signaling
2	High priority data
1	Medium priority data
0	Best effort data

The same three priority bit values are used in the ISL and MPLS headers. They represent the same levels of service, and also can be mapped to the same values in the IP precedence marking at Layer 3.

IP Precedence

The IP precedence value uses the first three bits of the ToS field in the IP header. The value (and level of service) can be directly translated to the CoS values in the Layer 2 headers. The same eight levels of service are defined for IP precedence as were used in Layer 2. The biggest difference between the Layer 2 and Layer 3 implementation is that this field does not change, is not removed, and remains valid end-to-end on the network, unlike like Layer 2 headers that are lost when the trunking header is removed.

Differentiated Services Code Point (DSCP)

The DSCP type of marking can be a little harder to understand. The marking has changed slightly over time. I'll first break down the fields and bits that are used for the Layer 3 markings.

Take a look at Figure 18.1. Eight bits make up the ToS field in the IP header. In the figure, each of the blocks in the ToS row represents one bit. Remember that only the most significant bits are used as traffic markers.

In the IP precedence row, I show only the three high-order bits that are used set IP precedence value. They are often referred to as bits 5 through 7. Bits 0 through 4 are not used and set to 0.

Then in the DSCP row, I show the six bits most often used to set the DSCP value. They are often just called bits 2 through 7. Bits 0 and 1 are used for some other flow control features that are beyond the scope of this book.

FIGURE 18.1   Comparing Marking Types

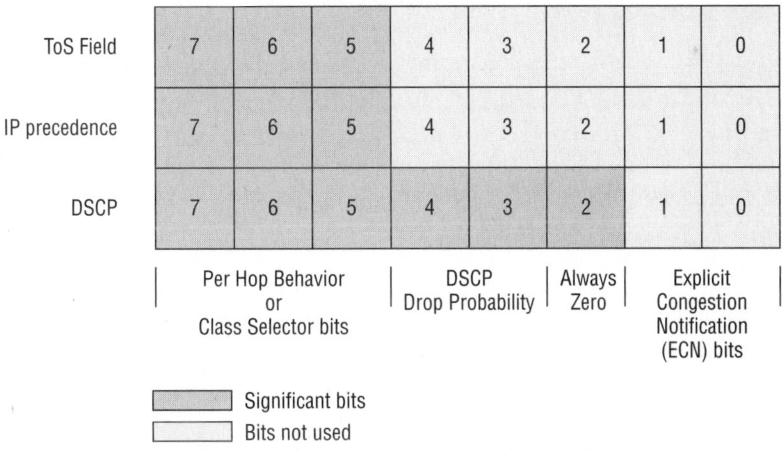

DSCP replaced IP precedence as the standard for Layer 3 marking. However, DSCP or DiffServ maintains interoperability with non–DiffServ-compliant devices. Non–DiffServ-compliant devices are those that still use IP precedence. Because of this backward compatibility, DiffServ can be deployed gradually in large networks.

The meaning of the eight bits in the DiffServ field of the IP packet has changed over time to meet the expanding requirements of IP networks. Originally, the field was referred to as the ToS field just as it was with IP precedence, and the first three bits of the field (bits 7 to 5) defined a packet IP precedence value. You can see what I am talking about if you look at Figure 18.2. A packet could be assigned one of six priorities based on the IP precedence value (eight total values minus two reserved ones). IP precedence 5 (101) was the highest priority that could be assigned under RFC 791.

FIGURE 18.2 DiffServ Class Selector Bits

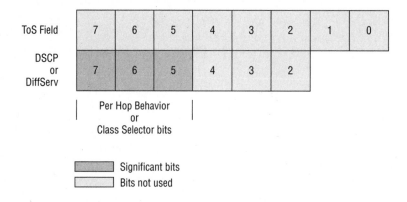

Concept: The DiffServ Field

RFC 2474 replaced the ToS field with the DiffServ field. DSCP uses the six most significant bits in the field. The three most significant bits specify a range of eight class selector PHB values that are used for backward compatibility with IP precedence. The next three bits specify forwarding behavior, also known as drop probability. The two least significant bits in the DiffServ field specify other traffic flow options.

The class selector PHB was defined to provide backward compatibility for DSCP with ToS-based IP precedence. RFC 1812 simply prioritized packets according to the precedence value. The PHB is defined as the probability of timely forwarding. Packets with higher IP precedence should be (on average) forwarded in less time than packets with lower IP precedence.

When the last three bits (bits 2 to 4) of the DSCP are set to zero, the value identifies a backward-compatible class selector PHB.

So that you can start to see these values, I am going to break them out in a table. Table 18.3 shows you the bit-by-bit values of the class selector values. In the bit-by-bit values only bits 2 through 7 are expressed; bits 0 and 1 are represented by *xx* variables, because they specify other traffic flow options.

Concept: PHB Notation

Class selector PHB values are represented in a couple of ways, depending on where and how you're using them.

When you are writing and configuring QoS policies, the values are represented by a CS prefix and the decimal equivalent of the PHB value.

As defined by the IETF, PHB values are written using a prefix that identifies the way forwarding should be handled: expedited forwarding (EF) or assured forwarding (AF). The AF class has four separately defined values, AF1 through AF4. The nice thing about the 1 through 4 values is that they are the same numbers as the IP precedence numbers for the same class.

TABLE 18.3   Class Selector PHB Values

Bit-by-Bit Value	CS Value	PHB Value
111000xx	Reserved	Reserved
110000xx	Reserved	Reserved
101000xx	CS5	EF (expedited forwarding)
100000xx	CS4	AF4 (assured forwarding)
011000xx	CS3	AF3 (assured forwarding)
010000xx	CS2	AF2 (assured forwarding)
001000xx	CS1	AF1 (assured forwarding)
000000xx	Default	Default

Now that you have a handle on the class selector values, let's take a look at the drop probability portion of the DSCP. Again, the full DSCP values are for devices that are fully compatible with the DiffServ standards. If you look at Figure 18.3, I have identified bits 3 and 4 as the drop probability bits. These two bits are used in the DSCP standard to identify the likelihood of a marked packet being dropped. As defined in the standard, bit 2 is always set to 0.

FIGURE 18.3   DSCP with Drop Probability

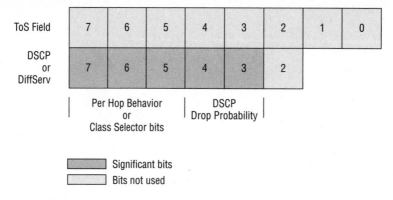

The hardest thing normally about understanding the DSCP value is that you must look at each section of the value separately. Bits 5 through 7 always tell you whether the PHB is EF, AF, or not used. For traffic identified as AF, they also tell you the specific class (AF4, AF3, AF2, AF1). For example, looking at just those three bits, if the bits are set to 101, the value is 5. When determining PHB classes, use standard binary counting for the three PHB bits.

The next two bits in the DiffServ field (bits 3 and 4) are the drop probability bits. When traffic is classified EF, both of the drop bits are set to one and they specify no drop. EF traffic will not be dropped unless the interface is completely congested and all traffic is being dropped (tail dropping).

In the AF classes, the drop bits can take on three different values and each has a different meaning:

- 01 means a low drop probability.
- 10 means a medium drop probability.
- 11 means a high drop probability.

Again, you have to look at just those two bits in the whole field and you get the drop probability. As another example, for a packet with the DSCP set to 100010:

- The first three bits tell you that you are in the AF4 class. That is spoken A-F-4.
- The two drop bits give you have a low drop value of 1.

So the whole spoken value is A-F-4-1. Sometimes you'll hear A-F-41, but remember that each of the numbers has its own meaning.

Now the kicker is that you haven't even learned the real DSCP value yet! The DSCP value is expressed as a single decimal number. It isn't very hard, just a little more binary counting. Let's try one and see how you do. Take this example: a packet has the DSCP set t0101110. You can see that the decimal equivalent of the first three bits, 101, is 5. Added from right to left:

$$1 + 0 + 4 = 5$$

That means that the PHB is EF, and for EF class traffic, the drop bits can only be set one way, 11.

Now, if you look at the decimal equivalent of all six DSCP bits, you'll find that it is 46. You might be asking how I got that. Look at the number values. I will add them from right to left by their binary placeholders:

$$0 + 2 + 4 + 8 + 0 + 32 = 46$$

Tell Yourself, "Six Bits, Only Six Bits!"

The hardest thing for some people remember, when they are given all eight of the bits from the ToS field, is to use only the six DSCP bits to determine the DSCP. So, for a ToS field set to 10111000, remember that you don't use bits 0 and 1 when determining the DSCP. If you used all eight of the bits, you would get:

$$0 + 0 + 0 + 8 + 16 + 32 + 0 + 128 = 184$$

and you would be wrong!

Take a look at Table 18.4; it lists all of the DSCP values for you. In the DSCP column, you can see the bit values and bolded above them is the actual DSCP value.

TABLE 18.4   DSCP Values

| PHB Value | With Drop | | | DSCP | | |
	Low	Med	High	Low	Med	High
EF	No Drop				**46** 101110	
AF	AF41	AF42	AF43	**34** 100010	**36** 100100	**38** 100110
	AF31	AF32	AF33	**26** 011010	**28** 011100	**30** 011110
	AF21	AF22	AF23	**18** 010010	**20** 010100	**22** 010110
	AF11	AF12	AF13	**10** 001010	**12** 001100	**14** 001110
Default				000000		

Queuing

Queuing mechanisms are designed to help with temporary congestion on a device's interface. It does this by storing excess packets in buffers until bandwidth becomes available.

The queuing types that I cover are:

- First-In-First-Out (FIFO)
- Priority Queuing (PQ)
- Weighted round robin (WRR)
- Weighted fair queuing (WFQ)
- Class-based weighted fair queuing (CBWFQ)
- Low latency queuing (LLQ)

First-In-First-Out (FIFO)   FIFO is the default queuing method on most interfaces on Cisco routers (only serial interfaces that are 2.048 Mbps and lower do not use FIFO by default). FIFO does not provide any type of priority access. Whatever traffic reaches the buffer first is transmitted out the interface first. This type of queuing is the most efficient and is suitable for higher capacity links that do not have very much delay or congestion.

Priority Queuing (PQ)   PQ gives the strictest priority to higher priority traffic. Using PQ, you can define up to four queues. Then, using a policy or filter, you can assign traffic to be placed into each of the queues.

The major problem with PQ is that lower priority traffic can starve; meaning traffic from the lower priority queues may never actually get transmitted. This is why: Traffic that is placed into the first queue has the highest priority. Queue number 1 is allowed to send traffic until the queue is empty. Once the queue is empty, queue number 2 is allowed to send one packet. Once the one packet has been sent from queue number 2, queue number 1 is checked again and allowed to send packets until it is empty. Queue number 3 is only allowed to send one packet when both queue number 1 and queue number 2 are empty—same for queue number 4. It can only send when the first 3 are empty. The lower priority queues may not ever be allowed to send their traffic, especially if there is a constant flow of traffic being placed into queue number 1.

Weighted Round Robin (WRR)   WRR queuing grew out of simple round robin (RR) queuing. In RR queuing, there are four queues and one packet from each queue is transmitted in succession, one queue after the next. The problem with RR queuing is that there is no prioritization. You basically break traffic up into four queues and then send the traffic out evenly multiplexed.

With WRR queuing a prioritization feature has been placed back into the algorithm by allowing a different weight (amount of traffic to be sent from each queue when it is that queue's turn). For example, let's say you assign a weight of 4 to queue number 1. The weight represents 1500 bytes' worth of data (one max-sized packet). The weight of the other queues can be set too. Queue 2 might have a weight of 2 and queues 3 and 4 a weight of 1. Now when traffic is to be sent, queues 3 and 4 will send one max-sized packet on their turns, but queue 2 will send two and queue 1 will send four.

Weighted Fair Queuing (WFQ)   WFQ is the default queuing technique on interfaces that have a bandwidth lower the 2.048 Mbps. WFQ is a flow-based queuing algorithm that provides you with two primary features: First, it schedules (allows traffic to be passed) interactive traffic to the front of the queue. Second, it fairly shares the remaining bandwidth with the other flows of traffic. This prevents traffic flows that have a high volume from using all the bandwidth on the outgoing interface.

You have to configure very few things to use WFQ. The WFQ algorithm sets up each of the flows with a separate queue. The idea of WFQ is to have a dedicated queue for each flow without introducing starvation, delay, or jitter. You may have to configure the number of queues. One last note about WFQ: it can make use of the IP precedence bits to apply weights when the algorithm allocates bandwidth.

Class-Based Weighted Fair Queuing (CBWFQ)   CBWFQ takes the standard WFQ functionality and goes beyond; you, the administrator, can define traffic classes based on specified match criteria. The match criteria can include specific protocols, the use of ACLs, and incoming (source) interfaces. Packets that match the defined criteria for each class constitute the traffic for that class. Each class of traffic has a queue reserved for it, and traffic that belongs to each class is directed into queue reserved for that class.

After you create a class and define its match criteria, you can assign and configure the class with characteristics that control how much and how often traffic will be forwarded. The characteristics configured on a class are then used to assign bandwidth and maximum packet limits. The bandwidth assigned to a class is the minimum bandwidth delivered during congestion. You can also specify the queue limit for each class—the maximum number of packets allowed to accumulate in the class queue. The WFQ guarantees the minimum amount of bandwidth, but also gives a class unlimited access to more bandwidth when it is available.

Low Latency Queuing (LLQ)   With WFQ, you cannot provide guaranteed bandwidth and low delay to selected applications. For example, voice may still have to compete with other bandwidth-hogging flows in the WFQ queuing system. With CBWFQ, the weight (overall priority) for a packet in a specific class comes from the bandwidth you configured for the class. All packets are given a fair service based on this internal weight; no class has strict priority. Like WFQ, this setup causes problems for real-time traffic (voice), which is largely intolerant of delay, especially variation in delay.

The LLQ was created specifically to reduce the jitter in voice conversations. LLQ does this by combining the idea of a strict priority queue for real-time traffic and CBWFQ for all the other classes of traffic. Multiple classes of traffic can be configured as priority classes, but only one priority queue can be made. This means that all traffic from any class that is set to priority is queued in the same, single, strict priority queue.

Traffic Conditioning

You can use traffic conditioners to control traffic rates. Traffic conditioning mechanisms can differentiate traffic by looking at the traffic's classification. By comparing the actual traffic rate to a configured policy rate, the flow of traffic (and congestion) can be controlled. The two primary means of implementing traffic conditioning are:

- Policing
- Shaping

Each of the mechanisms accomplishes its task differently and can be implemented in different places.

Policing   Traffic policing can drop traffic that exceeds the policy-defined rate or limit. The positive side of traffic policing is no additional delay to traffic that conforms to the policy is produced. The downside of traffic policing is the increase in TCP retransmissions. This is due to the traffic over the specified limits being dropped. However, without the drops, policing would not be fixing the bigger problem of too much traffic—then all traffic flows would be affected.

Within the realm of traffic policing are different ways to implement the mechanisms: class-based or committed access rate (CAR). These mechanisms not only allow you to rate-limit traffic, but you can re-mark traffic for lower priority transmission. Instead of just dropping all excess traffic, you can configure traffic policing to re-mark packets and send the excess, re-marked traffic at a lower priority rate.

Shaping   Traffic shaping's primary job is to control traffic bursts or excess traffic by buffering packets; this allows the overall traffic flow to stay within a desired rate. By smoothing out the traffic bursts you will have a steadier flow of traffic, which reduces congestion in the network. Traffic shaping, much like policing, has different mechanisms for implementing in different places, including class-based shaping, Frame Relay traffic shaping (FRTS), and virtual IP (VIP)-based distributed traffic shaping (DTS). Shaping mechanisms do not have the ability to re-mark traffic like policing does.

Shaping is most commonly used to prevent and manage congestion in ATM, Frame Relay, or Metro Ethernet networks. Shaping is used because the connections can have asymmetric bandwidths. Traffic shaping controls the amount of traffic being sent into a network; this is called bandwidth throttling. Traffic throttling should be implemented at the edge of your network, where the network connections enter. If you don't use shaping, you get excess buffering at the slow end of the link. This can cause additional queuing which, in turn, increases the delay and causes overflow and dropped packets.

Congestion Avoidance

If the outgoing interface of a router can't transmit a packet right away, the packet must sit in a queue until the interface can send it. The queue where the packet sits can be in the actual hardware queue for the interface, called the interface transmit (Tx) ring, or the router's memory buffer. If the transmit ring is full, the packet may be placed in the interface output hold queue (memory buffer).

When the amount of traffic being received on an interface exceeds the router's ability to send and buffer the traffic, the excess traffic will be dropped. Meet our old friend tail dropping, again.

The downside to tail dropping is that there is no differentiation of what traffic is dropped. So applications that are drop sensitive, such as voice and video, suffer more than all of the other types of data. The most common ways to prevent tail dropping and avoid congestion are:

- Random early detection (RED)

- Weighted random early detection (WRED)

Random Early Detection (RED)   To prevent tail dropping, mechanisms such as RED were developed. The standard type of RED does not drop traffic based on the type of traffic. It was first created to combat TCP synchronization; which occurs when multiple TCP flows increase their individual TCP window sizes simultaneously and cause congestion. The congestion then triggers a window size cut for all flows because tail dropping caused packet loss and retransmits.

Weighted Random Early Detection (WRED)   WRED has the ability to use IP precedence and DSCP markings to create a profile that allows traffic to be dropped based on a packet's classification. This allows WRED to drop packets that are lower priority and less drop sensitive before dropping flows of traffic that are real-time and drop sensitive.

Configuring QoS

Before I get into the actual processes of creating QoS policies, I want to give you a rundown on the different methods that exist for making a QoS policy. The four methods for implementing and managing a QoS policy are:

- Legacy Command-Line Interface (CLI)

- Modular QoS CLI (MQC)

- AutoQoS

- SDM QoS Wizard

Legacy CLI   In the past, the only way to implement a QoS policy in the network was by using the Command-Line Interface (CLI) to individually configure QoS policies at each interface. This was a time-consuming, tiresome, and error-prone task that involved cutting and pasting configurations from one interface to another. It also required someone with extensive networking expertise. I won't discuss this method any further in this book; if you require using this method because you still have old policies or old devices, I recommend upgrading to newer versions so that you can utilize the MQC.

Modular QoS CLI (MQC)   Cisco introduced the Modular QoS CLI (MQC) to simplify QoS configuration. With MQC, QoS can be configured in a building-block approach, using a single module repeatedly to apply policy to multiple interfaces. This is the process I cover in the most detail. It is also the recommend practice for creating policies; even the automated methods (AutoQoS and the SDM Wizard) create their policies using the MQC. The MQC also has the most versatile and powerful functions for editing and manipulating policies later.

AutoQoS   Cisco AutoQoS represents innovative technology that simplifies the challenges of network administration by reducing QoS complexity, cost, and deployment time. Cisco AutoQoS incorporates value-added intelligence in Cisco IOS software and Cisco Catalyst software to provision and assist in the management of large-scale QoS deployments.

The first phase of Cisco AutoQoS VoIP offers straightforward capabilities to automate VoIP deployments for customers who want to deploy IP telephony but lack the expertise and staffing to plan and deploy IP QoS and IP services. The second phase, AutoQoS Enterprise, which is supported only on router interfaces, uses NBAR to discover the traffic. After the discovery phase, the AutoQoS process can configure the interface to support up to ten traffic classes.

SDM QoS Wizard   You can easily configure, manage, and troubleshoot QoS deployments using the Cisco Security Device Manager (SDM) QoS Wizard. The SDM QoS Wizard provides centralized QoS design, administration, and traffic monitoring that scales to large QoS deployments.

 Real World Scenario

SOHO Offices Need Voice, Too

More and more companies have users who work from home and have a Small Office/ Home Office (SOHO) configuration. FutureTech is no different. Many of the company's engineers, researchers, and administrators (right up to some of the vice presidents) work from home. Not all of the users may have a need to send real-time traffic back and forth to the headquarters office, but some of them such as a VP will have that need.

One such FutureTech VP is located in Madison, Wisconsin. Mary Edditore is the VP of Marketing and Publications. She oversees the management of all documentation for FutureTech's product lines. This includes online content, reference manuals, technical manuals, and all the "how to" white papers.

She has a steady stream of documents and papers coming and going from her SOHO network. Mary is also on the phone a lot with individual engineers and authors who are preparing the documents for different product lines. She also has to accommodate conference calls, a necessary part of ensuring that all of the different projects are on schedule. (Some of the projects can fall a little behind and require attention from her level.)

Mary's SOHO configuration includes a business computer and phone that is tied into the FutureTech voice network and Communication Manager. Because her voice traffic is converged with her data traffic, it is necessary for you to configure QoS to control and prioritize the data across the connection. You can see the physical configuration of Mary's SOHO network in Figure 18.4.

A QoS policy is going to be needed at both ends of the connection. For the HQ side of the connection, you will configure the policy using the MQC. Then for the remote SOHO end, use the SDM Wizard to create the policy. That way you can see the difference in how the policies are made and compare the results when you are done.

FIGURE 18.4   SOHO Setup to Dallas HQ

Modular QoS CLI

Now that you have been introduced to many of the QoS mechanisms that can be implemented in your network, it is time to take you through the process of making an actual policy. You will create the Dallas router policies with the Modular QoS CLI (MQC). The two policies don't have to be created separately. You could create one policy that both classifies traffic by source/destination and that uses traffic markings to prioritize transmission. By creating separate policies for this exercise, though, I can highlight them individually and help you understand each one better. The traffic types that I want to classify and set policy for are voice, HTTP, FTP, and a business application that Mary is required to use. The business application is mission critical and uses a unique port because the program was created specifically for FutureTech; it is not a well known protocol or program.

In Figure 18.5, you can see on the Dallas router where I am going to place the policies to mark and prioritize the traffic leaving the HQ office.

FIGURE 18.5   Dallas Router Policy Placement

Concept: MQC

The MQC was created to allow network engineers to write QoS policies in small, interchangeable pieces. The modular part of the name is defining the fact that with this type of policy the classification and the feature configuration are now separated. Attaching the policy to an interface is also a separate part of the configuration. The three pieces or modules that are created in a policy are.

- Class-map (for traffic classification)

- Policy-map (QoS component assignment)

- Service-policy (for applying to an interface)

Incoming Class-Map Configuration

The first piece of the policy that I am going to configure is the class-map. Class-maps identify the traffic for classification. To create a new class-map the command is `class-map`. You then can apply an optional parameter to specify how the `class-map` will use the `match` commands that you specify. The options are `match-all` (default) or `match-any`. The `match-all` option performs a Boolean logical AND; if you place multiple `match` statements into a `class-map`, the data classification must match all the criteria specified in the match statements. If you use the `match-any` option, it performs a Boolean logical OR; one of the `match` statements much match. You don't have to specify this option if you want to leave the default `match-all in place`. You must also specify a name for the `class-map`. For setting up the QoS policies for Mary's SOHO connection to DalRtr1, I am going to base the class-map names on the type of traffic they are searching for, `voice_mark`, `video_mark`, and so on. Here is an example of creating a `class-map`:

```
DalRtr1(config)#class-map voice_mark
DalRtr1(config-cmap)#
```

Once in `class-map` mode you can begin identifying the traffic you wish to classify. The `match` command is used to accomplish this task. The options for the `match` command are as follows:

```
DalRtr1(config-cmap)#match ?
access-group          Access group
any                   Any packets
class-map             Class map
cos                   IEEE 802.1Q/ISL class of      service/user priority values
destination-address   Destination address
discard-class         Discard behavior identifier
dscp                  Match DSCP in IP(v4) and IPv6 packets
```

fr-de	Match on Frame-relay DE bit
fr-dlci	Match on fr-dlci
input-interface	Select an input interface to match
ip	IP specific values
mpls	Multi Protocol Label Switching specific values
not	Negate this match result
packet	Layer 3 Packet length
precedence	Match Precedence in IP(v4) and IPv6 packets
protocol	Protocol
qos-group	Qos-group
source-address	Source address

The most commonly used option is access-group, which allows you to identify traffic using an access-list. The access-list must be separately configured and then applied to the class-map using the access-group option. Another common option is the protocol option, which allows you to configure the class-map to automatically search for traffic that matches a protocol's characteristics, such as port number.

Now remember, this first policy just classifies traffic on the incoming interface so that you can mark it. Other options you saw in the output (for each of the different marking types) could be used as well; I will show you those on the outgoing interface.

By using a policy to mark traffic on the incoming interface, you then know that all traffic on the outgoing interface will be marked and you can match for the policies. The following output shows my class-map statements and the protocols that I want to mark for Mary's SOHO office:

```
DalRtr1(config)#class-map voice_mark
DalRtr1(config-cmap)#match protocol rtp audio
DalRtr1(config)#class-map http_mark
DalRtr1(config-cmap)#match protocol http
DalRtr1(config-cmap)#exit
DalRtr1(config)#class-map ftp_mark
DalRtr1(config-cmap)#match protocol ftp
DalRtr1(config-cmap)#exit
DalRtr1(config)#class-map business_app_mark
DalRtr1(config-cmap)#match acccess-group 101
DalRtr1(config)#access-list 101 permit tcp any any eq 16384
```

Notice that the business-critical application had to have an access-list specified because it cannot identify interesting traffic using a standard port or protocol.

Incoming Policy-Map Configuration

Now that all of the traffic is being identified by the class-map, you must configure a policy-map that will set the actions for the traffic that matches. In this policy I will mark the traffic so all the downstream routers and devices that are configured with a QoS policy can use the markings and will not have to separately classify the traffic by protocol.

Begin with the `policy-map` command. The `policy-map` must be given a name, just as the `class-map` was. You only create one `policy-map`—all of the `class-map`s you created will be placed into that `policy-map`, so name your policy accordingly. I just named mine `mark_traffic`. The following output shows you the commands that you can configure in the `policy-map` mode. The only one you really need to worry about right now is the `class` command.

```
DalRtr1(config)#policy-map mark-traffic
DalRtr1(config-pmap)#?
QoS policy-map configuration commands:
class         policy criteria
description   Policy-Map description
exit          Exit from QoS policy-map configuration mode
no            Negate or set default values of a command
rename        Rename this policy-map
```

The `class` command links the `class-map` and the traffic that is identified by the `class-map` to this `policy-map`. The option that you will use after the `class` command is the name of the `class-map` that you are associating. Yours should be similar to the following output:

```
DalRtr1(config-pmap)#class voice_mark
DalRtr1(config-pmap-c)#
```

Notice that assigning a `class-map` to the policy moved you to the `class policy-map-c` mode. In this mode, you can assign a marking value to the class of traffic. Look at the commands you can now configure at this mode:

```
DalRtr1(config-pmap-c)#?
QoS policy-map class configuration commands:
bandwidth       Bandwidth
compression     Activate Compression
drop            Drop all packets
estimate        estimate resources required for this class
exit            Exit from QoS class action configuration mode
netflow-sampler NetFlow action
no              Negate or set default values of a command
police          Police
priority        Strict Scheduling Priority for this Class
queue-limit     Queue Max Threshold for Tail Drop
random-detect   Enable Random Early Detection as drop policy
service-policy  Configure Flow Next
set             Set QoS values
shape           Traffic Shaping
```

Most of these commands can be used to configure QoS features for each of the classes. Because the purpose of this policy is just to mark the traffic, I am going to use the set command. In the policy on the outgoing interface, I will show you some of the other commands. The other commands such as priority and bandwidth are used to set queuing types.

The set command has quite a few options as well. Here's the output for them:

```
DalRtr1(config-pmap-c)#set ?
atm-clp        Set ATM CLP bit to 1
cos            Set IEEE 802.1Q/ISL class of service/user priority
discard-class  Discard behavior identifier
dscp           Set DSCP in IP(v4) and IPv6 packets
fr-de          Set FR DE bit to 1
ip             Set IP specific values
mpls           Set MPLS specific values
precedence     Set precedence in IP(v4) and IPv6 packets
qos-group      Set QoS Group
```

For this exercise, mark all of your traffic with a DSCP value. If you look under the dscp option, you can see all of the possible values. You were introduced to each of these values in the section named "Differentiated Services Code Point (DSCP)" of this chapter.

```
DalRtr1(config-pmap-c)#set dscp ?
<0-63>     Differentiated services codepoint value
af11       Match packets with AF11 dscp (001010)
af12       Match packets with AF12 dscp (001100)
af13       Match packets with AF13 dscp (001110)
af21       Match packets with AF21 dscp (010010)
af22       Match packets with AF22 dscp (010100)
af23       Match packets with AF23 dscp (010110)
af31       Match packets with AF31 dscp (011010)
af32       Match packets with AF32 dscp (011100)
af33       Match packets with AF33 dscp (011110)
af41       Match packets with AF41 dscp (100010)
af42       Match packets with AF42 dscp (100100)
af43       Match packets with AF43 dscp (100110)
cos        Set packet DSCP from L2 COS
cs1        Match packets with CS1(precedence 1) dscp (001000)
cs2        Match packets with CS2(precedence 2) dscp (010000)
cs3        Match packets with CS3(precedence 3) dscp (011000)
cs4        Match packets with CS4(precedence 4) dscp (100000)
cs5        Match packets with CS5(precedence 5) dscp (101000)
cs6        Match packets with CS6(precedence 6) dscp (110000)
cs7        Match packets with CS7(precedence 7) dscp (111000)
```

```
default   Match packets with default dscp (000000)
ef        Match packets with EF dscp (101110)
qos-group Set packet dscp from QoS Group.
```

The output that follows shows how I assigned a value to each of the types of traffic the rest of the policy-map will look for. Voice has the highest priority, followed by the mission-critical business application, and then HTTP and FTP follow behind that:

```
DalRtr1(config)#policy-map mark_traffic
DalRtr1(config-pmap)#class voice_mark
DalRtr1(config-pmap-c)#set dscp ef
DalRtr1(config-pmap-c)#exit
DalRtr1(config-pmap)#class busisnness_app_mark
DalRtr1(config-pmap-c)#set dscp af31
DalRtr1(config-pmap-c)#exit
DalRtr1(config-pmap)#class http_mark
DalRtr1(config-pmap-c)#set dscp af21
DalRtr1(config-pmap-c)#exit
DalRtr1(config-pmap)#class ftp_mark
DalRtr1(config-pmap-c)#set dscp af21
```

Incoming Service-Policy Configuration

The last piece of this configuration is the service-policy. The service-policy simply applies the policy-map to an interface in a given direction. The commands that follow apply this policy inbound on the interface so the incoming traffic can be classified. The commands look like this:

```
DalRtr1(config-pmap-c)#exit
DalRtr1(config)#int fa0/0
DalRtr1(config-if)#service-policy input mark_traffic
```

Now that you have seen many of the commands required to create a QoS policy, I want to show you what the policy looks like for the outgoing interface. In this outgoing policy, traffic is classified based on the DSCP markings that you set on the traffic in the incoming policy. Next you configure a queuing type for the policy-map so that the traffic will be prioritized when it leaves the interface. Lastly, you apply the policy to the outgoing interface of the router with the service-policy command.

Outgoing Class-Map Configuration

In this policy for the outgoing class-maps, classify the traffic using the markings that were set up on the incoming interface. Your class-maps for this policy should look like this:

```
DalRtr1(config)#class-map queue_voice
DalRtr1(config-cmap)#match dscp ef
```

```
DalRtr1(config-cmap)#exit
DalRtr1(config)#class-map queue_business_app
DalRtr1(config-cmap)#match dscp af31
DalRtr1(config-cmap)#exit
DalRtr1(config)#class-map queue_http_ftp
DalRtr1(config-cmap)#match dscp af21
```

Outgoing Policy-Map Configuration

The policy-map now needs to have those class-maps applied and then a queuing mechanism added. To enable LLQ for the voice class the command is priority. You have a couple of options to configure an amount of bandwidth under LLQ. You can specify an amount (in Kbps) or a percent of total bandwidth.

When I specify bandwidth for LLQ, I choose to use a percentage of the total bandwidth. The benefit to using percent comes when you change the speed of the link; the policy automatically modifies the bandwidth without having to be rewritten.

Here is the command and the options available to you:

```
DalRtr1(config)#policy-map queue_traffic
DalRtr1(config-pmap)#class queue_voice
DalRtr1(config-pmap-c)#priority ?
<8-2000000>  Kilo Bits per second
percent      % of total bandwidth
DalRtr1(config-pmap-c)#priority percent 35
```

For the other two classes, let's configure CBWFQ. The command to configure CBWFQ is bandwidth. The CBWFQ bandwidth command has the two options that are available for priority and a new one, the remaining percentage of bandwidth. The remaining command is useful when the actual bandwidth on a link varies and you want the same relative amount of bandwidth to be used for each class, regardless of what that link bandwidth might be. Here is the bandwidth command and options:

```
DalRtr1(config-pmap)#class queue_business_app
DalRtr1(config-pmap-c)#bandwidth ?
<8-2000000>  Kilo Bits per second
percent      % of total Bandwidth
remaining    % of the remaining bandwidth
DalRtr1(config-pmap-c)#bandwidth percent 25
```

Here in the last class, I am also assigning CBWFQ queuing using a percent of bandwidth:

```
DalRtr1(config-pmap)#class queue_http_ftp
DalRtr1(config-pmap-c)#bandwidth ?
```

```
<8-2000000>  Kilo Bits per second
percent      % of total Bandwidth
remaining    % of the remaining bandwidth
DalRtr1(config-pmap-c)#bandwidth percent 15
```

Outgoing Service-Policy Configuration

Finally, you have to take this policy-map and apply it to the outbound interface so that it can queue and prioritize the traffic. Applying the policy-map is done again with the service-policy command. This time the service-policy will be applied in the output direction.

```
DalRtr1(config-pmap-c)#exit
DalRtr1(config)#int fa0/1
DalRtr1(config-if)#service-policy output mark_traffic
```

SDM QoS Wizard

Now, let's configure a QoS policy on the SOHO router using the SDM. Remember that SDM uses preconfigured logic and can't (or won't) pick up every type of traffic or work for every situation that you might have. The SDM Wizard does, however, give you a great place to start. Most people have a much easier time modifying a configuration that is already done than starting one from scratch.

It doesn't matter if you do configure QoS through the SDM or using the CLI, but before you start the wizard you have to have the interface where you plan to place the policy configured as an interface and enabled. Once the interface is up, start the QoS Wizard. If you look at Figure 18.6, you can see what I mean. The SDM is going to place the policy on the outgoing interface, in this case the interface that is going toward Dallas.

FIGURE 18.6 Policy Placement by SDM

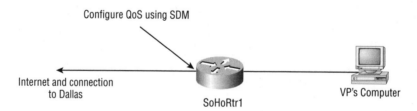

Now, open up your SDM interface and click the Configure button. Once you are in the configure screen you can select the Quality of Service button from the Task bar on the left side of the window. Figure 18.7 shows the Create QoS Policy tab. Click the Launch QoS Wizard button to start the wizard.

FIGURE 18.7   SDM QoS Screen

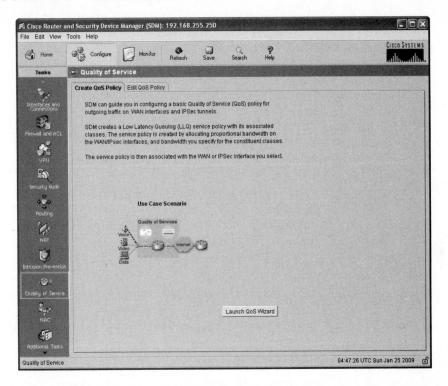

Figure 18.8 shows the opening screen for the QoS Wizard. This wizard is going to guide you through the process of creating a QoS policy for a WAN interface. The SDM will create a policy that handles two main types of traffic. The first is real-time traffic, which handles voice traffic and its signaling traffic. The second is business-critical traffic. The business-critical traffic is broken down into three subcategories:

- Transactional
- Management
- Routing

You will see once you get further into the wizard which protocols fall into each of those categories.

Click Next to begin configuring your policy using the wizard.

The first real step in the wizard is to choose the interface where you want the policy to be placed. Remember, for Mary's SOHO, you are configuring the outgoing interface, where you are going to be sending the traffic. You have to have the interface configured already or it won't show up in the drop-down. Figure 18.9 shows the drop-down list box. After you have selected the interface, click Next.

FIGURE 18.8 QoS Wizard Opening Screen

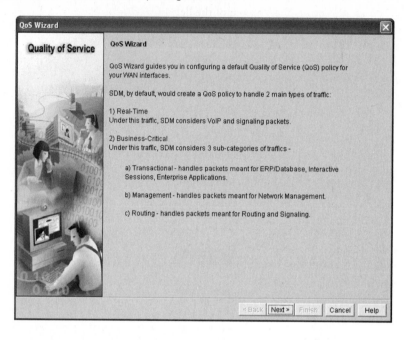

FIGURE 18.9 Interface Selection

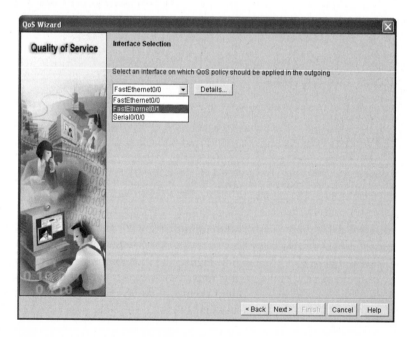

When the QoS Policy Generation dialog box opens, you have to configure the bandwidth (in percent) that you want to assign to each of the defined categories of traffic. By default the wizard assigned 72 percent for Mary's voice traffic and 2 percent for business-critical data traffic. Figure 18.10 shows the QoS Policy Generation dialog box. I recommend adjusting those percentages to make them a little more balanced because of the business application Mary is required to run and the high volumes of FTP and HTTP traffic that she sends. I suggest 40 percent for voice and 30 percent for business-critical. In Figure 18.11, you can see that this is what I configured. Click Next to continue.

The bandwidth percentages might have to be adjusted later if Mary has problems with a specific type of traffic or the bandwidth she is actually getting through her Internet connection.

FIGURE 18.10 Default Percentage Settings

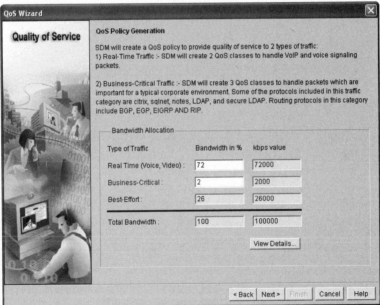

The wizard then prompts you to confirm enabling NBAR for protocol discovery. Click Yes. The discovery results can later be used to improve the policy configuration. Look at the pop-up screen in Figure 18.12.

The SDM will now create the QoS policy. Figures 18.13 through 18.17 show you the complete output of the Summary pages. It is important to review all of the class-maps that are made by SDM. Notice that not all of them are enabled by default. Once you scroll through the output and see each of the class-maps that were created, you can click Finish to complete the process.

FIGURE 18.11   Configured Percentage Settings

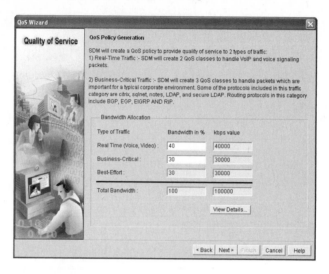

FIGURE 18.12   Enabling NBAR

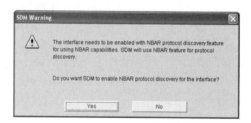

FIGURE 18.13   Voice and Video Classes

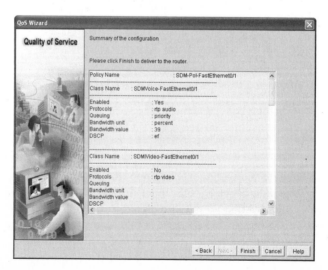

FIGURE 18.14   Signaling and Streaming Video Classes

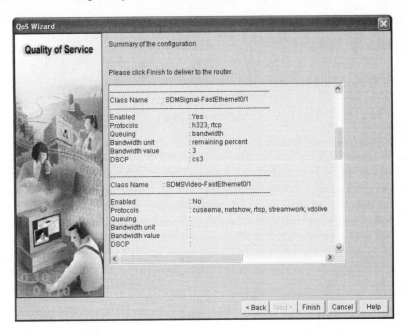

FIGURE 18.15   Transactional and Management Classes

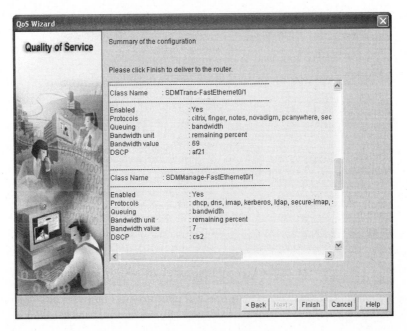

FIGURE 18.16   Routing and Bulk Classes

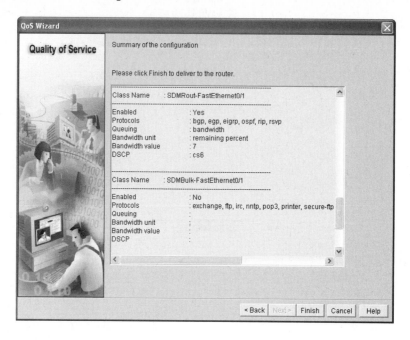

FIGURE 18.17   Scavenger Class

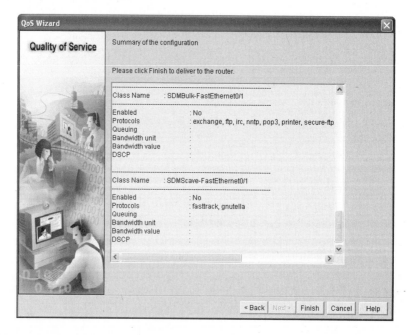

When the popup telling you that SDM is going to deliver an enormous amount of commands to your router appears, wait until you see that all the commands have been delivered and then click OK. For Mary's SOHO, the wizard delivered 94 commands, as you can see in Figure 18.18.

FIGURE 18.18   Command Delivery Screen

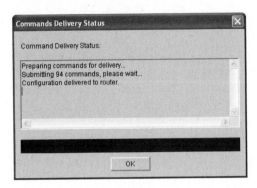

Now, take a look at a code output from the running-config that SDM configured and saved to the router. Compare it to the configuration that you did using the MQC.

```
class-map match-any SDMScave-FastEthernet0/1
match protocol fasttrack
match protocol gnutella
class-map match-any SDMTrans-FastEthernet0/1
match protocol citrix
match protocol finger
match protocol notes
match protocol novadigm
match protocol pcanywhere
match protocol secure-telnet
match protocol sqlnet
match protocol sqlserver
match protocol ssh
match protocol telnet
match protocol xwindows
class-map match-any SDMVoice-FastEthernet0/1
match protocol rtp audio
class-map match-any SDMSVideo-FastEthernet0/1
match protocol cuseeme
match protocol netshow
match protocol rtsp
match protocol streamwork
```

```
match protocol vdolive
class-map match-any SDMIVideo-FastEthernet0/1
match protocol rtp video
class-map match-any SDMManage-FastEthernet0/1
match protocol dhcp
match protocol dns
match protocol imap
match protocol kerberos
match protocol ldap
match protocol secure-imap
match protocol secure-ldap
match protocol snmp
match protocol socks
match protocol syslog
class-map match-any SDMRout-FastEthernet0/1
match protocol bgp
match protocol egp
match protocol eigrp
match protocol ospf
match protocol rip
match protocol rsvp
class-map match-any SDMSignal-FastEthernet0/1
match protocol h323
match protocol rtcp
class-map match-any SDMBulk-FastEthernet0/1
match protocol exchange
match protocol ftp
match protocol irc
match protocol nntp
match protocol pop3
match protocol printer
match protocol secure-ftp
match protocol secure-irc
match protocol secure-nntp
match protocol secure-pop3
match protocol smtp
match protocol tftp
!
policy-map SDM-Pol-FastEthernet0/1
class SDMManage-FastEthernet0/1
bandwidth remaining percent 7
```

```
set dscp cs2
class SDMVoice-FastEthernet0/1
priority percent 39
set dscp ef
class SDMRout-FastEthernet0/1
bandwidth remaining percent 7
set dscp cs6
class SDMTrans-FastEthernet0/1
bandwidth remaining percent 69
set dscp af21
class SDMSignal-FastEthernet0/1
bandwidth remaining percent 3
set dscp cs3
!
interface FastEthernet0/1
ip address 192.168.20.1 255.255.255.0
ip nbar protocol-discovery
duplex auto
speed auto
service-policy output SDM-Pol-FastEthernet0/1
```

Summary

Once again you have gone through a tremendous amount of material. I started you off showing you many of the potential problems that can and do occur on a network. Then, you moved through ways that each of those things could be handled or prevented.

Next, I took you through the process for implementing QoS, from planning and assessment all the way through setting up the policy. I then introduced you to quite a few different QoS components that can be used to correct problems that might arise on your network.

Finally, I showed you how a QoS policy could be implemented. Specifically, you used the MQC to configure a policy for a WAN-connected router. You also used the SDM QoS Wizard to configure a policy for the router on the other end of the WAN.

Review Questions

1. What are the problems that can occur on a network that QoS can help fix?
    A. Bandwidth
    B. Delay
    C. Packet loss
    D. Administrator error

2. What is the most expensive but often the best solution to a bandwidth problem?
    A. Queuing
    B. Upgrade the link
    C. Congestion avoidance
    D. Compression

3. What is the first step that must be done when preparing to implement QoS?
    A. Classify the traffic
    B. Write a policy
    C. Divide the traffic
    D. Assess the network

4. What feature is built into a router to help collect traffic statistics for a network assessment?
    A. inaBAR
    B. NBAR
    C. Traffic collector
    D. Interface watch

5. What is the most scalable model for implementing QoS?
    A. IntServ
    B. Best Effort
    C. DiffServ
    D. MostServ

6. What protocol does IntServ use to signal to the network?
    A. RSTV
    B. RSTP
    C. RSUP
    D. RSVP

7. What type of traffic marking is used for Layer 2 marking?
    A. ToS
    B. CoS
    C. IP precedence
    D. DSCP

8. What is the old standard for marking traffic before DSCP?
    A. CoS
    B. IP precedence
    C. DSCP
    D. DE

9. What type of queuing was made specifically to handle the requirements of voice and real-time traffic?
    A. PQ
    B. CQ
    C. WFQ
    D. LLQ

10. What method for implementing QoS has the most flexible and modular interface for configuration?
    A. Legacy CLI
    B. MQC
    C. AutoQoS
    D. SDM Wizard

Answers to Review Questions

1. A, B, C. Bandwidth, delay, and packet loss are the three biggest problems on a network that QoS can help to fix.

2. B. Upgrading the link will solve problems with lack of bandwidth and congestion, but costs the most.

3. D. Assessing the network is required so that you know what traffic you have and how much. A policy cannot be made until you know that information.

4. B. NBAR collects data on an interface, per direction, per protocol, and gives the statistics for what it finds.

5. C. DiffServ allows for the classification of traffic to make decisions through the network. This allows a large amount of data to flow.

6. D. RSVP is used to signal the network so that guarantees of service can be made for traffic flows.

7. B. CoS is the marking method used at Layer 2.

8. B. IP precedence is the standard marking that was used before DSCP was introduced.

9. D. LLQ is a combination of PQ and CBWFQ and was made to handle real-time traffic.

10. B. The MQC offers the best flexibility and most configuration modification ease of any type of configuration method.

Chapter

19

Wireless Devices and Topologies

IN THIS CHAPTER, YOU WILL LEARN HOW TO DO THE FOLLOWING:

✓ Describe the components and operations of WLAN topologies such as AP and bridge

✓ Describe the features of client devices, network unification, and mobility platforms, including CCX and LWAPP

✓ Configure a wireless client using the ADU suite

Wireless networking is one of the fastest growing and most exciting parts of networking in years. This chapter starts off with the fundamentals of wireless transmission and wireless networks. I show you the frequency ranges, governing agencies, modulation techniques, and standards. Then I take you through some of the basic devices that are required to make a wireless network. You learn about wireless clients and wireless access points (AP), how to configure them, and how they operate. You will see that an AP is much like a hub for a wired network—even the fact that they are both half-duplex. Finally, I show you the newest implementation strategy for wireless devices. In the past, you had APs and, to a small degree, those APs could be managed. The new implementation strategy mandates centralized control of APs through the use of a Wireless LAN Controller (WLC). Cisco calls the new strategy the Cisco Unified Wireless Network (CUWN); more commonly though, it is called the lightweight architecture.

For up-to-the-minute updates on this chapter, check out www.sybex.com/go/CiscoProGuidetoInternetworking or www.lammle.com.

Wireless Fundamentals

Signal transmission using the typical 802.11 specifications works a lot like transmitting does with a basic Ethernet hub: They're both two-way forms of communication and they both use the same frequency to both transmit and receive. The technique is often referred to as half-duplex, as I mentioned in the chapter introduction. Wireless LANs (WLANs) use radio frequencies (RFs) that are radiated into the air from an antenna that creates radio waves. These waves can be absorbed, refracted, or reflected by walls, water, and metal surfaces, resulting in low signal strength. So because of this innate vulnerability to surrounding environmental factors, it's pretty apparent that wireless will never offer us the same robustness as a wired network can, but that doesn't mean you're not going to run wireless. Believe me, you definitely will!

To improve signal strength, you can increase the transmitting power and gain transmitting distance, but doing so can create some nasty distortion, so it has to be done carefully. By using higher frequencies, you can attain higher data rates, but the gain is, unfortunately, at the cost of decreased transmitting distance. Likewise, if you use lower frequencies, you get to transmit greater distance but at lower data rates. This should make it pretty clear to you that understanding all the various types of WLANs you can implement is imperative to creating the LAN solution that best meets the specific requirements of each unique situation you deal with.

The 802.11 specifications were developed so that there would be no licensing required in most countries—to ensure the user the freedom to install and operate without any licensing or operating fees. This means that any manufacturer can create wireless networking products and sell them at a local computer store or wherever. It also means that all our computers should be able to communicate wirelessly without configuring much, if anything at all.

Various agencies govern the use of wireless devices, frequencies, standards, and specify how the frequency spectrums are used. Table 19.1 shows the current agencies that help create, maintain, and even enforce wireless standards worldwide.

TABLE 19.1   Wireless Agencies and Standards

Agency	Purpose	Web Site
Institute of Electrical and Electronics Engineers (IEEE)	Creates and maintains operational standards	www.ieee.org
Federal Communications Commission (FCC)	Regulates the use of wireless devices in the U.S.A.	www.fcc.gov
European Telecommunications Standards Institute (ETSi)	Chartered to produce common standards in Europe	www.etsi.org
Wi-Fi Alliance	Promotes and tests for WLAN interoperability	www.wi-fi.com
WLAN Association (WLANA)	Educates and raises consumer awareness regarding WLANs	www.wlana.org

Because WLANs transmit over radio frequencies, they're regulated by the same types of laws used to govern things like AM/FM radios. In the United States, it's the FCC that regulates the use of wireless LAN devices. The IEEE takes it from there and creates standards based on the frequencies the FCC releases for public use.

The FCC has released three unlicensed bands for public use: 900MHz, 2.4GHz, and 5GHz. The 900MHz and 2.4GHz bands are referred to as the Industrial, Scientific, and Medical (ISM) bands, and the 5GHz band is known as the Unlicensed National Information Infrastructure (UNII) band. Figure 19.1 shows where the unlicensed bands sit within the RF spectrum.

So, it follows that if you opt to deploy wireless in a range outside of the three public bands shown in Figure 19.1, you need to get a specific license from the FCC to do so. Once the FCC opened the three frequency ranges for public use, many manufacturers were able to start offering myriad products that flooded the market. 802.11b/g is the most widely used wireless network found today.

FIGURE 19.1 Unlicensed Frequencies

AM Broadcast
Cellular
(840MHz)
Visible
light
Sonar
(extremely low)
FM Broadcast
Infrared
Wireless
LAN
X-rays
900MHz
band
2.4GHz
band
5GHz
band

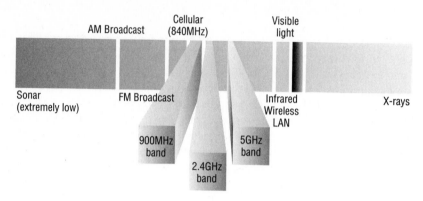

Figure 19.2 shows the WLAN history that is important to network administrators and engineers. Although wireless transmissions date back many, many years, the type we really care about is wireless as related to WLANs starting in the 1990s. Use of the ISM band started in early 1990 and it's deployed today in multiple environments, including outdoor links, mesh networks, office buildings, healthcare, warehousing, and homes.

FIGURE 19.2 Wireless LAN History

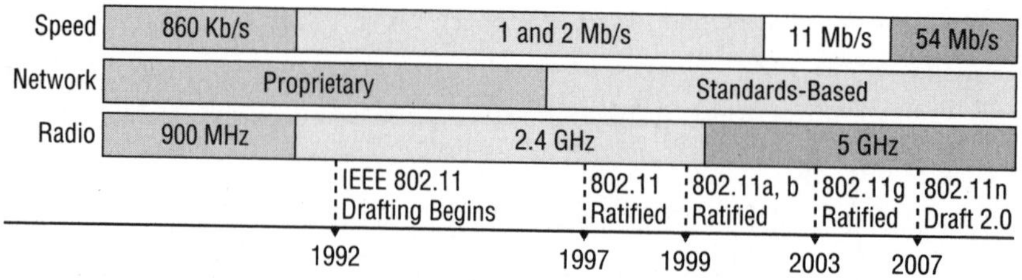

Speed
860 Kb/s
1 and 2 Mb/s
11 Mb/s
54 Mb/s
Network
Proprietary
Standards-Based
Radio
900 MHz
2.4 GHz
5 GHz
IEEE 802.11
Drafting Begins
802.11
Ratified
802.11a, b
Ratified
802.11g
Ratified
802.11n
Draft 2.0
1992
1997
1999
2003
2007

The Wi-Fi Alliance grants certification for interoperability among 802.11 products offered by various vendors. This certification provides a sort of comfort zone for the users purchasing the many types of products, although in my personal experience, it's just a whole lot easier if you buy all your access points from the same manufacturer.

In the current U.S. WLAN market, several accepted operational standards and drafts have been created and are maintained by the IEEE. I'll take you through these standards and then talk about how the most commonly used standards work.

The 802.11 Standards

Wireless networking has its own 802 standards group; you may remember Ethernet's committee is 802.3. Wireless starts with 802.11. Various other up-and-coming standard groups exist as well, like 802.16 and 802.20. And even cellular networks are becoming huge players in the wireless experience. But for now, I'm going to concentrate on the 802.11 standards committee and subcommittees.

Concept: So What Is Wi-Fi?

You may have seen products that are 802.11 compliant with a small sticker on them that says "Wi-Fi." You might be able to guess that this rather odd phrase stands for Wireless Fidelity, but you may not know what its implications are. Simply put, that sticker indicates that the product in question has passed certification testing for 802.11 interoperability by the Wi-Fi Alliance. This nonprofit group was formed to ensure that all 802.11a/b/g/n wireless devices would communicate seamlessly. So, Wi-Fi is a good thing.

IEEE 802.11 was the first, original standardized WLAN at 1 and 2Mbps. It runs in the 2.4GHz radio frequency. Although it was ratified in 1997, we didn't see many products pop up until around 1999 when 802.11b was introduced. All the committees listed in Table 19.2 made amendments to the original 802.11 standard, except for 802.11F and 802.11T, which produced stand-alone documents.

TABLE 19.2 802.11 Committees and Subcommittees

Committee	Purpose
IEEE 802.11a	54Mbps, 5GHz standard
IEEE 802.11b	Enhancements to 802.11 to support 5.5 and 11Mbps
IEEE 802.11c	Bridge operation procedures; included in the IEEE 802.1D standard
IEEE 802.11d	International roaming extensions
IEEE 802.11e	Quality of Service
IEEE 802.11F	Inter-Access Point Protocol
IEEE 802.11g	54Mbps, 2.4GHz standard (backward compatible with 802.11b)
IEEE 802.11h	Dynamic Frequency Selection (DFS) and Transmit Power Control (TPC) at 5Ghz
IEEE 802.11i	Enhanced security
IEEE 802.11j	Extensions for Japan and U.S. public safety

TABLE 19.2 802.11 Committees and Subcommittees *(continued)*

Committee	Purpose
IEEE 802.11k	Radio resource measurement enhancements
IEEE 802.11m	Maintenance of the standard; odds and ends
IEEE 802.11n	Higher throughput improvements using Multiple-Input-Multiple-Output (MIMO) antennas
IEEE 802.11p	Wireless Access for the Vehicular Environment (WAVE)
IEEE 802.11r	Fast roaming
IEEE 802.11s	ESS Extended Service Set Mesh Networking
IEEE 802.11T	Wireless Performance Prediction (WPP)
IEEE 802.11u	Internetworking with non-802 networks (cellular, for example)
IEEE 802.11v	Wireless network management
IEEE 802.11w	Protected management frames
IEEE 802.11y	3650–3700 operation in the U.S.

Concept: IrDA Wireless

One type of wireless networking that doesn't get a whole lot of attention is infrared wireless. Infrared wireless uses the same basic transmission method as many television remote controls—that's right, infrared technology. Infrared is used primarily for short distance, point-to-point communications, like those between a peripheral and a PC, with the most widely used for peripherals being the IrDA standard.

Okay, now let's consider some important specifics of the most popular 802.11 WLANs.

2.4GHz (802.11b)

First on the menu is the 802.11b standard. It was the most widely deployed wireless standard, and it operates in the 2.4GHz unlicensed radio band that delivers a maximum data rate of

11Mbps. The 802.11b standard has been widely adopted by both vendors and customers who found that its 11Mbps data rate worked pretty well for most applications. But now that 802.11b has a big brother (802.11g), no one goes out and just buys an 802.11b card or access point anymore—why would you buy a 10Mbps Ethernet card when you can score a 10/100 Ethernet card for the same price?

Concept: Data Rate Shifting

An interesting thing about all Cisco 802.11 WLAN products is that they have the ability to data-rate-shift while moving. This allows the person operating at 11Mbps to shift to 5.5Mbps, then 2Mbps, and finally still communicate farthest from the access point at 1Mbps. And furthermore, this rate shifting happens without losing connection and with no interaction from the user. Rate shifting also occurs on a transmission-by-transmission basis. This is important because it means that the access point can support multiple clients at varying speeds depending upon the location of each client.

The problem with 802.11b lies in how the Data Link layer is dealt with. In order to solve problems in the RF spectrum, Carrier Sense Multiple Access with Collision Avoidance (CSMA/CA), a type of Ethernet collision detection, is used. To get a clear picture of this, check out Figure 19.3.

FIGURE 19.3   802.11b CSMA/CA

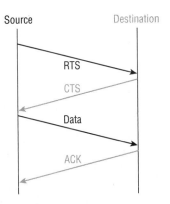

CSMA/CA is also called a Request to Send, Clear to Send (RTS/CTS) because of the way that hosts must communicate with the AP. For every packet sent, an RTS/CTS and acknowledgment must be received; because of this rather cumbersome process, it's kind of hard to believe it all actually works!

2.4GHz (802.11g)

The 802.11g standard was ratified in June 2003 and is backward compatible to 802.11b. The 802.11g standard delivers the same 54Mbps maximum data rate as you'll find in the 802.11a range, but it runs in the 2.4GHz range—the same as 802.11b.

Because 802.11b/g operates in the same 2.4GHz unlicensed band, migrating to 802.11g is an affordable choice for organizations with existing 802.11b wireless infrastructures. Just keep in mind that 802.11b products can't be "software upgraded" to 802.11g. This limitation is because 802.11g radios use a different chipset in order to deliver the higher data rate.

But still, much like Ethernet and Fast Ethernet, 802.11g products can be commingled with 802.11b products in the same network. Yet, for example, and completely unlike Ethernet, if you have four users running 802.11g cards and one user starts using an 802.11b card, everyone connected to the same access point is then forced to run the 802.11b CSMA/CA method—an ugly fact that really makes throughput suffer badly. So, to optimize performance if you never had 802.11b products on your network or have completed your staged upgrade, I recommend that you disable the 802.11b-only modes on all your access points.

To explain this further, 802.11b uses a modulation technique called Direct Sequence Spread Spectrum (DSSS) that's just not as robust as the Orthogonal Frequency Division Multiplexing (OFDM) modulation used by both 802.11g and 802.11a. (Modulation techniques are discussed later in this chapter.) 802.11g clients using OFDM enjoy much better performance at the same ranges as 802.11b clients do, but—and remember this—when 802.11g clients are operating at the 802.11b rates (11, 5.5, 2, and 1Mbps), they're actually using the same modulation 802.11b does.

Figure 19.4 shows the 14 different channels (each 22MHz wide) that the FCC released in the 2.4GHz range.

FIGURE 19.4   ISM 2.4GHz Channels

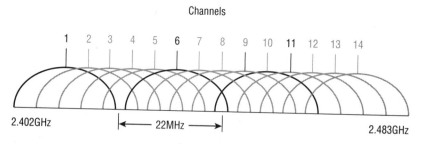

In the U.S.A., only 11 channels are configurable, with channels 1, 6, and 11 being non-overlapping. This allows you to have three access points in the same area without experiencing interference.

5GHz (802.11a)

The IEEE ratified the 802.11a standard in 1999, but the first 802.11a products didn't begin appearing on the market until late 2001—and boy, were they pricey! The 802.11a standard delivers a maximum data rate of 54Mbps with 12 non-overlapping frequency channels. Figure 19.5 shows the UNII bands.

FIGURE 19.5 UNII 5GHz band has 12 non-overlapping channels (U.S.A.).

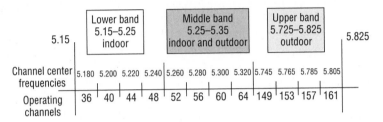

Operating in the 5GHz radio band, 802.11a is also immune to interference from devices that operate in the 2.4GHz band, like microwave ovens, cordless phones, and Bluetooth devices. 802.11a isn't backward compatible with 802.11b because they are different frequencies, so you don't get to just upgrade part of your network and expect everything to work together in perfect harmony. But no worries—plenty of dual-radio devices are available that will work in both types of networks. A definite plus for 802.11a is that it can work in the same physical environment without interference from 802.11b users.

Similar to the 802.11b radios, all 802.11a products also have the ability to data-rate-shift while moving. The 802.11a products allow the person operating at 54Mbps to shift to 48Mbps, 36Mbps, 24Mbps, 18Mbps, 12Mbps, and 9Mbps, and finally, still communicate farthest from the AP at 6Mbps.

There's also an extension to the 802.11a specifications called 802.11h, which is described next.

5GHz (802.11h)

The FCC added 11 new channels in February 2004; and now, we finally get to begin using these channels based on manufacturers' releases of more 802.11a 5GHz products. This means that we gain access to up to 23 non-overlapping channels! And there are even two new features to the 5GHz radio that are part of the 802.11h specification: Dynamic Frequency Selection (DFS) and Transmit Power Control (TPC).

Dynamic Frequency Selection (DFS)   This cool feature continuously monitors a device's operating range for any radar signals that are allowed to operate in portions of the 5GHz band, as well as 802.11a before transmitting. If DFS discovers any radar signals, it'll either abandon the occupied channel or mark it as unavailable to prevent interference from occurring on the WLAN.

Transmit Power Control (TPC)   Even though it's been employed by the mobile phone industry for a long time, this technology has some handy new uses. You can set the client machine's adapter and the access point's transmit power to cover various size ranges—a feature that's useful for many reasons. For one, setting the access point's transmit power to 5mW reduces cell range, which works great if you've got a compact area with high-density usage.

Further advantages include the fact that TPC enables the client and the access point to communicate. This means the client machine can fine-tune its transmit power dynamically so it uses just enough energy to preserve its connection to the access point, conserve its battery power, plus reduce interference on the neighboring WLAN cells—sweet!

2.4GHz/5GHz (802.11n)

802.11n builds on previous 802.11 standards by adding Multiple-Input-Multiple-Output (MIMO), which employs multiple transmitters and receiver antennas to increase data throughput. 802.11n allows up to eight antennas, but most of today's access points use four. These are sometimes referred to as smart antennas and, if you did have four of them, two would be used for transmitting simultaneously with the other two receiving simultaneously. This setup would allow for much higher data rates than 802.11a/b/g.

Keep in mind that the 802.11n standard hasn't yet been ratified and isn't expected to be until sometime in 2009. This means that the products on the shelf today are proprietary, and they are called pre-N products. In some large, outdoor Cisco proprietary networks that I'm currently working on, the Cisco N products work great. But keep in mind that all the devices are Cisco and the network won't tolerate other vendor's products working within it—at least, not today.

Listed next are some of the primary components of 802.11n that give people reason to say 802.11n has greater reliability and predictability:

40MHz Channels   802.11g and 802.11a use 20MHz channels and tones on the sides of each channel are not used to protect the main carrier, which means that 11 Mbps are unused or wasted. 802.11n aggregates two carriers to double the speed from 54Mbps to 108, plus the 11Mbps that we gain from not wasting the side tones = 119Mbps.

MAC Efficiency   802.11 protocols require acknowledgment of each and every frame. 802.11n can pass many packets before an acknowledgment is required, which saves you on overhead. This is called *block acknowledgment*.

Multiple-Input Multiple-Output (MIMO)   Several frames are sent by several antennae over several paths and are then recombined by another set of antennae to optimize throughput and multipath resistance. This is called *spatial multiplexing*.

Concept: 3G and 4G

You've heard various cell phone companies touting their 3G networks, so why isn't it covered here? Simple—3G and 4G aren't Wi-Fi. Wi-Fi uses unlicensed bands for all devices and transmissions. So all of the wireless devices that you have (except your cell phone) use part of this unlicensed band. When you start talking about 3G and 4G you are getting into what is called cellular data. The biggest difference is that cell phone providers buy and own the frequency bands that are used for phones. All of that data is transmitted using licensed frequencies, and therefore does not fall into the realm of wireless LANs that I am discussing in this book. There is a small discussion of these differences in the CCNA wireless objectives so if you need this information be looking for my CCNA wireless book.

Wireless LAN Modulation Techniques

I'm not going to go into a complete discourse of the technical workings of the wireless modulation techniques because doing so is beyond the scope of the objectives of this book. But it's still important for you to be aware of how these techniques match their corresponding 802.11 standards.

Direct-Sequence Spread Spectrum (DSSS)

First, there's DSSS. It's one of the modulation techniques specified by the original IEEE 802.11 standard and also happens to be the one chosen for use in the widely accepted IEEE 802.11b standard. IEEE 802.11 uses Differential Binary Phase Shift Keying (DBPSK) for 1Mbps DSSS, and Differential Quadrature Phase Shift Keying (DQPSK) for 2Mbps DSSS. The DSSS defined in IEEE 802.11b uses the Complementary Code Keying (CCK) modulation technique that gives us both 5.5Mbps and 11Mbps data rates. The cool thing is that all three modulation schemes are compatible and can coexist by using 802.11-standardized rate-switching procedures. Also important is that DSSS creates a redundant bit pattern for each bit that's transmitted, increasing DSSS's resistance to interference. A nice benefit of this is that if any bits in the bit pattern are damaged in transmission, you've got a chance at recovering the original data from the redundant bits.

Frequency-Hopping Spread Spectrum (FHSS)

Even though it's the original modulation technique specified by the IEEE 802.11 standard, Frequency-Hopping Spread Spectrum (FHSS) isn't the technique of choice for either vendors or the 802.11 working group. A big reason for this is that because so few vendors support FHSS in 802.11 products, DSSS has become the favored flavor instead. Plus, continued developments within 802.11 also favor DSSS.

FHSS modulates the data signal with a carrier signal that changes (hops) in a random but, over time, predictable sequence of frequencies. These changes also occur over a wide frequency band, with a spreading, or hopping, code establishing the transmission frequencies used. The receiver is set to the same code, allowing it to listen to the incoming signal at the right time and frequency so it can receive the signal properly. Manufacturers use 75 or more frequencies per transmission channel. The maximum *dwell time* (time spent during a hop at a particular frequency) has been established by the FCC at 400ms.

Orthogonal Frequency Division Multiplexing (OFDM)

802.11a/g uses OFDM with a system of 52 carriers (sometimes referred to as *subcarriers*) that are modulated by BPSK or QPSK. OFDM's spread-spectrum technique distributes the data over these 52 carriers, which are spaced apart at precise frequencies. This spacing approach helps prevent demodulators from seeing frequencies other than their own. OFDM is resistant to RF interference, and it presents lower multipath distortion—big reasons why we use it in our higher-speed wireless networks.

Range Comparisons

Take a look at Figure 19.6, which delimits the range comparisons of each 802.11 standard and shows these different ranges using an indoor open-office environment as a factor, using default power settings.

FIGURE 19.6   Range Comparisons of 802.11 Standards

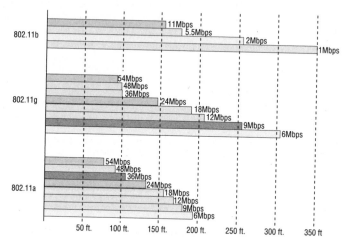

You can see that to get the full 54Mbps benefit of both 802.11a and 802.11g, you need to be between 50 feet and 100 feet (at the furthest) away, and likely even less if there happen to be any obstructions between the client and the access point.

Wireless Devices

Now that you have the basic fundamentals of wireless down, you have to dive into the devices that make it possible. Wireless client devices can connect directly together and talk—just as if you connected two devices together with a crossover cable. To make your wireless network more scalable and secure, though, you need to add APs. APs serve much the same purpose as switches and hubs for wired networks; they allow you to connect multiple wireless devices to the network. The following is a list of the basic required devices for creating and connecting to a wireless network.

- Wireless access points (WAP or AP)
- Wireless network interface card (NIC)
- Wireless antennas

Wireless Access Points

In the vast majority of wired networks, you'll find a central component—like a hub or switch—that serves to connect hosts together and allow them to communicate with each other. It's the same idea with wireless networks. The component that connects all wireless devices together is known as a wireless access point (WAP) or just AP. Wireless access points have at least one antenna, sometimes two for better reception (when two are used it's called diversity), and a port to connect them to a wired network.

You can think of an AP as a bridge between the wireless clients and the wired network. In fact, an AP can be used as a wireless bridge (depending on the settings) to bridge two wired network segments together.

Wireless Network Interface Card (NIC)

Every host that wants to connect to a wireless network needs a wireless network interface card (NIC) to do so. Basically, a wireless NIC does the same job as a traditional NIC; but instead of having a socket to plug some cable into, the wireless NIC has a radio antenna. In addition to the different types of wireless networking (I talk about those in a minute), wireless NICs (like other NICs) can differ in the type of connection they use to connect to the host computer.

Wireless Antennas

Wireless antennas act as both transmitters and receivers. Two broad classes of antennas are available on the market today:

- Omni (short for omni-directional, also known as point-to-multipoint)
- Yagi (or point-to-point).

Yagi Antennas   Yagi antennas usually provide greater range than Omni antennas of equivalent gain. Why? Because Yagis focus all their power in a single direction, whereas Omnis must disperse the same amount of power in all directions at the same time. A downside to using a directional antenna is that you've got to be much more precise when aligning communication points. This is why a Yagi is really only a good choice for point-to-point bridging of access points. It's also why most APs use Omnis, because often, clients and other APs could be located in any direction at any given moment.

Omni Antennas   To get a picture of this, think of the antenna on your car. Yes, it's a non-networking example, but it's still a good one because it clarifies the fact that your car's particular orientation doesn't affect the signal reception of whatever radio station you happen to be listening to. Well, most of the time, anyway. If you're in the Boonies, you're out of range—something that also applies to the networking version of Omnis.

The television aerials that *some* of us are old enough to remember rotating into a specific direction for a certain channel (how many of you labeled your set-top antenna dial for the actual TV stations you could receive?) are examples of Yagi antennas. Believe it or not, they still look the same to this day!

Both Omnis and Yagis are rated according to their signal gain with respect to an actual or theoretical laboratory reference antenna. These ratings are relative indicators of the corresponding production antenna's range. Range is also affected by the bit rate of the underlying technology, with higher bit rates extending shorter distances. Remember, a Yagi will always have a longer range than an equivalently rated Omni; but as I said, the straight-line Yagi will be very limited in its coverage area.

Both antennas are also rated in units of decibel isotropic (dBi) or decibel dipole (dBd), based on the type of reference antenna (isotropic or dipole) of equivalent frequency that was initially used to rate the production antenna. A positive value for either unit of measure represents a gain in signal strength with respect to the reference antenna.

Concept: Isotropic Reference Antenna

An isotropic antenna is a perfect antenna; it cannot be made in the real world. Isotropic antennas have perfect and equal transmission strength in all directions. Even though this antenna cannot be made, it can be used for reference when creating other antennas.

As a practical example, I'm going to use the Cisco Systems series of Aironet Access Point (indoor) and Bridge (outdoor) antennas. Table 19.4 describes the effect that gain ratings and attempted bit rates have on range limitations.

TABLE 19.4 Wireless Antenna Types and Ranges

Model	Gain	Indoor Range at 1Mbps	Indoor Range at 11Mbps	Outdoor Range at 2Mbps	Outdoor Range at 11Mbps
AIR-ANT2410Y-R	10dBi	800ft	230ft	Not specified	Not specified
AIR-ANT1728	5.2dBi	497ft	142ft	Not specified	Not specified
AIR-ANT4941	2.2dBi	350ft	130ft	Not specified	Not specified
AIR-ANT2506	5.2dBi	Not specified	Not specified	5,000ft	1,580ft
AIR-ANT24120	12dBi	Not specified	Not specified	24,288ft	7,392ft

It's pretty much a given that antennas operating with frequencies below 1GHz are measured in dBd, whereas those operating above 1GHz are measured in dBi. But because this rule doesn't always work definitively, sometimes we have to compare the strength of one antenna measured in dBd with another measured in numerically equivalent dBi in order to determine which one is stronger. This is exactly why it's important to know that a particular numerical magnitude of dBd is more powerful than the same numerical magnitude of dBi.

I know this sounds pretty complicated, but because the relationship between these two values is linear, it really makes the conversion a lot easier than you might think. Here's how it works.

Concept: Converting dBi to dBd

At the same operating frequency, a dipole antenna has about 2.2dBd gain over a 0dBi theoretical isotropic antenna, which means you can easily convert from dBd to dBi by adding 2.2 to the dBd rating. Conversely, subtract 2.2 from the dBi rating, and you get the equivalent dBd rating.

Okay—armed with what you've learned about the difference between Omni and Yagi antennas and the difference between dBd and dBi gain ratings, you should be able to compare the relative range of transmission of one antenna with respect to another based on a combination of these characteristics. For example, the following four antenna ratings are given in relative order from greatest to least range:

- 7dBd Yagi (equivalent to a 9.2dBi Yagi)
- 7dBi Yagi (longer range than 7dBi Omni)
- 4.8dBd Omni (equivalent to a 7dBi Omni)
- 4.8dBi Omni (equivalent to a 2.6dBd Omni)

Wireless Topologies

WLANs replace the Layer 1 transmission medium of a traditional wired network (usually Category 5 cable) with radio transmission over the air. The topologies that I cover first are the topologies that define how the APs will be connected together or connected to the wired network. Wireless extends the wired physical network to one that travels through the airwaves, allowing clients and devices to interoperate without wires. The devices used to do this include access points, bridges, repeaters, work group bridges (WGB), and wireless clients.

Client Access   Cisco wireless products can be directly connected to your wired network and function as an overlay to traditional or wired LANs, or they can be used as independent LANs where having a wired network may not be feasible.

Bridging   Wireless bridges allow you to connect two or more networks that are physically separated (maybe in different buildings) to form one internetwork. This can be done without the cost of dedicated cables or ISP connections.

Mesh Networking   Mesh networking is the combination of the two previous topologies. Mesh networks provide dynamic, redundant, fault-tolerant links for building and client access. Some APs are connected to the wired network and some are not. The APs that are not connected use a separate radio connection to form wireless links to the APs that are connected to the wired network.

Concept: Adaptive Wireless Path Protocol (AWPP)

In a mesh network, each access point runs the Cisco AWP protocol. This protocol was designed specifically for a wireless mesh network. AWPP communicates between the APs and determines the best path back to an AP that is connected to the wired network. The APs that are connected to the wired network are called Root Access Points (RAPs). The APs that are not connected to the wired network are called Mesh Access Points (MAPs). AWP keeps running to establish alternative paths back to the RAPs. Cisco AWPP takes into consideration factors such as interference and characteristics of the radio so that the mesh can be self-configuring and self-healing. AWPP ensures that the mesh network is not disruptive and provides consistent coverage.

A couple of other topologies can be used for specific purposes in your network:

- Repeater
- Work Group Bridge (WGB)

These additional topologies are not supported by all Cisco wireless devices, and typically each vendor that implements them has extensions or proprietary communication that happens when the APs are configured this way. That means for you that you probably won't be able to mix vendor equipment if you have to use the following topologies for some reason.

Repeater   If you have a need to cover an area in your environment, but there is no wired connection available, you can use a wireless repeater. A wireless repeater is simply an access point that is not connected to the wired network. This topology requires a 50 percent overlap of the access point coverage area. The receive-and-retransmit time involved decreases the throughput by approximately half.

The Service Set IDentifier (SSID) of the root access point must be configured on the repeater access point. The repeater access point uses the same channel as the root access point.

Work Group Bridge (WGB)   If you have a device that does not have a wireless radio connection and you can't add one to it for some reason (peripheral devices like printers, or old servers have this issue sometimes), a Cisco WGB allows you to connect to the wireless network. The WGB acts as the independent wireless device; your non-wireless device to connect to it, usually through an Ethernet connection.

Client Access

The following modes (sometimes called a type of topology) define how the client devices are going to connect to the wireless network, or use the wireless network:

- Ad hoc mode
- Infrastructure mode, with its two subsets
    - Basic service set
    - Extended services set

You will see in the first mode, using a wireless connection does not always mean having a connection to the rest of the wired network.

Ad Hoc Mode   This mode is called Independent Basic Service Set (IBSS). Mobile clients connect directly without an access point. Think of this like a wireless crossover cable. People use this sometimes for directly sharing data, or for gaming parties.

Infrastructure Mode   In infrastructure mode, clients connect through an access point; it has two modes:

Basic Service Set   Mobile clients use a single access point for connectivity to each other or to wired network resources.

Extended Services Set   In this mode, two or more Basic Service Sets are connected by a common distribution system (wired network typically). An Extended Services Set generally includes a common SSID to allow roaming from access point to access point without requiring client configuration.

Service Areas

Once a topology has been decided upon and APs have been deployed in the network, you will have coverage areas. These coverage areas can be defined by the number of APs that are deployed. Let's take a look at the ways you can define a coverage or service area.

Basic Service Area (BSA)   The basic service area is the area of radio frequency (RF) coverage provided by a single access point. This area is also referred to as a microcell. As the name access point indicates, this device is the point at which wireless clients can access the network.

The access point attaches to the Ethernet backbone and communicates with all the wireless devices in the cell area. The access point is the master for the cell and controls traffic flow to and from the network. The remote devices do not communicate directly with each other; they communicate with the access point.

Extended Service Area (ESA)   If a single AP does not provide enough coverage, more APs can be added to extend the range. This range is known as an extended service area (ESA).

It is recommended that the ESA cells have 10 to 15 percent overlap to allow remote users to roam without losing RF connections. For wireless voice networks, an overlap of 15 to 20 percent is recommended.

Cells that border or are next to each other should be configured with different non-overlapping channels. Using channels that do not overlap will provide you will the best performance and reduce interference.

Many wireless designs are moving from a microcell design to a pico cell design. Pico cells actually reduce the coverage area of an AP by reducing the output power. To cover the same amount of area, the number of access points that you deploy will have to increase.

You are probably asking why you would do something like that. The answer is that you get better coverage, less interference, higher data rates, and fault tolerance through convergence. If one access point were to go down, its neighboring access points could expand their coverage by increasing the output power. This would then cover the hole that was left by the access point that went down.

Concept: Roaming

One of the major benefits of a wireless network is many types of devices can connect. These devices give your users the ability to move around the office or area that you have covered with the wireless network. When you have a well covered area (using multiple devices usually), it is possible for the users to move from one AP to another without dropping any of their connections. This movement from one AP to the next is called *roaming*. Roaming provides other benefits such as reduced power usage on devices (keeping the power turned down saves the battery) because they can swap between APs. Dynamic load balancing gives the users better throughput. Finally, with more than one AP you have some fault tolerance.

Configuring Wireless Clients

I am now going to take you through the configuration of a Cisco client adapter. You can get a couple of different types of adapters depending on your needs: a CardBus, a PCMCIA card, is available for laptops or a PCI card can installed in a desktop.

The Cisco 802.11a/b/g wireless client adapters are supported by Windows 2000, Windows XP, and Windows Vista.

The Cisco Aironet 802.11a/b/g Wireless LAN Client Adapters (CB21AG and PI21AG) support IEEE 802.11a, IEEE 802.11b, and IEEE 802.11g (2.4GHz and 5GHz).

Two LED indicators, LED0 and LED1, provide information about the state of the adapters, as described in Table 19.3.

TABLE 19.3   CardBus and PCI Client Adapter Card State Indicators

State	Indicator Description
Power save mode	Slow blink, off
Awake from power save mode	On, off (can be used to indicate power is applied; the hardware automatically enters this state after exiting from power save mode before any other activity)
Looking for network association	Alternate blink between LED 1 and LED 0
Associated or joined with network, no activity	Slow simultaneous blink
Associated or joined with network, activity	Fast simultaneous blink (blink rate increases with activity)

Installing Cisco Client Adapters

In this section I show you the install process for a Cisco Client Adapter on a Windows XP laptop. For this installation, I am using WinClient-802.11a-b-g-Ins-Wizard-v42.exe software; at install, be sure to check Cisco's website to see if there is a newer version for your operating system.

Start the installation EXE file. When it opens, you will see a standard program installation screen, as shown in Figure 19.7.

The next step in the process is to select the software you want to install. You can choose to install just the driver or install Cisco Aironet Desktop Utility (ADU), the full software suite. For this exercise, choose the default and install both the ADU suite and the drivers for the card. Highlight Install Client Utilities and Driver, as shown in Figure 19.8, and click Next.

FIGURE 19.7   Client Installation Startup

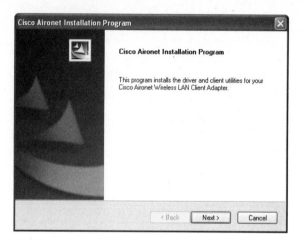

FIGURE 19.8   Software Selection

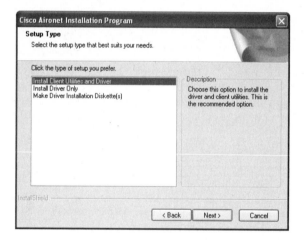

The next decision you have to make is whether to install the Cisco Aironet Site Survey utility. I won't go over using this in this text, but it can be very useful for gathering information about your wireless network. The default is not to install this software. You can see in Figure 19.9 that I have checked the box to install it. I suggest that you install the utility and try using it. Click Next to continue.

The next step is to select the installation path and installation directory name, as shown in Figures 19.10 and 19.11. I have just left them the defaults, but if you wish to change them you can at this point.

FIGURE 19.9 Site Survey Utility

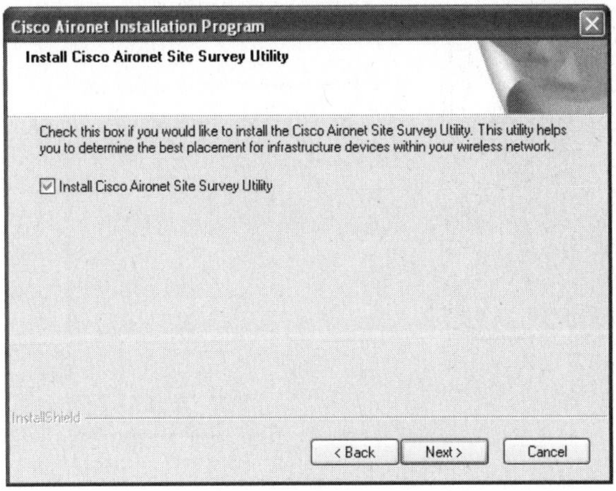

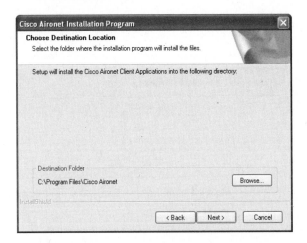

FIGURE 19.10 Destination Location

As shown in Figure 19.12, it is possible for you to have Windows or a third-party software control the operation of your wireless client card. I highly recommend against this. The functionality and options for configuration that you have in the ADU are far superior to other software suites that could control the card. Click Next to continue.

Choose which software you want to have control over the card. The default option is to have the ADU control the card. You can see that is what I have selected in Figure 19.13. I recommend you do the same.

As shown in Figure 19.14, a reboot of your computer will be required when the software is done loading. The reboot allows the card drivers to be fully loaded. Click Yes to continue.

FIGURE 19.11   Folder Naming

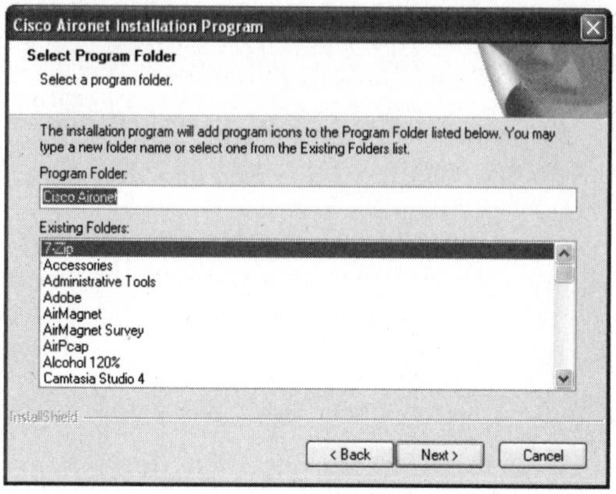

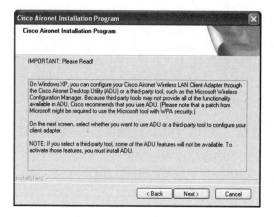

FIGURE 19.12   Important Note

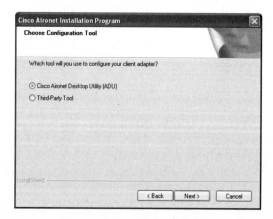

FIGURE 19.13   Software Control Selection

FIGURE 19.14   Reboot Prompt

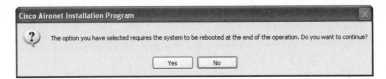

As you know, sometimes you have to install drivers before you physically install devices in the computer. That is not the case with the Cisco wireless card. As shown in Figure 19.15, you must have the card installed in the computer before you click OK and continue the installation.

FIGURE 19.15   Physical Install Prompt

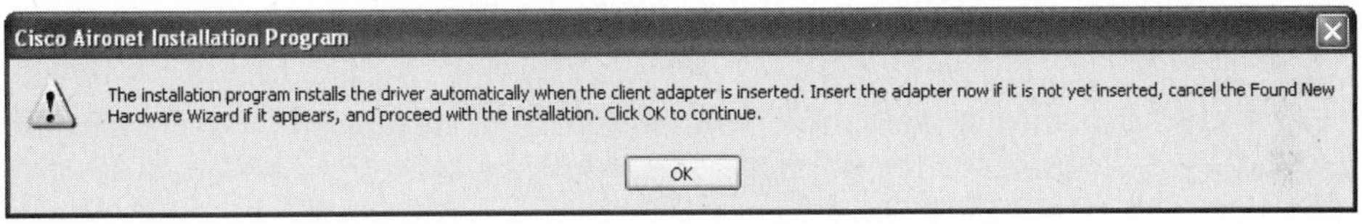

Once the installation is complete, you will get a standard prompt telling you that the computer needs to be rebooted, as shown in Figure 19.16. Click OK to reboot.

FIGURE 19.16   Reboot Prompt

When your computer comes back up, you will see an icon on the desktop called Aironet Desktop Utility. Double-click the icon to open the ADU and view the main status page. As shown in Figure 19.17, right now you have a default profile and are not associated with any wireless network.

Configuring a Profile

To associate your computer with a wireless network, you have to configure a profile. You can configure the default profile with the correct network information, but I recommend that you configure a new profile. One of the benefits of having separate profiles is that the profile can be imported or exported as a file. Think about this in your network; I am going to use the FutureTech network. If you have users that travel between different sites you are going to have different wireless networks in each one of the sites. You can easily help the user get connected to the appropriate network by giving them a file that has the correct profile information already configured. Click the Profile Management tab.

FIGURE 19.17   Default ADU Status Page

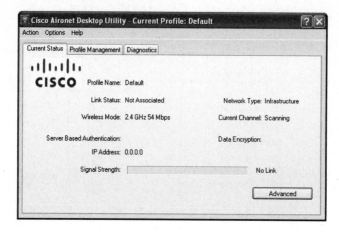

Figure 19.18 shows the Profile Management tab. Click the New button so that you can create a new profile with me.

FIGURE 19.18   Profile Management Tab

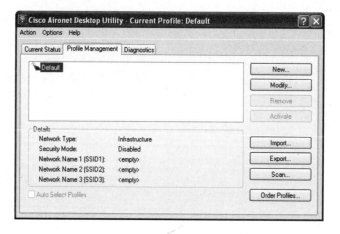

The General tab, shown in Figure 19.19, is where you begin; configure a profile name. I have called mine FutureTech. Be descriptive when you configure names for each of the sites in your network; configure unique names for each site. For example, when configuring the profile for FutureTech's Bangalore office, I would make the profile name FutureTech - Bangalore.

The second thing that you have to configure on this tab is the SSID for the wireless network. I have set up a sample network to allow the client card to connect to a network so I can show you a real status.

FIGURE 19.19   General Tab Configuration

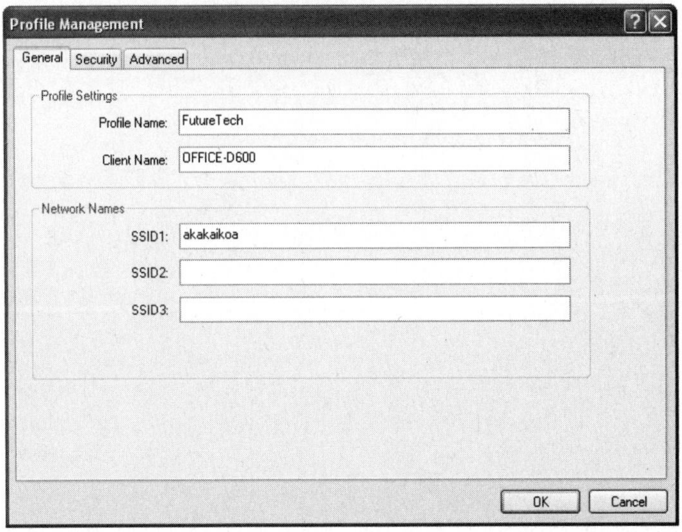

Once you have named your profile and entered the SSID for your network, click the Security tab. You can see you have quite a few different security setting to choose from. Don't worry about not knowing what all of the settings are at this point. I cover wireless security in Chapter 20, "Wireless Management and Security." Figure 19.20 shows the Security tab as I set it up for my client.

FIGURE 19.20   Security Tab

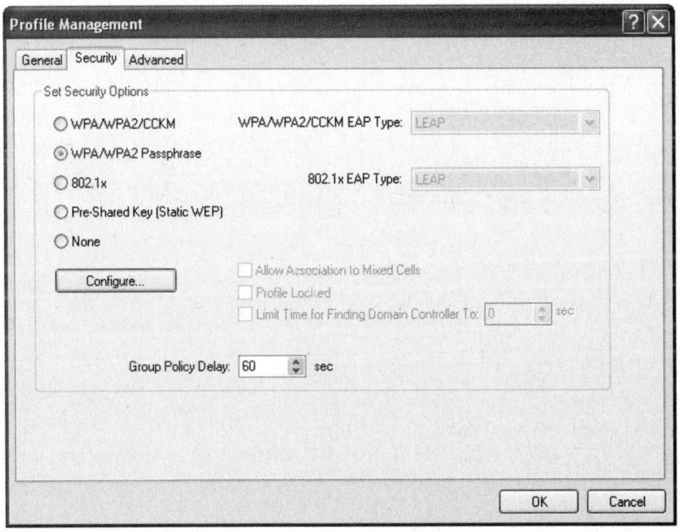

The next thing I want you to do is click over and look at the Advanced tab, shown in Figure 19.21. Typically on this tab, you will change the power setting for the client card and change the wireless mode that the card is scanning in. For example, if you know that your AP is only operating in the 802.11b/g range, you can uncheck the 802.11a box and save some time when the card is associating to the network. This will save time because the card won't have to scan through that spectrum.

FIGURE 19.21   Advanced Tab

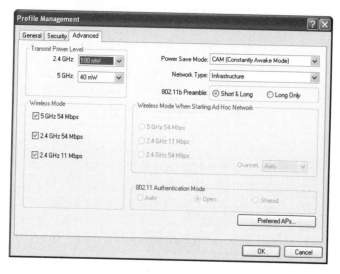

Once you have all of the settings configured for the profile, click OK. You may still be on the Profile Management tab. If you are, great; if not, go to that tab and click the new profile that you just created. The new profile name should show up in the list where there was just Default listed before.

Checking the Status of Your Connection

Once you have selected the new profile name, click the Current Status tab, shown in Figure 19.22. If you have all of the options configured properly, you should be connected to the wireless network.

If You're Not Connected . . .

When you click into the Current Status tab, if the Link Status is listed as Associated or is blank and the Signal Strength is blank, you are not connected to the wireless network. Typically, the problem is an incorrectly entered security code. Verify that the SSID was correctly entered.

FIGURE 19.22   Current Status for a Connected Wireless Network

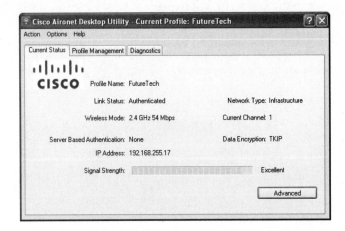

Once you verify that you're connected, click the Advanced button on the Current Status tab. The Advanced Status page (Figure 19.23 shows what mine looks like) will give you all of the status settings and show the operating status of the card, as it is connected to your network. Click OK when you are done reviewing the information about your connection.

FIGURE 19.23   Advanced Status Page

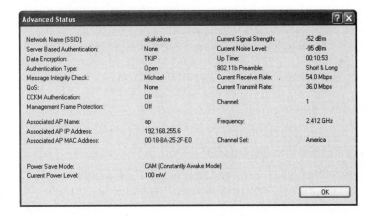

Diagnostics

The options on the Diagnostics tab, shown in Figure 19.24, are very useful if you are having problems and need to do some troubleshooting. From the Diagnostics tab you can access:

- Adapter information
- Advanced statistics
- Client and network managed tests

FIGURE 19.24   Diagnostics Tab

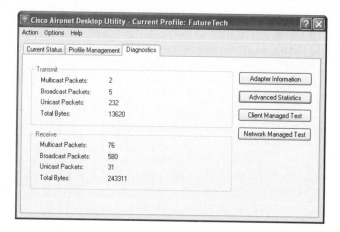

Click the Adapter Information button. As shown in Figure 19.25, Adapter Information opens a status window that provides information about the client card itself. Having ready access to the MAC address of the card can be very handy, if you need it for MAC address filtering or something. You also have information about the card's serial number and details about the driver installed at your fingertips. Click OK to close the window and return to the Diagnostics tab.

FIGURE 19.25   Adapter Information

Adapter Information	
Card Name:	Cisco Aironet 802.11a/b/g Wireless Adapter
MAC Address:	00-40-96-A3-94-D3
Driver:	C:\WINDOWS\system32\DRIVERS\csco21.sys
Driver Version:	4.2.0.297
Driver Date:	2/13/2008 4:39:36 PM
Client Name:	OFFICE-D600
Serial Number:	AMB08130V2K

Now, click the Advanced Statistics button. This again gives you access to some very good information. You can see how many frames have been sent and received. You can see if you are having a lot of drops or if the authentication is being rejected. You can see the statistics for my card in Figure 19.26. After you've had a chance to review the information available for your card, click OK to return to the Diagnostics tab.

Now, click the Client Managed Test button. You can see the screen that comes up in Figure 19.27. Notice that the figure shows that I have already run the test. You can simply click the Start Test button and the client will go through each of the tests for your card. Hopefully, they all pass for you. If not, the diagnostics provide information about where to start looking to resolve your problems. Click Close to return to the Diagnostics tab.

FIGURE 19.26   Advanced Statistics

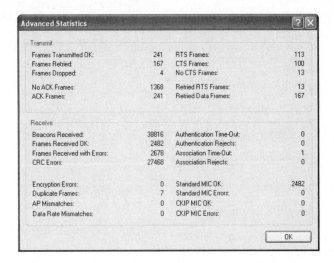

FIGURE 19.27   Client Managed Test Results

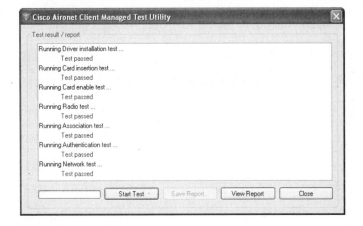

Network Managed Test

The Network Managed Test can be used when connected to a Cisco Wireless LAN Controller (WLC). This feature allows diagnostic troubleshooting from end-to-end on a Cisco Unified Wireless Network (CUWN). I further discuss WLC and CUWN in the upcoming section called "Wireless Implementation Strategies."

The last thing that I want to show you is something you probably won't use unless you are somewhere trying to connect to a network that you don't normally connect to. Click back to the Profile Management tab. If you click the Scan button, located at the bottom right of the screen, you will see a screen similar to what I have in Figure 19.28. The Available Infrastructure and Ad Hoc Networks dialog provides a list of all of the wireless networks that your client card can see at the time. If you don't see the network that you are looking for, you know it might not be available. Either you are not in range or there is something wrong with your card.

FIGURE 19.28   Available Networks Screen

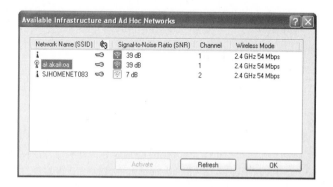

Wireless Implementation Strategies

In the past few years the strategy for implementing wireless devices has changed quite a bit. In the past, you simply had APs and those APs connected to switches and the rest of the wired network. No other devices were required to make them function. A new breed of wireless devices has been released, though, and they are typically referred to as the lightweight architecture. Lightweight APs now have an additional required device in order to operate on the network; this device is called the Wireless LAN Controller (WLC). The old APs are now called autonomous APs; they are called autonomous because they don't require any other device to operate and a new name was needed for comparison's sake. I'll take you through each of the different implementations with a particular focus on the new lightweight solution—just because it's new and cool.

Autonomous Solution

The autonomous solution is composed of the same devices that you have been using from Cisco for years. The only reason for the new name is the new solution to compare it to. You may have also heard the name Aironet; this the brand name that Cisco has used for years with most of its wireless devices. The name came from the Aironet Company that Cisco acquired.

Here is a rundown of the devices and features offered by the autonomous solution.

Autonomous AP   The AP is still the heart of either wireless solution; without the AP the client devices have nothing to connect to. The autonomous AP can operate on its own because it has a fully functioning IOS loaded on it. You can console or telnet to an autonomous AP and configure it.

Wireless Domain Services (WDS)   WDS is not so much a device but a collection of management functions. You can configure a single AP or switch to act as the WDS master for a larger group of APs. The WDS master can then coordinate functions such as roaming and client logon features. WDS is an optional configuration.

Wireless LAN Solution Engine (WLSE)   The WLSE is a separate device that can be configured and placed onto your network. The WLSE provides a central control point for autonomous APs. Again, it is not required but the WLSE is very useful when you have tens or hundreds of APs that you are trying to operate. The WLSE allows you to push out configuration changes and IOS upgrades without having to go to each of the separate APs and perform the task.

I won't go through each and every AP that Cisco makes that can operate as an autonomous AP. You do need to be aware that many of the new series of APs can be purchased in an autonomous or lightweight configuration. The physical device that is the AP does not typically define it as autonomous or lightweight. That is defined by the type of code you have running on the AP and of course the licensing that you purchased for the AP. You can convert an AP from autonomous to lightweight and back again.

Lightweight Solution

The lightweight solution is composed of devices and technology that was acquired by Cisco in the purchase of Airespace. The reason I bring up names like Airespace and Aironet is because you will encounter them in documentation and even configurations. One major configuration that comes to mind is in the Cisco Secure Access Control Server (CSACS); RADIUS extensions exist for each of the different lines of devices when you configure them in the AAA properties. So, let's look at the devices that make up a lightweight solution and then I'll cover more of its operation.

Lightweight Access Point   Lightweight APs don't have a full IOS version of code and therefore can't be configured directly at the AP. Instead, all code upgrades and configuration information is received from the WLC. Only a couple of the older models of APs that Cisco has can't be converted to lightweight. On the opposite side of that coin, only a few models of APs (models that came from Airespace) can't be converted to autonomous.

Wireless LAN Controller   WLCs provide centralized control and management for multiple lightweight APs. WLCs come in multiple models; all provide the same services just for a larger number of APs. I will come back to the models shortly, but I want to look at the services first.

WLCs are where you configure all of the wireless settings for your APs, including the SSIDs, security settings, and radio settings. WLCs also provide services such as roaming, radio management, mobility, redundancy, and the connection point to the wired network.

Table 19.4 describes you all the models and the number of APs each one supports.

TABLE 19.4   WLC Models

Model Series	Number of APs	Description
2006	6	Small desktop form factor, replaced by the 2100 series.
2100	6, 12, 25	Small desktop form factor, comes in three models—2106, 2112, and 2125.
3750G	25, 50	Integrated into 3750G rack mount switch, comes in two licensed configurations for 25 and 50 APs.
4400	12, 25, 50, 100	Rack mount, comes in two models—4402 and 4404 (the 2 and the 4 represent the number of Gigabit Ethernet ports on the device). The 4402 can have through license 12, 25, or 50 APs. The 4404 can have up to 100 APs.
WiSM	300	Wireless Service Module, integrates into the 6500 switch or the 7600 router. The WiSM blade is logically 2 4404 controllers but supports up to 300 APs.
WLCM	6, 8, 12, 25	WLC module is a network module (NM) that goes into an ISR router (2800, 3800 series) and supports by license 6, 8, 12, or 25 APs.

Wireless Control System   The Wireless Control System (WCS) is a browser-based management suite. WCS is entirely software; there is no device to purchase. This means that you have to purchase a sufficiently powerful server to load and run WCS. The software can be loaded on Windows Server 2003 or Linux. WCS is optional but provides tons of valuable services, including:

- Centralized management of multiple WLCs and APs
- Reporting
- Asset tracking (on-demand)
- Location services (with the Location appliance)
- Rogue AP detection

- Advanced security including IDS

- Maps of the campus and individual buildings and floors that help you locate APs, clients, and rogues

- Spectrum Intelligence (with Spectrum Expert)

Location Appliance   The 2700 series location appliance works solely with the WCS. All of the configuration and data management for this device is done through the WCS interface. The 2700 provides the software and processing capability to locate and track in real-time 2500 client devices.

LWAPP

The lightweight solution differs from the autonomous solution because the APs require a WLC to operate. The AP and WLC also communicate using a new protocol that allows them to encapsulate all of the data passed back and forth. This new protocol is called LightWeight Access Point Protocol (LWAPP). LWAPP encapsulates all of the data (control data and client data) between the WLC and the AP; this encapsulation logically makes the WLC and AP look directly connected regardless of where they are physically connected. This logical connection allows the WLC to perform some of the functions that would normally fall on the AP. The separation of functions between the WLC and the AP is called the Split MAC architecture.

The Split MAC architecture gets its name because it splits the Layer 2 (MAC layer) processing of the 802.11 protocol between two devices, the AP and a WLC. The AP and WLC share the processing of data and management protocols, as well as the AP functionality.

The AP handles the portions that have real-time requirements, which include:

- The handshake between a client and AP when transferring a frame over the air

- Transmitting Beacon frames

- The buffering and transmission of frames for clients in power save operation

- The response to Probe Request frames from clients

- Forwarding notification of received Probe Requests to the controller

- Providing real-time signal quality information to the controller with every received frame

- Monitoring each of the radio channels for noise, interference, and other WLANs

- Monitoring for the presence of other APs

The non–time-sensitive functions and processes that require data to pass between multiple APs is done by the WLC. Some of the MAC-layer functions provided in the WLC include:

- 802.11 authentication

- 802.11 association and reassociation (mobility)

- 802.11 frame translation and bridging

Summary

You have now had the opportunity to explore the exciting world of wireless networking. I started by explaining the fundamentals of wireless transmissions and how RF energy behaves. Then you learned about the standards for wireless networks and the regulating bodies.

Then, I described the different types of devices that are required to make a wireless network, and the topologies that those devices can be used in. Next, I took you through the coverage areas and how wireless cells are defined. That took you straight into how to set up and configure a wireless client using the ADU.

Finally, I showed you the two implementation strategies for Cisco wireless networks. The first and older one is now called the autonomous solution and the new solution is called lightweight. I also described the devices that make up each of the solutions.

Review Questions

1. An AP is much like a hub because it operates how?
   - **A.** Full duplex
   - **B.** Three quarter duplex
   - **C.** Half duplex
   - **D.** Quarter duplex

2. Higher frequencies travel what distance compared to lower frequencies?
   - **A.** Longer
   - **B.** The same
   - **C.** Shorter
   - **D.** Almost the same

3. What agency in the U.S. controls what frequencies can be used?
   - **A.** IEEE
   - **B.** WI-FI
   - **C.** WLANA
   - **D.** FCC

4. What standard operates in the 2.4GHz range with speeds up to 11Mbps?
   - **A.** 802.11a
   - **B.** 802.11b
   - **C.** 802.11g
   - **D.** 802.11n

5. What standard operates in the 2.4GHz range with speeds up to 54Mbps?
   - **A.** 802.11a
   - **B.** 802.11b
   - **C.** 802.11g
   - **D.** 802.11n

6. What do you call a perfect un-producible antenna?
   - **A.** Endotropic
   - **B.** Isotropic
   - **C.** Hawaiiantropic
   - **D.** Tropic

7. What do you call the coverage area created by a single AP?

    A. DSA

    B. BSA

    C. ESA

    D. FSA

8. The WLSE is used in what implementation strategy?

    A. Autonomous

    B. Lightweight

    C. Neither

    D. Both

9. The WLC is used in what implementation strategy?

    A. Autonomous

    B. Lightweight

    C. Neither

    D. Both

10. The WCS is used in what implementation strategy?

    A. Autonomous

    B. Lightweight

    C. Neither

    D. Both

Answers to Review Questions

1. C. APs operate in half duplex like a hub.

2. C. Higher frequencies travel shorter distances with higher data rates.

3. D. The FCC controls the frequencies that can be used.

4. B. 802.11b operates at 11Mbps in the 2.4 range.

5. C. 802.11g operates at 54Mbps in the 2.4 range.

6. B. An isotropic antenna cannot be made and is perfect.

7. B. A Basic service area is the coverage area of a single AP.

8. A. WLSE is used to control autonomous APs.

9. B. WLCs are used to control lightweight APs.

10. B. WCS is used to control WLCs and APs in the lightweight solution.

Chapter

20

Wireless Management and Security

IN THIS CHAPTER, YOU WILL LEARN HOW TO DO THE FOLLOWING:

✓ Describe and configure wireless security on Cisco clients and APs, including SSID, WEP, EAP, and the like

✓ Describe basic wireless management and WCS

✓ Configure and verify basic WCS configuration (login, add/review controller/AP status, security, and import/review maps)

✓ Describe and configure WLAN QoS

Our world is a complicated place, so it follows that our security solutions would have to be as well. Most administrators have come to a point where the wireless network has gone from a nice feature to a mission-critical component that must be supported and must provide high up-time. This shift in thinking about the wireless network, as well as the inclusion of wireless phones and video endpoints, has forced us to rethink what is required out of the wireless LAN. To support all of the new devices and requirements, a whole new line of management devices and software have been created to help you implement and control the wireless LAN. Devices such as the Wireless LAN Controller (WLC), Wireless Control System (WCS), and the 2700 Location Appliance give you the ability to control, monitor, track, and provide differentiated service to wireless clients. This chapter explores the basic configuration of the WLC and WCS to show you how to accomplish these tasks.

For up-to-the-minute updates on this chapter, check out www.sybex.com/go/CiscoProGuidetoInternetworking or www.lammle.com

Wireless Security

Okay—so wireless security is not very reassuring. The number of hacks added to the fact that many of the security standards are easily overcome has not provided the best outlook for wireless security. The original 802.11 committee just didn't imagine that wireless hosts would one day outnumber bounded media hosts, but that's actually where we're headed now. Also unfortunately, just like with the IPv4 routed protocol, engineers and scientists didn't include security standards that are robust enough to work in a corporate environment. So, we're left with proprietary solution add-ons to aid us in our quest to create a secure wireless network. And no—I'm not sitting here bashing the standards committees, because the security problems we're experiencing were also created by the U.S. government because of export issues with its own security standards. Our world is a complicated place, so it follows that our security solutions would have to be as well.

Out of that complication and the need to secure the wireless medium has come a whole new set of wireless security implementations. Many of these implementations require the use of some sort of extensible authentication protocol (EAP). You can use EAP to provide authentication for your wireless clients using certificates or tunnel-type security for the exchange of data and authentication credentials. I talk about these different flavors of EAP and security methods after I discuss some of the older and not so secure types of protocols.

Concept: War Driving

It's a fact—wireless networks are pretty much everywhere these days. You can get your hands on a wireless access point for less than $100, and they're flying off the shelves. You can find APs in public places like shopping malls, coffee shops, airports, and hotels; and in some cities, you can just hang out in a downtown area and zero in on a veritable menu of APs operating in almost every nearby business.

Predictably, this proliferation of APs has led to a new hobby for those with enough skill: It's called war driving. Not for the technologically challenged, war driving involves driving around in a car with a laptop, a wireless NIC, and a high-gain antenna, trying to locate open APs. If one with high-speed Internet access is found, it's like hitting the jackpot. People do this aided by various software programs and Global Positioning Systems (GPSs) to make their game even easier. But it's not always innocent—war drivers can be a serious security threat because they can potentially access anything on your wireless LAN, as well as anything it's attached to! Even though they're not a sinister threat most of the time, realize that in the very least, they're consuming precious resources from your network. So, if you happen to notice unusually slow-moving vehicles outside your home or business—especially those with computer equipment inside—know that you're the potential target of a war driver.

A good place to start discussing Wi-Fi security is by talking about the standard basic security that was incorporated into the original 802.11 standards and why those standards are still way too flimsy and incomplete to create a secure wireless network relevant to today's challenges.

Open Access

All Wi-Fi-certified wireless LAN products are shipped in open-access mode, with their security features turned off. Although open access or no security may be appropriate and acceptable for public hot spots such as coffee shops, college campuses, and maybe airports, it's definitely not an option for an enterprise organization, and it's probably not even adequate for your private home network.

With what I've told you so far, I'm sure you agree that security needs to be enabled on wireless devices during their installation in enterprise environments. Yet surprisingly, many companies actually don't enable any WLAN security features. Obviously, the companies that do this are exposing their networks to tremendous risk.

The reason that the products are shipped with open access is so that any person who knows absolutely nothing about computers can just buy an access point, plug it into their cable or DSL modem, and voilà—they're up and running. It's marketing, plain and simple, and simplicity sells.

Older Wireless Security Types

The original designers of 802.11 used service set identifiers (SSIDs), open or shared-key authentication, static wired equivalent privacy (WEP), and optional media access control (MAC) authentication to secure wireless networks. Sounds like a lot, but none of these really offer any type of serious security solution, although they may be close to adequate for use on a common home network. But I'll go over them anyway.

SSID is a common network name used by the devices to associate with a WLAN system. An SSID prevents access by any client device that doesn't have the SSID. The thing is, by default, an access point broadcasts its SSID in its beacon many times a second. And even if SSID broadcasting is turned off, a bad guy can discover the SSID by monitoring the network and just waiting for a client response to the access point. Why? Because, believe it or not, that information, as regulated in the original 802.11 specifications, must be sent in the clear—how secure!

Two types of authentication were specified by the IEEE 802.11 committee: open and shared-key authentication. Although open authentication involves little more than supplying the correct SSID, it's the most common method in use today. With shared-key authentication, the access point sends the client device a challenge-text packet that the client must then encrypt with the correct WEP key and return to the access point. Without the correct key, authentication fails and the client won't be allowed to associate with the access point. But shared-key authentication is still not considered secure because all an intruder has to do to get around this is detect both the clear-text challenge and the same challenge encrypted with a WEP key and then decipher the WEP key. Surprise—shared key isn't used in today's WLANs because of clear-text challenge.

With open authentication, even if a client can complete authentication and associate with an access point, the use of WEP prevents the client from sending and receiving data from the access point unless the client has the correct WEP key. A WEP key is composed of either 40 or 128 bits; and in its basic form, it's usually statically defined by the network administrator on the access point and all clients that communicate with that access point. When static WEP keys are used, a network administrator must perform the time-consuming task of entering the same keys on every device in the WLAN. Obviously, we now have fixes for this because tackling this would be administratively impossible in today's huge corporate wireless networks!

Last, client MAC addresses can be statically typed into each access point, and any device that attempts access and is not in the MAC address list or filter table will be denied access. Sounds good, but of course all MAC layer information must be sent in the clear—anyone equipped with a free wireless sniffer can just read the client packets sent to the access point and spoof their MAC address.

WEP can actually work if administered correctly. But basic static WEP keys are no longer a viable option in today's corporate networks without some of the proprietary fixes that run on top of it.

So, what should you use today? The answer lies in the size of your wireless network and how tight your security needs to be. Let's discuss this further now.

Temporal Key Integrity Protocol (TKIP)

Put up a fence, and it's only a matter of time until bad guys find a way over, around, and through it. And true to form, they indeed found ways to get through WEP's defenses, leaving Wi-Fi networks vulnerable—stripped of their Data Link layer security! So, someone had to come to the rescue. In this case, it happened to be the IEEE 802.11i task group and the Wi-Fi Alliance, joining forces for the cause. They came up with a solution called Temporal Key Integrity Protocol (TKIP). The Wi-Fi Alliance unveiled it back in late 2002 and introduced it as Wi-Fi Protected Access (WPA). This little beauty even saved us lots of money because TKIP—pronounced, "tee kip"—didn't make us upgrade all our legacy hardware equipment in order to use it. Then, in the summer of 2004, the IEEE put its seal of approval on its final version and added even more defensive muscle with goodies like 802.1x and Advanced Encryption Standard-Counter Mode CBC-MAC Protocol (AES-CCMP) upon publishing IEEE 802.11i-2004. The Wi-Fi Alliance responded positively by embracing the now-complete specification and dubbing it WPA2 for marketing purposes.

A big reason that TKIP doesn't require buying new hardware to run is because it really just kind of a wraps around the pre-existing WEP encryption key (which was way too short) and upgrades it to a much more impenetrable 128-bit encryption. Now I know that I told you a WEP key can have a 128-bit key, but the original WEP standard only allowed a 40-bit key. The upgrade to 128-bit keys came later after the TKIP improvement was designed. Another reason for TKIP's innate compatibility is that both its encryption mechanism and the RC4 algorithm used to power and define WEP, respectively, remained the same.

But significant differences exist that help make it the seriously tough shield it is, one of them being that it actually changes each packet's key. Let me explain… Packet keys are made up of three things: a base key, the transmitting device's MAC address, and the packet's serial number. It's an elegant design because although it doesn't place a ton of stress on workstations and APs, it serves up some truly formidable cryptographic force.

Here's how it works: Remember the packet serial number part of the transmission key? Well, it's not just your average serial number; it's special—very special. TKIP-governed transmission ensures that each packet gets its very own 48-bit serial number, which is augmented with a sequence number that increments whenever a new packet gets sent out. These two elements not only serve as part of the key, but also act as the initialization vector for the encryption process. And the good news doesn't end there—because each packet is now uniquely identified, the collision attacks that used to be performed using WEP are also history. Plus, the fact that part of the packet's serial number is also the initialization vector prevents something called replay attacks. It takes an ice age for a 48-bit sequence repeat, so replaying packets from some past wireless connection is just not going to happen; those recycled packets won't be in sequence, but they will be identified, thus preventing the attack.

Okay—now for what may be the truly coolest thing about TKIP keys: the base key. Because each base key that TKIP creates is unique, no one can recycle a commonly known key over and over again to gain access to a formerly vulnerable WEP wireless LAN. TKIP throws the base key into the mix when it assembles each packet's unique key, meaning that even if a device has connected to a particular access point a bunch of times, it won't be permitted access again unless it has a completely new key granting it permission.

Even the base key itself is a fusion of something called *nonces*—an assortment of random numbers gleaned from the workstation, the access point, and each of these devices' MAC addresses. The nonces are also referred to as a session secret. So basically, if you've got IEEE 802.1x authentication working for you, rest assured that a session secret absolutely will be transmitted securely to the each machine every time it initiates a connection to the wireless LAN by the authentication server—unless you're using pre-shared keys. If you happen to be using pre-shared keys, that important session secret always remains the same. Using TKIP with pre-shared keys is kind of like closing an automatically locking security door but not enabling its security settings and alarm—anyone who knows where the secret latch is can get right in!

> **WARNING**   When it comes to security, don't just rest on your laurels. Each and every security measure that's been brought into being has been compromised at one time or another. If someone can invent it, someone else will eventually hack it.

WPA and WPA 2 PSK

Wi-Fi Protected Access (WPA) and WPA 2 Pre-Shared Key (PSK) are essentially another form of basic security—really just an add-on to the specifications. Even though you can totally lock the vault, as I mentioned in the previous section, WPA/WPA2 PSK is a better form of wireless security than any other basic wireless security method I've talked about so far—and note that I did say basic!

WPA is a standard that was developed by the Wi-Fi Alliance, formerly known as Wireless Ethernet Compatibility Alliance (WECA). WPA provided a standard for authentication and encryption of WLANs that was intended to solve known security problems. The standard took into account the well-publicized AirSnort and man-in-the-middle WLAN attacks that ravaged WEP and RC4. Unfortunately, the TKIP protocol used in WPA was also based on the RC4 algorithm, which left it vulnerable to a new set of attacks. WPA does allow for a full range of EAP types of authentication, just as the new standard WPA2. WPA2 conforms to the new 802.11i standard for wireless security. WPA2 improves on the past shortcomings and vulnerabilities by utilizing AES encryption. AES encryption has yet to be compromised, so it is the securest type of security for use today. Of course, then you will want to use WPA2 to help you deal with today's security issues.

The PSK verifies users via a password or identifying code (also called a passphrase) on both the client machine and the access point. A client gains access to the network only if its password matches the access point's password. The PSK also provides keying material that TKIP or AES uses to generate an encryption key for each packet of transmitted data.

Although more secure than static WEP, PSK still has a lot in common with static WEP; the PSK is stored on the client station and can be compromised if the client station is lost or stolen (even though finding this key isn't all that easy to do). It's a definite recommendation to use a strong PSK passphrase that includes a mixture of letters, numbers, and non-alphanumeric characters. With WPA, it's actually possible to specify the use of dynamic encryption keys that change each time a client establishes a connection.

The benefit of WPA over a static WEP key is that WPA can change dynamically while the system is used.

WPA is a step toward the IEEE 802.11i standard and uses many of the same components, with the exception of encryption—802.11i (WPA2) uses AES-CCMP encryption. The IEEE 802.11i standard replaced WEP with a specific mode of AES known as the CCMP, as I mentioned earlier in this chapter. This allows AES-CCMP to provide both data confidentiality (encryption) and data integrity.

WPA's mechanisms are designed to be implementable by current hardware vendors, meaning that users should be able to implement WPA on their systems with only a firmware/software modification.

Wireless QoS

QoS in a wireless network has the same goals as in a wired network. When you place real-time traffic on wireless network, it still has the same requirements of bandwidth, delay, and packet loss as it does on the rest of the network. QoS gives you a way to provide a specific level of service to traffic that is classified as high priority. If you need a more detailed review of QoS for wired networks go back and look at Chapter 18, "DiffServ Quality of Service (QoS)."

With a little review of wired QoS and given that there is a need to have QoS in the wireless part of the network, you should be asking, "Does QoS have to be implemented differently for wireless traffic?" The answer is, "Yes." But why does it have to be different? For that answer, you have to think about how and on what devices wireless traffic is transmitted.

Let's think about how QoS information is carried and used on a wired network. To maintain QoS end-to-end on a network, you have to use DSCP for packet marking. You know that because Layer 2 markings (CoS) typically are carried in the 802.1p header. If that header is removed, which happens on links that are not trunks, that information is lost unless restored by a capable device.

Now, consider: What layer in the OSI model do all of our wireless devices operate in though? If you said, "They operate at Layer 2," you are right.

Wireless RF historically could only use Layer 2 marking. In fact, based on some of deployment models that Cisco set forth, the traffic destined for APs does not contain 802.1p QoS tag information because the APs do not connect to a switch port using a trunk. That means that packets sent by the wireless network will not have Layer 2 QoS markings. Because of this it is important to be able to utilize the Layer 3 DSCP information for QoS.

Queuing and Marking for Wireless

In the Cisco Unified Wireless Network design, the WLAN controllers (after code version 3.2) ensure that packets receive proper QoS handling end-to-end. WLAN controllers ensure the packet will maintain its QoS information as it moves back and forth from the wired and wireless networks. The way traffic is identified and how it is handled in the RF wireless network is different from a wired network. In wireless, because the AP is a half-duplex device and uses congestion avoidance, the queuing strategy that is employed is called distributed coordination function (DCF).

When you add wireless QoS, the queuing strategy becomes enhanced DCF (EDCF), also called Enhanced Distributed Channel Access Function (EDCAF). The markings or mappings for wireless traffic use either the IEEE 802.11e marking standard or the wireless multi-media (WMM) mapping standard.

802.11e   The IEEE 802.11e standard amendment is specifically written to expand the 802.11 standard's explanation of wireless QoS. As I described in Chapter 19, "Wireless Devices and Topologies," many of the standards were rolled up into an updated version of the 802.11 standard, now known as the 802.11-2007 standard.

The standard defines eight different priority levels that are comparable to the eight priority levels of CoS and IP precedence. Table 20.1 shows the correlation between the wired and wireless priority mappings.

TABLE 20.1   Wired to Wireless Priority Mappings

Traffic Type	DCSP	802.1p	802.11e
Reserved	52-62	7	7
IP routing	48	6	7
Voice	46 (EF)	5	6
Video	34 (AF41)	4	5
Voice signaling	26 (AF31)	3	4
High	18 (AF21)	2	2
Medium	10 (AF11)	1	1
Best Effort	0 (BE)	0	0 or 3

Wireless Multi-Media (WMM)   Because there was a commercial need for QoS in the wireless environment before the actual 802.11e standard was finished, the Wi-Fi Alliance developed the WMM standard to provide priority access categories to traffic traversing wireless devices.

Only four access categories are defined in the WMM standard. Cisco named the categories Platinum, Gold, Silver, and Bronze. Platinum is the highest priority and Bronze is less than best effort. Table 20.2 lists the levels of priority and describes the use for each.

TABLE 20.2 WMM Access Categories

Category	Level of Priority
Platinum	Highest, for voice traffic
Gold	Video traffic
Silver	Best effort
Bronze	Background, or less than best effort

Table 20.3 compares of the WMM categories to the eight priority levels of 802.11e. You see that background has values of 1 or 2 so that you can identify traffic that is worse than best effort. Best-effort data can be marked with either a 0 or a 3 so that traffic in that category can be marked either above or below that of background data.

TABLE 20.3 WMM Compared to 802.11e

WMM Category	802.11e Priority
Platinum—voice	6 or 7
Gold—video	4 or 5
Silver—best effort	0 or 3
Bronze—background	1 or 2

Implementing Wireless QoS

I want to talk about the process of how the data is actually marked and carried across the network so that all of the devices have the proper QoS information to handle the traffic. For this discussion, I am going to be using Cisco's Unified Wireless Network design. That means that the wireless network will be operating with lightweight access points communicating to a Wireless LAN Controller (WLC) using Lightweight Access Point Protocol (LWAPP) tunnels. In this type of setup the APs do not connect to the switches using a trunk link. Not using a trunk link means that the Layer 2 QoS markings are lost. For the QoS information to be maintained all the way to and from the AP there must be a way to map and carry the marking in the LWAPP header. Let's take a look.

Real World Scenario

Wireless QoS in the Dallas Headquarters

FutureTech has implemented a lightweight wireless solution in the headquarters office. The wireless network has greatly improved the way that many people work and collaborate in the building. Now, people can stay connected on their laptops and PDAs while they go to meetings or go to talk to other workers.

With all of this improvement could there possibly be more that FutureTech could do for their users? Yes! They can add wireless VoIP phones to the network so that employees can talk while not right at their desks. But, by adding wireless phones to the network, they are adding the same difficulties you looked at in Chapter 17, "Voice." You now have to think about the fact the voice data is time- and drop-sensitive. A few years ago, there was little that you could have done about this in a wireless network. Now, you have the ability to configure QoS on the wireless network.

This time, FutureTech has asked you to deploy a wireless phone for each of the directors in the Dallas office. The directors spend the most amount of time out of their offices and in meetings that are located somewhere else. This deployment will require that you understand how QoS in the wireless network operates. You have to make sure that you understand how the traffic markings transfer from the wireless to the wired sides of the network.

So, here is the process for how traffic will be marked and re-marked as it moves from the wired to the wireless network and vice versa. I am going to start this process with a packet coming from the wired network going to the wireless and then back. Take a look at Figure 20.1. You can see that the wireless network connects to the wired with the WLC. The WLC communicates to all of the APs over LWAPP. Then, of course, the APs communicate using RF to the wireless clients.

FIGURE 20.1   QoS from Wired to Wireless

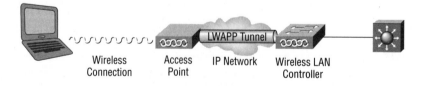

Wireless Connection   Access Point   IP Network   Wireless LAN Controller

Switch to WLC   When a packet is received by the WLC from the wired network (directly from the switch), the controller reads the DSCP value that is contained in the incoming packet header. The WLC must then translate that DSCP value into the Layer 2 or 802.1p priority value. Both of these values are then placed into the header of the LWAPP frame. The LWAPP frame encapsulates the original packet, so the 802.1p and DSCP values the WLC wrote into the frame are now the furthest outside header. This allows the AP to read and use the information. LWAPP control packets are always tagged with an 802.1p of seven, whereas the LWAPP data packets derive the DSCP and 802.1p value from the original packet. The LWAPP packet is then carried from the WLC to the AP. Remember, the packet is physically being carried over the same network infrastructure (switches and routers) as any other traffic, but because it is encapsulated in LWAPP it virtually travels directly from the WLC to the AP.

AP to Wireless Client   For a WMM-compliant client, the AP translates the DSCP value of the incoming LWAPP packet to the 802.11e priority value. The AP must also police the traffic flow to make sure it does not exceed the maximum value allowed based on the WLAN QoS policy assigned to that client. Then, the AP places packet in the 802.11e transmit queue appropriate for that WMM access category or 802.11e priority level.

For a regular (non-WMM) client, the AP places the packet in the default 802.11e or WMM transmit queue based on the WLAN QoS policy assigned to that client.

Wireless Client to AP   If the AP receives an 802.11 frame from a WMM-compliant client, it must first police the 802.11e priority value to ensure it does not exceed the maximum value allowed for the QoS policy assigned to that client. Then it translates the 802.11e priority value to the DSCP value.

If the AP receives a frame from a regular non-WMM client, it uses the default 802.11e priority or WMM value. The default value comes from the QoS policy assigned to that client or WLAN ID. Once the AP has that value, it translates the value to the DSCP value.

The traffic leaving the AP toward the WLC will again be encapsulated into LWAPP. The AP is not trunked to the switch that it is connected to. This means when the LWAPP packet leaves the AP, the 802.1p information will not be mapped back to the outside of the LWAPP header. The DCSP value will, however, be mapped from the inside header to the outside LWAPP header.

WLC to Wired Client   When the WLC receives the LWAPP packet, it generates the IEEE 802.1p priority value for the wired side, using the incoming DSCP value that was placed in the outside LWAPP header.

The outer 802.1p value from AP does not exist anymore because the AP does not send NULL VLAN ID frames.

The WMM or 802.11e policy for the wireless clients is configured at the WLAN ID (SSID) on the WLC. You configure the WLAN ID with an access category, as well as allot an amount of RF usage or time that it can have to send traffic.

When the traffic is being mapped back and forth between the wired and wireless side, there can be a difference in the markings. When a difference is discovered, the WLAN ID configuration takes priority for the QoS marking. When packets are received from the wired LAN with a tag that is lower than the configured QoS, the AP will queue the packet at the lower access category. For packets received from the wireless side, if the 802.11e access category is lower than the configured QoS value, the lower 802.1p tag will be applied.

Configuring Wireless Management Devices

In this section I recap the components of the Cisco Unified Wireless Network, commonly called the lightweight wireless network. Then, I show you how to install and set up processes for the WCS software. After that, I show you the steps for adding a WLC to the interface and how to monitor the network, show alerts, and set up a map. After you are done in the WCS interface I show you how to configure QoS and security in the WLC interface.

The two components that provide central control and management of the wireless network are the Wireless LAN Controller (WLC) and the Wireless Control System (WCS). The WLC is required to manage and operate lightweight APs in your network. You can use the WLC to configure both the QoS settings and the security for each one of your WLANs.

The Wireless Control System

The WCS is an optional component in your wireless network. However, I recommend that you use it wherever you can and I wish that it was a required component. The amount of control and the functions that the WCS provide to you are truly awesome. WCS gives you the ability to centrally manage up to 50 WLCs and 1500 APs. You can configure maps of your campus or building, orient the APs to their locations, and (with the right version of software and license of course) provide location services for clients and devices. The WCS also allows you to do network modeling, a small degree of site survey type functions, and provides a central point for all of your wireless network monitoring and data gathering.

Installing WCS

The first thing that you have to do is download the version of WCS that you are going to install and use. You can do this from Cisco's website in the Software Center. You can download a 30-day trial of the software so that you can evaluate the functions that it provides.

Tips for a Successful Deployment of WCS

If you plan to use the WCS permanently and are going to buy the software, here are a couple of things that you need to know. These are tips that I had to learn the hard way—setting this product up for my clients.

1. WCS can be a bit of a beast in terms of the resources that it consumes on a server. If you are using maps, monitoring multiple WLCs, and especially if you are doing location services, I recommend more than the minimum requirements for the server hardware.

2. Know the operating system you are going to run on the server before you download. You download different software depending on whether your server is running Windows Server 2003 or Linux.

3. Once you have actually purchased a license for WCS from your local Cisco vendor, you now have to contact the Cisco licensing team so that the license file for your software can be created. You have to have the server built, or at least know what the hostname of the server is going to be, because when you contact the licensing team, they need the name of the server to create the license file. The license file is tied to a single server with that name and that name only.

4. If you are upgrading WCS, back up the FTP and TFTP server files that are in the root directories on the WCS server; the files can be deleted during the installation process.

So, assuming that you have a server and have the software downloaded to that server, let's get on with the installation:

1. Double-click the WCS software file to begin the installer program and wait for the initial setup screen to appear. This could take a couple of minutes. You will see the initial configuration screen as shown in Figure 20.2. Read the information and click Next to continue.

FIGURE 20.2   WCS Initial Setup Screen

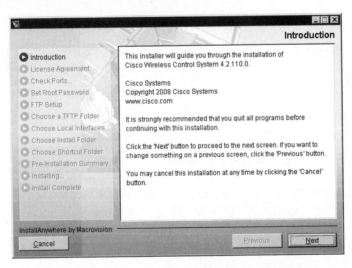

2. Read and agree to the software license and click Next to continue.
3. When the Check Ports dialog (Figure 20.3) opens, enter the HTTP and HTTPS ports for your server. The default is HTTP port 80 and HTTPS port 443. Click Next to continue.

FIGURE 20.3 Check Ports

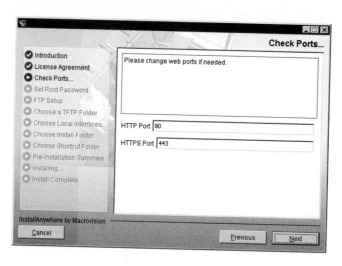

4. When the Password Restrictions information appears, read the restrictions, devise a root password that meets all of the requirements, and click Next to continue.

5. Enter the root password and click Next to continue.

6. Verify the root password by re-entering it. Figure 20.4 shows the Verify Root Password dialog.

FIGURE 20.4 Verify Root Password

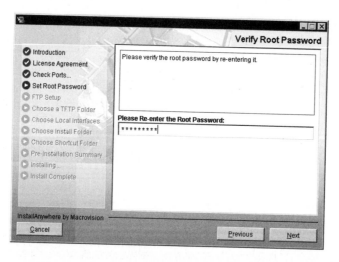

7. Devise a new password that meets all of the password restrictions. This will be the password that secures the root FTP server. Enter the FTP password on the Enter FTP Password dialog, shown in Figure 20.5, and click Next.

FIGURE 20.5   Enter FTP Password

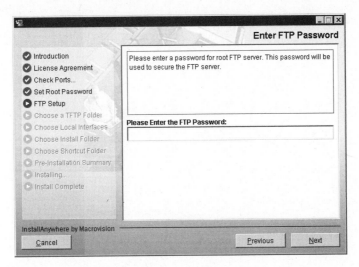

8. Specify the folder to be used for the FTP server files. Cisco recommends that the folder be located on a path different from that of the WCS installation. This preserves your FTP server files should you ever uninstall WCS. The default path, as shown in Figure 20.6, is C:\. Click Choose and specify a different path, one that is appropriate for your system. When you are finished, click Next to continue.

FIGURE 20.6   FTP Server File Location

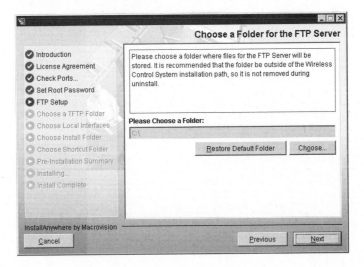

9. Specify the folder to be used for TFTP server files. Again, Cisco recommends that the folder be located on a path different from that of the WCS installation. This preserves files uploaded from or downloaded to controllers should you ever uninstall WCS. The default path, as shown in Figure 20.7, is C:\. Click Choose and specify a different path, one that is appropriate for your system. When you are finished, click Next to continue.

FIGURE 20.7   TFTP Server File Location

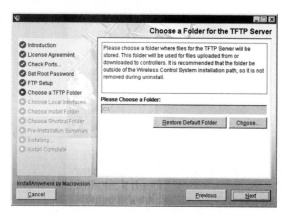

10. Specify the installation path for the WCS software. Typically, the default installation path, shown in Figure 20.8, is appropriate for most systems. Click Choose if you need to change the path for your system. When you are finished, click Next.

FIGURE 20.8   WCS Installation Path

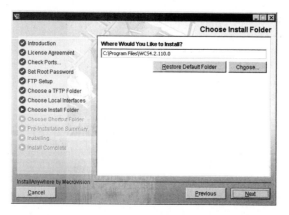

11. Specify the shortcut folder for the WCS software. Typically, the default new program group, shown in Figure 20.9, is appropriate for most systems, but you have other options. You can drop the shortcut into:

   ▪ An existing program group

   ▪ The Start menu

- The Quick Launch bar

- Another location you specify

You can also choose to create icons for all users or create no icons at all. Click Next when you are finished.

FIGURE 20.9 WCS Shortcut Options

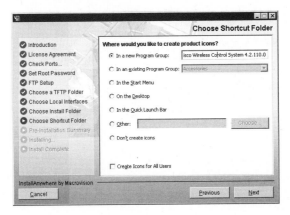

12. When the Pre-Installation Summary opens, double-check your settings and make sure that your system has enough disk space for the installation. Figure 20.10 shows the settings for the system in my test network. Click Next to begin the software installation.

FIGURE 20.10 Pre-Installation Summary

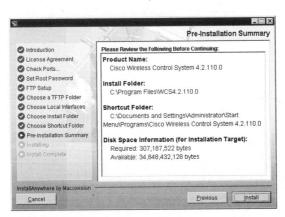

13. Wait while the software installs. Installation messages and a progress bar, shown in Figure 20.11, allow you to monitor the installation. If necessary, you can use the Cancel button to cancel the installation.

FIGURE 20.11 Monitoring the Software Installation

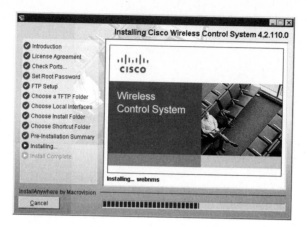

14. Once the installation is complete, a message box, shown in Figure 20.12, opens and allows you to choose whether to begin service immediately. Click Yes.

FIGURE 20.12 Starting Wireless Control

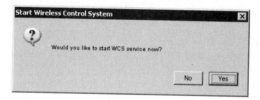

15. Wait while WCS starts. Once WCS is started, you will be returned to the installer. Review the on-screen information, shown in Figure 20.13, and click Done to exit the installer.

FIGURE 20.13 Installation Complete

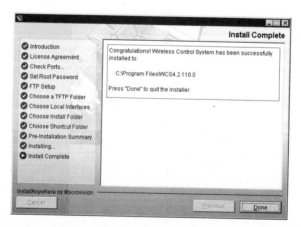

Starting the WCS

The next step is to log in to the WCS interface. WCS is entirely a Web-based application. You need only open a browser and navigate to the IP address of the server where you just installed the software. Look at Figure 20.14 and you can see an example of the login page. The default username is root and the password is whatever you set during the installation process.

FIGURE 20.14   WCS Login Page

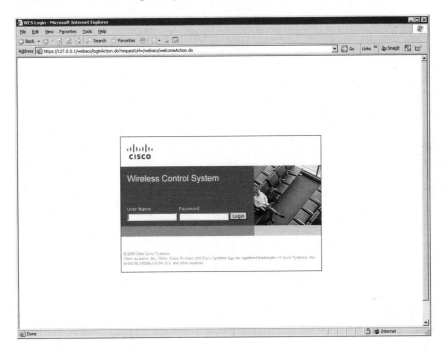

Configuring the WCS

As soon as you log in, the WCS interface notifies you that the interface is completely customizable and you can modify the interface to provide easy access to the most important information for your network and environment. Read and then close the message box.

Now that the interface is open you can begin to navigate through the WCS software. Notice that there is no information about your wireless network—or anything really. That is because WCS is a management suite and by default it isn't connected to any of your devices that might already be on the network.

With that understanding, the first thing that you have to do with WCS is add a WLC so the WLC and the WCS can begin sharing information. WCS gets most of its data from the WLCs on the network.

You can't add APs directly into the WCS interface. This is because all APs require a WLC to operate on the network. What happens is that all of the APs associate to a WLC; then when you add each of the WLCs to the WCS interface, all of the APs and network data are passed by the WLCs up to the WCS. You end up with a hierarchical structure and WCS truly becomes a central management application.

I want to take you through the process of configuring and adding devices and information to the WCS interface now. The first device that must be added to the WCS is the WLC.

Adding a WLC to the WCS

Adding a WLC to the WCS interface is a very straightforward and easy process. As you can see in Figure 20.15, I am on the main Home page of the WCS server. This is where I am going to start the process for showing you how to add a WLC.

FIGURE 20.15   Home Page

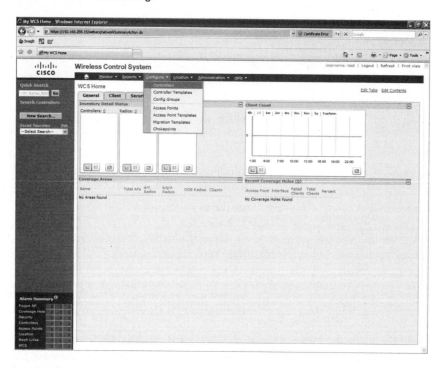

1.   Select Controllers from the Configure menu, as shown in Figure 20.15. This brings you to the All Controllers page shown in Figure 20.16.

FIGURE 20.16   All Controllers Page

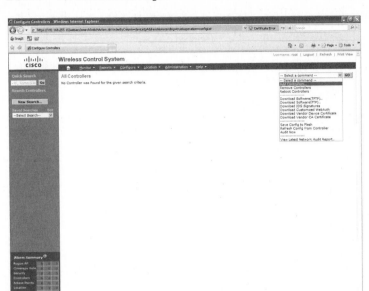

2. Choose Add Controllers from the Action drop-down list box, as shown in Figure 20.16, and click Go.

Below the menu bar, on the right side of the screen, you will find the Action drop-down list box. The Action box always contains a list of the actions that can be accomplished from whatever page you're on.

3. When the Add Controllers page (shown in Figure 20.17) opens, enter the IP address and subnet mask for the WLC that you are adding. Click OK to add the WLC to WCS.

The IP address and subnet mask provide the minimum information required to add a WLC. From this screen, you can also change the Simple Network Management Protocol (SNMP) version to match your implementation and tweak the SNMP options, but changing this information is optional. You can see the options in Figure 20.17.

The WCS defaults to the current and most secure version of SNMP. Unless you have an older server that only supports an earlier version, leave the default version in place.

4. Once the WLC is added, you will see it listed at the top of the Add Controllers page. In Figure 20.18, you can see that the WLC has been successfully added.

The catch is that you are still on the Add Controllers page—a handy place to be if you have another controller to add. (You can simply enter the new IP address and subnet mask and click OK again.) But, if you don't need to enter another WLC and just click OK thinking that this will navigate you to another page—well, it won't. You will get a message saying that the controller has already been added.

FIGURE 20.17   Add Controllers Page

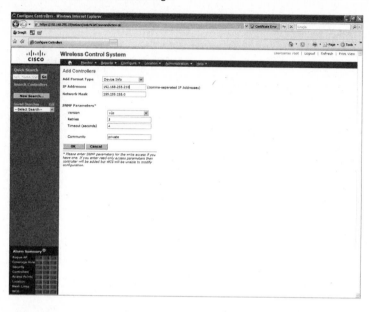

FIGURE 20.18   Successfully Added WLC

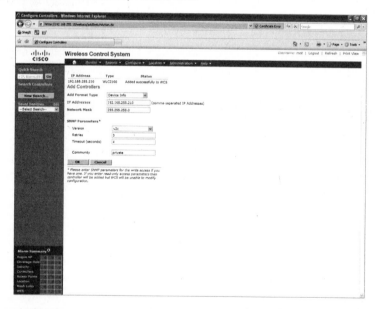

5. Go back up to the Configure menu and click Controllers again.

When the All Controllers page opens, you will see the WLC that you added. Figure 20.19 shows the All Controllers page with the WLC that I added.

FIGURE 20.19 All Controllers with a WLC

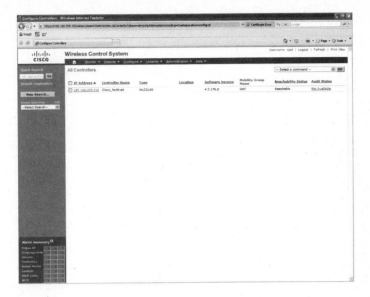

6. Click the hyperlinked IP address to bring up the WLCs Controller Properties page (shown in Figure 20.20).

7. Add the hostname, location, and contact information for your WLC. This page, once again, gives you an opportunity to modify the SNMP details. When you're finished, click OK.

FIGURE 20.20 Controller Properties Page

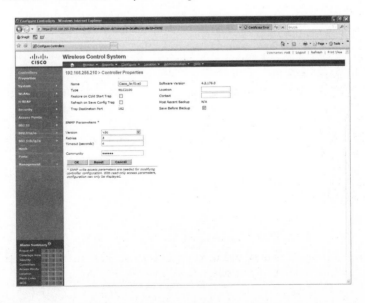

8. To access the WLC, see the summary, and make configuration changes, select the Controllers from the Monitor menu.

9. When the Search Results page opens (it looks pretty much the same as the All Controllers page), click the WLC IP address hyperlink. The WLCs summary page is similar to the one shown in Figure 20.21.

FIGURE 20.21   Controller Summary Page

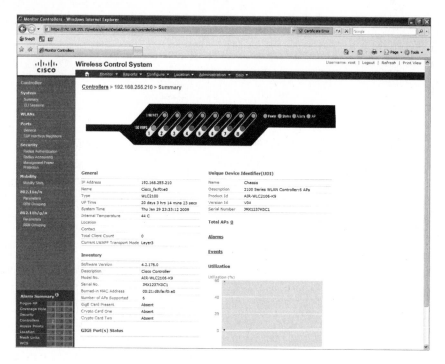

Adding a Map to the WCS

Much of the WCS's power and centralized control comes from having a configured campus map and being able to place and track your APs and clients on that map. The base for your map will be an existing site plan drawing, aerial photograph, or satellite photograph. With that image in place and dimensioned for the WCS, you can orient the APs to their physical location and configure the type of antenna they have. Once the APs are in place, the map displays their coverage and allows you to see possible interference issues. You can do a ton of cool things with the Maps section.

So, let's go through the process of adding a map to this WCS:

1. Select the Maps from the Monitor menu. This will bring up the Maps page, as shown in Figure 20.22.

FIGURE 20.22   Maps Page

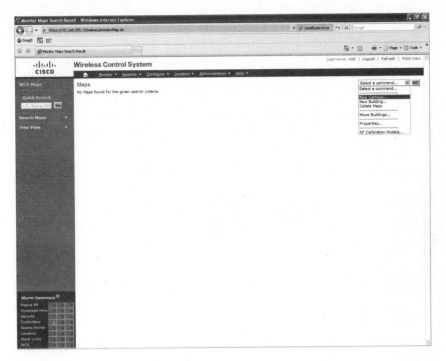

2. Select New Campus from the Action drop-down list box and click Go.

3. When the New Campus page opens, you can configure a campus name and the contact for the campus. Enter a descriptive name for the campus itself and the name of the contact person who can provide information about that campus.

4. Browse to an image of the campus and select the file to be included in the configuration. You can see my configuration in Figure 20.23. Click Next when you are finished.

To add an image to your configuration, you must select an existing plan or picture. The image file can be a JPEG, GIF, BMP, or PNG file. Site plans or satellite photos work well. I have found (at least for campus images) that online mapping services that offer satellite pictures of your area are good sources for appropriate campus images. The photo you see in Figure 20.24 is a satellite photo of my office complex. Be sure the Maintain Aspect Ratio check box on the New Campus page is checked. You want the image to reflect accurate dimensions for your campus. By default, campus maps are dimensioned using the English measure, feet. You can modify the WCS to accept metric measurements.

5. Dimension your campus map.

When you see the image you added to the campus map on the New Campus page, you can enter the dimensions of the area shown in the image. Use an accurate measurement of the overall area shown in the image. These distances will be used for showing scale and how far the RF in the network is going. You can see my map in Figure 20.24. When you are done, click OK to create the map.

FIGURE 20.23 Adding Map File

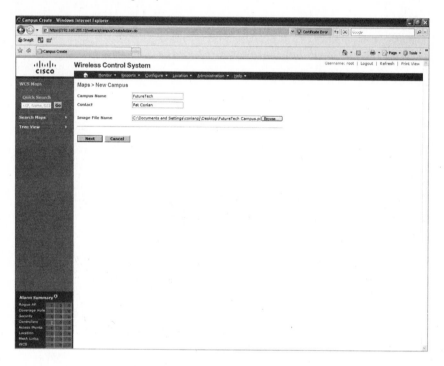

6. When the MAP page opens, select New Building from the Action drop-down list box and click Go.

7. Choose a building to be placed in the campus map. Enter the building name, building contact for your network, dimensions, and building characteristics.

Choosing a building creates a link for a new building map. The building map is typically a floor plan of the building you selected. You can then use the floor plan to more closely locate your APs.

Configuring buildings in this way creates a hierarchy with the maps. Once all of the maps are loaded, you can select a building map from the campus map and drill down for details about each of the buildings. You can see the building placement page in Figure 20.25.

FIGURE 20.24   Configuring Map

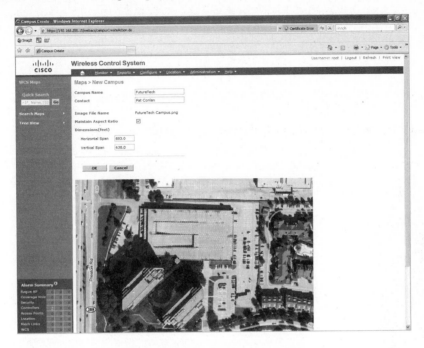

FIGURE 20.25   New Building Page

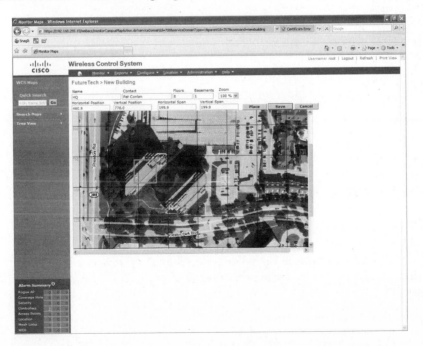

One last thing—clicking the house icon in the upper-left corner of any page brings you back to the WCS Home page. Click it now and you can see that you have added one controller to the interface. If that controller has any APs associated with it, you will also see those on the Home page. You can see my Home page in Figure 20.26.

FIGURE 20.26 Home Page

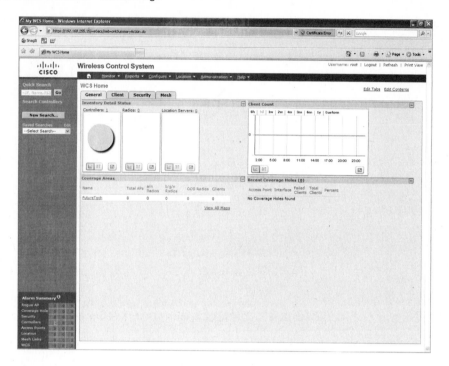

The Wireless LAN Controller

Now I want to take you through a couple of configuration options on a WLC. Log in to a WLC. I am going to take you through and show you the options for configuring QoS and security options on the WLC.

Configuring Options for QoS

1. On the opening screen, click the Wireless tab at the top of the screen.

2. On the Wireless page, click QoS in the task list (you'll find it at the bottom of the list on the left side of the screen).

3. Click the Profiles option under the QoS header. This brings you to the QoS Profiles page shown in Figure 20.27. Here you'll find a listing of the current QoS profiles.

FIGURE 20.27   QoS Profiles Page

4. To change or configure one of the profiles, click the hyperlink for that profile. For example, if you wanted to configure the platinum profile to add voice to your wireless network, click the platinum hyperlink. When you click the hyperlink, an Edit QoS Profile page opens. Figure 20.28 shows the Edit QoS Profile page for the platinum profile you created earlier.

FIGURE 20.28   Edit QoS Profile Page

5. On the Edit QoS Profile page you can configure/edit the:

    ▪ Per user bandwidth contracts

    ▪ Over the air QoS

    ▪ Wired QoS protocol

    Edit the amounts of bandwidth that you want to reserve for this type of traffic by adding values (in Kbps) to the data rate option boxes.

Select the wired CoS marking by selecting a protocol from the Wired QoS Protocol drop-down list box.

You can see the Edit Qos Profile screen with a wired QoS protocol selected in Figure 20.29.

FIGURE 20.29   Wired QoS Protocol

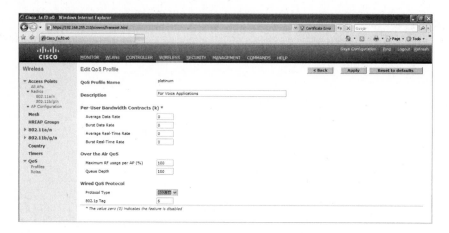

6.   Once you have the profile configured the way you want it, click the Apply button.

7.   Now, you will want to apply the QoS profile to a particular WLAN (SSID). For example, you might want to apply the configuration to the Voice SSID where all of your wireless phones are going to connect.

To select a WLAN to configure, click the WLANs tab on the horizontal menu bar.

8.   When the WLANs page opens, click the hyperlink for the WLAN you wish to configure with QoS. Figure 20.30 shows the hyperlink for my Test network.

FIGURE 20.30   WLANs Screen

9. When the WLANs Edit page opens, chose the QoS tab. You can see the QoS tab on the WLANs Edit page in Figure 20.31.

FIGURE 20.31   WLAN Edit QoS Tab

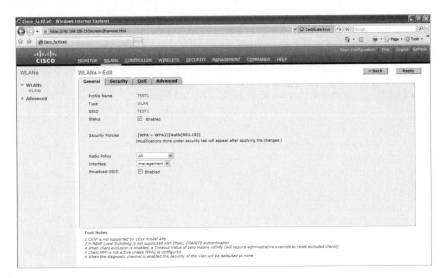

10. Select the appropriate profile from the Quality of Service (QoS) drop-down list box.

11. You can also edit the wireless multimedia setting from this tab. The WMM Policy is selected by default. If your network requires backward compatibility, you can enable 7920 AP CAC or 7920 Client CAC.

Configuring Options for Security

While you are on the WLAN Edit Page, I want to show you where you can configure the security options for a WLAN. Click the Security tab (you'll find it next to the QoS tab on the Edit page). This is where I am going to start off from.

Once on the Security tab, the Layer 2 (WPA+WPA2) sub tab opens by default. In Figure 20.32, you can see the other security options available through the WLC:

- 802.1x
- Static WEP
- Static WEP plus 802.1x
- CKIP

The appropriate option to choose here depends on the features supported by your clients and the level of security required for your network.

FIGURE 20.32 Layer 2 Security Tab

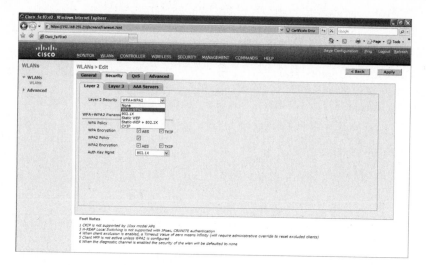

In Figure 20.33, you can see options available from the Auth Key Mgmt drop-down list box:

- 802.1x
- CCKM
- PSK
- 802.1x plus CCKM

Again, the appropriate option to choose here depends on the features supported by your clients and the level of security required for your network.

FIGURE 20.33 Auth Key Mgmt

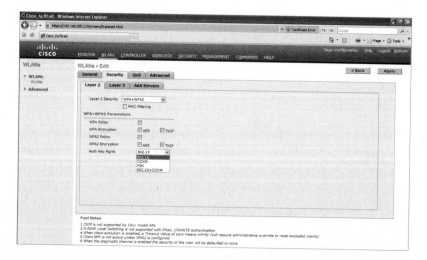

Now, let's take a look at the security options available on Layer 3 sub tab. Click the Web Policy check box so you can see all of the options shown in Figure 20.34.

The Layer 3 Security drop-down list box provides future options for IPsec VPN passthrough. Leave it set to None for now.

The main option here allows you to choose whether or not you want to use Web authentication. Web authentication is very useful for controlling guest access to the wireless network. You can choose any one of the following:

- Authentication

- Passthrough

- Conditional Web Redirect

You can also enable a preauthentication ACL or override the global config on this tab.

FIGURE 20.34   Layer 3 Security Tab

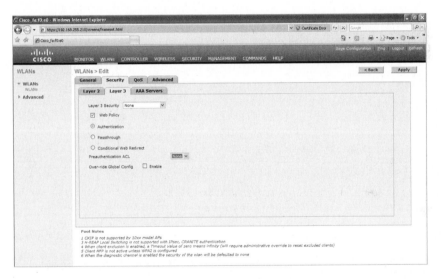

Summary

It is sad but true—you have to come to the end of the final chapter. Yes, you have made it. You should now be well armed, whether for day-to-day network administration or for your CCNP certification.

I hope that this chapter has whetted your appetite for wireless networks. I started off taking you through many of the wireless security standards that are available. I showed you the authentication and encryption options, as well as the different ways to implement them.

Next, you went through how QoS is implemented in the wireless world. The implementation is different in the wireless world, but it looks toward the same goal as QoS in the wired world. That goal is to prioritize traffic and, based on those priorities, give some better access or more bandwidth.

Then, I introduced you to the WCS and showed you how to set up and configure some of the features this exciting product has to offer; you can finally manage an entire wireless network from one central location. The maps that I showed you are a huge improvement over older management tools. Finally, I showed you how to configure QoS and security features on a WLAN. Those configurations have to be done from the WLC.

Review Questions

1. What is the first type of security that was implemented for wireless networks?
   A. WEP
   B. WPA
   C. WPA2
   D. 802.11i

2. What is the encryption algorithm that is used in WEP?
   A. AES
   B. DES
   C. 3DES
   D. RC4

3. What IEEE standard is used to provide EAP type authentication for wireless clients?
   A. 802.1a
   B. 802.1d
   C. 802.1x
   D. 802.1z

4. What encryption algorithm is used for WPA?
   A. AES
   B. DES
   C. 3DES
   D. TKIP

5. What is the Wi-Fi Alliance standard for implementing QoS?
   A. 802.11e
   B. WMDs
   C. WMM
   D. WWM

6. What is the IEEE standard for the QoS?
   A. 802.11e
   B. WMDs
   C. WMM
   D. WWM

7. How many access categories are there for WMM?

   A. 1

   B. 2

   C. 3

   D. 4

8. What operating system platforms can WCS be loaded on?

   A. Windows XP

   B. Windows Vista

   C. MAC OS X

   D. Windows Server 2003

9. What must you know in order to license your WCS software?

   A. Hostname

   B. IP address

   C. Number of APs

   D. Serial number of server

10. What kind of interface can you access the WCS with?

   A. CLI

   B. Program interface

   C. Browser

   D. From the WLC

Answers to Review Questions

1. A. WEP is the first standard that was set forth in the 802.11 standard.

2. D. The RC4 algorithm was used by WEP.

3. C. 802.1x provides EAP and certificate-based authentication for wireless clients.

4. D. TKIP is used for WPA, even though is it based on the RC4 algorithm.

5. C. Wireless multi-media (WMM) is the QoS standard set by the Wi-Fi Alliance.

6. A. 802.11e is the standard for QoS set by the IEEE.

7. D. Four categories (Platinum, Gold, Silver, and Bronze) are set by WMM.

8. D. Windows Server 2003 and Linux are the two OSs that WCS can be loaded on.

9. A. The hostname must be known when the license file is created by Cisco for your WCS instance.

10. C. WCS is entirely controlled via a web browser interface.

Appendix

About the Companion CD

IN THIS APPENDIX:

✓ What you'll find on the CD

✓ System requirements

✓ Using the CD

✓ Troubleshooting

What You'll Find on the CD

The following sections are arranged by category and summarize the software and other goodies you'll find on the CD. If you need help with installing the items provided on the CD, refer to the installation instructions in the "Using the CD" section of this appendix.

Some programs on the CD might fall into one of these categories:

Shareware programs are fully functional, free, trial versions of copyrighted programs. If you like particular programs, register with their authors for a nominal fee and receive licenses, enhanced versions, and technical support.

Freeware programs are free, copyrighted games, applications, and utilities. You can copy them to as many computers as you like—for free—but they offer no technical support.

GNU software is governed by its own license, which is included inside the folder of the GNU software. There are no restrictions on distribution of GNU software. See the GNU license at the root of the CD for more details.

Trial, *demo*, or *evaluation* versions of software are usually limited either by time or by functionality (such as not letting you save a project after you create it).

Sybex Test Engine

For Windows

The CD contains the Sybex test engine, which includes all of the assessment test and chapter review questions in electronic format, as well as two bonus exams located only on the CD.

PDF of the Book

For Windows

We have included an electronic version of the text in .pdf format. You can view the electronic version of the book with Adobe Reader.

Adobe Reader

For Windows

We've also included a copy of Adobe Reader so you can view PDF files that accompany the book's content. For more information on Adobe Reader or to check for a newer version, visit Adobe's website at www.adobe.com/products/reader/.

System Requirements

Make sure your computer meets the minimum system requirements shown in the following list. If your computer doesn't match up to most of these requirements, you may have problems using the software and files on the companion CD. For the latest and greatest information, please refer to the ReadMe file located at the root of the CD-ROM.

- A PC running Microsoft Windows 98, Windows 2000, Windows NT4 (with SP4 or later), Windows Me, Windows XP, or Windows Vista
- An Internet connection
- A CD-ROM drive

Using the CD

To install the items from the CD to your hard drive, follow these steps:

1. Insert the CD into your computer's CD-ROM drive. The license agreement appears.

Windows users: The interface won't launch if you have autorun disabled. In that case, click Start ➤ Run (for Windows Vista, Start ➤ All Programs ➤ Accessories ➤ Run). In the dialog box that appears, type D:\Start.exe. (Replace *D* with the proper letter if your CD drive uses a different letter. If you don't know the letter, see how your CD drive is listed under My Computer.) Click OK.

2. Read the license agreement, and then click the Accept button if you want to use the CD.

The CD interface appears. The interface allows you to access the content with just one or two clicks.

Troubleshooting

Wiley has attempted to provide programs that work on most computers with the minimum system requirements. Alas, your computer may differ, and some programs may not work properly for some reason.

The two likeliest problems are that you don't have enough memory (RAM) for the programs you want to use or you have other programs running that are affecting installation or running of a program. If you get an error message such as "Not enough memory" or

"Setup cannot continue," try one or more of the following suggestions and then try using the software again:

Turn off any antivirus software running on your computer. Installation programs sometimes mimic virus activity and may make your computer incorrectly believe that it's being infected by a virus.

Close all running programs. The more programs you have running, the less memory is available to other programs. Installation programs typically update files and programs; so if you keep other programs running, installation may not work properly.

Have your local computer store add more RAM to your computer. This is, admittedly, a drastic and somewhat expensive step. However, adding more memory can really help the speed of your computer and allow more programs to run at the same time.

Customer Care

If you have trouble with the book's companion CD-ROM, please call the Wiley Product Technical Support phone number at (800) 762-2974. Outside the United States, call +1(317) 572-3994. You can also contact Wiley Product Technical Support at http:// sybex.custhelp.com. John Wiley & Sons will provide technical support only for installation and other general quality-control items. For technical support on the applications themselves, consult the program's vendor or author.

To place additional orders or to request information about other Wiley products, please call (877) 762-2974.

Glossary

10BaseT   Part of the original IEEE 802.3 standard, 10BaseT is the Ethernet specification of 10 Mbps baseband that uses two pairs of twisted-pair, Category 3, 4, or 5 cabling—using one pair to send data and the other to receive. 10BaseT has a distance limit of about 100 meters per segment. *See also: Ethernet* and *IEEE 802.3.*

100BaseT   Based on the IEEE 802.3u standard, 100BaseT is the Fast Ethernet specification of 100 Mbps baseband that uses UTP wiring. 100BaseT sends link pulses (containing more information than those used in 10BaseT) over the network when no traffic is present. *See also: 10BaseT, Fast Ethernet,* and *IEEE 802.3.*

100BaseTX   Based on the IEEE 802.3u standard, 100BaseTX is the 100 Mbps baseband Fast Ethernet specification that uses two pairs of UTP or STP wiring. The first pair of wires receives data; the second pair sends data. To ensure correct signal timing, a 100BaseTX segment cannot be longer than 100 meters.

A

A&B bit signaling   Used in T1 transmission facilities and sometimes called "24th channel signaling." Each of the 24 T1 subchannels in this procedure uses one bit of every sixth frame to send supervisory signaling information.

AAA   Authentication, authorization, and accounting: A system developed by Cisco to provide network security. *See also: authentication, authorization,* and *accounting.*

AAL   ATM Adaptation Layer: A service-dependent sublayer of the Data Link layer, which accepts data from other applications and brings it to the ATM layer in 48-byte ATM payload segments. CS and SAR are the two sublayers that form AALs. Currently, the four types of AAL recommended by the ITU-T are AAL1, AAL2, AAL3/4, and AAL5. AALs are differentiated by the source-destination timing they use, whether they are CBR or VBR, and whether they are used for connection-oriented or connectionless mode data transmission. *See also: AAL1, AAL2, AAL3/4, AAL5, ATM,* and *ATM layer.*

AAL1   ATM Adaptation Layer 1: One of four AALs recommended by the ITU-T, it is used for connection-oriented, time-sensitive services that need constant bit rates, such as isochronous traffic and uncompressed video. *See also: AAL.*

AAL2   ATM Adaptation Layer 2: One of four AALs recommended by the ITU-T, it is used for connection-oriented services that support a variable bit rate, such as compressed voice traffic. *See also: AAL.*

AAL3/4   ATM Adaptation Layer 3/4: One of four AALs (a product of two initially distinct layers) recommended by the ITU-T, supporting both connectionless and connection-oriented links. Its primary use is in sending SMDS packets over ATM networks. *See also: AAL.*

AAL5   ATM Adaptation Layer 5: One of four AALs recommended by the ITU-T, it is used to support connection-oriented VBR services primarily to transfer classical IP over ATM and LANE traffic. This least complex of the AAL recommendations uses SEAL, offering lower bandwidth costs and simpler processing requirements but also providing reduced bandwidth and error-recovery capacities. *See also: AAL*.

AARP   AppleTalk Address Resolution Protocol: The protocol in an AppleTalk stack that maps data link addresses to network addresses.

AARP probe packets   Packets sent by the AARP to determine whether a given node ID is being used by another node in a nonextended AppleTalk network. If the node ID is not in use, the sending node appropriates that node's ID. If the node ID is in use, the sending node will select a different ID and then send out more AARP probe packets. *See also: AARP*.

ABM   Asynchronous Balanced Mode: When two stations can initiate a transmission, ABM is an HDLC (or one of its derived protocols) communication technology that supports peer-oriented, point-to-point communications between both stations.

ABR   Area Border Router: An OSPF router that is located on the border of one or more OSPF areas. ABRs are used to connect OSPF areas to the OSPF backbone area.

access layer   One of the layers in Cisco's three-layer hierarchical model. The access layer provides users with access to the internetwork.

access link   A link used with switches that is part of only one virtual LAN (VLAN). Trunk links carry information from multiple VLANs.

access control list   A set of test conditions kept by routers that determines "interesting traffic" to and from the router for various services on the network.

access method   The manner in which network devices approach gaining access to the network itself.

access rate   Defines the bandwidth rate of the circuit. For example, the access rate of a T1 circuit is 1.544 Mbps. In frame relay and other technologies, there may be a fractional T1 connection—256 Kbps, for example—however, the access rate and clock rate are still 1.544 Mbps.

access server   Also known as a "network access server," it is a communications process connecting asynchronous devices to a LAN or WAN through network and terminal emulation software, providing synchronous or asynchronous routing of supported protocols.

accounting   One of the three components in AAA. Accounting provides auditing and logging functionalities to the security model.

acknowledgment   Verification sent from one network device to another signifying that an event has occurred. May be abbreviated as ACK. *Contrast with: NAK*.

ACR   Allowed cell rate: A designation defined by the ATM Forum for managing ATM traffic. Dynamically controlled using congestion control measures, the ACR varies between the minimum cell rate (MCR) and the peak cell rate (PCR). *See also: MCR and PCR*.

active monitor   The mechanism used to manage a token ring. The network node with the highest MAC address on the ring becomes the active monitor and is responsible for management tasks such as preventing loops and ensuring that tokens are not lost.

active state   In regard to an EIGRP routing table, a route will be in active state when a router is undergoing a route convergence.

address learning   Used with transparent bridges to learn the hardware addresses of all devices on a network. The switch then filters the network with the known hardware (MAC) addresses.

address mapping   By translating network addresses from one format to another, this methodology permits different protocols to operate interchangeably.

address mask   A bit combination descriptor identifying which portion of an address refers to the network or subnet and which part refers to the host. Sometimes simply called the mask. *See also: subnet mask.*

address resolution   The process used for resolving differences between computer addressing schemes. Address resolution typically defines a method for tracing Network layer (Layer 3) addresses to Data Link layer (Layer 2) addresses. *See also: address mapping.*

adjacency   The relationship made to exchange routing information between defined neighboring routers and end nodes using a common media segment.

administrative distance (AD)   A number between 0 and 255 that expresses the level of trustworthiness of a routing information source. The lower the number, the higher the integrity rating.

administrative weight   A value designated by a network administrator to rate the preference given to a network link. It is one of four link metrics exchanged by PTSPs to test ATM network resource availability.

ADSU   ATM Data Service Unit: The terminal adapter used to connect to an ATM network through an HSSI-compatible mechanism. *See also: DSU.*

advertising   The process whereby routing or service updates are transmitted at given intervals, allowing other routers on the network to maintain a record of viable routes.

AEP   AppleTalk Echo Protocol: A test for connectivity between two AppleTalk nodes where one node sends a packet to another and receives an echo, or copy, in response.

AFI   Authority and Format Identifier: The part of an NSAP ATM address that delineates the type and format of the IDI section of an ATM address.

AFP   AppleTalk Filing Protocol: A presentation layer protocol, supporting AppleShare and Mac OS File Sharing, that permits users to share files and applications on a server.

AIP   ATM Interface Processor: Supporting AAL3/4 and AAL5, this interface for Cisco 7000 series routers minimizes performance bottlenecks at the UNI. *See also: AAL3/4 and AAL5.*

algorithm   A set of rules or processes used to solve a problem. In networking, algorithms are typically used for finding the best route for traffic from a source to its destination.

alignment error   An error occurring in Ethernet networks, in which a received frame has extra bits—that is, a number not divisible by eight. Alignment errors are generally the result of frame damage caused by collisions.

all-routes explorer packet   An explorer packet that can move across an entire SRB network, tracing all possible paths to a given destination. Also known as an all-rings explorer packet. *See also: explorer packet, local explorer packet,* and *spanning explorer packet.*

AM   Amplitude modulation: A modulation method that represents information by varying the amplitude of the carrier signal. *See also: modulation.*

AMI   Alternate Mark Inversion: A line-code type on T1 and E1 circuits that shows zeros as 01 during each bit cell and ones as 11 or 00, alternately, during each bit cell. The sending device must maintain ones density in AMI but not independently of the data stream. Also known as binary-coded, alternate mark inversion. *Contrast with: B8ZS. See also: ones density.*

amplitude   An analog or digital waveform's highest value.

analog transmission   Signal messaging whereby information is represented by various combinations of signal amplitude, frequency, and phase.

ANSI   American National Standards Institute: The organization of corporate, government, and volunteer members that coordinates standards-related activities, approves U.S. national standards, and develops U.S. positions in international standards organizations. ANSI assists in the creation of international and U.S. standards in disciplines such as communications, networking, and a variety of technical fields. It publishes over 13,000 standards for engineered products and technologies ranging from screw threads to networking protocols. ANSI is a member of the International Electrotechnical Commission (IEC) and International Organization for Standardization (ISO).

anycast   An ATM address that can be shared by more than one end system, allowing requests to be routed to a node that provides a particular service.

AppleTalk   Currently in two versions, the group of communication protocols designed by Apple Computer for use in Macintosh environments. The earlier Phase 1 protocols support one physical network with only one network number that resides in one zone. The later Phase 2 protocols support more than one logical network on a single physical network, allowing networks to exist in more than one zone. *See also: zone.*

Application layer   Layer 7 of the OSI reference network model, supplying services to application procedures (such as electronic mail and file transfer) that are outside the OSI model. This layer chooses and determines the availability of communicating partners along with the resources necessary to make the connection, coordinates partnering applications, and forms a consensus on procedures for controlling data integrity and error recovery. *See also: Data Link layer, Network layer, Physical layer, Presentation layer, Session layer,* and *Transport layer.*

ARA   AppleTalk Remote Access: A protocol for Macintosh users establishing their access to resources and data from a remote AppleTalk location.

area   A logical, rather than physical, set of segments (based on CLNS, DECnet, or OSPF) along with their attached devices. Areas are commonly connected to others using routers to create a single autonomous system. *See also: autonomous system.*

ARM   Asynchronous Response Mode: An HDLC communication mode using one primary station and at least one additional station, in which transmission can be initiated from either the primary or one of the secondary units.

ARP   Address Resolution Protocol: Defined in RFC 826, the protocol that traces IP addresses to MAC addresses. *See also: RARP.*

AS   autonomous system: A group of networks under mutual administration that share the same routing methodology. Autonomous systems are subdivided by areas and must be assigned an individual 16-bit number by the IANA. *See also: area.*

AS path prepending   The use of route maps in BGP to lengthen the autonomous system path by adding false ASNs.

ASBR   Autonomous System Boundary Router: An Area Border Router placed between an OSPF autonomous system and a non-OSPF network that operates both OSPF and an additional routing protocol, such as RIP. ASBRs must be located in a non-stub OSPF area. *See also: ABR, non-stub area,* and *OSPF.*

ASCII   American Standard Code for Information Interchange: An 8-bit code for representing characters, consisting of 7 data bits plus 1 parity bit.

ASICs   Application-specific integrated circuits: Used in Layer 2 switches to make filtering decisions. The ASIC looks in the filter table of MAC addresses and determines which port the destination hardware address of a received hardware address is destined for. The frame will be allowed to traverse only that one segment. If the hardware address is unknown, the frame is forwarded out all ports.

ASN.1   Abstract Syntax Notation One: An OSI language used to describe types of data that are independent of computer structures and depicting methods. Described by ISO International Standard 8824.

ASP   AppleTalk Session Protocol: A protocol employing ATP to establish, maintain, and tear down sessions as well as sequence requests. *See also: ATP.*

AST   Automatic Spanning Tree: A function that supplies one path for spanning explorer frames traveling from one node in the network to another, supporting the automatic resolution of spanning trees in SRB networks. AST is based on the IEEE 802.1d standard. *See also: IEEE 802.1* and *SRB.*

asynchronous transmission   Digital signals sent without precise timing, usually with different frequencies and phase relationships. Asynchronous transmissions generally enclose individual characters in control bits (called start and stop bits) that show the beginning and end of each character. *Contrast with: isochronous transmission* and *synchronous transmission.*

ATCP   AppleTalk Control Program: The protocol for establishing and configuring AppleTalk over PPP, defined in RFC 1378. *See also: PPP.*

ATDM   Asynchronous Time-Division Multiplexing: A technique for sending information, it differs from normal TDM in that the time slots are assigned when necessary rather than pre-assigned to certain transmitters. *Contrast with: FDM, statistical multiplexing,* and *TDM.*

ATG   Address Translation Gateway: The mechanism within Cisco DECnet routing software that enables routers to route multiple, independent DECnet networks and to establish a user-designated address translation for chosen nodes between networks.

ATM   Asynchronous Transfer Mode: The international standard, identified by fixed-length 53-byte cells, for transmitting cells in multiple service systems, such as voice, video, or data. Transit delays are reduced because the fixed-length cells permit processing to occur in the hardware. ATM is designed to maximize the benefits of high-speed transmission media, such as SONET, E3, and T3.

ATM ARP server   A device that supplies logical subnets running classical IP over ATM with address-resolution services.

ATM endpoint   The initiating or terminating connection in an ATM network. ATM endpoints include servers, workstations, ATM-to-LAN switches, and ATM routers.

ATM Forum   The international organization founded jointly by Northern Telecom, Sprint, Cisco Systems, and NET/ADAPTIVE in 1991 to develop and promote standards-based implementation agreements for ATM technology. The ATM Forum broadens official standards developed by ANSI and ITU-T and creates implementation agreements before official standards are published.

ATM layer   A sublayer of the Data Link layer in an ATM network that is service independent. To create standard 53-byte ATM cells, the ATM layer receives 48-byte segments from the AAL and attaches a 5-byte header to each. These cells are then sent to the physical layer for transmission across the physical medium. *See also: AAL.*

ATMM   ATM Management: A procedure that runs on ATM switches, managing rate enforcement and VCI translation. *See also: ATM.*

ATM user-user connection   A connection made by the ATM layer to supply communication between at least two ATM service users, such as ATMM processes. These communications can be uni- or bidirectional, using one or two VCs, respectively. *See also: ATM layer* and *ATMM.*

ATP   AppleTalk Transaction Protocol: A transport-level protocol that enables reliable transactions between two sockets; one requests the other to perform a given task and to report the results. ATP fastens the request and response together, assuring a loss-free exchange of request-response pairs.

attenuation   In communication, weakening or loss of signal energy, typically caused by distance.

AURP   AppleTalk Update-based Routing Protocol: A technique for encapsulating AppleTalk traffic in the header of a foreign protocol that allows the connection of at least two noncontiguous AppleTalk internetworks through a foreign network (such as TCP/IP) to create an AppleTalk WAN. The connection made is called an AURP tunnel. By exchanging routing information between exterior routers, the AURP maintains routing tables for the complete AppleTalk WAN. *See also: AURP tunnel.*

AURP tunnel   A connection made in an AURP WAN that acts as a single, virtual link between AppleTalk internetworks separated physically by a foreign network such as a TCP/IP network. *See also: AURP.*

authentication   The first component in the AAA model. Users are typically authenticated via a username and password, which are used to uniquely identify them.

authority zone   A portion of the domain-name tree associated with DNS for which one name server is the authority. *See also: DNS.*

authorization   The act of permitting access to a resource based on authentication information in the AAA model.

Autoconfiguration   The stateless means of an IPv6 host to get a link local address from its local router. Autoconfiguration uses router advertisements and router solicitation messages for the process.

auto-detect mechanism   Used in Ethernet switch, hub, and interface cards to determine the duplex and speed that can be used.

auto duplex   A setting on Layer 1 and Layer 2 devices that sets the duplex of a switch or hub port automatically.

automatic call reconnect   A function that enables automatic call rerouting away from a failed trunk line.

autonomous confederation   A collection of self-governed systems that depend more on their own network accessibility and routing information than on information received from other systems or groups.

autonomous switching   The ability of Cisco routers to process packets more quickly by using the CiscoBus to switch packets independently of the system processor.

autonomous system   *See: AS.*

autoreconfiguration   A procedure executed by nodes within the failure domain of a token ring wherein nodes automatically perform diagnostics, trying to reconfigure the network around failed areas.

auxiliary port   The console port on the back of Cisco routers that allows you to connect a modem and dial the router and make console configuration settings.

B

B8ZS   Binary 8-Zero Substitution: A line-code type, interpreted at the remote end of the connection, that uses a special code substitution whenever eight consecutive zeros are transmitted over the link on T1 and E1 circuits. This technique assures ones density independent of the data stream. Also known as bipolar 8-zero substitution. *Contrast with: AMI. See also: ones density.*

backbone   The basic portion of the network that provides the primary path for traffic sent to and initiated from other networks.

back end   A node or software program supplying services to a front end. *See also: server.*

bandwidth   The gap between the highest and lowest frequencies employed by network signals. More commonly, it refers to the rated throughput capacity of a network protocol or medium.

bandwidth on demand (BoD)   This function allows an additional B channel to be used to increase the amount of bandwidth available for a particular connection.

baseband   A feature of a network technology that uses only one carrier frequency. Ethernet is an example. Also named "narrowband." *Compare with: broadband.*

baseline   Baseline information includes historical data about the network and routine utilization information. This information can be used to determine whether there were recent changes made to the network that may contribute to the problem at hand.

Basic Management Setup   Used with Cisco routers when in setup mode. Only provides enough management and configuration to get the router working so someone can telnet into the router and configure it.

baud   Synonymous with bits per second (bps), if each signal element represents 1 bit. It is a unit of signaling speed equivalent to the number of separate signal elements transmitted per second.

B channel   Bearer channel: A full-duplex, 64 Kbps channel in ISDN that transmits user data. *Compare with: D channel, E channel, and H channel.*

BDR   Backup designated router: This is used in an OSPF network to back up the designated router in case of failure.

beacon   An FDDI frame or token ring frame that points to a serious problem with the ring, such as a broken cable. The beacon frame carries the address of the station thought to be down. *See also: failure domain.*

BECN   Backward Explicit Congestion Notification: BECN is the bit set by a frame relay network in frames moving away from frames headed into a congested path. A DTE that receives frames with the BECN may ask higher-level protocols to take necessary flow control measures. *Compare with: FECN.*

BGP4   BGP version 4: Version 4 of the interdomain routing protocol most commonly used on the Internet. BGP4 supports CIDR and uses route-counting mechanisms to decrease the size of routing tables. *See also: CIDR.*

BGP Identifier   This field contains a value that identifies the BGP speaker. This is a random value chosen by the BGP router when sending an OPEN message.

BGP neighbors   Two routers running BGP that begin a communication process to exchange dynamic routing information; they use a TCP port at Layer 4 of the OSI reference model. Specifically, TCP port 179 is used. Also known as "BGP peers."

BGP peers   *See: BGP neighbors.*

BGP speaker   A router that advertises its prefixes or routes.

bidirectional shared tree   A method of shared tree multicast forwarding. This method allows group members to receive data from the source or the RP, whichever is closer. *See also: RP (rendezvous point).*

binary   A two-character numbering method that uses ones and zeros. The binary numbering system underlies all digital representation of information.

binding   Configuring a Network layer protocol to use a certain frame type on a LAN.

BIP   Bit Interleaved Parity: A method used in ATM to monitor errors on a link, sending a check bit or word in the link overhead for the previous block or frame. This allows bit errors in transmissions to be found and delivered as maintenance information.

BISDN   Broadband ISDN: ITU-T standards created to manage high-bandwidth technologies such as video. BISDN presently employs ATM technology along SONET-based transmission circuits, supplying data rates typically between 155 Mbps and 622 Mbps and now even into the gigabyte range (if you have the big bucks). *See also: BRI, ISDN, and PRI.*

bit   One binary digit; either a 1 or a 0. Eight bits make a byte.

bit-oriented protocol   Regardless of frame content, the class of Data Link layer communication protocols that transmits frames. Bit-oriented protocols, as compared with byte-oriented, supply more efficient and trustworthy full-duplex operation. *Compare with: byte-oriented protocol.*

block size   Number of hosts that can be used in a subnet. Block sizes typically can be used in increments of 4, 8, 16, 32, 64, and 128.

Boot ROM   Used in routers to put the router into bootstrap mode. Bootstrap mode then boots the device with an operating system. The ROM can also hold a small Cisco IOS.

boot sequence   Defines how a router boots. The configuration register tells the router where to boot the IOS from as well as how to load the configuration.

bootstrap protocol   A protocol used to dynamically assign IP addresses and gateways to requesting clients.

border gateway protocol BGP   A router that facilitates communication with routers in different autonomous systems.

border peer   The device in charge of a peer group; it exists at the edge of a hierarchical design. When any member of the peer group wants to locate a resource, it sends a single explorer to the border peer. The border peer then forwards this request on behalf of the requesting router, thus eliminating duplicate traffic.

border router   Typically defined within open shortest path first (OSPF) as a router that connected an area to the backbone area. However, a border router can be a router that connects a company to the Internet as well. *See also: OSPF.*

BPDU   Bridge Protocol Data Unit: A Spanning Tree Protocol initializing packet that is sent at definable intervals for the purpose of exchanging information among bridges in networks.

BRI   Basic Rate Interface: The ISDN interface that facilitates circuit-switched communication between video, data, and voice; it is made up of two B channels (64 Kbps each) and one D channel (16 Kbps). *Compare with: PRI. See also: BISDN.*

bridge   A device for connecting two segments of a network and transmitting packets between them. Both segments must use identical protocols to communicate. Bridges function at the Data Link layer, Layer 2 of the OSI reference model. The purpose of a bridge is to filter, send, or flood any incoming frame, based on the MAC address of that particular frame.

bridge group   Used in the router configuration of bridging, bridge groups are defined by a unique number. Network traffic is bridged between all interfaces that are members of the same bridge group.

bridge identifier   Used to elect the root bridge in a Layer 2 switched internetwork. The bridge ID is a combination of the bridge priority and base MAC address.

bridge priority   Sets the STP priority of the bridge. All bridge priorities are set to 32768 by default.

bridging loop   Loops occur in a bridged network if more than one link to a network exists and the STP protocol is not turned on.

broadband   A transmission methodology for multiplexing several independent signals onto one cable. In telecommunications, broadband is classified as any channel with bandwidth greater than 4 kHz (typical voice grade). In LAN terminology, it is classified as a coaxial cable on which analog signaling is employed. Also known as "wideband."

broadcast   A data frame or packet that is transmitted to every node on the local network segment (as defined by the broadcast domain). Broadcasts are known by their broadcast address, which is a destination network and host address with all the bits turned on. Also called "local broadcast." *Compare with: directed broadcast.*

broadcast address   Used in both logical addressing and hardware addressing. In logical addressing, the host addresses will be all ones. With hardware addressing, the hardware address will be all ones in binary (all Fs in hex).

broadcast domain   A group of devices receiving broadcast frames initiating from any device within the group. Because routers do not forward broadcast frames, broadcast domains are not forwarded from one broadcast to another.

broadcast (multi-access) networks   Broadcast (multi-access) networks such as Ethernet allow multiple devices to connect to (or access) the same network, as well as provide a broadcast ability in which a single packet is delivered to all nodes on the network.

broadcast storm   An undesired event on the network caused by the simultaneous transmission of any number of broadcasts across the network segment. Such an occurrence can overwhelm network bandwidth, resulting in timeouts.

buffer   A storage area dedicated to handling data while in transit. Buffers are used to receive/ store sporadic deliveries of data bursts, usually received from faster devices, compensating for the variations in processing speed. Incoming information is stored until everything is received prior to sending data on. Also known as an "information buffer."

bursting   Some technologies, including ATM and frame relay, are considered burstable. This means that user data can exceed the bandwidth normally reserved for the connection; however, it cannot exceed the port speed. An example of this would be a 128 Kbps frame relay CIR on a T1—depending on the vendor, it may be possible to send more than 128 Kbps for a short time.

bus   Any common physical path, typically wires or copper, through which a digital signal can be used to send data from one part of a computer to another.

BUS   Broadcast and unknown servers: In LAN emulation, the hardware or software responsible for resolving all broadcasts and packets with unknown (unregistered) addresses into the point-to-point virtual circuits required by ATM. *See also: LANE, LEC, LECS, and LES.*

bus topology   A linear LAN architecture in which transmissions from various stations on the network are reproduced over the length of the medium and are accepted by all other stations. *Compare with: ring topology* and *star topology.*

BX.25   AT&T's use of X.25. *See also: X.25.*

bypass mode   An FDDI and token ring network operation that deletes an interface.

bypass relay   A device that enables a particular interface in the token ring to be closed down and effectively taken off the ring.

byte   Eight bits. *See also: octet.*

byte-oriented protocol   Any type of data link communication protocol that, in order to mark the boundaries of frames, uses a specific character from the user character set. These protocols have generally been superseded by bit-oriented protocols. *Compare with: bit-oriented protocol.*

C

cable range In an extended AppleTalk network, the range of numbers allotted for use by existing nodes on the network. The value of the cable range can be anywhere from a single network number to a sequence of several touching network numbers. Node addresses are determined by their cable range value.

CAC Connection Admission Control: The sequence of actions executed by every ATM switch while connection setup is performed in order to determine if a request for connection is violating the guarantees of QoS for established connections. Also, CAC is used to route a connection request through an ATM network.

call admission control A device for managing traffic in ATM networks, determining the possibility of a path containing adequate bandwidth for a requested VCC.

call establishment Used to reference an ISDN call setup scheme when the call is working.

call priority In circuit-switched systems, the defining priority given to each originating port; it specifies in which order calls will be reconnected. Additionally, call priority identifies which calls are allowed during a bandwidth reservation.

call setup Handshaking scheme that defines how a source and destination device will establish a call to each other.

call setup time The length of time necessary to effect a switched call between DTE devices.

CBR Constant bit rate: An ATM Forum QoS class created for use in ATM networks. CBR is used for connections that rely on precision clocking to guarantee trustworthy delivery. *Compare with: ABR* and *VBR*.

CD Carrier detect: A signal indicating that an interface is active or that a connection generated by a modem has been established.

CDP Cisco Discovery Protocol: Cisco-proprietary protocol that is used to tell a neighbor Cisco device about the type of hardware, software version, and active interfaces the Cisco device is using. It uses a SNAP frame between devices and is not routable.

CDP holdtime The amount of time a router will hold Cisco Discovery Protocol information received from a neighbor router before discarding it if the information is not updated by the neighbor. This timer is set to 180 seconds by default.

CDP timer The amount of time between Cisco Discovery Protocol advertisements transmitted out of all router interfaces, by default. The CDP timer is 90 seconds by default.

CDVT Cell Delay Variation Tolerance: A QoS parameter for traffic management in ATM networks specified when a connection is established. The allowable fluctuation levels for data samples taken by the PCR in CBR transmissions are determined by the CDVT. *See also: CBR* and *PCR*.

cell   In ATM networking, the basic unit of data for switching and multiplexing. Cells have a defined length of 53 bytes, including a 5-byte header that identifies the cell's data stream and 48 bytes of payload. *See also: cell relay.*

cell payload scrambling   The method by which an ATM switch maintains framing on some medium-speed edge and trunk interfaces (T3 or E3 circuits). Cell payload scrambling rearranges the data portion of a cell to maintain the line synchronization with certain common bit patterns.

cell relay   A technology that uses small packets of fixed size, known as cells. Their fixed length enables cells to be processed and switched in hardware at high speeds, making this technology the foundation for ATM and other high-speed network protocols. *See also: cell.*

Centrex   A local exchange carrier service providing local switching that resembles that of an on-site PBX. Centrex has no on-site switching capability. Therefore, all customer connections return to the central office (CO). *See also: CO.*

CER   Cell error ratio: In ATM, the ratio of transmitted cells having errors to the total number of cells transmitted within a certain span of time.

CGMP   Cisco Group Management Protocol: A proprietary protocol developed by Cisco. The router uses CGMP to send multicast membership commands to Catalyst switches.

channelized E1   Operating at 2.048Mpbs, an access link that is sectioned into 29 B channels and one D channel, supporting DDR, frame relay, and X.25. *Compare with: channelized T1.*

channelized T1   Operating at 1.544 Mbps, an access link that is sectioned into 23 B channels and one D channel of 64 Kbps each, where individual channels or groups of channels connect to various destinations, supporting DDR, frame relay, and X.25. *Compare with: channelized E1.*

CHAP   Challenge Handshake Authentication Protocol: Supported on lines using PPP encapsulation, it is a security feature that identifies the remote end, helping keep out unauthorized users. After CHAP is performed, the router or access server determines whether a given user is permitted access. It is a newer, more secure protocol than PAP. *Compare with: PAP.*

checksum   A test for ensuring the integrity of sent data. It is a number calculated from a series of values taken through a sequence of mathematical functions, typically placed at the end of the data from which it is calculated, and then recalculated at the receiving end for verification. *Compare with: CRC.*

choke packet   When congestion exists, it is a packet sent to inform a transmitter that it should decrease its sending rate.

CIDR   Classless Inter-Domain Routing: It allows a group of IP networks to appear to other networks as a unified, larger entity. In CIDR, IP addresses and their subnet masks are written as four dotted octets, followed by a forward slash and the number of masking bits (a form of subnet notation shorthand). *See also: BGP4.*

CIP   Channel Interface Processor: A channel attachment interface for use in Cisco 7000 series routers that connects a host mainframe to a control unit. This device eliminates the need for an FBP to attach channels.

CIR   Committed information rate: Averaged over a minimum span of time and measured in bps, a frame relay network's agreed-on minimum rate of transferring information.

circuit switching   Used with dial-up networks such as PPP and ISDN. Passes data, but needs to set up the connection first—just like making a phone call.

Cisco FRAD   Cisco Frame Relay Access Device: A Cisco product that supports Cisco IPS Frame Relay SNA services, connecting SDLC devices to frame relay without requiring an existing LAN. May be upgraded to a fully functioning multiprotocol router. Can activate conversion from SDLC to Ethernet and token ring, but does not support attached LANs. *See also: FRAD.*

CiscoFusion   Cisco's name for the internetworking architecture under which its Cisco IOS operates. It is designed to "fuse" together the capabilities of its disparate collection of acquired routers and switches.

Cisco IOS   Cisco Internet Operating System software. The kernel of the Cisco line of routers and switches that supplies shared functionality, scalability, and security for all products under its CiscoFusion architecture. *See also: CiscoFusion.*

CiscoView   GUI-based management software for Cisco networking devices, enabling dynamic status, statistics, and comprehensive configuration information. Displays a physical view of the Cisco device chassis and provides device-monitoring functions and fundamental troubleshooting capabilities. May be integrated with a number of SNMP-based network management platforms.

Class A network   Part of the Internet protocol hierarchical addressing scheme. Class A networks have only 8 bits for defining networks and 24 bits for defining hosts and subnets on each network.

Class B network   Part of the Internet protocol hierarchical addressing scheme. Class B networks have 16 bits for defining networks and 16 bits for defining hosts and subnets on each network.

Class C network   Part of the Internet protocol hierarchical addressing scheme. Class C networks have 24 bits for defining networks and only 8 bits for defining hosts and subnets on each network.

classful routing   Routing protocols that do not send subnet mask information when a route update is sent out.

classical IP over ATM   Defined in RFC 1577, the specification for running IP over ATM that maximizes ATM features. Also known as "CIA."

classless routing   Routing that sends subnet mask information in the routing updates. Classless routing allows variable-length subnet masking (VLSM) and supernetting. Routing protocols that support classless routing are RIP version 2, EIGRP, and OSPF.

CLI   Command line interface: Allows you to configure Cisco routers and switches with maximum flexibility.

CLP   Cell Loss Priority: The area in the ATM cell header that determines the likelihood of a cell being dropped during network congestion. Cells with CLP = 0 are considered insured traffic and are not apt to be dropped. Cells with CLP = 1 are considered best-effort traffic that may be dropped during congested episodes, delivering more resources to handle insured traffic.

CLR   Cell Loss Ratio: The ratio of discarded cells to successfully delivered cells in ATM. CLR can be designated a QoS parameter when establishing a connection.

CO   Central office: The local telephone company office where all loops in a certain area connect and where circuit switching of subscriber lines occurs.

collapsed backbone   A nondistributed backbone where all network segments are connected to each other through an internetworking device. A collapsed backbone can be a virtual network segment at work in a device such as a router, hub, or switch.

collision   The effect of two nodes sending transmissions simultaneously in Ethernet. When they meet on the physical media, the frames from each node collide and are damaged. *See also: collision domain.*

collision domain   The network area in Ethernet over which frames that have collided will be detected. Collisions are propagated by hubs and repeaters, but not by LAN switches, routers, or bridges. *See also: collision.*

composite metric   Used with routing protocols, such as IGRP and EIGRP, that use more than one metric to find the best path to a remote network. IGRP and EIGRP both use bandwidth and delay of the line by default. However, maximum transmission unit (MTU), load, and reliability of a link can be used as well.

compression   A technique to send more data across a link than would be normally permitted by representing repetitious strings of data with a single marker.

configuration register   A 16-bit configurable value stored in hardware or software that determines how Cisco routers function during initialization. In hardware, the bit position is set using a jumper. In software, it is set by specifying specific bit patterns used to set startup options, configured using a hexadecimal value with configuration commands.

congestion   Traffic that exceeds the network's ability to handle it.

congestion avoidance   To minimize delays, the method a network uses to control traffic entering the system. Lower-priority traffic is discarded at the edge of the network when indicators signal it cannot be delivered, thus using resources efficiently.

congestion collapse   The situation that results from the retransmission of packets in ATM networks where little or no traffic successfully arrives at destination points. It usually happens in networks made of switches with ineffective or inadequate buffering capabilities combined with poor packet discard or ABR congestion feedback mechanisms.

connection ID   Identifications given to each Telnet session into a router. The show sessions command will give you the connections a local router will have to a remote router. The show users command will show the connection IDs of users telnetted into your local router.

Connectionless   Data transfer that occurs without the creation of a virtual circuit. It has low overhead, uses best-effort delivery, and is not reliable. *Contrast with: connection-oriented. See also: virtual circuit.*

Connectionless Network Service (CLNS)   See *connectionless.*

connection oriented   Data transfer method that sets up a virtual circuit before any data is transferred. Uses acknowledgments and flow control for reliable data transfer. *Contrast with: connectionless. See also: virtual circuit.*

console port   Typically an RJ-45 (8-pin modular) port on a Cisco router and switch that allows command line interface capability.

control direct VCC   One of two control connections defined by Phase I LAN emulation; a bidirectional virtual control connection (VCC) established in ATM by an LEC to an LES. *See also: control distribute VCC.*

control distribute VCC   One of two control connections defined by Phase 1 LAN emulation; a unidirectional virtual control connection (VCC) set up in ATM from an LES to an LEC. Usually, the VCC is a point-to-multipoint connection. *See also: control direct VCC.*

convergence   The process required for all routers in an internetwork to update their routing tables and create a consistent view of the network using the best possible paths. No user data is passed during an STP convergence time.

core layer   Top layer in the Cisco three-layer hierarchical model, which helps you design, build, and maintain Cisco hierarchical networks. The core layer passes packets quickly to distribution layer devices only. No packet filtering should take place at this layer.

cost   Also known as path cost, an arbitrary value, based on hop count, bandwidth, or another calculation, that is typically assigned by a network administrator and used by the routing protocol to compare different routes through an internetwork. Routing protocols use cost values to select the best path to a certain destination: the lowest cost identifies the best path. Also known as "path cost." *See also: routing metric.*

count to infinity   A problem occurring in routing algorithms that are slow to converge where routers keep increasing the hop count to particular networks. To avoid this problem, various solutions have been implemented into each of the different routing protocols. Some of those solutions include defining a maximum hop count (defining infinity), route poising, poison reverse, and split horizon.

CPCS   Common Part Convergence Sublayer: One of two AAL sublayers that is service dependent, it is further segmented into the CS and SAR sublayers. The CPCS prepares data for transmission across the ATM network; it creates the 48-byte payload cells that are sent to the ATM layer. *See also: AAL* and *ATM layer.*

CPE   Customer premises equipment: Items such as telephones, modems, and terminals installed at customer locations and connected to the service provider network.

crankback   In ATM, a correction technique used when a node somewhere on a chosen path cannot accept a connection setup request, blocking the request. The path is rolled back to an intermediate node, which then uses GCAC to attempt to find an alternate path to the final destination.

CRC   Cyclic redundancy check: A methodology that detects errors, whereby the frame recipient makes a calculation by dividing frame contents with a prime binary divisor and compares the remainder to a value stored in the frame by the sending node. *Contrast with: checksum.*

crossover cable   Type of Ethernet cable that connects a switch to switch, host to host, hub to hub, or switch to hub.

CSMA/CD   Carrier Sense Multiple Access with Collision Detection: A technology defined by the Ethernet IEEE 802.3 committee. Each device senses the cable for a digital signal before transmitting. Also, CSMA/CD allows all devices on the network to share the same cable, but one at a time. If two devices transmit at the same time, a frame collision will occur and a jamming pattern will be sent; the devices will stop transmitting, wait a predetermined as well as a self-imposed random amount of time, and then try to transmit again.

CSU   Channel service unit: A digital mechanism that connects end user equipment to the local digital telephone loop. Frequently referred to along with the data service unit as CSU/DSU. *See also: DSU.*

CSU/DSU   Channel service unit/data service unit: Physical layer device used in wide area networks to convert the CPE digital signals to what is understood by the provider's switch. A CSU/DSU is typically one device that plugs into a RJ-45 (8-pin modular) jack, known as the demarcation point.

CTD   Cell Transfer Delay: For a given connection in ATM, the time period between a cell exit event at the source user-network interface (UNI) and the corresponding cell entry event at the destination. The CTD between these points is the sum of the total inter-ATM transmission delay and the total ATM processing delay.

cumulative interface delay   This is a Cisco term for delay of the line. The composite metric in IGRP and EIGRP is calculated by using the bandwidth and delay of the line by default.

cut-through frame switching   A frame-switching technique that flows data through a switch so that the leading edge exits the switch at the output port before the packet finishes entering the input port. Frames will be read, processed, and forwarded by devices that use cut-through switching as soon as the destination address of the frame is confirmed and the outgoing port is identified.

D

data circuit-terminating equipment   DCE is used to provide clocking to DTE equipment.

data compression   *See: compression.*

data direct VCC   A bidirectional point-to-point virtual control connection (VCC) set up between two LECs in ATM and one of three data connections defined by Phase 1 LAN emulation. Because data direct VCCs do not guarantee QoS, they are generally reserved for UBR and ABR connections. *Compare with: control distribute VCC and control direct VCC.*

data encapsulation   The process in which the information in a protocol is wrapped, or contained, in the data section of another protocol. In the OSI reference model, each layer encapsulates the layer immediately above it as the data flows down the protocol stack.

data frame   Protocol Data Unit encapsulation at the Data Link layer of the OSI reference model. Encapsulates packets from the Network layer and prepares the data for transmission on a network medium.

datagram   A logical collection of information transmitted as a Network layer unit over a medium without a previously established virtual circuit. IP datagrams have become the primary information unit of the Internet. At various layers of the OSI reference model, the terms *cell, frame, message, packet,* and *segment* also define these logical information groupings.

Data Link Control layer   Layer 2 of the SNA architectural model, it is responsible for the transmission of data over a given physical link and compares somewhat to the Data Link layer of the OSI model.

Data Link layer   Layer 2 of the OSI reference model, it ensures the trustworthy transmission of data across a physical link and is primarily concerned with physical addressing, line discipline, network topology, error notification, ordered delivery of frames, and flow control. The IEEE has further segmented this layer into the MAC sublayer and the LLC sublayer. Also known as the link layer. Can be compared somewhat to the data link control layer of the SNA model. *See also: Application layer, LLC, MAC, Network layer, Physical layer, Presentation layer, Session layer,* and *Transport layer.*

data terminal equipment   *See: DTE.*

DCC   Data Country Code: Developed by the ATM Forum, one of two ATM address formats designed for use by private networks. *Compare with: ICD.*

DCE   Data communications equipment (as defined by the EIA) or data circuit-terminating equipment (as defined by the ITU-T): The mechanisms and links of a communications network that make up the network portion of the user-to-network interface, such as modems. The DCE supplies the physical connection to the network, forwards traffic, and provides a clocking signal to synchronize data transmission between DTE and DCE devices. *Compare with: DTE.*

D channel   (1) Data channel: A full-duplex, 16K bps (BRI) or 64 Kbps (PRI) ISDN channel. *Compare with: B channel, E channel,* and *H channel.* (2) In SNA, anything that provides a connection between the processor and main storage with any peripherals.

DDP   Datagram Delivery Protocol: Used in the AppleTalk suite of protocols as a connection-less protocol that is responsible for sending datagrams through an internetwork.

DDR   Dial-on-demand routing: A technique that allows a router to automatically initiate and end a circuit-switched session per the requirements of the sending station. By mimicking keepalives, the router fools the end station into treating the session as active. DDR permits routing over ISDN or telephone lines via a modem or external ISDN terminal adapter.

DE   Discard Eligibility: Used in frame relay networks to tell a switch that a frame can be preferentially discarded if the switch is too busy. The DE is a field in the frame that is turned on by transmitting routers if the committed information rate (CIR) is oversubscribed or set to 0.

dedicated line   Point-to-point connection that does not share any bandwidth.

de-encapsulation   The technique used by layered protocols in which a layer removes header information from the Protocol Data Unit (PDU) from the layer below. *See: encapsulation.*

default route   The static routing table entry used to direct frames whose next-hop is not otherwise spelled out in the routing table.

delay   The time elapsed between a sender's initiation of a transaction and the first response they receive. Also, the time needed to move a packet from its source to its destination over a path. *See also: latency.*

demarc   The demarcation point between the customer premises equipment (CPE) and the telco's carrier equipment.

demodulation   A series of steps that return a modulated signal to its original form. When receiving, a modem demodulates an analog signal to its original digital form (and, conversely, modulates the digital data it sends into an analog signal). *See also: modulation.*

demultiplexing   The process of converting a multiplexed signal comprising more than one input stream back into separate output streams. *See also: multiplexing.*

designated bridge   In the process of forwarding a frame from a segment to the root bridge, the bridge with the lowest root path cost.

designated port   Used with the Spanning Tree Protocol (STP) to designate forwarding ports. If there are multiple links to the same network, STP will shut a port down to stop network loops.

designated router (DR)   An OSPF router that creates LSAs for a multi-access network and is required to perform other special tasks in OSPF operations. Multi-access OSPF networks that maintain a minimum of two attached routers identify one router that is chosen by the OSPF Hello protocol, which makes possible a decrease in the number of adjacencies necessary on a multi-access network. This in turn reduces the quantity of routing protocol traffic and the physical size of the database.

desktop layer   The access layer is sometimes referred to as the desktop layer. The access layer controls user and workgroup access to internetwork resources.

destination address   The address for the network device(s) that will receive a packet.

DHCP   Dynamic Host Configuration Protocol: DHCP is a superset of the BootP protocol. This means that it uses the same protocol structure as BootP, but it has enhancements added. Both of these protocols use servers that dynamically configure clients when requested. The two major enhancements are address pools and lease times.

dial backup   Dial backup connections are typically used to provide redundancy to frame relay connections. The backup link is activated over an analog modem or ISDN.

directed broadcast   A data frame or packet that is transmitted to a specific group of nodes on a remote network segment. Directed broadcasts are known by their broadcast address, which is a destination subnet address with all the host bits turned on.

discovery mode   Also known as dynamic configuration, this technique is used by an AppleTalk interface to gain information from a working node about an attached network. The information is subsequently used by the interface for self-configuration.

Distance vector protocols   The distance vector protocols find the best path to a remote network by judging distance. Each time a packet goes through a router, that's called a hop. The route with the least number of hops to the network is determined to be the best route. However, Cisco's IGRP is considered distance vector and uses a composite metric of bandwidth and delay of the line to determine the best path to a remote network.

Distance vector routing algorithm   In order to find the shortest path, this group of routing algorithms reports on the number of hops in a given route, requiring each router to send its complete routing table with each update, but only to its neighbors. Routing algorithms of this type tend to generate loops, but they are fundamentally simpler than their link state counterparts. *See also: link state routing algorithm* and *SPF.*

distribution layer   Middle layer of the Cisco three-layer hierarchical model, which helps you design, install, and maintain Cisco hierarchical networks. The distribution layer is the point where access layer devices connect. Routing is performed at this layer.

DLCI   Data Link Connection Identifier: Used to identify virtual circuits in a frame relay network.

DLSw   Data Link Switching: IBM developed Data Link Switching (DLSw) in 1992 to provide support for SNA (Systems Network Architecture) and NetBIOS protocols in router-based networks. SNA and NetBIOS are nonroutable protocols that do not contain any logical Layer 3 network information. DLSw encapsulates these protocols into TCP/IP messages that can be routed and is an alternative to Remote Source-Route Bridging (RSRB).

DLSw+   Cisco's implementation of DLSw. In addition to support for the RFC standards, Cisco added enhancements intended to increase scalability and to improve performance and availability.

DNS   Domain Name System: Used to resolve hostnames to IP addresses.

DSAP   Destination Service Access Point: The service access point of a network node, specified in the destination field of a packet. *See also: SSAP and SAP.*

DSR   Data Set Ready: When a DCE is powered up and ready to run, this EIA/TIA-232 interface circuit is also engaged.

DSU   Data service unit: This device is used to adapt the physical interface on a data terminal equipment (DTE) mechanism to a transmission facility such as T1 or E1 and is also responsible for signal timing. It is commonly grouped with the channel service unit and referred to as the CSU/DSU. *See also: CSU.*

DTE   Data terminal equipment: Any device located at the user end of a user-network interface serving as a destination, a source, or both. DTE includes devices such as multiplexers, routers, protocol translators, and computers. The connection to a data network is made through data communication equipment (DCE) such as a modem, using the clocking signals generated by that device. *See also: DCE.*

DTR   Data Terminal Ready: An activated EIA/TIA-232 circuit communicating to the DCE the state of preparedness of the DTE to transmit or receive data.

DUAL   Diffusing Update ALgorithm: Used in Enhanced IGRP, this convergence algorithm provides loop-free operation throughout an entire route's computation. DUAL grants routers involved in a topology revision the ability to synchronize simultaneously, while routers unaffected by this change are not involved. *See also: Enhanced IGRP.*

DVMRP   Distance Vector Multicast Routing Protocol: Based primarily on the Routing Information Protocol (RIP), this Internet gateway protocol implements a common, condensed-mode IP multicast scheme, using IGMP to transfer routing datagrams between its neighbors. *See also: IGMP.*

DXI   Data Exchange Interface: DXI defines the effectiveness of a network device such as a router, bridge, or hub to act as an FEP to an ATM network by using a special DSU that accomplishes packet encapsulation.

dynamic entries   Used in Layer 2 and Layer 3 devices to dynamically create a table of either hardware addresses or logical addresses dynamically.

dynamic routing   Also known as "adaptive routing," this technique automatically adapts to traffic or physical network revisions.

dynamic VLAN   An administrator will create an entry in a special server with the hardware addresses of all devices on the internetwork. The server will then report the associated VLAN to a switch that requests it based on the new device's hardware address.

E

E1   Generally used in Europe, a wide-area digital transmission scheme carrying data at 2.048 Mbps. E1 transmission lines are available for lease from common carriers for private use.

E.164   (1) Evolved from standard telephone numbering system, the standard recommended by ITU-T for international telecommunication numbering, particularly in ISDN, SMDS, and BISDN. (2) Label of field in an ATM address containing numbers in E.164 format.

EBGP   External border gateway protocol: Used to exchange route information between different autonomous systems.

E channel   Echo channel: A 64 Kbps ISDN control channel used for circuit switching. Specific description of this channel can be found in the 1984 ITU-T ISDN specification, but it was dropped from the 1988 version. *See also: B channel, D channel,* and *H channel.*

edge device   A device that enables packets to be forwarded between legacy interfaces (such as Ethernet and token ring) and ATM interfaces based on information in the Data Link and Network layers. An edge device does not take part in the running of any Network layer routing protocol; it merely uses the route description protocol in order to get the forwarding information required.

EEPROM   Electronically erasable programmable read-only memory: Programmed after their manufacture, these nonvolatile memory chips can be erased if necessary using electric power and reprogrammed. *See also: EPROM* and *PROM.*

EFCI   Explicit Forward Congestion Indication: A congestion feedback mode permitted by ABR service in an ATM network. The EFCI may be set by any network element that is in a state of immediate or certain congestion. The destination end system is able to carry out a protocol that adjusts and lowers the cell rate of the connection based on value of the EFCI. *See also: ABR.*

EIGRP   *See: Enhanced IGRP.*

EIP   Ethernet Interface Processor: A Cisco 7000 series router interface processor card, supplying 10 Mbps AUI ports to support Ethernet Version 1 and Ethernet Version 2 or IEEE 802.3 interfaces with a high-speed data path to other interface processors.

ELAN   Emulated LAN: An ATM network configured using a client/server model in order to emulate either an Ethernet or token ring LAN. Multiple ELANs can exist at the same time on a single ATM network and are made up of a LAN emulation client (LEC), a LAN emulation server (LES), a broadcast and unknown server (BUS), and a LAN emulation configuration server (LECS). ELANs are defined by the LANE specification. *See also: LANE, LEC, LECS,* and *LES.*

ELAP   EtherTalk Link Access Protocol: In an EtherTalk network, the link-access protocol constructed above the standard Ethernet Data Link layer.

encapsulation   The technique used by layered protocols in which a layer adds header information to the Protocol Data Unit (PDU) from the layer above. As an example, in Internet terminology, a packet would contain a header from the Data Link layer, followed by a header from the Network layer (IP), followed by a header from the Transport layer (TCP), followed by the application protocol data.

encryption   The conversion of information into a scrambled form that effectively disguises it to prevent unauthorized access. Every encryption scheme uses some well-defined algorithm, which is reversed at the receiving end by an opposite algorithm in a process known as decryption.

endpoints   *See: BGP neighbors.*

end-to-end VLANs   VLANs that span the switch fabric from end to end; all switches in end-to-end VLANs understand about all configured VLANs. End-to-end VLANs are configured to allow membership based on function, project, department, and so on.

Enhanced IGRP (EIGRP)   Enhanced Interior Gateway Routing Protocol: An advanced routing protocol created by Cisco combining the advantages of link state and distance vector protocols. Enhanced IGRP has superior convergence attributes, including high operating efficiency. *See also: IGP, OSPF,* and *RIP.*

enterprise network   A privately owned and operated network that joins most major locations in a large company or organization.

EPROM   Erasable programmable read-only memory: Programmed after their manufacture, these nonvolatile memory chips can be erased if necessary using high-power light and reprogrammed. *See also: EEPROM* and *PROM.*

ESF   Extended Superframe: Made up of 24 frames with 192 bits each, with the 193rd bit providing other functions including timing. This is an enhanced version of SF. *See also: SF.*

Ethernet   A baseband LAN specification created by the Xerox Corporation and then improved through joint efforts of Xerox, Digital Equipment Corporation, and Intel. Ethernet is similar to the IEEE 802.3 series standard and, using CSMA/CD, operates over various types of cables at 10 Mbps. Also called DIX (Digital/Intel/Xerox) Ethernet. *See also: 10BaseT, Fast Ethernet,* and *IEEE.*

EtherTalk   A data link product from Apple Computer that permits AppleTalk networks to be connected by Ethernet.

excess burst size   The amount of traffic by which the user may exceed the committed burst size.

excess rate   In ATM networking, traffic exceeding a connection's insured rate. The excess rate is the maximum rate less the insured rate. Depending on the availability of network resources, excess traffic can be discarded during congestion episodes. *Compare with: maximum rate.*

EXEC session   Cisco term used to describe the command line interface. The EXEC session exists in user mode and privileged mode.

expansion   The procedure of directing compressed data through an algorithm, restoring information to its original size.

expedited delivery   Specified by one protocol layer communicating either with other layers or with the identical protocol layer in a different network device, an option that requires that identified data be processed faster.

explorer frame   Used with source route bridging to find the route to the remote bridged network before a frame is transmitted.

explorer packet   An SNA packet transmitted by a source token ring device to find the path through a source-route-bridged network.

extended IP access list   IP access list that filters the network by logical address, protocol field in the Network layer header, and even the port field in the Transport layer header.

extended IPX access list   IPX access list that filters the network by logical IPX address, protocol field in the Network layer header, or even socket number in the Transport layer header.

Extended Setup   Used in setup mode to configure the router with more detail than Basic Setup mode. Allows multiple-protocol support and interface configuration.

external EIGRP route   Normally, the administrative distance of an EIGRP route is 90, but this is true only for what is known as an internal EIGRP route. These are routes originated within a specific autonomous system by EIGRP routers that are members of the same autonomous system. The other type of route is called an external EIGRP route and has an administrative distance of 170, which is not so good. These routes appear within EIGRP route tables courtesy of either manual or automatic redistribution, and they represent networks that originated outside of the EIGRP autonomous system.

F

failure domain   The region in which a failure has occurred in a token ring. When a station gains information that a serious problem, such as a cable break, has occurred with the network, it sends a beacon frame that includes the station reporting the failure, its NAUN and everything between. This defines the failure domain. Beaconing then initiates the procedure known as autoreconfiguration. *See also: autoreconfiguration* and *beacon.*

fallback   In ATM networks, this mechanism is used for scouting a path if it isn't possible to locate one using customary methods. The device relaxes requirements for certain characteristics, such as delay, in an attempt to find a path that meets a certain set of the most important requirements.

Fast Ethernet   Any Ethernet specification with a speed of 100 Mbps. Fast Ethernet is 10 times faster than 10BaseT while retaining qualities such as MAC mechanisms, MTU, and frame format. These similarities make it possible for existing 10BaseT applications and management tools to be used on Fast Ethernet networks. Fast Ethernet is based on an extension of IEEE 802.3 specification (IEEE 802.3u). *Compare with: Ethernet. See also: 100BaseT, 100BaseTX,* and *IEEE.*

fast switching   A Cisco feature that uses a route cache to speed packet switching through a router. *Contrast with: process switching.*

fault tolerance   The extent to which a network device or a communication link can fail without communication being interrupted. Fault tolerance can be provided by added secondary routes to a remote network.

FDDI   Fiber Distributed Data Interface: A LAN standard, defined by ANSI X3T9.5, that can run at speeds up to 200 Mbps and uses token-passing media access on fiber-optic cable. For redundancy, FDDI can use a dual-ring architecture.

FDM   Frequency-Division Multiplexing: A technique that permits information from several channels to be assigned bandwidth on one wire based on frequency. *See also: TDM, ATDM,* and *statistical multiplexing.*

FECN   Forward Explicit Congestion Notification: A bit set by a frame relay network that informs the DTE receptor that congestion was encountered along the path from source to destination. A device receiving frames with the FECN bit set can ask higher-priority protocols to take flow-control action as needed. *See also: BECN.*

FEIP   Fast Ethernet Interface Processor: An interface processor employed on Cisco 7000 series routers, supporting up to two 100 Mbps 100BaseT ports.

filtering   Used to provide security on the network with access lists. LAN switches filter the network by MAC (hardware) address.

firewall   A barrier purposefully erected between any connected public networks and a private network—made up of a router or access server or several routers or access servers—that uses access lists and other methods to ensure the security of the private network.

fixed configuration router   A router that cannot be upgraded with any new interfaces.

flapping   Term used to describe a serial interface that is going up and down.

Flash   Electronically erasable programmable read-only memory (EEPROM). Used to hold the Cisco IOS in a router by default.

flash memory   Developed by Intel and licensed to other semiconductor manufacturers, it is nonvolatile storage that can be erased electronically and reprogrammed, physically located on an EEPROM chip. Flash memory permits software images to be stored, booted, and rewritten as needed. Cisco routers and switches use flash memory to hold the IOS by default. *See also: EPROM* and *EEPROM.*

flat network   Network that is one large collision domain and one large broadcast domain.

floating routes   Used with dynamic routing to provide backup routes (static routes) in case of failure.

flooding   When traffic is received on an interface, it is then transmitted to every interface connected to that device except the interface from which the traffic originated. This technique can be used for traffic transfer by bridges and switches throughout the network.

flow control   A methodology used to ensure that receiving units are not overwhelmed with data from sending devices. Pacing, as it is called in IBM networks, means that when buffers at a receiving unit are full, a message is transmitted to the sending unit to temporarily halt transmissions until all the data in the receiving buffer has been processed and the buffer is again ready for action.

forward/filter decisions   When a frame is received on an interface, the switch looks at the destination hardware address and finds the exit interface in the MAC database. The frame is only forwarded out the specified destination port.

FQDN   Fully qualified domain name: Used within the DNS domain structure to provide name-to-IP-address resolution on the Internet. An example of an FQDN is bob.acme.com.

FRAD   Frame relay access device: Any device affording a connection between a LAN and a frame relay WAN. *See also: Cisco FRAD and FRAS.*

fragment   Any portion of a larger packet that has been intentionally segmented into smaller pieces. A packet fragment does not necessarily indicate an error and can be intentional. *See also: fragmentation.*

fragmentation   The process of intentionally segmenting a packet into smaller pieces when sending data over an intermediate network medium that cannot support the larger packet size.

FragmentFree   LAN switch type that reads into the data section of a frame to make sure fragmentation did not occur. Sometimes called modified cut-through.

frame   A logical unit of information sent by the Data Link layer over a transmission medium. The term often refers to the header and trailer, employed for synchronization and error control, that surround the data contained in the unit.

frame filtering   Frame filtering is used on a Layer 2 switch to provide more bandwidth. A switch reads the destination hardware address of a frame and then looks for this address in the filter table, built by the switch. It then sends the frame out only the port where the hardware address is located, and the other ports do not see the frame.

frame identification (frame tagging)   VLANs can span multiple connected switches, which Cisco calls a switch fabric. Switches within this switch fabric must keep track of frames as they are received on the switch ports, and they must keep track of the VLAN they belong to as the frames traverse this switch fabric. Frame tagging performs this function. Switches can then direct frames to the appropriate port.

Frame relay   A more efficient replacement of the X.25 protocol (an unrelated packet relay technology that guarantees data delivery). Frame relay is an industry-standard, shared-access, best-effort, switched Data Link layer encapsulation that services multiple virtual circuits and protocols between connected mechanisms.

Frame relay bridging   Defined in RFC 1490, this bridging method uses the identical spanning-tree algorithm as other bridging operations but permits packets to be encapsulated for transmission across a frame relay network.

Frame relay switching   Packet switching for frame relay packets that is provided by a service provider.

frame tagging   *See: frame identification.*

frame types   Used in LANs to determine how a packet is put on the local network. Ethernet provides four different frame types. These are not compatible with each other, so for two hosts to communicate, they must use the same frame type.

framing   Encapsulation at the Data Link layer of the OSI model. It is called framing because the packet is encapsulated with both a header and a trailer.

FRAS   Frame Relay Access Support: A feature of Cisco IOS software that enables SDLC, Ethernet, Token ring, and Frame relay–attached IBM devices to be linked with other IBM mechanisms on a frame relay network. *See also: FRAD.*

frequency   The number of cycles of an alternating current signal per time unit, measured in hertz (cycles per second).

FSIP   Fast Serial Interface Processor: The Cisco 7000 routers' default serial interface processor, it provides four or eight high-speed serial ports.

FTP   File Transfer Protocol: The TCP/IP protocol used for transmitting files between network nodes, it supports a broad range of file types and is defined in RFC 959. *See also: TFTP.*

full duplex   The capacity to transmit information between a sending station and a receiving unit at the same time. *See also: half duplex.*

full mesh   A type of network topology where every node has either a physical or a virtual circuit linking it to every other network node. A full mesh supplies a great deal of redundancy but is typically reserved for network backbones because of its expense. *See also: partial mesh.*

G

global command   Cisco term used to define commands that are used to change the router configuration and that affect the whole router. In contrast, an interface command only affects the interface on which it's configured.

GMII   Gigabit MII: Media Independent Interface that provides 8 bits at a time of data transfer.

GNS   Get Nearest Server: On an IPX network, a request packet sent by a customer for determining the location of the nearest active server of a given type. An IPX network client launches a GNS request to get either a direct answer from a connected server or a response from a router disclosing the location of the service on the internetwork to the GNS. GNS is part of IPX and SAP. *See also: IPX and SAP.*

grafting   A process that activates an interface that has been deactivated by the pruning process. It is initiated by an IGMP membership report sent to the router.

GRE   Generic Routing Encapsulation: A tunneling protocol created by Cisco with the capacity for encapsulating a wide variety of protocol packet types inside IP tunnels, thereby generating a virtual point-to-point connection to Cisco routers across an IP network at remote points. IP tunneling using GRE permits network expansion across a single-protocol backbone environment by linking multiprotocol subnetworks in a single-protocol backbone environment.

guardband   The unused frequency area found between two communications channels, furnishing the space necessary to avoid interference between the two.

H

half duplex   The capacity to transfer data in only one direction at a time between a sending unit and receiving unit. *See also: full duplex.*

handshake   Any series of transmissions exchanged between two or more devices on a network to ensure synchronized operations.

H channel   High-speed channel: A full-duplex, ISDN primary rate channel operating at a speed of 384 Kbps. *See also: B channel, D channel, and E channel.*

HDLC   High-Level Data Link Control: Using frame characters, including checksums, HDLC designates a method for data encapsulation on synchronous serial links and is the default encapsulation for Cisco routers. HDLC is a bit-oriented synchronous Data Link layer protocol created by ISO and derived from SDLC. However, most HDLC vendor implementations (including Cisco's) are proprietary. *See also: SDLC.*

helper address   The unicast address specified, which configures the Cisco router to change the client's local broadcast request for a service into a directed unicast to the server.

hierarchical addressing   Any addressing plan employing a logical chain of commands to determine location. IP addresses are made up of a hierarchy of network numbers, subnet numbers, and host numbers to direct packets to the appropriate destination.

hierarchy   Term used in defining IP addressing; in hierarchical addressing, some bits are used for networking and some bits for host addressing. Also used in the DNS structure and the Cisco design model.

HIP   HSSI Interface Processor: An interface processor used on Cisco 7000 series routers, providing one HSSI port that supports connections to ATM, SMDS, frame relay, or private lines at speeds up to T3 or E3.

holddown   The state a route is placed in so that routers can neither advertise the route nor accept advertisements about it for a defined time period. Holddowns are used to avoid accepting bad information. The actual information might be good, but it is not trusted. A route is generally placed in holddown when one of its links fails.

hop   The movement of a packet between any two network nodes. *See also: hop count.*

hop count   A routing metric that calculates the distance between a source and a destination based on the number of routers in the path. RIP employs hop count as its sole metric. *See also: hop and RIP.*

host address   Logical address configured by an administrator or server on a device. Logically identifies this device on an internetwork.

Host-to-Host layer   Layer in the Internet protocol suite that is equal to the Transport layer of the OSI model.

HSCI   High-Speed Communication Interface: Developed by Cisco, a single-port interface that provides full-duplex synchronous serial communications capability at speeds up to 52 Mbps.

HSRP   Hot Standby Router Protocol: A protocol that provides high network availability and nearly instantaneous hardware fail-over without administrator intervention. It generates a Hot Standby router group, including a lead router that lends its services to any packet being transferred to the Hot Standby address. If the lead router fails, it will be replaced by any of the other routers—the standby routers—that monitor it.

HSSI   High-Speed Serial Interface: A network standard physical connector for high-speed serial linking over a WAN at speeds of up to 52 Mbps.

hubs   Physical layer devices that are really just multiple port repeaters. When an electronic digital signal is received on a port, the signal is reamplified or regenerated and forwarded out all segments except the segment from which the signal was received.

hybrid routing protocol   Routing protocol that uses the attributes of both distance vector and link state. Enhanced Interior Gateway Routing Protocol (Enhanced IGRP).

I

ICD   International Code Designator: Adapted from the subnetwork model of addressing, this assigns the mapping of Network layer addresses to ATM addresses. ICD is one of two ATM formats for addressing created by the ATM Forum to be utilized with private networks. *See also: DCC.*

ICMP   Internet Control Message Protocol: Documented in RFC 792, it is a Network layer Internet protocol for the purpose of reporting errors and providing information pertinent to IP packet procedures.

IEEE   Institute of Electrical and Electronics Engineers: A professional organization that, among other activities, defines standards in a number of fields within computing and electronics, including networking and communications. IEEE standards are the predominant LAN standards used today throughout the industry. Many protocols are commonly known by the reference number of the corresponding IEEE standard.

IEEE 802.1   The IEEE committee specification that defines the bridging group. The specification for STP (Spanning Tree Protocol) is IEEE 802.1D. The STP uses STA (spanning tree algorithm) to find and prevent network loops in bridged networks. The specification for VLAN trunking is IEEE 802.1Q.

IEEE 802.3   The IEEE committee specification that defines the Ethernet group, specifically the original 10 Mbps standard. Ethernet is a LAN protocol that specifies physical layer and MAC sublayer media access. IEEE 802.3 uses CSMA/CD to provide access for many devices on the same network. Fast Ethernet is defined as 802.3U, and Gigabit Ethernet is defined as 802.3Q. *See also: CSMA/CD.*

IEEE 802.5   IEEE committee that defines token ring media access.

IGMP   Internet Group Management Protocol: Employed by IP hosts, the protocol that reports their multicast group memberships to an adjacent multicast router.

IGP   Interior gateway protocol: Any protocol used by an internetwork to exchange routing data within an independent system. Examples include RIP, IGRP, and OSPF.

IGRP   Interior Gateway Routing Protocol: Cisco-proprietary distance vector routing algorithm. Upgrade from the RIP protocol.

ILMI   Integrated (or Interim) Local Management Interface. A specification created by the ATM Forum, designated for the incorporation of network-management capability into the ATM UNI. Integrated Local Management Interface cells provide for automatic configuration between ATM systems. In LAN emulation, ILMI can provide sufficient information for the ATM end station to find an LECS. In addition, ILMI provides the ATM NSAP (Network Service Access Point) prefix information to the end station.

in-band management   In-band management is the management of a network device "through" the network. Examples include using Simple Network Management Protocol (SNMP) and Telnet directly via the local LAN. *Compare with: out-of-band management.*

in-band signaling   In-band signaling is the use of the bearer channel to deliver signaling, as call waiting in analog POTS lines. This is as opposed to out-of-band signaling, as in the case of the D channel being used to present a second active call in an ISDN circuit.

inside network   In NAT terminology, the inside network is the set of networks that are subject to translation. The outside network refers to all other addresses—usually those located on the Internet.

insured burst   In an ATM network, it is the largest, temporarily permitted data burst exceeding the insured rate on a PVC and not tagged by the traffic policing function for being dropped if network congestion occurs. This insured burst is designated in bytes or cells.

interarea routing   Routing between two or more logical areas. *Contrast with: intra-area routing. See also: area.*

interface configuration mode   Mode that allows you to configure a Cisco router or switch port with specific information, such as an IP address and mask.

interface processor   Any of several processor modules used with Cisco 7000 series routers. *See also: AIP, CIP, EIP, FEIP, HIP, MIP, and TRIP.*

Intermediate System to Intermediate System (IS-IS)   Intermediate System-to-Intermediate System: An OSI link state hierarchical routing protocol.

internal EIGRP route   Routes originated within a specific autonomous system by EIGRP routers that are members of the same autonomous system.

Internet   The global "network of networks," whose popularity has exploded starting in the mid-1990s. Originally a tool for collaborative academic research, it has become a medium for exchanging and distributing information of all kinds. The Internet's need to link disparate computer platforms and technologies has led to the development of uniform protocols and standards that have also found widespread use within corporate LANs. *See also: TCP/IP and MBONE.*

internet   Before the rise of the Internet, this lowercase form was shorthand for "internetwork" in the generic sense. Now rarely used. *See also: internetwork.*

Internet layer   Layer in the Internet Protocol suite of protocols that provides network addressing and routing through an internetwork.

Internet protocol (IP)   Any protocol belonging to the TCP/IP protocol stack. *See also: TCP/IP.*

internetwork   Any group of networks interconnected by routers and other mechanisms, typically operating as a single entity.

internetworking   Broadly, anything associated with the general task of linking networks to each other. The term encompasses technologies, procedures, and products. When you connect networks to a router, you are creating an internetwork.

intra-area routing   Routing that occurs within a logical area. *Contrast with: interarea routing.*

Inverse ARP   Inverse Address Resolution Protocol: A technique by which dynamic mappings are constructed in a network, allowing a device such as a router to locate the logical network address and associate it with a permanent virtual circuit (PVC). Commonly used in frame relay to determine the far-end node's TCP/IP address by sending the Inverse ARP request across the local DLCI.

IP   Internet protocol: Defined in RFC 791, it is a Network layer protocol that is part of the TCP/IP stack and offers connectionless service. IP furnishes an array of features for addressing, type-of-service specification, fragmentation and reassembly, and security.

IP address   Often called an Internet address, this is an address uniquely identifying any device (host) on the Internet (or any TCP/IP network). Each address consists of four octets (32 bits), represented as decimal numbers separated by periods (a format known as "dotted-decimal"). Every address is made up of a network number, an optional subnetwork number, and a host number. The network and subnetwork numbers together are used for routing, while the host number addresses an individual host within the network or subnetwork. The network and subnetwork information is extracted from the IP address using the subnet mask. There are five classes of IP addresses (A–E), in which classes A through C allocate different numbers of bits to the network, subnetwork, and host portions of the address. *See also: CIDR, IP,* and *subnet mask.*

IPCP   IP Control Program: The protocol used to establish and configure IP over PPP. *See also: IP* and *PPP.*

IP multicast   A technique for routing that enables IP traffic to be reproduced from one source to several endpoints or from multiple sources to many destinations. Instead of transmitting one packet to each individual point of destination, one packet is sent to a multicast group specified by only one IP endpoint address for the group.

IPX   Internetwork Packet eXchange: Network layer protocol (Layer 3) used in Novell NetWare networks for transferring information from servers to workstations. Similar to IP and XNS.

IPXCP   IPX Control Protocol: The protocol used to establish and configure IPX over PPP. *See also: IPX* and *PPP.*

IPXWAN   Protocol used for new WAN links to provide and negotiate line options on the link using IPX. After the link is up and the options have been agreed on by the two end-to-end links, normal IPX transmission begins.

ISDN   Integrated Services Digital Network: Offered as a service by telephone companies, a communication protocol that allows telephone networks to carry data, voice, and other digital traffic. *See also: BISDN, BRI,* and *PRI.*

IS-IS   *See: Intermediate System-to-Intermediate System (IS-IS)*

ISL routing   Inter-Switch Link routing: A Cisco-proprietary method of frame tagging in a switched internetwork. Frame tagging is a way to identify the VLAN membership of a frame as it traverses a switched internetwork.

isochronous transmission   Asynchronous data transfer over a synchronous data link, requiring a constant bit rate for reliable transport. *Compare with: asynchronous transmission* and *synchronous transmission.*

ITU-T   International Telecommunication Union-Telecommunication Standardization Sector: This is a group of engineers that develops worldwide standards for telecommunications technologies.

K

Kerberos   An authentication and encryption method that can be used by Cisco routers to ensure that data cannot be "sniffed" off of the network. Kerberos was developed at MIT and was designed to provide strong security using the Data Encryption Standard (DES) cryptographic algorithm.

L

LAN   Local area network: Broadly, any network linking two or more computers and related devices within a limited geographical area (up to a few kilometers). LANs are typically high-speed, low-error networks within a company. Cabling and signaling at the Physical and Data Link layers of the OSI are dictated by LAN standards. Ethernet, FDDI, and token ring are among the most popular LAN technologies. *Compare with: MAN.*

LANE   LAN emulation: The technology that allows an ATM network to operate as a LAN backbone. To do so, the ATM network is required to provide multicast and broadcast support, address mapping (MAC-to-ATM), and SVC management, in addition to an operable packet format. Additionally, LANE defines Ethernet and token ring ELANs. *See also: ELAN.*

LAN switch   A high-speed, multiple-interface transparent bridging mechanism, transmitting packets between segments of data links, usually referred to specifically as an Ethernet switch. LAN switches transfer traffic based on MAC addresses. *See also: multilayer switch* and *store-and-forward packet switching.*

LAPB   Link Accessed Procedure, Balanced: A bit-oriented Data Link layer protocol that is part of the X.25 stack and has its origin in SDLC. *See also: SDLC* and *X.25.*

LAPD   Link Access Procedure on the D channel: The ISDN Data Link layer protocol used specifically for the D channel and defined by ITU-T Recommendations Q.920 and Q.921. LAPD evolved from LAPB and is created to comply with the signaling requirements of ISDN basic access.

latency   Broadly, the time it takes a data packet to get from one location to another. In specific networking contexts, it can mean either (1) the time elapsed (delay) between the execution of a request for access to a network by a device and the time the mechanism actually is permitted transmission, or (2) the time elapsed between when a mechanism receives a frame and the time that frame is forwarded out of the destination port.

layer   Term used in networking to define how the OSI model works to encapsulate data for transmission on the network.

Layer 3 switch   *See: multilayer switch.*

layered architecture   Industry standard way of creating applications to work on a network. Layered architecture allows the application developer to make changes in only one layer instead of the whole program.

LCP   Link Control Protocol: The protocol designed to establish, configure, and test data link connections for use by PPP. *See also: PPP.*

leaky bucket   An analogy for the generic cell rate algorithm (GCRA) used in ATM networks for checking the conformance of cell flows from a user or network. The bucket's "hole" is understood to be the prolonged rate at which cells can be accommodated, and the "depth" is the tolerance for cell bursts over a certain time period.

learning bridge   A bridge that transparently builds a dynamic database of MAC addresses and the interfaces associated with each address. Transparent bridges help to reduce traffic congestion on the network.

LE ARP   LAN Emulation Address Resolution Protocol: The protocol providing the ATM address that corresponds to a MAC address.

leased line   Permanent connection between two points leased from the telephone companies.

LEC   LAN emulation client: Software providing the emulation of the link layer interface that allows the operation and communication of all higher-level protocols and applications to continue. The LEC runs in all ATM devices, which include hosts, servers, bridges, and routers. *See also: ELAN and LES.*

LECS   LAN emulation configuration server: An important part of emulated LAN services, providing the configuration data that is furnished on request from the LES. These services include address registration for Integrated Local Management Interface (ILMI) support, configuration support for the LES addresses and their corresponding emulated LAN identifiers, and an interface to the emulated LAN. *See also: LES and ELAN.*

LES   LAN emulation server: The central LANE component that provides the initial configuration data for each connecting LEC. The LES typically is located on either an ATM-integrated router or a switch. Responsibilities of the LES include configuration and support for the LEC, address registration for the LEC, database storage and response concerning ATM addresses, and interfacing to the emulated LAN. *See also: ELAN, LEC, and LECS.*

link   A link is a network or router interface assigned to any given network. When an interface is added to the OSPF process, it's considered by OSPF to be a link. This link, or interface, will have state information associated with it (up or down) as well as one or more IP addresses.

Link state database (LSDB)   The database used by a link state routing protocol to store all of the routing data for its area and the information known outside of its area. The Dijkstra algorithm uses all of this data to create routes to destination networks.

Link state protocols   In link state protocols, also called shortest path first protocols, the routers each create three separate tables. One of these tables keeps track of directly attached neighbors, one determines the topology of the entire internetwork, and one is used as the routing table. Link state routers know more about the internetwork than any distance vector routing protocol.

Link state routing algorithm   A routing algorithm that allows each router to broadcast or multicast information regarding the cost of reaching all its neighbors to every node in the internetwork. Link state algorithms provide a consistent view of the network and are therefore not vulnerable to routing loops. However, this loop-free network is achieved at the cost of somewhat greater difficulty in computation and more widespread traffic (compared with distance vector routing algorithms). See also: distance vector routing algorithm.

Link state packet (LSP)   Used by link state routing protocols to communicate information between adjacent routers. An LSP packet is specifically used by IS-IS as its update packet, similar to a LSU that is used by OSPF.

Link State Update (LSU)   An update packet used by OSPF to carry routing information to adjacent routers. An LSU carries link state advertisements (LSA) which are the actual pieces of routing information.

LLAP   LocalTalk Link Access Protocol: In a LocalTalk environment, the data link–level protocol that manages node-to-node delivery of data. This protocol provides node addressing and management of bus access, and it also controls data sending and receiving to ensure packet length and integrity.

LLC   Logical Link Control: Defined by the IEEE, the higher of two Data Link layer sublayers. LLC is responsible for error detection (but not correction), flow control, framing, and software-sublayer addressing. The predominant LLC protocol, IEEE 802.2, defines both connectionless and connection-oriented operations. *See also: Data Link layer and MAC.*

LMI   Local Management Interface: An enhancement to the original frame relay specification. Among the features it provides are a keepalive mechanism, a multicast mechanism, global addressing, and a status mechanism.

LNNI   LAN Emulation Network-to-Network Interface: In the Phase 2 LANE specification, an interface that supports communication between the server components within one ELAN.

load   Like IGRP, EIGRP uses only bandwidth and delay of the line to determine the best path to a remote network by default. However, EIGRP can use a combination of bandwidth, delay, load, and reliability in its quest to find the best path to a remote network. Load refers to the amount of data on the link.

load balancing   The act of balancing packet load over multiple links to the same remote network.

local explorer packet   In a token ring SRB network, a packet generated by an end system to find a host linked to the local ring. If no local host can be found, the end system will produce one of two solutions: a spanning explorer packet or an all-routes explorer packet.

local loop   Connection from a demarcation point to the closest switching office.

LocalTalk   Utilizing CSMA/CD, in addition to supporting data transmission at speeds of 230.4 Kbps, LocalTalk is Apple Computer's proprietary baseband protocol, operating at the Data Link and Physical layers of the OSI reference model.

logical address   Network layer address that defines how data is sent from one network to another. Examples of logical addresses are IP and IPX.

loop avoidance   If multiple connections between switches are created for redundancy purposes, network loops can occur. Spanning Tree Protocol (STP) is used to stop network loops while still permitting redundancy.

loopback address   The IP address 127.0.0.1 is called the diagnostic or loopback address, and if you get a successful ping to this address, your IP stack is then considered to be initialized. If it fails, then you have an IP stack failure and need to reinstall TCP/IP on the host.

loopback interface   Loopback interfaces are logical interfaces, which means they are not real router interfaces. They can be used for diagnostic purposes as well as OSPF configuration.

LPD   Line Printer Daemon: Used in the Unix world to allow printing to an IP address.

LSA   Link state advertisement: Contained inside of link state packets (LSPs), these advertisements are usually multicast packets, containing information about neighbors and path costs, that are employed by link state protocols. Receiving routers use LSAs to maintain their link state databases and, ultimately, routing tables.

LUNI   LAN Emulation User-to-Network Interface: Defining the interface between the LAN emulation client (LEC) and the LAN emulation server (LES), LUNI is the ATM Forum's standard for LAN emulation on ATM networks. *See also: LES* and *LECS.*

M

MAC   Media Access Control: The lower sublayer in the Data Link layer, it is responsible for hardware addressing, media access, and error detection of frames. *See also: Data Link layer* and *LLC.*

MAC address   A Data Link layer hardware address that every port or device needs in order to connect to a LAN segment. These addresses are used by various devices in the network for accurate location of logical addresses. MAC addresses are defined by the IEEE standard and their length is six characters, typically using the burned-in address (BIA) of the local LAN interface. Variously called hardware address, physical address, burned-in address, or MAC layer address.

MacIP   In AppleTalk, the Network layer protocol encapsulating IP packets in Datagram Delivery Protocol (DDP) packets. MacIP also supplies substitute ARP services.

MAN   Metropolitan area network: Any network that encompasses a metropolitan area; that is, an area typically larger than a LAN but smaller than a WAN. *See also: LAN.*

Manchester encoding   A method for digital coding in which a mid-bit-time transition is employed for clocking, and a 1 (one) is denoted by a high voltage level during the first half of the bit time. This scheme is used by Ethernet and IEEE 802.3.

maximum burst   Specified in bytes or cells, the largest burst of information exceeding the insured rate that will be permitted on an ATM permanent virtual connection for a short time and will not be dropped even if it goes over the specified maximum rate. *Compare with: insured burst. See also: maximum rate.*

maximum hop count   Number of routers a packet is allowed to pass before it is terminated. This is created to prevent a packet from circling a network forever.

maximum rate   The maximum permitted data throughput on a particular virtual circuit, equal to the total of insured and uninsured traffic from the traffic source. Should traffic congestion occur, uninsured information may be deleted from the path. Measured in bits or cells per second, the maximum rate represents the highest throughput of data the virtual circuit is ever able to deliver and cannot exceed the media rate. *Compare with: excess rate. See also: maximum burst.*

Mbone   The multicast backbone of the Internet, it is a virtual multicast network made up of multicast LANs, including point-to-point tunnels interconnecting them.

MBS   Maximum Burst Size: In an ATM signaling message, this metric, coded as a number of cells, is used to convey the burst tolerance.

MCDV   Maximum Cell Delay Variation: The maximum two-point CDV objective across a link or node for the identified service category in an ATM network.

MCLR   Maximum Cell Loss Ratio: The maximum ratio of cells in an ATM network that fail to transit a link or node compared with the total number of cells that arrive at the link or node. MCLR is one of four link metrics that are exchanged using PTSPs to verify the available resources of an ATM network. The MCLR applies to cells in VBR and CBR traffic classes whose CLP bit is set to zero. *See also: CBR, CLP, and VBR.*

MCR   Minimum cell rate: A parameter determined by the ATM Forum for traffic management of the ATM networks. MCR is specifically defined for ABR transmissions and specifies the minimum value for the allowed cell rate (ACR). *See also: ACR and PCR.*

MCTD   Maximum Cell Transfer Delay: In an ATM network, the total of the maximum cell delay variation and the fixed delay across the link or node. MCTD is one of four link metrics that are exchanged using PNNI topology state packets to verify the available resources of an ATM network. There is one MCTD value assigned to each traffic class. *See also: MCDV.*

media translation   A router property that allows two different types of LAN to communicate—for example, Ethernet to token ring.

MIB   Management Information Base: Used with SNMP management software to gather information from remote devices. The management station can poll the remote device for information, or the MIB running on the remote station can be programmed to send information on a regular basis.

MII   Media Independent Interface: Used in Fast Ethernet and Gigabit Ethernet to provide faster bit transfer rates of 4 and 8 bits at a time. Contrast to AUI interface, which is 1 bit at a time.

MIP   Multichannel Interface Processor: The resident interface processor on Cisco 7000 series routers, providing up to two channelized T1 or E1 connections by serial cables connected to a CSU. The two controllers are capable of providing 24 T1 or 30 E1 channel groups, with each group being introduced to the system as a serial interface that can be configured individually.

mips   Millions of instructions per second: A measure of processor speed.

MLP   Multilink PPP: A technique used to split, recombine, and sequence datagrams across numerous logical data links.

MMP   Multichassis Multilink PPP: A protocol that supplies MLP support across multiple routers and access servers. MMP enables several routers and access servers to work as a single, large dial-up pool with one network address and ISDN access number. MMP successfully supports packet fragmenting and reassembly when the user connection is split between two physical access devices.

modem   Modulator-demodulator: A device that converts digital signals to analog and vice versa so that digital information can be transmitted over analog communication facilities such as voice-grade telephone lines. This is achieved by converting digital signals at the source to analog for transmission and reconverting the analog signals back into digital form at the destination. *See also: modulation* and *demodulation.*

modem eliminator   A mechanism that makes possible a connection between two DTE devices without modems by simulating the commands and physical signaling required.

modulation   The process of modifying some characteristic of an electrical signal, such as amplitude (AM) or frequency (FM), in order to represent digital or analog information. *See also: AM.*

MOSPF   Multicast OSPF: An extension of the OSPF unicast protocol that enables IP multicast routing within the domain. *See also: OSPF.*

MPOA   Multiprotocol over ATM: An effort by the ATM Forum to standardize how existing and future Network layer protocols such as IP, IPv6, AppleTalk, and IPX run over an ATM network with directly attached hosts, routers, and multilayer LAN switches.

MTU   Maximum transmission unit: The largest packet size, measured in bytes, that an interface can handle.

multicast   Broadly, any communication between a single sender and multiple receivers. Unlike broadcast messages, which are sent to all addresses on a network, multicast messages are sent to a defined subset of the network addresses; this subset has a group multicast address, which is specified in the packet's destination address field. *See also: broadcast* and *directed broadcast.*

multicast address   A single address that points to more than one device on the network by specifying a special nonexistent MAC address transmitted in that particular multicast protocol. Identical to group address. *See also: multicast.*

multicast group   Multicast works by sending messages or data to IP multicast group addresses. The group is a defined set of users or hosts that are allowed to read or view the data sent via multicast.

multicast send VCC   A two-directional point-to-point virtual control connection (VCC) arranged by an LEC to a BUS, it is one of the three types of informational links specified by phase 1 LANE. *See also: control distribute VCC* and *control direct VCC.*

multilayer switch   A highly specialized, high-speed, hardware-based type of LAN router, the device filters and forwards packets based on their Layer 2 MAC addresses and Layer 3 network addresses. It's possible that even Layer 4 can be read. Sometimes called a Layer 3 switch. *See also: LAN switch.*

multilink   Used to combine multiple async or ISDN links to provide combined bandwidth.

multiplexing   The process of converting several logical signals into a single physical signal for transmission across one physical channel. *Contrast with: demultiplexing.*

N

NAK   Negative acknowledgment: A response sent from a receiver, telling the sender that the information was not received or contained errors. *Compare with: acknowledgment.*

named access list   Used in both standard and extended lists to help with administration of access lists by allowing you to name the lists instead of using numbers. This also allows you to change a single line of an access list, which isn't possible in regular, numbered access lists.

NAT   Network Address Translation: An algorithm instrumental in minimizing the requirement for globally unique IP addresses, permitting an organization whose addresses are not all globally unique to connect to the Internet nevertheless by translating those addresses into globally routable address space.

native VLAN   Cisco switches all have a native VLAN called VLAN 1. This cannot be deleted or changed in any way. All switch ports are in VLAN 1 by default.

NBP   Name Binding Protocol: In AppleTalk, the transport-level protocol that interprets a socket client's name, entered as a character string, into the corresponding DDP address. NBP gives AppleTalk protocols the capacity to discern user-defined zones and names of mechanisms by showing and keeping translation tables that map names to their corresponding socket addresses.

neighboring routers   Two routers in OSPF that have interfaces to a common network. On networks with multi-access, these neighboring routers are dynamically discovered using the hello protocol of OSPF.

neighbors   EIGRP and OSPF routers become neighbors when each router sees the other's Hello packets.

neighborship table   In OSPF and EIGRP routing protocols, each router keeps state information about adjacent neighbors. When newly discovered neighbors are learned, the address and interface of the neighbor is recorded. This information is stored in the neighbor data structure and the neighbor table holds these entries. Neighborship table can also be referred to as neighbor table or neighborship database.

NetBEUI   NetBIOS Extended User Interface: An improved version of the NetBIOS protocol used in a number of network operating systems including LAN Manager, Windows NT, LAN Server, and Windows for Workgroups, implementing the OSI LLC2 protocol. NetBEUI formalizes the transport frame not standardized in NetBIOS and adds more functions. *See also: OSI.*

NetBIOS   Network Basic Input/Output System: The API employed by applications residing on an IBM LAN to ask for services, such as session termination or information transfer, from lower-level network processes.

NetView   A mainframe network product from IBM used for monitoring SNA (Systems Network Architecture) networks. It runs as a VTAM (Virtual Telecommunications Access Method) application.

NetWare   A widely used NOS created by Novell, providing a number of distributed network services and remote file access.

Network Access layer   Bottom layer in the Internet protocol suite that provides media access to packets.

network address   Used with the logical network addresses to identify the network segment in an internetwork. Logical addresses are hierarchical in nature and have at least two parts: network and host. An example of a hierarchical address is 172.16.10.5, where 172.16 is the network and 10.5 is the host address.

network control protocol   A method of establishing and configuring different Network layer protocols. NCP is designed to allow the simultaneous use of multiple Network layer protocols. Some examples of protocols here are IPCP (Internet Protocol Control Protocol) and IPXCP (Internetwork Packet Exchange Control Protocol).

Network layer   In the OSI reference model, it is Layer 3—the layer in which routing is implemented, enabling connections and path selection between two end systems. *See also: Application layer, Data Link layer, Physical layer, Presentation layer, Session layer,* and *Transport layer.*

network segmentation   Breaking up a large network into smaller networks. Routers, switches, and bridges are used to create network segmentation.

NFS   Network File System: One of the protocols in Sun Microsystems's widely used file system protocol suite, allowing remote file access across a network. The name is loosely used to refer to the entire Sun protocol suite, which also includes RPC, XDR (External Data Representation), and other protocols.

NHRP   Next-Hop Resolution Protocol: In a non-broadcast multi-access (NBMA) network, the protocol employed by routers in order to dynamically locate MAC addresses of various hosts and routers. It enables systems to communicate directly without requiring an intermediate hop, thus facilitating increased performance in ATM, frame relay, X.25, and SMDS systems.

NHS   Next-Hop Server: Defined by the NHRP protocol, this server maintains the next-hop resolution cache tables, listing IP-to-ATM address maps of related nodes and nodes that can be reached through routers served by the NHS.

nibble   Four bits.

NIC   Network interface card: An electronic circuit board placed in a computer. The NIC provides network communication to a LAN.

NLSP   NetWare Link Services Protocol: Novell's link state routing protocol, based on the IS-IS model.

NMP   Network Management Processor: A Catalyst 5000 switch processor module used to control and monitor the switch.

node address   Used to identify a specific device in an internetwork. Can be a hardware address, which is burned into the network interface card, or a logical network address, which an administrator or server assigns to the node.

non-broadcast multi-access (NBMA) networks   Non-broadcast multi-access (NBMA) networks are types such as frame relay, X.25, and Asynchronous Transfer Mode (ATM). These networks allow for multi-access, but have no broadcast ability like Ethernet. So, NBMA networks require special OSPF configuration to function properly and neighbor relationships must be defined.

non-designated port   A switch port that will not forward frames in order to prevent a switching loop. Spanning Tree Protocol (STP) is responsible for deciding whether a port is designated (forwarding) or non-designated (blocking).

non-stub area   In OSPF, a resource-consuming area carrying a default route, intra-area routes, interarea routes, static routes, and external routes. Non-stub areas are the only areas that can have virtual links configured across them and exclusively contain an autonomous system border router (ASBR). *Compare with: stub area. See also: ASBR and OSPF.*

NRZ   Nonreturn to zero: One of several encoding schemes for transmitting digital data. NRZ signals sustain constant levels of voltage with no signal shifting (no return to zero-voltage level) during a bit interval. If there is a series of bits with the same value (1 or 0), there will be no state change. The signal is not self-clocking. *See also: NRZI.*

NRZI   Nonreturn to zero inverted: One of several encoding schemes for transmitting digital data. A transition in voltage level (either from high to low or vice versa) at the beginning of a bit interval is interpreted as a value of 1; the absence of a transition is interpreted as a 0. Thus, the voltage assigned to each value is continually inverted. NRZI signals are not self-clocking. *See also: NRZ.*

NT   Network termination: A point in an ISDN network. *See: NT1 and NT2.*

NT1   NT1 is the device that converts the two-wire "U" interface to the four-wire "S/T."

NT2   NT2 is an ISDN-compliant switching device, like a PBX, that splits the "S/T" bus into two separate, but electrically equivalent, interfaces. The "T" interface connects to the NT1, while the "S" interface connects to TE1 devices.

NVRAM   Nonvolatile RAM: Random-access memory that keeps its contents intact while power is turned off.

O

OC   Optical Carrier: A series of physical protocols, designated as OC-1, OC-2, OC-3, and so on, for SONET optical signal transmissions. OC signal levels place STS frames on a multimode fiber-optic line at various speeds, of which 51.84 Mbps is the lowest (OC-1). Each subsequent protocol runs at a speed divisible by 51.84. *See also: SONET.*

octet   Base-8 numbering system used to identify a section of a dotted decimal IP address. Also referred to as a byte.

ones density   Also known as pulse density, this is a method of signal clocking. The CSU/DSU retrieves the clocking information from data that passes through it. For this scheme to work, the data needs to be encoded to contain at least one binary 1 for each 8 bits transmitted. *See also: CSU and DSU.*

OSI   Open Systems Interconnection: International standardization program designed by ISO and ITU-T for the development of data networking standards that make multivendor equipment interoperability a reality.

OSI reference model   Open Systems Interconnection reference model: A conceptual model defined by the International Organization for Standardization (ISO), describing how any combination of devices can be connected for the purpose of communication. The OSI model divides the task into seven functional layers, forming a hierarchy with the applications at the top and the physical medium at the bottom, and it defines the functions each layer must provide. *See also: Application layer, Data Link layer, Network layer, Physical layer, Presentation layer, Session layer,* and *Transport layer.*

OSPF   Open Shortest Path First: A link state, hierarchical routing algorithm derived from an earlier version of the IS-IS protocol, whose features include multipath routing, load balancing, and least-cost routing. OSPF is the suggested successor to RIP in the Internet environment. *See also: Enhanced IGRP, IGP,* and *IP.*

OSPF area   An OSPF area is a grouping of contiguous networks and routers. All routers in the same area share a common Area ID. Because a router can be a member of more than one area at a time, the Area ID is associated with specific interfaces on the router. This would allow some interfaces to belong to area 1, while the remaining interfaces can belong to area 0. All of the routers within the same area have the same topology table.

OUI   Organizationally unique identifier: Code assigned by the IEEE to an organization that makes network interface cards. The organization then puts this OUI on each and every card it manufactures. The OUI is 3 bytes (24 bits) long. The manufacturer then adds a 3-byte identifier to uniquely identify the host. The total length of the address is 48 bits (6 bytes) and is called a hardware address or MAC address.

out-of-band management   Management "outside" of the network's physical channels— for example, using a console connection not directly interfaced through the local LAN or WAN or a dial-in modem. *Compare to: in-band management.*

out-of-band signaling   Within a network, any transmission that uses physical channels or frequencies separate from those ordinarily used for data transfer.

outside network   In NAT terminology, the inside network is the set of networks that are subject to translation. The outside network refers to all other addresses—usually those located on the Internet.

P

packet   In data communications, the basic logical unit of information transferred. A packet consists of a certain number of data bytes, wrapped or encapsulated in headers and/or trailers that contain information about where the packet came from, where it's going, and so on. The various protocols involved in sending a transmission add their own layers of header information, which the corresponding protocols in receiving devices then interpret.

packet switch   A physical device that makes it possible for a communication channel to share several connections; its functions include finding the most efficient transmission path for packets.

packet switching   A networking technology based on the transmission of data in packets. Dividing a continuous stream of data into small units—packets—enables data from multiple devices on a network to share the same communication channel simultaneously but also requires the use of precise routing information.

PAP   Password Authentication Protocol: In Point-to-Point Protocol (PPP) networks, a method of validating connection requests. The requesting (remote) device must send an authentication request, containing a password and ID, to the local router when attempting to connect. Unlike the more secure CHAP (Challenge Handshake Authentication Protocol), PAP sends the password unencrypted and does not attempt to verify whether the user is authorized to access the requested resource; it merely identifies the remote end. *See also: CHAP.*

parity checking   A method of error checking in data transmissions. An extra bit (the parity bit) is added to each character or data word so that the sum of the bits will be either an odd number (in odd parity) or an even number (even parity).

partial mesh   A type of network topology in which some network nodes form a full mesh (where every node has either a physical or a virtual circuit linking it to every other network node), but others are attached to only one or two nodes in the network. A typical use of partial-mesh topology is in peripheral networks linked to a fully meshed backbone. *See also: full mesh.*

passive state   Regarding an EIGRP routing table, a route is considered to be in the passive state when a router is not performing a route convergence.

PAT   Port Address Translation: This process allows a single IP address to represent multiple resources by altering the source TCP or UDP port number.

PCM   Pulse code modulation: Process by which an analog signal is converted into digital information.

PCR   Peak cell rate: As defined by the ATM Forum, the parameter specifying, in cells per second, the maximum rate at which a source may transmit.

PDN   Public data network: Generally for a fee, a PDN offers the public access to a computer communication network operated by private concerns or government agencies. Small organizations can take advantage of PDNs, aiding them to create WANs without investing in long-distance equipment and circuitry.

PDU   Protocol Data Unit: The processes at each layer of the OSI model. PDUs at the Transport layer are called segments; PDUs at the Network layer are called packets or datagrams; and PDUs at the Data Link layer are called frames. The Physical layer uses bits.

PGP   Pretty Good Privacy: A popular public-key/private-key encryption application offering protected transfer of files and messages.

phantom router   Used in a Hot Standby Routing Protocol (HSRP) network to provide an IP default gateway address to hosts. Also called the virtual router.

Physical layer   The lowest layer—Layer 1—in the OSI reference model, it is responsible for converting data frames from the Data Link layer (Layer 2) into electrical signals. Physical layer protocols and standards define, for example, the type of cable and connectors to be used, including their pin assignments and the encoding scheme for signaling 0 and 1 values. *See also: Application layer, Data Link layer, Network layer, Presentation layer, Session layer,* and *Transport layer.*

PIM   Protocol Independent Multicast: A multicast protocol that handles the IGMP requests as well as requests for multicast data forwarding.

PIM-DM   Protocol Independent Multicast Dense Mode: PIM-DM utilizes the unicast route table and relies on the source root distribution architecture for multicast data forwarding.

PIM-SM   Protocol Independent Multicast Sparse Mode: PIM-SM utilizes the unicast route table and relies on the shared root distribution architecture for multicast data forwarding.

Ping   Packet Internet Groper: A Unix-based Internet diagnostic tool consisting of a message sent to test the accessibility of a particular device on the IP network. The term's acronym reflects the underlying metaphor of submarine sonar. Just as the sonar operator sends out a signal and waits to hear it echo ("ping") back from a submerged object, the network user can ping another node on the network and wait to see if it responds.

pinhole congestion   A problem associated with distance vector routing protocols if more than one connection to a remote network is known, but they are different bandwidths.

plesiochronous   Nearly synchronous, except that clocking comes from an outside source instead of being embedded within the signal as in synchronous transmissions.

PLP   Packet Level Protocol: Occasionally called X.25 level 3 or X.25 Protocol, a Network layer protocol that is part of the X.25 stack.

PNNI   Private Network-Network Interface: An ATM Forum specification for offering topology data used for the calculation of paths through the network, among switches and groups of switches. It is based on well-known link state routing procedures and allows for automatic configuration in networks whose addressing scheme is determined by the topology.

point-to-multipoint connection   In ATM, a communication path going only one way, connecting a single system at the starting point, called the "root node," to systems at multiple points of destination, called "leaves." *See also: point-to-point connection.*

point-to-point connection   In ATM, a channel of communication that can be directed either one way or two ways between two ATM end systems. Also refers to a point-to-point WAN serial connection. *See also: point-to-multipoint connection.*

poison reverse updates   These update messages are transmitted by a router back to the originator (thus ignoring the split-horizon rule) after route poisoning has occurred. Typically used with DV routing protocols in order to overcome large routing loops and offer explicit information when a subnet or network is not accessible (instead of merely suggesting that the network is unreachable by not including it in updates). *See also: route poisoning.*

polling   The procedure of orderly inquiry used by a primary network mechanism to determine if secondary devices have data to transmit. A message is sent to each secondary, granting the secondary the right to transmit.

POP   (1) Point of presence: The physical location where an interexchange carrier has placed equipment to interconnect with a local exchange carrier. (2) Post Office Protocol: A protocol used by client e-mail applications for recovery of mail from a mail server.

port security   Used with Layer 2 switches to provide some security. Not typically used in production because it is difficult to manage. Allows only certain frames to traverse administrator-assigned segments.

port numbers   Used at the transport layer with TCP and UDP to keep track of host-to-host virtual circuits.

positive acknowledgment with retransmission   A connection-oriented session that provides acknowledgment and retransmission of the data if it is not acknowledged by the receiving host within a certain time frame.

POTS   Plain old telephone service: This refers to the traditional analog phone service that is found in most installations.

PPP   Point-to-Point Protocol: The protocol most commonly used for dial-up Internet access, superseding the earlier SLIP. Its features include address notification, authentication via CHAP or PAP, support for multiple protocols, and link monitoring. PPP has two layers: the Link Control Protocol (LCP) establishes, configures, and tests a link; and then any of various Network Control Protocols (NCPs) transport traffic for a specific protocol suite, such as IPX. *See also: CHAP, PAP,* and *SLIP.*

prefix routing   Method of defining how many bits are used in a subnet and how this information is sent in a routing update. For example, RIP version 1 does not send subnet mask information in the route updates. However, RIP version 2 does. This means that RIP v2 updates will send /24, /25, /26, etc., with a route update, which RIP v1 will not.

Presentation layer   Layer 6 of the OSI reference model, it defines how data is formatted, presented, encoded, and converted for use by software at the Application layer. *See also: Application layer, Data Link layer, Network layer, Physical layer, Session layer,* and *Transport layer.*

PRI   Primary Rate Interface: A type of ISDN connection between a PBX and a long-distance carrier, which is made up of a single 64 Kbps D channel in addition to 23 (T1) or 30 (E1) B channels. *See also: ISDN.*

priority queuing   A routing function in which frames temporarily placed in an interface output queue are assigned priorities based on traits such as packet size or type of interface.

privileged mode   Command line EXEC mode used in Cisco routers and switches that provides both viewing and changing of configurations.

Process/Application layer   Upper layer in the Internet protocol stack. Responsible for network services.

process switching   As a packet arrives on a router to be forwarded, it's copied to the router's process buffer, and the router performs a lookup on the Layer 3 address. Using the route table, an exit interface is associated with the destination address. The processor forwards the packet with the added new information to the exit interface, while the router initializes the fast-switching cache. Subsequent packets bound for the same destination address follow the same path as the first packet.

PROM   Programmable read-only memory: ROM that is programmable only once, using special equipment. *Compare with: EPROM*.

propagation delay   The time it takes data to traverse a network from its source to its destination.

protocol   In networking, the specification of a set of rules for a particular type of communication. The term is also used to refer to the software that implements a protocol.

protocol-dependent modules   The protocol-dependent modules, used in the EIGRP routing protocol, are responsible for network layer, protocol-specific requirements that allow multiple protocol support for IP, IPX and AppleTalk.

protocol stack   A collection of related protocols.

Proxy Address Resolution Protocol   Proxy ARP: Used to allow redundancy in case of a failure with the configured default gateway on a host. Proxy ARP is a variation of the ARP protocol in which an intermediate device, such as a router, sends an ARP response on behalf of an end node to the requesting host.

pruning   The act of trimming down the shortest-path tree. This deactivates interfaces that do not have group participants.

PSE   Packet switching exchange: The X.25 term for a switch.

PSN   Packet-switched network: Any network that uses packet-switching technology. Also known as packet-switched data network (PSDN). *See also: packet switching*.

PSTN   Public switched telephone network: Colloquially referred to as "plain old telephone service" (POTS). A term that describes the assortment of telephone networks and services available globally.

PVC   Permanent virtual circuit: In a frame relay or ATM network, a logical connection, defined in software, that is maintained permanently. *Compare with: SVC. See also: virtual circuit*.

PVP   Permanent virtual path: A virtual path made up of PVCs. *See also: PVC.*

PVP tunneling   Permanent virtual path tunneling: A technique that links two private ATM networks across a public network using a virtual path, wherein the public network transparently trunks the complete collection of virtual channels in the virtual path between the two private networks.

Q

QoS   Quality of service: A set of metrics used to measure and manipulate the quality of transmission and service availability of any given transmission system.

queue   Broadly, any list of elements arranged in an orderly fashion and ready for processing, such as a line of people waiting to enter a movie theater. In routing, it refers to a backlog of information packets waiting in line to be transmitted over a router interface.

R

R reference point   Used with ISDN networks to identify the connection between an NT1 and an S/T device. The S/T device converts the four-wire network to the two-wire ISDN standard network.

RADIUS   Remote Authentication Dial-In User Service: A protocol that is used to communicate between the remote access device and an authentication server. Sometimes an authentication server running RADIUS will be called a RADIUS server.

RAM   Random-access memory: Used by all computers to store information. Cisco routers use RAM to store packet buffers and routing tables, along with the hardware addresses cache.

RARP   Reverse Address Resolution Protocol: The protocol within the TCP/IP stack that maps MAC addresses to IP addresses. *See also: ARP.*

RARP server   A Reverse Address Resolution Protocol server is used to provide an IP address from a known MAC address.

rate queue   A value, assigned to one or more virtual circuits, that specifies the speed at which an individual virtual circuit will transmit data to the remote end. Every rate queue identifies a segment of the total bandwidth available on an ATM link. The sum of all rate queues should not exceed the total available bandwidth.

RCP   Remote Copy Protocol: A protocol for copying files to or from a file system that resides on a remote server on a network, using TCP to guarantee reliable data delivery.

redundancy   In internetworking, the duplication of connections, devices, or services that can be used as a backup in the event that the primary connections, devices, or services fail.

reference model   Used by application developers to create applications that work on any type of network. The most popular reference model is the Open Systems Interconnection (OSI) model.

reliability   Like IGRP, EIGRP uses only bandwidth and delay of the line to determine the best path to a remote network by default. However, EIGRP can use a combination of bandwidth, delay, load and reliability in its quest to find the best path to a remote network. Reliability refers to the reliability of the link to each remote network.

reliable multicast   When EIGRP sends multicast traffic it uses the Class D address 224.0.0.10. As I said, each EIGRP router is aware of who its neighbors are, and for each multicast it sends out, it maintains a list of the neighbors who have replied. If EIGRP doesn't get a reply from a neighbor, it will switch to using unicasts to resend the same data. If it still doesn't get a reply after 16 unicast attempts, the neighbor is declared dead. People often refer to this process as reliable multicast.

Reliable Transport Protocol (RTP)   The reliable transport protocol, used in the EIGRP routing protocol, is responsible for guaranteed, ordered delivery of EIGRP packets to all neighbors.

reload   An event or command that causes Cisco routers to reboot.

RIF   Routing Information Field: In source-route bridging, a header field that defines the path direction of the frame or token. If the Route Information Indicator (RII) bit is not set, the RIF is read from source to destination (left to right). If the RII bit is set, the RIF is read from the destination back to the source, so the RIF is read right to left. It is defined as part of the token ring frame header for source-routed frames, which contains path information.

ring   Two or more stations connected in a logical circular topology. In this topology, which is the basis for token ring, FDDI, and CDDI, information is transferred from station to station in sequence.

ring topology   A network logical topology comprising a series of repeaters that form one closed loop by connecting unidirectional transmission links. Individual stations on the network are connected to the network at a repeater. Physically, ring topologies are generally organized in a closed-loop star. *Compare with: bus topology* and *star topology.*

RIP   Routing Information Protocol: The most commonly used interior gateway protocol in the Internet. RIP employs hop count as a routing metric. *See also: Enhanced IGRP, IGP, OSPF,* and *hop count.*

RJ connector   Registered jack connector: Used with twisted-pair wiring to connect the copper wire to network interface cards, switches, and hubs.

rolled cable   Type of wiring cable that is used to connect a PC's COM port to a router or switch console port.

ROM Read-only memory: Chip used in computers to help boot the device. Cisco routers use a ROM chip to load the bootstrap, which runs a power-on self-test, and then find and load the IOS in flash memory by default.

root bridge Used with Spanning Tree Protocol to stop network loops from occurring. The root bridge is elected by having the lowest bridge ID. The bridge ID is determined by the priority (32,768 by default on all bridges and switches) and the main hardware address of the device.

route flap A route that is being announced in an up/down fashion.

route poisoning Used by various DV routing protocols in order to overcome large routing loops and offer explicit information about when a subnet or network is not accessible (instead of merely suggesting that the network is unreachable by not including it in updates). Typically, this is accomplished by setting the hop count to one more than maximum. *See also: poison reverse updates.*

route summarization In various routing protocols, such as OSPF, EIGRP, and IS-IS, the consolidation of publicized subnetwork addresses so that a single summary route is advertised to other areas by an area border router.

routed protocol Routed protocols (such as IP and IPX) are used to transmit user data through an internetwork. By contrast, routing protocols (such as RIP, IGRP, and OSPF) are used to update routing tables between routers.

router A Network layer mechanism, either software or hardware, using one or more metrics to decide on the best path to use for transmission of network traffic. Sending packets between networks by routers is based on the information provided on Network layers. Historically, this device has sometimes been called a gateway.

Router ID (RID) The Router ID (RID) is an IP address used to identify the router. Cisco chooses the Router ID by using the highest IP address of all configured loopback interfaces. If no loopback interfaces are configured with addresses, OSPF will choose the highest IP address of all active physical interfaces.

routing The process of forwarding logically addressed packets from their local subnetwork toward their ultimate destination. In large networks, the numerous intermediary destinations a packet might travel before reaching its destination can make routing very complex.

routing domain Any collection of end systems and intermediate systems that operate under an identical set of administrative rules. Every routing domain contains one or several areas, all individually given a certain area address.

routing metric Any value that is used by routing algorithms to determine whether one route is superior to another. Metrics include such information as bandwidth, delay, hop count, path cost, load, MTU, reliability, and communication cost. Only the best possible routes are stored in the routing table, while all other information may be stored in link state or topological databases. *See also: cost.*

routing protocol   Any protocol that defines algorithms to be used for updating routing tables between routers. Examples include IGRP, RIP, and OSPF.

routing table   A table kept in a router or other internetworking mechanism that maintains a record of only the best possible routes to certain network destinations and the metrics associated with those routes.

RP   Route processor: Also known as a supervisory processor; a module on Cisco 7000 series routers that holds the CPU, system software, and most of the memory components used in the router.

RSP   Route/Switch Processor: A processor module combining the functions of RP and SP used in Cisco 7500 series routers. *See also: RP and SP.*

RTS   Request To Send: An EIA/TIA-232 control signal requesting permission to transmit data on a communication line.

S

S reference point   ISDN reference point that works with a T reference point to convert a four-wire ISDN network to the two-wire ISDN network needed to communicate with the ISDN switches at the network provider.

sampling rate   The rate at which samples of a specific waveform amplitude are collected within a specified period of time.

SAP   (1) Service Access Point: A field specified by IEEE 802.2 that is part of an address specification. (2) Service Advertising Protocol: The Novell NetWare protocol that supplies a way to inform network clients of resources and services availability on network, using routers and servers. *See also: IPX.*

SCR   Sustainable cell rate: An ATM Forum parameter used for traffic management, it is the long-term average cell rate for VBR connections that can be transmitted.

SDH   Synchronous Digital Hierarchy: One of the standards developed for Fiber Optics Transmission Systems (FOTS).

SDLC   Synchronous Data Link Control: A protocol used in SNA Data Link layer communications. SDLC is a bit-oriented, full-duplex serial protocol that is the basis for several similar protocols, including HDLC and LAPB. *See also: HDLC and LAPB.*

seed router   In an AppleTalk network, the router that is equipped with the network number or cable range in its port descriptor. The seed router specifies the network number or cable range for other routers in that network section and answers to configuration requests from nonseed routers on its connected AppleTalk network, permitting those routers to affirm or modify their configurations accordingly. Every AppleTalk network needs at least one seed router physically connected to each network segment.

sequencing   Used in virtual circuits and segmentation to number segments so they can be put back together again in the correct order.

serial transmission   WAN serial connectors use serial transmission, which takes place one bit at a time, over a single channel.

server   Hardware and software that provide network services to clients.

Session layer   Layer 5 of the OSI reference model, responsible for creating, managing, and terminating sessions between applications and overseeing dataexchange between presentation layer entities. *See also: Application layer, Data Link layer, Network layer, Physical layer, Presentation layer,* and *Transport layer.*

set-based   Set-based routers and switches use the set command to configure devices. Cisco is moving away from set-based commands and is using the command line interface (CLI) on all new devices.

setup mode   Mode that a router will enter if no configuration is found in nonvolatile RAM when the router boots. Allows the administrator to configure a router step by step. Not as robust or flexible as the command line interface.

SF   A super frame (also called a D4 frame) consists of 12 frames with 192 bits each, and the 193rd bit providing other functions including error checking. SF is frequently used on T1 circuits. A newer version of the technology is Extended Super Frame (ESF), which uses 24 frames. *See also: ESF.*

shared tree   A method of multicast data forwarding. Shared trees use an architecture in which multiple sources share a common rendezvous point.

Shortest Path First (SPF)   A type of routing algorithm. The only true SPF protocol is Open Shortest Path First (OSPF).

signaling packet   An informational packet created by an ATM-connected mechanism that wants to establish connection with another such mechanism. The packet contains the QoS parameters needed for connection and the ATM NSAP address of the endpoint. The endpoint responds with a message of acceptance if it is able to support the desired QoS, and the connection is established. *See also: QoS.*

silicon switching   A type of high-speed switching used in Cisco 7000 series routers, based on the use of a separate processor (the Silicon Switch Processor, or SSP). *See also: SSE.*

simplex   A mode at which data or a digital signal is transmitted. Simplex is a way of transmitting in only one direction. Half duplex transmits in two directions but only one direction at a time. Full duplex transmits both directions simultaneously.

sliding window   The method of flow control used by TCP, as well as several Data Link layer protocols. This method places a buffer between the receiving application and the network data flow. The "window" available for accepting data is the size of the buffer minus the amount of data already there. This window increases in size as the application reads data from it and decreases as new data is sent. The receiver sends the transmitter announcements of the current window size, and it may stop accepting data until the window increases above a certain threshold.

SLIP Serial Line Internet Protocol: An industry standard serial encapsulation for point-to-point connections that supports only a single routed protocol, TCP/IP. SLIP is the predecessor to PPP. *See also: PPP.*

SMDS Switched Multimegabit Data Service: A packet-switched, datagram-based WAN networking technology offered by telephone companies that provides high speed.

SMTP Simple Mail Transfer Protocol: A protocol used on the Internet to provide electronic mail services.

SNA System Network Architecture: A complex, feature-rich, network architecture similar to the OSI reference model but with several variations; created by IBM in the 1970s and essentially composed of seven layers.

SNAP Subnetwork Access Protocol: SNAP is a frame used in Ethernet, token ring, and FDDI LANs. Data transfer, connection management, and QoS selection are three primary functions executed by the SNAP frame.

snapshot routing Snapshot routing takes a point-in-time capture of a dynamic routing table and maintains it even when the remote connection goes down. This allows the use of a dynamic routing protocol without requiring the link to remain active, which might incur per-minute usage charges.

SNMP Simple Network Management Protocol: This protocol polls SNMP agents or devices for statistical and environmental data. This data can include device temperature, name, performance statistics, and much more. SNMP works with MIB objects that are present on the SNMP agent. This information is queried, then sent to the SNMP server.

socket (1) A software structure that operates within a network device as a destination point for communications. (2) In AppleTalk networks, an entity at a specific location within a node; AppleTalk sockets are conceptually similar to TCP/IP ports.

software address Also called a logical address. This is typically an IP address, but can also be an IPX address.

SOHO Small office/home office: A contemporary term for remote users.

SONET Synchronous Optical Network: The ANSI standard for synchronous transmission on fiber-optic media, developed at Bell Labs. It specifies a base signal rate of 51.84 Mbps and a set of multiples of that rate, known as Optical Carrier levels, up to 2.5 Gbps.

source tree A method of multicast data forwarding. Source trees use the architecture of the source of the multicast traffic as the root of the tree.

SP Switch processor: Also known as a ciscoBus controller, it is a Cisco 7000 series processor module acting as governing agent for all CxBus activities.

span A full-duplex digital transmission line connecting two facilities.

SPAN Switched Port Analyzer: A feature of the Catalyst 5000 switch, offering freedom to manipulate within a switched Ethernet environment by extending the monitoring ability of the existing network analyzers into the environment. At one switched segment, the SPAN mirrors traffic onto a predetermined SPAN port, while a network analyzer connected to the SPAN port is able to monitor traffic from any other Catalyst switched port.

spanning explorer packet Sometimes called limited-route or single-route explorer packet, it pursues a statically configured spanning tree when searching for paths in a source-route bridging network. *See also: all-routes explorer packet, explorer packet,* and *local explorer packet.*

spanning tree A subset of a network topology, within which no loops exist. When bridges are interconnected into a loop, the bridge, or switch, cannot identify a frame that has been forwarded previously, so there is no mechanism for removing a frame as it passes the interface numerous times. Without a method of removing these frames, the bridges continuously forward them—consuming bandwidth and adding overhead to the network. Spanning trees prune the network to provide only one path for any packet. *See also: Spanning Tree Protocol* and *spanning-tree algorithm.*

spanning-tree algorithm (STA) An algorithm that creates a spanning tree using the Spanning Tree Protocol (STP). *See also: spanning tree* and *Spanning Tree Protocol.*

Spanning Tree Protocol (STP) The bridge protocol (IEEE 802.1D) that enables a learning bridge to dynamically avoid loops in the network topology by creating a spanning tree using the spanning-tree algorithm. Spanning-tree frames called Bridge Protocol Data Units (BPDUs) are sent and received by all switches in the network at regular intervals. The switches participating in the spanning tree don't forward the frames; instead, they're processed to determine the spanning-tree topology itself. Cisco Catalyst series switches use STP 802.1D to perform this function. *See also: BPDU, learning bridge, MAC address, spanning tree,* and *spanning-tree algorithm.*

SPF Shortest Path First algorithm: A routing algorithm used to decide on the shortest-path. Sometimes called Dijkstra's algorithm and frequently used in link state routing algorithms. *See also: link state routing algorithm.*

SPID Service Profile Identifier: A number assigned by service providers or local telephone companies and configured by administrators to a BRI port. SPIDs are used to determine subscription services of a device connected via ISDN. ISDN devices use SPID when accessing the telephone company switch that initializes the link to a service provider.

split horizon Useful for preventing routing loops, a type of distance vector routing rule where information about routes is prevented from leaving the router interface through which that information was received.

spoofing (1) In dial-on-demand routing (DDR), where a circuit-switched link is taken down to save toll charges when there is no traffic to be sent, spoofing is a scheme used by routers that causes a host to treat an interface as if it were functioning and supporting a session. The router pretends to send "spoof" replies to keepalive messages from the host in an effort to convince the host that the session is up and running. *See also: DDR.* (2) The illegal act of sending a packet labeled with a false address, in order to deceive network security mechanisms such as filters and access lists.

spooler   A management application that processes requests submitted to it for execution in a sequential fashion from a queue. A good example is a print spooler.

SPX   Sequenced Packet Exchange: A Novell NetWare transport protocol that augments the datagram service provided by Network layer (Layer 3) protocols, it was derived from the Switch-to-Switch Protocol of the XNS protocol suite.

SQE   Signal Quality Error: In an Ethernet network, a message sent from a transceiver to an attached machine that the collision-detection circuitry is working.

SRB   Source-Route Bridging: Created by IBM, the bridging method used in token ring networks. The source determines the entire route to a destination before sending the data and includes that information in routing information fields (RIF) within each packet. *Contrast with: transparent bridging.*

SRT   Source-Route Transparent bridging: A bridging scheme developed by IBM, merging source-route and transparent bridging. SRT takes advantage of both technologies in one device, fulfilling the needs of all end nodes. Translation between bridging protocols is not necessary. *Compare with: SR/TLB.*

SR/TLB   Source-Route Translational Bridging: A bridging method that allows source-route stations to communicate with transparent bridge stations aided by an intermediate bridge that translates between the two bridge protocols. Used for bridging between token ring and Ethernet. *Compare with: SRT.*

SSAP   Source Service Access Point: The SAP of the network node identified in the Source field of the packet identifying the Network layer protocol. *See also: DSAP and SAP.*

SSE   Silicon Switching Engine: The software component of Cisco's silicon switching technology, hard-coded into the Silicon Switch Processor (SSP). Silicon switching is available only on the Cisco 7000 with an SSP. Silicon-switched packets are compared to the silicon-switching cache on the SSE. The SSP is a dedicated switch processor that offloads the switching process from the route processor, providing a fast-switching solution, but packets must still traverse the backplane of the router to get to the SSP and then back to the exit interface.

standard IP access list   IP access list that uses only the source IP addresses to filter a network.

standard IPX access list   IPX access list that uses only the source and destination IPX address to filter a network.

star topology   A LAN physical topology with endpoints on the network converging at a common central device (known as a hub) using point-to-point links. A logical ring topology can be configured as a physical star topology using a unidirectional closed-loop star rather than point-to-point links. That is, connections within the hub are arranged in an internal ring. *See also: bus topology* and *ring topology.*

startup range   If an AppleTalk node does not have a number saved from the last time it was booted, then the node selects from the range of values from 65,280 to 65,534.

state transitions   Digital signaling scheme that reads the "state" of the digital signal in the middle of the bit cell. If it is five volts, the cell is read as a one. If the state of the digital signal is zero volts, the bit cell is read as a zero.

static route   A route whose information is purposefully entered into the routing table by an administrator and takes priority over those chosen by dynamic routing protocols.

static VLAN   A VLAN that is manually configured port-by-port. This is the method typically used in production networks.

statistical multiplexing   Multiplexing in general is a technique that allows data from multiple logical channels to be sent across a single physical channel. Statistical multiplexing dynamically assigns bandwidth only to input channels that are active, optimizing available bandwidth so that more devices can be connected than with other multiplexing techniques. Also known as statistical time-division multiplexing or stat mux.

STM-1   Synchronous Transport Module Level 1. In the European SDH standard, one of many formats identifying the frame structure for the 155.52 Mbps lines that are used to carry ATM cells.

store-and-forward packet switching   A technique in which the switch first copies each packet into its buffer and performs a cyclic redundancy check (CRC). If the packet is error-free, the switch then looks up the destination address in its filter table, determines the appropriate exit port, and sends the packet.

STP   (1) Shielded twisted-pair: A wiring scheme, used in many network implementations, that has a layer of shielded insulation to reduce EMI. (2) Spanning Tree Protocol.

straight-through cable   Type of Ethernet cable that connects a host to a switch, host to a hub, or router to a switch or hub.

stub area   An OSPF area carrying a default route, intra-area routes, and interarea routes, but no external routes. Configuration of virtual links cannot be achieved across a stub area, and stub areas are not allowed to contain an ASBR. *See also: non-stub area, ASBR,* and *OSPF.*

stub network   A network having only one connection to a router.

STUN   Serial Tunnel: A technology used to connect an HDLC link to an SDLC link over a serial link.

subarea   A portion of an SNA network made up of a subarea node and its attached links and peripheral nodes.

subarea node   An SNA communications host or controller that handles entire network addresses.

subchannel   A frequency-based subdivision that creates a separate broadband communications channel.

subinterface   One of many virtual interfaces available on a single physical interface.

subnet   *See: subnetwork.*

subnet address   The portion of an IP address that is specifically identified by the subnet mask as the subnetwork. *See also: IP address, subnetwork,* and *subnet mask.*

subnet mask   Also simply known as mask, a 32-bit address mask used in IP to identify the bits of an IP address that are used for the subnet address. Using a mask, the router does not need to examine all 32 bits, only those indicated by the mask. *See also: address mask* and *IP address.*

subnetting   Used in IP networks to break up larger networks into smaller subnetworks.

subnetwork   (1) Any network that is part of a larger IP network and is identified by a subnet address. A network administrator segments a network into subnetworks in order to provide a hierarchical, multilevel routing structure, and at the same time protect the subnetwork from the addressing complexity of networks that are attached. Also known as a subnet. *See also: IP address, subnet mask,* and *subnet address.* (2) In OSI networks, the term specifically refers to a collection of ESs and ISs controlled by only one administrative domain, using a solitary network connection protocol.

summarization   Term used to describe the process of summarizing multiple routing table entries into one entry.

supernetting   *See: summarization.*

SVC   Switched virtual circuit: A dynamically established virtual circuit created on demand and dissolved as soon as transmission is over and the circuit is no longer needed. In ATM terminology, it is referred to as a switched virtual connection. *See also: PVC.*

switch   (1) In networking, a device responsible for multiple functions such as filtering, flooding, and sending frames. It works using the destination address of individual frames. Switches operate at the Data Link layer of the OSI model. (2) Broadly, any electronic/mechanical device allowing connections to be established as needed and terminated if no longer necessary.

switch block   A combination of Layer 2 switches and Layer 3 routers. The Layer 2 switches connect users in the wiring closet into the access layer and provide 10 or 100 Mbps dedicated connections. 1900/2820 and 2900 Catalyst switches can be used in the switch block.

switch fabric   Term used to identify a Layer 2 switched internetwork with many switches. More commonly, it is a term used to identify the inner workings of a switch itself. Thus, it is the matrix of pathways that any frame or cell might be able to traverse as it is switched from input port to output port.

switched LAN   Any LAN implemented using LAN switches. *See also: LAN switch.*

synchronous transmission   Signals transmitted digitally with precision clocking. These signals have identical frequencies and contain individual characters encapsulated in control bits (called start/stop bits) that designate the beginning and ending of each character. *See also: asynchronous transmission* and *isochronous transmission.*

syslog   A protocol used to monitor system log messages by a remote device.

T

T reference point   Used with an S reference point to change a 4-wire ISDN network to a two-wire ISDN network.

T1   Digital WAN that uses 24 DS0s at 64K bps each to create a bandwidth of 1.536Mbps, minus clocking overhead, providing 1.544 Mbps of usable bandwidth.

T3   Digital WAN that can provide bandwidth of 44.763 Mbps.

TACACS+   Terminal Access Controller Access Control System Plus: An enhanced version of TACACS, this protocol is similar to RADIUS. *See also: RADIUS.*

tagged traffic   ATM cells with their cell loss priority (CLP) bit set to 1. Also referred to as Discard Eligible (DE) traffic in frame relay networks. Tagged traffic can be eliminated in order to ensure trouble-free delivery of higher priority traffic, if the network is congested. *See also: CLP.*

TCP   Transmission Control Protocol: A connection-oriented protocol that is defined at the transport layer of the OSI reference model. Provides reliable delivery of data.

TCP/IP   Transmission Control Protocol/Internet Protocol. The suite of protocols underlying the Internet. TCP and IP are the most widely known protocols in that suite. *See also: IP* and *TCP.*

TDM   Time Division Multiplexing: A technique for assigning bandwidth on a single wire, based on preassigned time slots, to data from several channels. Bandwidth is allotted to each channel regardless of a station's intent to send data. *See also: ATDM, FDM,* and *multiplexing.*

TE   Terminal equipment: Any peripheral device that is ISDN-compatible and attached to a network, such as a telephone or computer. TE1s are devices that are ISDN-ready and understand ISDN signaling techniques. TE2s are devices that are not ISDN-ready and do not understand ISDN signaling techniques. A terminal adapter must be used with a TE2.

TE1   Terminal Equipment Type 1. A device with a four-wire, twisted-pair digital interface is referred to as terminal equipment type 1. Most modern ISDN devices are of this type.

TE2   Terminal Equipment Type 2. Devices known as terminal equipment type 2 do not understand ISDN signaling techniques, and a terminal adapter must be used to convert the signaling.

telco   A common abbreviation for the telephone company.

Telnet   The standard terminal emulation protocol within the TCP/IP protocol stack. Method of remote terminal connection, enabling users to log in on remote networks and use those resources as if they were locally connected. Telnet is defined in RFC 854.

terminal adapter (TA)   A hardware interface between a computer without a native ISDN interface and an ISDN line. In effect, a device to connect a standard async interface to a non-native ISDN device, emulating a modem.

terminal emulation   The use of software, installed on a PC or LAN server, that allows the PC to function as if it were a "dumb" terminal directly attached to a particular type of mainframe.

TFTP   Trivial File Transfer Protocol: Conceptually, a stripped-down version of FTP; it's the protocol of choice if you know exactly what you want and where it's to be found. TFTP doesn't provide the abundance of functions that FTP does. In particular, it has no directory browsing abilities; it can do nothing but send and receive files.

TFTP host/server   A host or server on which Trivial File Transfer Protocol is used to send files using IP at the Network layer and UDP at the Transport layer, which makes it unreliable.

thicknet   Also called 10Base5. Bus network that uses a thick coaxial cable and runs Ethernet up to 500 meters.

thinnet   Also called 10Base2. Bus network that uses a thin coax cable and runs Ethernet media access up to 185 meters.

three-way handshake   Term used in a TCP session to define how a virtual circuit is set up. It is called a "three-way" handshake because it uses three data segments.

token   A frame containing only control information. Possessing this control information gives a network device permission to transmit data onto the network. *See also: token passing.*

token bus   LAN architecture that is the basis for the IEEE 802.4 LAN specification and employs token-passing access over a bus topology. *See also: IEEE.*

token passing   A method used by network devices to access the physical medium in a systematic way based on possession of a small frame called a token. *See also: token.*

token ting   IBM's token-passing LAN technology. It runs at 4 Mbps or 16 Mbps over a ring topology. Defined formally by IEEE 802.5. *See also: ring topology and token passing.*

toll network   WAN network that uses the public switched telephone network (PSTN) to send packets.

topology database   A topology database (also called a topology table) contains all destinations advertised by neighboring routers. Associated with each entry is the destination address and a list of neighbors that have advertised the destination.

Traceroute   Also Trace; IP command used to trace the path a packet takes through an internetwork.

transparent bridging   The bridging scheme used in Ethernet and IEEE 802.3 networks, it passes frames along one hop at a time, using bridging information stored in tables that associate end-node MAC addresses with bridge ports. This type of bridging is considered transparent because the source node does not know it has been bridged, because the destination frames are addressed directly to the end node. *Contrast with: SRB.*

Transport layer   Layer 4 of the OSI reference model, used for reliable communication between end nodes over the network. The transport layer provides mechanisms used for establishing, maintaining, and terminating virtual circuits, transport fault detection and recovery, and controlling the flow of information. *See also: Application layer, Data Link layer, Network layer, Physical layer, Presentation layer,* and *Session layer.*

trap   Used to send SNMP messages to SNMP managers.

TRIP   Token Ring Interface Processor: A high-speed interface processor used on Cisco 7000 series routers. The TRIP provides two or four ports for interconnection with IEEE 802.5 and IBM media with ports set to speeds of either 4 Mbps or 16 Mbps set independently of each other.

trunk link   Link used between switches and from some servers to the switches. Trunk links carry traffic for many VLANs. Access links are used to connect host devices to a switch and carry only VLAN information that the device is a member of.

TTL   Time to live: A field in an IP header, indicating the length of time a packet is valid.

TUD   Trunk Up-Down: A protocol used in ATM networks for the monitoring of trunks. Should a trunk miss a given number of test messages being sent by ATM switches to ensure trunk line quality, TUD declares the trunk down. When a trunk reverses state and comes back up, TUD recognizes that the trunk is up and returns the trunk to service.

tunneling   A method of avoiding protocol restrictions by wrapping packets from one protocol in another protocol's frame and transmitting this encapsulated packet over a network that supports the wrapper protocol. *See also: encapsulation.*

U

U reference point   Reference point between a TE1 and an ISDN network. The U reference point understands ISDN signaling techniques and uses a 2-wire connection.

UDP   User Datagram Protocol: A connectionless transport layer protocol in the TCP/IP protocol stack that simply allows datagrams to be exchanged without acknowledgments or delivery guarantees, requiring other protocols to handle error processing and retransmission. UDP is defined in RFC 768.

unicast   Used for direct host-to-host communication. Communication is directed to only one destination and is originated only from one source.

unidirectional shared tree   A method of shared tree multicast forwarding. This method allows only multicast data to be forwarded from the RP.

unnumbered frames   HDLC frames used for control-management purposes, such as link startup and shutdown or mode specification.

user mode   Cisco IOS EXEC mode that allows an administrator to perform very few commands. You can only verify statistics in user mode; you cannot see or change the router or switch configuration.

UTP   Unshielded twisted-pair: Copper wiring used in small-to-large networks to connect host devices to hubs and switches. Also used to connect switch to switch or hub to hub.

V

VBR   Variable bit rate: A QoS class, as defined by the ATM Forum, for use in ATM networks that is subdivided into real time (RT) class and non–real time (NRT) class. RT is employed when connections have a fixed-time relationship between samples. Conversely, NRT is employed when connections do not have a fixed-time relationship between samples, but still need an assured QoS.

VCC   Virtual channel connection: A logical circuit that is created by VCLs (virtual channel links). VCCs carry data between two endpoints in an ATM network. Sometimes called a virtual circuit connection.

VIP   (1) Versatile Interface Processor: An interface card for Cisco 7000 and 7500 series routers, providing multilayer switching and running the Cisco IOS software. The most recent version of VIP is VIP2. (2) Virtual IP: A function making it possible for logically separated switched IP workgroups to run Virtual Networking Services across the switch port.

virtual circuit (VC)   A logical circuit devised to assure reliable communication between two devices on a network. Defined by a virtual path identifier/virtual channel (really the only time "channel" is used) identifier (VPI/VCI) pair, a virtual circuit can be permanent (PVC) or switched (SVC). Virtual circuits are used in frame relay and X.25. Known as virtual channel in ATM. *See also: PVC and SVC.*

virtual ring   In an SRB network, a logical connection between physical rings, either local or remote.

VLAN   Virtual LAN: A group of devices on one or more logically segmented LANs (configured by use of management software), enabling devices to communicate as if attached to the same physical medium, when they are actually located on numerous different LAN segments. VLANs are based on logical instead of physical connections and thus are tremendously flexible.

VLAN ID   Sometimes referred to as VLAN color, the VLAN ID is tagged onto a frame to tell a receiving switch which VLAN the frame is a member of.

VLSM   Variable length subnet mask: Helps optimize available address space and specify a different subnet mask for the same network number on various subnets. Also commonly referred to as "subnetting a subnet."

VMPS   VLAN Management Policy Server: Used to dynamically assign VLANs to a switch port.

VPN   Virtual private network: A method of encrypting point-to-point logical connections across a public network, such as the Internet. This allows secure communications across a public network.

VTP   VLAN Trunking Protocol: Used to update switches in a switch fabric about VLANs configured on a VTP server. VTP devices can be a VTP server, client, or transparent device. Servers update clients. Transparent devices are only local devices and do not share information with VTP clients. VTP devices send VLAN information down trunked links only.

VTP transparent mode   Switch mode that receives VLAN Trunking Protocol VLAN information and passes it on, but doesn't read the information.

W

WAN   Wide area network: Is a designation used to connect LANs together across a DCE (data communications equipment) network. Typically, a WAN is a leased line or dial-up connection across a PSTN network. Examples of WAN protocols include frame relay, PPP, ISDN, and HDLC.

wildcard   Used with access lists and OSPF configurations. Wildcards are designations used to identify a range of subnets.

windowing   Flow-control method used with TCP at the Transport layer of the OSI model.

WINS   Windows Internet Name Service: Name resolution database for NetBIOS names to TCP/IP address.

WinSock   Windows Socket Interface: A software interface that makes it possible for an assortment of applications to use and share an Internet connection. The WinSock software consists of a dynamic link library (DLL) with supporting programs such as a dialer program that initiates the connection.

workgroup layer   The distribution layer is sometimes referred to as the workgroup layer and is the communication point between the access layer and the core. The primary functions of the distribution layer are to provide routing, filtering, and WAN access and to determine how packets can access the core, if needed.

workgroup switching   A switching method that supplies high-speed (100 Mbps) transparent bridging between Ethernet networks as well as high-speed translational bridging between Ethernet and CDDI or FDDI.

X

X Window

A distributed multitasking windowing and graphics system originally developed by MIT for communication between X terminals and Unix workstations.

X.25   An ITU-T packet-relay standard that defines communication between DTE and DCE network devices. X.25 uses a reliable Data Link layer protocol called LAPB. X.25 also uses PLP at the Network layer. X.25 has mostly been replaced by frame relay.

Z

ZIP   Zone Information Protocol: A Session layer protocol used by AppleTalk to map network numbers to zone names. NBP uses ZIP in the determination of networks containing nodes that belong to a zone. *See also: ZIP storm* and *zone.*

ZIP storm   A broadcast storm occurring when a router running AppleTalk reproduces or transmits a route for which there is no corresponding zone name at the time of execution. The route is then forwarded by other routers downstream, thus causing a ZIP storm. *See also: broadcast storm* and *ZIP.*

zone   A logical grouping of network devices in AppleTalk. Also used in DNS. *See also: ZIP.*

Acronyms

In case you hadn't noticed, reading about internetworking is a bit like taking a bath in alphabet soup. Here for your confusion-ending pleasure is a listing of the acronyms and abbreviations I use in this book.

A

AAA Authentication, Authorization, Accounting

AAL5 ATM Adaptation Layer 5

ABR Area Border Router

ACE Access Control Entry

ACK Acknowledgment

ACL Access Control Lists

ACS Access Control Server

AD Administrative Distance
Advertised Distance

ADSL2 Enhanced ADSL

ADSL2+ Further enhanced ADSL

ADU Aironet Desktop Utility

ADV Advertised

AES Advanced Encryption Standard

AF Assured Forwarding

AFI Authority and Format Identifier

AH Authentication Header

AM Amplitude Modulation

AM/FM Amplitude Modulation/Frequency Modulation

ANSI American National Standards Institute

AP Aggregation Point
Access Point

ARA Appletalk Remote Access

ARAP Appletalk Remote Access Protocol

ARIN American Registry for Internet Numbers

ARP Address Resolution Protocol

AS Autonomous System

ASA American Standards Association (now ANSI)

ASBR Autonomous System Boundary Router

ASCII American Standard Code for Information Interchange

ASDL Asymmetric Digital Subscriber Line

ASIC Application Specific Integrated Circuit

ATM Asynchronous Transfer Mode

ATOMIC.IP AtomIC Systems IP Ltd

ATU-C ADSL Terminal Unit-Central Office

ATU-R ADSL Terminal Unit-Remote Unit

AV Attribute Value-Pairs

AVF Active Virtual Forwarder

AVG Active Virtual Gateway

AWP Adaptive Wireless Path

AWPP Adaptive Wireless Path Protocol

B

BDR   Backup Designated Router
Baud Rate

BE   Best Effort

BGP   Border Gateway Protocol

BGP/TCP   Border Gateway Protocol Transmission Control Protocol

BGP4   BGP version 4

BID   Bridge ID

BPDU   Bridge Protocol Data Unit

BPSK   Binary Phase Shift Keying

BRI   Basic Rate ISDN

BSA   Basic Service Area

C

CAC   Call Admission Control

CAM   Content-Addressable Memory

CAP   Carrierless Amplitude Phase modulation

CAS   Channel Associated Signaling

CATV   Community Antenna Television
Cable Television

CB21AG   Cisco Aironet 802.11a/b/g Wireless LAN Client Adapters

CBAC   Context-Based Access Control

CBC-MAC   Cipher Block Chaining Message Authentication Code

CBWFQ   Class Based Weighted Fair Queuing

CCK   Complementary Code Keying

CCMP   Counter Mode CBC-MAC Protocol

CCNA   Cisco Certified Network Administrator

CCNP   Cisco Certified Network Professional

CCO   Cisco Connection Online

CCS   Common Channel Signaling

CCX   Cisco Compatible Extensions

CDP   Cisco Discovery Protocol

CE   Customer Edge

CEF   Cisco Express Forwarding

CGMP   Cisco Group Management Protocol

CHAP   Challenge Handshake Authentication Protocol

CIDR   Classless Inter-domain Routing

CIR   Committed Information Rate

CLI   Command Line Interface

CLNS   Connectionless Network Service

CM   Cable Modem

CMTS   Cable Modem Termination System

CNTL/Z   Cntrl + Z key combination

CO   Central Office (also Cables Originate)

CPE   Customer Premises Equipment

CPU   Central Processing Unit

CRC   Cyclic Redundancy Check

CS   Class Selector

CS-MARS   Cisco Security Monitoring Analysis and Response System

CSA Cisco Secure Agent

CSAMC Cisco Secure Agent Management Center

CSMA/CA Carrier Sense Multiple Access/Collision Avoidance

CST Common Spanning Tree

D

DAI Dynamic ARP Inspection

DBD Database Descriptor

DBPSK Differential Binary Phase Shift Keying

DCC Data Country Code

DCF Distributed Coordination Function

DCSP Domain Central Service Provider

DDOS Distributed Denial Of Service

DDR Dial-on-Demand Routing

DEC Digital Equipment Corporation

DEMARC Demarcation Point

DFS Dynamic Frequency Selection

DHCP Dynamic Host Configuration Protocol

DHCPACK DHCP Acknowledgment

DHCPNAK DHCP Negative Acknowledgement

DMT Discrete Multitone

DMZ Demilitarized Zone

DNS Domain Name System

DOCSIS Data Over Cable Service Interface Specification

DOD Department of Defense

DPD Dead Peer Detection

DQPSK Differential Quadrature Phase Shift Keying

DR Designated Router

DR/BDR Designated Router Backup Designated Router

DSCP DiffServ Code Point

DSL Digital Subscriber Line

DSLAM Digital Subscriber Line Access Multiplexer

DSP Domain Specific Part

DSSS Direct Sequence Spread Spectrum

DTP Dynamic Trunking Protocol

DTV Digital Television standard

DUAL Diffused Update ALgorithm

DVMRP Distance Vector Multicast Routing Protocol

E

E&M Earth and Magneto
            Ear and Mouth

E1 E-carrier standard circuit 1

E2 E-carrier standard circuit 2

EAP Extensible Authentication Protocol

EAP-MD5 Extensible Authentication Protocol Message Digest 5

EAPOL Extensible Authentication Protocol Over LAN

EBGP External Border Gateway Protocol

EDCAF   Enhanced Distributed Channel Access Function

EDCF   Enhanced DCF

EF   Expedited Forwarding

EGP   Exterior Gateway Protocol

EIGRP   Enhanced Interior Gateway Routing Protocol

ES   End System

ES-IS   End System-to-Intermediate System

ESA   Extended Service Area

ESH   End System Hello

ESP   Encapsulating Security Protocol

ETH-LAN   Ethernet-Local Area Network

EX   External

EXP   Experimental field

F

FCC   Federal Communications Commission

FCS   Frame Check Sequence

FD   Feasible Distance

FDDI   Fiber-optic Data Distribution Interface

FDM   Frequency-Division Multiplex

FHSS   Frequency-Hopping Spread Spectrum

FIB   Forwarding Information Base

FIFO   First In First Out

FM   Frequency Modulation

FTP   File Transfer Protocol

FWD   Forward

FXO   Foreign eXchange Office

FXS   Foreign eXchange Station

G

G.dmt   ITU 992.1

G.lite   ITU 992.2

GBIC   Gigabit Interface Converters

GGP   Gateway-to-Gateway Protocol

GLBP   Gateway Load Balancing Protocol

GOSIP   U.S. Government OSI Profile

GRE   Generic Routing Encapsulation

GUI   Graphical User Interface

H

HDLC   High-Level Data Link Control

HDSL   High-Speed Digital Subscriber Line

HDTV   High-Definition Television

HFC   Hybrid Fibre-Coax

HIDS   Host Based Intrusion Detection System

HIPS   Host Based Intrusion Prevention System

HLEN   Header Length

HMAC   Hash Message Authentication Code

HO-DSP   High-Order Domain Specific Part

HQ   Headquarters

HSA   High System Availability
High Speed Access

HSRP Hot Standby Router Protocol

HTTP Hypertext Transfer Protocol

HWIC High-Performance WAN Interface Card

Hz Hertz

HMAC Hash Message Authentication Code

I

IA OSPF Inter Area

IANA Internet Assigned Numbers Authority

IAS Internet Authentication Service

IBSS Independent Basic Service Set

ICD International Code Designator

ICMP Internet Control Message Protocol

ICSA International Computer Security Association

ID Interface Device also Identification Number or Identifier

IDI Initial Domain Identifier

IDP Initial Domain Part

IDRP Inter-Domain Routing Protocol

IDS Intrusion Detection System

IDS/IPS Intrusion Detection System/ Intrusion Prevention System

IDSL ISDN Digital Subscriber Line

IEEE Institute of Electrical & Electronics Engineers, Inc.

IETF Internet Engineering Task Force

IEV IPS Event Viewer

IFS IOS File System

IGMP Internet Group Management Protocol

IGP Interior Gateway Protocol

IGRP Interior Gateway Routing Protocol

IIH IS-IS Hello

IIN Intelligent Information Network

IKE Internet Key Exchange

IOS Internetwork Operating System

IP Information Protocol

IPCP Internet Protocol Control Protocol

IPS Internet Protocol Suite

IPS/IDS Intrusion Prevention System/Intrusion Detection System

IPSec Internet Protocol Security

IPX Internetwork Packet Exchange

IRB Integrated Routing and Bridging

IS Intermediate System

IS-IS Intermediate System-to-Intermediate System

ISAKMP Internet Security Association and Key Management Protocol

ISDN Integrated Services Digital Network

ISH Intermediate System Hello

ISL Inter-Switch Link

ISM Industrial Scientific and Medical

ISO International Organization for Standardization Organisation internationale de normalisation

ISP   Internet Service Provider

ISR   Integrated Services Router

IST   Internal Spanning Tree

IT   Information Technology

ITIL   Information Technology Infrastructure Library

ITU   International Telecommunication Union

K

KE   Key Exchange

kHz   kilohertz

L

LACP   Link Aggregation Control Protocol

LAN   Local Area Network

LAP   Lightweight Access Point

LCP   Link Control Protocol

LDP   Label Distribution Protocol

LEAP   Learning Automata-Based Polling Lightweight Extensible Authentication Protocol

LED   Light Emitting Diode

LFIB   Label Forwarding Information Base

LIB   Label Information Base

LLS   Local Link Signaling

LRE   Long Reach Ethernet

LSA   Link State Advertisement

LSDB   Link State Database

LSP   Link State Protocol

LSP   Label Swapping Protocols

LSR   Link State Routing

LSU   Link State Update

LWAPP   Lightweight Access Point Protocol

M

M-ID   Mode ID

MAC   Media Access Control

MARS   Monitoring Analysis and Response System

MCU   Multipoint Control Units

MD5   Message Digest 5

MHz   megahertz

MIMO   Multiple-Input Multiple-Output

MISTP   Multiple Instance Spanning Tree Protocol

MOP   Maintenance Operation Protocol

MP-BGP   Multi-Protocol BGP

MPLS   Multi-Protocol Label Switching

MPLS TE   MPLS Traffic Engineering

MRU   Maximum Receive Unit

MS-CHAP   Microsoft Challenge Handshake Authentication Protocol

MSS   Maximum Segment Size

MST   Multiple Spanning Tree

MSTI   MST instance

MSTP Multiple Spanning Tree Protocol

MSTP Multiple Spanning Tree

MTU Maximum Transmission Unit

MUX Multiplexer (also Muldex)

N

N1 NSSA 1

N2 NSSA 2

NAC Network Admission Control

NAS Network Access Server

NAT Network Address Translation

NAT-PT Network Address Translation - Protocol Translation

NAT-T Network Address Translation-Traversal

NBMA Non-Broadcast Multi-Access

NBNS NetBIOS Name Service

NCP Network Control Program

NET Network Entity Title

NIC Network Interface Card

NID Network Interface Device

NIDS Network Intrusion Detection Systems

NIPS Network Intrusion Prevention System

NM Network Module

NO Nonegotiate Option

NRAM Nonvolatile Random Access Memory

NSAP Network Service Access Point

NSEL Network Selector

NSSA Not So Stubby Area

NTP Network Time Protocol

NTSC National Television Standards Committee

O

ODR On-Demand Routing

OFDM Orthogonal Frequency Division Multiplexing

OS Operating System

OSI Open Systems Interconnection

OSPF Open Shortest Path First

OSPF-TE Open Shortest Path First-Traffic Engineering

P

PACL Port Access Control List

PAD Packet Assembler and Disassembler

PADI PPPoE Active Discovery Initiation

PADO PPPoE Active Discovery Offer

PADR PPPoE Active Discovery Request

PADS PPPoE Active Discovery Session-Confirmation

PADT PPPoE Active Discovery Terminate

PAL Phase Alternating Line

PAM Pulse Amplitude Modulation

PAP Password Authentication Protocol

PASV Passive Mode
Password Verification

PAT   Port Address Translation

PBX   Private Branch eXchange

PC   Protocol Control
Personal Computer

PCI   Peripheral Component Interconnect

PCMCIA   Peripheral Component
MicroChannel Interconnect
Architecture
Personal Computer Memory
Card International Association

PDA   Personal Digital Assistant

PDU   Protocol Data Unit

PE   Provider Edge

PE1   Priority Exchange 1

PE2   Priority Exchange 3

PFS   Personal File Sharing

PHB   Per-Hop Behavior

PHP   Penultimate Hop Popping

PI21AG   Cisco Aironet 802.11a/b/g Wireless
LAN Client Adapters

PID   Protocol ID

PIM   Protocol Independent Multicast

PIM-DM   PIM Dense Mode

PIM-SM   PIM Sparse Mode

PIX   Private Internet eXchange

PIX/ASA   Private Internet eXchange
Adaptive Security Appliance

PMTU-D   Path Maximum Transmission
Unit Discovery

POP   Point of Presence
Post Office Protocol

POTS   Plain Old Telephone System

PPP   Point-to-Point Protocol

PPP/IP   Point-to-Point IP

PPPoA   PPP over ATM

PPPoE   PPP over Ethernet

PRI   Primary Rate Interface

PSK   Pre-Shared Key

PSTN   Public Switched Telephone
Network

PVACL   Per-Port and VLAN Access
Control List

PVC   Permanent Virtual Circuit

PVLAN   Private VLAN

PVRST   Per VLAN Rapid Spanning Tree

PVST   Per VLAN Spanning Tree

Q

QoS   Quality of Service

R

R&D   Research and Development

RA   Router Advertisement

RACL   Router Access Control Lists

RADAR   Radio Detection And Ranging

RADIUS   Remote Authentication Dial-In
User Service

RADSL   Rate Adaptive Digital
Subscriber Line

RAM   Random Access Memory

RF   Radio Frequency

RFC   Request for Comments (a memorandum published by the Internet Engineering Task Force)

RFID   Radio Frequency Identification

RIB   Routing Information Base

RID   Router Identity

RIP   Routing Information Protocol
Ripv2 Is Pretty

RJ-11   Registered Jack type 11

RLQ   Root Link Query

RP   Rendezvous Point

RPC   Remote Procedure Call

RPF   Reverse Path Forwarding

RPVST   Rapid Per VLAN Spanning Tree

RS   Router Solicitation

RSA   Router Security Audit

RSS   Really Simple Syndication

RST   Reset

Restart

RSTP   Rapid Spanning Tree Protocol
Real-Time Streaming Protocol

RSVP   Resource Reservation Protocol

RSVP-TE   Resource Reservation Protocol-Traffic Engineering

RTMP   Real Time Messaging Protocol
Routing Table Maintenance Protocol

RTO   Retransmission Timeout

RTP   Real-Time Transport Protocol

RTS/CTS   Request to Send Clear to Send

RUE   Resume Updating Event

S

S-CDMA   Synchronous Code Division Multiple Access

SA   isakmp Security Association

SAID   Security Association Identifier

SAP   Session Announcement Protocol

SDEE   Security Device Event Exchange

SDF   Signature Definition File

SDM   Secure Device Manager

SDP   Session Description Protocol

SDSL   Synchronous Digital Subscriber Line

SECAM   Sequential Couleur avec Mémoiré

SFP   Small Form-Factor Pluggable

SHA   Secure Hash Algorithm

SHA-1   Secure Hash Algorithm

SHDSL   Single-Pair High-Speed Digital Subscriber Line

SIA   Stuck-in-Active

SIP   Session Initiation Protocol
SPA Interface Processor
Serial Interface Processor

SLIP   Serial Line Internet Protocol

SMB   Small- and Medium-Sized Businesses

SMTP   Simple Mail Transfer Protocol

SNMP   Simple Network Management Protocol

SOHO   Small Office/Home Office

SONA   Services-Oriented Network Architecture

SPF   Shortest Path First

SPT   Shortest Path Tree

SRTT   Smoothed Round Trip Time

SSH   Secure Shell

SSID   Service Set Identifier
Service Set Identification
Secure Set Identifier

SSL   Secure Sockets Layer

SSM   Source Specific Multicast

ST   Stream Protocol

STP   Spanning Tree Protocol

SVC   Switched Virtual Circuit

SVI   Switched Virtual Interface

SYN   Synchronize

SYN-ACK   Synchronize Acknowledgment

SYSLOG   System Log

T

T1   Digital Signal 1 leased line standard

TAC   Terminal Access Controller

TACACS   Terminal Access Controller Access Control System

TC   Topology Change

TCA   Topology Change Acknowledgement

TCAM   Ternary Content Addressable Memory

TCN   Topology Change Notification

TCP   Transmission Control Protocol

TCP/IP   Transmission Control Protocol Internet Protocol Suite

TDMA   Time Division Multiple Access

TDP   Tag Distribution Protocol

TFTP   Trivial File Transport Protocol

TKIP   Temporal Key Integrity Protocol

TLV   Type Length Value

TPC   Transmit Power Control

TTL   Time to Live
Transistor-to-Transistor Logic

TV   Transparent VPN
Television

U

UDLD   Uni-Directional Link Detection

UDP   User Datagram Protocol

UHF   Ultra High Frequency

UNII   Unlicensed National Information Infrastructure

UNIX   Universal Network Information Exchange
Uniplexed Information and Computing System

URL   Uniform Resource Locator

UTC   Coordinated Universal Time

V

VC   Virtual Circuit

VCI   Virtual Circuit Identifier

VCR   Videocassette Recorder

VDSL   Very-High-Bit-Rate Digital Subscriber Line

VHF   Very High Frequency

VID   Virtual ID

Video

VLAN ID   Virtual Local Area Network Identifier

VLAN   Virtual Local Area Network

VLSM   Variable Length Subnet Masking

VOIP   Voice Over Internet Protocol

VP   Voice Packets

VPDN   Virtual Private Dialup Network

VPI   Virtual Path Indicator

VPI/VCI   Virtual Path Indicator/Virtual Circuit Identifier

VPN   Virtual Private Network

VPN/GRE   Virtual Private Network Generic Routing Encapsulation

VSA   Vendor Specific Attribute

VTP   VLAN Trunk Protocol

VTY   Virtual Teletype Terminal

VWIC   Voice WAN Interface Cards

W

WAN   Wide Area Network

WAP   Wireless Access Point

WCS   Wireless Control System

WDS   Wireless Domain Services
Wide-area Data Services
Wireless Distribution Services

WECA   Wireless Ethernet Compatibility Alliance

WEP   Wired Equivalent Privacy

WFQ   Weighted Fair Queuing

WGB   Work Group Bridge

WIC   WAN Interface Card

Wi-Fi   Wireless Fidelity

WINS   Windows Internet Name Service

WLAN   Wireless Local Area Network

WLANA   WLAN Association

WLC   Wireless LAN Controller

WLSE   Wireless LAN Solution Engine

WMM   Wireless Multimedia

WPA   Wi-Fi Protected Access

WPA2   Wi-Fi Protected Access as adopted by the Wi-Fi Alliance

WRED   Weighted Random Early Detection

WRR   Weighted Round Robin

X

XML   Exchange Markup Language
Extensible Markup Language

XTACACS   Extended Terminal Access Controller Access Control System

XP   Microsoft Windows XP (Experience)

Index

Note to the Reader: Throughout this index **boldfaced** page numbers indicate primary discussions of a topic. *Italicized* page numbers indicate illustrations.

A

AAA (authentication, authorization, and accounting), **495–497**, *496*
  accounting, **507–508**
  authentication, 477, 480, **505–506**
  authorization, **506–507**
  Cisco Easy VPN, 453
  configuring, **503–508**
  Layer 2 security, **528**
  RADIUS, **498–500**, *498*
  TACACS+, **500–503**, *501*
aaa accounting command, **507–508**
aaa accounting exec default command, 508
aaa accounting exec pats_list command, 508
aaa authentication login command, 505
aaa authentication login default command, 506
aaa authentication login pats_list command, 506
aaa authorization command, 506
aaa authorization exec default command, 507
aaa authorization exec pats_list command, 507
aaa new-model command, **503–504**
About Your Router tab, 437
ABRs (Area Border Routers), 195
ACCEPT response in TACACS+, **501–502**
acceptable service traffic levels, 633
Access-Accept messages, 499
Access-Challenge messages, 499
access control entries (ACEs), 531
access layer in hierarchical design model, 3, *3*
access links in VLANs, 34
access-list command, 651
access-list permit ip command
  PAT, 405
  VPNs, 436, 444
access-list remark command, 566
access lists
  Cisco IOS Firewall, **563**
  distribution lists, 140
access points. *See* wireless access points (WAPs)
access ports
  LANs, **46–47**
  VLANs, **34**
Access-Reject messages, 499
Access-Request messages, 499

accounting in AAA, 496, **507–508**
ACEs (access control entries), 531
ACK (acknowledgment) packets, 153
ACL attribute in TACACS+, 502
ACS Solution Engine, 497
active routers in HSRP, 342
active state
  EIGRP, 157
  HSRP, 344
active timers in HSRP, **342**
active virtual forwarder (AVF), 367–369
active virtual gateway (AVG), 367–369
AD (advertised distances), 148, **150–152**
ad hoc mode in wireless topologies, 685, 698, *698*
Ad Hoc Networks dialog, 698, *698*
Adapter Information screen, 696, *696*
adapters
  in diagnostics, 696, *696*
  wireless client configuration, **687–691**, *688–691*
Adaptive Wireless Path Protocol (AWPP), 684
Add a Signature Location dialog, 590, *590*
Add Controllers page, 727–728
Add Group Policy page, 458–461, *459–461*
Add Telnet/SSH Account dialog, 488, *488*
ADDR attribute in TACACS+, 502
Addr-pool attribute in TACACS+, 503
address resolution protocol (ARP)
  DAI, **534**
  ICMP, 325
  Proxy ARP, 339, *339*
  spoofing, **524–525**, *525*
addresses
  BGP, **275–277**, *277*
  IP. *See* IP addresses
  IP Source Guard filters, 534
  IPv6. *See* Internet Protocol Version 6 (IPv6)
  IS-IS, **235–237**, *236*
  Layer 2 switching, **31**
  MAC. *See* Media Access Control (MAC) addresses
  multicasts, **295–299**, *298*
adjacency tables, **55**
adjacent routers, 193
administrative distance in routing, **116–117**

administrative keys setting, 59
administratively scoped multicast addresses, **297**
ADSL. *See* asymmetric digital subscriber
    line (ADSL)
ADSL terminal unit-central office (ATU-C), 396
ADSL terminal unit-remote (ATU-R), 396
ADU (Aironet Desktop Utility), 687, 691,
    695–696, *696*
Advanced Distance Vector Protocol, 123
Advanced Encryption Standard (AES), 712
Advanced Encryption Standard-Counter Mode
    CBC-MAC Protocol (AES-CCMP), 711, 713
Advanced Firewall
    configuring, **552–560**, *552–560*
    verifying, **564–568**
Advanced Firewall Configuration Wizard, 490,
    490, 553, *554–555*
Advanced Firewall DMZ Service Configuration
    dialog, 553, *555*, 557, *557*
Advanced Firewall Interface Configuration
    screen, 553, *554*
Advanced Firewall Security Configuration
    Wizard, 558, *558*
Advanced Statistics screen, 696, *697*
Advanced Status page, 695, *695*
Advanced tab for wireless client profiles, 694, *694*
advertised distances (AD), 148, **150–152**
advertisements
    intervals, 365
    link state, 127, **198–199**
    router, 321, *321*
AES (Advanced Encryption Standard), 712
AES-CCMP (Advanced Encryption Standard-
    Counter Mode CBC-MAC Protocol),
    711, 713
AF (assured forwarding), 641
AFI (Authority and Format Identifier), 236, *236*
aggressive mode in UDLD, 101
AHs (Authentication Headers), 431–432, *431*
Aironet Desktop Utility (ADU), 687, 691,
    695–696, *696*
Aironet Site Survey utility, 688, *689*
AirSnort, 712
alarms in IPS, 577, **584–585**
alerts in EIGRP, 162
All Controllers page, 726–728, *729*
alternate ports in RSTP, 90
alternative wireless hardware in case study, 23
AM radio interference, 394
amplifiers, cable, 380
AND function with match command, 273–274
anomaly-based IPS approach, **580–581**

antennas
    cable systems, 381, 384
    wireless systems, **681–683**
anycast communications, 316, 319
AP (access points). *See* wireless access
    points (WAPs)
Application Security tab, 550, *551*
application servers for voice, 605
application-specific integrated circuits (ASICs), 53
area addresses in IS-IS, 237
Area Border Routers (ABRs), 195
area boundaries, **239**
area command, 219
Area ID field, 197, 201
area stub command, 221, 226
area stub no-summary command, 221, 226–227
areas in OSPF, 197, 201
    description, 194
    designations, **194**
    vs. IS-IS, 240
ARP (address resolution protocol)
    DAI, **534**
    ICMP, 325
    Proxy ARP, 339, *339*
    spoofing, **524–525**, *525*
AS (Autonomous System)
    dynamic routing, 122
    EIGRP, **158–159**, *160*
AS-path attribute in BGP, **266–267**, *266*
ASBRs (Autonomous System Boundary
    Routers), 195
ASICs (application-specific integrated circuits), 53
assured forwarding (AF), 641
asterisks (*) in BGP, 283
asymmetric digital subscriber line (ADSL),
    390–392, *390*
    benefits, **396**
    data, **398**
    details, **395–396**
    equipment, 396
    modulating, 397
    PPP over ATM, **401–402**
    PPPoE. *See* PPP over Ethernet (PPPoE)
    RFC 1483 bridging, **398**
ATM interface
    CPE configuration with PPPoE, **408–409**
    PPP over, **401–402**
attacks, Layer 2, **517–519**
    MAC layer, **519–520**
    spoofing, **523–525**, *525*
    switch device, **525–526**
    VLAN, **520–523**, *521*

attenuation in DSL, 394
ATU-C (ADSL terminal unit-central
    office), 396
ATU-R (ADSL terminal unit-remote), 396
Auth Key Mgmt in WLC, 738, *738*
authentication
    AAA, 477, 480, 495, 505–506
    AutoSecure, 477, 480
    dialer interface, 405
    enterprise teleworkers, 379
    PPPoE, 399–400
    RADIUS, **498–500**, *498*
    servers, 529
    VPN connections, 440
    wireless, 710
authentication, authorization, and accounting.
    See AAA (authentication, authorization,
    and accounting)
Authentication field in OSPF, 197
Authentication Headers (AHs), 431–432, *431*
Authentication password field in OSPF, 201
authentication pre-share command, 436, 443
authentication proxy, **540**
Authentication type field in OSPF, 197
authenticators, *529*
Authority and Format Identifier (AFI), 236, *236*
authorization, 495–496, **506–507**
auto-cost reference-bandwidth command, 213
auto option in dot1x port-control, *530*
Auto-RP, 307
auto secure command, 474–476
auto-summary command, 163
Autocmd attribute in TACACS+, *503*
autoconfiguration in IPv6, **320–322**, *321*
automatic bundling protocols, 58–60
automatic summarization
    disabling, **169–170**
    RIP, 132
Autonomous System (AS)
    dynamic routing, 122
    EIGRP, **158–159**, *160*
Autonomous System Boundary Routers
    (ASBRs), 195
autonomous wireless solutions, **698–699**
AutoQoS feature, **648**
AutoSecure feature, **472–473**
    configuring, 474–482
    lockdown items, **473**
    rollback, **473–474**
auxiliary VLANs, **614–616**
AV-pairs in RADIUS, 499–500
Available Networks Screen, 698, *698*

AVF (active virtual forwarder), 367–369
AVG (active virtual gateway), 367–369
AWPP (Adaptive Wireless Path Protocol), 684

B

backbone areas in OSPF, **194**, 239
backbone routers in OSPF, 195
BackboneFast feature, 81, **84–87**, *86*, **106**
backbones in case study, **13**
Backup Designated Routers (BDRs), 195
backup ports in RSTP, 90
bandwidth
    delay, **629**, 631
    dynamic routing, 121
    EIGRP, 166–167
    IGRP, 137
    Layer 2 switching, 31
    QoS, **626–628**
    STP, 80
    voice, 603
bandwidth command
    CBWFQ, 655
    EIGRP, 176
bandwidth percent command, 655–656
base keys in WEP, 711–712
Basic Firewall
    configuring, **545–551**, *545–551*
    verifying, **560–564**
Basic Firewall Configuration Wizard, 547–549,
    547–549
basic routing, **112–116**, *115–116*
Basic Service Area (BSA), **686**
basic service sets, 685
BDRs (Backup Designated Routers), 195
best-effort QoS model, **634–635**
best routes in EIGRP, 150
BGP. *See* border gateway protocol (BGP)
bgp always-compare-med command, 268
BGP/TCP keepalive messages, 254
BID (Bridge ID) field, 69–71, 73–75
bidirectional PIM mode, 304–305
black holes in IBGP routing, 260
block acknowledgment in 2.4GHz/5GHz, 678
blocking traffic in IPS, 577, 585
border gateway protocol (BGP), 128
    appropriate uses, **249–250**
    attributes
        AS-path, **266–267**, *266*
        local preference, **264–265**, *265*

multi-exit discriminator,
  267–268, *267*
next-hop, **268**
origin, 265–266
path, 262–263
route maps for, 270
weight, 263–264, *264*
configuring, 274–275, 280–283, *281*
connections, 250–252, 257–258
IBGP, **258–261**, *259–261*
inappropriate uses, **249**
message types, 254–256
neighbors, 257, **275**
network command, 280
next-hop issues, 278
operations, 248–249
path vectors, 252–253
paths, 268–269
peer groups, 278–280, *279*
peers, 257, **276**
review questions, 287–289
route maps, 270–274
source and destination IP addresses,
  275–277, *277*
summary, **286**
tables, **254**
transmissions, **253**
verifying, 283–286
BPDU Guard, 97, **517**
Bridge ID (BID) field, 69–71, 73–75
Bridge Protocol Data Units (BPDUs),
  68–70, *69*
filtering, **98–99**, *99*
Loop Guard, 100
RSTP, 91
bridge taps in DSL, 394
bridges
RSTP, 91
STP, 70
wireless, 684–685
broadband cable, 377, *379*
broadcasts
IPv6, 316
OSPF networks, **216**
transmissions, **293**
Bronze category in WMM, 714–715
BSA (Basic Service Area), **686**
bundle-enable command, 409
bundling protocols, 61
business traffic requirements, 633
busy signals, 608

C

cable modem termination system (CMTS), 382
cable modems (CMs), 382
cable technologies, 379
  benefits, 384–385, *385*
  broadband, 377, *379*
  components, 381
  data over, 386–387, *387*
  DOCSIS, 381–382
  downstream data transfers, 387–388
  fiber, 385–386
  HFC architecture, 386, *386*
  original systems, 384
  provisioning cable modems, 388–389
  radio waves, 382–384, *382*
  standards, 380
  terms, 379–380
  upstream data transfers, 388
CAC (Call Admission Control), 605–606
cache-based CEF, 55
cache switching, **414–415**
Call Admission Control (CAC), 605–606
call agents for voice, 605
call control, **606**
  centralized, **608–609**, *609*
  distributed, **607–608**, *608*
Call Manager, 602
CAM (content-addressable memory) tables
  Layer 2 switching, 31
  MAC layer attacks, 519–520
  multilayer switching, 53
campus core, 6
Campus Infrastructure Module, **6–7**
campus module, 5, 6, 376–377
CAP (Carrierless Amplitude and Phase)
  modulation, 397
CAR (committed access rate), 646
CardBus adapters, 687
Carrier Sense Multiple Access with Collision
  Avoidance (CSMA/CA), 675–676, *675*
Carrierless Amplitude and Phase (CAP)
  modulation, 397
CAS (channel associated signaling), 605–606
case study overview, **10–11**
  background, **11–16**, *12*
  test network, 16–21, *17*
  wireless equipment, **21–23**
CATV (Community Antenna Television), 379, 384
CBAC (Content-based Access Control),
  541–543, *541*, *543*

CBWFQ (class-based weighted fair queuing), 626, **645**

CCK (Complementary Code Keying) modulation, 679

CCS (channel signaling), 605

CDP (Cisco Discovery Protocol), 615

CEF (Cisco Express Forwarding)
MPLS, **415–416**
overview, **54–55**

centralized call control, **608–609**, *609*

CGMP (Cisco Group Management Protocol), **300–301**

change process in LSDBs, **210**

channel associated signaling (CAS), 605

channel-group command, **60–61**

channel-protocol lacp command, 61

channel signaling (CCS), 605

channels in 2.4GHz, 676, *676*

CHAP authentication, 405

Check Ports dialog, 719, *720*

Checksum field, 197

Cisco Discovery Protocol (CDP), 615

Cisco Easy VPN, **452–453**
configuring, **453–463**, *454–463*
Dead Peer Detection, 464
redundant connections and equipment, **463**
redundant routes, **464**

Cisco Express Forwarding (CEF)
MPLS, **415–416**
overview, **54–55**

Cisco Group Management Protocol (CGMP), **300–301**

Cisco IOS Firewall, **539–540**
authentication proxy, 540
configuring, 545
advanced, **552–560**, *552–560*
basic, **545–551**, *545–551*
DDOS protection, 544
review questions, **570–572**
setup, 490, *490*
stateful packet inspection, **541–543**, *541*, *543*
summary, **569**
transparent firewall, **541**
verifying
advanced, **564–568**
basic, **560–564**

Cisco Secure Access Control Server (CSACS), 699

Cisco Secure Agent Management Center (CSAMC), 579

Cisco Secure Agents (CSA), 579

Cisco Unified Wireless Network (CUWN), 670, 697, 713

class-based weighted fair queuing (CBWFQ), 626, **645**

class busisnness_app_mark command, 654

class ftp_mark command, 654

class http_mark command, 654

class-map business_app_mark command, 651

class-map ftp_mark command, 651

class-map http_mark command, 651

class-map queue_business_app command, 655

class-map queue_voice command, 654

class-map voice_mark command, **650–651**

Class of Service (CoS), 625
markings, 613
network traffic, 634
QoS, **638**

class queue_business_app command, 655

class queue_http_ftp command, 655

class queue_voice command, 655

class voice_mark command, 652, 654

classifications
QoS, **612–613**
traffic, **633–634**

CLI (Command-Line Interface)
MQC. *See* Modular QoS CLI (MQC)
QoS, 647

client mode
Cisco Easy VPN, 453
VTP, **41**

Client Settings tab, 458, *460*

clients
Cisco Easy VPN, 458, *460*
IEEE devices, 529
PPPoE, 399, *399*
redundancy issues, **338–339**, *338–339*
wireless access, **685**
wireless configuration, **687**
adapters, **687–691**, *688–691*
connection status, **694–695**, *695*
diagnostics, **695–698**, *696–698*
profiles, **691–694**, *692–694*

CLNS (Connectionless Network Service), **235–236**

clock rate command, 444

clock synchronization, **509–510**

CMD attribute in TACACS+, 502

CMTS (cable modem termination system), 382

coaxial cable, 379

codecs, voice, 604

coexistence of applications in QoS, 612

collision detection, **675–676**

collision domains, 30

colons (:) in IPv6 addresses, **316–318**

color encoding systems, 380
Command Delivery Status screen, 663, *663*
Command-Line Interface (CLI)
    MQC. *See* Modular QoS CLI (MQC)
    QoS, **647**
Commands Delivery Status screen
    Cisco Easy VPN, 462, *462*
    Cisco IOS Firewall, 549, *549*, 559, *559*
    IOS IPS, 592, *592*
commands level option
    AAA accounting, 507
    AAA authorization, 506
committed access rate (CAR), 646
Common Spanning Tree (CST), 81–82
Community Antenna Television (CATV),
    379, 384
community ports in PVLANs, 532
community VLANs, 532
Complementary Code Keying (CCK)
    modulation, 679
compression
    QoS, **627**, **629–630**
    voice transmission, 610
config-commands option in AAA
    authorization, 506
Configuration screen in IPS, 586
configure terminal command, 53, 56
configure terminal vlan command, 45
Configure tool, 437
congestion avoidance, 625, 631, **646–647**
congestion control in multicasts, 295
connected parameter for stub routers, 172
Connection option in AAA accounting, 507
connection signatures, 583
Connectionless Network Service (CLNS),
    235–236
connections
    BGP, 250–252, 257–258
    EIGRP, **148**
    resetting, 577, 585
    wireless clients, **694–695**, *695*
consolidated voice networks, 603
content-addressable memory (CAM) tables
    Layer 2 switching, 31
    MAC layer attacks, 519–520
    multilayer switching, 53
Content-based Access Control (CBAC), **541–543**,
    541, *543*
CONTINUE response in TACACS+, 501
control planes in MPLS, **416–417**, *416*
Controller Properties page, **729–730**, *729*

convergence
    case study, **14–15**
    EIGRP, **147**
    traffic, **603–604**
converting voice, **609–611**
Coordinated Universal Time (UTC), 509
core layer
    case study, **13**
    three-layer hierarchical design model, *3*, *4*
CoS (Class of Service), 625
    markings, 613
    network traffic, 634
    QoS, 638
costs
    EIGRP routes, **151–152**
    OSPF, **212–213**
    STP paths, **72–74**, *74*, *79*
    voice transmission, 603
counting to infinity, 126
CPE (customer premises equipment) configuration
    as PPPoA client, **409–411**, *409*
    with PPPoE and ATM interface,
        408–409
    as PPPoE client, **402–403**, *402*
CRC (cyclic redundancy check), 36
Create Firewall tab, 552–553, *553*
Create IPS tab, 586, *587*
Create QoS Policy tab, 656
Create Site to Site VPN tab, 437, *439*
crosstalk in DSL, 394
crypto ip-sec transform-set command, 436
crypto isakmp policy command, 436, 443
crypto isakmp sa command, 445
crypto map, checking, **444–445**
crypto map command, 444
CSA (Cisco Secure Agents), 579
CSACS (Cisco Secure Access Control
    Server), 699
CSAMC (Cisco Secure Agent Management
    Center), 579
CSMA/CA (Carrier Sense Multiple Access with
    Collision Avoidance), 675–676, *675*
CST (Common Spanning Tree), 81–82
Current Status tab, 694, *695*
customer premises equipment (CPE) configuration
    as PPPoA client, **409–411**, *409*
    with PPPoE and ATM interface, **408–409**
    as PPPoE client, **402–403**, *402*
CUWN (Cisco Unified Wireless Network), 670,
    697, 713
cyclic redundancy check (CRC), 36

D

DAI (Dynamic ARP inspection), 526, **534**
data
    ADSL, **398**
    over cable, **386–387**, *387*
data and voice
    ADSL, 396
    DSL, 392
Data field in OSPF, **197**
Data Link Layer in traffic marking, 637
data loss in multicasts, 295
Data Over Cable Service Interface Specification
    (DOCSIS), 381–382
data planes in MPLS, **416–417**, *416*
data rate shifting, 675
DBD packets
    LSDBs, **209**
    OSPF, 197
DBPSK (Differential Binary Phase Shift
    Keying), 679
DCF (distributed coordination function), 714
DDOS (Distributed Denial of Service)
    attacks, **544**
dead intervals in OSPF, 201
Dead Peer Detection (DPD), **464**
debug crypto ipsec command, 445
debug crypto isakmp command, 445
debug ip rip command, **134–136**
debug standby command, 346, 350
dedicated bandwidth in Layer 2 switching, 31
Default ADU Status page, *692*
default gateway routers, 338, *338*
default-router command, 407
default routes
    BGP, **251–252**
    EIGRP, **167–169**, *168*
delay
    bandwidth, **629**, 631
    BPDU, 70
    EIGRP, 166–167
    QoS, **628–630**
Delivery Screen, 494, *494*
demarcation point (DEMARC), 396
dense PIM mode, **302–305**, *304*
Deny Action on IPS Interface option, 592
deny ip any any log command, 563
designated ports
    RSTP, 90
    STP, 71
Designated Routers (DRs) in OSPF
    description, 195
    elections, **204–208**, *205–207*

Designing Large-Scale IP Internetworks
    document, 213
destination addresses in BGP, **275–277**, 277
destination-pattern command, 617–619
deterministic failures, 2
device security, **469–470**
    AAA. *See* AAA (authentication, authorization,
        and accounting)
    AutoSecure feature, **472–473**
        configuring, 474–482
        lockdown items, 473
        rollback, **473–474**
    management, 508–510
    purpose, 470–472
    RADIUS, **498–500**, *498*
    review questions, 511–513
    Security Audit Wizard, 482–495
    summary, 510
    TACACS+, 500–503, *501*
DFS (Dynamic Frequency Selection), 677
DHCP (Dynamic Host Configuration Protocol)
    local VLANs, 40
    snooping, **533**
    spoofing, 523–524
DHCP servers, Ethernet interface configuration
    as, **406–407**
DHCPv6 (Dynamic Host Configuration Protocol
    for IPv6), **322–324**
diagnostics for client wireless devices, **695–698**,
    696–698
Diagnostics tab, 695–696, *696*
diagrams, network, 74
dial-peer voice command, 617–619
dialer interface configuration, 403–405
dialer lists, 404
dialer pool command, 404–405
dialer pool-member command, 410
diameter option in STP, 78
Differential Binary Phase Shift Keying
    (DBPSK), 679
Differential Quadrature Phase Shift Keying
    (DQPSK), 679
Differentiated Services Code Point (DSCP)
    marking, 613, 625, **639–643**,
    639–640, *642*
Diffie-Hellman Groups, 443
DiffServ field, 640, *640*
DiffServ Quality of Service. *See* Quality of
    Service (QoS)
Diffused Update ALgorithm (DUAL), 127,
    147–148, 150
digital interfaces for voice, 605
digital signal processors (DSPs), 605

digital subscriber line (DSL), 377, **389–390**
    categories, **391**
    characteristics, **391–392**
    issues, **394–395**
    speed vs. distance limitations, **393–394**
    types, **392–393**
Digital Subscriber Line Access Multiplexer
    (DSLAM), 391
digital television (DTV), 380
Dijkstra's algorithm
    IS-IS, 212, 235
    OSPF, 200, 213–214
Direct-Sequence Spread Spectrum (DSSS), 676, **679**
disabling automatic summarization, 170
discovery stage in PPPoE, 400
Discrete Multitone (DMT) modulation, **397**
discretionary attributes in BGP, 262–263
distance
    administrative, **116–117**
    DSL limitations, 393–394
    EIGRP, 148, **150–152**
distance vector protocols, 123
    EIGRP. *See* Enhanced Interior Gateway
        Routing Protocol (EIGRP)
    IGRP, **137–138**
    overview, **124–128**, *125*
    RIP. *See* Routing Information Protocol (RIP)
distribute-list command, 140
distribute-list out command, 140
distribute lists, **139–140**
distributed applications, 294
distributed call control, **607–608**, *608*
distributed coordination function (DCF), 714
Distributed Denial of Service (DDOS)
        attacks, **544**
distributed traffic shaping (DTS), 646
distribution layer, **3–4**, *3*
distribution networks, 381
DMT (Discrete Multitone) modulation, **397**
DMZ interface, 553, *555–557*, *556–559*, 564–566
DMZ Service Configuration dialog, *556*, 556
DNS (Domain Name System) servers, 524
dns-server command, 324
DNS/WINS screen, 458, *459*
do command, 45
DOCSIS (Data Over Cable Service Interface
        Specification), **381–382**
domain-name command, 324
Domain Name System (DNS) servers, 524
domain names in AutoSecure, 480
Domain-Specific Part (DSP) in IS-IS addresses,
        236, 237

DoS signatures, 583
dot1q protocol, **36–37**, *36*
dot1x port-control command, 529–530
double tagging in VLAN attacks, **523**
downstream cable transmissions, 380, **387–388**
DPD (Dead Peer Detection), **464**
DQPSK (Differential Quadrature Phase Shift
        Keying), 679
DR and BDR IP addresses field in OSPF, 201
drop probability bits, 641–643, *642*
dropped packets in PPPoE, **412–413**
DRs (Designated Routers) in OSPF
    description, 195
    elections, **204–208**, *205–207*
DSCP (Differentiated Services Code Point)
        marking, 613, 625, **639–643**,
        639–640, 642
DSL. *See* digital subscriber line (DSL)
dsl operating-mode command, 408–409
dsl operating-mode auto command, 410
DSLAM (Digital Subscriber Line Access
        Multiplexer), 391
DSP (Domain-Specific Part) in IS-IS addresses,
        236, 237
DSPs (digital signal processors), 605
DSSS (Direct-Sequence Spread Spectrum),
        676, **679**
DTP (Dynamic Trunking Protocol)
    overview, 37, *38*
    switch spoofing, 520–522
DTS (distributed traffic shaping), 646
DTV (digital television), 380
DUAL (Diffused Update ALgorithm), 127,
        147–148, 150
dual stacking, **329–330**
duplicate multicast packets, 295
dwell time, 680
Dynamic ARP inspection (DAI), 526, **534**
dynamic auto mode in DTP, 37
dynamic desirable mode in DTP, 37
Dynamic Frequency Selection (DFS), 677
Dynamic Host Configuration Protocol (DHCP)
    local VLANs, 40
    snooping, **533**
    spoofing, 523–524
Dynamic Host Configuration Protocol for IPv6
        (DHCPv6), **322–324**
dynamic NAT-PT, 333
dynamic routing
    EGP, 128
    IGP, **123–128**
    overview, **121–123**, *123*

Dynamic Trunking Protocol (DTP)
    overview, **37**, *38*
    switch spoofing, *520–522*
dynamic tunnels, **332**

E

E&M ports, 605
EAP (extensible authentication protocol), 708
EAPOL (Extensible Authentication Protocol over
    LAN) traffic, *528–530*
Easy VPN Server Wizard, **453–458**, *454–458*,
    461–463, *461–463*
eavesdropping issues in multicasts, 295
EBGP (external BGP), **257**, 266–269, 275, **277**
EDCAF (Enhanced Distributed Channel Access
    Function), 714
EDCF (enhanced DCF), 714
edge LSRs, 420
edge ports, 91
edge routers, 119, *119*
Edit Firewall Policy/ACL tab, 549, *550–551*,
    560, *560*
Edit IPS tab, 592, *593–594*
Edit page for WLANs, 737
Edit QoS Profile page, 735–736, *735*
Edit Signature screen, 594, *595–596*
EF (expedited forwarding), 641
efficiency
    multicasts, 294
    OSPF vs. IS-IS, 239
efficient resource utilization in GLBP, 368
EGPs (Exterior Gateway Protocols), **128**, **247–248**
    BGP. *See* border gateway protocol (BGP)
    dynamic routing, 122
    overview, **128**
80/20 rule for end-to-end VLANs, 39
802.1Q tagging, **36–37**, *36*, **523**
802.1x standards. *See* Institute of Electrical and
    Electronics Engineers (IEEE) standards
EIGRP. *See* Enhanced Interior Gateway Routing
    Protocol (EIGRP)
eigrp stub command, 172
EIGRPv6 protocol, **327**
election process
    IGMP, 300
    OSPF, **204–208**, *205–207*
    STP, 71
enable authentication method, 505
enabling EIGRP, **158**
Encapsulating Security Payload (ESP), **431–433**

encapsulation
    GRE, **433–435**, *433*
    ISL, **35–36**, *36*
    trunk, 47–48
    voice overhead, **610–611**
encapsulation aa15mux ppp dialer command, 410
encapsulation dot1q command, 53
encapsulation ppp command, 404
encoding voice transmission, 610
encryption
    AES, 712
    ESP, 433
    VPNs, 443
    WEP, 711
    WPA, 713
End System Hello (ESH) packets, 235
end-to-end VLANs, **38–39**
enhanced DCF (EDCF), 714
Enhanced Distributed Channel Access Function
    (EDCAF), 714
Enhanced Interior Gateway Routing Protocol
    (EIGRP), 120, 123
    capabilities, **147–148**
    configuring, **159–161**, 163–166
    default routing, **167–169**, *168*
    description, **127–128**
    enabling, 158
    features, **146–147**
    interface control, **161–162**
    load balancing, **173–175**, *175*
    message types, 153
    metrics, **166–167**
    query propagation, 171
    remote sites, **177–178**, *177*
    review questions, **188–190**
    route costs, **151–152**
    stub routers, **171–173**
    successor and feasible successor routes, 152
    summary, **187**
    summary routes, **169–171**
    tables, **155–158**
    terms, **148–151**, *150*
    verifying and troubleshooting, **179–186**
    over WANs, **176–178**
Enterprise Branch, 376–377
Enterprise Campus module, 5, 6, 376–377
Enterprise Composite Network Model, **4–5**, *5*
    Campus Infrastructure Module, **6–7**
    Enterprise Campus Module, 5, 6
    Enterprise Edge, **7–8**
    Network Management Block, 7
    Server Farm Block, 7
    service provider edge, **9**

Enterprise Edge, 7–8, 13
enterprise network design, **1**
    case study, **10–23**, *12, 17*
    Enterprise Composite Network Model. *See*
        Enterprise Composite Network Model
    IIN and SONA, **9**
    three-layer hierarchical design model, **2–4**, *3*
enterprise teleworkers, **378–379**
    cable technologies. *See* cable technologies
    DSL technologies, **389–395**, *390*
enterprise WANs, **413**
equal-cost load balancing, **173–174**
ERROR response in TACACS+, 501
ESA (Extended Service Area) in wireless
    topologies, **686**
ESH (End System Hello) packets, 235
ESP (Encapsulating Security Payload), 431–433
EtherChannel feature, 3, **57–58**
    automatic bundling protocols, **58–60**
    configuring, **60–62**
Ethernet interface configuration as DHCP servers,
    406–407
European Telecommunications Standards
    Institute (ETSi), 671
exec option
    AAA accounting, 507
    AAA authorization, 506
exit command, 96
expedited forwarding (EF), 641
exploit signatures, 583
Express SDM, 21
Extended Service Area (ESA) in wireless
    topologies, **686**
extended services sets, 685
Extended User Authentication (XAuth), 456, *457,*
    461, *461*
extensible authentication protocol (EAP), 708
Extensible Authentication Protocol over LAN
    (EAPOL) traffic, 528–530
Exterior Gateway Protocols (EGPs), **128**, 247–248
    BGP. *See* border gateway protocol (BGP)
    dynamic routing, 122
    overview, **128**
external BGP (EBGP), **257**, 266–269, 275, 277
external modems with PPPoE, 400

F

failure, deterministic, 2
FCC (Federal Communications Commission), 671
FCS (frame check sequence), 36

feasible distances (FD), 148, **150–152**
feasible successors, 148, 150, **152**
Federal Communications Commission (FCC), 671
feeder cables, 381
FHSS (Frequency-Hopping Spread Spectrum),
    679–680
FIB (forwarding information base) tables
    building, 55
    description, 415–416
    MPLS, 420–421
fiber cable systems, **385–386**
FIFO (First-In-First-Out) queuing, 626, 644
filters
    BPDU, **98–99**, *99*
    IP Source Guard, 534
firewall option, 474
Firewall Wizard, 490, *490–492*
firewalls
    AutoSecure, 474
    Cisco Easy VPN, 458
    Cisco IOS Firewall. *See* Cisco
        IOS Firewall
    Security Audit Wizard, 490, *490–492*
First-In-First-Out (FIFO) queuing, 626, 644
5GHz standards, **677–678**, *677*
Fix It page, 485, *487*
Flags field in BPDU, 69
flat architectures, 32
floating static routes, 117, 120, *120*
flood attacks, 519–520
flush timers, **129**
force-authorized option, 530
force-unauthorized option, 530
foreign exchange offices (FXO), 605
foreign exchange stations (FXS), 605
40MHz channels in 2.4GHz/5GHz, 678
Forward Delay field in BPDU, 70
forwarding, priority, **626, 629**, 631
forwarding information base (FIB) tables
    building, 55
    description, 415–416
    MPLS, 420–421
forwarding lookups, 53–54
forwarding planes, **473–474**
4G networks, 679
frame check sequence (FCS), 36
frame errors, 630
Frame Relay traffic marking, 637
Frame Relay traffic shaping (FRTS), 646
Frequency-Hopping Spread Spectrum (FHSS),
    679–680
FTP Password dialog, 720–721, *721*

full-duplex mode
    Layer 2 switching, 30
    RSTP, 91
full mesh
    IBGP, 260–261, *261*
    and TCP, **262**
full option in AutoSecure, 474
full route tables in BGP, **252**
FutureTech Corporation case study
    overview, **10–11**
    background, **11–16**, *12*
    test network, **16–21**, *17*
    wireless equipment, **21–23**
FXO (foreign exchange offices), 605
FXS (foreign exchange stations), 605

G

G.991.2 single-pair high-speed digital subscriber
    line (G.SHDSL), 390, **393**
g.lite standard, 398
gatekeepers, voice, 605
Gateway Load Balancing Protocol (GLBP),
    340, 367
    configuring, **371**
    features, **368–369**
    functions, **367–368**
    per-host traffic balancing, **369**
gateway routers, 338, *338*
Gateway-to-Gateway Protocol (GGP), 128
gateways, voice, 604
    configuring, **616–619**, *617*
    interfaces, **605**
GBIC (gigabit interface converters), 101
General tab
    Cisco Easy VPN, 458, *459*
    wireless client profiles, 692, *693*
Generic Routing Encapsulation (GRE),
    433–435, *433*
geographic issues for VLANs, 39–40
GGP (Gateway-to-Gateway Protocol), 128
gigabit interface converters (GBIC), 101
GLBP. *See* Gateway Load Balancing
    Protocol (GLBP)
glbp ip command, 371
glbp priority command, 371
glbp timers command, 371
global multicast addresses, **297**
Global Setting page, 592, *593*
global UDLD configuration, 101
global unicast addresses, 318

Gold category in WMM, 714–715
GRE (Generic Routing Encapsulation),
    433–435, *433*
group authentication method, 505
Group Authorization and User Group Policies
    screen, 458, *458*
Group Policy creation page, 458–461, *459–461*
group radius option
    AAA accounting, 507
    AAA authorization, 506
group-specific queries, 299–300
group tacacs+ option
    AAA accounting, 507
    AAA authorization, 506
groups
    Cisco Easy VPN, 456–458, *457*
    HSRP
        communication and configuration,
        344–353, *345, 347, 349–352*
        roles, **342–343**
    VRRP, **363**, *363*

H

H.323 protocol, 607
half-duplex mode in RSTP, 91
half-open connections, 544
hard QoS, 635
HDSL (high-bit-rate digital subscriber line),
    390, 393
HDTV (high-definition television), 380
headends, cable, 381
Hello frames in STP, 69
Hello intervals in OSPF, 201
Hello messages in HSRP, **346–352**, *349–352*
Hello packets
    EIGRP, 153, 167
    link state routing protocols, 127
    OSPF, 197, 200, 202–203, *203*
Hello Time field in BPDU, 70
Hello timers
    HSRP, **341**
    RSTP, 91
hellotime value in standby timers, 356
HFC (Hybrid Fiber-Coax), 380, **386**, *386*
hierarchy
    OSPF, **214–215**, *214*
    three-layer hierarchical design model, **2–4**, *3*
high availability for local VLANs, 40
high-bit-rate digital subscriber line (HDSL),
    390, 393

high-definition television (HDTV), 380

High-Order Domain-Specific Part (HO-DSP) of IS-IS addresses, *236, 237*

high-performance WAN interface cards (HWIC), 21

HIPS sensors, 579

hold timers in HSRP, 342

holddown timers in RIP, **129–130**

holddowns in IGP, **126**

holdtime value in standby timers, 356

Home screen for SDM, **437**, 483, *483*, **586**, *586*

honeypot systems, 581

hop counts
  IGP, **125–126**
  IGRP, 137

host-based IDS sensors, 579

host-dependent load-balancing algorithm, 369

hostnames in AutoSecure, 480

Hot Standby Router Protocol (HSRP), **340–341**
  groups
    communication and configuration, **344–353**, *345, 347, 349–352*
    roles, **342–343**
  interface tracking, **356–362**, *357, 359*
  standby preempt command, **354–355**, *354*
  standby priority, **353**
  states, **343–344**
  timers, **341–342**, 356
  virtual MAC addresses, **343**
  vs. VRRP, 362

HTTP connections for IPv6 devices, **317**

HTTPS application for Cisco IOS Firewall, **561**

hub-and-spoke network topologies, 171

HWIC (high-performance WAN interface cards), 21

Hybrid Fiber-Coax (HFC), 380, **386**, *386*

I

IBGP (internal BGP)
  full and partial mesh, **260–261**, *261*
  neighbors, 257
  nontransit AS, **258–260**, *260*
  transit AS, **258**, *259*

ICMP (Internet Control Message Protocol)
  for IPv6, **325–326**
  packets, 114

ICSA (International Computer Security Association), 482

identifying codes in WPA, 712

IDI (Initial Domain Identifier), *236, 237*

IDP (Initial Domain Part), *236, 236*

IDRP (Inter-domain Routing Protocol), 238

IDS (Intrusion Detection System). *See also* Intrusion Prevention System (IPS)
  benefits and drawbacks, **578**
  functions, **574–575**, *575*
  sensors, **578–581**

IDSL (ISDN digital subscriber line), 390, *390*, **393**

IEEE. *See* Institute of Electrical and Electronics Engineers (IEEE) standards

IEV (IPS Event Viewer), 584

if-authenticated option, 506

IGMP (Internet Group Management Protocol)
  CGMP, **300–301**
  snooping, **301**
  versions, **299–300**

IGP (Interior Gateway Protocols), **123–124**
  BGP origin, 266
  distance vector protocols, **124–128**, *125*
  dynamic routing, 122
  link state routing protocols, **126–127**

IGRP (Interior Gateway Routing Protocol), **123–124**, **137–138**

IIN (Intelligent Information Network), **9**

IKE phases in VPNs, **435–436**

images in WCS configuration, 731

impedance mismatch in DSL, 394

import all command, 406–407

InACL attribute in TACACS+, 503

inbound ACL for Cisco IOS Firewall, **562**, 566

incoming class-map configuration, **650–651**

incoming policy-map configuration, **651–654**

incoming service-policy configuration, **654**

Incomplete option for BGP origin, 266

infrastructure mode for wireless clients, 685

Initial Domain Identifier (IDI), *236, 237*

Initial Domain Part (IDP), *236, 236*

initial state in HSRP, 344

inside interface for Cisco IOS Firewall, **562**, 565

inspection process in Cisco IOS Firewall, **561**, 565

instance vlan command, 96

Institute of Electrical and Electronics Engineers (IEEE) standards
  Layer 2 security, **528–530**
  wireless, **671–674**
    2.4GHz, **674–676**, *675–676*
    2.4GHz/5GHz, **678**
    5GHz, **677–678**, *677*
    QoS, 714

int fa command, **46–48**

int tunnel command, 331

Integrated Routing and Bridging (IRB), 398

Intelligent Information Network (IIN), **9**
Inter-domain Routing Protocol (IDRP), 238
Inter-Switch Link (ISL)
    trunk protocols, **35–36**, *36*
    VLAN attacks, 520
inter-VLAN routing
    CEF, **54–55**
    configuring, **56–57**
    multilayer switching, **53–54**
    router on a stick, **51–53**, *52*
interactive mode for Auto Secure, 472
interface atm command, 408–410
interface dialer command, 403, 406
interface FastEthernet command, 330, 616, 618
interface port-channel channel-group number
    command, 60
interface range command, 60–61
Interface Selection option, 440
interface tracking in HSRP, **356–362**, *357, 359*
interface tunnel command, 434
interface vlan vlan-id command, *56*
Interfaces and Connections dialog, 484, *484*
interference in DSL, 394
Interior Gateway Protocols (IGP), **123–124**
    BGP origin, 266
    distance vector protocols, **124–128**, *125*
    dynamic routing, 122
    link state routing protocols, **126–127**
Interior Gateway Routing Protocol (IGRP),
    123–124, 137–138
Intermediate System Hello (ISH) packets, 235
Intermediate System to Intermediate System
    (IS-IS), 123, **234**
    addresses, **235–237**, *236*
    configuring, **240–241**
    features, **235**
    vs. OSPF, **238–240**
    routing levels, **237–238**
    routing types, **238**
internal BGP (IBGP)
    full and partial mesh, **260–261**, *261*
    neighbors, 257
    nontransit AS, **258–260**, *260*
    transit AS, **258**, *259*
internal modems for PPPoE, 400
internal routers with OSPF, 195
Internal Spanning Tree (IST), 94
International Computer Security Association
    (ICSA), 482
Internet connections
    case study, **13**
    Enterprise Edge, **8**

Internet Control Message Protocol (ICMP)
    for IPv6, **325–326**
    packets, 114
Internet Firewall Configuration Summary dialog,
    559, *559*
Internet Group Management Protocol (IGMP)
    CGMP, **300–301**
    snooping, **301**
    versions, **299–300**
Internet Protocol Version 6 (IPv6), **313–314**
    addressing, **316–320**, *316*
    autoconfiguration, **320–322**, *321*
    benefits, **315–316**
    in case study, **15–16**
    DHCPv6, **322–324**
    dual stacking, **329–330**
    ICMP for, **325–326**
    IPv4 interoperability, **329–333**, *331*
    NAT-PT, **332–333**
    operating, **314–315**
    review questions, **334–336**
    routing protocols, **326–328**
    summary, **333**
    tunneling, **330–332**, *331*
internetworks, IPv6 in, **320–324**, *321, 323*
Intrusion Detection System (IDP). *See also*
    Intrusion Prevention System (IPS)
    benefits and drawbacks, **578**
    functions, **574–575**, *575*
    sensors, **578–581**
Intrusion Prevention System (IPS), **573–574,**
    576–577, *577*
    alarms, **584–585**
    benefits and drawbacks, **578**
    configuring, **585–596**, *586–596*
    review questions, **598–600**
    sensors, **578–581**
    signatures, **581–585**
    summary, **597**
Intrusion Prevention System (IPS) page, 586,
    587, 595
IntServ QoS model, **635–636**
invalid timers, **129**
IOS firewall. *See* Cisco IOS Firewall
ip access-group command, 562
ip address command
    dual stacking, 330
    EIGRP, **162–165**
    EtherChannel, 61
    GRE tunnels, 434
    inter-VLAN routing, 53, 56
    voice, 616, 618

ip address negotiated command, 404
IP addresses
    BGP, **275–277**, *277*
    blocking, *585*
    end-to-end VLANs, *39*
    IP Source Guard, *534*
    IPv6 interoperating with IPv4, **329–333**, *331*
    mapping to multicast MAC, **297–299**, *298*
    summary masks, **170**
    unicast reverse-path forwarding, *547*
ip adjust-mss command, 412
ip bandwidth-percent eigrp command, 176, 179
ip default-network command, 167–169
ip dhcp excluded-address command, 407
ip dhcp pool command, 406
IP header fields in OSPF, **196–197**
ip ips fail closed command, 592
ip local pool command, 566
ip mtu command, 405
ip multicast-routing command, 307
ip nat inside command, 405–406
ip nat inside source list command, 405
ip nat outside command, 406
ip ospf cost command, 212
ip pim rp-address ip-address command, 307
ip pim send-rp-announce command, 307
ip pim send-rp-discovery command, 307
ip pim version command, 307
ip policy route-map command, 274
IP precedence
    DSCP, **639–643**, *639–640, 642*
    QoS, **625**, **639**
ip route command, 117–119, 121, 407
ip router isis command, 241
ip routing command, 56
IP Source Guard, **533–534**
ip summary-address eigrp command, 170
ip summary-address rip command, 132
ip tcp adjust-mss command, 412
ip verify unicast reverse-path command, 562
IPS. *See* Intrusion Prevention System (IPS)
IPS Event Viewer (IEV), 584
IPS Policies Wizard, *585–586, 588–589, 591*
IPsec VPNs
    enterprise teleworkers, *378*
    overview, **431–433**, *431, 433*
    site-to-site and remote-access with, *377*
IPv6. *See* Internet Protocol Version 6 (IPv6)
ipv6 address command, 322
ipv6 dhcp pool command, 323
ipv6 dhcp server command, 324
ipv6 eigrp command, 327

ipv6 enable command, 322
ipv6 ospf command, 328
ipv6 rip enable command, 326
ipv6 router eigrp command, 327
ipv6 router ospf command, 328
ipv6 router rip command, 327
ipv6 unicast-routing command, 322, 330
IRB (Integrated Routing and Bridging), 398
IrDa wireless, 674
IS-IS. *See* Intermediate System to Intermediate
    System (IS-IS)
is-type command, 241
ISAKMP policy, 443
ISDN digital subscriber line (IDSL), 390, *390*, **393**
ISH (Intermediate System Hello) packets, 235
isis metric command, 241
ISL (Inter-Switch Link)
    trunk protocols, **35–36**, *36*
    VLAN attacks, *520*
ISM band, 672
isolated ports in PVLANs, 532
isolated VLAN, 532
isotropic reference antennas, 682
ISPs for BGP default routes, **251**
IST (Internal Spanning Tree), 94

K

keepalive messages
    BGP, **256**
    BGP/TCP, 254
keys
    WEP, 711
    WPA, 712
krb5 authentication method, 505

L

Label Distribution Protocol (LDP), 420, 422
Label Forwarding Information Base (LFIB) tables,
    417, **421–424**, *423–424*
Label Information Base (LIB) tables,
    420–422, *422*
Label Switch Router (LSR), 420
    MPLS packets, 420
    OSPF packets, 198
Label Switched Path (LSP) tunnels, 419
labels, MPLS, **417–424**, *418–419, 421–424*
LACP (Link Aggregation Control Protocol), **59**

LANs (local area networks)
    access ports, **46–47**
    setting up, 44–46
    virtual. *See* virtual local area
        networks (VLANs)
    wireless, **679–680**
last mile, 390–391
Layer 1 and 2 in case study, **11–13**
Layer 3 in case study, **13–14**
Layer 2 security, 515–516
    AAA, **528**
    attacks, 517–519
        MAC layer, **519–520**
        spoofing, **523–525**, *525*
        switch device, **525–526**
        VLAN, **520–523**, *521*
    DAI, **534**
    DHCP snooping, **533**
    IEEE 802.1x standard, **528–530**
    introduction, 516–517
    IP Source Guard, **533–534**
    port security, **526–528**
    private VLANs, **531–533**
    review questions, **536–538**
    rogue devices, **517**
    summary, **535**
    VACLs, **530–531**
Layer 2 switching, 30–31
Layer 3 in case study, **13–14**
LDP (Label Distribution Protocol), 420, 422
learn state in HSRP, 344
leave group messages in IGMP, 300
LED indicators for adapter states, 687
levels in IS-IS routing, 237–238
LFIB (Label Forwarding Information Base) tables,
    417, **421–424**, *423–424*
LIB (Label Information Base) tables,
    420–422, *422*
LightWeight Access Point Protocol (LWAPP), **701**,
    715–717
lightweight wireless solutions, **699–701**
line authentication method, 505
line coding technology property, 392
line console command, 506
Link Aggregation Control Protocol (LACP), **59**
link-local addresses, 318
link state advertisements (LSAs), 127, **198–199**
link state databases (LSDBs), 208
    change process, **210**
    creating, 208–209
    DBD information, 209
    OSPF, 196
    updating, **210–211**

link state packets (LSP), 127
link state protocols, 123, **126–127**, **191–192**
    improvements, **192–193**
    IS-IS. *See* Intermediate System to Intermediate
        System (IS-IS)
    OSPF. *See* Open Shortest Path First
        (OSPF) protocol
    review questions, **243–245**
    summary, **241–242**
link types
    OSPF, 193, **215–218**
    VLANs, **34–35**
listen state, HSRP, 344
LLQ (low latency queuing), 626, **645**
load balancing
    EIGRP, 148, **173–175**, *175*
    GLBP, **367–371**
    STP, **79–81**, *80*
    VRRP, **364**, *364*
load coil in DSL, 394
loading in EIGRP, 166
local area networks (LANs)
    access ports, **46–47**
    setting up, 44–46
    virtual. *See* virtual local area
        networks (VLANs)
    wireless, **679–680**
local authentication method, 505–506
local-case authentication method, 505
local loop, 390–391
local multicast addresses, **296–297**
local preference attribute in BGP, **264–265**,
    265, 284
local VLANs, **39–40**
location appliances, 701
lockdown
    AutoSecure, **473**
    one-step, **493–495**, *493–494*
logical functions with match command, 273–274
login authentication command, 506
login option, 474
login page, 725
logins
    AutoSecure, 474
    Security Audit Wizard, 489–490, *489*
    WCS, 725
Long Reach Ethernet (LRE), 393
loop avoidance in IGP, 125, *125*
Loop Guard feature, **100**
loopback addresses in BGP, **276–277**
low latency queuing (LLQ), 626, **645**
LRE (Long Reach Ethernet), 393

LSAck packets, 198
LSAs (link state advertisements), 127, **198–199**
LSDBs. *See* link state databases (LSDBs)
LSP (Label Switched Path) tunnels, 419
LSP (link state packets), 127
LSR (Label Switch Router), 420
   MPLS packets, 420
   OSPF packets, 198
LSU packets, 198
LWAPP (LightWeight Access Point Protocol), **701**,
   715–717

M

MAC addresses. *See* Media Access Control
   (MAC) addresses
MAC layer
   attacks, **518–520**
   DOCSIS, 382
macros
   defining, 77
   STP priorities, 77–78
Maintain Aspect Ratio option, 731
maintenance of phone calls, **606**
malicious traffic identification approaches,
   579–581
man-in-the-middle WLAN attacks, 712
management
   enterprise teleworkers, 379
   Layer 2 switching, 31
   securing, **508–510**
management indicators in QoS, 612
management planes in AutoSecure, 473–474
mandatory attributes in BGP, 262–263
map queue_http_ftp command, 655
maps
   BGP routes, 270–274
   crypto, **444–445**
   WCS, **730–734**, *731–734*
MAPs (Mesh Access Points), 684
Maps page, 730–731, *731*
marking, QoS, **613–614**, *614*, **639–643**,
   639–640, **713–715**
master down intervals in VRRP, 365
match command, **271–272**
match access-group command, 651
match address command, 436, 444
match-all option, 650
match dscp command, 654–655
match ip address command, 273–274
match protocol ftp command, 651

match protocol http command, 651
match protocol rtp audio command, 651
Maximum Age field, 70
maximum data rate property, 392
maximum distance property, 392
maximum hop count, **126**
maximum-path command, 173
Maximum Segment Size (MSS) field, 412
maximum transmission units (MTUs)
   EIGRP, 167
   IGRP, 137
   PPPoE, 412
Mbone, 297
MCU (Multipoint Control Units), 604
MED (multi-exit discriminator) attribute,
   267–268, *267*, 284
Media Access Control (MAC) addresses
   2.4GHz/5GHz, 678
   ARP spoofing, 524
   CGMP, 301
   filters, 534
   HSRP, **343**
   ICMP, 325
   IPv6, 320
   Layer 2 switching, 31
   multicast, **297–299**, *298*
   port security, **526–527**
   Proxy ARP, 339
   RSTP, 91
   STP, 71, 75
   UplinkFast, 89
   wireless authentication, 710
media gateway control protocol (MGCP),
   605, 608
membership in end-to-end VLANs, 39
Mesh Access Points (MAPs), 684
mesh networking, 684
Message Age field, 70
Message Type field, 69
messages
   BGP, **254–256**
   BPDU, 69–70
   EIGRP, **153**
   OSPF, **196–198**
metric command, 241
metrics
   EIGRP, 148, **166–167**
   OSPF vs. IS-IS, 240
MGCP (media gateway control protocol),
   605, 608
microengines, **581–582**
microfilters, 396

MIMO (Multiple-Input Multiple-Output), 678
Mission-critical traffic class, 634
mls qos trust command, 616
modes, VTP, **41**
Modular QoS CLI (MQC), 625, **649–650**, *649*
    incoming class-map configuration, **650–651**
    incoming policy-map configuration, **651–654**
    incoming service-policy configuration, **654**
    outgoing class-map configuration, **654–655**
    outgoing policy-map configuration, **655–656**
    outgoing service-policy configuration, **656**
    QoS, **647**
modulation
    ADSL, **397**
    LAN techniques, **679–680**
MP-BGP (MPLS VPNs Multi-protocol BGP), 419
MPLS (Multi-protocol Label Switching), **413–414**
    labels, **417–424**, *418–419*, *421–424*
    router architecture, **416–417**, *416*
    switching types, **414–416**
mpls ip command, 421
mpls label protocol tdp command, 422
MQC. *See* Modular QoS CLI (MQC)
MST (Multiple Spanning Tree), **93–96**
MST instance (MSTI), 94
MTUs (maximum transmission units)
    EIGRP, 167
    IGRP, 137
    PPPoE, 412
multi-exit discriminator (MED) attribute,
    267–268, *267*, 284
Multi-protocol Label Switching (MPLS), **413–414**
    labels, **417–424**, *418–419*, *421–424*
    router architecture, **416–417**, *416*
    switching types, **414–416**
multicast listener discovery, 326
multicasts, **291–292**
    addressing, **295–299**, *298*
    case study, **15**
    EIGRP, 148
    IGMP, **299–301**
    IPv6 addresses, **318–319**
    operation and configuration, **305–307**
    PIM, **302–305**, *303–305*
    pros and cons, **294–295**
    review questions, **310–312**
    summary, **309**
    transmission types, **292–294**, *293–294*
    verifying, **307–309**
multilayer switching, **53–54**
Multiple-Input Multiple-Output (MIMO), 678

multiple network-layer protocol support, **147**
multiple OSPF processes, 225
Multiple Spanning Tree (MST), **93–96**
multiple virtual routers in GLBP, 368
Multipoint Control Units (MCU), 604

N

NAC (Network Admission Control), 9
name command
    MST, 95
    VLANs, 45
NAPT-PT (Network Address Port Translation-
    Protocol Translation), 333
NAT overload configuration, **405–406**
NAT-PT (Network Address Translation-Protocol
    Translation), 16, 329, **332–333**
National Television System Committee (NTSC)
    standard, 380
nature property in DSL, 392
NBAR (Network Based Application Recognition),
    625, **633**
NBMA (non-broadcast multi-access) networks
    EIGRP, 148, 176
    OSPF, **216–218**
neighbor command, 257
neighbor discovery
    EIGRP, 148
    ICMP, 325
    OSPF, **200–203**, *203*
neighbor ebgp-multihop command, 277
neighbor next-hop-self command, 278–279
neighbor peer-group command, 278–282
neighbor remote-as command, 279–280
neighbor shutdown command, 275
neighbors and neighbor tables
    BGP, 257, **275**
    EIGRP, 153, **156**
    link state routing protocols, **127**
    OSPF, 193, 196, 201
Neighbors field, 201
net command, IS-IS, 241
Network Address Port Translation-Protocol
    Translation (NAPT-PT), 333
Network Address Translation-Protocol
    Translation (NAT-PT), 329, **332–333**
Network Admission Control (NAC), 9
Network Based Application Recognition (NBAR),
    625, **633**
network-based IDS sensors (NIPS), 578

network command
  BGP, **280–282**
  EIGRP, **159–161**
  IGRP, 139
  OSPF, **225–226**
  RIP, **129–132**, 134
network extension mode in Cisco Easy VPN, 453
network extension plus mode in Cisco Easy VPN, 453
network interface cards (NICs), **681**
network interface devices (NIDs), 396
Network Layer in traffic marking, 637
Network Managed Test, 697
Network Management Block, 7
network mask command, 283
network module (NM) bays, 21
network network-number command, 280
network option
  AAA accounting, 507
  AAA authorization, 506
Network Service Access Point (NSAP) addresses, 235–236
Network Time Protocol (NTP), **509–510**
networks
  BGP connections, **250–252**
  case study, **14–15**
  LANs. *See* local area networks (LANs)
  VLANs. *See* virtual local area networks (VLANs)
  voice. *See* voice
  WANs. *See* Wide Area Networks (WANs)
New Campus page, 731–732
next-hop attribute in BGP, **268**, 278
NICs (network interface cards), **681**
NIDs (network interface devices), 396
NIPS, 578
NM (network module) bays, 21
no atm ilmi-keepalive command, 409
no auto-summary command, 132, 163, 170
no cdp enable command, 404
no-interact option, 474
no ip directed-broadcast command, 409
no neighbor shutdown command, 275
no network command, 282
no passive-interface command, 139
no shutdown command
  EIGRPv6, 327
  HSRP, 344
no standby group track command, 358
no standby priority command, 353
no switchport command, 56, 61
no vlan command, 46

no vtp pruning command, 51
noise, quantization, 610
non-broadcast multi-access (NBMA) networks
  EIGRP, 148, 176
  OSPF, **216–218**
non-edge ports in RSTP, 92
non-root switches, 74–75, 76
nonces, 712
nondesignated ports in STP, 71
nonegotiate mode in DTP, 37
noninteractive mode in Auto Secure, 473
nonstatistical anomaly-based detection systems, **581**
nontransit AS, IBGP in, **258–260**, *260*
nontransitive attributes in BGP, **262–263**
normal mode in UDLD, 101
not-so-stubby areas (NSSAs), **221–224**, *222*
notification messages in BGP, **256**
NSAP (Network Service Access Point) addresses, 235–236
NSEL field, *236*, 237
NSSAs (not-so-stubby areas), **221–224**, *222*
NTP (Network Time Protocol), **509–510**
ntp option in AutoSecure, 474
NTSC (National Television System Committee) standard, 380
Nyquist theorem, 610

O

OFDM (Orthogonal Frequency Division Multiplexing), 676, 680
Omni antennas, **682–683**
One-Step Lockdown, **493–495**, *493–494*
One-Step LockDown Wizard, 493–494, *493*
one-to-all transmissions, **293**
one-to-many transmissions. *See* multicasts
one-to-one transmissions, **292–293**, *293*
open-access wireless mode, 709
open messages in BGP, **255–256**
Open Shortest Path First (OSPF) protocol, 123, 192
  benefits, **213–214**
  configuring, **224–227**, *224*
  costs, **212–213**
  DR elections, **204–208**, *205–207*
  drawbacks, 213
  hierarchy, **214–215**, *214*
  vs. IS-IS, **238–240**
  link state advertisements, **198–199**
  link types, **215–218**

LSDBs, 208–211
neighbor discovery, 200–203, *203*
operation, 199–200
packet types, 196–198
RID, 203–204
routing tables, **211–212**
stub type areas, **218–224**, *220–222*
tables, **195–196**
terms, **193–195**
verifying, **227–234**
open wireless authentication, 710
optimized multicast processing, 294
optional attributes in BGP, 262–263
OR function with match command, 273–274
organization-local multicast scope, 297
origin attribute in BGP, **265–266**
Orthogonal Frequency Division Multiplexing
   (OFDM), 676, 680
OSPF. *See* Open Shortest Path First
   (OSPF) protocol
OSPFv3 protocol, **328**
out-of-sequence multicast delivery packets, 295
OutACL attribute in TACACS+, 503
outbound ACL for Cisco IOS Firewall, **562**, 565
outgoing class-map configuration, **655–656**
outgoing service-policy configuration, **656**
outside interface for Cisco IOS Firewall, **562**, 566
Overview tab, 437

P

packet dropping
   IPS, 577, *585*
   QoS, **630–631**
packet fragmentation in ICMP, 325
packet serial numbers, 711
packets
   OSPF, **196–198**
   stateful inspection, 196, **541–543**, *541, 543*
PACLs (Port Access Control Lists), 531
PADI (PPPoE Active Discovery Initiation)
   packets, 400
PAgP (Port Aggregation Protocol), 58–59
PAL (Phase Alternating Phase) standard, 380
partial mesh in IBGP, **260–261**, *261*
partial route tables, 251–252
partial updates in EIGRP, **147**
passive-interface command, 139
passive state in EIGRP, 157
passphrases in WPA, 712

passwords
   WCS, 720–721, *720*
   WPA, 712
PAT (port address translation), **405–406**
paths
   BGP
      attributes, **262–263**
      selecting, **268–269**
      vectors, **252–253**
   STP, **72–75**, *74–76*, 79
payload compression, 627
PBR (policy-based routing), 270
PBX (private branch exchange), 602
PDMs (Protocol Dependent Modules), 127, 147
Peer Identity option, 440
peers in BGP, 257, **276**, **278–280**, *279*
Penultimate Hop Popping (PHP), 424
Per-Hop Behavior (PHB), 636, **641**
per-host traffic balancing, **369**
Per-VLAN Spanning Tree Plus (PVST+), **82**
Perfect Forward Secrecy option, 458
permanent virtual circuits (PVCs), 409–410
Phase Alternating Phase (PAL) standard, 380
PHB (Per-Hop Behavior), 636, **641**
phone calls, **606**
phone features, 604
phone line spectrum, 390, *390*
PHP (Penultimate Hop Popping), 424
physical layer in DOCSIS, 382
PIM (Protocol Independent Multicast), **302–305**,
   303–305
plain old telephone systems (POTS)
   bandwidth 390, *390*
   setup, 617
   splitters, 396
Platinum category in WMM, 714–715
point-to-multipoint connections
   EIGRP, 177–178, *177*
   OSPF NBMA networks, **217–218**
point-to-point (PP) connections
   EIGRP, **178–179**
   OSPF, **216**, 218
   RSTP, 91
poison reverse in IGP, **126**
policing traffic, **646**
policy-based IPS approach, **580**
policy-based routing (PBR), 270
policy-map command, 652, 655
policy-map mark-traffic command, 652, 654
policy-map queue_traffic command, 655
Port Access Control Lists (PACLs), 531
port address translation (PAT), **405–406**

Port Aggregation Protocol (PAgP), 58–59
port command for voice, 618–619
Port IDs
    BPDU, 70
    STP, 73–74, 75, 79
port negotiation mode, 61
port priority setting
    LACP, 59
    STP, 79
Port Security feature, 526–528
PortFast feature, 81–84, 97
ports
    LANs, 46–47
    PVLANs, 532–533
    RSTP, 90–92
    security, 526–528
    STP, 70–71, 104–105
    VLANs, 34–35
    WCS, 719, 720
POTS (plain old telephone systems)
    bandwidth 390, 390
    setup, 617
    splitters, 396
power save mode, 687
PP (point-to-point) connections
    EIGRP, 178–179
    OSPF, 216, 218
    RSTP, 91
ppp authentication chap command, 405
ppp chap password command, 405
PPP over ATM, 401–402
PPP over Ethernet (PPPoE), 398–401, 399
    CPE configuration, 402–403, 402, 408–409
    dialer interface configuration, 403–405
    dropped packets, 412–413
    Ethernet interface as DHCP servers, 406–407
    outside Ethernet interface configuration, 403
    overall configuration, 407–408
    PAT configuration, 405–406
    static default route, 407
PPPoA clients, 409–411, 409
PPPoE Active Discovery Initiation (PADI)
    packets, 400
pppoe-client command, 403
pppoe-client dial-pool-number command, 408
pppoe enable command, 403
PQ (Priority Queuing), 644
Pre-Installation Summary screen, 723, 723
Pre-Shared Key (PSK), 712
predetermined traffic flow, 40
Predictor algorithm, 627
preemption in GLBP, 368

prefix-delegation command, 324
primary VLANs, 532
priorities
    Hello messages, 348
    HSRP, 353–354, 354
    QoS, 612, 626, 629, 631
    STP, 76–78
priority command, 655
priority forwarding, 626, 629, 631
Priority Queuing (PQ), 644
Priv-lvl attribute in TACACS+, 502
private branch exchange (PBX), 602
private VLANs (PVLANs), 520, 526, 531–533
private WAN Layer 2 technologies, 377
process switching
    CEF, 55
    MPLS, 414
processing delay, 628
Profile Management dialog, 692–694, 693–694
Profile Management tab, 691–692, 692
profiles for wireless clients, 691–694, 692–694
promiscuous ports in PVLANs, 532–533
propagation delay, 629
protecting spanning tree, 96–97
protocol changes, OSPF vs. IS-IS, 239
Protocol Dependent Modules (PDMs),
    127, 147
Protocol Identifier field, 69
Protocol Independent Multicast (PIM), 302–305,
    303–305
protocol usage in voice, 610–611
provisioning cable modems, 388–389
Proxy Address Resolution Protocol (Proxy ARP),
    339, 339
pruning VTP, 42–43, 42, 50–51
PSK (Pre-Shared Key), 712
public switched telephone network (PSTNs), 602
pvc command, 408
pvc vpi/vci command, 410
PVCs (permanent virtual circuits), 409–410
PVLANs (private VLANs), 520, 526, 531–533
PVST+ (Per-VLAN Spanning Tree Plus), 82
PVSTs, 81

Q

Q-in-Q tunneling, 523
QoS Policy Generation dialog, 659, 659–660
QoS Profiles page, 734, 735
QoS tab, 737
QoS Wizard, 656–665, 656–663

Quality of Service (QoS), 531, **611–612**, **623–624**
    ACLs, 531
    bandwidth, **626–628**
    classification, **612–613**
    configuring
        methods, **647–649**, *649*
        MQC, **649–656**
        SDM QoS Wizard, **656–665**, *656–663*
    congestion avoidance, **646–647**
    CoS, **638**
    delay, **628–630**
    dynamic routing, 121
    enterprise teleworkers, 379
    implementing, **631**
    introduction, **624–625**
    IP precedence, **639**
    marking, **613–614**, *614*, **637–638**, 713–715
    models, **635–637**
    packet loss, **630–631**
    problems, **625–626**
    queuing, **644–645**, 713–715
    review questions, **666–668**
    summary, **665**
    traffic
        classification, **633–634**
        conditioners, **645–646**
        identification, **632–633**
        marking, **637–638**
    voice. *See* voice
    wireless, **713–717**
    WLC options, **734–737**, *735–737*
quantizing voice transmission, **610**
querier election in IGMP, 300
query-interval response time in IGMP, 300
query packets in EIGRP, 153
query propagation in EIGRP, **171**
question marks (?) in BGP, 284
queuing delay, 628
queuing in QoS, 625, **644–645**, 713–715

R

RA (router advertisements), 321, *321*
RACLs (Router Access Control Lists), 531
radio frequencies (RFs)
    data transmission, **382–384**, *382*
    wireless devices, 670
radio frequency identification (RFID) tags, 22
radio interference, 394

RADIUS (Remote Authentication Dial-In
    User Service)
    Cisco Easy VPN configuration, 456
    configuring, **503–504**
    device security, **498–500**, *498*
radius-server command, 503
radius-server host command, 504
radius-server key command, 504
RADSL (rate adaptive digital subscriber line),
    390, 392
Random Early Detection (RED), 647
range comparisons for wireless topologies,
    680, *680*
Rapid Per-VLAN Spanning Tree Plus
    (RPVST+), 92
Rapid Spanning Tree Protocol (RSTP), **90–93**
RAPs (Root Access Points), 684
rate adaptive digital subscriber line (RADSL),
    390, 392
Real-Time Transport Protocol (RTP), 627
receive-only parameter for stub routers, 172–173
recovery mechanism in EIGRP, 148
RED (Random Early Detection), 647
redundancy in Cisco Easy VPN, **463–464**
redundancy protocols, **337–338**
    client redundancy issues, **338–339**, *338–339*
    GLBP, **367–371**
    HSRP. *See* Hot Standby Router
        Protocol (HSRP)
    overview, **340**
    review questions, **372–374**
    summary, **371**
    VRRP. *See* virtual router redundancy
        protocol (VRRP)
regular areas in OSPF, 214
REJECT response in TACACS+, **501–502**
reliability
    EIGRP, 166
    multicasts, 295
reliable transport protocol (RTP), 148, 156, 627
remote-access
    Enterprise Edge, **8**
    IPSec VPNs, 377
remote-as command, 275
Remote Authentication Dial-In User
    Service (RADIUS)
    Cisco Easy VPN configuration, 456
    configuring, **503–504**
    device security, **498–500**, *498*
remote sites in EIGRP, **177–178**, *177*
removing VLANs, 46
rendezvous points (RPs) in PIM, 302

repeaters, **684–685**
reply packets in EIGRP, 153
reporting in IPS, **584**
Request to Send, Clear to Send (RTS/CTS),
    675–676, *675*
Resource Reservation Protocol (RSVP), **635–636**
reverse-access option, 506
reverse path forwarding (RPF), 302
revision command, 95
RFC 1483 bridging, **398**
RFID (radio frequency identification) tags, 22
RFs (radio frequencies)
    data transmission, **382–384**, *382*
    wireless devices, 670
RID (Router Identity), 195, **203–204**
RIP. *See* Routing Information Protocol (RIP)
RIP next generation (RIPng), **326–327**
RIP version 1 (RIPv1), 128
RIP version 2 (RIPv2), 128, **130–132**
RLQs (Root Link Queries), 85
roaming wireless topologies, **686**
rogue devices, **517**
rollback in AutoSecure, **473–474**
Root Access Points (RAPs), 684
root bridges
    RSTP, 91
    STP, 70
Root Guard, 88, **97–98**, 517
Root ID field, 69
Root Link Queries (RLQs), 85
Root Path Cost field, 69
root ports
    RSTP, 90–91
    STP, 70, 74, *75*
root properties in STP, **105**
round-robin load-balancing algorithm, 369
Route attribute in TACACS+, *503*
route-map command, 271
route-map test permit command, 273–274
route maps in BGP, **270**
    configuring, **271–273**
    implementing, **274**
    match statements, **273**
    set command, **271–274**
route poisoning, **126**
route update timers, **129**
Router Access Control Lists (RACLs), 531
router advertisements (RA), 321, *321*
router bgp command, 275, **279–282**
router eigrp command, 158–159
router-id command, 204, 328
Router ID field, 197, **201**

Router Identity (RID), 195, 197, **201, 203–204**
router igrp command, 138
router isis command, 241
router on a stick, **51–53**, *52*
router ospf command, 225–227
Router priority field, 201
router rip command, 129, 131–132, 134
router solicitation (RS) requests, 321, *321*
routers
    case study, **20–21**
    gateway, 338, *338*
    MPLS architecture, **416–417**, *416*
    OSPF, 195
    standby, 342
    stub, 118, *118*, **171–173**
routing, **111–112**
    administrative distance, **116–117**
    basic, **112–116**, *115–116*
    distribute lists, **139–140**
    dynamic, **121–128**, *123*, *125*
    EIGRP, **151–152**, **167–169**, *168*
    IGRP, **137–138**
    inter-VLAN, **51–57**, *52*
        CEF, **54–55**
        configuring, **56–57**
        multilayer switching, **53–54**
        router on a stick, **51–53**, *52*
    IPv6 protocols, **326–328**
    IS-IS, **237–238**
    link state protocols. *See* link state protocols
    passive interface, **139**
    review questions, **142–144**
    RIP. *See* Routing Information Protocol (RIP)
    route manipulation, **138–140**
    static, **117–121**, *118–120*
    summary, **141**
Routing Information Protocol (RIP), 123–124,
    128–129
    vs. IGRP, 138
    RIP Version 2, **130–132**
    routing configuration, **129–130**
    summarization, **132**
    timers, **129**
    troubleshooting, **133–137**
    verifying, **132–133**
routing loops
    IBGP, **260**
    IGP, 124, *125*
routing tables
    EIGRP, **158**
    MPLS, 420
    OSPF, 196, **211–212**

RPF (reverse path forwarding), 302
RPs (rendezvous points) in PIM, 302
RPVST+ (Rapid Per-VLAN Spanning Tree
    Plus), 92
RS (router solicitation) requests, 321, *321*
RSTP (Rapid Spanning Tree Protocol), **90–93**
RSVP (Resource Reservation Protocol), **635–636**
RTP (reliable transport protocol), 148, 156, 627
RTS/CTS (Request to Send, Clear to Send),
    675–676, *675*

S

S-CDMA (Synchronous Code Division Multiple
    Access), 382
sampling in voice transmission, **610**
SAP (Session Announcement Protocol), 306
scalability of local VLANs, 40
Scavenger traffic class, 634
scope
    IDS sensors, **578**
    multicast, 297
sd (Session Directory) applications, 306
SDEE (Security Device Event Exchange), 577,
    584, 586, *588*
SDF Locations page, 589, *589*
SDFs (signature definition files), **583–584**
SDM. *See* Security Device Manager (SDM)
SDP (Session Description Protocol), 306
SDSL (synchronous digital subscriber line), 390,
    390, **393**
seamless connectivity in EIGRP, **148**
Search Results page, 730
SECAM color system, 380
Secure Shell Protocol (SSH)
    AutoSecure, 474, 478, 480
    SDM, 488, *488*
    switch device attacks, 526
security
    case study, **14–15**
    device. *See* device security
    enterprise teleworkers, 378–379
    IPS. *See* Intrusion Prevention System (IPS)
    multicasts, 295
    switch. *See* Layer 2 security
    VLAN access ports, 47
    wireless. *See* wireless management
        and security
security associations, **445–452**
Security Audit dialog, 484, *484*

Security Audit Interface Configuration dialog,
    485, *486*
Security Audit Wizard, **482–483**
    One-Step Lockdown, **493–495**, *493–494*
    working with, **483–493**, *485–489*
Security Dashboard tab, 595, *596*
Security Device Event Exchange (SDEE), 577,
    584, 586, *588*
Security Device Manager (SDM), 20
    Cisco Easy VPN configuration, **453–463**,
        454–463
    Cisco IOS Firewall configuration, 545, *545*
        advanced, **552–560**, *552–560*
        basic, **545–551**, *545–551*
    Express, 21
    IPS configuration, **585–596**, *586–596*
    QoS Wizard, **656–665**, *656–663*
    Security Audit Wizard, **482–483**
        One-Step Lockdown, **493–495**, *493–494*
        working with, **483–493**, *485–489*
    VPN site-to-site configuration, **436–441**,
        438–442
Security tab
    wireless client profiles, 693, *693*
    WLC, 737–739, *738–739*
Select Interfaces screen, *588*
Select Signature Definition File (SDF) field, 595
self-contained AAA, 497
seniority in STP, 71
sensors, IPS and IDS, **578–581**
serialization delay, 629
Server Edit tab, 463, *463*
Server Farm Block, 7
server mode in VTP, **41**
service areas in wireless topologies, **686**
service-policy command, 654
service-policy input mark_traffic command, 654
service-policy output mark_traffic command, 656
service provider edge, **9**
service provider MPLS-based IP VPNs, 377
Service Set Identifiers (SSIDs), 685, 710
Services-Oriented Network Architecture
    (SONA), **9**
Session Announcement Protocol (SAP), 306
Session Description Protocol (SDP), 306
Session Directory (sd) applications, 306
session initiation protocol (SIP), 607
session target command, 619
session target ipv4 command, 618
sessions in PPPoE, **400–401**
set command
    MQC, 653
    route maps, **271–274**

set dscp command, 653–654

set dscp ef command, 654

set peer command, 444

set serial command, 274

set transform-set command, 436, 444

setup for phone calls, **606**

SFP (small form-factor pluggable) modules, 101

shaping traffic, **646**

shared-key authentication, 710

shared mode in RSTP, 91

shared trees in PIM, 302

shortcuts in WCS, 722, *723*

shortened IPv6 addresses, **317–318**

Shortest Path First (SPF) algorithm, 127

shortest path trees (SPTs), **302–303**, *303*

show crypto ipsec sa command, 446

show crypto map command, VPNs, 444–445

show debug command, 445

show interface command, 167

show interface trunk command, 48–49

show interfaces fastethernet command, 62

show interfaces interface-id switchport command, 616

show ip bgp command, 268, 283

show ip bgp summary command, **284–286**

show ip eigrp interfaces command, **185–186**

show ip eigrp neighbors command, **179–180**

show ip eigrp topology command, **180–182**

show ip eigrp traffic command, **186**

show ip interface brief command, 134, 160

show ip mroute command, 308

show ip nbar protocol-discovery command, 633

show ip ospf database command, 227–228

show ip ospf interface command, 229–231

show ip ospf neighbor command, 227

show ip ospf statistics command, 231–232

show ip ospf traffic command, 232–234

show ip pim interface command, 308

show ip pim neighbor command, 308

show ip pim rp command, 309

show ip protocols command
    dynamic routing, **184–185**
    RIP, **132–134**

show ip route command, 114–115
    EIGRP, **182–184**
    OSPF, 229
    RIP, 137

show mls qos interface interface-id command, 616

show pending command, 96

show running-config command, 61, 160

show running-configuration command, 565

show spanning-tree command, 74, 102

show spanning-tree backbonefast command, 86–87, 106

show spanning-tree detail command, 104

show spanning-tree uplinkfast command, 106

show spanning-tree vlan bridge command, 105

show spanning-tree vlan root command, 105

show spanning-tree vlan summary command, 105

show vlan command, 44–45

shutdown command for BGP neighbors, 275

SIA (stuck-in-active) state, 158, 172

signal attenuation in DSL, 394

signature definition files (SDFs), **583–584**

signature microengines (SME), **581–582**

signatures in IPS
    alarms, 584–585
    SDFs, **583–584**
    traffic identification, **579–582**
    types, **583**

Silver category in WMM, 714–715

Simple Network Management Protocol (SNMP)
    securing, 508
    WLC, 727, 729

SIP (session initiation protocol), 607

site-local addresses, 318

site-local multicast scope, 297

Site-to-Site VPN Wizard, 437, 439–441, *439–442*

site-to-site VPNs, 377, **436–441**, *438–442*

6t04 tunneling, 329–332

skew time in VRRP, 365

small form-factor pluggable (SFP) modules, 101

SME (signature microengines), **581–582**

SNMP (Simple Network Management Protocol)
    securing, 508
    WLC, 727, 729

snooping
    DHCP, **533**
    IGMP, **301**

soft QoS, 636

SONA (Services-Oriented Network Architecture), **9**

source IP addresses
    BGP, **275–277**, 277
    blocking, 585
    IP Source Guard sources, 534

source-specific multicast (SSM), 304–305

spanning-tree bpdufilter enable command, 99

spanning-tree bpduguard enable command, 97

spanning-tree guard loop command, 100

spanning-tree guard root command, 98

spanning-tree link-type point-to-point command, 93

spanning-tree loopguard default command, 100

spanning-tree mode mst command, *95*
spanning-tree mode rapid-pvst command, *93*
spanning-tree mst configuration command, *95*
spanning-tree portfast command, *93*
spanning-tree portfast bpdufiltering default command, *99*
spanning-tree portfast bpduguard default command, *97*
spanning-tree portfast default command, *82–83*
spanning-tree portfast disable command, *84*
spanning-tree priority command, *76*
Spanning Tree Protocol (STP), **67–68**
    BackboneFast, 84–87, *86*, **106**
    BPDU filtering, **98–99**, *99*
    BPDU Guard, **97**
    components, **69–71**, *69*
    configuring, *76–78*
    history, **81**
    Loop Guard, **100**
    MST, **93–96**
    operation, **68**
    paths, 72–75, *74–76*, *79*
    PortFast, **82–84**
    ports, **104**
    protecting, **96–97**
    PVST+, **82**
    review questions, *107–109*
    root and port properties, **105**
    Root Guard, **97–98**
    RSTP, **90–93**
    summary, **106**
    switch identification, **71–72**
    UDLD, **100–102**
    UplinkFast, 87–90, *88*, **106**
    verifying and troubleshooting, **102–106**
spanning-tree uplinkfast command, *89*
spanning-tree vlan command, *76–81*
sparse PIM mode, 303–305, *305*
spatial multiplexing, 678
speak state in HSRP, 344
speakers in BGP, 257
special addresses in IPv6, **319–320**
speed limitations in DSL, **393–394**
SPF (Shortest Path First) algorithm, 127
split horizon
    IGP, **126**
    RIP Version 2, 130
Split MAC architecture, 701
Split Tunneling tab, 458, *460*
splitters, POTS, 396
spoofing
    ARP, 524–525, *525*
    description, 518–519

DHCP, **523–524**
    switch, 520–522, *521*
SPTs (shortest path trees), 302–303, *303*
SSH (Secure Shell Protocol)
    AutoSecure, 474, 478, 480
    SDM, 488, *488*
    switch device attacks, 526
SSIDs (Service Set Identifiers), 685, 710
SSM (source-specific multicast), 304–305
Stacker algorithm, 627
standard areas in OSPF, **194**
standards
    cable, **380**
    IEEE. *See* Institute of Electrical and Electronics Engineers (IEEE) standards
standby ip command, 345–346, 349
standby preempt command, 354–355, *354*, 360
standby priority command, 353, 355
standby priority in HSRP, 353
standby routers in HSRP, 342
standby state in HSRP, 344
standby timers command, 356
standby timers in HSRP, **342**
standby track command, 357–358
start-stop option in AAA accounting, 507
stateful packet inspection, **541–543**, *541*, *543*
stateless DHCP servers, 323
states
    adapter, 687
    HSRP, **343–344**
    link. *See* link state protocols
    OSPF, 193
static default routes, 407
static NAT-PT, 333
static parameter for stub routers, 172
static routing, **117–121**, *118–120*
statistical anomaly detection, **580–581**
status codes in BGP, **283–284**
sticky MAC addresses, 527
stop-only option in AAA accounting, 507
STP. *See* Spanning Tree Protocol (STP)
string signatures, 583
Stub area flag field, 201
stub routers, 118, *118*, **171–173**
stub type areas in OSPF, 194, 201, **218–219**
    not-so-stubby areas, **221–224**, *222*
    stub areas, **219**, *220*
    totally stubby areas, **220–221**, *221*
stuck-in-active (SIA) state, 158, 172
subcarriers, 680
subnets in EIGRP, **169**
subscriber drops, 381
successors in EIGRP, 148, 150, **152**

summarization
  disabling, **169–170**
  EIGRP, **169–171**
  IGP, 124
  RIP, 132
summary masks in EIGRP, **170**
Summary page
  IP Policies Wizard, 591, *591*
  Security Audit Wizard, 492, *492*
summary parameter in stub routers, 172
SVCs (switched VCs), 410
SVIs (switched virtual interfaces), 54
switch blocks, 6–7
switch fabric in STP, 69
switched VCs (SVCs), 410
switched virtual interfaces (SVIs), 54
switches, 29–30
  attacks, 519, 525–526
  case study, 19–20
  EtherChannel, 57–62
  IEEE devices, 529
  Layer 2, 30–31
  MPLS, 413–414
    labels, 417–424, *418–419, 421–424*
    router architecture, 416–417, *416*
    switching types, 414–416
  review questions, 63–66
  security. *See* Layer 2 security
  spoofing, 520–522, *521*
  STP, 71–72
  summary, 62
  VLANs. *See* virtual local area
    networks (VLANs)
  voice, **614–616**
  VTP, 41
switchport command, 56
switchport access vlan command, 46
switchport mode access command, 47
switchport mode dynamic command, 49
switchport mode trunk command, 48
switchport port-security command, 527–528
switchport priority command, 616
switchport trunk encapsulation command, 48
switchport voice vlan command, 47, 615–616
symmetrical DSL, 391
SYN packets, 544
SYN-ACK packets, 544
synchronizing clocks, 509–510
Synchronous Code Division Multiple Access
    (S-CDMA), 382
synchronous digital subscriber line (SDSL), 390,
    390, 393

Syslog protocol, **508–509**
System IDs in IS-IS addresses, *236, 237*
System option in AAA accounting, 507
system priority
  LACP, *59*
  STP, *71*

T

tables
  adjacency, *55*
  BGP, **251–252**, 254
  CAM, 31, 53, 519–520
  EIGRP, **155–158**
  FIB, 55, 415–416, 420–421
  LIB, 420–422, *422*
  OSPF, **195–196**
TAC (Technical Assistance Center), 482
TACACS+ protocol, **500–504**, *501*
tacacs-server host command, 504
tacacs-server key command, 504
Tag Distribution Protocol (TDP), 422
tagging in 802.1Q, 36–37, *36*
tail dropping, 625, 630
taps, cable, 379
TCAM (ternary content-addressable memory), 53
TCN (topology change notification), 83
TCP
  for BGP, 253–254
  Cisco IOS Firewall, 542, *543*
  full mesh, **262**
  header compression, 627
  voice, **610–611**
tcp-intercept option, 474
TDM (time-division multiplexing), 602
TDMA (Time Division Multiple Access), 382
TDP (Tag Distribution Protocol), 422
teardown of phone calls, **606**
Technical Assistance Center (TAC), 482
teleworkers, enterprise, **378–379**
  cable technologies. *See* cable technologies
  DSL technologies, **389–395**, *390*
templates, virtual interface, 410
Temporal Key Integrity Protocol (TKIP), **711–712**
Teredo, 332
terminal monitor command, 134–135
ternary content-addressable memory (TCAM), 53
test networks in case study, **16–21**, *17*
TFTP (Trivial File Transfer Protocol)
  securing, **509**
  server files, 722, *722*

three-layer hierarchical design model, 2–4, *3*
3DES encryption, 443
3G networks, 679
Time Division Multiple Access (TDMA), 382
time-division multiplexing (TDM), 602
timers
    HSRP, **341–342**, 356
    RIP, 129–130
    RIP Version 2, 130
    VRRP, **365**
TKIP (Temporal Key Integrity Protocol), **711–712**
topology-based switching, 55
topology change notification (TCN), 83
topology tables
    EIGRP, **156–157**
    link state routing protocols, **127**
ToS (type of service) field, 613, 639–640, *640*, 643
totally stubby areas, **220–221**, *221*
TPC (Transmit Power Control), **678**
traffic blocking in IPS, *577*, 585
traffic flow in local VLANs, 40
traffic in QoS
    classification, **633–634**
    conditioning, 625, **645–646**
    identification, **632–633**
    marking, **637–638**
traffic management in case study, 15
Traffic to Encrypt option, 440
Transactional traffic class, 634
transform-set command, 443
Transform Set screen, *456*, *456*
transit areas in OSPF, 214
transit AS, IBGP in, 258, *259*
transitive attributes in BGP, 262–263
transmissions
    BGP, **253**
    multicasts, **292–294**, *293–294*
    voice, 603, **609–611**
Transmit Power Control (TPC), **678**
transparent feature in Cisco IOS Firewall, **541**
transparent mode in VTP, **41**
transport mode in VPNs, 432
transportation networks for cable, 381
triggered updates, 147
Trivial File Transfer Protocol (TFTP)
    securing, **509**
    server files, 722, *722*
troubleshooting
    EIGRP, **179–186**
    RIP, **133–137**
    STP, **102–106**
    VPNs, **444–452**

trunk links in VLANs, 35, **47–49**
trunk ports in VLANs, 35
trunk protocols, 35
    802.1Q tagging, **36–37**, *36*
    DTP, 37, *38*
    ISL encapsulation, **35–36**, *36*
tunnel command, 331
tunnel destination command, 434
tunnel mode command, 434
tunnel mode for VPNs, 432
tunnel source command, 434
tunnels
    GRE, **433–435**, *433*
    IPv6, **330–332**, *331*
    Q-in-Q, *523*
2.4GHz standards, **674–676**, *675–676*
2.4GHz/5GHz standard, **678**
Type field in OSPF, 196
type of service (ToS) field, 613, 639–640, *640*, 643

U

UDLD (UniDirectional Link Detection), **100–102**
udld aggressive command, 101–102
udld disable command, 102
udld enable command, 101–102
UDP (User Data Protocol)
    Cisco IOS Firewall, 542, *543*
    multicasts, 295
    voice, 611
Ultra High Frequency (UHF) range, 383
unequal-cost load balancing, 148, **174–175**, *175*
unicast transmissions
    description, **292–293**, *293*
    EIGRP, 148
    IPv6, 316, 318
UniDirectional Link Detection (UDLD), **100–102**
Unique-local addresses in IPv6, 318
Unlicensed National Information Infrastructure (UNII) band, 671, 672, 677
update-source command, **276–277**, *277*
update timers, **129**
updates
    BGP, **256**
    EIGRP, **147**, 153
    LSDBs, **210–211**
    OSPF vs. IS-IS, **239**
UplinkFast feature, 81, **87–90**, *88*, 106
upper layer applications in case study, **14–15**
upstream bandwidth in STP, 80
upstream cable transmissions, 380, **388**

Use Built-In Signatures (As Backup) option, 590, 592
User Data Protocol (UDP)
   Cisco IOS Firewall, 542, *543*
   multicasts, 295
   voice, 611
user traffic problems, 632
UTC (Coordinated Universal Time), 509

V

VACLs (VLAN access control lists), 520, 526, 530–531
variable length subnet masks (VLSMs), 124, 131, **147**
variance command, 174
VCs (virtual circuits), 410
VDSL (very-high-bit-rate digital subscriber line), 390, 392–393
vectors for BGP path, 252–253
vendor support, OSPF vs. IS-IS, 240
Verify Root Password dialog, 720, *720*
verifying
   BGP, 283–286
   Cisco IOS Firewall
      advanced, **564–568**
      basic, **560–564**
   EIGRP, 179–186
   multicast, 307–309
   OSPF, 227–234
   RIP, **132–133**
   STP, **102–106**
   trunk links, 48–49
   VPNs, **442–444**
version 2 command, 132
Version field
   BPDU, 69
   OSPF, 196
very-high-bit-rate digital subscriber line (VDSL), 390, 392–393
Very High Frequency (VHF) range, 383–384
VID field, 35
video endpoints, 605
video in case study, **15**
VIP (virtual IP)-based DTS, 646
virtual circuits (VCs), 410
virtual interface templates, 410
virtual IP (VIP)-based DTS, 646
virtual local area networks (VLANs), 7, 32–33, *32–33*
   attacks, **518**, 520–523, *521*
   auxiliary, **614–616**

configuring, **43**, *43*
end-to-end, 38–39
implementing, 38
inter-VLAN routing, 51–57, *52*
link types, 34–35
local, 39–40
PVLANs, 520, 526, 531–533
trunk links, 47–49
trunk protocols, 35–37, *36*, *38*
VTP, 40–43, *42*, 49–51
virtual MAC addresses, 343
Virtual Private Dialup Network (VPDN), 403
virtual private networks (VPNs), **429–430**
   case study, **14**
   Cisco Easy VPN, **452–453**
      configuring, 453–463, *454–463*
      Dead Peer Detection, **464**
      redundant connections and equipment, **463**
      redundant routes, **464**
   Enterprise Edge connections, **8**
   GRE, 433–435, *433*
   introduction, **430**
   IPsec, 431–433, *431*, *433*
   MPLS, 419
   operation, **435–436**
   review questions, 465–467
   site-to-site, 436–441, *438–442*
   summary, **464**
   troubleshooting, **444–452**
   verifying, **442–444**
virtual router redundancy protocol (VRRP), 340, 362
   characteristics, 364–365
   configuring, 366–367
   group setup, 363, *363*
   vs. HSRP, 362
   load balancing, 364, *364*
   timers, 365
   transition, 366
virtual routers in HSRP, 342
VLAN access control lists (VACLs), 520, 526, 530–531
vlan command, 45
vlan-id command, 53
VLAN Trunk Protocol (VTP), **40–41**
   configuring, 49–51
   modes, **41**
   operation, **42**
   pruning, 42–43, *42*, 50–51
VLANs. *See* virtual local area networks (VLANs)
VLSMs (variable length subnet masks), 124, 131, **147**

voice, 601–602
    call control, 606–609, *608–609*
    components, 604–605
    converting and transmitting, 609–611
    gateway configuration, 616–619, *617*
    phone calls, **606**
    protocol usage and encapsulation overhead, 610–611
    QoS, 611–614, *614*
    review questions, 620–622
    summary, **619**
    switch configuration, 614–616
    traffic convergence, 603–604
    VLANs, **34**
voice bearer traffic, 608
voice over IP (VoIP) systems, **8**, 602
Voice traffic class, 634
VPDN (Virtual Private Dialup Network), 403
VPNs. *See* virtual private networks (VPNs)
VRRP. *See* virtual router redundancy protocol (VRRP)
vrrp ip command, 366
vrrp priority command, 367
vrrp timers advertise command, 367
vrrp timers learn command, 367
VTP (VLAN Trunk Protocol), **40–41**
    configuring, **49–51**
    modes, **41**
    operation, **42**
    pruning, 42–43, *42*, 50–51
vtp command, 49
vtp domain domain-name command, 50
vtp mode client command, 50
vtp mode server command, 50
vtp password command, 50
vtp pruning command, 51

W

wait-start option in AAA accounting, 507
WAN interface card (WIC) slots, 21
WANs. *See* Wide Area Networks (WANs)
WAPs (wireless access points), **681**
    autonomous solutions, **699**
    case study, 23
    Layer 2 security, 517
    lightweight solutions, **699–700**
war driving, 709
WCS. *See* Wireless Control System (WCS)
WDS (Wireless Domain Services), 699
WECA (Wireless Ethernet Compatibility Alliance), 712

weight attribute in BGP, **263–264**, *264*, 284
weighted fair queuing (WFQ), 626, **645**
weighted load-balancing algorithm, 369
weighted random early detection (WRED), 631, **647**
weighted round robin (WRR), 626, **644**
well-known attributes in BGP, 262–263
WEP (wired equivalent privacy), 710–711
WFQ (weighted fair queuing), 626, **645**
WGBs (Work Group Bridges), 684–685
Wi-Fi, description, 673
Wi-Fi Alliance, 671–673, 711–712
Wi-Fi Protected Access (WPA) and WPA2, **711–713**
WIC (WAN interface card) slots, 21
Wide Area Networks (WANs), **14**, 375–376
    case study, **14**
    EIGRP over, 176–178
    enterprise, **413**
    Enterprise Campus module, 376–377
    Enterprise Edge connections, **8**
    enterprise teleworkers, 378–379
        cable technologies. *See* cable technologies
        DSL technologies, 389–395, *390*
    MPLS, **413–414**
        labels, **417–424**, *418–419*, *421–424*
        router architecture, 416–417, *416*
        switching types, 414–416
    review questions, 426–428
    summary, **425**
wire gauge for DSL, 394
wired equivalent privacy (WEP), 710–711
wireless access points (WAPs), **681**
    autonomous solutions, **699**
    case study, 23
    Layer 2 security, 517
    lightweight solutions, **699–700**
Wireless Control System (WCS), **22**, 700–701
    configuring, **725–726**
    installing, **718–724**, *719–724*
    maps added to, **730–734**, *731–734*
    starting, **725**, *725*
    WLC added to, **726–730**, *726–730*
wireless devices and topologies, 669–670
    access points, **681**
    antennas, **681–683**
    autonomous solutions, 698–699
    case study, **21–23**
    client access, **685**
    client configuration, **687**
        adapters, **687–691**, *688–691*
        connection status, **694–695**, *695*

diagnostics, **695–698**, *696–698*
profiles, **691–694**, *692–694*
fundamentals, **670–672**, *672*
IEEE standards. *See* Institute of Electrical and
    Electronics Engineers (IEEE) standards
LAN modulation techniques, **679–680**
lightweight solutions, **699–701**
LWAPP, 701
NICs, 681
range comparisons, **680**, *680*
review questions, **703–705**
security. *See* wireless management and security
service areas, 686
summary, 702
topology overview, **684–685**
Wireless Domain Services (WDS), 699
Wireless Ethernet Compatibility Alliance
    (WECA), 712
Wireless LAN Controllers (WLCs), 670, 697–700,
    715–718
    QoS options, **734–737**, *735–737*
    security options, **737–739**, *738–739*
    WCS added to, **726–730**, *726–730*
Wireless LAN Solution Engine (WLSE), 699
Wireless LANs (WLANs), **16**, 670, 712
wireless management and security, **707–709**
    configuring
        WCS. *See* Wireless Control System (WCS)
        WLC. *See* Wireless LAN
            Controllers (WLCs)
    older types, 710
    open-access mode, 709
    QoS, **713–717**
    review questions, **741–743**
    summary, **739–740**
    TKIP, **711–712**
    WCS. *See* Wireless Control System (WCS)
    WPA, **712–713**
wireless multi-media (WMM) mapping
    standard, 714

Wireless tab, 734
WLANA (WLAN Association) standards, 671
WLANs (wireless local area networks), **16**,
    670, 712
WLCs (Wireless LAN Controllers), 670, 697–700,
    715–718
    QoS options, **734–737**, *735–737*
    security options, **737–739**, *738–739*
    WCS added to, **726–730**, *726–730*
WLSE (Wireless LAN Solution Engine), 699
WMM (wireless multi-media) mapping
    standard, 714
Work Group Bridges (WGBs), **684–685**
WPA (Wi-Fi Protected Access) and WPA2,
    711–713
WRED (weighted random early detection),
    631, 647
WRR (weighted round robin), 626, **644**

X

X-OR operation in EtherChannel, 57
XAuth (Extended User Authentication), 456, *457*,
    461, *461*
XAuth Options tab, 461, *461*
XTACACS protocol, 497

Y

Yagi antennas, **682–683**

Z

zeros in IPv6 addresses, 317–318

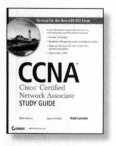

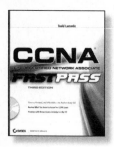